HISTORICAL DICTIONARIES OF ASIA, OCEANIA, AND THE MIDDLE EAST
Edited by Jon Woronoff

Asia

1. *Vietnam*, by William J. Duiker. 1989. *Out of print. See No. 57.*
2. *Bangladesh*, 2nd ed., by Craig Baxter and Syedur Rahman. 1996. *Out of print. See No. 48.*
3. *Pakistan*, by Shahid Javed Burki. 1991. *Out of print. See No. 61.*
4. *Jordan*, by Peter Gubser. 1991.
5. *Afghanistan*, by Ludwig W. Adamec. 1991. *Out of print. See No. 47.*
6. *Laos*, by Martin Stuart-Fox and Mary Kooyman. 1992. *Out of print. See No. 67.*
7. *Singapore*, by K. Mulliner and Lian The-Mulliner. 1991.
8. *Israel*, by Bernard Reich. 1992. *Out of print. See No. 68.*
9. *Indonesia*, by Robert Cribb. 1992. *Out of print. See No. 51.*
10. *Hong Kong and Macau*, by Elfed Vaughan Roberts, Sum Ngai Ling, and Peter Bradshaw. 1992.
11. *Korea*, by Andrew C. Nahm. 1993. *Out of print. See No. 52.*
12. *Taiwan*, by John F. Copper. 1993. *Out of print. See No. 64.*
13. *Malaysia*, by Amarjit Kaur. 1993. *Out of print. See No. 36.*
14. *Saudi Arabia*, by J. E. Peterson. 1993. *Out of print. See No. 45.*
15. *Myanmar*, by Jan Becka. 1995. *Out of print. See No. 59.*
16. *Iran*, by John H. Lorentz. 1995. *Out of print. See No. 62.*
17. *Yemen*, by Robert D. Burrowes. 1995. *Out of print. See No. 72*
18. *Thailand*, by May Kyi Win and Harold Smith. 1995. *Out of print. See No. 55.*
19. *Mongolia*, by Alan J. K. Sanders. 1996. *Out of print. See No. 42.*
20. *India*, by Surjit Mansingh. 1996. *Out of print. See No. 58.*
21. *Gulf Arab States*, by Malcolm C. Peck. 1996. *Out of print. See No. 66.*
22. *Syria*, by David Commins. 1996. *Out of print. See No. 50.*
23. *Palestine*, by Nafez Y. Nazzal and Laila A. Nazzal. 1997.
24. *Philippines*, by Artemio R. Guillermo and May Kyi Win. 1997. *Out of print. See No. 54.*

42. *Mongolia*, 2nd ed., by Alan J. K. Sanders. 2003.
43. *Cambodia*, by Justin Corfield and Laura Summers. 2003.
44. *Iraq*, by Edmund A. Ghareeb with the assistance of Beth K. Dougherty. 2004.
45. *Saudi Arabia*, 2nd ed., by J. E. Peterson. 2003.
46. *Nepal*, by Nanda R. Shrestha and Keshav Bhattarai. 2003.
47. *Afghanistan*, 3rd ed., by Ludwig W. Adamec. 2003.
48. *Bangladesh*, 3rd ed., by Craig Baxter and Syedur Rahman. 2003.
49. *Kyrgyzstan*, by Rafis Abazov. 2004.
50. *Syria*, 2nd ed., by David Commins. 2004.
51. *Indonesia*, 2nd ed., by Robert Cribb and Audrey Kahin. 2004.
52. *Republic of Korea*, 2nd ed., by Andrew C. Nahm and James E. Hoare. 2004.
53. *Turkmenistan*, by Rafis Abazov. 2005.
54. *Philippines*, 2nd ed., by Artemio Guillermo. 2005.
55. *Thailand*, 2nd ed., by Harold E. Smith, Gayla S. Nieminen, and May Kyi Win. 2005.
56. *New Zealand*, 2nd ed., by Keith Jackson and Alan McRobie. 2005.
57. *Vietnam*, 3rd ed., by Bruce Lockhart and William J. Duiker, 2006.
58. *India*, 2nd ed., by Surjit Mansingh. 2006.
59. *Burma (Myanmar)*, by Donald M. Seekins. 2006.
60. *Hong Kong SAR and the Macao SAR*, by Ming K. Chan and Shiu-hing Lo. 2006.
61. *Pakistan*, 3rd ed., by Shahid Javed Burki. 2006.
62. *Iran*, 2nd ed., by John H. Lorentz. 2007.
63. *People's Republic of China*, 2nd ed., by Lawrence R. Sullivan. 2007.
64. *Taiwan (Republic of China)*, 3rd ed., by John F. Copper. 2007.
65. *Australia*, 3rd ed., by James C. Docherty. 2007.
66. *Gulf Arab States*, 2nd ed., by Malcolm C. Peck. 2008.
67. *Laos*, 3rd ed., by Martin Stuart-Fox. 2008.
68. *Israel*, 2nd ed., by Bernard Reich and David H. Goldberg. 2008.
69. *Brunei*, 2nd ed., by Jatswan S. Sidhu, 2010.
70. *Postwar Japan*, by William D. Hoover, 2009.
71. *Malaysia*, by Ooi Keat Gin, 2009.
72. *Yemen*, 2nd ed., by Robert D. Burrowes, 2010.

Historical Dictionary of Yemen

Second Edition

Robert D. Burrowes

Historical Dictionaries of Asia, Oceania, and the Middle East, No. 72

The Scarecrow Press, Inc.
Lanham • Toronto • Plymouth, UK
2010

R
953.3
B9724 h
2010

Published by Scarecrow Press, Inc.
A wholly owned subsidiary of The Rowman & Littlefield Publishing Group, Inc.
4501 Forbes Boulevard, Suite 200, Lanham, Maryland 20706
http://www.scarecrowpress.com

Estover Road
Plymouth PL6 7PY
United Kingdom

British Library Cataloguing in Publication Information Available

Library of Congress Cataloging-in-Publication Data

Burrowes, Robert D.
    Historical dictionary of Yemen / Robert D. Burrowes. — 2nd ed.
        p. cm. — (Historical dictionaries of Asia, Oceania, and the Middle East ; no. 72)
    Includes bibliographical references.
    ISBN 978-0-8108-5528-1 (hardcover: alk. paper) —
    ISBN 978-0-8108-7080-2 (ebook)
    1. Yemen (Republic)—History—Dictionaries. I. Title.
DS247.Y45B87 2010
953.3003—dc22   2009027643

Printed in the United States of America

∞ ™ The paper used in this publication meets the minimum requirements of
American National Standard for Information Sciences—Permanence of Paper for
Printed Library Materials, ANSI/NISO Z39.48-1992.

To Yemen
and a Yemeni People
not yet free enough to decide their fate
and again to
Ron Hart and Leigh Douglas,
too young to die or be killed
and to my first Yemeni mentor and friend,
Muhammad Anaam Ghaleb
and another dear friend,
Muhammad Abdullah al-Shami

Contents

Editor's Foreword

Yemen is one of the most remote, and least known, countries in the Middle East . . . at present, at least. Hundreds (and sometimes thousands) of years back, due to its location on major trade routes, it was almost at the center of things, but its earlier kingdoms flourished and then collapsed, remembered today mainly by historians. As a modern state, it is much newer, having achieved independence shortly after World War II—first as one state, then as two, and again as one with the unification as the Republic of Yemen in 1990. That renewed unity has managed to hold better than some expected, tensions still affect the country as a whole. Moreover, its economy has suffered, and its political situation is far from stable. This means that Yemen could remain a failing state, or even become a failed state, unless its people sort out their difficulties and its government makes greater progress toward national unity, order and security within the country, and improved relations with Yemen's neighbors. This is particularly important in light of Yemen's strategic location: south of Saudi Arabia, bordering the Red Sea and Gulf of Aden (through which much of the world's oil flows), and not far from Sudan, Ethiopia, and Somalia, three of the world's hot spots.

This makes the task of the *Historical Dictionary of Yemen* more daunting. It is not just enough to provide information, bits of facts and figures that are very hard to come by elsewhere. It is also necessary to create some balance, to show just how poorly the nation's starting position was and how much has been achieved in the years since then—as well as how much more remains to be done. This is one of the tasks of the introduction; the other is simply to put us in contact with this constantly changing country. Because the changes have been so radical, it will be helpful to rely for context and clarity on the chronology, which follows the countless twists and turns more closely. But the dictionary is the main source of information. Its entries describe Yemen's many different political units—especially the more recent ones—and tell us of leaders of whom we rarely hear, a nation so varied that just lumping its populace together as Yemeni is a meaningless exercise, Yemen's one religion, Islam, which itself comes in infinite variations, the bevy of political parties in what has hardly been a model democracy, and the economic and cultural factors that underlie them all. Long as this book is, still more remains to be learned; the bibliography will point readers who want to know more in the right direction.

This impressive volume was written by one of the best possible guides, Robert D. Burrowes. First of all, Dr. Burrowes is a scholar. Since 1961, he has taught at New York University, then at the American University of Beirut, and, until recently, at the Political Science Department and Henry M. Jackson School of International Studies at the University of Washington. During this time, he has researched North Yemen and then the united Republic of Yemen, producing numerous articles in learned and professional journals and even a book: *The Yemen Arab Republic: The Politics of Development, 1962–1986*. But that is only one side of his career. Dr. Burrowes has become fascinated by the intriguing country in which he has lived and taken part in development projects and to which he has returned repeatedly for long and short stays for over three decades. Even though much of the information in this dictionary is derived from printed sources available to all, Dr. Burrowes has studied much more of them than most, and he brings with him extensive experience of how things are on the ground. This second edition (he also wrote the first), considerably longer and extensively updated, is an excellent starting point for those unfamiliar with Yemen and a wonderful source of information even for those who know it well.

Jon Woronoff
Series Editor

Preface

The differences in Yemen between the time I signed off on the first edition in late 1994 and today are great and, at first glance, somewhat contradictory. In my mind and memory, the mid-1970s to the end of the 1980s were the halcyon years, a period of unprecedented hope and prosperity fed by employment abroad, the massive inflow of widely scattered remittances, and increasing amounts of external aid from many sources. Bulldozers were cutting dirt roads to previously isolated, almost inaccessible villages, and a great number of mostly mustard-colored four-wheel-drive Toyotas were hauling people and goods to and from those villages. Common people had things, new things, for the first time. Who comes to mind is a *shayba*, an old man, walking along with a bundle of qat under one arm and carrying a battery-powered radio-cassette player and a gaudy Chinese thermos of tea. The times were good, and they promised to get better.

I remember sadly telling a younger researcher in Yemen in 1995, the year the first edition came out, that over the past decade Yemen had become just another third-world country. The forces that were working to erase the North Yemen of the 1970s and 1980s were obvious: the sudden and massive drop in remittances, the expelled remitters who came home to unemployment, and the corrupting effect of new oil revenues that went via the coffers of the state unequally—primarily into the pockets of the well-positioned and well-connected.

And yet, even then, I regarded Yemen's glass as half full. President Ali Abdullah Salih had been firmly in office for 15 years—this after the last years and overthrow of the imamate, the Yemeni Civil War and al-Sallal era, the several-year al-Iryani and al-Hamdi eras and the al-Ghashmi interlude, and their attendant coups and assassinations. President Salih pushed hard for Yemeni unification in 1989–1990 and preserved it in the War of Secession in 1994. He and his chief advisers seemed to recognize in 1995 the need for drastic economic and other reforms to restore Yemen's viability.

In mid-2009, President Salih had been in office for 31 years; when and if he completes his current term, his tenure will amount to 35 years. But now the glass appears half empty, not half full; in truth, I think it less than half empty. For the most part, the Salih regime has failed to keep its promise of reform, a promise repeated during and after the 2006 presidential campaign. The corruption that most distinguishes the regime seems to have rendered it unwilling and unable to do what has to be done to make Yemen viable and sustainable—i.e., to act in the nation's self-interest. At the risk of using terms too often wrongly applied to other cases since 2000, Yemen has became a failing state that could easily become a failed state in the very near future. Of course, as a lover of Yemen and the Yemenis, I hope it doesn't.

I want to thank again those Yemenis who taught me so much and who have been such good friends of mine from 1975 to the present. In addition to those to whom this book is dedicated is the friend whom I regard as the greatest and most intelligent living Yemeni: Dr. Abd al-Karim al-Iryani. A generation younger, but also very bright and politically astute, is his nephew, Abd al-Ghani al-Iryani, my best younger Yemeni friend. And then there are my first friend in Taiz in 1975, Amin Abd al-Wahid; my student at NYU in 1972, and then longtime friend, Ambassador Abdullah al-Ashtal, now deceased; and Hamoud al-Salahi, a dear friend in Sanaa since about 1980. And so many others deserve mention for helping and befriending me. My thanks go, too, to my colleagues in the Henry M. Jackson School of International Studies (JSIS) and the Middle East Center at the University of Washington for their support and encouragement—especially to Jere Bacharach, former JSIS director, and current director Anand Yang. Last of all, thanks to Jon Woronoff, the series editor, for prodding me on and for putting up with countless excuses for extensions.

Reader's Note

No formal system of transliteration is used in this volume to render Arabic words into English. Instead, I have tried to render these words in a form understandable to both the Arabist and the non-Arabist. For example, the plural of "sayyid," or descendent of the Prophet, is "sadah," but I have chosen to use "sayyids." Again, because it is the rendering known to two generations of Middle East specialists and nonspecialists alike, "Nasser" rather than "Nasir." By contrast, the leader of South Yemen in the 1980s is referred to as "Ali Nasir Muhammad." In cases of likely confusion regarding terms, names, and things, I have tried to use cross-references to direct readers seeking particular entries.

Public figures and ordinary persons are known by a given or a family name—or even a place name. For example, the South Yemeni leader Chairman Abd al-Fattah Ismail was known by all as "Chairman Abd al-Fattah," and President Ali Nasir Muhammad al-Hasani as "President Ali Nasir Muhammad," or even "President Ali Nasir." By contrast, President Abdullah al-Sallal was always referred to as "President al-Sallal." These possible confusions are dealt with by means of cross-references. For example, the reader is led to the entry for Abd al-Fattah Ismail by the cross-reference "Ismail, *see* Abd al-Fattah." Honorifics, such as "qadi" or "shaykh," are defined in the text when appropriate.

Finally, cross-references to relevant entries are indicated in **bold** within the entry or are listed at the entry's end under *See also*.

Acronyms and Abbreviations

AAIA	Aden–Abyan Islamic Army
ACC	Arab Cooperation Council
ACT	Aden Container Terminal
ADB	Abyan Development Board
AFESD	Arab Fund for Economic and Social Development
AFZ	Aden Free Zone
ANM	Arab Nationalist Movement
ATUC	Aden Trade Union Congress
b/d (bpd)	barrels (of oil) per day
BP	British Petroleum
CBY	Central Bank of Yemen
CC	Consultative Council
CPO	Central Planning Organization
CSO	Central Statistical Organization
CYDA	Confederation of Yemeni Development Associations
DFLP	Democratic Front for the Liberation of Palestine
DRY	Democratic Republic of Yemen
EAP	Eastern Aden Protectorate (the Hadhramawt, Mahrah, sometimes the Wahida Sultanate)
ECWA	Economic Commission for Western Asia, UN
ELF	Eritrean Liberation Front
FAAS	Federation of Arab Amirates of the South
FBI	Federal Burea of Investigation
FLOSY	Front for the Liberation of Occupied South Yemen
FRG	Federal Republic of Germany (West Germany)
FSA	Federation of South Arabia
GCC	Gulf Cooperation Council
GDP	gross domestic product
GDR	German Democratic Republic (East Germany)

GFYLU	General Federation of Yemeni Labor Unions
GIA	General Investment Authority
GPC	General People's Congress
GUYW	General Union of Yemeni Women
GUYW	General Union of Yemeni Workers
HBL	Hadhrami Bedouin Legion
HCCO	Higher Coordination Council for the Opposition
ICC	International Criminal Court
ICU	Islamic Courts Union
IDA	International Development Association
IMF	International Monetary Fund
JMP	Joint Meeting Parties
KFAED	Kuwait Fund for Arab Economic Development
LC	local council
LCCD	Local Council for Cooperative Development
LDA	Local Development Association
LDC	less developed country
LNG	liquefied natural gas
LPC	Local People's Council
MAN	Movement of Arab Nationalists
MAWJ	National Association of Opposition Groupings
MCC	Millennium Challenge Corporation
MECO	Military Economic Corporation (later renamed the Yemeni Economic Corporation)
MP	Member of Parliament
NBY	National Bank of Yemen
NCB	National Commercial Bank
NCFT	National Corporation for Foreign Trade
NDC	National Dialogue Committee
NDF	National Democratic Front
NDI	National Democratic Institute
NF	National Front
NFPO	National Front Political Organization
NGO	non-governmental organization
NHTC	National Home Trade Company
NIPA	National Institute for Public Administration
NLF	National Liberation Front
NSO	National Security Organization

NYU	National Yemeni Union
OECD	Organization of Economic Cooperation and Development
OLOS	Organization for the Liberation of the Occupied South
OPEC	Organization of Petroleum Exporting Companies
PCA	People's Constituent Assembly
PDFLP	Popular Democratic Front for the Liberation of Palestine
PDRY	People's Democratic Republic of Yemen
PDU	Popular Democratic Union
PFLO	Popular Front for the Liberation of Oman
PFLOAG	Popular Front for the Liberation of the Occupied Arab Gulf
PFLP	Popular Front for the Liberation of Palestine
PLO	Palestine Liberation Organization
PONF	Political Organization, National Front
PRF	People's Resistance Forces
PRSY	People's Republic of South Yemen
PSA	Port of Singapore Authority
PSC	People's Supreme Council
PSO	Political Security Organization
PSP	People's Socialist Party (Abdullah al-Asnag's party)
PVP	People's Vanguard Party (Vanguard Party)
RAF	Royal Air Force
RAY	League of the Sons of Yemen (Rabita), al-Jifri's party
RC	Republican Council
RDC	Religious Dialogue Council
RDP	Revolutionary Democratic Party
ROY	Republic of Yemen
SAAF	South Arabian Armed Forces
SAL	South Arabian League (League of the Sons of the Arab South)
SCER	Supreme Committee for Elections and Referendums
SDF	Social Development Fund
SFD	Saudi Fund for Development
SPC	Supreme People's Council
SYC	Supreme Yemeni Council

TDA	Tihama Development Authority
TEU	twenty-foot equivalent unit
UAE	United Arab Emirates
UAR	United Arab Republic (the union of Egypt and Syria)
UAS	United Arab States (the loose association of the YAR and the Yemeni imamate)
UK	United Kingdom
UN	United Nations
UNDP	United Nations Development Fund
UNESCO	United Nations Education, Scientific, and Cultural Organization
UNF	United National Front
UNICEF	United Nations Children's Fund
UNYOM	United Nations Yemen Observation Mission
UPF	Union of Popular Forces
UPONF	United Political Organization, National Front
U.S.	United States
USD	United States dollar
USSR	Union of Soviet Socialist Republics
WAP	Western Aden Protectorate (states in Aden's hinterland)
WB	World Bank
WHO	World Health Organization
YAR	Yemen Arab Republic
YBRD	Yemen Bank for Reconstruction and Development
YD	Yemeni Dinar, PRDY currency (about USD3.00 in 1980)
YEMCO	Yemen Economic Corporation
YHOC	Yemen Hunt Oil Company
YIJ	Yemeni Islamic Jihad
YJS	Yemeni Journalists Syndicate
YLNG	YemenLNG
YOMINCO	Yemen Oil and Mineral Company
YPC	Yemen Petroleum Company
YR	Yemeni Rial, YAR currency (about USD0.20 in 1980)
YSP	Yemeni Socialist Party
YWU	Yemen Women's Union

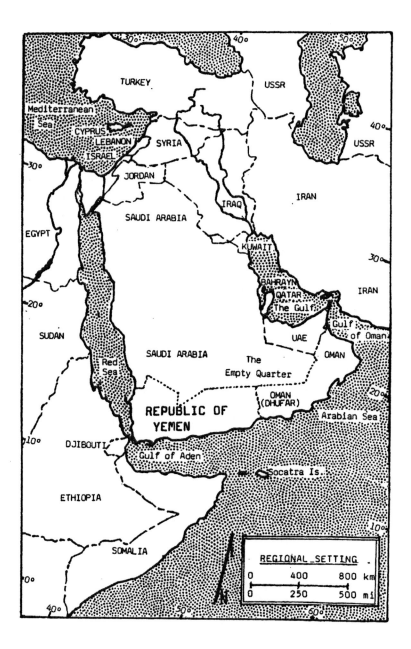

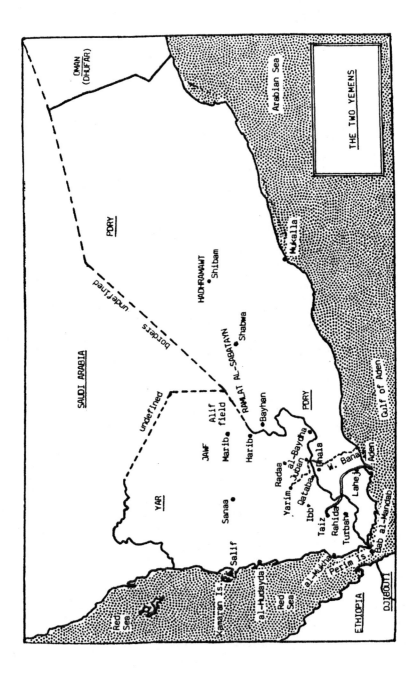

THE TWO YEMENS

Chronology

***ca.* 1200 B.C.–630 A.D.** The period of the great pre-Islamic trading kingdoms along the Frankincense Trail on the edge of the desert that for about 2,000 years linked Egypt and the Mediterranean world to the riches of South Arabia, East Africa, the Indian subcontinent, and points east. The first of these kingdoms was the Main (Minean) kingdom, which was followed and superseded by the Sabean trading kingdom (Saba), based in Marib on the overland trade route and best known to the world in subsequent centuries for the great Marib dam and for Bilqis, Queen of Sheba (Saba). The kingdom persisted for much of the first millennium B.C., to be paralleled in the later centuries by the lesser trading kingdoms of Hadhramawt (Shabwa), Qataban (Timna), and Awsan. From ***ca.* 400–100 B.C.** a reinvigorated Egypt under the Ptolemies controls the commerce of the Red Sea and the coast of East Africa as the South Arabian kingdoms continue to control the overland caravan trade with the East. The Himyarite kingdom that emerged in ***ca.* 110 B.C.** was to be the last of the great South Arabian kingdoms and the only one centered in the Yemeni highlands and not on the trade routes on the edge of the desert. Rome conquers Egypt and ***ca.* A.D. 100** Roman sailors discover the secret of the monsoon winds, causing overland trade to plummet and the kingdoms of South Arabia to decline forever. In **A.D. 490**, after generations of economic stagnation and political decline, the enfeebled Himyarite state is seized by Dhu Nuwas, who converts to Judaism and proceeds to persecute Christians encroaching on Yemen from the north. In **A.D. 525**, Christian Abyssinia (Ethiopia) invades and occupies Himyaritic Yemen, overthrowing the indigenous Dhu Nuwas regime. In turn, in ***ca.* A.D. 575**, the ruler of Persia helps a Himyarite prince overthrow Abyssinian Christian rulers only to proceed to make South Arabia a distant province of the Sassanid empire.

ca. **600–1400 A.D.** The Prophet Muhammad moves from Mecca to Medina **A.D. 622**, the formal beginning of the Islamic era. Over the next couple of decades, answering the call issued by Muhammad from Medina, Yemenis are among the earliest converts to Islam—and mosques are built in Yemen before Muhammad's death in A.D. 632 Far to the north, focusing on Damascus and Baghdad, the new regional Islamic politics play out. In **A.D. 822**, in Yemen, Muhammad ibn Ziyad founds the Banu Ziyad dynasty in the new city of Zabid in the Red Sea coastal desert, which in effect cuts Yemen off from the Abbasid empire and the Arab Islamic mainstream, making it more likely that Yemen would remain more distinctively Yemeni than otherwise. The **mid-to late-800s** is a period of struggle between the Banu Ziyad of the Tihama and the Yufirids of the highlands, as well as intense Ismaili (Fatimid) missionary efforts in Yemen. In **893**, Al-Hadi ila al-Haqq (al-Hadi), invited to the North Yemeni town of Saada to mediate local disputes, proceeds to found there the Zaydi imamate that, based on Zaydi Shii teachings, was to hold sway over at least part of North Yemen nearly continuously until the 1962 Revolution. In **1037**, Ali al-Sulayhid, acting for the Ismaili Fatimid caliphate in Cairo, founds the Sulayhid dynasty, which based itself in Sanaa and then Jibla, lasts for a century, and concludes with the long rule of fabled Queen Arwa. In **1173**, Saladin's brother Turanshah conquers nearly all of Yemen except for the Zaydi far north and founds the short-lived Ayyubid dynasty, thereby providing a precedent for one Yemen and, more immediately, a foundation upon which the longer-lived Rasulid dynasty could build. In **1232**, Nur al-Din ibn al-Rasul replaces the Ayyubid dynasty with the new Rasulid dynasty, which will last for 200 years, compete with the Zaydi imamate for predominance in Yemen, and firmly establish Shafii Sunnism as the dominant form of Islam in South Yemen and the southern part of North Yemen for future generations down to the present. In **1323**, the Zaydi imamate retakes Sanaa from the Rasulids, an event denoting the modest revival of the former and the faltering of the latter. Aden-based Tahirids, Rasulid vassals, take over much of the territory of declining Rasulids in *ca.* **1400** and rule over most of it for more than a century, taking Sana from the Zaydi imamate in 1505.

1507–1840 The Portuguese occupy Socotra island in **1507**, signaling the start of Europe's imperial interest in South Arabia as well as the beginning of the end of medieval Yemen's isolation. In **1515**, Mamluks of Egypt invade Yemen, and in the **1520s**, the Ottoman Turks, having only recently overthrown the Mamluks in Egypt, take over from the Mamluks in Yemen and begin to consolidate their rule there—a rule that will last for a century. In **1598**, Qasim ibn Muhammad becomes imam, marking the beginning of a long era in which a reinvigorated Zaydi imamate—the Qasimi imamate—eventually ousts the Turks from the highlands. In **1636**, Ottoman forces quit the Tihama for the Hijaz, thus ending the first Ottoman occupation of Yemen and leaving most of the country temporarily and nominally united under the Qasimi imamate extending from Asir in the North to Dhufar in Oman in the east. One result is that the interior of Yemen is again and for generations all but completely isolated from the outside world. In the **early 1600s**, coffee, a drink from Yemen introduced to Europe via the Turks and Constantinople, begins to attract English and Dutch merchants to the Red Sea port of al-Mukha (Mocha), thereby beginning the coffee trade. In **1720–1740**, al-Mukha participates in the golden age of the coffee trade, dominated by English, Dutch, French, and American traders—and all the while the Zaydi imam succeeds in isolating the interior of North Yemen from the outside world. Carsten Niebuhr, a European, pierces the secrecy of imamate Yemen and the Yemeni highlands in **1763**, traveling throughout the Tihama, to Taiz, and then up to Sanaa. From **1798–1840**, events in Egypt and in the lands along the Red Sea coast of Arabia, including the designs of Muhammad Ali and the occupation of portions of Yemen by the Wahhabi sect, rekindle British and Ottoman Turkish interest in the area. The age of the steamship also arrives, and with it the need for coaling depots.

1839–1918 Britain occupies Aden, a tiny fishing village, launching its rise as a great port in world trade in **1839**, and the second Ottoman Turkish occupation of much of North Yemen begins with the seizure of al-Hudayda in **1849**. These events begin the process of bifurcation that culminates in the creation of two Yemeni states in the second half of the 20th century. In **1869**, the Suez Canal opens, conferring new geopolitical significance on the Red Sea, North Yemen, and Aden and its hinterland. In **1873**, clashes between Britain and the Ottomans over lands and people between North Yemen's Hujariyya and Aden's hinterland focus attention on spheres of imperial interest and hasten the bifurcation of

Yemen. In **late 1880s–1890s**, British authorities in Aden conclude formal treaties of friendship and protection with 10 or so of the surrounding tribes and mini-states, beginning what will become a protracted process of establishing some claim and control over the fragmented hinterland of Aden, known thereafter as the Aden Protectorates. In **1904**, Imam Yahya ibn Muhammad succeeds his father, the first of the Hamid al-Din imams, and continues the Yemeni opposition to Ottoman imperial rule as he simultaneously begins efforts to strengthen and extend the imamate. In **1905**, Britain and the Ottomans demarcate and accept a boundary between their respective territories from the Bab al-Mandab Straits at the foot of the Red Sea eastward to a point near Harib. In **1911**, in the Treaty of Daan, the embattled Ottoman Turks and Imam Yahya effectively agree to split the rule of North Yemen between themselves. In **1918**, the Turks withdraw from North Yemen for the second time, the result of the dismemberment of the defeated Ottoman Empire after World War I, leaving the way open to Imam Yahya's efforts to extend his rule to virtually all of modern North Yemen by the mid-1930s.

Mid-1920s–1936   Iman Yahya drives his Idrisi rival, based to the north, in Asir, out of al-Hudayda in the **mid-1920s** and then continues to consolidate his rule over the Tihama and the rest of North Yemen. In **1934**, the Treaty of Sanaa between Great Britain and imamate Yemen recognized the territorial status quo and implicitly accepts the Anglo–Turkish line of 1905. After a short war, the Treaty of Taif in **1934** sets imamate Yemen's northern border with the newly proclaimed Kingdom of Saudi Arabia, and Imam Yahya accepts Saudi jurisdiction over the Asir, Najran, and Jizan as the price of defeat. Organized "modernist" opposition to the rule of Imam Yahya and the Hamid al-Din family begins in **1935** with the formation of a secret organization, Hayat al-Nidal, and in **1936**, Imam Yahya sends 13 boys to Iraq for military and technical training, Abdullah al-Sallal and other future leaders of the 1962 Revolution among them, only to abort the mission after second thoughts only a year later.

1936–1937   The "Peace of Ingrams," a truce negotiated with dozens of tribal leaders by Harold Ingrams and Abu Bakr al-Kaf, brings peace to the Hadhramawt for the first time in decades—and marks the beginning of a more intrusive, interventionist approach by Britain to this vast area east of Aden. In **1937**, formal responsibility for the governance of Aden passes from the Government of India to the Colonial Office and the Aden Protectorate is divided into the Western Aden Protectorate (WAP), with a British agent in Aden, and the Eastern Aden Protectorate (EAP), with a resident adviser in Mukalla in the Hadhramawt.

1944–1948 The Free Yemeni movement is established by North Yemenis in Aden in **1944**, marking the start of sustained, organized "modernist" opposition to the policies and later the very existence of the Zaydi imamate. In **1947**, Imam Yahya sends the young, ill-prepared "Famous Forty" abroad for modern education, thereby beginning what by the mid-1950s was to become a flood of educational emigrants, most of whom returned years later full of modern social and political ideas. Also in **1947**, a general strike and disturbances to protest the perceived pro-Zionist policy of the British in Palestine provide the first clear evidence of serious discontent with British rule in Aden. In **1948**, the aborted 1948 Revolution begins with the assassination of Imam Yahya and ends after only weeks with the overthrow of his successor from the al-Wazir family and modernist allies—and the re-establishment of the Hamid al-Din imamate under Imam Ahmad, Yahya's eldest son. Several future republican leaders are jailed together in Hajja prison, an experience that only sharpens republican and "revolutionary" sensibilities. The creation of Israel in **1948** sets the stage for a mass exodus by air of Yemeni Jews from the two Yemens in Operation Flying Carpet after 1950.

1949–1962 In the first elections ever in Aden, in **1949**, a narrow electorate participates in choosing only partially elective township authorities. In the **early 1950s**, political organizations appear openly in Aden and in a few places in the Protectorates, urging political solutions ranging from an independent Aden city-state to the merger of Aden with North Yemen, the Protectorates, and even Muscat and Oman. Important among them is the South Arabian League (SAL). In **1952**, British Petroleum (BP) decides to build an oil refinery at Little Aden, triggering a boom in jobs, small businesses, and growth generally. In **1956**, the Aden Trade Union Congress (ATUC) is formed under the leadership of Abdullah al-Asnag. Pro-Nasser, pan-Arab sentiment increases among Arabs in Aden after the Anglo–French–Israeli attack on Egypt in **1956**, causing the first bloodshed in a protest against authorities in Aden since 1947. The Defense White Paper in **1957** envisaged that Aden ·····

Singapore and the United Kingdom itself, would be one of the British bases in the Western defense system, causing the service population of Aden to increase four-fold by **1960**, triggering a new boom and expansion. In **1959**, the formation of a Federation of South Arabian Amirates is declared in a treaty signed by the rulers of six states in the Western Aden Protectorate (WAP) and the governor of Aden. (Four more states in the WAP join by early 1960.) In **mid-1962**, al-Asnag, the leader of the ATUC, announces plans to create the People's Socialist Party (PSP) to oppose the proposed inclusion of Aden Colony with the renamed Federation of South Arabia (FSA). Meanwhile, now based in Taiz, Imam Ahmad in **1955** puts down a serious coup attempt. In **1957**, opening slightly to the outside world, Imam Ahmad receives arms from the Soviet Union via Czechoslovakia, ostensibly for use against the British to the south. In **1958**, Imam Ahmad joins with Egypt and Syria, recently merged into the United Arab Republic (UAR), to form the new United Arab States, thereby gaining temporary protection from revolutionary Arab nationalism by hiding under its wing. By the **late 1950s**, the Soviet Union, China, and the United States are competing for influence in Yemen with modest aid programs, most notably with each of them undertaking to build the highway on one side of the Sanaa–Hudayda–Taiz triangle. In **1959**, after granting safe conduct for a meeting with them, Imam Ahmad, in a rage, orders the execution of the paramount shaykh of the Hashid tribal confederation and his eldest son, alienating the Hashids from the imamate. In **1961**, Imam Ahmad takes Yemen out of the largely fictitious United Arab States and ridicules Egypt's President Gamal Abdul Nasser in a published poem, thereby launching a war of words between the two states.

1962–1963 Imam Ahmad dies on **19 September** and is succeeded by his son, Muhammad al-Badr. A week later, on 26 September, the imamate in North Yemen is overthrown in an army-led coup and replaced by the Yemen Arab Republic (YAR) and a regime led by President Abdullah al-Sallal, political events that quickly expose North Yemen for the first time—and forever—to the modern world beyond its borders. In **late 1962**, a long civil war begins in North Yemen that is soon regionalized and then internationalized, with Soviet-backed Egyptian forces fighting on the republican side against royalists headed by deposed Imam al-Badr and strongly backed by Saudi Arabia and, to a lesser degree, the West.

Meanwhile, on **26 September 1962**, a divided Legislative Council in Aden votes to merge Aden with the FSA against a background of public disturbances by those opposed to the merger, and in **January 1963**, Aden Colony is merged with the FSA, despite intense popular opposition from Adenis. In **fall 1963**, the "Third Force" emerges in the YAR, calling for some sort of compromise between the republicans and royalists and for the end of all foreign intervention in Yemeni affairs—an authentic, albeit partly Saudi-subsidized, cry of "Yemen for the Yemenis." In South Yemen, fighting in the Radfan Mountains north of Aden on **14 October 1963** marks the start of armed struggle against Britain by the National Liberation Front (NLF).

1965–1967 The Organization for the Liberation of the Occupied South (OLOS) is formed out of al-Asnag's PSP and the old South Arabian League in **1965** as the British governor in Aden, faced with growing opposition, civil unrest, and violence, suspends the constitution and reimposes direct colonial rule. In **1966**, the Defense White Paper states Britain's intention to grant independence to the Federation of South Arabia (FSA) by the end of 1968 and not to retain military facilities there after that time, thereby ending its military presence "East of Suez." Also in **1966**, the Front for the Liberation of Occupied South Yemen (FLOSY) is created out of the union of al-Asnag's and Abd al-Qawi Makkawi's OLOS and the NLF, although the latter quickly bows out of what it perceives as an attempt by Egypt's President Nasser to control the local opposition to Britain in South Yemen. In **1966–1967**, the NLF and FLOSY wage an independence struggle against Britain as well as a civil war against each other to determine the successor to departing British. In **June 1967**, blockage of the Suez Canal during the Six-Day War reduces the Port of Aden's economic activity to practically nothing. In **fall 1967**, after defeat in the Six-Day War, Egyptian forces withdraw from the YAR in accordance with the Khartoum Agreement that finally reconciles Egypt and Saudi Arabia. On **5 November**, the al-Sallal regime is ousted after five years and replaced by one headed by Qadi Abd al-Rahman al-Iryani that is committed to both the YAR and reconciliation with the moderate royalists. **30 November 1967** is declared South Yemen's independence day, the day on which the last British forces leave Aden and the NLF assumes power and declares the birth of the People's Republic of Southern Yemen (PRSY).

1968–1970   In **February 1968**, the 70-day Siege of Sana by royalist tribes is broken by the heroic, embattled republicans, ending the royalists' last good chance of overturning the republic and the new regime led by Qadi al-Iryani. In **August**, conservative republican elements in the army subdue and expel the republican left from the army and body politic, thereby solidifying the center-right nature of the regime. In **June 1969**, the "Corrective Move" in Aden marks the triumph of the left wing in the NLF, resulting in the start of a major shift to the left in the PRSY as well as to both the adoption of major nationalization laws and an increase in the flow of refugees to the YAR. In **1969**, the YAR breaks the Arab boycott of West Germany and recognizes that country in return for generous aid, marking the first major success in the al-Iryani regime's efforts toward an opening to the West and a lessening of the civil war–caused dependence on the East Bloc for aid. In **spring 1970**, republican–royalist reconciliation finally ends the civil war. Moderate royalists are allowed to return and assume their place in society and their positions in the republican state and government. Later that year, the YAR adopts the 1970 Constitution, which calls for a largely elected Consultative Council. "President" al-Iryani continues as chairman of the plural executive, the Republican Council, and the YAR establishes diplomatic relations with Saudi Arabia and with Britain and France. South Yemen adopts the 1970 State Constitution and changes its name to the People's Democratic Republic of Yemen (PDRY), a change whose implications bring protests from the YAR.

1971–1973   In **early 1971**, the YAR holds elections for the Consultative Council called for in the 1970 Constitution, the first popular elections in the country's history. By **1971**, relations between the two Yemens, already showing signs of strain in 1969, worsen as the YAR drifts right and the PDRY lurches left. In **August 1971**, Prime Minister M. Ali Haytham is purged in Aden, and the regime, now completely under the control of the NLF left and the uneasy co-leadership of Salim Rubay Ali and Abd al-Fattah Ismail, soon takes major steps toward both a socialist organization of economic and social life, and closer identification with the socialist camp and revolutionary movements around the world. The PDRY, in keeping with its new stance, supports and serves as a conduit for the aid of others to the Dhufar Rebellion in neighboring Oman and also provides sanctuary to members of various leftist "terrorist" groups.

In **summer–fall 1972**, the two Yemens wage an intermittent civil war, the northern side taken largely by tribal forces supplied and encouraged by Saudi Arabia; on the southern side, regular PDRY forces are aided by guerrillas led by YAR leftist dissidents in exile. In **November**, the two Yemens end their border war with a cease-fire and then the Cairo Agreement and the Tripoli summit, in which they agree to a plan for political unification. Despite this agreement, Inter-Yemeni relations deteriorate again by **mid-1973**, especially after the murky murder of YAR leader Muhammad Ali Uthman. In **1973**, the local development association (LDA) movement is provided national organization and a boost through the creation of the Confederation of Yemeni Development Associations (CYDA) under the leadership of Col. Ibrahim al-Hamdi.

1974–1977 On **13 June**, President al-Iryani is respectfully sent into exile, and his regime is replaced by one headed by a Command Council chaired by Col. al-Hamdi, who immediately suspends the Consultative Council and the 1970 Constitution. In **January 1975**, President al-Hamdi consolidates his position by replacing the ambitious Muhsin al-Aini as prime minister with Abd al-Aziz Abd al-Ghani, and by expelling most of the leading tribal leaders from the regime. In **June**, President al-Hamdi launches the "13 June Correction Movement," reviving his year-old call to reform the government and the state and to focus on Yemeni development. In the PDRY, in **fall 1975**, the Unified Political Organization, National Front (UPONF), a coalition consisting of the dominant NLF and the People's Democratic Union and Baath Party, is formed and hailed as a step toward creation of a vanguard party for the building of socialism. Closed since the Six-Day War in 1967, the Suez Canal is reopened in **mid-1975**, improving the economic prospects for the port of Aden and giving added strategic importance to the Red Sea and Horn of Africa. (In a couple of years, after the 1974 Ethiopian Revolution, Somalia will realign with the United States, Ethiopia will realign with the Soviet Union and Cuba, and Somalia and Ethiopia will clash violently in the Ogadan rebellion.) In **1976**, a rapprochement between the PDRY and Saudi Arabia begins and, although it largely stalls after a year, results in Saudi aid for the regime in Aden and a cutback in Saudi aid to the domestic enemies of the PDRY; in return, the PDRY ends all but verbal support for the Dhufar rebellion against Oman. In **summer 1976**, several dissident leftist groups from the YAR create the National

Democratic Front (NDF), in part with the hope of persuading President al-Hamdi to readmit the left to the YAR, perhaps with the NDF as his partner, a hope that is not realized. Also in **summer 1976**, al-Hamdi begins the re-equipment of the YAR's armed forces through a triangular deal in which Saudi Arabia pays for light arms from the United States at the same time that negotiations for F-5E fighters, tanks, and other heavy equipment proceed. In **March 1977**, President al-Hamdi, seeking stature and leverage in his dealings with a demanding Saudi Arabia, hosts the Taiz Summit on Red Sea security, bringing together the heads of state of Somalia, Sudan, and the two Yemens in discussions that, given the absence of Ethiopia and the drift toward war between Ethiopia and Somalia in the Ogadan, were to lead nowhere. On **11 October 1977**, President al-Hamdi and his brother are assassinated and Col. Ahmad al-Ghashmi succeeds him in an atmosphere charged with recrimination and lamentation over the popular leader's demise.

1978–1979   Al-Ghashmi restores most of the 1970 Constitution but creates the appointed People's Constituent Assembly (PCA) in place of the suspended Consultative Council and re-creates the singular presidency of the al-Sallal era—and is promptly chosen to fill that new post. But in **June 1978**, President al-Ghashmi is assassinated in Sanaa by an agent of one of the two fiercely competing factions in the PDRY regime. In **July**, Lt. Col. Ali Abdullah Salih succeeds him as president amid worsening relations between the two Yemens and predictions of deteriorating domestic political and economic conditions in the YAR. Over **June–July**, the ongoing intraparty struggle in the PDRY leads to armed clashes and, only one day after Ghashmi's assassination, climaxes in the execution of Salim Rubay Ali in Aden, thereby allowing his co-ruler, Abd al-Fattah Ismail, to purge the regime and consolidate power in his hands. In **October**, the ruling coalition of parties in the PDRY, the UPONF, is transformed into the Yemeni Socialist Party (YSP), in line with Ismail's conception of a vanguard party and correct socialist evolution. In **October**, a coup attempt by pro-Hamdi "Nasirites" against President Salih fails—but just barely. In **February-March 1979**, the YAR and the PDRY, assisted by the NDF, fight a short border war that ends with a cease-fire, a reaffirmation of the goal of Yemeni unification, and a new schedule for the unification process. The United States increases and greatly accelerates its military assistance to the YAR in the **spring**, citing as the reasons the alleged Soviet-supported aggression of the PDRY against the YAR and the threat this posed to an ally, Saudi Arabia. Then, in **September**, President Salih turns successfully to the Soviet Union for a major new supply of arms, a move prompted by dissatisfaction with both the amount of U.S. arms and the extent to which Saudi Arabia was able to control the flow of this Saudi-funded U.S. aid. In **October**, the PDRY signs a 20-year Treaty of Friendship and Cooperation with the USSR and then signs similar ones with East Germany and Marxist Ethiopia.

1980–1981 The NDF gives up on efforts to cut a deal with the Salih regime and again escalates its simmering dissidence into open rebellion—and with the full backing of the PDRY. In **April**, Ali Nasir Muhammad al-Hasani, longtime PDRY prime minister, assumes the highest party and state offices on the occasion of Abd al-Fattah Ismail's "medical" exile to Moscow. President Salih receives the draft of a National Pact in **mid-1980**, providing the basis for both a national dialogue on the nature of the Yemeni polity and for the holding of a General People's Congress (GPC) to endorse the National Pact and plan its implementation. This dialogue based on the pact, orchestrated by the National Dialogue Committee, takes place over the next 18 months. The Tripartite Agreement is signed by the PDRY, Ethiopia, and Libya in **August 1981**, a move interpreted by some as an effort by the PDRY to bring about a radical regroupment in the region. In **October**, President Salih welcomes ex-presidents al-Sallal and al-Iryani upon their return home for the first time since they were deposed, the occasion being the anniversary of the 1962 Revolution. In **December**, President Salih visits Aden—the first time ever for a YAR head of state—and positive discussions with Chairman Ali Nasir Muhammad lead to creation of the Supreme Yemeni Council and renewed talk of Yemeni unification—but no sure end to the NDF rebellion against the YAR.

1982–1985 In **April**, heavy flooding in South Yemen places new burdens on a regime already in difficult economic circumstances. In the **spring**, YAR forces defeat NDF forces in battle, and the Salih regime invites NDF members to return and assume a role in the political life of the nation, an invitation accepted by many. A summit meeting between President Salih and Chairman Ali Nasir Muhammad in **May** marks the end of the long PDRY-supported NDF rebellion and the beginning of improved relations and cooperation between the two Yemens. In the **summer**, on the occasion of the Israeli invasion of Lebanon, the two Yemens undertake a major joint initiative to find a unified Arab approach to aiding the embattled PLO and to providing havens for PLO forces evacuating from Beirut. Also in the **summer**, through Kuwaiti mediation, the PDRY and Oman reach and sign an agreement on principles, a major step in normalizing relations that had hit bottom in the 1970s with Aden's support of the Dhufar rebellion. Again, in the **summer**, nationwide elections to the General People's Congress are held, and then the GPC convenes, adopts the National Pact, declares itself a permanent body that will meet biennially and be elected every four years, and elects a 75-member Standing Committee headed by President Salih to act on its behalf between biennial meetings. A severe earthquake in the YAR's Dhamar province in **December 1982** causes great loss of life and property, strains the capacity of the regime for relief and reconstruction, and rallies the nation around this natural disaster. **August 1984**, the YAR announces both the discovery of oil by the Hunt Oil Company in the Marib region and preliminary plans for its rapid commercial development. In **1985**, indicative of their increasingly good working relationship, the heads of state of the two Yemens meet in Taiz and defuse a tense armed standoff in the disputed border area between the Marib region where the YAR recently discovered oil and the Shabwa region where the PDRY was searching for the same. In 1983–1984, relations between the two Yemens improve greatly, one measure being the positive results of the semiannual meetings of the new Supreme Yemeni Council.

1986–1987 On **13 January**, the intraparty struggle in the PDRY, worsening over the past couple of years, erupts in a bloodbath that results in the virtual decapitation of the YSP, the exile of Ali Nasir Muhammad and his surviving colleagues, and the emergence of a new, second-tier leadership headed by Ali Salim al-Baydh. **In early 1986**, the YAR refuses to embrace either the new leaders in Aden or their call for a renewal of the stalled Yemeni unification process. The failure of the winners in the PDRY to reconcile with the losers, and thereby to open the way to easing the refugee burden on the YAR, places severe new strains on relations between the two Yemens. The PDRY announces in **1986** that Technoexport of the Soviet Union has discovered oil in commercial quantities in Block 4 in the Shabwa region and that oil would be trucked to Aden Refinery until a pipeline to the coast is completed. In **June 1987**, a special YSP conference is only partially successful in an effort to come to terms with the leadership crisis that culminated in the previous year's bloodbath, settling for a condemnation of both "left" and "right" extremism. The YAR celebrates in **September** its silver jubilee with oil about to flow from Marib down to the new Red Sea terminus at Ras Isa, with President Salih in his 10th year in office. In **November**, the PDRY, experiencing grave economic difficulties and continuing political isolation, celebrates the 20th anniversary of independence from Britain. In **December**, the export of oil from Ras Isa begins just months after completion of the pipeline over the mountains from Marib.

1988 In **May**, the two Yemens end a new period of tension along their undemarcated border with a summit meeting at which they agree to open their border, to neutralize and jointly search for oil in the disputed borderlands, and to revive the unification process through the Supreme Yemeni Council. Less publicized, progress was apparently also made on leadership reconciliation in the PDRY and on the easing of the refugee problem across the border in the YAR. In **July**, the YAR's 1970 Constitution, reinstated only in part by al-Ghashmi in 1978, is virtually restored in full with national elections for a new Consultative Council that, in turn, elects President Salih to a third five-year term and votes approval of the new government and its program. This marks the first time since 1974 that the head of state and government were chosen in accordance with the constitution.

1989 Early in the year, the overstretched Soviet Union informs the PDRY that it is no longer able to provide the kind and degree of political and economic support that it had provided over the past 20 years, thereby increasing the PDRY's isolation and dimming further its short-term prospects. In mid-year, the moderates in the YSP decisively prevail over the militant left in another round of program review and self-criticism. The joint YAR–PDRY committee for a unified political organization meets in late **October** for the first time since it was authorized in 1972, and its proposals lead to a flurry of visits, talks, and statements about imminent Yemeni unification. On **30 November**, President Salih and Chairman al-Baydh hold a summit in Aden, and the two Yemens, according to the 30 November Agreement, decide to unite and specify the steps through which a unified Republic of Yemen (ROY) could be declared by November 1990.

1990 In **April**, the leaders of the two Yemens decide to advance the unification date to mid-May 1990, follow this with a 30-month transition period, and defer parliamentary elections for unified Yemen until the end of the transition in late 1992. They also accept the recommendation of the joint committee for a unified political organization so that a unified Yemen can embrace political pluralism and multiparty politics. On **22 May**, after the new constitution is ratified by the legislatures of the two Yemens on the previous day, the ROY with its capital in Sanaa is proclaimed, the constitution is declared in force, the two governments and legislatures are merged, and Ali Abdullah Salih and Ali Salim al-Baydh are declared president and vice president, respectively, to hold office for the 30-month transition period before new legislative elections. The ROY makes its debut at the Arab summit in Baghdad later that month. On **2 August**, Iraq suddenly invades and occupies Kuwait, precipitating the First Gulf Crisis and the U.S.-led international coalition to get Iraq out of Kuwait. Later that month, the ROY states its case for an "Arab" diplo-political solution to the crisis that would involve withdrawal of both Iraq from Kuwait and "foreign forces" from the Arabian Peninsula, thereby placing it increasingly at odds with the United States, Saudi Arabia and others. In **September**, Saudi Arabia, in response to this stand, forces hundreds of thousands of Yemeni workers and merchants to leave—which quickly and massively causes remittances to fall and unemployment to rise. At about this time, Shaykh Abdullah ibn Husayn al-Ahmar, the tribal leader, announces the creation of the Islah (the Reform Grouping) party; he asserts that the new ROY constitution is insufficiently Islamic and criticizes the regime for siding with Iraq. In **late November**, very visible as a UN Security Council member, the ROY votes against the U.S.-sponsored resolution authorizing the use of force to eject Iraq from Kuwait. In **December**, the United States threatens to cut aid to the ROY and withdraws all non-essential personnel. Also in December, Canadian Occidental Petroleum (CanOxy, but soon to be Nexen) makes a major oil strike in the Masila region of the Hadhramawt and announces plans for a pipeline down to Mukalla.

1991 In **mid-January**, Operation Desert Storm is launched against Iraq, and the ROY expresses concern for the Iraqi people and reiterates its commitment to an Arab diplo-political solution. At about this time, and paralleling the cutoff of far larger amounts of aid from Saudi Arabia and the Gulf states, the United States slashes aid to the ROY for 1990–1991 from $20.5 million to $2.9 million, calling aid into question for 1991–1992. In **May**, a nationwide plebiscite in the ROY endorses the new constitution by a large margin, but the turnout is low, partly because of a call for a boycott by Islah and other Islamic and conservative opponents. On **22 May**, the first anniversary of Yemeni unification, Aden, the designated economic capital, is declared a free zone. During the year, despite the turmoil, several oil companies driven by increased interest in Yemen, sign new exploration and production-sharing agreements that contain good terms and fat signing bonuses for the ROY. Included are agreements covering the "neutral zone" created in 1988 and the reassigned Block 4 in Shabwa, which is now connected to Bir Ali by a newly completed pipeline.

1992   The old border dispute with Oman is settled in **early 1992**, opening the door to good relations between them and providing a possible model for Saudi–Yemeni relations. Also in **early 1992**, what remains of the ROY's domestic political honeymoon is in tatters. The economic crisis caused by the loss of remittances, massive unemployment, and the cutoff of external aid increasingly triggers strikes and protests. At the same time, politics is marked more and more by conflict between the two ruling parties and between them and the other parties—and by a spate of bombings and assassination attempts aimed mostly at YSP figures. In the **summer**, Vice President al-Baydh goes to Aden, beginning a several-month-long boycott of the regime of which he is a part. Also in the **summer**, the ROY and Saudi Arabia hold the first of a series of inconclusive talks on their decades-old border dispute, this a few months after the Saudis issue warnings to several oil companies against operating in Saudi-claimed border areas under concessions from the ROY. Breaking rank with its long-time ally, the United States objects publicly to the Saudis' harsh approach. In **November**, amid opposition cries of foul play, the ruling parties announce they will extend the transition period and agree to hold the ROY's first parliamentary elections on 27 April 1993. In **December**, serious rioting throughout the country and a fatal bombing in Aden lead the GPC and YSP to put aside their differences, close ranks against the opposition, and renew efforts to cooperate in the government and in the coming elections. In **late December**, targeting U.S. military personnel, Yemen Islamic Jihad bombs Aden's *Goldmur Hotel* and fails in an attempt to bomb the bigger Aden Hotel.

1993 In **January 1993**, the ROY blames the hotel bombing in Aden on the Yemeni Islamic Jihad (YIJ). Its leader, Tarik al-Fadhli, an "Afghani Arab" and member of a former ruling family in old South Yemen, is besieged, arrested, "escapes," and soon aligns himself with President Salih; some members of the YIJ who are not co-opted then form the Aden–Abyan Islamic Army. In **March**, the two ruling parties in the ROY agree to merge but defer implementation until after the elections. On **27 April**, after a month's campaigning, the relatively open, fair elections yield results in which the GPC, the big winner, wins about 40 percent of the seats and the YSP and Islah each win about 20 percent, with a few seats going to minor parties and independents. In **mid-May**, the new parliament meets and elects Shaykh al-Ahmar, Islah leader, its speaker. On **22 May**, the ROY celebrates its third anniversary amid hope for the future and concern over delays in forming a post-election, post-transition government. In **late May**, the GPC, YSP, and Islah do form a tripartite coalition government in which the GPC has just over half of the positions and the YSP has more than half of the remaining positions. The ROY launches a major campaign in **June** to restore good relations with the Gulf states, a campaign that especially bears fruit with the UAE and Qatar as well as Oman. In **August**, the fifth round of Yemeni–Saudi border talks is amicable, but the Saudis again warn Western oil companies about operating in disputed border territory. Also by **August**, and casting new doubt on the ability of YSP and GPC to work together, the YSP issues an 18-point reform program and Vice President al-Baydh again goes "home" to Aden and resumes his boycott. In **early fall**, Total of France announces that its oil find in the "neutral zone" in East Shabwa is of commercial quantity and that it plans to connect its field with the pipeline CanOxy has built down to the coast. At its Masila field, CanOxy goes into full production, aiming near term at 120,000 barrels per day (b/d) that would bring total ROY production to more than 300,000 b/d. In **October**, President Salih hosts a visit of Oman's Sultan Qaboos, and the two reaffirm plans for a road link and several other projects. In **November**, the ROY picks the United States' Enron Corp. as partner in developing large natural gas reserves that could cost $5.5 billion and produce 5.5 million tons of liquefied natural gas (LNG)/year, but this action is disputed by the consortium headed by Hunt Oil. Delayed by bitter wrangling, the re-election of President Salih and Vice President al-Baydh finally takes place in **October**, but al-Baydh boycotts the swearing-in ceremonies; he repeats reform demands and claims that 150 YSP members have been assassinated since May 1990. Yemeni leaders and institutions as well as several foreign leaders attempt without success over the next two months to end the political strife between Salih (and the GPC) and al-Baydh (and the YSP). The crisis renders the regime unable to deal with Yemen's growing problems. Whispers of possible violence and an end to unification mix with YSP statements that the north has reaped the lion's share of the power and benefits, that unification has become annexation, and that the GPC and Islah seek to marginalize the YSP. In **November**, ROY's armed forces, still consisting of completely separate northern and southern units, pledge neutrality in the ongoing political crisis amid rumors of troop movements, re-supplying of the forces, and of unauthorized checkpoints. In **December,** the YSP floats the idea of federation as an alternative to the current unitary system for Yemen, and the GPC charges that the YSP really seeks secession and a mini oil-state. The Political Forces Dialogue Committee, with members from parties in the government and in the opposition, is formed to find a solution to the crisis.

1994   The crisis deepens, and on **9 January** Al-Baydh refuses to come north for a meeting with President Salih sponsored by Yemen's religious leaders, citing continuing political violence. Through the efforts of many, Salih and al-Baydh meet on **20 February** for the first time in months, in Amman and under King Husayn' auspices; there they sign the Document of Pledge and Accord, a set of reforms hammered out and agreed to by all sides on the Dialogue Committee. The next day, rather than return to Sanaa with Salih, al-Baydh and his colleagues begin visits to Saudi Arabia, Kuwait, and other Arab states, on the same day that a serious clash occurs between northern and southern army units in Abyan. In **late February**, efforts are made to defuse the tense military situation by a joint military commission from the two Yemens, Jordan, Oman, France, and the United States, even as Jordan and Oman continue efforts to broker a political settlement. In **early April**, in Oman, under Sultan Qaboos' auspices, another meeting between Salih and al-Baydh occurs but fails to bring accord. Northern and southern army units start a bloody four-day battle in Amran on **27 April**, the first anniversary of the legislative elections. On **4 May**, continuous, widespread fighting erupts in both parts of Yemen, marking the onset of the War of Secession and rendering moot new efforts by Egypt and the UAE. In **mid-May**, northern forces gain upper hand, push south toward Aden, and attempt to cut Aden off from Abyan, Shabwa, and the Hadhramawt. On **21 May**, on the day before the ROY's fourth anniversary, al-Baydh proclaims secession and the creation of the Democratic Republic of Yemen (DRY). Although no state grants recognition, Egypt, Saudi Arabia, and all the other Arabian Peninsula states but Qatar lean toward the DRY. Salih then declares that union will prevail and that al-Baydh and 15 others will be tried as traitors. In **late May**, fighting in the south continues sporadically and inconclusively. On **1 June**, the UN Security Council passes a resolution calling for an immediate cease-fire and a fact-finding mission to Yemen. The ROY, fearing that a ceasefire and disengagement of troops would mean *de facto* partition, stalls. In **mid-late June**, UN fact-finders visit Yemen, several cease-fire attempts fail, the north makes gains on the ground and siege of Aden tightens—and casualties mount. On **7 July**, Mukalla and then Aden fall to northern unionist forces and southern leaders flee Yemen, marking the end of both the War of Secession and the DRY. The Salih regime makes concerted efforts in **July–September** to get economics and politics (external as well as domestic) back to "normal," most notably by granting amnesty to all but the 16 top leaders of the secession. In **early October**, a constitutional amendment abolishes the multiple executive, President Salih is elected to a new term by the legislature, and a new coalition government consisting of the GPC and Islah—but not the YSP—is formed. In **September**, attention returns to the old border dispute between Yemen and Saudi Arabia, the creation of the National Front for the Liberation of Najran and Asir is announced, and, over the next few months, clashes between Saudi and Yemeni forces occur.

1995 In **late January**, after reports of fighting on the border, President Salih says for the first time that Yemen is prepared to accept all provisions of the Taif Treaty of 1934. In **early 1995**, the "south" gains representation in the government by the appointment of four cabinet members in addition to Vice President Abed Rabbo Mansour Hadi, but all are members of the Ali Nasir Muhammad faction of the YSP and now members of the GPC. In **early February**, a loose confederation of 13 opposition parties is formed to oppose the reconstituted government and adopts the Document of Pledge and Accord as its platform. In June, after the GPC's first General Congress since 1988, the deputy prime minister for foreign affairs, Abd al-Karim al-Iryani, is appointed secretary general of the GPC and charged with readying the party for the 1997 elections. In **late 1995**, the ROY and the International Monetary Fund (IMF) and the World Bank negotiate and sign a complex, multi-year package of stabilization measures and structural reforms in which the ROY can expect aid from those international organizations and others in exchange for its step-by-step implementation of the package. These almost draconian measures seemed required by the economy's collapse and GDP being halved, results of the costs of both unification and the War of Secession and, above all, the loss of the remittances upon which Yemen had become so dependent. In **mid-November**, a car-bombing in Riyadh that kills five American military trainers alert the Saudis and the United States to the terrorist threat—and to the danger of the porous border with Yemen and the vast area of Yemen beyond state control. In **December**, a dispute with newly independent Eritrea unexpectedly erupts into fighting when Eritrea occupies the largest of the Hanish Islands. After a tense stalemate of some months, the conflict de-escalates and the two sides seek a settlement.

1996 In **early 1996**, the ROY begins implementing the IMF/World Bank stabilization and structural reform package and signs an aid agreement with the Kuwait-based Arab Fund for Economic and Social Development, the latter an indication of some success in campaign to improve relations with, and get aid from, the GCC states. In **early April**, other major economic steps are taken: a donors' conference in The Hague secures major funding, the IMF agrees to a stand-by credit facility, indications point to an easing and rescheduling of debt by the Paris Club, and further steps are taken to realize the ROY's flagship development project, the Aden container port and free zone. In **early May**, the ROY and Eritrea agree to a French-initiated plan for settlement by arbitration of the conflict over the Hanish Islands, and the dispute is defused. Also in **May**, rioting in towns in the Hadhramawt over the raping of two women in Mukalla by policemen is indicative of the continuing—and perhaps growing—southern resentment against northern "occupation" that continues over the coming months of the year. In the **last quarter of 1996**, politics heat up as focus turns to the upcoming April 1997 parliamentary elections, with efforts at coalition-building and positioning and disputes over provincial boundaries, election supervision, registration, and monitoring. In **late June**, another more serious bombing of a U.S. facility in Saudi Arabia—this time at the Khubar Towers, which houses U.S. military personnel in Dhahran—kills 19 Americans and further raises concerns about terrorism and conditions in Yemen. In **late 1996**, the ROY officially applies for membership in the GCC. In **December**, the kidnapping of foreign workers and tourists continues with the taking of three Dutch, and later five Polish, tourists hostage.

1997 In **February**, the GCC informs the ROY that its application for membership was rejected. At this time, relations with the Saudis are running hot and cold; those with Oman improve markedly. In **April**, the still-reeling YSP boycotts the parliamentary elections and Islah does well, but the GPC wins a commanding majority. The GPC chooses to form a new government on its own, thus making Islah the major opposition party both in and outside the parliament. In **May**, President Salih appoints the 59 members of the Shura Council, the new second chamber that will add to his style of ruling through co-optation. In **late June**, the increase in oil production at CanOxy's Masila block in recent years is underlined by a one-day high of 210,000 b/d. In **late June/early July**, already strained relations with Saudi Arabia are worsened by border clashes. In **August**, opposition figures are arrested across the south, and in **late October**, eight bombs go off in Aden. Also in **October**, farmers with the backing of local tribal chiefs blockade roads at strategic locations in the north to protest a rise in diesel fuel prices. On **31 October**, the faltering and politically challenged economic reform program does get a boost with the announcement of a new IMF facility and its promise of social "safety net" funding. In the **last quarter of 1997** there occur a number of tribally related kidnappings in the north, a number of bombings in and around Aden, and numerous arrests by the government in Sanaa, Aden, and the Hadhramawt. In **late November**, one of those arrested, a Syrian with Spanish citizenship, confesses to having been recruited by Saudi intelligence to recruit and train "Afghani Arabs" to destabilize the country and to assassinate Foreign Minister al-Iryani. In **early December**, after further clashes between Saudi and Yemeni forces on the border, the ROY threatens to submit their border dispute to arbitration, an option it claims is provided for in the 1934 Taif Treaty.

1998 On **March 23**, a Sanaa court sentences in *absentia* the 15 secession leaders in exile; five of them, including V.P. Ali Salim al-Baydh and P.M. Haydar Abu Bakr al-Attas, are sentenced to death. In **late March**, Total of France says that the global economic downturn in Asia has made it hard to find the needed long-term customers for Yemen's LNG project and that, consequently, the start of construction will be delayed from 1999 until 2001. Despite fits and starts in 1997, the vital Aden container port and free zone gets a boost with the Port of Singapore Authority (PSA) taking over operations and a 49 percent stake in the enterprise. In **late April**, a demonstration against the sentencing of the 15 southern leaders takes place and, in **mid-May**, a new group issues a communiqué calling for southern independence. In **early May**, despite the lack of progress on border talks, the Saudis issues over 36,000 work visas for Yemenis. Also in **May**, after the short, stormy tenure of technocrat Faraj bin Ghanim, longtime foreign minister Abd al-Karim al-Iryani takes over as prime minister and is charged with carrying out the third phase of the economic reform package. The task is complicated by the fact that, although oil production in 1998 continued the upward trend of past years, the price of Brent crude continued to be below \$12/b. On **June 18**, the new government adheres to the reform package and lifts key subsidies, leading to large protests throughout the north and the deaths of dozens of protesters as well as military and security personnel. The government blames the political opposition and even Saudi Arabia for fostering the demonstrations. To make matters worse, from **early June** through **mid-July**, low-level violence, including bombings and armed clashes, occurs in the south in Aden and its environs. On **1 August**, amid ongoing tensions and rising frustration, President Salih says that Yemen would favor outside arbitration as called for in the 1934 Taif Treaty if a border agreement cannot be reached bilaterally. In **early August**, suicide bombers allegedly tied to al-Qaida strike the U.S. embassies in Kenya and Tanzania with great force and effect, emphasizing the threat of terrorism to the United States. The ROY and Eritrea accept the arbitration panel's ruling, which awards the bulk of the Hanish Islands to Yemen, and in **early October**, Eritrea yields control of the largest of the islands to Yemen. In **late November**, under the leadership of Ali Salih Ubad, the YSP holds its first party congress since the mid-1980s. In **late December**, as a result of a bizarre string of events involving the earlier arrest of relatives of the London-based Islamic cleric, Abu Hamza al-Masri, hostage-taking in the south by the Aden–Abyan Islamic Army (AAIA) results in the death of four tourists. The hostage-takers are captured, and the head of the AAIA is quickly tried and executed.

1999   In **January**, as President Salih denies that the ROY will permit the United States a military presence on Socotra Island, a U.S. military vessel refuels in Aden under a new agreement between the United States and the ROY. In **mid-May**, marking the restoration of relations with Kuwait, the ROY foreign minister re-opens the long-closed embassy in Kuwait. In **mid-year**, kidnapping by the tribes continues in the north, as do bombings and protest in the south. Also in **mid-year**, the Salih regime, promoting itself, hosts the Emerging Democracy Conference in Sanaa. In **late July**, the GPC-dominated parliament denies the YSP candidate the right to run in Yemen's first direct presidential election. In **September**, with Islah's endorsement, President Salih runs virtually unopposed and wins big in an election that many regard as a sham.

2000   In **late January**, the long-delayed local authorities law is passed, providing for elected assemblies at the district and governorate levels and for the appointment by the president of executives at both levels. In **early March**, the Polish ambassador is kidnapped by tribesmen, a reminder that more than 100 foreigners have been taken hostage over the past several years, mostly in the north; low-level political violence has been nearly as persistent, although mostly in the south. In **early 2000**, President Salih's eldest son, Ahmad, is appointed head of the Republican Guard. (This, added to his appointment months earlier as first head of the Special Forces and his election to parliament in 1977, raises questions of his being groomed to succeed his father, and of growing nepotism in Yemen in general.) In **mid-May**, the autonomy and power of the Central Bank of Yemen is increased, possibly making it less a mere extension of President Salih's power. In **late May**, President Salih cancels the plan to permit Israelis of Yemeni descent to visit Yemen, a plan adopted early in the year and at the height of the revived Arab–Israeli peace process. In **June**, and quite unexpectedly, the Saudi–Yemeni Border Agreement is signed, removing a major source of serious and often lethal conflict over two generations; although some nationalists and members of the opposition raise objections, most Yemenis accept it and hope it will yield benefits. In **July**, in a response to growing demands to fight corruption, President Salih announces a plan to create a special anti-corruption agency and has the cabinet raise the pay of corruption-vulnerable military personnel and civil servants. On **12 October**, in Aden harbor, suicide bombers blow a hole in the side of the U.S.S. *Cole*, killing 17 U.S. sailors, and al-Qaida claims credit; the next day, a blast targets the British embassy in Sanaa, but there are no casualties. Although an aggressive, insensitive investigation of the *Cole* bombing by the Federal Bureau of Investigation strains relations with Yemeni authorities, security cooperation between the United States and the ROY increase by year's end. Indeed, the United States rewards ROY with the renewal of economic aid frozen in Gulf crisis in 1990–1991. In **late November**, parliament approves constitutional amendments favored by President Salih that would, among other things, extend the terms of parliament and the presidency to six and seven years, respectively, and increase the size of the presidentially appointed Shura Council from 59 to 111 members. In **mid-December**, Saudi Arabia and Yemen hold a meeting of their joint cooperation council for the first time in more than a decade. In **late December**, President Salih announces that the first local elections and the referendum on the constitutional amendments will be held together on 20 February. Subsequently, the Supreme Opposition Council (SOC), the loose coalition of opposition parties, says that it will vote "no" on the referenda and that it will participate in the local council election in an effort to lessen the number of seats won by the GPC and Islah.

2001   In **early January**, the new year is greeted by tribal kidnappings and an explosion in Aden. In **February**, a national referendum approves amendments that extend the president's and the parliament's terms to seven and six years, respectively, also doubling the size of the presidentially appointed Shura Council to 111 and allowing it to vote with the elected parliament on issues chosen by the president. While this enhances executive power at the expense of that of the legislature, in the local elections held simultaneously, the opposition parties, especially Islah, do surprisingly well. Opposing the GPC on the local level, where it has some grassroots support, Islah begins to act like an opposition party. Also in **February**, after a hiatus of 18 months, the IMF conditionally resumes lending to the ROY. In **early 2001**, the budget for the year projects revenues based on the price of crude oil rising to $22 per barrel, this reflecting the recovery and sharp rise in oil prices over the past few years. (The price projected in the budget for 2000 was only $17 per barrel.) In **March**, after a popular pushback against the earlier lifting of subsidies called for in the IMF/WB structural reform package, Abd al-Qadr Bajammal forms a new government and is charged by President Salih with somehow reinvigorating the reform effort. Indeed, agreement is reached with the IMF to extend lending to the ROY in exchange for a renewed commitment to reforms. In response to the events of **11 September**—forever dubbed 9/11—the United States launches its attack on al-Qaida and Taliban in Afghanistan. In **October**, amid speculation that Yemen might be next, the U.S. ambassador reassures Yemen that it is "a partner and not a target." In **late November**, President Salih goes to Washington, D.C., and pledges Yemen's support of the just-declared "War on Terror." In **mid-December** in an attempt to follow through, near Marib, nearly 20 soldiers are killed by tribal fighters in a failed effort to capture or kill a reputed top al-Qaida leader involved in the *Cole* bombing, Qaed Salim al-Harithi. At about the same time, a group of ex-ministers and intellectuals create a forum to defend the rights of citizens of the former PDRY and the grievances of southerners become the source of some tension between the president and Vice President Abdel Rabbu Mansour Hadi. In **late December**, the ROY is admitted to four of the non-political institutions of the GCC, and it is said that all six members now favor full membership for the ROY—eventually.

2002 In **early 2002**, security cooperation between the United States and the ROY becomes more apparent, although failure to capture al-Harithi and another key al-Qaida suspect, Muhammad Hamdi al-Ahdal, raise questions about the ability of the ROY to deliver. In

April, three bombings occur in Sanaa by a group calling itself "al-Qaida Sympathizers," accompanied by large demonstrations protesting ties with the United States and its support of Israel. In mid-**May**, Prime Minister Bajammal declares that al-Qaida and its sympathizers are now not present in Yemen but, in **June**, bombings and protests against the United States continue. In **early August**, the National Security Organization (NSO), a new agency, is rolled out. On **October 6**, the French-flagged supertanker *Limburg* is rammed offshore near Mukalla by a small explosives-laden boat, returning the terrorist threat to Yemen. Almost immediately, maritime insurance rates for the region around Aden soared, compromising efforts to restore Aden as a major hub for transit trade and manufacture. Also in **October**, the heads of state of the ROY, Sudan, and Ethiopia meet in Sanaa and address pressing Horn of Africa issues in general and concerns about Eritrea in particular. In **mid-October**, a donors' conference in Paris, led by the World Bank, provides Yemen with a package worth $2.3 billion, an amount that is more than one-fourth of Yemen's current GDP and more than all aid to Yemen since 1990. At about the same time, however, the IMF indicated the likelihood that it would take a tough line on the ROY's failure to meet the schedule set out in its poverty reduction strategy. Also in **mid-October**, with full membership clearly a long way off, the ROY signs an agreement giving it associate status in GCC organizations associated with education, information, labor, health, youth, and sports. In **early November**, in the desert near Marib, a missile from a drone controlled by the Central Intelligence Agency from its base in Djibouti kills al-Harithi, the al-Qaida leader involved in the *Cole* bombing. This breach of Yemeni sovereignty strained the Salih regime's relations with both the United States and many Yemeni domestic political players. Also in **November**, several parties that have been working together in opposition to the GPC and the Salih regime form an opposition coalition, the Joint Meeting Parties (JMP); the JMP evolves to include Islah and the YSP, the two leading parties, and the Nasirites and two small Zaydi parties. On **28 December**, the chief architect of the JMP and a top YSP leader, Jarallah Omar, is assassinated by an Islamic militant after speaking at an Islah conference. Two days later, an alleged associate of Jarallah's killer kills three American hospital workers in Jibla.

2003 In **early January**, a well-known imam from a mosque in Sanaa and a figure in Islah, Shaykh Ali Hassan al-Moayyad, is caught in a sting operation in Frankfurt, Germany, by U.S. anti-terrorist forces; the ROY protests the action and demands his release. In **February and March**, many officially sanctioned anti-war demonstrations occur on the eve of the U.S. invasion of Iraq, revealing much antipathy toward the United States. In **April**, the 10 main suspects in the *Cole* bombing escape from an Aden jail; collusion is suspected. (The United States had requested their extradition.) Also in **April**, and on the eve of parliamentary elections, opposition parties demand abrogation of painful and, according to them, counterproductive IMF/World Bank reforms. In the elections on **27 April**, amid charges of fraud, the GPC wins overwhelmingly, Islah holds its own, and the YSP makes a very modest comeback. The GPC chooses to form a government by itself, pushing Islah more decidedly into the opposition coalition with the YSP. In **early May**, the new cabinet headed by Bajammal includes a woman, Amat al-Alim al-Suswa, as minister of the newly created Ministry of Human Rights. In **early June**, the ROY and Saudi Arabia sign a pact designed to coordinate border control, and, a month later, Crown Prince Abdullah visits Yemen; still, Saudi Arabia remains reluctant to allow Yemeni workers to enter the kingdom easily or in significant numbers. In **late June**, extensive fighting in Abyan region involving government forces marks the reemergence of the Aden–Abyan Islamic Army. About this time, in a conciliatory gesture to the old YSP, President Salih appoints Salim Salih Muhammad his special adviser and grants amnesty to the 16 YSP leaders previously convicted of treason. In **midyear**, riots break out over cuts in subsidies on oil products adopted as part of an effort to reduce the burden on the budget and to revive the IMF-backed reforms that have been on the back burner for more than a year. In **mid-July**, Germany approves extradition of Shaykh al-Moayyad to the United States, further heightening Yemeni protest against the entire action. In **August**, it is reported that 34 persons arrested as Islamic militants have been released after they went through the "dialogue process" conducted by the Dialogue Committee and its leader, Qadi Hamoud al-Hitar, and designed to "re-educate" militants in true Islam; the United States expresses skepticism and alarm regarding this approach. In September, the issue of corruption comes to the forefront as the World Bank representative in Sanaa pointedly addresses the issue and Yemen is ranked for the first time, and poorly, on Transparency International's "Corruption Perception Index." In **November**, Shaykh al-Moayyad is extradited to the United States, where he is subsequently charged with raising funds and otherwise aiding "terrorist" activities of al-Qaida and Hamas, thereby further staining U.S.–Yemeni relations. In **late November**, the government arrests Muhammad al-Ahdal, the reputed successor to al-Harithi as head of al-Qaida in Yemen. In **December**, over the objections of Eritrea, the series of meetings among the ROY, Ethiopia, and Sudan leads to the creation of the Sanaa Forum for Cooperation with its focus on Horn of Africa issues.

2004 In **early 2004**, the U.S. Treasury's placing Shaykh Abd al-Majid al-Zindani on the list of those supporting terrorism puts a strain on U.S.–Yemeni relations, and this at a time when Yemenis were already angered by U.S. treatment of Shaykh al-Moayyad. In **February**, the ROY's improving relations with Saudi Arabia are strained over border security issues, reflecting the Saudis' heightened concerns after bomb-ings in Riyadh in May 2003. Also in **February**, the government's approval of a further lifting of the diesel subsidy, on top of earlier parliamentary approval of a general sales tax, signals again the desire to reinvigorate the IMF-monitored reform process. In **March**, the ROY signs a one-year contract with a Singapore group for the operation of the Aden container port. Also in **March**, Yemeni security forces catch 30 terrorism suspects, including 8 of the 10 *Cole* bombing suspects who had escaped from jail in Aden in 2003. Shortly thereafter, they catch the other 2, including Jamal al-Badawi, Yemen's most wanted fugitive, as well as 2 other al-Qaida and Islamic Jihad figures. In **April**, Prime Minister Bajammal asserts that the authorities have "managed to subdue 90 percent of al-Qaida cells in the country" and that coopera-tion with the United States on security and development matters has increased greatly in recent months. In **early May**, trials of the men accused of the *Cole* and *Limburg* bombings begin after delays and amid confusion. In **June 2004**, an armed rebellion of sayyid Zaydis led by Husayn al-Houthi erupts in the north, in Saada. (It is triggered initially by the opposition of his Believing Youth movement to the Salih regime's alleged support of the United States and Israel, beneath which lay old, deep-seated grievances of sayyid Zaydis against repub-lican Yemen.) In **late June**, spurred by the rebellion, the Salih regime begins its long-delayed plan to regulate licensed religious schools and to close unlicensed ones. In **June and July**, the government postpones both the long-delayed lifting of diesel subsidies and the introduction of the general sales tax. Shortly thereafter, a World Bank report harshly criticizes the ROY's shortcomings in planning and carrying out reforms; it also says ominously that poverty breeds terrorism. In **July**, amid an upsurge of government corruption charges and after parliament raises questions about an especially egregious case, the government agrees to freeze the sale of government shares in an oil block to two Arab-owned oil companies. (There is growing public concern over the fact that, while the rising price of oil is increasing oil revenues, oil production in the first half of 2004 was 10% lower than in the comparable period in 2003.) In **September**, after a harsh crackdown by the regime and many deaths, injuries and destruction of property—and the death of Husayn al-Houthi—the rebellion in Saada is put down and a shaky cease-fire and amnesty are achieved. Also in **September**, the sentencing of Abd al-Karim al-Khaiwani, editor of *Al-Shura*, to a year in prison focuses attention on both the growing adversarial relationship between the Salih regime and the press and the growing domestic and global criticism of the regime over free speech and press issues. (Al-Khaiwani was convicted of giving support to the al-Houthi rebellion, an indication that the regime has become very sensitive to criticism by the press for its harsh response to the "Houthis".) Again in **September**, the trials of those accused of involvement in the *Cole* and the *Limburg* violence end with some of the convicted sentenced to death. In **November**, the government releases over 100 "reformed" Islamic militants, bringing to nearly 350 the number who have completed the "dialogue process" and satisfied the Dialogue Committee in 2003 and 2004.

2005 In **mid-February**, the building of the LNG facility at Balhaf and the pipeline from the Marib gas field down to Balhaf on the coast finally moves forward with Total of France signing the 20-year LNG purchase agreement. In **early March**, bids are received for the long-term build–operate–transfer contract for the Aden Container Terminal. In **late March**, in a large reversal, the ROY cancels the extension of Hunt Oil Co.'s production sharing agreement for the old Marib field; Hunt plans to seek a reversal through arbitration. Also in **March**, mass demonstrations occur against the planned general sales tax and other reforms seen by the public as raising prices for essentials but seen by the IMF as necessary if Yemen is to prepare for a post-oil economy. In **late March**, the al-Houthi rebellion erupts again, now under the spiritual and military leadership of Husayn's father and brother, respectively. At the **end of March**, editor al-Khaiwani is pardoned, but the harassment of journalists continues, and the conflict between them and the government finds focus in the latter's desire to amend the press law. In **mid-April**, the fiercest fighting in the latest round of the rebellion ends, but skirmishes around Saada continue and even spread to Sanaa, where grenade attacks occur. In **early July**, parliament approves the development of the Yemen LNG project by a consortium headed by Total of France. Also in **early July**, the Joint Meeting Parties (JMP) proposes major political reforms, including the strengthening of the Shura Council and the abolition of the Ministry of Information. Later in **July**, President Salih says he will not run in the presidential elections in September 2006, saying it is time for a new generation of "young leaders." In the **second half of July**, riots break out in many locations after price hikes follow cuts in the subsidies for petroleum products, causing the regime to partially backtrack. By **September**, the rebels seem beaten or exhausted, and the pardoning of several hundred of them by President Salih briefly holds out the possibility of peace. In **October**, Transparency International ranks Yemen low on its Corruption Perceptions Index, this after an earlier low ranking by Freedom House on transparency and a low ranking by the Fund for Peace on its Failed State Index. In **November**, during President Salih's visit to the United States, the United States' Millennium Challenge Corporation suspends Yemen's eligibility for millions of U.S. dollars in aid because of its failure to deal with corruption and to improve regulatory quality and trade and fiscal policy. At the **end of November**, the al-Houthi rebellion erupts yet again. At about the same time, the JMP unveils the details of its economic and political reform program, calling for, among other things, severely curtailed presidential power. Then, in **December**, at its annual conference, the GPC adopts its reform program for the 2006 presidential elections, selects President Salih as GPC chairman, and replaces Dr. al-Iryani as GPC secretary general with Prime Minister Bajammal. (The appointment of Salih as chairman suggests to many that he will run again for president, and the appointment of Bajammal as secretary general suggests that this now unpopular prime minister will be removed from this post.) Also in **December**, the World Bank reiterates its decision to reduce aid to the ROY because of its dissatisfaction with Yemen's implementation of reforms, its lack of transparency, and its high level of corruption. In **late 2005**, a number of kidnappings of tourists in Marib and Shabwa further harms Yemen's image as a tourist destination.

2006   By **early 2006**, reform of the regime-controlled Supreme Commission for Elections and Referenda (SCER) has become a primary concern of the JMP in light of the upcoming presidential elections. (It was a part of the JMP's Agenda for Reform in November 2005.) In **January** and **February**, clashes continue in Saada province, this despite the pardon of most prisoners in September 2005. On another front in **February**, 25 hard-line Islamic militants stage a dramatic escape from a top security prison in Sanaa, probably with inside help. (Some of the escapees had been convicted of the *Cole* and *Limburg* bombings and, of these, some were involved in a jailbreak in Aden in 2003, among them Jamal al-Badawi. Another, Jabr al-Banna, was a U.S. citizen close to the "Lackawanna Six" and wanted by the United States for supporting a "terrorist organization.") This and other events over the next few months cause President George H. Bush to write to President Salih and complain that his handling of leading terrorists "casts doubt on [his] commitment to the war on terrorism." In **March**, Qatar brokers a ceasefire with the "houthis," and prisoners are released and promises of compensation and reconstruction aid are made. Still, in **April**, tensions remain high, accusations fly, violent incidents occur and the conflict broadens as other dissident and disaffected groups in Yemen come to support the "houthis." On the other side, the regime has recruited militant Salafi or Wahhabi Sunnis to fight the Shii "houthis." By this time, moreover, the ideology of the struggle has evolved from protest against the Salih regime into a challenge to the legitimacy of the 1962 Revolution and Republicanism itself—indeed, the al-Houthi fringe is calling for restoration of a sayyid Zaydi imamate. Internationally, the Salih regime charged the Libyans and the Iranians with supporting the rebellion, and Iraq's Grand Ayatollah Ali al-Sistani condemns the conflict as a Sunni "jihad" against Yemen's Shii. On another front, the ROY in **mid-2006** hosts an unsuccessful reconciliation meeting among Somali factions, an effort prompted by both the costs to Yemen of waves of refugees from Somalia and the political dangers to Yemen of an Islamic regime in Somalia opposed by the United States. Also by **mid-2006**, the Aden Container Terminal and Aden Free Zone begin to contribute to Yemen's GDP, but at a level lower than earlier expected. Also in **mid-2006**, President Salih reverses himself and accedes to "popular pressure" to run again, about the same time that the JMP chooses an independent, Faisal bin Shamlan, as its candidate. For the next few months, surprisingly vibrant campaigns for the presidency and local council seats ensue, despite the fact that the resources of the state bias the process against the JMP. In **mid-September**, only days before the voting, security forces thwart attacks by militants on oil installations in Marib and the Hadhramawt, and the GPC tries to implicate the opposition in the attacks. While Salih wins handily in **late September**, bin Shamlan makes a respectable showing with 22 percent of the vote. In the local council elections, however, the JMP parties do poorly, and surprisingly so. After the elections, the president promises to deliver on reforms and the JMP pledges to monitor and challenge the GPC on a day-to-day basis, as well as to prepare itself for the parliamentary elections in 2009 and the next presidential contest in 2013. In **November**, the ROY garners pledges of loans and grants worth up to $5 billion at a donors' conference in London. **In late 2006**, the United States' Millennium Challenge Corporation (MCC) decides to reinstate the ROY's eligibility for its Threshold Program, suspended in 2005. The MCC's likely initial grant of about $30 million could lead thereafter to a multi-year award of $500–700 million.

2007 In **January–April**, the al-Houthi rebellion escalates into all-out warfare, resulting in perhaps a thousand killed or wounded, tens of thousands displaced, and many homes and much infrastructure destroyed. In **early January**, the president chooses to increase use of lethal force and, in **late January**, when the "houthis" ignore his warning to lay down their arms, he launches a major and lethal offensive through **mid-February**. President Salih goes on the political offensive and secures strong parliamentary backing at the same time that the rebels threaten to "open new fronts." Despite another warning and a two-day ultimatum from the president, the rebels intensify operations; the authorities use fighter aircraft and helicopter gun-ships through **March** and into **late April**. Also in **March**, Ali Muhammad Mujawer, former minister of electricity, replaces Bajammal as prime minister and forms a new cabinet pledged to change, reform, and the fight against corruption. In **June**, journalist Khaiwani is rearrested on charges of ties to persons linked to "terrorist activities" and, in **mid-July**, a protest sit-in of human rights activists, journalists, and opposition politicians is broken up by thugs, two incidents that again focus attention on the issue of the freedom of speech and of the press. On **18 June**, a cease-fire between the government and the "houthis" mediated by Qatar is implemented, ending the five-month-long fourth round of the rebellion. But incidents, bickering, and intransigence occur from the start and, in **late July**, frustrated, the Qatari mediators suspend their efforts. Also in **July**, eight Spanish tourists and two Yemenis are killed in a suicide bombing in Marib, suggesting to some a resurgence of al-Qaida in Yemen. In **early September**, a demonstration in Mukalla by former PDRY military officers who claim to have been forced to retire and take inadequate pensions after the War of Secession in 1994 is suppressed. This quickly leads to a series of demonstrations and riots in southern regions to the north of Aden. Throughout **September** and **October**, these actions by southern dissidents—and their suppression—spread across the south and into the north and broaden to include the unemployed in general and disaffected youth who are angry at economic conditions in Yemen. In **October**, the Salih regime shifts from repression to accommodation, authorizing reinstatement of sacked southern officers and pledging to speed up efforts designed to help the poor and unemployed in general. In **mid-October**, the release of Jamal al-Badawi, the convicted *Cole* and *Limburg* participant, angers the United States and causes it to cancel the 31 October ceremony that was to mark the ROY's reinstatement into the MCC's Threshold Program—and its generous funding. In **late November**, the ROY and Dubai Ports World finally sign the agreement on the operation and further development of Aden Container Terminal. By this time, the LNG project is also on track and progressing. In **mid-November**, the seizure of a Saudi supertanker by pirates focuses regional and international attention on the growing, year-old problem of Somali piracy in the Gulf of Aden and beyond. In **mid-December**, as skirmishes going back to September continue and increase tensions in Saada, the top leader of the "houthis" appeals to the opposition JMP to help prevent "an unprecedented catastrophe." Also in **December**, *Oil Market Report* says quarterly oil production was the lowest since early 1994. On **29 December**, Shaykh al-Ahmar, the personification of the tribal dimension of Yemeni politics and a major political player since the 1960s, dies.

2008   In **January**, fighting breaks out in Saada, ending the uneasy, imperfect cease-fire of the past six months. On **1 February**, after talks again brokered by Qatar, the two sides agree to implement the cease-fire; armed incidents occur a few days later amid accusations and acrimony. In **mid-January**, a rally in Aden calling for redress of past injustices and equal treatment of southerners turns violent. Also in **mid-January**, two Belgium tourists are killed in the Hadhramawt, and al-Qaida claims responsibility. On **18 March**, mortars miss the U.S. embassy in Sanaa and hit a neighboring high school for girls and, on **6 April**, rockets are fired on a residential complex for American and other foreigners in Sanaa. Al-Qaida takes credit for both acts. In **late March**, the southern officers' Retired Army Association calls for more demonstrations, and the protests that follow are dealt with harshly by the authorities. At the **end of March**, the release by Yemen of a second terror suspect wanted by the United States further strains relations. In **April**, alleged al-Qaida terrorists in Sanaa fire missiles at a Western residential compound and business office and kill three policemen in Marib. In **early April**, the intermittent fighting in the north increases and the rebel leader raises doubts about the cease-fire. In **early May**, the JMP boycotts the elections for governors, and the GPC candidates win 18 of the 21 posts. In **May**, a mosque bombing and clashes between the military and the "houthis" in Saada raise fears that fighting on the order of that in early 2007 might recur; the "houthis" then extend the fighting south to within 20 miles of Sanaa. Also in **May**, a court in Lahj sentences nine to prison for participating in southern protests. At the **end of May**, discontent in the south increases in advance of the trial of three YSP leaders accused of inciting the conflict. On **7 July**, police break up protests in Dhala and Aden on both the 1st anniversary of the southern protests and the 14th anniversary of the defeat of the "secessionists" in 1994. On **17 July**, President Salih declares the al-Houthi rebellion over and the "houthis" agrees to his peace plan; government and rebel forces continue to hamper efforts to get relief aid to the needy, and many think more fighting is likely. On **17 September**, a complex suicide bombing and attack on the U.S. embassy in Sanaa takes 18 lives. In **early November**, the government identifies the embassy suicide squad as linked to al-Qaida, trained in camps in Yemen and including young, more militant returnees from Iraq. In **mid-November**, several policemen and al-Qaida suspects die in a clash in a southern town. Also in **November**, Dubai's DP World takes over operation and expansion of Aden's container port operations and President Salih inaugurates a key phase of the LNG project, noting that the first LNG shipment is set for May 2009. In **late 2008**, the GPC and the JMP increasingly focus their attentions on the April 2009 parliamentary elections; they negotiate over the electoral laws and their supervision, and the JMP threatens to boycott the elections if the negotiations fail. At **end of December**, the Sanaa Forum for cooperation meets to address the issues of Somali piracy, and the international community's increasing military presence in the region in response to it.

2009   Throughout January, strained U.S.–ROY relations focus on whether Yemeni prisoners in Guantanamo will be sent to a U.S.-financed rehabilitation center in Yemen or one in Saudi Arabia. Also in **January**, the GPC and JMP continue to negotiate on electoral procedures and accuse each other of blocking agreement; a JMP boycott seems a possibility. In the **last half of January**, a wide manhunt results in the arrest or death of several al-Qaida suspects, and a new al-Qaida on the Arabia Peninsula is announced. On **3 February**, President Salih calls on tribal leaders to stop harboring terrorists; on **19 February**, the new al-Qaida on the Arabian Peninsula urges the tribes to wage jihad against the regime. On **27 February**, the GPC and JMP give up and agree to both a two-year postponement of the April elections and a package of electoral and constitutional changes. On **4 March**, the U.S. embassy is attacked, with no reported casualties. On **7 March**, two soldiers and one "houthi" rebel are killed in Saada. In **mid-March**, the trial begins for al-Qaida suspects accused of 13 terrorist acts throughout Yemen in 2008. On **15 March**, a suicide bomber kills four South Korean tourists in the Hadhramawt. On **27–29 March**, soldiers and "houthis" are killed in a fight in Saada. On **28 March**, 4 policemen are killed and 10 Islamic militants are arrested in a police raid in Abyan. On **2 April**, southerner Tarik al-Fadhli breaks with the Salih regime and declares that it has used unity to occupy and plunder the south; on **15 April**, he announces that he has joined the Southern Mobilization Movement and shares its goal of full independence. Also on **15 April**, two civilians and a policeman are killed when police clash with southerners in Lahij. On

25 April, President Salih delivers a stark warning to leaders that any division of Yemen would lead to many states, not just two. In **late April**, as the southern protest movement grows bigger and more violent, over 50 are arrested and about 10 soldiers and civilians are killed. On **3 and 4 May**, many civilians and police or soldiers are killed or injured in a rash of incidents across the south. In **early May**, a government report shows oil revenues in the first quarter of 2009 to be down almost 75 percent from 2008. Also in **early May**, the regime cracks down on eight newspapers for "anti-unity" reporting. Over **5–9 May**, one soldier, four pro-government tribesmen and four "houthis" are killed in an upsurge of fighting in Saada province; in **mid-May**, 3 "houthis" are sentenced to prison and 25 other "houthis" are charged with having formed an "armed gang" in Sanaa in 2008. On **13 May**, the leader of al-Qaida on the Arabian Peninsula declares its support for the southern secessionist revolt against the Salih regime. On **21 May**, the 19th anniversary of unification, President Salih declares at a celebration in Sanaa that unity will prevail and, in Aden, the breakup of a counter-demonstration leaves 3 dead and 25 wounded. Also on **21 May**, Ali Salim al-Baydh, the ex-vice president of the ROY, vows from exile to return to politics to lead the new secession effort.

Introduction

A small, extremely poor Islamic country, the Republic of Yemen (ROY) is located on an edge of the Arab world, the southernmost corner of the Arabian Peninsula. It was the product of the unification of the Yemen Arab Republic (YAR) and the People's Democratic Republic of Yemen (PDRY) in May 1990.

The location of the two Yemens on the world's busiest sea lane at the southern end of the Red Sea, where Asia almost meets Africa, gave them strategic significance from the start of the age of imperialism through the Cold War. More vital today is the fact that the ROY shares a long border with oil-rich Saudi Arabia, and is a key to efforts both to spread and to end global revolutionary Islam and its use of terror. Arguably, the near future of Saudi Arabia and much of the rest of the Middle East turns significantly on the political stability and economic development of impoverished Yemen, results that were by no means assured in the first decade of the new millennium.

LAND AND PEOPLE

The ROY is bounded on the west by the Red Sea and on the southeast by the Gulf of Aden and the Arabian Sea. It points west toward Africa and is separated from Djibouti and Eritrea only by the narrow Bab al-Mandeb straits; to the north and northeast is Saudi Arabia and to the east is Oman, its only contiguous neighbors. Yemen is small in area, roughly 150,000 square miles, making it about the size of Oregon and California combined, or less than three-fourths the size of France. Although dwarfed by Saudi Arabia, which has four-and-one-half times its area, the ROY's population of about 24 million may be as much as twice the indigenous population of this neighbor and more than half that of the entire Arabian Peninsula.

The Land

Geographically, Yemen is marked by a high, steep, jagged mountain range that forms the western and southern edge of a high plateau that then descends gradually north and east until it is lost in the desert interior, on the edge of the Empty Quarter of Saudi Arabia. The mountains rise abruptly about 25 miles inland from a low, flat coastal desert plain, the Tihama; they parallel the Red Sea, running north to south the length of North Yemen, abruptly turn 90 degrees near the old border between the two Yemens, and then go east parallel to the Gulf of Aden for part of the length of South Yemen. Averaging several thousand feet—at one point rising to about 12,400 feet, the highest point on the peninsula— the northern highlands and southern uplands have a largely semi-arid, but otherwise temperate climate, despite their location well south of the Tropic of Cancer. By contrast, the Tihama and Aden are hot and humid much of the year, at times extremely so.

Thanks to the annual monsoon winds that blow inland after crossing the water, picking up moisture on the way, the mountains mean seasonal rainfall as they force the warm air to rise, cool, and drop its moisture. It is this considerable, albeit erratic, rainfall that accounts for the considerable cultivation and the relatively dense population that has resided in much of Yemen for millennia. In North Yemen, the highlands and uplands are loftier and more extensive than in South Yemen, hence its greater rainfall, more intensive and extensive agriculture, and considerably larger population. By contrast, the eastern two-thirds of South Yemen are all but uninhabitable, except for coastal fishing villages, the port of Mukalla, and, deep in the interior, the densely populated Wadi Hadhramawt. Half again larger in area than North Yemen, South Yemen has less than one-third as many people—roughly 6 million to 18 million. In the north, nearly all of the population is sedentary, and this is only slightly less the case in the south. What nomadic pastoralists there are can be found mostly on the edge of the desert near the eastern border with Saudi Arabia.

The ROY has four major cities, Sanaa, the capital, and Aden, al-Hudayda, and Taiz. Aden and al-Hudayda are the major ports, with

Aden being a world-class natural port. There are several large towns: Saada, far to the north; Dhamar, Yarim, and Ibb in the middle region; Mukalla, on the southern coast; and, in Wadi Hadhramawt, the trio of Shibam, Seiyun, and Tarim. The population of the former PDRY is highly concentrated in a few places—in Mukalla and the towns of Wadi Hadhramawt, in the highlands north and east of Aden, and, above all, in Aden proper and its immediate environs. By contrast, the far larger population of the former YAR is much more widely scattered over a great many towns, villages, and hamlets. Thus, in the late 1980s, the combined populations of Sanaa, Taiz and al-Hudayda made up roughly only 15 percent of the YAR's total population. Since then, however, their rapid growth has far outstripped that of the rest of the country.

The People

Virtually the entire indigenous population of the ROY is Arab and Muslim. The Christian community that existed in Yemen in pre-Islamic times disappeared early in the Islamic era. All but several hundred of the once sizable Jewish community, which may have had a continuous presence in Yemen since pre-Islamic times, emigrated *en masse* to Israel shortly after its creation in 1948. The once large and powerful Ismaili Shii Muslim population was reduced through persecution over the centuries to an insignificant, but now reviving, minority in the mountains west of Sanaa.

There remains an old and still politically and socially salient schism between the rest of Yemen's Muslims, between its Zaydi Shiis and Shafii Sunnis. Although at most only a large minority, the Zaydis dominated politics and cultural life in North Yemen for centuries through the tribes and the imamate. With Yemeni unification in 1990, and with the addition of South Yemen's almost totally Shafii population, the numerical balance has shifted dramatically to the Shafiis. Nevertheless, the Zaydis are still overrepresented in the government, and especially in the military. Although a movement and mixing of people has occurred over the past 40 years, the Zaydi–Shafii schism is a north–south geographic divide, with the divide roughly passing through the Dhamar region, where the northern highlands plunge to North Yemen's southern uplands.

Extremely rugged terrain and primitive means of transportation and communications made for some diversity in the largely homogeneous Yemeni people. Although Arabic is spoken by nearly all, there are several different dialects, most notably that of the North Yemeni highlands and that of the southern part of North Yemen and South Yemen. Beyond language, other regional socio-cultural differences abound. In South Yemen, many of the people of the Hadhramawt reflect the influence of distant Southeast Asia, with which they have had commercial and familial ties for centuries; even farther to the east, toward Oman, the people of Mahra, as well as those of nearby Socotra Island, are culturally distinct and speak a pre-Arabic South Arabian tongue. Finally, the people of North Yemen's Tihama and around Aden reflect the long racial and cultural influences of nearby Africa. Culturally, Aden also still displays hints of the Indian subcontinent, a legacy of British colonial rule.

HISTORICAL BACKGROUND

Yemen has been dotted with human settlements for several thousand years, perhaps since humans first came out of Africa; indeed, it has been suggested recently that Yemen was the initial crossover point from Africa to Asia. Neolithic sites abound and, literally, the surface has barely been scratched regarding these sites and those of later prehistoric ages.

Early History

Geography largely determined the history of Yemen after the rise of the great ancient civilizations to the north and east in Egypt, Mesopotamia, and the Mediterranean basin. During this long period, roughly from 1000 BC to 500 AD, this corner of Arabia provided the overland commercial link between these civilizations and the highly prized goods of South Arabia, East Africa and the Indian subcontinent. These were the centuries of the several pre-Islamic trading kingdoms astride the "frankincense trail." That trail followed the edge of the desert all the way from the coast of the Arabian Sea northwest to Najran, Petra, and other entrepots to the rich, higher civilizations to the north.

The first of these kingdoms was the Main (Minean) kingdom. Then there was the kingdom of Saba (the Sabean kingdom), ruled from Marib by, among others, Bilqis, allegedly the Queen of Sheba (Saba). Farther south and east were the Qataban and Hadhramawt kingdoms. The last of the great pre-Islamic kingdoms, that of Himyar, was the only one ruled from the central highlands rather than the desert's edge. At their heights, the Sabean and Himyarite kingdoms embraced much of historic Yemen.

The prominence and prosperity of the states and societies of the interior of Yemen, captured in the Roman place name Arabia Felix, depended upon the ability of those astride the trade routes to control and tax the passage of luxury goods sought by others. When the Romans occupied Egypt in the first century BC, they learned both the secret of the monsoon winds and the true source of the goods they desired. They then made the Red Sea their primary avenue of commerce, causing the interior of Yemen to go into a decline from which it never recovered. Indicative of this decline, in the centuries just before the rise of Islam, weakened indigenous regimes were unable to prevent the invasion and occupation of Yemen by Christian Abyssinia (Ethiopia) and, from the east, the Sassanids of Persia.

Probably over these early centuries emerged the ideas of Yemen as a place and of the Yemeni people, in their consciousness and that of outsiders. However, with the disappearance of the last of the trading kingdoms, Yemen ceased forever to have much impact on the fortunes and thinking of the rest of the world. The growing Red Sea traffic sailed past the Tihama and the mountains, and what sea-borne commerce Yemen engaged in had little impact on the interior of the country. The malarial, hot, humid, hazy, windy, and sand-blasted coastal desert served to isolate, hide, and render inaccessible the comparatively well-watered, verdant, and populous highlands of Yemen.

The Islamic era, which began in the seventh century AD, contains many events critical to the making of Yemen and the Yemenis. The force with which Islam exploded out of Mecca and Medina in the nearby Hijaz made almost inevitable the Islamization of nearby Yemen in a matter of decades. Yemen's converts to Islam provided many of the first soldiers of Islam, those who marched north and then both west across North Africa and east to Iraq. In the ninth century AD, the founding of an indigenous dynasty in Yemen ended Abbasid rule from distant

Baghdad, and this in turn served to free Islamic Yemen to develop in relative isolation its own variant of Arab-Islamic culture and civilization. In the late ninth century AD, the establishment of the Zaydi imamate in Yemen's far north, and its persistence almost continuously down to the 1962 Revolution, forever stamped the northern highlands and their towns and tribes with the Zaydi brand of Shii Islam. By contrast, it was the two-century rule of the Rasulids, beginning in the 12th century and initially based in Aden, which stamped the Tihama and the south with the Shafii form of Sunni Islam.

The occupation of Yemen by the Ottoman Turks in the 16th century, and their expulsion after a long struggle led by the Zaydi imamate in the next century, served to deepen a sense of Yemeni identity among the people and to usher in another long period of Zaydi rule. Despite the rapid growth of the coffee trade on the coast at al-Mukha (Mocha), the interior highlands of Yemen remained almost completely isolated from, and ignored by, the rest of the world from the mid-17th to nearly the mid-19th century. During this period western Europe was both transformed by modern thought and technology and came to exercise control over much of the rest of the world. All this passed Yemen by.

Modern History

The process by which one Yemen and Yemeni people, albeit still vaguely defined, became two Yemens began with both Great Britain's seizure of Aden in 1839 and the start of the second occupation of North Yemen by the Ottoman Turks in 1849. The bifurcation of historic Yemen was virtually inevitable. In the north, Ottoman rule was again opposed by many Yemenis, and the opposition was again led by the Zaydi imamate. Defeat in World War I forced Ottoman withdrawal in 1918, and an ambitious imam seized the opportunity to lay claim to all of Yemen. Britain thwarted this claim to the south, and gradually extended its sway well beyond Aden and its immediate environs.

During the first six decades of the 20th century, two willful and able imams of the Hamid al-Din family, Yahya and his son Ahmad, acted to forge a king-state much as the kings of England and France had done centuries earlier. They strengthened the state, thereby enabling them to expand their domain, secure the borders, and pacify the interior to a considerable degree. The two imams used their credentials as defenders of Yemen against both the Ottoman occupier in the north and the continuing British presence in the south to strengthen their claim to authority over the land and people of Yemen. This served to foster a nascent modern Yemeni nationalism.

The two imams used the strengthened imamate to revive and protect North Yemen's traditional Islamic culture and society; this at a time when traditional societies around the world were crumbling under the weight of modernity backed by imperial power. The result was a "backward" Yemen, more frozen in time than not, and a small but increasing number of Yemenis exposed to the modern world who wanted change—and blamed the imamate for its absence. This produced the chain of events that resulted in the 1962 Revolution: First, the births of the Free Yemenis and the Yemeni Union in the 1940s; second, the aborted 1948 Revolution that left Imam Yahya dead and brought Ahmad to power; and third, the aborted 1955 coup against Imam Ahmad. The 1962 Revolution deposed Muhammad al-Badr, Ahmad's son who had just become imam, abolished the imamate, and created the YAR.

In retrospect, the history of the YAR can best be divided into three periods: first, the al-Sallal era (1962–1967), the wrenching first five years under President Abdullah al-Sallal, marked by the revolution that began it, the long civil war and foreign intervention that quickly followed, and—above all—the rapid and irreversible opening of the country to the modern world; second, a 10-year transition period (1967–1977), distinguished by the end of both Egypt's military presence and the civil war, the republican–royalist reconciliation under President Abd al-Rahman al-Iryani, and the attempt by President Ibrahim al-Hamdi to strengthen the state and foster development; and third, the Salih era (1978–1990), a 12-year period marked with both the long tenure of President Ali Abdullah Salih and the change from political weakness and economic uncertainty at the outset to political stability, the discovery of oil, and the prospect of oil-based development and prosperity. The YAR's history ended with the Yemeni unification and the birth of the ROY in 1990.

Of the many important political and socioeconomic changes that took place in the YAR after 1962, most of the positive ones were compressed into the years since the republic's 15th anniversary in 1977. Nevertheless, the decade from the late 1960s to the late 1970s was also important, a transitional period in which much-needed time was bought by a few modest but pivotal acts and, most important, by economic good fortune. Above all, events over which the YAR had no control facilitated a huge flow of funds into the country in the form of both foreign aid and, especially, remittances from Yemenis working abroad. This interlude was much needed because the changes that had buffeted Yemen in the five years following the 1962 Revolution had left it both unable to retreat into the past and ill equipped to go forward. The ability to move forward in the 1980s was enhanced by the breather afforded by the 1970s.

The path taken by—or, more correctly, imposed upon—South Yemen after the British occupation of Aden in 1839 was quite different. Of critical importance was Britain's focus on the port of Aden and its neglect of the dozen or so statelets in the hinterland with which it signed treaties of protection only in the last quarter of the 19th century. As a consequence, no single political entity except the belated and stillborn Federation of South Arabia of the early 1960s embraced even most of what was to become independent South Yemen in late 1967. Instead, what existed was the 75-square-mile Aden Colony—a city-state, a partly modern urban enclave, and, by some measures, the world's second or third busiest port in the late 1950s—and a vast, mostly distant, politically fragmented hinterland that was, for the most part, based on subsistence agriculture and traditional socio-cultural and political institutions. Neither the British administration nor the nationalists who first stirred in Aden in the 1940s had much knowledge of, interest in, or impact on this hinterland, this despite Britain's adoption of a new "forward policy" during the last decades of imperial rule.

At independence in 1967, the infrastructure barely holding together the scattered settlement areas consisted of dirt tracks, unpaved roads, a number of airstrips, and the telegraph. The country consisted of many micro-economies, most of them agriculturally based and largely self-sufficient. Isolated Wadi Hadhramawt was an odd case, dependent as it was upon emigration to and remittances from Southeast Asia, East Africa, Saudi Arabia, and the rest of the Persian Gulf. What little market economy existed during the British period mostly centered on the port of Aden and its environs, and this in turn was plugged less into its hinterland than into the international economic system via its sea lanes. This fragile modern sector was dealt devastating blows in 1967, at the time of independence. The blocking of the Suez Canal during the Six-Day War that year nearly brought port activities to a halt, and Britain's rapid withdrawal ended both subsidies from London and the significant economic activity tied to the large British presence.

The history of South Yemen since independence is marked by four periods: first, the period of takeover and consolidation (1967–1969), the initial phase in which the National Liberation Front (NLF) established control in Aden and over the hinterland at the same time that power within the NLF passed from the nationalists to its left wing; second, the period of uneasy leftist co-leadership of Salim Rubay Ali and Abd al-Fattah Ismail (1969–1978), distinguished by the efforts of these two rivals to transform the Yemeni Socialist Party (YSP) into a vanguard party, to organize the country in terms of their Marxist "scientific socialism" and to align the renamed PDRY with the socialist camp and liberation movements around the world; third, the era of Ali Nasir Muhammad (1980–1985), the period in which the consolidation of power in a single leader was paralleled by growing moderation in both domestic affairs and external relations, especially with the YAR; and fourth, a period of collective leadership (1986–1999) after the violent end of the Ali Nasir's era in which a weak, decapitated YSP had to cope with worsening economic conditions and the end of aid from the Soviet Bloc.

The period of co-leadership ended in 1978 in armed conflict between two rival factions within the YSP and the execution of Salim Rubay Ali by the victorious Abd al-Fattah. The era of Ali Nasir, beginning in 1980 with the temporary exile of Abd al-Fattah, ended in January 1986 with an intra-party bloodbath that included the assassination of Abd al-Fattah and his top colleagues and Ali Nasir's flight into exile. Despite this pattern of bitter and sometimes lethal conflict, the regime over the years had some notable successes. It maintained its rule and order in the country, made good use of very limited resources in efforts to develop a very poor country, made progress in bridging the vast gap between Aden and the rest of the country, and advanced such social goals as literacy and health care.

Unification and War of Secession

Despite the emergence of two independent Yemens with different political systems and differing political problems and goals, the idea of one Yemen and one Yemeni people remained alive in many quarters in both places. The persistence of the goal of a unified Yemen, and the difficulty of its realization, is attested to by the fact that in 1972 and 1979 two border wars between the Yemens were concluded with agreements to unify—agreements that were quickly placed on the shelf. Indeed, the 1979 agreement was followed by a PDRY-backed rebellion against the Salih regime.

Inter-Yemeni relations improved during Ali Nasir's tenure in the first half of the 1980s—and then worsened with his exile in 1986. However, in mid-1988, after new border tensions beginning in late 1987 in an area where both Yemens had recently found oil, President Salih and the new secretary-general of the YSP, Ali Salim al-Baydh, signed major inter-Yemeni agreements in May 1988. New factors at play were the confidence and relative strength of the Salih regime and the weakening of the YSP as a result of its decapitation in 1986.

The pattern of improving inter-Yemeni relations was transformed dramatically—and, for most, unexpectedly—into the politics of Yemeni unification in late 1989. On November 30, after intense negotiations, the two leaders committed "the two parts of Yemen" to a time schedule and steps that would result in creation of the "Republic of Yemen." Subsequently, in a flurry of bargaining that changed the schedule and some of the details, it was decided that the ROY would come into being in May 1990 after the draft unity constitution, on the shelf since the early 1980s, was approved by the two parliaments. Elections for a new parliament would come in late 1992 after a 30-month transition period during which the merged parliaments would sit in the new capital, Sanaa, the General People's Congress (GPC) and the YSP would be equal partners in the transitional government, and the top posts would be filled by Ali Abdullah Salih as president and Ali Salim al-Bayalh as vice president. The ROY would be a unitary state—not a federation or confederation— and multiparty politics and pluralism would be the order of the day.

New political parties, non-government organizations, newspapers and magazines sprang up like weeds at about this time, and the government came in for unprecedented scrutiny and criticism by these entities as well as in the merged parliament, the Council of Deputies. The Yemenis took to the rights to speak, write, and organize with a vengeance, and the new regime got more democratic politics than planned for.

Caught up in the task and excitement of unification, the Yemenis were blindsided less than three months later, in early August, by Iraq's invasion of Kuwait. When the ROY called for an Arab diplomatic–political solution and opposed the U.S.- and Saudi-led effort to expel Iraq by force, the United States, Saudi Arabia, and other Gulf Arab states chose to punish the ROY by slashing their considerable aid to unified Yemen. Far more damaging was Saudi Arabia's expulsion of about 800,000 Yemeni workers, thereby both dealing a near-fatal blow to the remittance system upon which Yemen depended and creating for Yemen a huge unemployment problem. Relations between the ROY and Saudi Arabia became extremely tense over the next few years, and the Saudis resisted efforts by the Yemenis to undo the damage. All this was piled atop the myriad economic and administrative—and political—problems attendant to unification.

The referendum on the new constitution was held in May 1991, a few days before the ROY's first anniversary. Although it was approved by a great majority of those voting, less than half of the eligible voters turned out—in part because of a boycott called by Islamists and other conservatives who demanded changes in a constitution that they regarded as insufficiently Islamic. Opposition to the regime's stand on the Gulf crisis, and support for the Saudis and Kuwaitis, tended to go hand-in-hand with demands for constitutional change. This opposition found its expression mainly in a new political party, the Reform Group (Islah), an odd mix of tribal and religious interests.

After the referendum, attention turned to the legislative elections scheduled for the end of the transition period in November 1992. Their collaboration notwithstanding, the two equal partners in the regime—the GPC and the YSP—competed against each other at the same time that they often closed ranks against the several other major parties. Increasingly, however, worsening economic conditions as well as problems in the effort to merge the two states and to reorganize politics heightened competition and strained cooperation between the ruling parties. In particular, the loss of remittances and increased unemployment produced dire economic conditions all over Yemen. This both distracted the government from the tasks facing it and poisoned the political atmosphere. Beginning in late 1991, day-to-day politics was increasingly marked by acrimony, popular protests, strikes, riots, and even bombings, kidnappings, and assassinations. Late in the summer of 1992, Vice President al-Baydh withdrew to Aden and began a long boycott of the government. The promised legislative elections were postponed until early 1993, further adding to the acrimony. Things came to a head in late 1992 with the violent suppression of widespread price riots in cities in the north and a series of grave terrorist acts in the south, apparently by militant Islamists.

These alarming events had a sobering effect on the unification regime and its moderate opponents, and then led to a closing of ranks and an easing of the political crisis. The successful holding of the elections in April 1993 served anew to legitimize unification and the regime, at home and abroad. No major players boycotted the elections, and the losers accepted the results after only some grumbling and cries of fraud—and appeared ready to assume the role of opposition.

Moreover, the election results produced a coalition government that seemed potentially able both to stay together and to address some of Yemen's pressing problems. President Salih and his centrist GPC were the big winners, as expected. The other half of the unification regime, the YSP, while much diminished, survived in good order; as important, the tribal and moderate Islamic critics of that regime, represented by Islah, made a strong showing, but not overly so. These results facilitated the formation of a tripartite coalition government ranging from center-left to center-right—from the YSP to the GPC to Islah—the "big tent" favored by President Salih.

During its first months the government emphasized new beginnings and, in particular, launched a concerted effort to restore good relations with Saudi Arabia and the other Arab Gulf states, an effort that produced only modest results. At the same time, however, demonstrations and strikes during the summer and fall of 1993, protesting inflation and the late payment of salaries and wages, placed the government under the gun to quickly meet campaign pledges to ease the "pains" of unification and hard times. Kidnappings by the tribes resumed, causing chagrin to a regime that had made the end of "lawlessness" another campaign promise. Most worrisome, sporadic political violence resumed.

It was quickly apparent that the elections had not provided passage to a more complete, more permanent stage of unification—and to more effective government. The tripartite government soon evidenced serious strain and discord. The longtime armed forces' chief of staff, a northerner, resigned over the failure of the minister of defense, a southerner, to proceed with the merger of the armed forces, another main electoral promise. Rumor had some YSP leaders urging the party to join the opposition rather than continue as junior partner in a coalition dominated by a suspected alliance between the GPC and Islah, the two "northern" parties.

In mid-August 1993, Vice President al-Baydh again retired to Aden and resumed his boycott—signaling the start of a second full-blown political crisis. He left behind a list of 18 conditions for his return, a full plate of administrative, economic, political, and military reforms.

Efforts to mediate by Arab friends and statements of concern by the United States, Russia, and others were of no avail. As a result, the political climate near the end of 1993 was as bad as or worse than a year earlier.

Moreover, unlike during the crisis of 1992 that preceded the elections, moderates inside the unification regime did not close ranks, put aside differences, and take joint action to save both the regime and Yemeni unity when danger signals appeared in early 1994. Instead, the political conflict worsened and, more important, a simmering military crisis erupted in a series of lethal fights between northern and southern units of the unmerged army.

Despite concerted efforts at mediation, by non-Yemenis as well as Yemenis, and despite the efforts and desires of many of the leaders of the GPC and the YSP, the crisis of 1993–1994 defied solution. Al-Baydh's refusal to come north and be inaugurated as vice president in October 1993, nearly six months after the elections, highlighted the continuing stalemate. Thereafter, an attempt by the religious leadership to bring al-Baydh and Salih together in early 1994 failed. By early January, moreover, the other YSP leaders in the regime had quietly left Sanaa and joined al-Baydh in Aden, adding further to the creation of a *de facto* separate government in the old capital of the PDRY. By this time the southern leaders were openly expressing their call for decentralization in terms of federation, and their northern counterparts were translating this as a call for the end of the ROY. Each side accused the other of resupplying and redeploying their military units along the former border.

The failed effort by the religious leaders was followed by the effort by King Husayn that led to the February 20 Amman meeting of "the two Alis" and their signing of the Document of Pledge and Accord, an agreement on reforms fashioned over the past year by all political forces to end the crisis. On the very day of the signing, however, the leaders of the two parts of Yemen launched what amounted to separate, opposing diplomatic initiatives in the Arab world. On the next day, fighting occurred between army units of the north and the south in Abyan province in the former South Yemen.

In early April, hastily arranged talks between the two Alis in Oman failed to get the reconciliation process back on course. Shortly after this, a serious incident involving a southern army unit occurred in Dhamar in the north. By this time, as the fiction of unity gave way to obvious physical division, the wagers of the war of words dropped the euphemisms of the recent past: al-Baydh accused Salih and his cronies of abandoning unification for "annexation," of conspiring to "marginalize" the YSP, and Salih charged al-Baydh and greedy "secessionists" with forsaking unified Yemen for "a mini oil-state."

Egypt and the United Arab Emirates (UAE) started another mediation effort, and talk turned to the possibility of a summit in Cairo in May. Then, on April 27, the first anniversary of the elections, a bloody four-day battle between northern and southern army units erupted in an army camp in Amran, north of Sanaa; tanks and artillery were involved at extremely close range, and the casualties, civilian as well as military, were high. Despite efforts to contain the conflict, fighting again broke out in Dhamar on May 4, a week after the start of the Amran battle. The War of Secession had begun.

After more than two weeks of fighting, during which northern forces got the upper hand and drove deep into the south, al-Baydh was welcoming outside mediation and urging an immediate ceasefire and separation of forces. For his part, Salih opposed efforts to "internationalize" an "internal" conflict and demanded surrender of the "secessionists" and the trial or exile of about 15 top "rebels," including al-Baydh. On May 21, with Aden and its environs increasingly cut off from the rest of the south, al-Baydh formally announced secession and the creation of the Democratic Republic of Yemen (DRY)—and Salih replied with a charge of "treason" and a pledge to crush the new state and to restore unity. It was the day before the ROY's fourth anniversary.

The fighting and the diplomatic effort for a ceasefire that might, if successful, have led to the *de facto* redivision of Yemen continued for another seven weeks. Then, at the end of the first week in July, both Mukalla and Aden fell to the northern forces and the southern leaders fled Yemen, marking the collapse of the secession and the DRY's demise.

From Late 1994 to 2009

The War of Secession over in mid-1994, the Salih regime was faced with the need both to deal with an economy in free fall and to reintegrate the just-defeated south into the ROY. The regime acted quickly on the latter, granting amnesty to all but the top 16 leaders in the secession and urging those who had fled abroad to return without fear to Yemen—and most of the latter did. Addressing the economic crisis, however, involved protracted negotiations with the International Monetary Fund (IMF) and World Bank over a package of economic reforms that led to a complex, demanding agreement in 1995.

Domestic political activity paralleled efforts to address these problems. By late 1994, President Salih was elected by the parliament to a new five-year term, this in accordance with a constitutional amendment abolishing the multi-member presidency. A new coalition government was approved which included members of the GPC and Islah—but not the YSP. In 1997, two-and-one-half years later, a still-reeling YSP chose perhaps unwisely to boycott the upcoming parliamentary elections. Winning with a huge majority, the Salih regime then chose not to form a coalition government and to rule alone, with the result that Islah became the major opposition party. In 1999, the GPC used its dominance of parliament to prevent a somewhat revived YSP from running it leader in the ROY's first direct popular presidential elections. As a result, President Salih ran virtually unopposed and was elected to a new term, one extended by another amendment from five to seven years.

These political events were promoted at home and abroad in the name of the broadening and deepening of Yemen's democracy—and, in mid-1999, President Salih did host a self-congratulatory conference for "emerging democracies." Indeed, the various elections were not unimportant and, after 1994, Yemenis were free to organize and speak out to a significant degree, in part because of the relative stability and popularity of the Salih regime. In fact, however, the regime and the oligarchy that supported and reaped benefits from it consolidated still further its power and wealth over these years. Moreover, these political events did nothing to reintegrate further the defeated south into the

ROY after the mid-1990s; in addition, northerners had occupied most military and top administrative positions in the south, and many used their positions to seize property and to reap other economic benefits. This caused many southerners now to see unification as little more than "occupation," and fed protest talk and action both at home and from abroad. This discontent persisted into the 21st century, when it began to erupt into demonstrations and other actions—and in harsh responses by the government.

During these years, the ROY improved frayed relations with—and increased aid from—the United States and the major countries of the European Union. More important, its dogged efforts resulted in the restoration of virtually broken relations with Saudi Arabia, Kuwait, and the UAE, major sources of aid in the past. Although its formal application to join the Gulf Cooperation Council (GCC) was firmly turned down, the GCC did admit the ROY to some of its agencies and did hold out the possibility of full membership in the future. The most important mark of improved relations between the ROY and its all-important Saudi neighbor was the long-sought agreement in mid-2000 on their long undemarcated border, a major bone of contention and cause of border fights since the 1930s.

The nature and salience of the ROY's relations with many countries, but especially the United States, changed dramatically with al-Qaida's terrorist attacks on the World Trade Center and the Pentagon on September 11, 2001. Actually, the change in relations with the United States was anticipated in reactions by both parties to the suicide bombing by al-Qaida of the U.S.S. *Cole* in Aden's port nearly a year earlier in October 2000. President Salih traveled to Washington, D.C., only days after "9/11" to pledge the ROY's full support to President George W. Bush's new "War on Terror." Thereafter, President Salih had to balance meeting the United States' demand for full support in this "war" against a domestic political landscape marked by Yemeni nationalism, strong Islamic sensibilities, and growing anti-American feeling. Perhaps most important, a number of military officers and politicians inside the Salih regime were themselves militant Islamists or tied to militant Islamist groups. From "9/11" on, as had been the case immediately after the U.S.S. *Cole* bombing, President Salih picked his way carefully but imperfectly and with difficulty through these often contradictory forces.

The seemingly endless turmoil in Somalia, and the U.S.'s growing tendency to view that and other events on the Horn of Africa in terms of its War on Terror, was of increasing concern to the Salih regime after "9/11." In 2002, it convened a meeting of the presidents of Sudan, Ethiopia, and Yemen. This led in the following year to the formation of the Sanaa Forum for Cooperation that thereafter met annually, later including the president of Djibouti and sometimes the president of Somalia. The Forum addressed, with little apparent effect, the turmoil in Somalia, Ethiopia's major and the U.S.'s limited intervention in Somalia, and Eritrea's conflicts with both Ethiopia and Djibouti. The increase in Somali piracy and the international community's response to it was high on the Forum's agenda late in the decade.

Despite both the complications posed by the War on Terror on domestic politics and increasing economic deprivation caused by the growing reluctance of the oligarchs to implement the reforms needed to restore Yemen's economic viability, the GPC won by a large majority in the parliamentary elections in 2003. While the YSP did make something of a comeback, Islah remained the only significant opposition party. In 2006, President Salih again decisively won a new seven-year term, this despite the relatively good showing by the candidate of the new five-party coalition dominated by Islah and the YSP, the Joint Meeting Parties (JMP). The GPC also had a big win in the local council elections that were also held at this time. The JMP remained intact after the elections, maintaining a unified opposition to the Salih regime, and planned for the parliamentary elections in 2009—and the next presidential contest in 2013. The Salih regime pledged to initiate political and economic reforms, and the JMP promised to hold it to those pledges.

Nevertheless, the conflicting demands of the War on Terror and the myriad problems facing Yemen's economy and society—and, in both policy domains, things done and left undone by the Salih regime—did cumulatively increase anger and dissatisfaction throughout Yemen over the years since 2000. The al-Houthi Rebellion was launched in mid-2004 in Saada in the far north by Zaydi sayyids who initially expressed their discontent with their social and political lot by condemning the Salih regime as pro-American and pro-Israeli. Between June and a truce in September, many lives were lost and homes and infrastructure were destroyed. In part as a result of the harshness of the regime's response, the rebellion re-erupted and more violently in three of the next four years, defying third-party efforts—especially by the ruler of Qatar—to reach a truce that would hold. While it appeared in late 2008 that the active rebellion had come to an end, many unmet grievances and great discontent remained. Indeed, acts of violence revived and escalated to open warfare in September 2009.

Beginning in mid-2007, an epidemic of protests and demonstrations, some of them turning violent, broke out over many months and in a large number of places across the old PDRY. These actions were initiated by angry military officers who objected to their forced retirement and meager pensions. These actions, and the often harsh responses by the regime, soon spread to civil servants, lawyers, teachers, professors, and unemployed youths protesting against what they saw as the systematic exploitation of the south since the end of the War of Secession in 1994. These actions and the regime's reactions continued throughout 2008, and increased significantly in 2009.

The rebellion in the north and the protests in the south evolved into a questioning of the legitimacy of the Salih regime, Yemeni unification, and even republicanism. Some protesting southerners, moving beyond charges of unfairness, again began openly questioning the notion of Yemeni unification itself, dismissing it as the occupation of the south by the north. Even more fundamental, some supporters of the al-Houthi rebellion questioned the idea of republicanism, and explicitly called for restoration of the imamate and rule by Zaydi sayyids.

If this were not enough, a number of bombings occurred in Sanaa's diplomatic quarter in the first half of 2008, at about the time that al-Qaida called upon its Yemeni supporters to pick up the pace and focus attacks on the western "crusaders" and their Yemeni allies. The outbreak of violent incidents claimed by or blamed on al-Qaida and its allies had also spread to Wadi Hadhramawt in the second half of the year, targeting tourists as well as security forces. The massive suicide bombing at the entrance to the U.S. embassy in Sanaa on September 17, taking 19 lives, was only the worst of this rash of events. The Salih regime's responses to this and the other "terrorist" acts in 2008 and early 2009 were swift and harsh.

Thus, by early 2009, the legitimacy and continuation of the regime and even the ROY itself were being challenged in the north, the south, and at the center and in the east—that is, from almost every quarter. Against this background, the GPC and the JMP had for months worked persistently but without success to agree on electoral and other political reforms in advance of the April 2009 parliamentary elections. In late February, with the threat of a JMP election boycott looming over the stalled negotiations, the GPC and the JMP agreed to a two-year post-ponement of the elections. Serious conflict between the Salih regime and both al-Qaida and the southern dissidents, and violent incidents in the north, in Saada, persisted late 2009.

ECONOMIC AND SOCIAL DEVELOPMENT

For centuries, North Yemen had a largely self-sufficient economy based on subsistence agriculture and animal husbandry in the interior and fishing on the coasts. The few needed imports to imamate Yemen were covered by modest exports of such things as livestock, hides, and coffee, and the overall economy generated little surplus; indeed, the country virtually had no currency and no banks. Today, although North Yemen moved quickly from self-sufficiency to growing dependence on the outside world after the 1962 Revolution, as did Aden, its environs, and Wadi Hadhramawt many decades earlier, the chief sources of live-lihood for most Yemenis continue to be farming, fishing, and animal husbandry. Traditional artisanship and trade and commerce also have remained important sources of livelihood, but modern industry contin-ues to be rare, marginal, and small in scale. The economy is now largely monetized and a banking system is firmly in place.

Economic Development

After the Civil War and the collapse of the artificial economy it had sustained, the YAR's economy began to grow and again become more viable in the 1970s, largely by becoming a remittance economy depen-dent upon the employment abroad of a large percentage of its adult male population. The growing inflow of external aid created another form of dependency. The PDRY, dependent on the Soviet Bloc for aid, also became increasingly dependent on worker remittances. Both Yemens came to rely heavily on the United Nations and other international orga-nizations for development aid.

Until the mid-1980s, the Yemens had no known natural resources of consequence other than the fruit of the sea. In 1984 and 1986, respectively, modest amounts of oil were discovered in the YAR and the PDRY, and the first oil was exported from the YAR in late 1987. As a result of further development, oil production reached about 300,000 barrels per day (b/d) in 1993, and projections were optimistically raised to nearly 500,000 b/d for 1998. Further, plans went forward in the second half of the 1990s to develop the significant gas reserves found in the north in the 1980s.

Unification in 1990 brought with it the major task of integrating the economies of the two Yemens. A few months after unification, however, this task was superseded by that of coping with the consequences of the loss of remittances and massive unemployment caused by Saudi Arabia's expulsion of Yemeni workers in the months before the first Gulf War in early 1991.

Consequently, the story of the ROY's economy and economic policy since the early 1990s was largely that of attempting to cope with the sudden loss of aid and remittances, an effort complicated by the economic costs of the political crisis that began in 1992 and ended in the War of Secession in 1994. The ROY's economy late that year was in free fall and no longer viable and sustainable as then constituted—this despite the increasing oil revenues. The main thread of the story from 1995 until late in the next decade was the largely failed attempt to restructure the economy according to the ambitious, multi-stage IMF/World Bank package of economic reforms first agreed to by the Salih regime and those bodies in 1995. The package consisted of stabilization measures and major structural reforms—and some governance reforms—which Yemen pledged to implement over a decade in exchange for generous amounts of international aid from many sources. A major goal was to make Yemen an attractive target for much-needed investment from abroad.

The ROY's political economy presented hurdles to this effort. In the 1980s, the Salih regime in the YAR had gradually crystallized into an oligarchy dominated by military officers, tribal shaykhs, and northern businessmen. Increasingly, though, it became a special kind of oligarchy, a kleptocracy, in which the state with access to oil revenues for the first time and increased external aid functioned primarily to enrich the oligarchs at the expense of the wider public through patronage, nepotism, bribery, fraud, and other corrupt practices. For the first time the Yemeni state became a collection of profit centers for the rulers and their associates. Over time, they came to regard these benefits as entitlements.

Set back by Yemeni unification and the power-sharing and political competition that came with it, this kleptocratic system was quickly restored and extended by the victorious Salih regime after the War of Secession. However, faced with economic collapse—for example, 1995's GDP was less than half that of 1990—the Salih regime did implement over the latter half of the 1990s the initial steps in the IMF/World Bank reform package. These involved currency, budget, and trade reforms, all of which involved economic sacrifices by the entire population. However, efforts to implement subsequent steps in the reform package ceased by the late 1990s, in large part because these more demanding economic and governance reforms directly threatened the economic and political interests of the ruling oligarchs and their clients. As a result, and despite threats and some actions by the IMF, World Bank, and the donor community, little progress was made after the year 2000 in implementing the reforms deemed necessary to attract investors to Yemen—and to create jobs and foster enterprise.

It would be hard to exaggerate the grimness of Yemen's situation and prospects late in the first decade of the 21st century. Despite some improvement over the last half of the 1990s, the economy soon plateaued at a low level, and as of 2005 was barely creating enough jobs and public services needed to keep up with a population growth rate of 3.8 percent. Unemployment held at about 40 percent, as did the rate for those malnourished and those living below the poverty line. Perhaps the only bright spot on the economic horizon in late 2009 was the initial liquefied natural gas (LNG) export, the limited supply of which would do little more than partially make up for declining oil production and revenue.

Social Development

Despite great differences in status, North Yemen's economy of scarcity under the imams until 1962 fostered a social system that was not marked by great inequality among males. The imams did live better than most of their fellow Yemenis, but not perceptibly that much better. Inequality increased after the 1962 Revolution, both within the modern sector and between parts of that sector and traditional Yemen, much as had happened in South Yemen under British colonial rule earlier in the 20th century.

The Marxist ideology of the regime in the PDRY, as well as a condition of economic scarcity, served after 1967 to temper the growing inequality that tends to accompany the early stages of development. The tendency over time of entrenched one-party states, socialist ones as well as others, to widen class divides was countered in the PDRY through the 1980s by wider access to education, health care, and housing, and by efforts to integrate the rest of the country into modern Aden and its environs.

In the YAR, the main force that tempered increasing inequality during the 1970s and early 1980s was the mass emigration of workers and the remittances they brought home. Nearly anyone who stayed home could find a job, and wages were pushed up to new levels by a labor shortage. More important, the remittances were distributed widely—as if magically sprinkled from above—with some going directly or indirectly to most families in nearly all parts of the country. Thanks to remittances, people had the capital to add a second story to their stone houses, to buy a four-wheel drive Toyota to use as a taxi, or to open a new store or shop. New local development associations, the LDAs, mixed remittances with other funds and often a sense of mission to build thousands of feeder roads, schools, clinics, and cisterns in towns and on the countryside.

By the mid-1980s, however, with the withering of the LDA movement, the economic gap between city and countryside ballooned. More important, as the Salih regime's pyramid of patronage topped by officers, shaykhs, and businessmen grew steeper and became more entrenched, the trend toward increasing inequality in North Yemen became greater and more dramatically apparent by decade's end. With Yemeni unification in 1990, moreover, this trend spread to include the south. By the mid-1990s, the loss of remittances and the massive unemployment of returning workers caused both inequality and poverty to increase at alarming rates throughout the ROY. The effect of the loss of remittance income was greatest in the north, but in the south it combined negatively with the dismantling of the all-encompassing socialist state and its economic agencies.

In the shrunken economy of the mid-1990s, urban workers and especially the new middle class that had grown up in both Yemens over the previous two decades were quickly pauperized; the modern institutions in which they worked, and on which they had come to place their hopes for a better future, were hollowed out. For example, the plight of professors was typical of most professionals and government employees. Increasingly they found themselves in dwellings far too small for growing families, in threadbare sport coats or suit jackets with torn pockets and collars, and in old cars that barely ran. By contrast, and increasingly, only the privileged few—mostly officers, shaykhs, businessmen, and their friends—had access to a growing share of the smaller economic pie and a hidden economy.

Late in the first decade of the 21st century, the middle class had shrunk even further and its pauperization had continued relentlessly. At the same time, the gap between the rich few and the many poor—on the countryside and in the towns and cities—grew still wider, and more visibly so. On the personal level, most people were just trying desperately to make ends meet; ground down and worn out by the effort, many had no hope for the future. For most, the previous decade had been one of pain and no gain.

Institutionally, the education and health systems had become quite dysfunctional, and many other social services had almost ceased to exist. In particular, illiteracy remained very high, especially in rural areas and among females, and medical services were in short supply and of poor quality throughout the country. In short, most institutions had decayed—had been starved and further hollowed out. And as much of modern Yemen withered, new villas continued to grow like weeds in Sanaa's new suburbs. Huge SUVs—and even Hummers—stood out in contrast to the Toyota pickups so widely seen in the 1970s and 1980s. Yemen at the end of 2008 was a fractured if not broken society.

PROBLEMS AND PROSPECTS

The performance of the Salih regime since 1995 does not augur well for Yemen's future. Bluntly put, the regime has demonstrated the lack of will and capacity, especially political capacity, to do what has to be done to make Yemen viable and sustainable—and to make it again a land of some promise for most of its people.

What makes this so ominous and alarming is that the regime had through its oil resources acquired the chance to do what had to be done.

North Yemenis, without much state or government, had made fairly good use of remittances in the 1970s and much of the 1980s; similarly, the PDRY had put its meager resources toward its socialist vision fairly well in the 1970s and 1980s. By contrast, the ROY has largely squandered the revenue from its modest and soon-to-be depleted oil reserves. (Declining oil production was masked since 2007 by soaring oil prices, oil prices that plunged in late 2008.) It has also failed to apply the more demanding reforms—those called for by the IMF/World Bank or others—required to make Yemen attractive for investors, Yemeni as well as non-Yemeni. The main culprit is the kleptocracy that the Salih regime became and the systemic corruption it spawned.

The ROY in 2009 qualified as a failing state, its support and legitimacy being drained away. If it is not very soon to become a failed state in a broken society, then a reformed Salih regime or a successor must institute needed reforms and make better use of modest gas reserves than it had in the case of modest oil reserves since the mid-1980s. And it is a race against time. More ominous than the imminent depletion of Yemen's oil reserves is the relentless depletion of its water resources. Its ancient and once ample aquifers are being drawn down far more rapidly than they are being recharged—this at the same time that Yemen's population continues to grow at a rate that probably cannot be easily brought under control over the next two decades. Simply put, Yemen risks running out of water over this period. A joke has it that Yemen need not worry about seepage from oil operations contaminating a pristine aquifer in Wadi Hadhramawt because the water table is falling more rapidly than the oil can seep down towards it. This, alas, is no laughing matter.

Again, the regime's abysmal stewardship of its oil resources since the late 1980s provides little cause for hope. The relevant political markers are the parliamentary elections in 2011 and the next presidential elections in 2013. Either the Salih regime will address the pyramid of patronage and the rampant corruption it supports and depends upon, or it will be replaced or reconfigured by political forces that will try to do what has to be done. It comes down to that. If the regime or a successor peacefully chosen proves unable to do this—if it lacks the required will and capacity—then the door will be opened to the possibility of state failure, serious violence, and even civil war or chaos. The models of Lebanon, Afghanistan, and even Somalia are not without relevance to the Yemeni case.

The Dictionary

– A –

ABBASIDS AND UMAYYADS. The Umayyads created and ruled the first Arab–Islamic kingdom from Damascus from the mid-seventh to the mid-eighth centuries. Despite Yemen's early conversion to Islam, this shift of the political and cultural center of Islam from neighboring **Hijaz** north to Damascus contributed to Yemen's soon becoming an idiosyncratic backwater on the edge of the Islamic world. The Umayyads were succeeded by the Abbasids, whose great, far-flung **Sunni** Arab–Islamic empire, founded in Baghdad in A.D. 750, flourished extravagantly for more than two centuries and then continued, more in form than in substance, until finally ended by the Mongol conquerors in 1258. The shift of the center of power in the Arab world from Damascus east to Baghdad served to marginalize Yemen further and made effective control of it and its Islam all the more difficult. By the early ninth century the rugged southwest corner of the Arabian Peninsula was free of Baghdad and was a haven for various strains of **Shii Islam** (i.e., the **Ismailis** and the **Zaydis**).

ABD AL-ALIM, LT-COL ABDULLAH. The YAR commando and paratroop commander and close colleague of President Ibrahim Muhammad **al-Hamdi** who fled south from Sanaa across the border into the PDRY in the spring of 1978 only several months after al-Hamdi's assassination, thereby ending the serious threat of a rebellion of pro-Hamdi supporters against the new regime headed by President Ahmad Hussayn **al-Ghashmi**. Abd al-Alim conspired with the **National Democratic Front** and others against al-Hamdi's successors for the next few years, and then withdrew from the political fray. A native of the **Hugariyya**, from around **Turba**, he had been

1

the highest-ranking **Shafii** in a military overwhelmingly dominated by northern **Zaydis**.

ABD AL-AZIZ BIN ABD AL-RAHMAN AL-SAUD. *See* AL-SAUD (BAYT SAUD).

ABD AL-FATTAH ISMAIL (1939–1986). Co-ruler of the PDRY with his rival Salim **Rubiyya Ali** from mid-1969 to mid-1978. Ismail served throughout this period as secretary general of the regime's evolving political organization, was one of the regime's most insistent and dogmatic proponents of "**scientific socialism**," and is rightly regarded as the father of what became the PDRY's well-developed ruling party, the **Yemeni Socialist Party**. Victorious in the lethal political struggle with Salim Rubiyya Ali in 1978, Abd al-Fattah was himself forced to leave for "health" reasons in 1980. He returned from his Moscow exile in late 1984 and became at least the symbolic leader of the party militants' opposition to moderate party chief and head of state **Ali Nasir Muhammad** al-Hasani, only to die in the bloodbath that marked the **13 January events** in 1986.

Abd al-Fattah migrated from **Hayfan** in North Yemen to **Aden**, where he worked as an unskilled port and refinery worker. A founding member of the **National Liberation Front**, and of its left wing, his absence of much formal education did not prevent him from developing into a Marxist ideologue and theorist of the PDRY's "scientific socialism," categorized by some as a "Stalinist" in contrast to Salim Rubiyya Ali, the "Maoist."

ABD AL-GHANI, ABD AL-AZIZ (1939–). The U.S.-educated technocrat of modest origins in the **Hujariyya** region in North Yemen who, after serving as minister of economics twice in the late 1960s and early 1970s and as founding head of the **Central Bank of Yemen** throughout the first half of the 1970s, served as YAR prime minister during all but three years between January 1975 and Yemeni **unification** in May 1990. During this interlude, 1980–1983, Abd al-Aziz served as second vice president, and between May 1990 and the summer of 1993 he was a member of the five-man **Presidential Council** of the newly created ROY. He was again named to the Presidential Council during the **War of Secession** in 1994, and again became prime minister in October of that year after the secessionists were defeated. He was then appointed chairman of the new **Shura Council** in 1997. In this position for more than a decade, he became one of the ROY's elder Statesmen.

A **Shafii** from **Hayfan**, Abd al-Aziz is arguably the youngest of North Yemen's first-generation **modernists**. He got his early education in **Aden** and Cairo, and then, as one of the first four Yemenis to be selected for a scholarship under the United States' Point IV aid program, went to the United States in 1958, where he earned a B.A. and an M.A. in economics at the University of Colorado. Back in Aden in the mid-1960s, he taught at **Bilqis Preparatory College** and then went home to the YAR at the time of the ouster of the **al-Sallal regime** in 1967 to begin his long career in government.

Abd al-Aziz served as prime minister under presidents **al-Hamdi**, **al-Ghashmi**, and **Salih**, serving almost continuously for nearly 15 years—and surviving in office the first two, who were assassinated. A technocrat who learned to play the game of politics and enjoyed public life, he has been criticized for being too inclined to accommodate and avoid conflict. As head of the Shura Council, however, Abd al-Aziz served well as elder statesman and adviser.

ABD AL-RABO MANSOUR HADI. The career soldier from the PDRY who became minister of defense and then vice president of the ROY after the **War of Secession** in 1994, remaining in the latter post through most of the first decade of the 21st century. A leader of the **Ali Nasir Muhammad** faction of the regime in **Aden**, he was the PDRY's military chief of staff until the **13 January events** forced Ali Nasir and many of his followers—Abd al-Rabo among them—to flee north to the YAR in 1986. In exile in the north, he joined the **General People's Party** about the time of Yemeni **unification**. During the War of Secession, Abd al-Rabo's knowledge of the south and its **armed forces** contributed to the war's outcome. Thereafter, he proved to be a loyal, non-threatening supporter of President Ali Abdullah **Salih** and used his position in the second half of the 1990s to protect and advance his fellow former followers of Ali Nasir, sometimes at the expense of Yemeni "**Afghani Arabs**" who had helped the Salih regime put down the southern secessionists. However, with rising southern protests against northern "occupation" in 2007–2009, it was rumored that relations between Abd al-Rabo and President Salih had become strained. Like Ali Nasir, he hails from **Abyan** province.

ABD AL-WAHHAB, ABD AL-RAQIB. The young **Shafii** commando leader and hero of the **Siege of Sanaa** in late 1967 and early 1968 who then led the **Sanaa Mutiny** in the fall of 1968 against plans of conservatives led by General Hasan **al-Amri** to purge the **armed forces** of Shafii leftists. He was sent in defeat into exile with a number of his colleagues and was then killed in Sanaa when he returned and failed in an attempted coup in early 1969. The demise of Abd al-Wahhab, who did have links with the leftist **National Liberation Front** that had recently come to power in South Yemen, was part of the drift in the late 1960s in which the YAR became more conservative and more dominated by the **Zaydis**.

ABDALI TRIBE, REGION, AND SULTANATE. The tribal region directly north of **Aden** that was the most important part of that city's hinterland and the only component of the Aden **Protectorates** integrated to a significant degree into Aden's expanding economic life during **Great Britain's** colonial era. The region and its tribes were ruled since the 18th century by the Abdali sultanate of **Lahej**, which owed its growing local influence and wealth from the mid-19th century onward to the British in Aden, upon whom it came to be completely dependent. Aden's British governors furnished the Abdali sultanate the material means with which to persuade or force neighboring tribes—e.g., the **Aqrabi**—to respect freedom of movement along the trade routes and also to expand its territory and influence at the expense of those areas. Indeed, the British sphere of interest beyond Aden that took shape in the late 19th century coincided with the existing political orbit of the sultans of Lahej, on whose advice the British relied heavily. As a result, the interdependence of Aden and Lahej became a permanent feature of the area's politics and economy, surviving to this day.

Sultan Sir Ali bin Abd al-Karim, the politically ambitious Abdali sultan of Lahej from 1952 to 1958, joined forces with the **al-Jifri** family to promote the **South Arabian League** and its goal of an independent federation uniting Aden and the Western Aden Protectorates. He aspired to rule this state, and to this end, he opposed a more limited federation of protectorate states and, in 1957, allied himself, quite improbably, to Egypt's President Gamel Abdul **Nasser**. All of this brought him into serious conflict with his British patrons, who deposed him in 1958. His successor, Sultan Fadhl bin Ali, lacked his political ambition.

ABDULLAH BIN ABD AL-AZIZ, KING. *See* AL-SAUD (BAYT SAUD).

ABDULLAH BIN YAHYA HAMID AL-DIN (?–1955). The brother of Imam **Ahmad** of North Yemen who on the occasion of the **1955 coup attempt** proclaimed himself imam, only to be put to death when Imam Ahmad forcefully thwarted the attempt. Although conspiracy between him and the army officer who moved to oust his brother was never established, Prince Abdullah did act with unseemly (and suspicious) haste to proclaim himself imam. At the time, he was serving as "foreign minister," and had previously served his father, Imam **Yahya**, as governor of **al-Hudayda**.

ABDULLAH ("MUHSIN"), MUHAMMAD SAID. *See* "MUHSIN," MUHAMMAD SAID ABDULLAH.

ABHA. The still quite traditional large town and provincial capital of the **Asir** region in the **Sarat** mountains in the southwest corner of **Saudi Arabia**, bordering on Yemen.

ABRAHA. The last ruler of the **Sabean** state based in **Marib**, a militant Christian who was defeated in A.D. 570 by **Sassanid** forces from **Persia** invited to Yemen by indigenous pagans to rid the country of **Ethiopian** Christian influences. Popularly called the "Year of the Elephant," allegedly this was the same year that the great **Marib Dam** burst and that the Prophet Muhammad was born in Mecca. Whatever the precise details of history, Abraha ruled on the eve of the rise of Islam in the 7th century, and his rule helps mark the divide between pre-Islamic and Islamic Yemen.

ABU DHABI. *See* UNITED ARAB EMIRATES (UAE).

ABU DHABI FUND. *See* ARAB REGIONAL FUNDS.

ABU LUHUM, SINAN (MID-1930s–). The minor shaykh of the **Nihm** tribe in the **Bakil** confederation who started out as little more than a leader of tribal mercenaries, opposed the **imamate** during its last years, joined the **republicans** during the **Yemeni Civil War**, and then went on to become arguably the most powerful and most successful tribal politician in the YAR from the late 1960s through the mid-1970s. The chief broker of Yemeni politics during these years, he could make and break governments almost at will.

A "republican tribalist" with one foot planted in the state, Sinan made the Nahm tribe and region a base of traditional power even as he derived much power and patronage from his position as longtime governor of **al-Hudayda** province—a post that gave him control of the YAR's main port and its custom duties during the **al-Iryani** era from the late 1960s through the mid-1970s. Several relatives from the Luhumi clan Sinan held key posts in the "tribalized" regular army at this time, among them his brothers Muhammad and Dirham and his cousin, Ali. Indeed, Ali became commander of an elite unit, the Reserves, in the early 1970s. At the same time, Sinan was patron and brother-in-law of the YAR's most prominent and successful modernist politician during the al-Iryani era, Muhsin **al-Aini**. Al-Aini was the modernist head of the **Baath Party** in Yemen, and a number of Sinan's younger relatives became Baathis. More easily than most tribal figures, Sinan bridged the modern and traditional political domains and drew strength from each. During these years, he seemed to have as much, if not more, power than his tribal rival, paramount shaykh of the **Hashid** confederation, Abdulla ibn Husayn **al-Ahmar**. This, however, was to prove short-lived.

In 1974, Sinan was a part of the plot to oust President al-Iryani and replace him with Ibrahim **al-Hamdi**. Then, in turn, in 1975, Sinan was stripped of power and ousted from the state by al-Hamdi along with the rest of the "Luhumis" and most other leading tribalists, including Shaykh al-Ahmar. Living in comfort during the long **Salih era** that followed the short al-Hamdi era, Sinan did make something of a comeback in the 1980s as an elder statesman. However, without the power and prestige of leadership over a united tribal base, he lacked both the capacity to make the big comeback and the staying power demonstrated by his old rival, Shaykh al-Ahmar.

In 1993, more than two years after Yemeni **unification**, Sinan formed with Mujahid **abu Shuwarib** a political group that sought to end the deepening political crisis and conflict between the two main parties in the ruling coalition. When this effort failed in March 1994, he and Mujahid went into exile in protest just weeks before the **War of Secession**. Soon back in Yemen, he was appointed to the new **Shura Council** in 1997 and has remained there.

ABU RAS FAMILY. Important members of the Dhu Muhammad tribe of the **Bakil** tribal confederation, the extended Abu Ras family had their roots in the mountainous Barat region in the far northeast but were also large landowners in the southern uplands of **Ibb** province. Shaykh Amin Abu Ras was a strong republican at the time of the **1962 Revolution** and was active in republican politics and the government in subsequent years. His son, Sadik Amin Abu Ras, was active in the **Local Development Association** movement in the 1970s and 1980s. With **Yemeni unification** in 1990, Sadik became minister of agriculture and then, in 1994, minister of civil service. In 1997, he became minister of local administration and remained in that post until early 2006. In the latter capacity, he was deeply involved in the major effort to enhance local government through elected and empowered **local councils**.

ABU SHUWARIB, MUJAHID (1938–2004). The longtime aide and protege of Abdullah ibn Husayn **al-Ahmar**, paramount shaykh of the **Hashid** tribal confederation, Shaykh Mujahid emerged as a **Yemeni Civil War** hero in the 1960s and went on to become an important political figure in the YAR in his own right beginning in the late 1970s, in the early years of the presidency of Ali Abdullah **Salih**. He served as deputy prime minister for internal affairs in the YAR from 1979 to 1990. He continued in that post after Yemeni **unification** in 1990, and later that year emerged as a leading critic of the coalition against **Iraq** led by the **United States** and **Saudi Arabia**. During the months before the **War of Secession** in 1994, he and Shaykh Sinan **Abu Luhum** joined forces to mediate in the growing conflict between the opposing political forces and then, with Shaykh Sinan, went into exile in protest over the failure to peacefully save unification. He returned in 1994 and in 1997 was appointed to the new

Shura Council and as adviser to President Salh. Imposing, forceful, and charismatic, Shaykh Mujahid had links to the **Baath** Party in his early years and is a good example of a tribal leader who adapted to modern politics by assuming a state office and then using that position to represent the tribes and their interests. He died in a car accident in Yemen in 2004.

ABYAN. The province comprised of rugged uplands and the fertile coastal delta of Wadi **Bana** northeast of **Aden.** The rich delta was developed by the **colonial administration** of **Great Britain** during World War II to grow cereals for Aden and, after the war, as an area for the cultivation of the long staple cotton highly prized on world markets. Historically, the tribes of **Fadhli** and Lower **Yafa** had shared the delta, and bitter disputes between them over water had been common. The Abyan scheme, administered from 1947 by the Abyan Development Board (ADB) introduced tribesmen to a new pattern of irrigated **agriculture** on a large scale. Since both the Fadhli and Lower Yafi sultanates and their tribal allies were represented on the ADB, the political relationship between them changed and became more collaborative. Zinjibar, on the coast and about 40 miles northeast of Aden was the capital of the Fadhli sultanate and, with the economic activity generated by the agricultural scheme, a more prosperous center of local commerce than most towns in the **Aden Protectorates**.

Politically, Abyan was important after the exodus of the British because of both its proximity to Aden and its role as the base of the power and popularity of **Ali Nasir Muhammad** al-Hassani, the man who dominated the PDRY from late 1980 until he was forced into exile in early 1986. Just as his Abyan supporters had benefited from his rule—e.g., **Abd al-Rabu** Mansour Hadi—some of them were again rewarded after Ali Nasir Muhammad had his forces in exile side with President **Salih** regime during the **War of Secession** in 1994. However, some of the militant Islamists from Abyan who had also supported the Salih regime during this crisis came to feel that they were not being rewarded. As a result, in the 1990s and beyond, Abyan also became a base for militant Islamic activity, first in the form of Tariq **al-Fadhli's** Yemeni Islamic Jihad and then the **Aden–Abyan Islamic Army**.

ABYSSINIA. *See* ETHIOPIA.

ADEN–ABYAN ISLAMIC ARMY (AAIA). The militant **political Islamist** group that grew out of the Yemeni Islamic Jihad (YIJ) in the early 1990s and that became best known for the kidnapping in **Abyan** in late 1998 in which 4 of 18 British and Australian **tourists** were killed. The AAIA emerged after the YIJ's founder, Tarik **al-Fadhli,** and some of his colleagues were co-opted by the **Salih** regime. Many members of YIJ and AAIA were fighters returning from **Afghanistan**—"Afghani Arabs"—who, upon returning, had sided with and helped the Salih regime in the **War of Secession** in 1994. Feeling insufficiently rewarded for this, even passed over for benefits that instead went to Abyan followers of **Ali Nasir Muhammad** al-Hassani, the AAIA engaged in skirmishes in Abyan with the local authorities and police throughout the rest of the 1990s, thereby becoming a problem for the regime.

By contrast, the fatal 1998 kidnapping incident did pose a serious threat to the regime, coming shortly after the bombings of the two American embassies in East Africa had focused the attentions of the United States and others on the Islamic terrorist threat. Most immediately, the death of the tourists sorely strained relations between the Salih regime and **Great Britain.** Only days after the latter severely criticized the regime publicly for mishandling the effort to free the hostages, it was learned that the tourists had been kidnapped by the AAIA on behalf of a radical Islamic cleric in London, Abu Hamza al-Masri. Al-Masri's son and stepson had been part of a group of young militants arrested near **Aden** in a car full of weapons just days before the kidnapping. When al-Masri asked the head of the AAIA for help in securing his relatives' release, the AAIA took the 18 tourists hostage, thereby setting the stage for the tragic and bizarre diplomatic episode.

Immediately after the kidnapping deaths, the head of the AAIA, Zain al-Abdin al-Mihdar, was captured, quickly tried and executed in 1999. Minor incidents between the AAIA and the regime continued episodically thereafter, but 2003 saw a large siege and bloody battle in the mountains of Abyan after the AAIA attacked a military medical convoy. This, and the lesser encounters, served to suppress the AAIA as a major actor by late in the decade.

ADEN, ADEN COLONY AND THE PORT OF ADEN. The cosmopolitan city on the southern tip of the Arabian Peninsula and Gulf of Aden that is most distinguished by a large natural harbor, the deep and protected waters of which are guarded by, in the words of Charles Johnson, "the two adjoining volcanic peninsulas of Aden and Little Aden which stick out into the sea like the claws of a lobster buried in the sand." Under **Great Britain's** administration, the 75-square-mile Aden Colony grew to consist of these two peninsulas, which defined the entrance of the Bay of Aden, as well as the low, narrow, curved littoral that connected the larger peninsula and the various commercial, residential, and military districts of Aden proper to the much smaller one that is home to the **Aden Refinery** and the factories, residences, and military facilities that make up Little Aden. The smaller volcanic formation lies a few miles west of the main crater at Aden. To the north and east of Aden Colony lay the vast area that came to be known as the **Aden Protectorates**.

With the potential for control of the narrow straits separating Asia from the **Horn of Africa**, long-inhabited Aden has served from time to time over many centuries as an important political as well as commercial center. It gave Yemen access to the outside world and was, as described by Yemeni historians long ago, "the eye of Yemen." It grew to be a major strategic and trade link in the British Empire from the mid-19th century to the mid-1960s, the capital of what became the Marxist PDRY from 1967 to 1990, and the designated "economic capital" of the ROY on the occasion of **unification** in 1990. Under British rule since 1839, Aden Colony and its immediate environs evolved into a sort of colonial city–state. The story of the PDRY was largely one of efforts to close the wide socioeconomic, political, and cultural gaps between this relatively modern, worldly wise city and its vast, highly fragmented, and much more traditional hinterland.

Modern Aden, with a population of nearly 800,000, consists of several markedly different towns that grew together over time. The old city is located in bits and pieces in and around the volcanic crater, rising some 550 meters, that forms Cape Aden. The oldest and biggest part is Crater, actually inside the crater of the dormant volcano. Crater was the longtime home to many old Adeni families, as well as home of the many Indians who came to Aden after Britain made it a colonial outpost; it remains one of the very distinct and most-densely populated neighborhoods of modern Aden. Facing the harbor, and distinguished by a mile-long stretch of divided roadway flanked on both sides by an unbroken wall of drab six-story concrete apartment and office buildings with bustling shops and restaurants on their first floors, is Maalla. In late colonial days, it catered to the families of British servicemen and civil servants and to other foreigners. Maalla, while remaining quite vibrant, became run down over the years of austerity since Britain's departure in 1967.

Around the tip of the cape that juts into the Bay of Aden are Steamer Point and al-Tawahi, the bustling transit tourist area of colonial **Aden**, jutting out into the great bay, where ocean liners were moored to its wharves. Then it was full of duty-free shops piled high with inexpensive products and other places to spend money frivolously, tasteless and exotic by turns. Steamer Point became quite shabby during the decades of socialist austerity and few tourists. Still, there remain a couple of majestic old hotels, a little replica of Big Ben and other traces of the British imperial era. Here, too, are the steep slopes of Jabal Shamsan on which the 18 ancient Cisterns of al-Tawahi can be found.

The closest suburb of the old city is Khormaksar, which is near the international airport and notable for its old military installations. Separated from Khomaksar by saltpans, and near old Aden colony's border with **Lahaj**, is Sheikh Othman. It is a big suburb, gateway to North Yemen. Indeed, it was temporary home for most of the migrants from the north, especially during the periods of increasing economic activity between World War I and the end of the 1960s. Halfway between Aden and Little Aden, on the Bay of Aden, is Madinat al-Shaab (or al-Ittihad), the post-British government center that also contains Aden University.

During the colonial era, Aden was transformed from a poor, sleepy fishing village, long in deep decline and with only several thousand dwellers, into a rather cosmopolitan, decidedly multiracial city of a couple hundred thousand residents and a port that was, by some measures, the third or fourth busiest in the world from the mid-1950s to the mid-1960s. Created in the 1890s through the efforts of private, locally based commercial companies that were dissatisfied with the efforts of British colonial civil servants, the Aden Port Trust operated, maintained and improved Aden Port over the decades, contributing much to the growth, competitiveness, and world-class status of the port over the first two-thirds of the 20th century. Under the PDRY, the Yemen Ports and Shipping Corporation was the state agency that exercised centralized control over all operations of the Port of Aden through its supervision of three subsidiaries: the Port of Aden Authority, responsible for port operations; the National Shipping Company, responsible for stevedoring, shipping, and shipping agency activities; and the National Dockyards Company, responsible for ship repairs.

Although in a state of socialist neglect and disrepair by the end of the 1980s, the city and its port still evidence traces of past beauty and grandeur and, more importantly, great potential for **tourism** and as a regional commercial and industrial center in the 21st century. Efforts since Yemeni unification to realize Aden's new role as economic capital of the ROY include the creation of the Aden container port and free zone, as well as the modernization and expansion of the rest of the port and the mid-1950's Aden Refinery. These and other efforts to revitalize and build the economy of Aden have proceeded slowly and with disappointing results because of difficulty in getting Aden and Adenis to adjust to the post-socialist system, the sense and reality of defeat after the **War of Secession** in 1994, and political events associated with the United States' **War on Terror** after 9/11. By the middle of the first decade of the 21st century, however, Adenis seemed to be getting over their hangover and engaging in a binge of business expansion and construction in Aden proper and in its suburbs. It may yet become the economic capital of the ROY, once again "the eye of Yemen." *See also* HAINES, COMMANDER A. B.

ADEN ASSOCIATION. One of the first modern political organizations in South Yemen, the Aden Association in the early 1950s called for the eventual independence of Aden within the Commonwealth and in cooperation with the British. Led by the prominent **Luqman** family, and armed with its own newspaper, its members included long-resident Indians and Somalis as well as Adeni Arabs. Although it accurately reflected the social reality produced over the colonial era—i.e., the cosmopolitan and separate nature of Aden—the Aden Association and its political agenda were overtaken by the late 1950s by political events that precluded the creation of a Singapore–like city–state of Aden, whatever the merits of the idea.

ADEN CONTAINER PORT AND FREE ZONE. Touted at **unification** in 1990 as the top non-petroleum economic projects and the keys to **Aden's** becoming the ROY's "economic capital," the separate but complementary Aden Container Terminal (ACT) and Aden Free Zone (AFZ) projects were still falling far short of hopes by late in the first decade of the new century. At the time that ACT opened in 1999, promoters were saying that Aden's possession of one of the world's best protected natural deepwater harbors and its location just a couple of miles from the main sea lanes linking Europe and Asia placed ACT in a position to overtake Dubai's Jebel Ali/Port Rashid and Oman's recently launched Salalah as the premier transshipment hub in the region. In 2005, however, the number of twenty-foot equivalent units (TEUs) using ACT was only small percentages of those using Dubai and Oman.

By 2007, however, ACT was beginning to live up to greatly scaled-back, but still high, expectations. Increasing rapidly after 1999, the use of ACT peaked at nearly 400,000 TEUs in 2002, only to plunge to about 125,000 TEUs in 2003. The primary cause was the suicide bombing of the supertanker *Limburg* in October 2002, an event that instantly raised questions about the ROY's ability to secure its waters and harbor and that caused maritime insurance rates to soar. As a result of increased maritime security, largely the result of United States and European aid, the ROY's new and well-equipped and trained coastguard, the number of TEUs in 2006 approached the 2002 peak in 2006—and surpassed it in 2007. In addition to security and security-driven insurance issues, this turnabout was also the result of increases in the capacity of the facilities and the sorting out of some issues of the ownership and operation of ACT.

From the outset, the Port of Singapore Authority (PSA) had been the majority owner and operator of ACT and in these capacities had devoted significant resources to increase greatly and quickly ACT's capacity. Concerned about the port's prospects in the wake of the **Limburg** bombing, and the problem of doing business in Yemen generally, PSA opted in late 2003 to sell its 60 percent stake back to the ROY, forcing the latter to seek a new operator and possible partners. In early 2004, the government appointed a Singapore consortium to operate ACT for one year.

In mid-2005, the ROY chose DP World (until recently Dubai Ports International) to run ACT as a long-term partner under a concession expected to last for up to 35 years. In mid-2007, faced with charges from parliament and elsewhere that DP World had reneged on a planned expansion of ACT and that its big role in the container port in Dubai posed a conflict of interest, the government pulled out of the agreement and called for new bidders on the contract. After months of confusion, including a major takeover proposal by former PSA employees and global investors, the ROY in late 2007 reversed itself and signed a Memorandum of Understanding (MoU) with DP World to operate and develop ACT. The MoU calls for creation of a joint United Arab Emirates (UAE)–Yemeni company to run the terminal, which will be half-owned by each partner. The ROY and DP World will also split investment costs equally, and for its part, DP World will invest $493 million over a 30-year period to raise ACT's capacity nearly fivefold and to link it closely to the AFZ. It seemed that DP World's strong brand and deep pockets, combined with the ROY's desire to build on improving relations with the UAE, won the day.

Created shortly after unification in 1991, and adjacent to the port and city of Aden, the AFZ was conceived and promoted as a major effort to create thousands of jobs (taking advantage of Yemen's cheap labor) and to take advantage of Aden's geographic location and make it an important regional fabrication, manufacturing and transshipment center. To this end, various incentives were to be included to attract Yemeni and foreign investment capital. The first chairman of the enterprise was Abd al-Qadr **Bajammal**.

The AFZ failed to get off the ground. The causes were epic mismanagement and corruption, as well as the domestic political crisis that led the **War of Secession** in 1994 and the effect of global **political Islam** and the **War on Terror** after 2001 on the investment climate in Yemen. Many of the questions hanging over the ACT at the time were also plaguing the free zone. Nevertheless, initial construction on Phase II of the AFZ—which was to include an "air cargo village" tied to the recently rehabilitated Aden Airport—began in January 2003. Bad luck continued to plague the free zone, however, and by the end of the year, the company managing the project, Yeminvest, had been dissolved amid allegations of rampant corruption. The phoenix rose, though, and at the end of 2006 the chairman of the

AFZ announced that $250 million of the funds pledged at the London donors' conference for Yemen in November was to go to reviving the second phase of the project.

ADEN PORT TRUST. *See* ADEN, ADEN COLONY AND THE PORT OF ADEN.

ADEN PROTECTORATES. The dozen or so traditional political units to the west, north, and east of **Aden** Colony with which Britain signed treaties of friendship and protection in the 19th century. This large, partly British-defined hinterland of Aden served primarily as a military and political buffer for the city, port, and military base and their environs. Consisting of an area huge relative to Aden Colony, the protectorates were defined and redefined geographically as well as administratively in an unplanned and ad hoc way over the century-and-a-quarter between the British occupation of Aden in 1839 and the British withdrawal and creation of an independent South Yemen in 1967.

The need to define Britain's claim and relationship to Aden's socially diverse and politically fragmented hinterland immediately to the north and west became urgent when the **Ottoman Turks** occupied the interior and southern parts of North Yemen in the 1870s. This prompted negotiation of a comprehensive network of treaties of protection between Britain and the rulers of several of the political entities in the hinterland and, in the early 1900s, a negotiated agreement between the British and the Turks on the **Anglo–Ottoman line** separating their spheres of interest.

Similarly, Britain was increasingly forced to define and extend its influence and presence east of Aden in the **Hadhramawt** and neighboring areas, beginning with the need to end the ill effects of the long **Quaiti–Kathiri war** in the second half of the 19th century. This culminated in the successful efforts by Harold **Ingrams** to effect a truce among the tribes of the Hadhramawt in the mid-1930s.

Later in the same decade, Britain divided South Yemen beyond Aden into the Western Aden Protectorate, with a British agent in Aden, and an Eastern Aden Protectorate, with a resident adviser in **Mukalla**. It was out of the many "independent" components of these jerrybuilt protectorates, eventually in combination with Aden Colony,

that the British in the 1960s sought to build the **Federat**
Arabia, the rickety ship of state they vainly hoped
them when they withdrew in 1967.

ADEN PROTECTORATE SECURITY FORCF

of security forces in the **Aden Protectorates** is   ...ure of
the evolution of the **"forward policy"** adopted by ᴕreat Britain after
the second decade of the 20th century. The emergence of an assertive,
expansive Yemeni **imamate** after World War I caused the British in
Aden, as an alternative to the costly stationing of their own troops
along the border, to provide arms, training, and funds to rulers in
what later became the Western Aden Protectorate. This did more than
just address the threat from the north. Through the small, but regular,
armed forces that this made possible, the local rulers' control over
their unruly tribes was enhanced at the same time that their dependence upon Britain also grew.

In the late 1920s, however, the **Royal Air Force** was given
responsibility for Aden's defense, and a single British-trained and
-officered local force—the Aden Protectorate Levies—was raised
in order to defend the entire western portion of the protectorates
from outside attack, constituting the first time that the British had
successfully treated the area as a single political entity. Beginning
in the 1930s, the Aden Protectorate Levies were supplemented by
two other forces: units of Tribal Guards, charged with policing trade
routes, and the Government Guards, charged with escorting the British **political officer** and other officials anywhere in the Protectorates. With the creation of the **Federation of Arab Amirates of the**
South (FASS) in 1959, the various tribal guards were combined as
the Federal National Guards, and the Aden Protectorate Levies were
expanded into the Federal Regular Army. In mid-1967, on the eve
of South Yemen's rushed independence and four years after Aden
had joined with the states of the (FAAS) to form the **Federation of**
South Arabia (FSA), the Federal National Guard and the Federal
Regular Army were merged to form the South Arabian Armed Forces
(SAAF). By this time, however, the national struggle had rendered
these forces unreliable—a matter of little real consequence, because
the power and authority of both the British and the FSA were fast
slipping away.

The course of events was different in what was to become the Eastern Aden Protectorate. In 1938, after **"Ingrams' Peace"** was secured, the British-officered Hadhrami Beduin Legion was formed along the lines of Glubb Pasha's Arab Legion in Transjordan and given the task of providing security in the Protectorate. With modifications, this security system was still in place when the **National Liberation Front** took over from the British in 1967, the states in the Eastern Aden Protectorate having remained aloof from the constitutional changes that led up to the FSA and its security arrangements. *See also* AIR CONTROL.

ADEN REFINERY. *See* REFINERIES, OIL.

ADEN TRADE UNION CONGRESS. *See* LABOR UNIONS.

ADEN UNIVERSITY. *See* EDUCATION.

ADNAN AND ADNANIS. *See* QAHTANIS AND ADNANIS.

ADVISORY COUNCIL. A small advisory body, originally of 15 notables, that was created by President **Salih** in mid-1979 as part of a broader effort designed to build regime support and legitimacy. Its specific purpose was to facilitate greater participation by elements of the elite previously outside or on the edges of the regime. Basically an instrument of co-optation, the council was reinvigorated or enlarged on a couple of occasions after its creation. Upon Yemeni **unification** in 1990, a 45-member version of it became a feature of the ROY. After the **War of Secession** in 1994, it was replaced by the 59-member **Shura Council**.

AELIUS GALLUS. The Roman prefect of Egypt, then only recently absorbed by the Roman Empire, who in 24 B.C. failed in his campaign deep into the **Arabian Peninsula** to conquer the Kingdom of **Saba** or to force it to ally with Rome. Rome and its historians derived much of their knowledge and lore about Arabia—Arabia Felix as well as Arabia Deserta—from the accounts of this ill-fated expedition.

AFGHANISTAN AND "AFGHANI ARABS." The country of Afghanistan is strikingly like the mountains and highlands of

Yemen in terms of geography, culture, social organization, level of economic development, and, until the second half of the 20th century, isolation from the modern world. Located east of Iran, distant Afghanistan's impact on Yemen today is less a function of these similarities than of its role as the principal incubator of global revolutionary **political Islam** since the mid-1980s. This incubator was created as a result of the effort led by the United States and Saudi Arabia to recruit, train, and arm young Muslims to wage jihad against the invasion of Afghanistan by the **Soviet Union** in 1979. When Soviet forces withdrew in defeat in 1989, the incubator was suddenly turned off—and the militants nurtured by it came home to roost, most notably to Egypt, Algeria, Bosnia, Chechnya, and Yemen. These returnees were dubbed "Afghani Arabs" and many of them, more militant and skilled as jihadists than when they first went to Afghanistan, continued their jihad in new venues. Usama **bin Ladin** and many of those who were soon to comprise al-Qaida were among them.

Meanwhile, back in Afghanistan, the Taliban emerged out of the warlord-induced chaos in the mid-1990s. The Taliban were inspired by the madrasas in neighboring Pakistan that were run by the Deobandi sect, a militant, anti-western school of fundamentalism that had been backed earlier as a source of mujahidiin to fight the Soviet occupiers. With the rise of the Taliban, the incubator was again turned on and nurtured a second generation of fighters, a process that continued after the overthrow of the Taliban in 2001, shortly after **9/11**. The Taliban's provision of a haven in 1995 for the newly created al-Qaida further fostered the creation of "Afghani Arabs," a process that continued in modified form after the U.S. invasion of Afghanistan in late 2001.

Given Yemen's proximity to Saudi Arabia and the Saudis' two decades effort to spread throughout the YAR its variant of Islamic fundamentalism, Wahhabism, it should not come as a surprise that, beginning in the early 1980s, Yemenis made up a disproportionate share of those recruited for jihad in Afghanistan. Because of Yemen's porous borders and vast areas beyond the reach of the state, a continuous stream of "Afghani Arabs," Yemeni and non-Yemeni, found haven and safe transit in Yemen from the late 1980s into the new millennium.

Evidence abounds of the important role that the Yemeni "Afghani Arabs" played in the era of global revolutionary Islam. After their success in Afghanistan, bin Laden and many of his colleagues returned to Saudi Arabia and Yemen, intent on making the anti-Islamic "communist" regime in South Yemen their next target for jihad. When Yemen **unification** in 1990 rendered this moot, Yemeni "Afghani Arabs" used assassination and bombing to settle old scores with members of the **Yemeni Socialist Party** (YSP) and then fought against the YSP during the **War of Secession** in 1994. They came to staff such organizations as Yemeni Islamic Jihad, the **Aden–Abyan Islamic Army**, and the local branch of al-Qaida. Their most notable acts of violence were the bombings of the Goldmur Hotel in 1992, the U.S.S. *Cole* in 2000, and the French supertanker *Limburg* in 2002. Increasingly, the Yemeni "Afghani Arabs" came to see their chief enemies as the United States and the **Salih** regime—the latter an ally of the former in the **War on Terror**.

AL-AFIF, AHMAD JABR. Several times minister of education in the 1970s who, since the beginning of the 1990s, became a leader and benefactor of Yemeni culture as founding chairman of the al-Afif Cultural Foundation and head of Yemen's largest and most vocal anti-**qat** organization. During his tenure as minister, al-Afif came to be associated with corruption and the misuse of foreign aid, and some critics pointed to him as one of the first Yemeni to use his position in government to enrich himself in the new era of international aid. Like Andrew Carnegie, he made amends—through his foundation and anti-qat campaign. During much of the 1960s, during the **Yemeni Civil War**, al-Afif was in exile in Beirut and a leader of the **Third Force**, opposed to both the **Egyptians** and the **royalists**.

AGRICULTURE. The **economy** of Yemen, once largely self-sufficient and based on subsistence agriculture, has become increasingly dependent on agricultural imports. At the same time, and as recently as 2005, more then 50 percent of Yemen's population still lived in rural areas and were largely dependent on domestic agricultural products for income and sustenance—thus the low per capita income. To lessen these dependences, and to address the issue of "food security," the governments of the YAR, PDRY and ROY devoted considerable attention to agricultural development over the past 40 to 45 years.

Given its considerably greater agricultural potential, the YAR has placed more emphasis on the agricultural sector than has the PDRY. The more limited agricultural development in the PDRY built upon the irrigated agricultural schemes launched by the British during and after World War II, particularly that in **Abyan**; thereafter, it was shaped by the Agrarian Reform Law of 1970 and the Cooperatives Law of 1972, which broke up large landholdings, limited the size of permissible holdings, and placed their greatest emphasis on the reation of cooperatives and state farms. The scope and depth of the effects of agricultural reform in the Wadi **Hadhramant** and elsewhere were significant, restructuring rural social life and improving living standards; less successful, however, were efforts to firmly ground these gains in increased agricultural productivity.

The PDRY's emphasis upon land reform and reorganization contrasts sharply with that of the YAR. Such notable exceptions as Wadi **Mawr** notwithstanding, small landholdings have been the norm in North Yemen. This condition and the more conservative orientation of successive regimes in the YAR explain the absence of land reform in the north. Large-scale agricultural development in North Yemen focused on the several **wadi** development schemes under the umbrella of the **Tihama Development Authority** (TDA), schemes beginning with the Wadi **Zabid** project. These projects have capitalized on the Yemenis' traditional skill with spate **irrigation**, although the careful channeling and use of flash floods is now secondary to pumped-water irrigation. Similar schemes outside the Tihama are being developed in the **Marib** and the Wadi **Jawf** areas far to the east, the former depending notably upon the rebuilding of the Marib Dam in the 1980s.

North Yemen had some agricultural successes. The towns and cities are full of fruit and vegetables produced in the countryside, something that was not the case until the early 1980s. Notable has been the production of bananas and citrus fruit, largely stimulated by the imposition of import controls at this time. (The tiny but sweet bananas were associated by the public with Dr. Abd al-Karim **al-Iryani**, prime minister at the time.) In another success, Yemen has become self-sufficient in poultry production, the major source of protein away from the coast. However, Yemen's greatest agriculture success story is the massive increase in **qat** production. Its big downsides notwithstanding, qat production has generated income for a huge number of Yemens, with the effect that people have remained on and preserved the land, particularly Yemen's famed terraces.

Despite these successes, and despite the oft-repeated theme of the Salih regime since Yemeni **unification** in 1990 that Yemen's future depends largely on the application of new **oil** revenues to the agricultural sector, the sector has largely been neglected and agricultural development has been spotty and disappointing. The wasteful use of scarce water and the precipitous drop in the water table are twin sources of concern. And if Yemen can grow and market dozens of varieties of qat so successfully, why has the country crucial to the birth of the **coffee** trade not been able to cash in on the rapidly growing boutique coffee market?

AL-AHDAL, MUHAMMAD HAMDI. *See* WAR ON TERROR.

AHMAD ALI ABDULLAH SALIH. *See* SALIH, ALI ABDULLAH, AND THE SALIH FAMILY.

AHMAD BIN YAHYA HAMID AL-DIN, IMAM (?–1962). Imam of North Yemen from 1948 until 1962 who, after a long apprenticeship to his father, Imam **Yahya**, dealt forcefully and even courageously with the forces, many of them aspects or expressions of modernity, that were challenging the **imamate** and traditional Yemen at home and from abroad. The end of the imamate came with the **1962 Revolution**, a week after Ahmad died of natural causes.

At home, Imam Ahmad led the armed forces that undid the **1948 Revolution** that had deposed the **Hamid al-Din** family on the occasion of his father's assassination; later, in the **1955 attempt coup**, he quite literally and single-handedly stared down his captors. In these and lesser cases, he harshly punished the offenders, many of them modernist political reformers. Short and stocky, he was known for his fearsome appearance, especially for his bulging eyes, the bulging of which some claimed he induced.

Abroad, Imam Ahmad tried diplomatically and militarily to counter a **Great Britain** that was increasing its presence in territory to the south and southeast that he regarded as Yemeni. On the Arab front, he tried politically to protect Yemen and the imamate from the rising tide of revolutionary Arab nationalism, especially as personified by Egypt's President Gamal Abdel **Nasser**. After the dramatic creation of the United Arab Republic (UAR), uniting revolutionary Egypt and Syria, he pushed the UAR to create, with him, the United Arab States (UAS). Something of a poet, he is best known in this regard for a poem attacking Nasserism on the occasion of the breakup of the on-paper-only UAS.

AL-AHMAR FAMILY AND SHAYKH ABDULLAH IBN HUSAYN AL-AHMAR (1932–2007). The paramount leader of the **Hashid** tribal confederation who for nearly a half century since the **1962 Revolution** was the leading tribal figure in Yemen and the personification of both the **tribal system** and its ambivalent, ambiguous relationship to the modern state and the non-tribal modernists most committed to it. Based in the northern town of **Khamr**, Shaykh Abdullah's family had provided the paramount shaykh of Hashid for generations. He assumed the position in 1960 when his father, then paramount shaykh, and his eldest brother were killed on orders from Imam **Ahmad** in a moment of anger during negotiations. This act, on the eve of the revolution and the creation of the YAR, made Shaykh Abdullah and his followers bitter enemies of the **Hamid al-Din** imamate. They then became supporters of the republic during the long **Yemeni Civil War** that followed the revolution.

Shaykh Abdullah's relationships with the YAR's five heads of state were strained as often as not, and his relationship with President Ibrahim **al-Hamdi** in the mid-1970s was unambiguously adversarial. In 1971, his election as speaker of the new **Consultative Council** symbolized both his special prominence and the inclusion of the tribal shaykhs in general in the conciliatory regime led by President Abd al-Rahman **al-Iryani** from 1967 to 1974. However, during the al-Hamdi era from mid-1974 to 1977, the attempt was made to lessen tribal influence in the name of state-building and development, and Shaykh Abdullah and other big shaykhs were stripped of their positions in the state and virtually expelled from **Sanaa**. The result was a virtual cold war between the state and the tribes.

The situation changed suddenly in 1978, after the assassination of al-Hamdi and with the presidency of Ali Abdullah **Salih**, a member of the **Sanhan** tribe, a lesser tribe in the Hashid confederation. The complex, sometimes strained relationship between these two leaders is implicit in a statement allegedly made by President Salih to Shaykh al-Ahmar early in the former's tenure: "You'll be my shaykh and I'll be your president." Shaykh Abdullah apparently agreed and the relationship was reaffirmed when he again became speaker of the reinstated Consultative Council after the 1988 **elections**.

With Yemeni **unification** in 1990, Shaykh Abdullah gained new prominence as the head of the newly created **Islah Party** that opposed the unification regime composed of President Salih's **General People's Congress** (GPC) and the southerners' **Yemeni Socialist Party** (YSP), charging it with being insufficiently Islamic and not a true friend of the tribes and tribalism. Nevertheless, with President Salih's approval, he became speaker of the new **Council of Deputies** after Islah did well in the April 1993 elections and went into a coalition government with the two unification parties. Conflict between the two unification partners and the **War of Secession** in 1994 resulted in a coalition government of Islah and the GPC—and the further increase in Shaykh Abdullah's importance.

Despite the GPC's decision to rule alone and not go into coalition with Islah after the 1997 elections, Shaykh Abdullah remained speaker of the Council—again, underlining the special relationship between these two leaders. This relationship continued into the new century, although strains between them became increasingly apparent. With the creation of the **Joint Meeting Parties** (JMP) in 2002, and with Islah's leading position in this opposition coalition, Shaykh Abdullah found himself caught between his president and the party he still headed. Things came to a head in the run-up to the 2006 presidential elections when the JMP chose a candidate to oppose President Salih and Shaykh Abdullah chose to support his president.

By this time, however, Shaykh Abdullah was old, in failing health, and less of a force to be reckoned with in Yemeni politics. Still, as evidence of his staying power, Shaykh Abdullah was reelected president of Islah in early 2007. He died of cancer on 29 December, 2007, at the age of 74.

The sons of Shaykh Abdullah have been conspicuously present in recent years, four of them currently as elected members of the council—revealingly, two representing Islah and two the GPC. Two of them, Hamid and Sadiq, are prominent businessmen, and Sadiq has assumed his father's duties as paramount shaykh of Hashid. However, dwarfed by their father during his lifetime, it is almost certain that not one of them—or, for that matter, any other tribal figure—will play the the role Shaykh Abdullah played over the decades.

AL-AHRAR. *See* FREE YEMENI PARTY.

AID, FOREIGN. *See* ARAB REGIONAL FUNDS; ARMS AND MILITARY AID; ECONOMY AND POLITICAL ECONOMY; EUROPEAN UNION (EU); GERMANY; GULF COOPERATION COUNCIL (GCC); IMF/WORLD BANK AID; IMF/WORLD BANK REFORMS; JAPAN; KUWAIT; SAUDI ARABIA, KINGDOM OF; UNITED NATIONS (UN); UNITED STATES.

AL-AINI (AL-AYNI), MUHSIN (1932–). A first-generation **modernist** and a member of the **Famous Forty**, al-Aini was North Yemen's leading and best-known "modern" civilian politician from the early 1960s to the mid-1970s and allegedly aspired to succeed President **al-Iryani**. A thoroughly political man, he was known on the Arab stage even before the **1962 Revolution** as the head of the Yemeni branch of the **Baath party**; probably for this reason, he was named foreign minister in the first government after the revolution. He went on to be prime minister and foreign minister jointly in three governments during the al-Iryani era and in the first government under President **al-Hamdi**.

The chief support for his political ambitions was his powerful brother-in-law, Shaykh Sinan **abu Luhum**, and together with the rest of the Luhumi clan they made for a formidable political group. It was President al-Hamid's successful effort in 1975 to eliminate as challengers the big **tribal** leaders in general and Shaykh Sinan in particular that cut short al-Aini's political career. Thereafter, from the mid-1970s into the 1990s, his career was reduced to a series of ambassadorial posts, albeit important ones—e.g., YAR ambassador to France, the United Nations, and the United States and then, in 1990, the first ambassador to the United States from the ROY. In 1997, an elder statesman, al-Aini was appointed to the new **Shura Council**.

AIR CONTROL. The policy and doctrine developed by the **Royal Air Force** and applied in the Aden **Protectorates** in the late 1920s and thereafter whereby control over territory and people was exercised through the threat and use of bombing and strafing by airplanes from strategically placed air bases in the rear, instead of through the positioning and use of ground forces in advance bases. Reported in the Arab media as the punitive bombing of defenseless villages, which it surely sometimes was, this modern military dimension of unobtrusive, indirect rule was abandoned as politically unacceptable by the early 1960s. According to its advocates in **Great Britain**, however, air control had been ritualized and codified by both sides to the point that the colonial power got its way, the offending locals saved face, and few lives were lost. One unintended effect of this policy was that the country cobbled together by the British was one held together by a network of small airfields and small planes rather than by motorable roads and lorries. *See also* ADEN PROTECTORATE SECURITY FORCES.

AIR TRANSPORT AND AIRPORTS. *See* INFRASTRUCTURE DEVELOPMENT.

AKHDAM CASTE. *See* SOCIAL SYSTEM AND STRUCTURE.

AKK TRIBAL CONFEDERATION. The ancient tribal lineage from which the warlike, fiercely independent tribes that make up much of the inland population of the **Tihama** are descended. Among them are the **Zaraniq** and Quhra tribes.

AKSUM. *See* ETHIOPIA.

AL-AKWA, QADI ISMAIL (1920–). A minor figure in the movement for political change in North Yemen from the 1940s through the 1960s who went on to play a prominent role in the intellectual and cultural life of Yemen for over a generation as the author of works on its traditional institutions, history and culture and as founder and head of the General Organization of Antiquities and Libraries from 1969 to 1990. In these capacities, he encouraged new research by Yemeni and foreign scholars and contributed much to the study and preservation of Yemen's pre-Islamic and Islamic heritage. As to his life in government and politics, he was an early Yemeni "revolutionary," a diplomat and, in 1968–1969, minister of information.

ALAWI. One of the roughly 10 **tribes** in the hinterland of **Aden** to which **Great Britain** extended treaty protection, as a member of the **Aden Protectorates**, in the last quarter of the 19th century as part of its growing effort to block expansion toward Aden by the **Ottoman Turkish** occupiers of North Yemen and, later, by the Zaydi **imamate** of North Yemen.

ALI ABDULLAH SALIH. *See* SALIH, ALI ABDULLAH, AND THE SALIH FAMILY.

ALI ANTAR (1939–1986). Ali Ahmad Nasir al-Antar was the very politically minded, power-oriented veteran of the **Radfan Rebellion** and member of the leadership of the left wing of the **National Liberation Front** who held high government and party posts in independent South Yemen from the late 1960s through the mid-1980s—among them minister of defense and Politburo member—and who always seemed at or near the center of the fierce political struggles and leadership changes during these years. Ali Antar was much involved in the intrigue that brought **Ali Nasir Muhammad** al-Hasani to power in 1980, and even more so in the escalating intrigue from 1984 forward that aimed at reining in or deposing Ali Nasir; he was shot to death in the **13 January events** in 1986, when Ali Nasir tried unsuccessfully to save himself through a preemptive ambush of several of his enemies. Ali Antar came from **al-Dhala** and enjoyed up-country support. He also found support in the military, both going back to **Radfan Rebellion** days and as a result of serving as commander-in-chief of the **armed forces** and as minister of defense in the 1970s.

AL-ALIM, LT.-COL. ABDULLAH ABD. *See* ABD AL-ALIM, LT-COL ABDULLAH.

ALI MUHSIN SALIH AL-AHMAR (*CA.* 1940–). The out-of-the-limelight relative and longtime colleague of President **Salih** who, as perhaps the second most powerful person after the president in the military of the YAR and then the ROY, has been since the late 1970s both the president's biggest supporter and his biggest challenger and threat. Allegedly, the two agreed at the outset that Ali Muhsin would back the president in exchange for being the president's chosen successor. This would explain why, as rumors had it, relations between them became strained after the 1990s when talk turned to the president's grooming his eldest son, Ahmad Ali Abdullah, to succeed him—and to the president's having made major changes in military command that seemed to reflect this. Talk of Ahmad as successor subsided by the time his father was elected to a new seven-year term in 2006. However, the place and future of Ali Muhsin remained unclear.

In terms of division of labor, Ali Muhsin has over the years become "Mr. Inside," paying greater attention to domestic politics, whereas President Salih has been "Mr. Outside," focusing on Yemen's external relations and image. With regard to domestic politics, Ali Muhsin has promoted and defended Yemen's militant **political Islamists**, on the one hand, and come to depend upon and draw strength from them, on the other. Starting in the late 1980s, he folded jihadists back from Afghanistan—the **"Afghani Arabs"**—into the YAR military and had these and other Islamists play a major role in defeating the southern "socialists" in the **War of Secession** in 1994. On another front, when the Salih regime cracked down on the **Shii** leaders of the **al-Houthi Rebellion** in 2004, Ali Muhsin was in command of the forces involved. Many claimed that the severity of the repression was a function of the **Salafi** inclinations that Ali Muhsin shared with troops under his command, and with some of the tribal fighters who joined them. On another front, the period after **9/11** made the Salafi reputations of Ali Muhsin and his colleagues awkward and embarrassing, given President George W. Bush's insistence on unambiguous support in the **War on Terror**.

ALI NASIR MUHAMMAD AL-HASANI (CA. 1940–). The forceful but moderate, pragmatic politician from **Abyan** who greatly consolidated power in the PDRY and served as head of state, prime minister, and secretary general of the **Yemeni Socialist Party** (YSP) from late 1980 to early 1986—a period distinguished by a more relaxed, eclectic, non-doctrinaire approach to domestic policy and broadly cooperative, moderate external relations, most notably with the country's immediate neighbors, the YAR, **Oman**, and **Saudi Arabia**. A **National Liberation Front** activist from its start, Ali Nasir had served as prime minister through the entire period of co-leadership of Salim **Rabbiya Ali** and **Abd al-Fattah Ismail** in the 1970s, sided with the latter in the violent elimination of the former in 1978, and then assumed power himself by forcing Ismail into exile in 1980. In turn, he and his supporters fled across the border into the YAR in early 1986 after the **13 January events**, when his attempt to eliminate his more radical challengers in the YSP, including the returned Ismail, backfired.

Given his role as an architect of close, friendly ties with the YAR and his warm personal relationship with President **Salih**, Ali Nasir's ouster seriously strained relations between the two Yemens from early 1986 to mid-1988. Indeed, when Yemeni **unification** came in 1990, it had been facilitated by Ali Nasir's formal announcement in exile of his withdrawal from politics and by the subsequent partial reconciliation between his followers and the leaders who had succeded him in the PDRY. In exile in Syria most of the time after 1986, where he founded and headed an Arab political think tank, Ali Nasir reappeared briefly on the Yemeni political stage in late 1993, when he tried to mediate the conflict between the YSP and President Salih's **General People's Congress** only months before the **War of Secession** in 1994. Many of his followers fought, with his blessing, on the GPC's side, and many were rewarded after victory in that war. There was some talk about his being the opposition candidate to President Salih in the 2006 presidential elections, but that came to naught.

ALI SALIM AL-BAYDH (AL-BID). *See* AL-BAYDH (AL-BID), ALI SALIM.

AMD, WADI. *See* HADHRAMAWT AND WADI HADHRAMAWT; QUAITIS AND QUAITI SULTANATE.

AMIRI TRIBE. *See* DHALA (DHALIA) TOWN, REGION, TRIBES, AND EMIRATE.

AMMAN ACCORD, 1994. *See* DOCUMENT OF PLEDGE AND ACCORD (AL-WATHIQA).

AMRAN. An important large, walled market town on the high plateau of North Yemen, on the main road to **Saada** some 30 miles north of **Sanaa**; the secondary road going west from Amran connected another major provincial town, **Hajja**, to the main north–south road. For about 15 years after the **1962 Revolution**, Amran was the YAR's northernmost major military outpost and government center except for the enclave at Saada, far to the north, most of the intervening territory being controlled by **tribes** often opposed to the state until the late 1970s. In April 1994, decades later and nearly four years after Yemeni **unification** and the birth of the ROY, a fierce clash between northern and southern armored units occurred at the large base in Amran, an event followed in a week by the onset of the **War of Secession**.

AL-AMRI, GENERAL HASAN (1916–1989). The YAR army officer who, despite his close association with President Abdullah **al-Sallal** and the high offices held in his regime, managed to sidestep al-Sallal's overthrow in 1967 and go on to be the military strongman during the first four years of the regime of President **al-Iryani**. Al-Amri came to be known informally as "the sword of the republic" for his leadership in the field during the **Yemen Civil War**, and especially during the **Siege of Sanaa** in 1967–1968. Only months after the siege was broken, he led the suppression of the **Sanaa Mutiny**, assuring that the victorious republic would be a conservative one. Al-Amri served over the next three years as either or both commander in chief and prime minister. His role in an argument in 1971, in which he killed a journalist, led President **al-Iryani** to force him to go into exile, ending his career on the eve of what many thought would have been his bid to oust and replace al-Iryani as head of state. Al-Amri never returned and died in Egypt in 1989.

Al-Amri was a fighter, possibly mentally unstable, and one observer has called him the YAR's General George Patton. From the Yemeni highlands, he and al-Sallal were two of the 13 "boys" sent by Imam **Yahya** to **Iraq** for military or technical training in 1936. As with al-Sallal, he was deeply involved in Yemeni politics in the 1940s and 1950s. Of modest origins, Hasan Al-Amri was not of the great al-Amri **qadi** family.

AL-AMRI QADI FAMILY. Abdullah al-Amri was the head of a prominent **qadi** family in Sanaa who from the 1930s onward served faithfully as Imam **Yahya**'s principal aide and adviser on domestic affairs—with the modern title of "prime minister." He died in the hail of assassins' bullets that also took Yahya's life in 1948. Qadi al-Amri was the quintessential representative of the qadi class in Yemen, the learned and loyal servant of the Zaydi **imamate**. Previously, he had been in the employ of the **Ottoman** administration in Sanaa.

By contrast, the qadi's son, Husayn Abdullah al-Amri, through education abroad during the decade following the **1962 Revolution**, acquired the skills and orientation needed to transition to modernity and to assume modern roles. He earned his PhD. from an English university, has authored books on Yemeni history, and has been a lecturer at **Sanaa University**. In addition, he served as a government minister during the 1980s, and was for many years ambassador to the United Kingdom. More recently, he has assumed the role of an elder stateman on the **Shura Council**.

ANGLO–OTTOMAN LINE OF 1904. The line separating the British and **Ottoman** spheres of influence in **South Arabia**, extending, as demarcated by a joint Anglo–Ottoman commission between 1901 and 1904, from the **Bab al-Mandab Straits** to the North Yemeni town of **Harib**. New and old issues raised by the Ottomans caused the ratification of the border demarcation agreement to be delayed until 1913, the eve of the world war that ended the Ottoman Empire. This demarcation line was later incorporated into the **Treaty of Sanaa** of 1934 between **Great Britain** and the Yemeni **imamate**. In later decades, it served as the border between the YAR and PDRY and was the scene of two border wars between them in the 1970s—all of which became moot with Yemeni **unification** in 1990.

The original line was the result of the Anglo–Ottoman Clash of 1873, which, in turn, was the result of Ottoman expansion south from Sanaa after 1870 and, in response, British expansion north from **Aden**. This intense but essentially nonviolent imperial confrontation, preceded by increasing frontier incidents, resulted in both the first major steps by Britain to organize Aden's large hinterland into the Western **Aden Protectorate** and the clear division of Yemen into two distinct territories separated by a boundary accepted by the local **tribes** and recognized by the international community.

AL-ANISI, ABD AL-AZIZ. *See* ISLAH (YEMENI REFORM GATHERING).

ANTAR, ALI AHMAD NASSER. *See* ALI ANTAR.

AQRABI TRIBE AND REGION. The **tribal** and political unit in **Aden's** hinterland that was closest to that port city and hence of considerable interest to those concerned about Aden's security and the safety of the trade routes from it to points beyond in the hinterland and to the southern uplands of North Yemen. Aqrabi was well within the British-supported sphere of influence of the **Abdali sultanate** in **Lahej** and became a unit in the Western **Aden Protectorate** and, later, the **Federation of South Arabia**.

ARAB COOPERATION COUNCIL (ACC). The mutual cooperation agreement reached in early 1988 to promote and defend the mutual interests of **Iraq, Egypt, Jordan**, and the YAR. The trouble was that the four members had little in the way of mutual interests and had formed the ACC out of very mixed motives. Egypt and Iraq, respectively, sought to put behind them the political effects of **Camp David** and the **Iraq–Iran War**, whereas Jordan sought to satisfy its old need for strong Arab friends. For its part, the YAR sought to attain a place in the Arab world commensurate with its new political stability and **oil** resources; indeed, in 1989, the YAR hosted the second ACC summit with much fanfare. In addition, it is clear that the ACC was set up in opposition to the older **Gulf Cooperation Council**, and the prior existence of the latter surely contributed to the decision to create the former.

In any case, the ACC ceased to exist, for all practical purposes, when Iraq invaded **Kuwait** in August 1990—and Egypt joined with **Saudi Arabia** and the **United States** to undo Iraq's aggression in the course of the crisis that led to the First **Gulf War**. With the realignment after Iraq's invasion of Kuwait, some Saudis and Egyptians even came to believe the improbable thesis that Egypt had been deceived by its ACC partners, and that Iraq, Jordan, and the YAR had conspired to create the alliance in order to dismember Saudi Arabia and to swallow up the oil-rich Arab Gulf states.

ARABIAN SEA. The body of water south of the long southern coast of Yemen, north and west of the **Indian Ocean** and east of the **Gulf of Aden** and the **Bab al-Mandab** entrance to the **Red Sea**. Because of its strategic location and the sea lanes crossing it, the Arabian Sea has for more than three millennia had—and today continues to have—commercial and transportation significance, and these give it political and cultural importance. *See also* TRADE ROUTES, ANCIENT.

ARABIC, YEMENI. Although virtually all Yemenis speak Arabic, there are important dialectical differences from place to place, a reflection of the barriers erected by geography to the free flow of communications, as well as movement, in pre-modern Yemen. The most important difference is between the Arabic of **Sanaa** and the highlands of North Yemen and that of **Aden** and the southern and coastal parts of North Yemen. The Arabic dialect of the **Hadhramawt** reflects its isolation from the rest of Yemen, and the language shared by **Mahra** and **Socotra** is considered a separate language, not an Arabic dialect. In addition to the many regional differences, there is also the considerable difference between the Arabic of the men and that which the **women** use when conversing among themselves—often disparagingly about the men.

ARAB–ISRAELI CONFLICT. Most Yemenis have sided with the **Palestinians** and other Arabs in their struggle with **Israel** since the latter's creation in 1948, years before the **1962 Revolution** that brought republicanism to North Yemen and years before South Yemen became independent from **Great Britain** in 1967. Indeed, the first political demonstration in Aden occurred in the late 1940s and was in protest against British policy in Palestine.

The two Yemens, while never direct participants, were significantly affected by the several Arab–Israeli wars, some more than others. The 1948 War and the Suez War in 1956 served to advance nationalist sentiment, Pan-Arab and parochial, in these two late-developing polities—and simply to help put them in contact politically with the outside world. But it was the Six-Day War in 1967 that had profound, immediate impacts. In the YAR, it led to the quick end to the long **Egyptian intervention** in the **Yemen Civil War** and to the creation of conditions that would permit the ending of that struggle, especially the ouster of the **al-Sallal** regime and its replacement by that of Qadi **al-Iryani.** In South Yemen, it led to the long closure of the **Suez Canal,** virtually shutting down the Port of **Aden,** the core of Aden's economic life, just six months before independence from Britain.

Preoccupied then with inter-Yemeni conflict, the two Yemens were not dramatically moved or affected by the October War of 1973. By contrast, the Israeli invasion of Lebanon in 1982, afforded both Yemens the opportunity to come to the aid of the **Palestine Liberation Organization** (PLO) and its need for havens for its armed forces. Fortuitously, this provided a convenient smokescreen behind which the two Yemens in the mid-1980s took politically controversial steps toward ending more than a decade of inter-Yemeni conflict.

With **unification** in 1990, the Yemenis continued to give strong moral support to Yasir **Arafat** and the PLO—and, after its creation in 1994, the Palestinian Authority (PA)—throughout the Oslo peace process and the Second Intifada. With Arafat's death in 2004, Yemeni support went to Mahmoud Abbas, his successor as president of the PA. After Hamas's victory in the parliamentary elections in 2005, the ROY extended support to both the leadership of that Islamist party in Gaza and to President Abbas in the West Bank. The ROY supported Hamas in its war with Israel in early 2009, as it had supported Hizbullah when Israel invaded Lebanon on 2006.

ARAB NATIONALIST MOVEMENT (ANM). Founded in 1952 by George Habash and others in Beirut, Lebanon, this was the region-wide Arab nationalist movement that was transformed in South Yemen in the early 1960s into the **National Liberation Front** (NLF), the movement that launched the **Radfan Rebellion** in 1963, assumed power in **Aden** upon **Great Britain**'s hasty exit in 1967, and evolved into the **Yemeni Socialist Party** (YSP) in the late 1970s. The left wing of the NLF moved to the left ideologically with George Habash in the late 1960s as his focus evolved from the Arab world and Arab nationalism to **Palestine** and the Marxist–Leninist internationalism embodied in his new Popular Front for the Liberation of Palestine (PFLP). The fact that the regime in the PDRY was the only one in the Arab world that could trace its ideological roots directly to the old ANM, as well as to the Marxism–Leninism of the PFLP, helps explain the special relationship and sense of kinship that existed between Habash and the leaders of the YSP in the PDRY through the 1980s.

ARAB REGIONAL FUNDS. Several oil-fueled Arab regional funding agencies provided considerable aid to the two Yemens, among them the **Kuwait** Fund for Arab Economic Development (KFAED), the Arab League's Kuwait-based Arab Fund for Economic and Social Development (AFESD), the Saudi Fund for Development, and the **Abu Dhabi** Fund for Arab Economic Development. Aid from the Kuwait Fund had the longest record of continuity: to the YAR from the mid-1960s and to the PDRY shortly thereafter. Aid from these several funds had risen sharply in the 1970s and leveled off in the 1980s.

Aid from both the Kuwait Fund and the Abu Dhabi Fund was viewed by the givers in part as a way of making the Yemens, especially the YAR, less dependent on **Saudi Arabia**—and therefore better able to serve as constraints from the other side of the Arabian peninsula on Saudi hegemonic designs. The Saudi Fund for Development was a major, continuous source of funds for the YAR from the mid-1970s through the 1980s and a key institutional link in the growing dependence of the YAR upon Saudi Arabia. Aid from this source to the PDRY was later in coming, smaller in amount, more episodic, and politically more problematical.

The Gulf crisis and First **Gulf War** in 1990–1991 caused a complete break in the flow of aid from Kuwait, Abu Dhabi, and Saudi Arabia to the newly unified ROY, a punishment of client by patrons for the tilt of the former toward Iraq after its occupation of Kuwait. Aid began to flow again from these sources to the ROY in the late 1990s, but it never regained its earlier relative magnitude or importance.

ARAB RENAISSANCE SOCIALIST PARTY, YEMENI. *See* BAATH PARTY (ARAB SOCIALIST RENAISSANCE PARTY).

ARAB SOCIALISM. *See* NASSER (NASIR), GAMAL ABDUL.

ARAFAT, YASIR (1929–2004). The founding head of al-Fattah, the chairman of the **Palestine** Liberation Organization (PLO) since 1969, and the president of the Palestinian Authority from 1994 until his death in 2004. Arafat on several occasions during the 1970s and 1980s sought in the interest of unity to mediate between the two Yemens; in return, he received rather strong and steady support from both Yemens in the **Arab–Israeli conflict**, support that continued after Yemeni **unification** in 1990. Arafat regarded the two Yemens as particularly good friends because they had closed ranks and provided havens for PLO fighters forced to evacuate Beirut in 1982. Arafat and the YAR regime were quite comfortable with each other because of a shared moderate, non-ideological stance, whereas the PDRY's kinship with the Palestinian Marxist left at times strained relations between it and Arafat.

ARCHITECTURE. The drama of Yemen's natural landscape is complemented by spectacular works of traditional residential architecture, whether they be the stone fortress villages that seem to grow out of the tops of pinnacles and sheer cliffs or the tall, several-storied gingerbread skyscrapers of **Sanaa** and mud-brick skyscrapers of **Shibam** in the **Hadhramawt.** Just as striking and beautiful are the very different sensuously serpentine mud tower houses and walls of **Saada** in the far north and the more subdued geometrically embellished mud brick buildings of **Zabid** on the **Tihama.** As fine as the mosques in **Taiz** and several other places are, the traditional public architecture of Yemen does not begin to match the residential—with the restored Amariya madrasa in Radaa clearly one of the exceptions.

AL-ARHABI, ABD AL-KARIM. The very able and apparently honest minister of labor and social affairs in the government formed in 2001 who then became minister of planning and international cooperation in the major cabinet reshuffle in February 2006. As minister of labor and social affairs he directed the **Social Development Fund**, the agency funded by the **World Bank** and created to design and operate programs to ease the painful effects of measures mandated by the economic reform package adopted in the mid-1990s. In the largely donor-induced cabinet reshuffle in 2006, he replaced Ahmad **Sufan**, who, along with Minister of Finance Alawi **al-Salami**, was suspected of enriching himself and his friends. Al-Arhabi was given much of the credit for the successful London donors' conference in November 2006. Partly because of this success, he retained his ministry and also became deputy prime minister for economic affairs in the new cabinet formed by Ali Muhammad **Mujawar** in April 2007.

ARHAB TRIBE AND AREA. A **Bakil** tribe and area located just north of Sanaa near **Amram** on the main route between Sanaa and **Saada**. Often a factor in the politics of the more remote past because of its strategic location, this was no less the case during the first two decades of insecure republican rule after the **1962 Revolution**. When challenged in the mid-1970s by tribal actions in the Arhab, President **al-Hamdi** unleashed the armed forces in reprisal, ordered the offending tribal leaders to pledge allegiance to him, and then ordered his government to redress many of their material grievances—a carrot-and-stick approach that some called al-Hamdi's "Arhab model" of dealing with the **tribes**.

AL-ARISHI, QADI ABD AL-KARIM (1934–2006). A traditionally trained **qadi** from one of North Yemen's major qadi families, al-Arishi occupied ministerial posts in the YAR in the first half of the 1970s and then went on to serve in the visible but mostly ceremonial posts of vice president, speaker of the **People's Constituent Assembly**, and member of the elected **Consultative Council** under Presidents Ahmad Husayn **al-Ghashmi** and Ali Abdullah **Salih** from 1978 to 1990. When President al-Ghashmi was assassinated in mid-1978, al-Arishi became the chairman of an interim four-member Presidential Council and considered a bid for the presidency, an office quickly preempted by Ali Abdullah Salih. On the occasion of Yemeni **unification** in 1990, Qadi al-Arishi became a member of the new five-member **Presidential Council** and then the head of the Supreme Election Committee that supervised the 1993 **elections**.

ARMED FORCES. In South Yemen, the Liberation Army of the **National Liberation Front** was merged after 1967 with the units inherited from the British colonial power to form what became the PDRY's regular armed forces, the People's Defense Forces. Intent on making it a united and loyal instrument of a revolutionary party-state, the victorious left proceeded to purge, retrain, and enlarge the armed forces—and political education went along with technical training and reequipment. In addition, however, a People's Militia of about 15,000 members, organized on a local basis, was created in the early 1970s to act as a political counterweight to what were to become regular armed forces numbering nearly twice that.

The result was a military divided along **tribal** and regional lines on the one hand and along ideological lines on the other. These different and competing loyalties were played upon by various elements in the fierce political battles from the late 1960s through the mid-1980s. Both the success and failure of this effort to create professional armed forces were evident during and after the **13 January events**, the intraparty bloodbath in 1986. Although the military did largely split along regional and tribal lines under extreme pressure during the fighting, it resisted temptations to seize power during the more than three years of very troubling politics that followed.

The soldiers who carried out the **1962 Revolution** in North Yemen were not heirs to much in the way of armed forces, since the **imam-ate** had relied in times of military need upon tribal levies, instead of a large standing army. More surprising, the Yemeni republicans did not end up with a very modern military establishment out of the long **Yemeni Civil War** over the 1960s. That long struggle was mostly fought by forces from **Egypt**, which both downplayed the enlargement and modernization of YAR forces and had almost exclusive use of the modern weaponry introduced into Yemen. The civil war over, major tribal leaders used their new positions of power inside the republican state headed by President Abd al-Rahman **al-Iryani** to maintain the fragmented, "tribalized" nature of the armed forces and to prevent reforms that might turn those armed forces into effective instruments of state power—possibly for future use against the tribes.

Consequently, steps toward creating modern armed forces were not taken in the YAR until the second half of the 1970s. At this time, under President Ibrahim **al-Hamdi**, the power of the tribal leaders was curtailed, and the modest reequipment of the armed forces was used to induce the modest reform and reorganization of those forces. The pace of the reequipment, enlargement, and reform of the military quickened after 1978 during the long tenure of President Ali

Abdullah **Salih**. The introduction of conscription and professional training of officers did strengthen the YAR military in the ranks and at the top. Still, the YAR military continued to draw heavily from and reflect the tribal system, and gains in the effort to professionalize it were compromised by the new privileges and presumptions of many members of the officers' corps.

The PDRY leadership made a transfer of forces a condition of Yemeni **unification**, and this did take place around the time of formal union in May, 1990: three southern units went north, and three northern units went south. Despite urgent calls for the merger of the two armed forces, this did not take place during the three-year transition period that followed, and the unmerged armed forces went on to be central to the waging and the outcome of the **War of Secession** in mid-1994. The defeat of the secessionists seems to have been less a function of the capabilities of the northern forces than of the surprisingly poor performance of the southern forces.

Since 1994, the ROY's military has been dominated by northern elements, with the notable exception of the followers of ex-PDRY president **Ali Nasir Muhammad**, who strongly opposed secession. The northern officers, mostly **Zaydis** from the highlands, are an integral part of the tribal–military–northern business complex that dominated the YAR in the 1980s and the ROY since 1994. Much of the continuing disaffection of southerners centers on their perception that the military has turned unification into occupation. Voicing very specific complaints, southern officers and troops forced from the military in 1994 took to the streets in force in the fall of 2007, demanding the restoration of careers and benefits. This southern protest continued and broadened through 2009.

ARMS AND MILITARY AID. The regular **armed forces** inherited by independent South Yemen were British-equipped, and lightly so. In the 1970s, the **Soviet Union** and its socialist allies replaced **Great Britain** as the source of virtually all arms through the 1980s. The reequipped and reorganized forces received Soviet—and, later, Cuban—training. The result was forces that were well equipped, trained, and disciplined, and better so than their YAR counterparts, at least through the early 1980s. As of the mid-1980s, these forces consisted of some 27,500 regulars (24,000 in the army, 2,500 in the air force, and 1,000 in the navy), a relatively large force for a poor country of about 3 million people.

The YAR armed forces were heir to a small supply of antiquated arms on the occasion of the **1962 Revolution**, among them, oddly enough, some Soviet arms secured by the **imamate** in the mid-1950s. During the **Yemeni Civil War**, the only resupply of these ill-equipped forces involved the transfer of a sizable amount of obsolete Soviet arms, along with a number of Soviet advisers, on the occasion of **Egypt**'s precipitous withdrawal from Yemen in 1967. After much effort, the YAR secured a modest supply of light arms from the **United States** in 1977, and then a much more important supply of heavy arms, with a training mission, from the **Carter** administration in 1979. Surprisingly, the YAR secured an even larger amount of arms from the Soviet Union later this same year. Additional Soviet arms were supplied in 1986 and again in 1988.

One major cost of the firm entrenchment of the northern tribal–military–business complex in the ROY since the **War of Succession** in 1994 was a buying binge for the military's infrastructure and arms, something made possible by new **oil** revenues. This has certainly helped assure the loyalty of the officers' corps to the **Salih regime**. But another effect is that Yemen, the Middle East's poorest country, ranks among the highest in the world in terms of defense expenses as a percentage of GDP.

ARWA, QUEEN. The wife of the son of the founder of the **Sulayhid Dynasty** who governed all of Yemen in the name of her husband for 50 years until her death in A.D. 1138. Al-Sayyida al-Hurra Bint Ahmad al-Sulahi was a gifted ruler and politician, a builder of public works, and a great patron of writers and architects, something evident even today in the remains of her new capital, **Dhu Jibla**. Traces of her stone-paved road running north from **Ibb** can still be seen. Queen Arwa is a great favorite among the Yemeni people, rivaling even the earlier Queen Bilqis of **Saba (Sheba)** for the honor of being Yemen's greatest **woman**—or, surprising for a patriarchy, even Yemen's greatest Yemeni. Plans were going forward in 2006 to restore her great palace in Jibla.

AL-ASHTAL, ABDULLAH SALEH (1938–2004). The bright, politically skillful Yemeni who became PDRY ambassador to the **United**

Nations in 1973 and then, after 17 years in that post, became UN ambassador from the newly proclaimed ROY in 1990. He served until 2002, making his tenure among the longest in UN history. Since ROY had a seat on the Security Council during the crisis ending in the First **Gulf War** 1991, it was al-Ashtal's lot to have to make Yemen's case often for a nonmilitary, Arab solution to the situation created by **Iraq**'s occupation of **Kuwait**. It was he who, with Cuba, voted against the **United States**' "all necessary means" resolution, bringing the wrath of the U.S. and **Saudi Arabia** down on the ROY.

Born in Ethiopia and of North Yemeni origins, al-Ashtal studied at the American University of Beirut in the mid-1960s, where he came under the spell of George Habash and his **Arab Nationalist Movement**. Upon graduation, now a member of the **National Liberation Front** (NLF), he took a job in the YAR. With the triumph of the NLF in South Yemen in 1967, he went south and joined the new revolutionary regime as an aide to Ali Salim **al-Baydh** in the **Hadhramawt**, where the early radical surge did not get much beyond al-Ashtal's nationalization of the cinema. On the losing side of one of the many political fights inside the NLF, he was appointed to the PDRY mission to the UN in the early 1970s.

ASIR. The quite mountainous region in the southwestern corner of **Saudi Arabia**, south of the **Hijaz**, and the most densely populated portion of this sparsely populated country. Most Asiris are hardworking farmers who till steep, terraced hillsides and live in small villages and towns in houses constructed of stone, just like the Yemenis just to the south. Indeed, the Asiris are culturally Yemeni, and the Asir has been governed by regimes of Yemeni origins from time to time throughout history. Like North Yemen and the Hijaz, Asir was part of the **Ottoman Empire** until its defeat in World War I. It was ruled thereafter by the **Idrisis** and then by the expanding Kingdom of **Saudi Arabia**. Conflicting claims to Asir by Yemen and Saudi Arabia led to the **Saudi–Yemeni War of 1934** and the **Treaty of Taif**, which decided the matter, on an interim basis, in the Saudis' favor. Although most Yemenis regarded Asir as rightfully part of Yemen, the issue of its status lay dormant for 40 years, only to erupt politically in the mid-1970s and again in the 1990s when Yemeni–Saudi relations soured badly over the crisis that resulted in the First **Gulf War** in 1991. The issue was finally settled in the Saudis' favor in the Saudi–Yemeni Border Treaty of 2000. *See also* BORDERS AND BORDER DISPUTES, WARS, AND AGREEMENTS.

AL-ASNAG, ABDULLAH (*CA.* 1930–). The founder and head of both the **Aden Trade Union Council** (ATUC) and the **People's Socialist Party** (PSP) who in the mid-1960s was defeated by the **National Liberation Front** (NLF) in his efforts to head the first independent South Yemeni government and who then, quite amazingly, went north to serve as foreign minister and adviser to four YAR heads of state between 1973 and 1979. Al-Asnag finally fell into disgrace and went into exile amid accusations by the **Salih regime** of treasonous dealings with a foreign power, presumably **Saudi Arabia**. Despite, or perhaps because of, his lack of a political base in the YAR, al-Asnag more than anyone else was the architect of the YAR's successful attempt to find its way between Saudi Arabia's economic power and the PDRY's political appeal in the 1970s. In total political eclipse for more than a decade, al-Asnag, with the blessings of the Saudis, improbably reappeared just before and during the **War of Succession** in 1994 as deputy prime minister and foreign minister in the hastily created and short-lived **Democratic Republic of Yemen**.

Al-Asnag's Achilles' heel in South Yemeni politics in the 1960s had been his totally **Adeni** base and vision, and hence his lack of any real support in or even links to the states and peoples of the **Aden Protectorates**. Still in his late twenties and early thirties when he headed the ATUC and the PSP, he was regarded as a hypnotic speaker and shrewd political tactician. From a family long established in **Crater**, the son of a government health inspector, he apparently did not let his labor and nationalist militancy prevent him from being a conscientious employee of Aden Airways. One of the tasks that he took on in the north in the late 1960s was the reorganization and expansion of the YAR's fledgling Yemen Airways.

ATAQ It is town up-country northeast of **Aden** and somewhat south of the town of **Shabwa**. The capital of and major town of Shabwa governorate, just to the west of the **Hadhramawt**.

AL-ATTAR, MUHAMMAD SAID (1927–2005). The Djibouti-born and -raised, French-educated Yemeni who founded the **Yemen Bank**

for **Reconstruction and Development** (YBRD) and served as minister of economics during the early years of the YAR after the **1962 Revolution**. He left the rightward-drifting YAR in 1968 for a 15-year career as a diplomat at the **United Nations** and as the head of the UN's Economic Commission for Western Asia in Beirut. Al-Attar then returned to the YAR at the dawn of its oil era in 1985 to serve as deputy prime minister, minister of development, and chairman of the Central Planning Organization. His falling out of favor in the late 1980s may account for his being named only minister of industry at **unification** in 1990. He was appointed acting prime minister by President **Salih** during the political crisis and the **War of Secession** in 1994, serving from May until October of that year. He became deputy prime minister and minister of industry in late 1994 and then was deputy prime minister and minister of petroleum and minerals in 1996–1997.

A young doctoral candidate just out from the Sorbonne to do his doctoral dissertation research in Aden, al-Attar got caught up and swept north in the 1962 Revolution, labored to set up the YBRD and the Ministry of Economics, took a short sabbatical from the revolution to write up his dissertation in Paris, and then returned to his economic and financial posts for the last years of the **al-Sallal** era and the first year of the **al-Iryani** era. Al-Attar viewed himself, and was regarded by many others, as a progressive or socialist intellectual and was the author of the best early book—a rewrite of his doctoral dissertation—on the economics of North Yemen on the eve of the 1962 Revolution. Originally from the **Hujariyya** in North Yemen, the very large, prominent family in which al-Attar was raised in comfort had business interests in Djibouti and Ethiopia.

AL-ATTAS, HAIDAR ABU BAKR. The **National Liberation Front** (NLF) and **Yemeni Socialist Party** (YSP) figure who became prime minister of the PDRY in 1985, its president from 1986 to 1990, prime minister of the ROY after Yemeni **unification** from 1990 to 1994, and, finally, prime minister in the stillborn **Democratic Republic of Yemen** during the brief **War of Secession** in 1994. Forced into exile in 1994, al-Attas was later tried and sentenced to death. Despite being pardoned, he has remained in exile in **Saudi Arabia**. Quite non-ideological, al-Attas also failed—as did his relative, Faisal al-Attas—to fit the NLF and YSP profile by virtue of being from an old, prestigious, influential **sayyid** family in the **Hadhramawt**.

During most of his years of public service, al-Attas was regarded primarily as a loyal, hard-working technocrat and only a second-level party figure. Prior to 1985, he had served almost continuously as minister of construction from shortly after independence. Out of the country and in the **Soviet Union** during the bloody **13 January events** of 1986, the PDRY's Soviet patrons pushed al-Attas as a conciliator during the turmoil, thereby making more likely a major role for him in the regime of survivors—and, indeed, he became PDRY head of state. With unification in 1990, al-Attas became prime minister and proved popular in the north as well as the south. Although his popularity fell during the transition period, he was again named to head the government formed after the April 1993 parliamentary **elections**.

AWDHALI REGION, TRIBES, AND SULTANATE. The border region and **tribal** group in South Yemen northeast of **Aden** and opposite the North Yemeni region and town of **al-Baydha**. The Awdhalis bore the brunt of Imam **Yahya**'s expansionism to the southeast from the mid-1920s to the late 1930s, as well as that of Imam **Ahmad** in the mid-1950s. Yahya's forces occupied the plateau and part of the lowlands of Awdhali in the mid-1920s and withdrew only under the threat of **Royal Air Force** action in the mid-1930s, a withdrawal formally acknowledged in the **Treaty of Sanaa** in 1934.

Although this border area became more peaceful over the years, Sultan Husayn al-Awdhali was killed repelling North Yemeni raiders across the border in 1938, and his son, Sultan Salih ibn Husayn al-Awdhali, had to deal with the hostile border actions of Imam Ahmad in 1956–1957. A strong, outspoken leader, Sultan Salih was a close friend of top officials in Aden, became a strong supporter of a continuing British connection, and was one of the original proponents of and an active leader and minister in the **Federation of South Arabia** and its predecessor organization in the 1950s and 1960s. Later, he became an outspoken critic of **Great Britain** when it announced plans to give up its military base at Aden and to no longer guarantee the security of the federation and its members.

AWLAQI TRIBES AND REGION. The large, resource-poor, and thinly populated area that extends from **Bayhan** south to the coast about halfway between **Aden** and the **Hadhramawt**. The Awlaqi consists of a number of tribal elements and three territorial political entities: the Lower Awlaqi sultanate, the Upper Awlaqi sultanate, and the Upper Awlaqi shaykhdom. The Upper Awlaqi shaykhdom became a strong supporter of the **Federation of South Arabia** (FSA), and one of their number, the Oxford-educated Muhammad Farid al-Awlaqi, served as the FSA's first foreign minister and key diplomat. By contrast, the Upper Awlaqi sultanate and its Upper Yafi neighbor were the two regions in the Western **Aden Protectorate** least under British influence and the only two never to join the FSA. An ancient lineage, the Upper Awlaqi sultanate made locally accepted claim to descent from pre-Islamic **Main** (Minean) rulers. During the last decades of the colonial era, **Great Britain** allowed the Awlaqis to become disproportionately represented and influential in the regular army that was reorganized as the South Arabian Armed Forces in mid-1967. This almost inevitably led to suspicion and antagonism between the Awlaqis and the **National Liberation Front** (NLF) when the FSA collapsed and the NLF took over from the British later that year.

AWSAN. *See* TRADING KINGDOMS, SOUTH ARABIAN.

AL-AYNI, MUHSIN. *See* AL-AINI (AL-AYNI), MUHSIN.

AYYUBIDS. The Kurdish clan of **Sunni** Muslims, headed by the famous Saladin (Salah al-Din bin Ayyub), that conquered **Egypt** and ended the **Fatimid Shii** caliphate there and then proceeded to overrun and rule most of Yemen from 1173 until 1229. Yemen was conquered by Saladin's brother, Turanshah, and was governed during the rest of this short period by another brother, two nephews, and a grandson of Saladin. Preoccupied with matters in **Syria** and Egypt, the Ayyubids lost control of Yemen to their former servants, the subsequently long-ruling **Rasulid** dynasty.

– B –

BAATH PARTY (ARAB SOCIALIST RENAISSANCE PARTY). Founded in **Syria** in the mid-1950s, this revolutionary Arab nationalist party that epitomized the pan-Arab and Arab socialist **ideologies** of the 1960s and 1970s had only a minor and diminishing role to play in each of the Yemens since the mid-1960s and in the ROY since 1990. Branches of the Baath Party in the two Yemens competed and cooperated with the **Arab Nationalist Movement** (ANM) and the **Nasirites** in their respective national struggles in the 1960s and thereafter, serving with these other parties as key mediums through which many young Yemenis were inducted into modern secular politics. Probably the YAR civilian politician best known outside Yemen in the 1960s and early 1970s was Muhsin **al-Ayni**, and he was known primarily as Yemen's leading Baath Party leader. During these years, such Yemeni figures as Mujahid **abu Shuwarib** and members of the **abu Luhum** clan were also "Baathis."

The Baath Party in Yemen was prone to division and, thereby, to weakness. In addition to the effects of two separate and different Yemeni national struggles, the Baath parties in both Yemens in the late 1960s and 1970s reflected the bitter split between the opposing ruling Baath regimes in Syria and **Iraq**. Generally, the Baath faction in both Yemens that identified with the Syrian Baath proved more durable than those identified with the Iraqi Baath. In each of the Yemens, the Yemeni branch of the Syrian Baath "Yemenized" itself and called itself the Vanguard (Al-Talia). In the YAR, the Vanguard was banned and opposed the regime beginning in the late 1960s; it even engaged in armed struggle against the regime as part of the **National Democratic Front** after the mid-1970s, only to be pressured to make peace with the regime in the early 1980s. By contrast, the Vanguard in the PDRY became a part of the ruling establishment at the end of the 1960s and remained so throughout the 1970s and 1980s, becoming as it did a minor constituent of the ruling **Yemeni Socialist Party** (YSP) in 1978.

By contrast, strains in South Yemen between the Iraqi Baath and the ruling **National Liberation Front** and then the YSP dated back to old conflicts in the region between the ANM and the founding generation of Baathis, conflicts that continued in new forms after South Yemen's independence in 1967. In the north, the YAR branch of the Iraqi Baath Party was in opposition during the **al-Iryani** era from the late 1960s to the mid-1970s, and rumors of a planned coup by it precipitated or provided an excuse for the coup by Ibrahim **al-Hamdi** in 1974. Warm relations between Iraq and the **Salih regime** from the late 1970s into the 1990s did finally yield modest benefits for Yemen's Iraqi Baath—and considerable financial benefits for Qassim Sallam, its longtime secretary general, who, after losing an intra-party fight in 1996, was appointed by President Salik to the new **Shura** Council in 1997.

With Yemeni unification in 1990 and the advent of political pluralism, the Vanguard wing of the Baath reemerged as a separate entity—only to split again into Syrian and Iraqi factions. By this time, however, the Baathists, even more so than the Nasirites, had become politically marginalized and irrelevant. Today they are cut off from the people and without popular support, living in the pan-Arab past and debating irrelevant issues with each other. Indicative of this, the Baathis chose not to join the five-party **Joint Meeting Parties**, the coalition formed in 2002 to provide more effective opposition to the Salih regime in upcoming parliamentary and presidential elections.

BAB AL-MANDAB STRAITS. The narrow waterway connecting the **Red Sea** and the **Gulf of Aden** that, because of its place on the sea lanes between Europe and the Indian Ocean, the **Gulf**, and points east, has been considered of strategic importance as a choke point at various times over the centuries, particularly with the building of the **Suez Canal** at the height of the British Empire and, more recently, with the dependence of Western Europe on Gulf oil. The two Yemens meet on the Asian side of the straits, and **Ethiopia** (now **Eritrea**) and **Djibouti** meet on the African side. This geography is a big part of the reason for the considerable interest of the two Yemens and the ROY in the politics of the **Horn of Africa** and the Red Sea. Indeed, since the 1990s, the straits have been seen less as a choke point than as a bridge between Arabia and the Horn of Africa for the passage of men, ideas—and weapons. *See also* RED SEA AND HORN OF AFRICA SECURITY ISSUES.

AL-BADAWI, JAMAL. *See* WAR ON TERROR.

BADHIB (BADHEEB) FAMILY. An Adeni, Abdullah Abd al-Razzaq was the founder of Yemeni communism and, in 1961, its political party, the **People's Democratic Union (PDU)**, Badhib worked closely with the left wing of the **National Liberation Front** (NLF) during and after the independence struggle in the 1960s. He became a minister in the government formed after the ouster in 1969 of the right wing of the NLF, led the PDU in 1975 into the **Unified Political Organization, National Front**, a coalition with the dominant NLF and the **Baath Party**, and, finally, in 1978, merged his old PDU into the new single vanguard party, the **Yemeni Socialist Party**. Indicative of the esteem in which he was held by the regime, the PDRY's major organ of political education was named the Abdullah Badhib Higher School for Scientific Socialism. Abu Bakr Abd al-Razzak Badhib and Abd al-Razzaq Badhib, his close relatives and political protégés, also held high party and government posts in the 1970s and 1980s. Closely identified with President **Ali Nasir** Muhammad al-Hasani in the 1980s, all three Badhibs lost political influence and position as a result of the leadership change following the bloody **13 January events** in 1986.

AL-BADR, IMAM MUHAMMAD (1926–1996). The last of North Yemen's **Hamid al-Din imams**, he fled **Sanaa** on the day of the **1962 Revolution**, 26 September, only a week after succeeding his father, Imam **Ahmad bin Yahya**. He had been named crown prince years before, an act that was not in accord with **Zaydi** political theory and that served to undermine the legitimacy of the Hamdi al-Din imamate. Al-Badr spent most of the next seven years leading, sometimes forcefully and sometimes halfheartedly or nominally, the unsuccessful royalist side in the **Yemen Civil War**. Thereafter he ceased to play any role in Yemeni politics, went into permanent exile in London, and died there in 1996.

Much more than his father or Imam **Yahya**, his grandfather, al-Badr was personally caught between traditional Yemen and the modern world. He seems to have been drawn to modernity and to have wanted to modernize Yemen and to work with the growing group of Yemeni **modernists**, ideas anathema to his two immediate predecessors. Indeed, with his father absent from Yemen for medical reasons in 1961, al-Badr tried to institute some modest reforms, only to have his father undo them upon his return. Al-Badr acceded to the imamate too late to be an agent of change—and history passed him by.

BAHARUN, SAYYID ZAYN. *See* FEDERATION OF SOUTH ARABIA (FSA).

BAJAMMAL, ABD AL-QADR (1947–). The loquacious, middle-level government figure in the PDRY who, after the 1994 **War of Secession**, became the most successful southern politician in the ROY, first as deputy prime minister and minister of planning and development from 1994 to 1997, deputy prime minister and foreign minister from 1998 to 2001, prime minister from 2001 to 2007, and, most recently, as secretary general of the ruling **General People's Congress** (GPC) since 2006. He had been reappointed prime minister after the 2003 parliamentary **elections** and again in the major cabinet reshuffle in February 2006—and then gave up that post in early 2007.

A native of Wadi **Hadhramawt** with a BA in commerce from Cairo University in the early 1970s, Bajammal thereafter joined the **Yemeni Socialist Party** (YSP) and, at that time, played a role in the **Dhufar Rebellion** against Oman. He was a lecturer in economics at Aden University in the late 1970s and then served as deputy minister of planning from 1979 to 1980, minister of industry and president of the oil and minerals authority from 1980 to 1985, and, finally, minister of energy and minerals in 1985. His close association with President **Ali Nasir Muhammad** cost him three years in jail after the bloody 13 January events in 1986.

No longer in the YSP, Bajammal joined the Central Committee of the GPC at Yemeni **unification** in 1990 and became the first chairperson of the **Aden Free Zone Authority** created amid great hope in May 1991. With the **War of Secession** in 1994, Bajammal stuck with the "unionists" in Sanaa and thereafter rose rapidly in the **Salih regime**, becoming prime minister in 2001. He was selected as secretary general of the GPC, despite vocal opposition, at a party congress in late 2005. His continuation as prime minister in the donor-induced reshuffle in February 2006 surprised some due to his past failure to take the lead in fighting corruption. Ceasing to be prime minister with the reshuffle in 2007, he continued as GPC secretary general.

BAKIL TRIBES. *See* HASHID AND BAKIL TRIBES AND CONFEDERATIONS.

BALANCE OF PAYMENTS AND TRADE. *See* IMPORTS AND EXPORTS.

BANA, WADI. The major **wadi** shared by the two Yemens, originating in North Yemen's middle region around **Yarim** and running in a southerly direction over the border and on to a point on the coast northeast of **Aden** near **Zinjibar**. For millennia, the wadi has been a major link and conduit between what became the two Yemens. In the mid-20th century, it facilitated movement of workers and students from **imamate** Yemen to Aden and abroad, as well as the flow of goods, contraband, rebels, and refugees in both directions.

BANKS. As **Aden** increasingly got plugged into international trade and commerce in the late 19th century, modern banks appeared there to meet the growing financial needs this created. The businessmen of the **Hadhramawt** were also linked to this system in Aden and East Asia. Meanwhile, governed by the **Ottoman** Turks and then the **Hamid al-Din** imamate, North Yemen during the first six decades of the 20th century was so self-contained and subsistence-based that its banking needs were minimal. During its last years, the modest needs of the **imamate** were met by a branch of a bank based in Saudi Arabia and owned by a Saudi of Hadhrami origins. During these years, the growing needs of the merchant families of the southern uplands of North Yemen were being met by banks in Aden.

The Yemen Bank for Reconstruction and Development (YBRD) was created only months after the **1962 Revolution**. Founded and first headed by Muhammad Said **al-Attar**, a young, French-trained Yemeni economist, the YBRD remains one of the most important acts of institution building in the early years of the YAR. A remarkably large number of the YAR's first- and second-generation **modernists** spent at least part of their careers at the YBRD. The YBRD has evolved from being the YAR's first and only bank, a protean institution rudimentarily performing all banking functions, to being after the late-1970s both a development bank and one of several commercial banks in the YAR and then the ROY. While still an important public agency, its significance has been diminished by these other commercial banks and, most importantly, by the **Central Bank of Yemen** (CBY).

In South Yemen, after independence in 1967, the National Bank of Yemen (NBY) was created to serve as a key institution in the centrally planned and administered economy. It was formed in Aden by the nationalization and combination of eight banks—seven of them foreign-owned—under the nationalization and banking laws of 1969 and 1972, respectively. Several years after Yemeni **unification** in 1991, the NBY was privatized, its public functions having been folded into the Central Bank of Yemen (CBY) in **Sanaa**.

Created in 1971, the CBY had consolidated and added much to existing rudimentary central banking functions in the YAR, thereby making possible the more prudent development and regulation of a modern commercial banking system. Abd al-Aziz **Abd al-Ghani** was founding governor and continued as head of the CBY after he became prime minister in 1975. The capabilities of the CBY did increase over the years, and under its supervision the banking system expanded rapidly and with only one major mishap. The number of member banks rose to five by the mid-1980s—the YBRD and four foreign-owned banks—with more Yemeni and non-Yemeni banks to come over the next two decades. By 2000, Islamic banks had become a vibrant part of the system.

The CBY played a key role throughout the 1980s in efforts to control inflation, exchange rates, and money supply, although these efforts continued to be compromised by the flood of worker remittances and other financial transactions that bypassed the banking system. Later innovations included the issuance of bonds to help regulate liquidity and, in the late 1990s, the adoptions of reforms designed to give the CBY more autonomy and to limit the ability of the government to dip at will into its resources. In 2000, a law gave the CBY even greater autonomy over monetary policy and the regulation of commercial banks. See also FINANCE, MINISTRY OF.

AL-BANNA (ELBANEH), JABR. *See* WAR ON TERROR.

BANU TAHIR. *See* TAHIRIDS.

BANU ZIYAD DYNASTY. *See* ZABID.

BANYANS. *See* SOCIAL SYSTEM AND STRUCTURE.

BARAKAT, AHMAD QAID (*CA.* 1935–). One of three north Yemenis to become engineers before the **1962 Revolution**. Barakat worked for the United States' Point 4 in **Taiz** and the **Kuwait Fund** in the 1960s and then held a number of YAR ambassadorial and ministerial posts in the 1970s and 1980s, among them foreign minister (1969–1970), minister of state for petroleum and mineral resources (1978–1980), and minister of economy and industry (mid-1980s). Barakat became deputy minister of **oil** and mineral resources at the time of Yemeni **unification** in 1990 and then, in early 1991, was also appointed president of the state oil company. One of the **Famous Forty**, he was educated in Egypt and England in the late 1940s and 1950s.

BARAQISH. The impressive until-recently unexcavated tell and exposed ruins of the ancient **Minean** trading center of Yathul, located to the east of **Sanaa** in **al-Jawf**, on the **trade route** north to **Najran**. An Italian team began excavation and restoration work on the site in the 1990s.

BARAT, JABAL. *See* HASHID AND BAKIL TRIBES AND CONFEDERATIONS.

BASINDWA, MUHAMMAD SALIM (*CA.* 1935–). The close colleague and subordinate of Abdullah **al-Asnag**, who fled from **Aden** north to the YAR with the defeated al-Asnag in the mid-1960s and thereafter occupied positions of importance in the YAR, among them adviser to the president, chairman of the Central Planning Organization, minister of information and culture and ambassador to the UN. On good terms with the leaders of **Saudi Arabia** and the Arab **Gulf** states, Basindwa was named foreign minister after the ROY's first national **elections** in April 1993 and tried with limited success to restore the relations that had been frayed by the First **Gulf War** in 1991; he remained in this post through the **War of Secession** in 1994. Basindwa was appointed to the **Shura Council** in 1977.

Long in the shadow of al-Asnag, in Aden and **Sanaa**, Basindwa came into his own somewhat in the YAR, especially after al-Asnag's fall from grace in 1981. An insecure, politically ambitious man, he continued to hope that changes in the PDRY would one day allow him to return home to South Yemen to a top leadership post. Adeniborn and -raised, his family's origins were in the **Hadhramawt**.

AL-BAYDANI (BAYDHANI), ABDUL RAHMAN (B. 1920s–) The part-Yemeni, Egyptian-born and -raised, and German-trained economist who had the ear and confidence of Gamal Abdul **Nasser** at the time of the **1962 Revolution** and who immediately became **Egypt**'s man in the new YAR and used his Egyptian connection to gain appointment as deputy prime minister with responsibility for economic affairs in the YAR's regime, headed by President Abdullah **al-Sallal**. Although he launched some reforms, set up new institutions and initiated studies, Baydani, an outsider in Sanaa and a **Shafii** without a Yemeni power base or network, soon fell victim to the parochial complexities and contradictions of a Yemeni political process increasingly dominated, as in the past, by **Zaydis**. Probably with Egyptian approval, al-Sallal soon dismissed him when he went to Cairo to mend his political fences.

Beidani was married to the sister of Anwar **Sadat**, and this surely was his entry to the Nasser regime. He had been active in Egypt's propaganda campaign against the Yemeni **imamate** during the months before the 1962 Revolution. Although he resurfaces from time to time—indeed, he said he might run for president in 2006—Baydani has played no role in Yemeni politics since he left for Cairo in the mid-1960s.

AL-BAYDHA. A province and small provincial capital in the southeast corner of North Yemen. The town of al-Baydha shared with its neighbor to the north, **Harib**, the distinction of being the easternmost towns of any consequence in the YAR, and both towns are very close to the old border with the PDRY. Given its location, Al-Baydha had an important role to play in conflict between the **republicans** and **royalists** in the **Yemen Civil War**, as well as between the two Yemens from the late 1960s through the 1980s. Earlier, it had an even more significant part in the conflict between **Great Britain** in Aden and, first, the **Ottoman Turks** and then the revived and expansive **imamate** in North Yemen.

The town of al-Baydha is at the end of the secondary road running east from **Dhamar** through **Rada**. Al-Baydha province is mostly very arid and affords little means of livelihood, with the results that the population density is extremely low and most of the people living there are women, children, and the elderly, most living on money from men working abroad or in Yemen's cities.

AL-BAYDH (AL-BID), ALI SALIM (*CA.* 1940–). A participant from the beginning in the struggle of the **National Liberation Front** against the British imperialists and local "feudalists" in South Yemen, al-Baydh survived intraparty struggles and rose from the second rank of party leaders and ministers to become the secretary general of the ruling **Yemeni Socialist Party** after the of 1986 **13 January events** that resulted in the death of many top leaders and the overthrow of **Ali Nasir Muhammad** al-Hasani.

The most influential member of the new collective leadership, it was al-Baydh who led the PDRY into Yemeni **unification** in 1990, at which time he became vice president of the **ROY**. Increasingly in conflict with his northern counterparts, especially President Ali Abdullah **Salih**, he led the south in mid-1994 in the **War of Secession** and announced the birth of the short-lived **Democratic Republic of Yemen**, with himself as president. Al-Baydh fled into exile in **Oman** when his forces were defeated in July 1994, and along with three others was convicted of treason and sentenced to death in absentia. Except for a brief flurry of talk and activity in the late 1990s and again in mid-2009, he has maintained a low political profile in exile. He has remained abroad, despite being pardoned by President Salih in mid-2003 and, a few days later, having a reconciliation meeting with President Salih in the United Arab Emirates.

During the earlier years of the PDRY, al-Baydh had held many posts, among them minister of defense, and took a special interest in Wadi **Hadhramawt**. Indeed, in the early years after independence, he led the fruitless effort to subject the Hadhramis to socialist transformation. His family came from the Wadi, having earlier migrated there from **Yafi**.

BAYHAN, BAYHAN EMIRATE AND WADI BAYHAN. A remote town and region of South Yemen lying 150 miles north-northeast of **Aden** and bordering on the YAR's "middle region" just east of the town of **Harib** and north of the town of **al-Baydha**. A salient of land between North Yemen, the **Hadhramawt**, and the **Empty Quarter**, the Bayhan region is roughly defined by the long Wadi Bayhan that drains the Yemeni highlands northeastward into the **Ramlat al-Sabatayn** desert and roughly traces part of the old undemarcated border between the two Yemens. In ancient times, the **Qataban** trading state was centered in Wadi Bayhan and the adjacent Wadi Harib.

In modern times, Wadi Bayhan's location gave it a significant role to play in conflict between the British and first the **Ottoman Turks** and then the expansive **Hamid al-Din imams**, as well as in conflict between the two Yemens from the late 1960s through the 1980s. The rulers of the Bayhan emirate, Hashimites with ties to the Jordanian royal family, entered into a treaty of protection with **Great Britain** in the early 20th century, and then into a closer advisory agreement in the early 1940s.

Sharif Husayn bin Ali Bayhan, the shrewd and forceful ruler of Bayhan throughout the decades after World War II, was a close friend of the able, experienced British political officer in the Western **Aden Protectorate**, Sir Kenneth Trevaski. Sharif Husayn openly sided with the royalists and **Saudi Arabia** against the **republicans** and **Egypt** in the **Yemen Civil War**, providing sanctuary and a conduit for arms and other support, and was a strong proponent and leader of the federation first proposed in the late 1950s and later transformed into the short-lived **Federation of South Arabia** in the mid-1960s. The Bayhan emirate was abolished in the turbulent fall of 1967 by the **National Liberation Front,** victor in the fight to succeed Britain. Sharif Husayn failed in a determined effort to recover Bayhan by force in early 1968—the only South Arabian ruler to try for a comeback.

BAYOOMI, HASAN ALI. *See* FEDERATION OF SOUTH ARABIA (FSA).

BAYT AL-FAQI. The well-known medieval center of trade and Islamic learning that, well-placed some 20 miles inland on the **Tihama** on the main road to the mountains and **Sanaa** and about halfway between **Zabid** and **al-Hudayda** on the main north–south road, remains a bustling market town and commercial center. Perhaps most memorable is the colorful and evocative dress of the town's **women.**

BAYT SAUD (HOUSE OF SAUD). *See* AL-SAUD (BAYT SAUD).

BEDOUIN (PL. BEDU). *See* TRIBES AND THE TRIBAL SYSTEM.

BELIEVING YOUTH, THE. *See* AL-HOUTHI (AL-HUTHI) REBELLION.

BENT, THEODORE AND MABEL. *See* TRAVELERS.

BESSE, ANTONIN (1877–1951). A. Besse and Company was created between the two world wars by the French national Antonin Besse and soon became a famous **Red Sea** trading and shipping empire. It was active in Aden, Ethiopia, and other neighboring countries and was the most advanced and successful of private European enterprises in the Aden of the last several decades of colonial rule. Harold **Ingrams** reports that in the mid-1930s, Besse, then in his sixties, relished the sights and silences of the heights above Aden town and waterfront and could scamper up and down them as no one else, European or native. A self-made man of limited formal schooling, the shrewd and very able Monsieur Besse was so impressed with the advantages in business of a good education that he gave Oxford £1 million pounds sterling to found St. Anthony's College.

From the 1950s through the 1960s, and up until the increasingly radical post-independence South Yemeni regime forced the discontinuation of activities in Aden, family operations there were in the hands of the founder's youngest son, Tony Besse, a cosmopolitan, urbane man whom his friend Governor Charles **Johnston** has described approvingly as "a keen, rather ruthless businessman and a devastating critic of the [British colonial] Government."

BILQIS PREPARATORY COLLEGE. The school in **Aden** inspired and founded by Ahmad Muhammad **Numan** at the end of the 1950s for the express goal of preparing boys from North Yemen and the **Aden Protectorates** to assume their sacred role in nation-building in their "backward" homeland. The school was felt necessary by virtue of a British policy that denied access to the colony's schools to students from outside the colony. The first principal of Bilqis was Husayn **al-Hubayshi**, and the early faculty included **Abd al-Aziz**

Abd al-Ghani and Muhammad Anaam **Ghaleb**, first-generation **modernists** who went north after the **1962 Revolution**.

BILQIS, QUEEN OF SABA (SHEBA). *See* SABA (SHEBA) AND SABEAN KINGDOM.

BIN GHANEM, DR. FAREG (1937–2007). The non-partisan economist and technocrat from Ghail ba Wazir in the **Hadhramawt** who was chosen by President **Salih** to be prime minister in the first cabinet after the April 1997 **elections** and who, after less than one year, resigned in protest very publicly when the president refused to increase his power over the cabinet and its composition in exchange for his carrying out the unpopular lifting of subsidies on petroleum products and other basic necessities. The president accepted his resignation at the end of April 1998, after his month-long protest, absent in Europe.

Bin Ghanem's brief foray into politics ended at this time, despite his popularity as an honest man of integrity—and despite some talk about him as a possible presidential candidate for the **Joint Meeting Parties** in 2006. In his last years he was the ROY's ambassador to Switzerland and permanent representative to the **United Nations** in Geneva. Previously, in the PDRY, he had served as minister of planning, a post he continued to hold in the first government in the ROY after **unification** in 1990. In the mid-1990s, he was the ROY's representative in Geneva.

BIN LADIN FAMILY AND USAMA BIN LADEN (1957–). The large Saudi family of Yemeni origins, the patriarch of which, Muhammad bin Awad bin Laden, migrated to **Saudi Arabia** from Wadi Duan in the **Hadhramawt** in the 1950s. Bin Laden started a construction company just at the beginning of the oil-fueled building boom, became the builder for the ruling house of **Saud**, and proceeded to build a vast family-run business conglomerate. When he died in a plane crash in 1969, just before the first decade of soaring oil revenues, he was succeeded by his son, Salim bin Laden, who proceeded to grow the conglomerate into one worth tens of billions of dollars by the end of the 20th century.

Salim's half-brother, Usama, roughly the 20th of about 50 children sired by Muhammad, gravitated away from the family business for which he had been educated and towards a life devoted to the defense and spread of a militant version of **Salafism** and, in particular, its Saudi variant, **Wahhabism**. To this end, he took himself and his wealth to Pakistan and **Afghanistan** in the 1980s to wage—and to finance—jihad against the forces of the Soviet Union that had invaded Islamic Afghanistan. With the "defeat" and withdrawal of the Soviet forces in 1989, bin Laden returned to Saudi Arabia—as many **"Afghani Arabs"** returned to their respective homelands—more militant than ever and intent on waging jihad against, among others, the Marxist PDRY regime. The First **Gulf War** in 1991 caused Usama to redirect his wrath against the **United States** and his Saudi homeland. For his activities, he was stripped of his Saudi citizenship, disowned by his family, and forced in the mid-1990s to flee to **Sudan** and the protection of its militant Islamic leader, Hassan al-Turabi. It was during this period that he joined with Ayman al-Zawahiri, a former leader of Egyptian Islamic Jihad, to create **al-Qaida**, the organization that soon came to symbolize the most violent, anti-Western variant of modern **political Islam** and the use of terror to achieve religio-political goals.

In 1995, pressured to leave the Sudan, bin Laden sought and was granted refuge by the **Taliban** in Afghanistan. From there he and his colleagues planned and executed their suicide bombings of the U.S. embassies in Kenya and Tanzania in 1998, the U.S.S. *Cole* in Aden harbor in 2000, the Twin Towers and Pentagon in 2001, and the French tanker *Limburg* off the southern coast of Yemen in 2002. The bombings in the United States in 2001—on **9/11**—precipitated the U.S. invasion of Afghanistan in late 2001, the overthrow of the Taliban regime, and the ongoing effort to capture or kill bin Laden. The U.S. invasion and occupation of **Iraq** in 2003, the next chapter in the United States' **War on Terror**, brought al-Qaida to that hapless country.

BIN MAHFOUZ. The prominent Saudi banking and merchant family of Yemeni—more precisely, **Hadhrami**—origins that provided **imamate** Yemen's only bank in the mid-20th century and that, since **unification** in 1990, has been active in various ways in development in Yemen. In particular, bin Mahfouz controlled the Nimr Petroleum Company that had acquired the Block 4 **oil** concession in **Shabwa**

with its Soviet-developed field, pipeline, and export terminus. In addition, the Nimr group acquired other oil concessions in Yemen and involved itself in plans to upgrade the **Aden Refinery**, develop the **Aden Free Zone**, and launch other enterprises.

The bin Mahfouz traces itself to the Bani Seyyar tribe that has long occupied part of the Yemeni–Saudi borderland on the northern reaches of the Hadhramawt. In the 1930s, the family founded the National Commercial Bank (NCB), destined to become **Saudi Arabia**'s biggest bank, and NCB's reach soon extended to imamate Yemen. The most prominent family member was the fabulously wealthy Khalid bin Mahfouz, who was very close to the Saudi royal family and who was sometimes called the banker to the king.

BIN SHAMLAN, FAYSAL UTHMAN (1934–). The British-trained engineer and technocrat from the **Council of Deputies**, well regarded for his honesty, who served in the council from Yemeni **unification** in 1990 until 2003, was briefly minister of **oil** after the **War of Secession** in 1994, and ran against President **Salih** as the candidate of the **Joint Meeting Parties** (JMP) in the 2006 presidential **elections**. Aged 71, bin Shamlan was the first opposition candidate to run for the presidency, and his campaign pitted his honesty and modest lifestyle against the wealth and corruption of the Salih regime; prior to nomination by the JMP, he considered himself an independent and had run as one for the council in 1997. Under the circumstances, he made a respectable showing against the president, getting 21.82 percent of the vote, and helped establish the JMP as a credible opposition.

In a long career of public service, bin Shamlan was minister of public works and transport in the first government after South Yemen became independent in 1967, executive chairman of the General Authority for Electric Power, and, in the 1980s, director of the **Aden Oil Refinery** Company. From 1991 to 1992, after unification, he was manager of oil marketing in the recently merged Ministry of Oil, and in 1997, he became a vice president of Nimr Petroleum.

Bin Shamlan was a member of the **People's Supreme Council** in the PDRY from 1971–1990. He had been a founder of the Muslim Brotherhood in pre-independence South Yemen and, with the flowering of pluralist politics at unification in 1990, he was one of the founders of the al-Minbar Party and the newspaper *al-Minbar.*

BIN TALIB, SAADALDEEN. *See* CORRUPTION.

BIR ALI. *See* OIL AND GAS EXPLORATION AND PRODUCTION.

BORDERS AND BORDER DISPUTES, WARS, AND AGREE-MENTS. In addition to their common border, the YAR and PDRY both bordered on **Saudi Arabia**, and the PDRY bordered on **Oman.** The two Yemens had more than their share of border problems, largely because they and the other states of the Arabian Peninsula were artifacts of the 20th century and because many of the borders of these states remained undemarcated until late in that century. Some of these problems turned on the arbitrary creation of two Yemens as a result of the **Ottoman** Turkish occupation of North Yemen in the mid-19th century and, at about the same time, **Great Britain**'s occupation of **Aden** and what later became the **Aden Protectorates.** Increasingly in conflict as a result of the Ottoman pushing south and the British pushing north, the two occupying powers in the Yemens drew and demarcated the **Anglo–Ottoman line** of 1904 (ratified in 1913), a border between their territories from the **Bab al-Mandab Straits** northeast to the vicinity of **Harib.** The Yemeni **imamate** state that succeeded the Turks immediately thereafter vigorously disputed but more or less lived with this border, and the British unilaterally extended this border without demarcation in a straight line from the vicinity of Harib northeast into the vast desert in the interior of the peninsula.

The two independent Yemeni states that emerged in the 1960s, the **YAR** and the **PDRY**, inherited but did not honor this common border. The result was a rise of tensions and incidents in the late 1960s that led to border wars in 1972 and 1979, the PDRY-supported **National Democratic Front (NDF) rebellion** in the borderlands of the YAR in the early 1980s, and military confrontations in the disputed border-lands between **Marib** and **Shabwa** in 1985 and 1987–1988. The 1972 border war, which the YAR lost, was largely promoted by YAR Prime Minister Muhsin **al-Aini**, with the blessings of **Saudi Arabia.** By contrast, the 1979 border war was more the result of the ideological fervor of the socialist regime in the PDRY and was closely tied up in the NDF rebellion. The border problems and conflict between the two Yemens in the 1980s were engines of the process that ended with Yemeni **unification** in 1990.

The border between British-protected South Yemen and British-protected **Oman** was never demarcated, and it was across this border that much of the **Dhufar Rebellion** was waged in the 1970s—and with the support of the PDRY. The end of the rebellion led to improved relations between the PDRY and Oman, and to a protracted but not intense effort to settle and demarcate their common border. This was achieved shortly after unification, and in 1991 a border treaty was signed between Oman and the **ROY**; in 1992, that border was delimited. The final demarcation maps were not signed by Oman and the ROY until 1997, by which time agreements had been reached on new air links and a new highway connecting the two neighbors.

With the border settlement with Oman, the ROY had outstanding border disputes only with Saudi Arabia. This, however, is a long border, and the differences between the two parties were great and involved very high stakes—and a lot of ancient and recent history. Providing context for the contemporary border issue was the old, widely held, but rarely articulated notion of **Greater Yemen**—the historic, cultural, or natural "bilaad al-yaman." As for the recent past, hanging over this dispute in the 1990s were memories of the **Saudi–Yemeni War of 1934** and the border agreement that issued from it, the **Taif Treaty of 1934**. This 20-year renewable treaty between the victorious and ascendant Kingdom of Saudi Arabia and the revived Imamate of Yemen drew a border that gave the victor control over **Asir**, **Najran**, and **Jizan**, regions in the northeast and east of the Red Sea that were culturally Yemen and that many Yemenis came to refer to as the "lost northern provinces."

Salt was rubbed in the wound in 1973, about 40 years later, when the prime minister of a virtually bankrupt YAR, Abdullah **al-Hajri**, felt compelled to reaffirm the Taif Treaty, which had been renewed earlier in the mid-1950s, in exchange for budgetary support and economic aid from oil-rich Saudi Arabia, the very country that had in the 1960s aided the royalists against the **republicans** in the **Yemeni Civil War**; the joint communiqué issued after the meeting said cryptically that the border covered by the treaty was "permanent and final." At the time, and for long thereafter, many Yemenis were angered at being taken advantage of unfairly in a moment of national weakness.

At about the same time, in the late 1960s and 1970s, Saudi Arabia was putting territorial pressure farther to the east on a newly independent South Yemen. Most notably, the Saudi forces in 1969 seized **al-Wadiah**, a town and area claimed by Yemen and located between the **Hadhramawt** and the **Empty Quarter**.

Despite the virulence of Yemeni nationalism in the 1970s and 1980s, the YAR and the PDRY did little to act on their claims and grievances against Saudi Arabia for another 20 years, until after unification in 1990. Neither of the two Yemens was in a position to press its border claims with its Saudi neighbors. Preoccupied with other problems—state-building and development, as well as inter-Yemeni conflict—most Yemeni nationalists put the border issues with the Saudis on the back burner.

In the case of the YAR, the state was weak and unable to exercise anything like sovereignty over much of the territory nominally under its control, especially on the periphery to the east and northeast, areas bordering Saudi Arabia. Moreover, the YAR needed the budgetary subsidies and aid secured by Prime Minister al-Hajri in 1973 to perform minimal government functions, much less pursue a program of economic development. Most important, the YAR increasingly depended on the inflow of **remittances** from the several hundred thousand Yemeni workers that Saudi Arabia, in the midst of the oil-fed growth boom of the 1970s, allowed to freely enter under special terms. For its part, the PDRY focused its attentions on the external "socialist camp" upon which it became wholly dependent for economic survival and on the politics and economics of its own experiment at socialist transformation.

At the same time, these years were punctuated by reports of Saudi efforts to create new facts in the disputed border areas—e.g., advancing a road here, placing a new frontier outpost there, and offering citizenship to **tribesmen** in the borderland. Even Yemenis not familiar with the legal principle of "effective occupancy" received these reports with concern. At the same time, armed clashes or other hostilities occurred between Yemenis and Saudis in the border areas, events that both sides denied or at least downplayed. All this left the impression that the Saudis were encroaching on Yemeni territory, albeit slowly and quietly, and that there was little that the two Yemens could do about it. As in 1973, the Yemenis felt that they were being taken advantage of in their weakness.

Yemeni unification in 1990, and the discovery of **oil** in both Yemens a few years earlier, brought the Yemeni–Saudi border question to the front burner and seemingly changed its political dynamics. Euphoric, the leaders of the newly created ROY thought that they now had the strength to stand up to their Saudi neighbor on a number of issues, including borders. Moreover, Yemeni leaders were aware that, in the past, attempts by either of the Yemens to press its territorial claims with the Saudis had been confounded by border disputes between the two Yemens. The Saudis could claim that they did not know whether they were negotiating with the right Yemen regarding the particular piece of border in question. Unification denied the Saudis this ploy.

Unfortunately for the ROY, its failure to line up with Saudi Arabia in the First **Gulf War** in 1991, less than a year after unification caused the Saudis to cut off economic aid to Yemen and, more damaging, expel several hundred thousand Yemeni workers. The result was a massive drop in the flow of remittances into Yemen as well as an equally massive upsurge in unemployment. Despite, or perhaps because of, the effects of the war on the ROY's economy and its relations with the Saudis, it was President Salih's public call in September 1991 for a final settlement of borders with its neighbors that started what was to prove to be the beginning of the end of the border dispute with Saudi Arabia. The Saudis responded positively, and bilateral negotiations began in July 1992 in Geneva. Both sides were motivated by uncertainty over whether their 1973 communiqué obviated the need for renewal of the Taif Agreement, as well as by new efforts to explore for oil reserves in their borderland. In March 1992, Saudi Arabia sent written warnings to several oil companies operating under recent Yemeni concessions in territory it claimed. The **United States** quickly upped the ante when it responded brusquely to the warnings, stating that the border issue should be settled by peaceful means and that Yemen Hunt Oil and Phillips Petroleum should ignore the warning and proceed.

Interrupted by the **War of Secession** in mid-1994, and complicated by Saudi support of the secessionists' cause, negotiations did resume shortly thereafter but took place against the background of armed clashes and confrontations in the border area, the further buildup of Saudi forces in the Empty Quarter, and the announced emergence of a National Front for the Liberation of Najran and Asir. Against this, the process seemingly got a boost in early 1995 with President Salih saying for the first time that Yemen was open to accepting all provisions of the Taif Treaty and with the signing by ROY and Saudi Arabia of a memorandum of understanding that established joint committees and a procedural framework for negotiating the rest of the border, including an unelaborated-upon provision for recourse to arbitration if the two sides could not reach agreement.

As it turned out, the ROY ended up preoccupied throughout 1995 with an unanticipated and serious territorial dispute with **Eritrea**. More generally, Saudi Arabia and the ROY seem to have opted for the long haul in 1995, both because of a reduced sense of urgency brought on by recent negative results in the search for oil in the border area and because increased anti-Saudi feeling in Yemen made probable territorial concessions by Yemen politically more dangerous. Moreover, the two sides settled into different priorities and strategies. The Saudis wanted a border settlement before addressing other outstanding issues, whereas the ROY wanted to hold off on the border agreement until agreement was reached on the right of Yemenis to go freely to Saudi Arabia to work and the restoration of significant Saudi economic aid to Yemen.

Prospects for a border agreement dimmed further in mid-1996 when, four years into negotiations, the ROY for the first time officially specified to the Saudis its claim to territory east of the Taif Treaty line. This claim to Yemen's "traditional boundary," a vague notion related to the idea of **Greater Yemen**, reached deep into desert area that the Saudis assumed to be theirs. The Yemenis backed up their claim with maps dating back to the early 20th century, but the Saudis would not even consider the claim. The situation turned nasty in 1997 and thereafter, what with border confrontations and armed clashes, as well as charges and counter-charges. In frustration, the ROY threatened at least twice to give up on bilateral negotiations and insist on arbitration, an option it insisted was provided for in the Taif Treaty. Nevertheless, despite the lack of signs of progress, President Salih on different occasions in 1999 declared that a final border settlement would come "soon," and on one occasion again said that Yemen was prepared to give up its claims to Asir, Najran, and Jizan.

Even insiders were surprised when, on 12 June, 2000, it was announced that the ROY and Saudi Arabia had reached a "final and permanent" border agreement—the Jidda Agreement—an agreement that covered their Red Sea maritime border, the border covered by the Taif Agreement and the long desert border east to the intersection of Oman with the ROY and Saudi Arabia. In the agreement, Yemen gave up its claim to the "lost provinces" and Saudi Arabia gave up a small amount of the disputed territory to the east. The rather sudden breakthrough was probably the result of strategic political decisions on both sides. For the Saudis, faced with a porous border with Yemen and the growing threat of militant **political Islam** at home and abroad, the rebuilding of bilateral relations with Yemen nearly 10 years after the First Gulf War made sense. For the Yemenis, the needs for Saudi aid, jobs for Yemeni workers in Saudi Arabia, regional peace as a precondition for foreign investment and the benefits of membership in the **Gulf Cooperation Council** were greater than ever.

The Jidda Agreement called for choosing an outsider party to demarcate the eastern three-quarters of the border, and a German company was soon engaged for this purpose. Renewed Saudi concerns about the openness of the border to terrorists, arms and bomb-making materials, heightened by the **terrorist** bombing deep within the kingdom in mid-2003, strained relations anew and caused Crown Prince Sultan to visit **Sanaa** in June. Work on a border security "wall," begun in haste by the Saudis, ceased when comparisons were made between it and the Israeli-built wall on the edge of the West Bank, and, in lieu of that, the ROY agreed to beef up its border forces as well as to conduct joint Yemeni–Saudi border patrols. The old concerns of the **Wailah** tribe regarding its historic right to move back and forth across the borderland, expressed anew and vigorously as the delineation proceeded, were addressed.

The border was finally delineated and new border crossings established by mid-decade. Both governments approved the demarcations and maps, and, finally, in March 2006, Crown Prince Sultan, the person who had been the harsh overseer of Saudi Arabia's relations with Yemen since the mid-1970s, signed the final maps fixing the final border.

BRITAIN. *See* GREAT BRITAIN.

BUNKERING. The provision of coal or oil to ships from onshore storage facilities, a need that came with the age of the steamship and the modern age of **imperialism**. This need both triggered much of the interest in **Aden** and other locations near the **Bab al-Mandab Straits** in the 19th century and made Aden the second or third busiest port in the world by the middle of the 20th century. Through major improvements in its port facilities, Aden had won, by the end of the 19th century, the long competition with **Perim Island** and other spots for the rapidly expanding bunkering trade. Further port improvements as well as the shift to oil and the opening of the **Aden refinery** in 1954 contributed to making Aden the world-class port that it became.

BURAYKAH. *See* ADEN, ADEN COLONY AND THE PORT OF ADEN.

BURY, WYMAN. *See* TRAVELERS.

AL-BUSHAIRI, BRIG. ABDULLAH HUSAYN. The senior YAR army officer who served as chief of staff of the **armed forces** from late 1978 until Yemeni **Unification** in 1990, at which time he became chief of staff of the armed forces of the ROY. Al-Bushairi is credited with saving the new regime of President **Salih** by acting quickly and forcefully on the occasion of the **October 1978 coup attempt**. He was then rewarded with the chief of staff post, replacing Ali al-Shayba, and remained a loyal member of the Salih regime until he resigned in 1993. His resignation in protest from that post in 1993 marked the growing tensions between the two partners in the ROY and the two unmerged Yemeni armed forces.

BUSH, GEORGE H. W. (1924–). The political figure who as **United States** vice president in 1987 visited the YAR to take part in the opening of **Yemen Hunt Oil Company's** refinery in **Marib** and who as the 41st president of the U.S. in 1990 suspended economic and military assistance to the newly created **ROY** because of the latter's refusal to join the anti-**Iraq** international coalition in the crisis that led to the First **Gulf War**. President Bush had hosted the upbeat visit of the YAR's President **Salih** in January 1990, about four and six months, respectively, before Yemeni **unification** and the onset of the Gulf crisis. Fellow Texans and connected to the petroleum industry, the Bush family was on very friendly terms with that of Ray Hunt, head of the Yemen Hunt Oil Company.

BUSH, GEORGE W. (1946–). The 43rd president of the **United States**, and son of President George H.W. Bush, whose relationship to the ROY was almost solely defined by **9/11** and his **War on Terror** during his two terms in office, 2001 to early 2009. President Bush courted and rewarded—and, implicitedly, threatened—President Ali Abdullah **Salih** in terms of his commitment to this war.

– C –

CAIRO AGREEMENTS ON UNIFICATION (1972). The two agreements reached in Cairo in October 1972 under which the two Yemens agreed to end their **border war** by agreeing on political **unification**. The first called for a cease-fire, withdrawal of forces from the borders, return of all territory occupied during the fighting, the ending of sabotage, the repatriation of all refugees wanting to go home, and the closure of all military training camps for refugees. The second was the actual unification agreement, which called for a single Yemeni state with one flag and unified legislative, executive, and judicial organs. **Joint unification committees** on key issues were to be set up and charged with completing their work within one year. The Cairo agreements, negotiated by the prime ministers of the YAR and the PDRY, **Muhsin al-Aini** and **Ali Nasir Muhammad** al-Hasani, respectively, were ignored shortly after they were reached, as were the results of the **Tripoli Summit** at the end of 1972. Nevertheless, the committees did begin their work, and the agreements were benchmarks in the episodic, nearly two-decade process that led to unification in 1990.

CANADIAN OCCIDENTAL OIL. *See* NEXEN.

CARAVAN ROUTES. *See* TRADE ROUTES, ANCIENT.

CARTER, PRESIDENT JIMMY (1924–). The administration of U.S. President Jimmy Carter (1977–1981) registered negatively with both Yemens due to Carter's key role in the **Arab–Israeli conflict**—specifically, the Camp David Agreement in 1979 that resulted in a separate peace between **Egypt** and **Israel**. The YAR and the PDRY joined the other Arab states in condemning the agreement and both Presidents Carter and Anwar **Sadat**, although the YAR's rejection was not as severe as that of the PDRY.

At about the same time, President Carter was being criticized at home and abroad for indecisiveness during the crisis surrounding the fall of the United States' longtime friend, the Shah of **Iran**. The president seized upon the 1979 **border war** between the two Yemens to demonstrate to a doubting **Saudi Arabia** and others that the United States was willing and able to come to the aid of its friends decisively and in a timely manner. It did so by declaring an emergency and ordering that the transfer of arms to the YAR be speeded up and increased.

The arms arrived too late to figure in the fighting, and President Carter came in for criticism in Congress and elsewhere for having suspended normal congressional review by declaring an emergency a situation that was nothing of the sort. Moreover, the YAR was not particularly thankful, because the triangular deal of Saudi-purchased American arms for the YAR, which put the actual transfer of the arms in the hands of the Saudis, was perceived as further evidence of the United States' willingness to deal with the YAR only through the Saudis and in accord with Saudi interests. Within a few months, the YAR turned successfully to the **Soviet Union** for an even larger infusion of arms. Nevertheless, the sizable amount of heavy arms from the United States did strengthen the YAR state and armed forces, as well as the new, and very shaky, regime of President Ali Abdullah **Salih**.

By chance, the one-term Carter presidency coincided with periods of tumult in each of the Yemens. In the YAR, two heads of state were assassinated in rapid succession, Ibrahim **al-Hamdi** and Ahmad **al-Ghashmi**, opening the way for the **Salih regime**; and, only a few months after coming to power, President Salih survived a serious coup attempt. In the PDRY, one head of state, Salim **Rubay Ali**, was executed, and his successor, **Abd al-Fattah** Ismail, was sent into exile, opening the way to **Ali Nasir Muhammad** al-Hasani—all in 1977–1980.

CASTE. *See* SOCIAL SYSTEM AND STRUCTURE.

CENTRAL BANK OF YEMEN (CBY). *See* BANKS.

CENTRAL PLANNING ORGANIZATION (CPO). Created in 1972 out of the much more modest **Technical Office**, and ably led for its first five years by Dr. Abd al-Karim **al-Iryani**, the CPO quickly became both the vital center of the YAR's mushrooming development activities and its model modern institution. Located in the Office of the Prime Minister, the CPO was charged with several tasks: the formulation of development priorities and strategies, the preparation of the national development plan and an annual development budget, the collection and processing of socioeconomic statistics, and the coordination and supervision of plan implementation by the ministries. In addition, the CPO was to assess and make recommendations on foreign aid proposals, to act on behalf of the government in negotiating and concluding aid agreements, and to monitor and otherwise deal with donors during the implementation of these agreements.

Under Dr. al-Iryani's leadership, and through the joint effort of an able Yemeni staff and foreign experts provided by the **World Bank**, the CPO was fashioned into a functioning institution in a very short time. Indeed, by 1974, it had become the main source of hard data on the **economy** and society, the focal point for development policy and planning, and, perhaps most crucial, the main interface between the Yemeni government and aid donors. The annual statistical yearbooks, the successive five-year-development plans, and the national censuses were key achievements.

In the late 1970s, the image of the CPO as the YAR's model modern institution became tarnished as its capabilities declined and other agencies involved in development found ways to bypass its procedures for the selection, supervision, and coordination of projects. An attempt was made with some success to revitalize the CPO and reassert its supervisory role in the early 1980s during the years when Dr. al-Iryani was prime minister.

With Yemeni **unification** in 1990, the CPO became the Central Statistical Organization (CSO). By this time, however, the planning functions of the old CPO had been ceded to the Ministry of Planning. As a result, the CSO had as its focus the gathering and analysis of statistical data, much as the predecessor of the CPO, the Technical Office, had done in the late 1960s and early 1970s.

CHINA, PEOPLE'S REPUBLIC OF. Since 1980, China has had a modest political and economic presence in the two Yemens and then the ROY, a marked change from its more active posture in North Yemen from 1960 through the 1970s and in South Yemen throughout the decade after independence in 1967. This commitment of greater effort and resources in the earlier period was largely a function of the three-cornered **Cold War** among China, the **United States** and the **Soviet Union,** a competition from which China largely withdrew by the late 1970s. The intense Sino–Soviet competition for influence in the Third World that marked those years, as well as the salience of China to the politics and economics of the PDRY's formative years, is suggested by the fact that the great internal political struggle in the late 1970s was portrayed by some as between the "Maoist" Salim **Rabiyya Ali** and the victorious "Stalinist" **Abd al-Fattah** Ismael.

In the YAR, Chinese aid efforts were highly regarded. North Yemenis still fondly recall Chinese laborers toiling side-by-side with Yemeni workers on projects, unlike the aid officials from Western countries or the Soviet Bloc. They also associate the Chinese with some of the biggest and most visible projects from the early, more heroic days of the republic—for example, the completion of the paved highway between **al-Hudayda** and **Sanaa** during the **Yemeni Civil War** in the 1960s, culminating in the **Siege of Sanaa** at the end of 1967. The then-modern textile plant and the vocational school in Sanaa, built and operated by the Chinese, were held up as embodiments of a modern Yemen.

CHRISTIANITY IN YEMEN. *See* RELIGION AND RELIGIOUS GROUPS IN YEMEN.

CIVIL SOCIETY ORGANIZATIONS. *See* INTEREST (PRESSURE) GROUPS.

CIVIL WAR, 1962–1970. *See* YEMENI CIVIL WAR.

CLASS AND CASTE. *See* SOCIAL SYSTEM AND STRUCTURE.

CLIMATE. *See* GEOGRAPHY AND CLIMATE.

COFFEE AND THE COFFEE TRADE. The refreshing, stimulating drink to which the world became addicted in its varied forms only a few centuries ago was originally made from the beanlike seeds of the coffee tree, first domesticated in the cool, well-watered, terraced highlands of Yemen and **Ethiopia**. Coffee was known in Constantinople by the mid-16th century, brought home by the **Ottoman Turkish** occupiers of Yemen. Its fame spread sufficiently to England and continental Europe in the next 50 years to make it a prized object of trade, putting the long-forgotten souce of highly prized **incense** back on the map of world commerce.

The English, Dutch, and French competed fiercely in the lucrative coffee trade, regularly stopping at the port of **al-Mukha**—hence the term "mocha"—to take on the sacks of beans purchased by their resident agents. However, by the early 19th century, ships and merchants from the **United States** came to dominate the Yemeni coffee trade. But the Yemeni coffee monopoly was soon broken, and coffee trees were grown in increasing quantities and more cheaply on great plantations in European colonies in East Asia, East Africa, and Latin America. Before long, Yemen's small coffee crop was priced out of the world market, and Yemen was again forgotten.

Yemeni coffee continues to be produced for domestic consumption and, still prized by connoisseurs, is exported in small quantities. Indeed, the willingness in the 1980s of Americans and Europeans to pay premium prices for quality and exotic coffees raised the possibility of a revival of Yemeni coffee production—and of the old Yemeni coffee trade. Unfortunately, issues of quality control and predictable supply caused Starbucks, for one, to give up on Yemeni coffee in the 1990s, only to try it again in the new century. These issues, and not the widely held view that coffee cultivation was crowded out by the cultivation of the more profitable **qat** plant, were the major causes of the decline in coffee production in Yemen. Although the two plants are grown at about the same elevation, coffee cultivation declined long before qat became widely and wildly popular.

COLD WAR. The post–World War II superpower confrontation between the **United States** and the **Soviet Union** was felt in the Yemens, but usually at a distance and in muted form. However, it was the end of the Cold War, signaled by the Soviet Union's global retrenchment in economic aid in the late 1980s, that jolted and virtually forced a nearly bankrupt and now-patronless PDRY to accept **unification** when the YAR made the offer in late 1989.

Although the Soviet Union had earlier provided Imam **Ahmad** with a small number of arms to face imperialist **Great Britain** in **Aden**, it was the late 1950s that brought the Cold War as well as the Sino–Soviet conflict to backward, despotic **imamate** Yemen in a visual and highly symbolic form. The United States, Soviet Union, and **China** competed head-to-head as each built a motorable highway on one side of the triangle formed by **Sanaa**, **Taiz**, and **al-Hudayda**. China was judged the clear winner, with the much admired paved "Chinese road" connecting Sanaa and al-Hudayda. Having unwisely refused to pave its Sanaa–Taiz–Mukha road, the United States was judged the loser by lorry drivers and Yemeni officials alike.

Coming on the heels of the **1962 Revolution**, the **Yemeni Civil War** was quickly regionalized and then internationalized, acquiring a Cold War veneer in the process. The Soviet Union supported the **Egyptians**, who supported the republicans against the **royalists**, who, in turn, were backed by **Saudi Arabia**, Britain, and, a bit later, the United States. With the end of that struggle in 1970, the Cold War became quite muted in the Yemens over the next two decades. However, the outpouring of Marxist revolutionary rhetoric from the PDRY continued and President Jimmy **Carter** did attempt to represent the 1979 **border war** between the Yemens as an East–West confrontation.

Both superpowers had strong but different constraints on whatever urge they may have had to make the Yemens more salient to the Cold War. The Soviet Union was the principal arms supplier for both Yemens, which put a damper on efforts by it to use the conflict by the one Yemen against the other for Cold War purposes. Moreover, while the Soviet Union desired to have the PDRY as a client, it was unwilling to have this at the financial costs of another **Cuba**. Reluctant to generously bankroll a revolutionary PDRY, Moscow counseled the PDRY to moderate sufficiently to get needed funds from Saudi Arabia and the other Arab Gulf states. Indeed, with the collapse of the Soviet Union imminent, its leaders told the PDRY in 1988 that thereafter it would have to fend for itself. In addition, political turmoil in Aden—culminating in the **13 January events** in 1986—had caused the Soviet Union to question the reliability of the PDRY leadership,

For its part, the Washington's "special relationship" with Saudi Arabia made it impossible for a strong U.S.–YAR patron–client relationship to develop, given the persistent tensions between these neighboring states. For example, instead of cementing U.S.–YAR ties, the large transfer of U.S. arms to the YAR in early 1979 angered the Yemenis because of the alleged control exerted by the Saudis over the process. The YAR sought and got an even larger arms transfer from the Soviet Union at the end of that same year.

***COLE* BOMBING, U.S.S.** The suicide bombing by **al-Qaida** of the destroyer U.S.S. *Cole* while refueling in **Aden** in October 2000 that, taking the lives of 19 servicemen, placed the issue of terrorism at the center of **U.S.**–Yemeni relations almost a full year before **9/11**. The start of the refueling of U.S. navel vessels in Aden almost a full year earlier, in August 1999, had marked the highpoint in the restoration of U.S.–Yemeni relations since the nadir reached at the time of the First **Gulf War** in 1991.

The months after the *Cole* bombing, beginning with the investigation into causes and perpetrators, saw U.S.–Yemeni relations become strained and complicated, a foretaste of a pattern that persisted through the first decade of the 21st century. Increasingly, the **Salih regime** found itself caught between U.S. demands that it commit itself in deed, as well as in word, to the U.S.-defined, post-9/11 **War on Terror** and the perspective and demands of major portions of its political base. The Federal Bureau of Investigation (FBI) agent in charge of the case dealt so undiplomatically with his Yemeni counterparts that the U.S. ambassador in Sanaa demanded his removal from the case. Ironically, and tragically, the agent resigned from the FBI, became security chief of New York's World Trade Center, and, a week after taking his new position, died when al-Qaida brought down the Twin Towers on 9/11.

COLONIAL ADMINISTRATION AND ADMINISTRATORS. An anomalous result of **Aden**'s seizure in 1839 by agents of British rulers in Bombay, the administration of **Aden Colony** and the territories that later became the **Aden Protectorates** was largely in the hands of the Bombay Presidency and its superior, the governor general of **India** in Delhi. This remained the case until full responsibility for these places far from India was finally transferred nearly a century later to the Colonial Office in 1937. Before this transfer, this locus of power and responsibility in India often produced a perspective and policies on Aden and South Arabia that were both at variance with those of the Foreign and Colonial Offices in London and oblivious to conditions in and the dynamics of the Near East and, in particular, the **Arabian Peninsula**. In this India-eyed view, the economic, political, and military needs of British India were paramount, and Aden and the rest of South Arabia were reduced to afterthoughts or means toward the end of economically maintaining the imperial umbilical cord between Britain and India.

Equally important, the transfer of responsibility to the Colonial Office followed 20 years of improvisation during which different offices in London and India were given responsibility for different functions in Aden and the Protectorates. As a result of divided and changing responsibilities, it was often hard to know who had responsibility for what, much less to plan for the whole or over the long term. In particular, the fragmented administrative setup militated against thinking about future relationships among **Great Britain**, South Arabia, and the rest of the Arab world, between Aden and the much bigger and more backward Protectorates, and between Britain in South Arabia and a North Yemen under the **Ottomans** and then the **imamate**.

Tangled administration and responsibility partly explains why British authorities in London and in Aden seemed so unprepared to deal with these crucial matters in the tumultuous 1950s and 1960s, a time when anti-colonialism, nationalism, and republicanism finally came to South Arabia. The colonialists seemed to be constantly playing catch-up only to again be overtaken by events: first, they set up the two protectorates separate from Aden Colony and then tried to integrate them into a single entity; second, they built up the military facilities of Aden as a linchpin of continuing imperial power "east of Suez" in the 1950s and then decided to abandon that policy, and South Yemen, in the mid-1960s.

Nevertheless, some of the colonial officers during the last generation of British rule in South Yemen were very able. Col. Sir Charles

Reilly was the highest-ranking British official in Aden during most of the 1930s, a key period in which jurisdiction over South Yemen was switched to the Colonial Office and it became apparent that the security of Britain's position in Aden required increased British involvement in the protectorate states. In 1933, he became the first resident of Aden to visit the **Hadhramawt**. The following year he guided the negotiations that resulted in the **Treaty of Sanaa**'s setting the boundary between the territories administered by the British and those ruled by the Yemeni imamate. Thereafter, as governor, he took a number of other measures to increase security and social welfare in the Protectorates. These several actions marked the real beginnings of Britain's **"forward policy"** in the Protectorates.

Harold **Ingrams** set the standard high for **political officers**. As the first resident adviser to the **Quaiti** sultanate in **Mukalla**, he organized the government of the newly created Eastern Aden Protectorate in the late 1930s. Previously, in 1936, he had guided the grand truce that brought the Hadhramawt out of a long period of anarchy and fighting and that came to be known as "Ingrams' Peace." A skilled Arabist and student of Arabia in the classic British imperial mold—almost the last of his kind—Ingrams wrote books of lasting value about South Arabia.

Coming closer to the time that colonial rule was seriously challenged in South Arabia, it was Sir Tom Hickinbotham who as governor of Aden from 1951 to 1956 pushed the idea of federal union as an instrument of rule and as a vehicle for the creation of a South Arabian nationalism as distinct from the Yemeni nationalism being promoted by Imam **Ahmad** of North Yemen. Unfortunately for him, the conference of rulers that he held in early 1954 failed because of London's insensitive effort to force upon the rulers its own prepackaged set of constitutional proposals.

During the late 1950s, Sir William Luce, the statesmanlike governor of Aden, did guide six of the states of the Western Aden Protectorate in the creation of the **Federation of Arab Amirates of the South** (FAAS) and then saw to its expansion and articulation. By his departure in late 1960, he had taken steps toward the proposed merger of Aden Colony with the federation.

From late 1960 into 1963, Sir Charles H. Johnson was the career diplomat in Aden who guided the mixed bag of Adeni and the

Western Aden Protectorate political leaders to the constitutional merger of Aden Colony and the new FAAS into the ill-fated **Federation of South Arabia** (FSA). In his account of these years, *The View From Steamer Point,* written fresh from this task in 1963, he expressed his strong beliefs that the FSA was the best way to square the interests of Britain and the various South Arabian entities and that its prospects were at least hopeful. As he wrote, however, the newly formed **National Liberation Front** (NLF) was dooming the new federation to failure.

Sir Kennedy Trevaski, an able colonial officer with great knowledge of and experience in the Western Aden Protectorate, having served as British agent there from 1951, succeeded Johnson as British high commissioner in Aden in 1963. Closely identified with and trusted by the conservative protectorate rulers and their desires for an independent FSA with security links with Britain, Trevaski's dismissal in 1965 signaled the fresh approach of London's new Labour government both to the conflict between the Adeni politicians and the protectorate rulers and to the issues of the independence and security of South Arabia. The NLF's **Radfan Rebellion** began early in Trevaski's short tenure, and political violence in Aden revived after a period of dormancy, forever changing the course of South Yemen's evolution. He wrote of his experiences in *Shades of Amber,* published in 1968.

Sir Richard Turnbill was British high commissioner in Aden from early 1965 until spring 1967, during which time the decision by the British government not to maintain military facilities in South Yemen after it became independent in 1968—announced in the **Defense White Paper of 1966**—made all but inevitable the failure of any independence formula based on the merger of Aden and the protectorate states in the FSA. Having earlier played a key role in bringing Tanzania to a peaceful birth, Turnbull's appointment in place of Trevaski was meant to signal a new start in South Yemen on the part of **Harold Wilson**'s Labor government, a new start that seemed to rely more upon such Adeni nationalists as Abdullah **al-Asnag** than upon the **Federalis** in the protectorate states. Perhaps Turnbull hastened the collapse of the FSA by not trying hard to persuade Sayyid Zayn Baharun, a friend of the federation, to stay on as chief minister in Aden and by appointing as his successor an opponent of the federation, Abd al-Qawi **Makkawi**. In any case, political stalemate and turmoil as well as terrorism increased and finally led Turnbull to dismiss the obstructionist Makkawi, suspend the constitution, and impose direct colonial rule on Aden.

The veteran ambassador Sir Humphrey Trevelyan was named high commissioner in Aden in the spring of 1967, shortly before the fiercest of the **Arab–Israeli** wars—the Six-Day War—sent shock waves through the Arab World, including South Arabia. His tenure of only several months was marked by the final collapse of the FSA and the last bloody battle between al-Asnag's fading **Front for the Liberation of Occupied South Yemen** and the ascendant NLF—and the departure of the last of the British forces and officials by late 1967.

COLONIALISM. *See* IMPERIALISM AND COLONIALISM.

COMMAND COUNCIL, YAR. The YAR's highest ruling body, the repository of all legislative and executive power, during the nearly four-year period from the **al-Hamdi coup** and the suspension of the **1970 Constitution** in 1974 to the abolition of the council by President Ahmad **al-Ghashmi** in 1978. The number of members of the Command Council declined from about a dozen to just a few, as President al-Hamdi consolidated power in his own hands and relegated the council to insignificance. "President" Al-Hamdi technically had the title "chairman" of the Command Council.

COMMERCE. *See* ECONOMY AND POLITICAL ECONOMY; IMPORTS AND EXPORTS.

COMMUNIST PARTY. *See* PEOPLE'S DEMOCRATIC UNION (PDU).

CONFERENCES (1960s), YEMENI OR REGIONAL. *See* YEMENI CIVIL WAR.

CONFERENCES (1990–1992), TRIBAL AND PARTY. The several conferences triggered by the growing political crisis after the short honeymoon period which followed Yemeni **unification** in 1990, each designed in a different way to save the project and to steer it in a particular party or ideological direction. Not all **tribal** and rural, this flurry of big meetings largely for modern political purposes built on a tradition of ad hoc participation in the tribal areas of Yemen. A famous modern precedent was the calling of a large tribal gathering in 1975 in **Khamir** by Abdullah ibn Husayn al-**Ahmar** in his unsuccessful effort to reverse President Ibrahim **al-Hamdi**'s effort to lessen the influence of the tribes vis-à-vis the state.

The Solidarity Conference of October 1990, the first of the large tribal meetings after unification, was held in the countryside and brought together thousands of tribal leaders and tribesmen. Other conferences of this sort were the National Cohesion Conference in November 1991 and the Saba (Sheba) Conference in October 1992. In addition to dealing with parochial issues, such as tribal dispute settlement, the discussions and resolutions (*bayan*) of these conferences addressed the major issues involved in the growing political crisis surrounding unification.

Late 1992 saw a series of large urban conferences, beginning on the occasion of North Yemen's revolution day, 26 September, with the National Conference (NC) organized by professionals in the modernist, progressive or radical opposition and chaired by the liberal intellectual, Umar **al-Jawi**. It brought together the modern political parties and organizations not tied to the two ruling parties, the **General People's Congress** (GPC) and the **Yemeni Socialist Party** (YSP), as well as key tribal figures. With the help of **Islah** and the **Baath Party**, the GPC held at the same time a counter-conference, the Conference of Parties and Popular Organizations; its resolutions and declarations were for the most part the mirror image off those of the NC. although originally billed as a non-partisan event, and coming after the delay of the legislative elections and amidst worsening economic conditions, The Taiz Conference in November 1992, ended up dominated by the YSP. Finally, the Islah-dominated Unity and Peace Conference was held in a stadium in **Sanaa** in December 1992.

The rash of conferences ended as attentions turned to the parliamentary **elections** rescheduled for April 1993 and to the short period of hope and cooperation that followed them. When the political crisis returned with a vengence later in that year, the instrument chosen to address it in late 1993 and early 1994 was the **National Dialogue Committee of Political Forces**, not conferences. The one exception was the **Hadhramawt** Conference in December 1993, organized by the "Sons of Hadhramawt" and focusing ominously on local autonomy and "Greater Hadhramawt." But the era of political conferences was over—and the **War of Secession** was just months away.

CONSTITUTIONAL CONFERENCES. The futile meetings between **Great Britain** and South Yemeni politicians in London in 1964 and 1965 for the purpose of reaching agreement on the form of governance of and transition to an independent **Federation of South Arabia** in which **Aden** was merged with the states of the **Aden Protectorates**. The British idea was to leave behind in South Arabia a single state, much as it was about to do in the Gulf with the creation of the **United Arab Emirates**. The political setting and constituent parts in South Arabia proved very different from those in the Gulf. Despite skillful negotiations and compromise, this effort at constitutional engineering was overtaken and doomed to failure by fast-moving, out-of-control political events in Aden and the Protectorates.

CONSTITUTIONS. *See* 1970 CONSTITUTION, YAR'S; 1970 STATE CONSTITUTION, PDRY'S; 1990 CONSTITUTION (ROY).

CONSULTATIVE COUNCIL (MAJLIS AL-SHURA). The 179-member (159 elected and 20 appointed) legislature provided for in the YAR's **1970 Constitution** that after the 1971 **elections** quickly asserted a strong role in the political and decision-making processes and, in particular, became the chief state institution through which tribal leaders and other conservative elements were able to dilute, if not block, efforts to strengthen the state and achieve other modernist goals. Largely for this reason, the Consultative Council was abolished little more than three years later by President **al-Hamdi** just after he came to power through a coup in 1974, and it was only restored a decade into the **Salih** era, in 1988, after new elections. With Yemeni **unification** and creation of the ROY in 1990, the Consultative Council was merged with the PDRY's **Supreme People's Council** to form the **Council of Deputies** (Majlis al-Nuwab). The ROY's **1990 constitution** provided for an appointed second chamber that was finally created in 1997. Although officially the "Consultative Council," it came to be known in common parlance as the "**Shura Council.**"

CONSUMPTION AND CONSUMERISM. *See* ECONOMY AND POLITICAL ECONOMY; IMPORTS AND EXPORTS.

COOPERATIVES AND COOPERATIVE MOVEMENT, YAR. *See* LOCAL DEVELOPMENT ASSOCIATIONS AND THE LDA MOVEMENT.

COOPERATIVES AND STATE FARMS, PDRY. These two forms of agricultural organization in the PDRY were firmly established by the end of the 1970s in an effort to end large-scale private ownership in accordance with principles of "**scientific socialism.**" At their height, some 45 cooperatives and 33 state farms covered 70 percent and 10 percent of all arable land, respectively. Although judged successful as means to deliver basic services to a rural peasantry previously denied even the minimal services available to residents of the **Aden** area, the state farm and the typically very large cooperative did not lead to large increases in **agricultural** production over their lifetime. Partly the result of the confusion and turmoil that came with the take-over or start-up process, these modest results were also a function of administrative inefficiencies and the lack of incentives to produce. By contrast, the PDRY was more successful with its fishing coopera-tives, which grew and became more productive over the years. Some of these continued after Yemeni **unification** and have even been rep-licated in the former YAR.

CORRECTION MOVEMENT, YAR. *See* 13 JUNE CORRECTION MOVEMENT.

CORRECTIVE MOVE, PDRY. *See* 22 JUNE CORRECTIVE MOVE.

CORRUPTION. In the North Yemen of old, petty corruption notwith-standing, there was little wealth over which to be corrupt, and this was true right on up to the **imamate** and **qadi** families. This began to change—but not much—after the **1962 Revolution** and for the next decade. Corruption increased markedly after the republican–royalist **reconciliation** in 1970 and, beginning in the mid-1970s, with the surge in the importation of goods and greatly increased development aid from the West, the wealthier Arab countries, and the United Nations and other international bodies. Development activity produced, among other things, resources needed for corruption.

In the 1980s, the Ali Abdullah **Salih regime** had evolved into an oligarchy in which the relatively small number of persons who got the most of what there was to get came from the northern highlands. Corruption increased greatly with this concentration of political and economic power in the hands of the **tribal** chiefs, military officers, and northern businessmen. This became even more so when, late in the 1980s, the YAR, for the first time, became the recipient of **oil** revenues as well as increased development aid.

Meanwhile, in South Yemen, corruption during the last decades of British rule seems to have been minimal, something that was apparently the case after independence in 1967 and the rapid evolution of the Marxist PDRY. In the 1970s and 1980s, this was probably a function of both very limited resources, domestic and external, and the moral constraints imposed by the regime's ideology.

Many hoped and believed that, with Yemeni **unification** in 1990, the order and law of the PDRY would prevail over the corruption of the YAR. On balance, however, corruption prevailed, quickly corrupting many southern politicians. This process accelerated after the 1994 **War of Secession** eliminated or weakened politicians from the former PDRY. Since then, the political culture of the YAR in its last days has become dominant in the ROY. The state quickly became a principal source of wealth and private gain for the well-placed few. As a result, the ROY is best described as a variant of oligarchy, a kleptocracy. The occupants of the key government posts through which oil-related revenues and development aid flow have been able to enrich themselves. They have used their positions in the state—"profit centers"—to extract a price for the rendering of services or granting of permission. The friends and relatives of occupants of key offices have also been enriched in this manner, the reaping of riches being a matter of connection as well as location.

The degree of corruption, not just the fact of it, has been key to understanding Yemen in the first decade of the 21st century. Graft, bribery, and other forms of thievery pervade all levels of a steep-sided pyramid of patronage. At the broad base of this pyramid are the hundreds of thousands of employees of the government and the military who are paid extremely low salaries and who have to take petty bribes—"eat money"—in order to barely make ends meet. Perhaps the most visible measures of this corruption high up the pyramid are the growing number of high-end SUVs and new villas—some virtual castles—on the outskirts of Sanaa, most owned by high-ranking government officials on modest salaries.

Most of this nouveau aristocracy of shaykhs, officers and business-men has motives and values that do not include an ethic of "public service" and noblesse oblige—and its newness is masked by a pervading, unquestioning sense of entitlement. The second generation of this aristocracy is now slipping into key positions, and most of its members are even surer and less questioning of their entitlement. This small part of the total population is on the take, and without apology; an even smaller part senses that this cannot last much longer, and that they must get as much as they can while the getting is still good. These are the kleptocrats of contemporary Yemen.

Against this, many public servants, high and low, have chosen not to participate in this system, or at least not to participate in it very much; indeed, many in government are simply not in posts through which much money flows. Moreover, many individuals and groups outside the state are opposed to corruption and committed to fighting it. The 2006 presidential **election** campaign was partly waged over the issue of corruption, with the opposition **Joint Meeting Parties** (JMP) condemning the Salih regime for rampant corruption and President Salih pledging to fight corruption. Since that election, the JMP stayed on this issue and President Salih appointed a Supreme National Anti-Corruption Comission that includes a number of longtime corruption fighters—for example, Saadaldeen bin Talib. How these words and deeds play out over the decade after the 2006 elections is crucial. Yemen is faced with huge problems surmountable only if it has a state willing and able to address these problems. Corruption at these levels incapacitates a state, and a state unable to address grave problems is a failing state, and one that could become a failed state such as Somalia or Afghanistan today, or Lebanon during its long civil war.

COUNCIL OF DEPUTIES (MAJLIS AL-NUWAB). The parliament provided for in the ROY's **1990 Constitution** and constituted on a transitional basis at **unification** in May of that year by merging the 159 members of the YAR's **Consultative Council** with the 111 members of the PDRY's **Supreme People's Council** (31 appointees brought the grand total up to 301). This transitional council was replaced by a fully elected 301-member Council of Deputies chosen in the 1993 **elections**. Thereafter, parliamentary elections were held in 1997 and 2003, the latter after the term was increased from four to six years.

The Council of Deputies initially attracted much popular attention, on TV and in the print media. However, the further consolidation of power in the hands of President **Salih** after the **War of Secession** in 1994 served to lessen interest in—and, hence, the power of—the Council. Still, the opposition has tried with limited success to use it to confront the regime on a number of issues, especially since the 2003 elections. The speaker of the council from the 1993 elections until his death in late 2007 was Shaykh Abdullah ibn Hussayn **al-Ahmar**. This both provided him with a state office with some leverage and, because of his close ties to President Salih, compromised efforts to make the council more of a check on presidential power.

COUP ATTEMPT, 1955. *See* 1955 COUP ATTEMPT.

CRAFTS. *See* ARTS.

CRANE, CHARLES R., AND KARL S. TWITCHELL. Heir to a bathroom-fixtures fortune, Charles R. Crane is best known as coleader of the King–Crane Commission to the Near East, the mission sent by President Woodrow Wilson to the former **Ottoman** Empire to gather the facts needed to apply his principle of self-determination at the Paris Peace Conference. Later, in 1926, Crane, an enthusiast of exotic places and their rulers, visited remote North Yemen, struck up a friendship with Imam **Yahya**, and then hired Karl S. Twitchell, a mining engineer, and made a gift of his services to the imam. Twitchell, an American who had been working in Ethiopia, conducted six expeditions to Yemen between 1926 and 1932, during which he undertook a range of projects that included searches for mineral wealth, distribution of gifts of farming and industrial machinery, and assistance in the building of roads, experimental farms, and the Arabian Peninsula's first steel truss bridge. He also reported to Imam Yahya the good possibility of **oil** under the desert to the east of Sanaa, a possibility that the imam refused to pursue out of fear that this would only bring western **imperialism** to Yemen.

In the mid-1930s, Crane put Twitchell in the service of a newer Arab friend, Abd al-Aziz **ibn Saud**, the then quite impoverished ruler of the newly formed Kingdom of **Saudi Arabia**. His survey and positive assessment of the oil prospects of Hasa province opposite Bahrayn Island were the first steps toward the momentous discovery later in the 1930s of what proved to be Saudi Arabia's fabulous oil reserves.

CRATER. *See* ADEN.

CUBA. Having gone through its own bigger-than-life socialist revolution less than a decade before South Yemen became independent, Cuba was a major ally, supporter, symbol, and source of inspiration for the PDRY throughout the 1970s and 1980s. The fact that President Fidel Castro and the Cuban Revolution could vie with President Gamal Abdul **Nasser** and the **Egyptian** Revolution—and that talk of Che Guevara, Franz Fanon, dependency, neo-colonialism, the Third World, and the Socialist Camp resonated with political South Yemenis—indicates the importance of when the PDRY came into existence and the place of Cuba in that era.

The brotherly relations and solidarity between the PDRY and Cuba go beyond the rhetoric of building socialism and confronting imperialism. By allowing themselves to be isolated so completely from the West, both Cuba and the PDRY made themselves clients of the **Soviet Union**, dependent on it for political support and aid. In addition, Cuba, poor but more developed than the PDRY, was the source of training for the PDRY's militia and air force and furnished some technical assistance. For its part, the PDRY helped Cuba and its Soviet patron by making it possible for both of them to gain easy air and sea access to politically important **Ethiopia** and Angola in the 1970s. In addition, the PDRY sent troops to fight with the Cubans on the Ethiopian side in the Ogadan Rebellion against **Somalia**. Deeply involved in the politics and diplomacy of the **Horn of Africa**, Castro visited the PDRY in the late 1970s and urged the formation of a socialist alliance for the area that would include the PDRY and endorsed the **Tripartite Alliance** of 1981 among the PDRY, Ethiopia, and Libya. In 1986, he mediated after the bloody **13 January events**, urging reconciliation between the two PDRY leadership factions in the interest of socialism.

The basis of the close relationship between Cuba and the PDRY changed in the late 1980s with the decline of their Soviet patron and the fading of the **Cold War**. In addition, Yemeni **unification** in 1990 diluted the socialism that had previously brought them together, and by 1991 Cuba was standing almost alone for the path long championed by the socialist camp. A faint glimmer of the old relationship was evident when the ROY and Cuba stood together—often by themselves—on votes in the United Nations Security Council on the crisis resulting in the first **Gulf War**, 1990–1991.

CURRENCY. *See* MONEY, CURRENCY, AND FOREIGN EXCHANGE.

– D –

DAAN, TREATY OF. The 1911 treaty between the **Ottoman** Turks and the Yemeni **imamate** that ended their armed conflict and, in effect, created an odd imamate–Ottoman condominium over North Yemen, one under which the **Hamid al-Din** imam had de facto control over the Yemeni highlands from **Amran** and **Hajja** south to **Taiz** and the Turks retained control of Sanaa and the **Tihama**. The Turks had recently suffered defeats at the hands of Yemeni rebels and, farther afield, were being battered by war in the Balkans and by Italy's seizure of Libya. The treaty provided a satisfactory basis for coexistence for the last years of the Ottoman occupation, which ended in 1919, and provided Imam **Yahya** with the political and territorial foundation needed to create a unified state in place of a politically fragmented North Yemen.

DAMASH, AHMAD. *See* AL-HAMDI, PRESIDENT IBRAHIM MUHAMMAD; 13 JUNE CORRECTION MOVEMENT.

DAMBARI TRIBE. *See* DHALA (DAHLIA) TOWN, REGION, TRIBES AND EMIRATE.

DAMMAJ, ZAID MUTTEE (1944–2002). The highly regarded author of, among many other works, *The Hostage*, a short novel of artistic and historical significance about a North Yemen just before the end of both the time of the **imamate** and the country's isolation from the outside world and the 20th century. From Ibb, Dammag was the son of a well-known revolutionary figure.

DATHINA AREA AND TRIBES. The small, remote area more than 100 miles northeast of **Aden** that is occupied by a loose confederation of tribes and hemmed in by the areas occupied by the more clearly defined **Awdhalis**, **Awlaqis**, and **Fadhlis**. The Dathini tribes vacillated for many generations over firm allegiance to either the Awlaqi ruler or the Fadhli ruler. Then, during World War II, they submitted to a British-imposed autonomous regime, this last artifact nothing more than another example of **Great Britain**'s effort to achieve administrative order by imposing clearly defined and bounded territorial entities on an age-old fluid **tribal** pattern. As with **Abyan**, Dathina was developed agriculturally by the colonial power to grow foodstuffs during World War II and cotton after the war.

DAWLA (DOULAH). A ruling house or family in the traditional scheme of governance in much of South Yemen and the adjacent parts of North Yemen that had acquired, over time and by various means, some limited power to decide or mediate in the affairs of the **tribes** or sections of tribes living in its area. Not to be confused with sovereigns having the power of the modern state, which is how the British often thought of them, the *doulah* and their heads frequently shared this limited power and authority with learned and wealthier **sayyid** families. Moreover, their rulership waxed and waned, was conditional, and depended as much on subsidies and services rendered as on respect and tradition.

DECENTRALIZATION. *See* LOCAL COUNCILS, ROY.

DEMOCRACY. *See* ECONOMY AND POLITICAL ECONOMY; YEMENI UNIFICATION.

DEMOCRATIC REPUBLIC OF YEMEN (DRY). The political system proclaimed by Ali Salim **al-Baydh** on the occasion of South Yemen's secession from the ROY on 21 May 1994, one day before the fourth anniversary of Yemeni **unification** and about three weeks after the beginning of the **War of Secession.** Al-Baydh declared that the borders of the DRY would be those of the old PDRY and created a 111-member council, charging it with selection of a Presidential Council and an interim Cabinet. Al-Baydh and Haidar Abu Bakr **al-Attas** became the president and the prime minister, respectively. In addition to members of **Yemeni Socialist Party**, the executive roster included strange bedfellows, united by ties to **Saudi Arabia**, including Abdel-Rahman **al-Jifri**, Abdullah **al-Asnag**, and even Abnd al-Qawi **al-Makkawi.** Al-Baydh promised multiparty elections within a year and said that Islamic sharia law would be the basis of legislation and that free-market economics would prevail. The DRY ceased to exist with its defeat in the war on 7 July.

DEMOCRATIC UNIONIST FRONT. The political party formed in 1989, during the rush toward Yemeni **unification** and pluralism, by many of the followers of **Ali Nasir Muhammad** al-Hasani, the PDRY president deposed in 1986. Upon unification in 1990, five members of this new party were appointed to the ROY's new merged legislature, the **Council of Deputies.** The party was soon absorbed by the **General People's Congress.**

DESERT SHIELD/DESERT STORM. *See* GULF WAR (1991), FIRST.

DEVELOPMENT PLANS. *See* PLANS AND PLANNING, ECONOMIC.

DHALA (DHALIA) TOWN, REGION, TRIBES, AND EMIRATE. A town and rugged mountainous region in South Yemen near the border with North Yemen, the region deriving much of its significance in past generations from the fact that a main route for goods and people between Aden to the south and main settlement areas in the southern half of North Yemen passed through it. Situated in the **Radfan Mountains**, the several tribes of Dhala, among them the Amiri, Qutaybi, and Dambari, at best only nominally paid allegiance to the Dhala emirate and over the centuries used their independence and geographic position to exact tribute from the passing travelers and caravan traffic to and from North Yemen. Indeed, they were effectively controlled by neither the local government, the *dawla*, nor by the competing outside hegemonic powers—the **Ottoman** Turks, the Yemeni **imamate**, or the British—that vied for the area in the 19th and 20th centuries.

The Dhala emirate entered into a treaty of protection with **Great Britain** in the late 19th century, received a stipend over the years from Britain, and was a member of the ill-fated **Federation of South Arabia** (FSA) during the last years of British rule. Tribal elements in the region—e.g., the Qutaybi tribe—were involved in the **Radfan Rebellion** that broke out in 1963, and the emirate was abolished when the **National Liberation Front** (NLF) assumed power on the occasion of Britain's withdrawal and the collapse of the FSA in 1967. Because of its location, the area had been a locus of major conflict between forces of the Yemeni imamate and Britain in the second half of the 1950s, British forces and those of the emerging NLF in the mid-1960s, and forces of the YAR and those of the PDRY-supported **National Democratic Front** in the 1970s and early 1980s on the border the North Yemeni fort at **Qataba** and Jabal Jihaf were was opposite another mountain in South Yemen.

DHAMAR PROVINCE AND TOWN. The province and provincial capital perceived of as in the middle of North Yemen, in its "middle region," located just north of **Yarim**, the **Samarra Pass** and the plunge from the pass down to "lower Yemen." Dhamar, a large, dusty, rough-edged town, is located on the expansive high Plain of Dhamar, an important agricultural area. In addition to being a provincial capital, the town has long been a center of commerce, located as it is on the intersection of North Yemen's main north–south road and the beginning of the road east to **Radaa** and **al-Baydha**. A once-main road up from **al-Hudayda** via **Bajil** also intersects with the north–south highway in Dhamar. Artisans in Dhamar were known in the recent past for their welded metal doors and other welded metal decorative objects. Long home to a major military garrison, the town was the site of two violent exchanges between northern and southern forces just prior to the outbreak of the **War of Secession** in May 1994.

DHUFAR (DHOFAR). The fairly well watered but mountainous and geographically isolated westernmost province of the Sultanate of **Oman**, adjacent to South Yemen's **Mahra** province. The link between Dhufar and Yemen goes far back in history. It was a key to the wealth of pre-Islamic Yemen, the source of most of the frankincense transported and protected by the Yemeni **trading kingdoms** along the Frankincense Trail. Throughout history, strong political systems based in Yemen have extended their rule for a time to include Dhufar, and some Yemenis today still think of it as part of "Greater Yemen." The border between Dhufar and Mahra—i.e., between Oman and South Yemen—was roughly drawn by the British, and its final demarcation was a bone of contention in recent years; it was finally demarcated in a treaty negotiated and ratified by Oman and the ROY in the early 1990s. New highways have been constructed and now meet at the new border, and hopes are high for **trade** and **tourism**. This is a far cry from the mid-1960s to the mid-1970s, when relations between Yemen and Oman were largely defined by the PDRY-backed **Dhufar rebellion** against the sultanate.

DHUFAR REBELLION. The long rebellion waged by elements in **Dhufar** province—with the help of the PDRY, **China**, and others—against the Sultanate of **Oman** from 1965 until it was virtually extinguished by late 1976 by Omani forces with military assistance from **Great Britain**, **Iran**, and **Jordan** and major financial help from **Saudi Arabia**. The Popular Front for the Liberation of Oman (PFLO), the political organization behind the rebellion at its height, had a complicated radical provenance. It was, like the **National Liberation Front** that succeeded Britain in neighboring South Yemen, a local offspring of the radical wing of the **Arab Nationalist Movement** (ANM). The Dhufar Liberation Front, the direct descendent of the ANM and the initiator of the rebellion in 1965, was succeeded by the PFLO in 1968.

The PFLO was portrayed by its opponents as a communist insurgency backed by a communist client state, the PDRY, which gave international communism a foothold in Arabia. For its part, the PDRY saw itself as aiding a kindred progressive force against a reactionary feudal regime backed by the former imperialist ruler and some oil-rich regional lackeys of a waning imperialism. Given its limited resources, the PDRY did give a lot of aid to the effort, providing sanctuary, covering for incursions over the border, propaganda facilities, and a channel for supplies from China, other socialist countries, and radical Arab regimes. In reprisal, Oman and its well-equipped allies shelled, bombed, and pursued PFLO insurgents over the border into PDRY. By the late 1970s, however, cross-border military exchanges became very sporadic, and the PDRY's support of the PFLO did not go much beyond the verbal.

DHU JIBLA. *See* JIBLA (DHU JIBLA).

DHU MUHAMMAD AND DHU HUSAYN. *See* HASHID AND BAKIL TRIBES AND CONFEDERATIONS.

DHU NUWAS, YUSUF ASHAR. The **Himyarite** king of the late 5th and early 6th centuries A.D., a convert to Judaism whose brutal persecution of Christians, especially in **Najran**, gave cause for Christian **Ethiopia** to reconquer Yemen and then for **Sassanid** Persia to occupy Yemen in the course of expelling the Ethiopians. This was a time of economic decline and religious change in South Arabia, and this series of events brought down the final curtain on the centuries-long run of the great **trading kingdoms** of pre-Islamic Yemen. It preceded by little more than a generation the rise of Islam and the beginning of a new age for Yemen.

"DIALOGUE PROCESS" AND RELIGIOUS DIALOGUE COUNCIL (RDC). The process that emerged in the ROY a few years after **9/11** and the United States' focus on the **War on Terror** by which—or so it was claimed—followers of militant **political Islam** could be "reprogrammed" to renounce armed "struggle" (jihad) through a dialogue with those expert on the Quran and Sunna. Chosen for the task by President Ali Abdullah **Salih** in 2002, Judge Hamoud **al-Hitar** of the Supreme Court was the person who developed, and is most closely associated with, the dialogue process and the RDC.

Although he did not claim it could convert the leaders of organizations like **al-Qaida**, Judge al-Hitar did assert success with most of the roughly 400 suspected jihadists subjected to the process and then released from custody between 2002 and 2006. From the outset, the **United States** was skeptical of the work of the RDC and the release of terror suspects, a skepticism reinforced when it was reported in late 2005 that a number of the reprogrammed ended up fighting in Iraq. It was later learned that the process administered by the RDC was requiring only that converts declare loyalty to President **Salih** and pledge not to commit violent acts inside Yemen. The more cynical saw President Salih's use of al-Hitar and the dialogue process as a way of both siding with the United States in the **War on Terror** and releasing a large number of Yemenis who may have had strong Yemeni patrons, even within the regime. In any case, the bad publicity led to suspension of the program in early 2006, despite al-Hitar's proposal in 2006 that the process be applied to Shii fighters captured in the **al-Houthi Rebellion**.

DIWAN AND "DIWAN MENTALITY." An institution in the traditional art of governance in Yemen in which rulers or leaders regularly held meetings or audiences where—in theory and, to a surprising degree, in practice—any subject or follower could make a claim, register a grievance, petition for aid, or merely state an opinion. **Imams**, tribal **shaykhs** and other notables alike used the diwan, and it could take place beneath a shade tree, in a public building, or at **qat** chew in a notable's *mafrag*. Many Yemeni modernists insist that the "diwan mentality," with its emphasis on personal contact and direct access to the top, is incompatible with the hierarchical bureaucratic organization required for modern governance, making for excess pressure at the top and idleness and irresponsibility in the middle and lower levels of governance.

DJIBOUTI. The former French Somaliland and, since 1977, an independent country—more appropriately, a small city–state—on the

Red Sea and wedged uneasily between **Ethiopia** (and now **Eritrea**) and **Somalia** and just across the **Bab al-Mandab Straits** from Yemen. The bustling port city of Djibouti has long been a temporary or permanent overseas home to Yemeni sailors and merchants, some of them prominent, such as the family of Muhammad Said **al-Attar**. The movement of business skills and capital to it increased when **Aden** became less hospitable after South Yemen's turn left in 1969. Open, French-influenced Djibouti is conveniently located for the smuggling of contraband, including alcoholic beverages, in dhows to deserted points along the North Yemeni coast, a fact not lost on enterprising Yemenis. In recent years, it has also been involved in the smuggling of subsidized petroleum products from Yemen.

Independence for an improbable Djibouti in 1977 was viewed by some as a wild card in the already dangerous game of Red Sea and **Horn of Africa** politics, but the city and its small hinterland have not proven to be a major source of instability or conflict in the area. Relative calm has persisted despite the addition of a new and volatile neighbor, Eritrea, the result of a long war of independence with Ethiopia that still yields episodic fighting between Eritrea and Ethiopia. Djibouti's relatively happy circumstances could easily come to an end. Still home to a contingent of the French Foreign Legion, Djibouti more recently became home to the Horn of Africa unit of the **United States**' Central Command. Part of the United States' **War on Terror**, this facility was the source of the unmanned drone and missile that the United States used to kill **al-Qaida** leader Qaid Salim **al-Harithi** deep in Yemeni airspace near **Marib** in 2002. Air strikes against a handful of alleged al-Qaida members in war-torn Somalia came from this same U.S. facility in early 2007.

DOCUMENT OF PLEDGE AND ACCORD (AL-WATHIQA). The reconciliation agreement signed under pressure by President **Salih**, Vice President **al-Baydh**, and Speaker **al-Ahmar** in Amman in the presence of Jordan's King **Husayn** and a number of Yemeni and other Arab notables on 20 February 1994, a document designed to salvage Yemeni **unification** and end the political crisis growing out of the conflict between al-Baydh, Salih and their respective parties. The result of three feverish months of work by the **National Dialogue Committee of Political Forces**, the document represented a broad consensus and an amalgam of earlier reform proposals, especially the **Yemeni Socialist Party's** "Eighteen Points," issued in August 1993, and the **General People's Party's** response to them. Adopted by the committee on 20 January 1994, it called for limits on executive power, the de-politicization and redeployment of military and security forces, administrative and financial decentralization, a bicameral legislature, judicial autonomy, and other reforms. Although it failed to prevent the **War of Secession** that began soon after the signing, the document contained most of the major reforms advocated for, and sometimes adopted by, the ROY over the next 15 years.

DUAN, WADI. *See* HADHRAMAWT AND WADI HADHRAMAWT.

DUBAI. *See* UNITED ARAB EMIRATES (UAE).

– E –

EASTERN ADEN PROTECTORATE. *See* ADEN PROTECTORATE.

EAST GERMANY. *See* GERMANY.

EAST INDIA COMPANY. *See* GREAT BRITAIN.

"EAST OF SUEZ." *See* SUEZ CANAL; GREAT BRITAIN.

ECONOMIC ORGANIZATION LAW. The sweeping framework law passed by the **National Liberation Front** in South Yemen in 1969 for the purpose of building socialism. Under this law, 12 private insurance companies were reorganized into the public sector Insurance and Reinsurance Company, 1 local and 7 foreign-owned **banks** were taken over and combined into the **National Bank of Yemen**, 5 major trading houses were expropriated and combined into either the National Corporation for Foreign Trade (NCFT) or the National Home Trade Company (NHTC), 5 petroleum distribution companies were seized and their functions entrusted to the Petroleum and Mineral's Board and its subsidiary, the **Yemen National Oil Company**, and the companies providing services (other than oil **bunkering**) to the port of Aden were nationalized and placed under the Yemen Ports and Shipping Company and its subsidiary, the Aden Ports Board.

The NCFT expropriated and reorganized the property and activities of the major locally and foreign-owned trading companies engaged in foreign **trade** in South Yemen. The NHTC was created to serve the same purpose in domestic trade. Although these corporations did help to give a regime with a radical agenda considerable control over the country's **economy**, they also served to stifle the vibrant and vital trade and commerce for which Aden had long been known.

South Yemen's biggest industrial facility, the **Aden Refinery**, continued to be owned by British Petroleum. After the PDRY took ownership of the refinery and all international telecommunications facilities in 1977 and 1978, respectively, the only foreign firms still operating were several international oil companies providing bunker fuel in the port.

ECONOMY AND POLITICAL ECONOMY. The economy of Yemen down to the mid-19th century amounted to many barely connected local economies. For the most part, these micro-economies were based on subsistence **agriculture** or **fishing** and had little economic contact with one another, much less with the outside world. True, in the north there was the much-diminished **coffee** trade centered on the **Red Sea** port of **al-Mukha** and the coffee-growing highlands. In the south and far to the east, Wadi **Hadhramawt** flourished through **emigration** and **remittances** that tied it to the Indian subcontinent, Malaysia, Singapore, and East Africa—but not to the rest of South Arabia. And **Aden** was a sleepy little port and fishing village when the British arrived in 1839.

After the mid-19th century, however, the economies of what were to become the two Yemens became more separate, differentiated and subject to new centripetal forces. In North Yemen, the driving forces were first the **Ottoman** Turkish occupation and second, after the withdrawal of the Turks at the end of World War I, the **Hamid al-Din** imamate. In South Yemen, the engine of change was the occupation of Aden by **Great Britain** and Aden's gradually expanding economic influence over its hinterland.

Aden's economy increasingly reflected the growing role of its port as a key link in the British imperial system and, more specifically, its strategic position on the sea lanes connecting the British Isles to the Indian subcontinent, Southeast Asia and East Africa. Essentially, Aden became more plugged into the international imperial system—its economy and even its politics, culture, and demogaphics—than to its own hinterland and the rest of South Yemen; indeed, its hinterland increasingly functioned to support Aden in its growing imperial role. Much of the rest of the south continued to constitute local self-sufficient, self-contained micro-economies. The economy of Wadi Hadhramawt continued to thrive apart on emigration and remittances.

In contrast to Britain's integration of Aden into the 20th century's global economy, Imams **Yahya** and **Ahmad** did all they could to insulate and isolate North Yemen from the corrupting influences of the modern world during the period from, say, 1918 to the **1962 Yemeni Revolution**. Economically, the result was a mainly self-contained and self-sufficient economic system, but one based largely on subsistence agriculture and fishing. Hides, some **coffee**, and a few other goods were exported to finance the imamate's modest import needs. In contrast to the ruler of **Saudi Arabia**, Imam Yahya refused to let international oil corporations prospect in Yemen, explicitly stating his unwillingness to trade Yemen's independence for possible **oil** wealth. The result was an economy that generated little wealth and surplus, even for the ruling family, its coterie, and the "big" merchants. There was inequality, but not that much—and, perhaps more important, not so visible. Imam Ahmad's "palace" in **Taiz**, now a museum, attests to this.

The opening of North Yemen to the outside world and the global economy began modestly with Imam Ahmad's approval in the late 1950s of the modernization of the port of **al-Hudayda** and some road construction in the interior. But it was the 1962 Revolution and the creation of the YAR—with a flood of foreigners, their governments and corporations and, above all, the consumer and capital goods of the modern world—that overwhelmed the traditional Yemen that Imam Yahya had sought to preserve. Two North Yemens emerged rather quickly, the one still local and based on subsistence agriculture and fishing and the other linked in a variety of ways to the modern world.

Not surprisingly, the efforts by inexperienced Yemenis to simultaneously create a "modern" state and society and fight the long **Yemeni Civil War** produced a YAR economy that in the 1960s was an ad hoc, non-sustainable mish-mash of programs and sectors. This was worsened by separate efforts—and competition—among **Egypt**, the **United States** and its allies, the **Soviet Union** and its allies, and even **China**. In any case, the largely self-contained, self-sufficient Yemen of imamate times soon became dependent on other nation states, **United Nations** organizations, and, after 1970, the International Monetary Fund (**IMF**) and World Bank. Many state corporations were set up, a few of which survive to this day—among them the National Tobacco and Matches Company, the Yemen Pharmaceutical Products Company, and the **Yemen Bank for Reconstruction and Development**.

Although the **republican–royalist Reconciliation** brought peace in 1970, the winding down of the externally fueled war economy led to economic woes and the **financial crisis of 1968–1971**. However, the **Central Planning Organization**, fashioned into the YAR's first modern institution under the leadership of Dr. Abd al-Karim **al-Iryani** in the mid-1990's served as the needed interface between Yemen and the donor community. Another, more important force rapidly kicked in in the mid-1970s: the relatively huge amount of remittances resulting from the oil-fueled emigration of a huge number of Yemeni workers to Saudi Arabia and, to a lesser extent, the other Arab Gulf oil states. In addition, because of this emigration, nearly anyone who stayed in Yemen and wanted to work could find a job, and wages in the cities and the countryside were pushed up to new levels by a labor shortage. The remittances sent or brought home were distributed widely—as if sprinkled from above—with some of it going directly or indirectly to nearly all families in all parts of the country. Throughout the 1970s, only a little of this money passed through the hands of gatekeepers in the state or the banks. Thus, paradoxically, the remittances both bought time for a Yemeni state that was severely limited in its capacity for economic development and denied to that state the revenue that would have given it more control over development. In addition, the rise in remittances in the mid-1970s was by chance paralleled by the rapid rise of **local development associations** (LDAs) throughout North Yemen. The LDAs helped channel part of the remittances into the construction of unpaved feeder roads that gave isolated towns and districts motorable access to main roads for the first time, as well as into building one- or two-room schools, clinics, wells, and cisterns. Generators meant electricity and electric lights for many towns, at least for a few hours a day.

On the individual and family level, the remittances were used to add a second story to a stone house, to open and stock a little shop, or to buy a Toyota to use as a taxi. Many Yemenis became consumers of goods previously unavailable and mostly imported. The main streets of small towns ended up nearly paved with crushed Chinese juice cans, and every family seemed to have at least one new thermos and a portable radio and cassette player. Before long, TV sets began to appear in public places and in some homes. Most visible, however, were the cars, vans, and trucks. Toyoto four-wheel drive vehicles were suddenly everywhere, in town and on the countryside. Not surprisingly, many older North Yemenis regard the period from the mid-1970s through the 1980s as their halcyon years, the best of times in living memory.

Beginning in 1978, the first decade of the long tenure of President Ali Abdullah **Salih** resulted in unprecedented political stability and optimism about the future, the latter based largely on the continuation of remittances and increasing external aid. Talk and some of the trappings of democracy notwithstanding, the YAR at this time was an oligarchy, and most of the relatively small number of persons and families that were politically powerful came from the northern highlands and had either or both strong tribal and military (or security) connections. To this military–tribal complex was added a northern commercial–business element in the 1980s, the result of an "affirmative action" program that favored these newcomers over their then-dominant counterparts from the southern uplands, especially Taiz. The wealthiest of these newcomers soon came to share in the political power enjoyed by the shaykhs and officers.

Until the mid-1980s, Yemen had no known natural resources of consequence other than the bounty of the sea, and this was but barely exploited. In 1984 and 1986, modest amounts of oil were discovered in North Yemen and South Yemen, respectively. As a result of the oil revenues that began to flow in 1987, as well as increased external economic aid, the state in North Yemen became for the first time a primary source of wealth and private gain for the well-placed and fortunate few. In the process, and by the mid-1980s, the YAR evolved into a special variant of oligarchy, a kleptocracy. Increasingly, the occupants of key government posts and offices through which flowed revenues and development aid were able to enrich themselves, usually at the expense of development and other policy goals. They used their positions in the state—"profit centers"—to extract a price for the rendering of services or granting of access, thereby increasing the cost of government and development. The associates, friends, and relatives of occupants of key posts and offices were also enriched in this manner, the reaping of riches being a matter of connection as well as location. Many, but by no means all, were associated with the ruling party, the **General Peoples's Congress** (GPC).

The path taken by South Yemen after it achieved independence from Britain in 1967 was very different. As the regime came to embrace a doctrinaire Marxism—its "scientific socialism"—the PDRY evolved into a state led by a "vanguard party" and featuring a centalized, planned command economy; the **Economic Organization Law** of 1969 was a major early step in this process. It was the Soviet Union and the other countries of the Communist Bloc who provided the PDRY with its model for economic growth and development. This said, what the PDRY lacked after 1967 were the resources this model required for implementation. Most notably, and only several months before South Yemen's independence, the long-term closure of the **Suez Canal** and the virtual shutdown of the Port of Aden, the mainstay of the economy of Aden and its hinterland, resulted from the latest eruption of the **Arab–Israeli conflict**, the Six-Day War. Far to the east, in Wadi Hadhramawt, a lot of talk about and a few steps toward "socialism" scared off Hadhrami emigrants and much of the money they would otherwise have remitted.

Consequently, and to a greater extent than Castro's Cuba, the PDRY became dependent on the Soviet Union and its allies and, to a lesser extent, the IMF, the World Bank, and UN organizations for sustenance and development. According to donors, the PDRY in the 1970s and 1980s made good use of development assistance and, unlike many other late-developing countries, was not known for **corruption** and great inequality. **Education** and medical care were made widely available, and a major effort was made to integrate the countryside and urban areas through infrastructure development and the provision of services.

Nevertheless, when the Soviet Union and its bloc began to implode and had to sharply cut external aid in the late 1980s, the economic viability of the PDRY built over the previous two decades was put to the test—and found wanting. As a result, the economy of the PDRY was increasingly marked by scarcity and privation. Still, the regime was able to hang on to the hope for a big oil discovery and sizable oil revenues. And, indeed, had the oil found in **Shabwa** been substantial, or had the sizable **Masila** field begun generating revenues a few years earlier, Yemeni **unification** probably would not have occurred in 1990.

In the late 1980s, the Salih regime felt itself on something of a roll and turned its attention to the old question of unification. For the first time in over two decades, the economic and political strength of the YAR versus that of the PDRY allowed it to initiate and dominate the unification process. A heady time, was witness to the creation of the ROY and the hope for a unified Yemen made even stronger and more prosperous by newly discovered oil, a Yemen able at last to stand up to such rich neighbors as Saudi Arabia.

In August 1990, just a few months later, things came tumbling down with **Iraq**'s occupation of **Kuwait** and the crisis that led to the First **Gulf War** in 1991. The ROY's failure to join the U.S.- and Saudi-led coalition against Iraq caused the United States, Saudi Arabia, and other nations to punish Yemen by cutting off nearly all economic aid. In the most punishing act by far, Saudi Arabia savaged Yemen's economy by expelling several hundred thousand workers, thereby denying Yemen the remittances upon which it depended, and creating a new, massive problem of Yemeni unemployment. This, when combined with the inevitable costs of unification and the costs of the **War of Secession** in 1994, devastated the Yemeni economy. By late 1994, the economy was in free fall and, as then structured, well on its way to becoming nonviable, despite the steady rise of oil revenues.

It would be hard to exaggerate how dire Yemen's situation and prospects were in 1995. The GDP for that year was less that half that of 1990, and the value of the Yemeni riyal had undergone a precipitous decline, raising the cost of goods, especially much needed imports. Due to the massive unemployment and loss of remittances, inequality and abject poverty increased at alarming rates throughout Yemen. In the shrunken economy, urban workers, and especially the new middle class, were quickly pauperized; the modern institutions in which they worked and had come to place their hopes for a better future were hollowed out. Only the privileged few had access by family or position to a constant or growing share of the smaller economic pie and the hidden economy.

The ROY in 1995 provided a textbook case of a country in such crisis as to require immediate triage followed by a regimen of long-term reform. Unfortunately, the men who had to address this situation were mostly the northern officers, shaykhs, and businessmen who, in the aggregate, had pushed the YAR from old-fashioned oligarchy to modern kleptocracy in the 1980s. The unification process, and power sharing with the leaders of the **Yemeni Socialist Party** (YSP), had merely interrupted the trend toward kleptocracy. The trend reappeared after the War of Secession eliminated most of the politicians from the old South Yemen and the YSP.

The degree of corruption, not just the fact of it, is key to understanding Yemen's political economy after the mid-1990s. Although many officials chose not to take advantage of their positions or simply were not in positions through which funds flowed, graft, bribery, and other forms of thievery came to pervade all levels of a steep-sided pyramid of patronage. At the broad base of this pyramid were the hundreds of thousands of employees of the government and the military who were paid extremely low salaries and had to take petty bribes—"eat money"—in order to barely make ends meet. High up the pyramid, perhaps the most visible measures of this corruption were the growing number of high-end SUVs and new villas—some virtual castles—on the outskirts of **Sanaa**, most owned by high-ranking government officials on modest salaries.

In mid-1995, the Salih regime agreed with the IMF and the World Bank on a program of economic stabilization followed by a multifaceted program of structural reform. The premise was that significant IMF/World Bank aid, and the program of stabilization and reforms upon which that aid was conditioned, would begin to turn the Yemeni economy around. This, and the stamp-of-approval of these international bodies, would begin to attract other aid donors—and, most important, private investors both Yemeni and non-Yemeni. The promise was that belt-tightening and other sacrifices required of the Yemeni people would create an economic environment that would attract from abroad the investment needed to create jobs, enterprise, and wealth.

Initially, the collaboration between the ROY and the IMF and World Bank followed very closely the adopted script and won praise from the United States, the **European Union** (EU), and **Japan**. From the outset, the relationship was collaborative, not adversarial. For the most part, the regime stuck to its agreements, and the IMF and the World Bank provided the promised aid. The latter were understanding of Yemen's political problems, making mid-course adjustments for some of them, and funded social "safety-net" projects for those least able to bear the burden of the reforms.

In late 1995 and 1996, the Salih regime put in place the stabilization measures and the initial set of structural reforms designed, among other things, to bring inflation under control; and, indeed, according to IMF figures, inflation fell by late 1996 to about 9 percent on an annualized basis from almost 48 percent at the beginning of the year. The several exchange rates for the Yemeni riyal were unified and allowed to float, and the riyal stabilized at about USD1:YR 125–130 in contrast to 1995, when it had fluctuated wildly between a high of USD1:YR 80 and a low of USD1:YR 160. The budget deficit was narrowed through a combination of spending restraint and increased oil revenues; imports were suppressed, with the results that the current accounts situation improved and foreign exchange reserves rose considerably. Then, in late 1996, the regime took a cautious first step toward lifting subsidies of essential goods, and in 1997 and 1998 it took further steps to cut these. In return, the IMF and World Bank lent the ROY roughly $1 billion to support reform projects over these years; in addition, they sponsored and organized two donors' conferences that yielded pledges of another $2 billion in aid. Further, the IMF pledge of financial support led to a large reduction of Yemen's debt owed to the Paris Club of creditor nations.

Although other efforts to revive and develop the Yemeni economy gained momentum into 1998—for example, the **Aden container port** and free zone—the ROY's implementation of the IMF/World Bank structural reform program faltered in late 1997. The government became deadlocked in late 1997 and resigned in early 1998.

From the outset, the successor government ran into serious popular protest against its effort at reform. In addition, the price of oil, which had held fairly steady at about $20/barrel for some years, temporarily plunged in 1998 to $10/barrel; the decline in revenues limited the government's ability to soften the effects of the reforms through social spending, causing more widespread unrest.

The new IMF/World Bank agreement negotiated with the ROY in 2000 was demanding, calling for the broadening and deepening of reforms in exchange for new credits worth hundreds of millions of dollars. The complete lifting of subsidies for essential goods was included, this despite the recent protests and evidence that in the first five years of reforms there had been a big increase in poverty and a widening of the income gap in Yemen. Borne by the people, belt-tightening had not triggered much new investment and job-creation. Moreover, the required downsizing of the civil service and the privatizing of bloated public corporations pointed to the loss of existing jobs for many Yemenis.

Perhaps more important politically, some of the new reforms reached beyond the poor and the working class and directly touched some of the prerogatives and benefits of the privileged and highly placed. Among them were measures designed to fight corruption, increase transparency in government, make the courts fairer and more efficient, and reform the banking and financial sectors. For many of the well-off, the reforms were getting too close for comfort; many lost whatever appetite they had for reform as it began to threaten their personal interests. In addition, by this time, the nouveau aristocracy of shaykhs, officers, and businessmen was marked by a pervading, unquestioning sense of entitlement. The second generation of this aristocracy was slipping silently into key positions and is even less doubtful of its entitlement.

By 2001, the reform program was virtually abandoned. Most of the measures in the 2000 agreement were not implemented or were done so partially and half-heartedly. Reforms of the judiciary and the civil service lagged, and the rampant corruption in the public and private sectors was barely addressed except verbally. Although dramatic events did upstage the reform program—e.g., the **U.S.S.** *Cole* bombing and **9/11** in 2000 and 2001, respectively—that program had already virtually collapsed.

Since this apparent failure of will to carry out the reform program, the **Salih regime** has resisted IMF/World Bank pressure to revive the process. In early 2004, these bodies expressed publicly their growing impatience and displeasure with Yemen, particularly regarding its failure to complete the final lifting of subsidies on petroleum products and to implement civil service reforms designed to address corruption and inefficiency. These criticisms were accompanied by not-so-veiled warnings that continued aid to Yemen remained contingent on Yemen's keeping its part of the old aid-for-reform bargain. A few months later, the Salih regime, caving in to domestic political pressure and fear of popular unrest, postponed the elimination of diesel fuel subsidies and the imposition of a sales tax, both scheduled to go into effect months earlier.

In mid-2004, the outgoing head of the UN Development Program noted that Yemen's almost total dependence on oil revenues inflated by high oil prices was made more dangerous by "signs of increasing budget deficits and, indeed, initial signs of fiscal difficulties." He asserted that, in addition, the government suffered from an absence of transparency and pervasive corruption. "A pessimistic scenario will include a situation whereby corruption not only continues but also expands, further taking resources away from development."

In addition to the reform program, major development projects failed to move forward rapidly or to live up to expectations after 2001. Yemen was told in the mid-1990s that the window for the development of its significant natural gas reserves was small; other producers, like Qatar and Oman, were pushing ahead to develop their reserves and to secure the long-term marketing agreements required to secure financing. It was widely believed that timely exploitation of Yemen's gas would more than make up for the decline in oil output expected in the near future. Nevertheless, fighting between two groups of Yemeni politicians, each with its preferred multinational gas developer as client, caused one delay after another; as a result, the window closed and the development of Yemen's gas was put on hold in about 2001.

The Aden container port and free zone, touted in the early 1990s as the ROY's most important development project, promised to create thousands of jobs and much wealth. These facilities were supposed to take advantage of location and go head-to-head with Jabal Ali in

Dubai and facilities then being built in Salala in Oman. Up and running in 2000, after numerous delays, the project soon fell far short of expectations. True, much of the problem resulted from soaring insurance costs and the drop in business in the port of Aden due to security concerns after the bombing of the U.S.S. *Cole* in 1990 and, more important, that of the French tanker **Limburg** in 2002. However, a big part of the problem apparently had to do with bad planning, mismanagement, and corruption.

Similarly, Yemen lost considerable time and money regarding the increase of refinery capacity that had promised both to lower the import of petroleum products and to capture some of the added value coming from downstream petroleum activities. Endless debate focused on whether the Aden Refinery should be privatized and on whether emphasis should be on upgrading and expanding Aden Refinery or on the construction of new facilities.

The failure to attract investment funds during these years is not explained primarily in terms of investors' being scared off by security issues after the U.S.S. *Cole* bombing, especially in the case of potential Yemenis investors at home and abroad. Wealthy Yemenis who had jumped in early, especially those with origins in Wadi **Hadhramawt**, quickly retreated because of bad personal experiences and others' tales of woe. Many potential foreign investors decided that the risks were too great relative to potential gains, based partly on a number of well-publicized cases of corruption, nepotism, and political favoritism.

As a result of what happened—or, as is often the case, what did not happen—since the late 1990s, Yemen's economy and society became increasingly dysfunctional. The problems and their causes were endemic and structural, not cyclical, and they had their origins in the collapse of the remittance economy, the corrupting and distorting effect of dependence on oil revenues, and the failure to implement in the late 1990s the economic reforms adopted earlier in the decade. The economy did stabilize at a low level of output and performance in the late 1990s, but did not rise much thereafter, if at all. Instead, it bounced along on the bottom of this low range of output and performance.

As of 2005, the Yemeni economy was barely creating enough jobs and economic activity to keep up with a 3.8 percent population growth rate. The unemployment rate had persistently held at about 40 percent, as had the percentages for the malnourished and those below the poverty line. The middle class shrank further, and—more important—its pauperization continued relentlessly. As a result, the gap between the rich few and the many poor became wider and more visibly so. The education and health systems were increasingly dysfunctional, and most other social services almost ceased to exist. In short, most institutions had decayed—had been hollowed out and starved. For most Yemenis, the past decade had been one of pain and no gain.

In addition, the poorly performing Yemeni economy had become very vulnerable. It became dangerously dependent on oil revenues and on the economic aid and other forms of assistance it received from the IMF and World Bank, as well as from the many donors who took their lead from those two bodies. Most worrisome, the oil revenues were increasingly less a function of increasing Yemeni oil production, which had leveled off and begun to decline by 2005, than they were of the price of oil per barrel, which fluctuated widely over time and which was determined by forces over which Yemen had no control.

The state of the economy, economic reform, and government performance became the main focuses of the 2006 presidential **election**, especially after the opposition coalition, the **Joint Meeting Parties** (JMP), selected a credible candidate, Faysal bin Shamlan, to run against President Salih. Bin Shamlan and the JMP hammered away at the corruption, self-enrichment, cronyism, and incompetence of the Salih regime—and at the unemployment, poverty, and inequality they produced—and put forward a sweeping program of reform. For his part, while claiming many past successes, President Salih acknowledged the need for major reforms, put forward an imposing reform package, and questioned the capacity of the JMP to effect reform. While President Salih won by a wide margin, bin Shamlan made a good showing and, more important, the JMP pledged to remain intact and to campaign for its reform agenda in the parliamentary elections in 2009 and the next presidential election in 2013.

After his swearing-in for his new term, the president frequently reiterated his pledges to fight corruption, create jobs, and end poverty. Concern about his legacy and his growing awareness of his and

Yemen's dependence on increasingly critical and impatient donors have added urgency to these pledges. The large, very successful donors' conference held in mid-November 2006 in London certainly contributed to this awareness, yielding as it did pledges of $4.7 billion over four years, as well as further signs that the donors were determined to make delivery of that aid conditional on demanding and often painful reforms. However, the political environment in which the regime and the JMP had to act was challenging. Adding urgency in 2007 and 2008 were popular protests throughout the country over rising food prices, as well as—and politically more ominous—many protests and demonstrations across South Yemen over lost jobs, income, and pension, as well as economic hardships generally. Indeed, some southern leaders and protestors questioned unification itself.

Even as the Salih regime seemed to begin to address some of the demands of the donors and the opposition, such as the effort to rein in corruption and to raise needed revenue by further cutting subsidies and imposing a sales tax, other domestic issues and international politics threatened to distract and divide the Salih regime and the country. The **al-Houthi Rebellion**, which had begun in 2004, reerupted with a vengeance at the beginning of 2007 and, despite a settlement a few months later, broke out again in early 2008, further complicating and heating up the domestic political scene. Similarly, the ongoing **War on Terror** and U.S. demands that Yemen clearly and forcefully stand with it placed great strain on relations within the Salih regime and between it and the JMP. Donor support for the ROY collided with the demands of the War on Terror in early 2008, when the U.S. suspended the recently restored Millennium Challenge Corporation funding after the Salih regime, responding to domestic political realities, failed to deal with a convicted participant in the U.S.S. *Cole* bombing, Jamal al-Badawi, in a fashion the United States deemed appropriate. Shortly thereafter, the Salih regime angered Washington by dealing gently with another alleged terrorist, a U.S. citizen, Jabr al-Banna.

By late 2008, it was not at all clear that the Salih regime had acquired the will and capacity to effect quickly the reforms required to make Yemen viable and sustainable again. Facing Yemen were the facts that reserves of both oil and water were being rapidly depleted at the same time that the population was growing relentlessly. The one big hope was that liquefied natural gas was to come online in 2009. The big question was whether Yemen would squander its finite gas reserves the way it had its oil reserves.

Although the Yemeni economy was in many ways less affected by the global recession of 2008–2009 than the economies of many more highly developed, "globalized" economies, the sharp decline in world oil prices and new declines in remittances and external aid further compromised Yemen's future. Already living on the edge, Yemen and the Yemenis could ill afford this added burden. And it will take more than rising oil prices and an inflow of gas revenues to get them back from the edge.

EDUCATION. Both parts of unified Yemen have had and still have great educational needs, but the PDRY was more successful than the YAR in meeting basic educational needs from the late 1960s through the 1980s. For example, the YAR in 1990 was still dependent on many foreign teachers, especially **Egyptians**, whereas the teacher-training program in the PDRY was producing a surplus of qualified teachers. The literacy rate in the PDRY, especially among females, was higher than that in the YAR, partly the result of successful **Cuban**-style literacy campaigns. Vocational education lagged in both Yemens, but especially in the YAR.

Both parts of Yemen benefited from major economic and technical aid programs for education from external sources in the 1970s and 1980s, and these programs, supplemented by new ones, continued after **unification** in 1990. Generally, however, education has not had the priority and funding needed to keep up with the extremely high growth rate of school-aged children. As a result, the access to and quality of education has eroded overall in the ROY since 1990. The literacy rate remains low, especially among females in rural areas. Vocational education continues to fail to meet needs.

Sanaa University was the only public university in the YAR at the time of its founding in 1970 and is by far the largest unit in the modern public university system in the ROY in the first decade of the 21st century. The university started on a modest ad hoc basis with a teachers' college and a law school in 1970. The first external aid for the university was secured from **Kuwait** during that first year, and

Kuwait remained its biggest benefactor until the 1990s. The university's arts and science faculties underwent rapid growth during its first two decades, and faculties of engineering, agriculture, and medicine were created during the 1980s. By 1990, it occupied two campuses and a vast number of buildings.

Partially staffed mostly by Egyptians, Kuwait-funded Sanaa University was for a long time something of a pale carbon copy of the Kuwait University that, in turn, was a copy of Cairo University. As a result, a theme at least since the mid-1970s has been the struggle to make the university more relevant to the needs of Yemen through the "Yemenization" of its program, faculty, and administration. The short tenure as acting president of British- and U.S.-educated exile from **Aden** Dr. Abdullah al-Maktari was an important early step in this long, frustrating process, as were the longer-term efforts of such faculty members as sociologist Abdu Ali Othman. In addition, classes have been coeducational from the outset, creating a continuing battleground in the 1990s and beyond between secularists and resurgent Islamic militants. Finally, since the mid-1990s, the **Political Security Organization** has deeply penetrated the university's faculty and staff, something that has taken a toll on the quality of its programs and the freedom of expression.

By the 1990s, Sanaa University had become merely the biggest unit of a national university system that had large units in all major cities, most notably **Taiz** and **al-Hudayda**. Moreover, after Yemeni **unification** in 1990, it had to share top billing with the large, long-established Aden University, many units of which were located just outside **Aden** in **Madinat al-Shaab**. More significantly, the failure of the ROY to join the international coalition against **Iraq** in the First **Gulf War** in 1991 led to the loss of Kuwait funding, a loss that was not subsequently made up by other sources. Moreover, since the early 1990s, the continuing rapid growth in the demand for higher education and a regime that did not make meeting this need a high priority has led to an erosion in the quality of education throughout the university system generally. Class size grows, the need for new offerings goes largely unmet, faculty members supplement their low incomes by moonlighting at a second teaching job or by tutoring, and many current and potential faculty members seek employment in other countries or professions. Higher education in Yemen was in a crisis after 2005, as was education in Yemen as a whole.

EGYPT AND EGYPTIANS. The impact of Egypt on Yemen goes back to pharaonic days and the demand for luxury goods that contributed to the growth and wealth of the **trading kingdoms** along the Frankincense Trail in eastern Yemen. Demand was especially strong from 400 to 100 B.C. under the rule of the Ptolemies, who reinvigorated Egypt. Although the Ptolemaic period was marked by firm control over the commerce of the **Red Sea** and the coast of East Africa, it was also a period of increased demand for luxury goods brought overland through Yemen.

After the rise of Islam, it was the **Fatimids** of Egypt who left their mark on Yemen in the 11th century. Later, the involvement of the **Mamluks** in Yemen led quite directly to the first occupation of Yemen by the **Ottoman** Turks in the 16th century. In the 19th century, the expansionism of the Khedive of Egypt, **Muhammad Ali**, raised concerns in **Great Britain** and among the Ottomans about the safety of their interests in Arabia and on the **Red Sea**. This triggered the British occupation of **Aden** and the second Ottoman occupation of North Yemen in the mid-19th century—and to the gradual bifurcation of Yemen in the modern era.

Modern Egypt and isolated North Yemen had little impact on one another until after the Egyptian Revolution—and the rise of Gamal Abdul **Nasser** and Nasserism. The Egyptian revolution challenged equally the conservative Yemeni **imamate** and Britain's position in Aden. One result in the late 1950s was the strange and brief interlude of the **United Arab States** that loosely associated imamate Yemen with that ill-fated union of Egypt and Syria, the **United Arab Republic**. Thereafter, the Nasser regime waged a political campaign and war of words against the imamate, encouraged the young Yemeni officers who were about to launch the **1962 Revolution**, and then intervened quickly and massively in an effort to defend the YAR militarily as well as politically against the Saudi-backed **royalists** in the long, grinding **Yemen Civil War**. Egypt's five-year venture was a failure, and it withdrew in defeat from Yemen in the summer of 1967 in the wake of the most disastrous of all **Arab–Israeli** conflicts, the Six-Day War. Field Marshall Hakim Amr, longtime revolutionary colleague of Nasser, was commander of the armed forces and directly responsible for their long, and losing, venture in Yemen. Anwar **Sadat**, Nasser's successor, alleged that Amr used the war for personal gain and to increase the power of the army within Egypt, and that Nasser was aware of this but unable to do anything about it.

For many Yemeni republicans, the Egyptians saved the YAR—but at the price of deforming it. The Egyptians came to defend the republic but ended up occupying Yemen as they took over the just-born republic and tried to remake it in their own image. Given the mixed feeling on both sides—the Egyptians were wont to call the intervention "our Vietnam"—it was to take years for relations between the YAR and Egypt to really warm up again. And just when they had begun to do so, they were put on hold by Arab reactions to another Arab–Israeli event, the Camp David Agreement and its separate peace between Egypt and Israel. Relations improved in the 1980s, reaching their high point with the formation of the **Arab Cooperation Council** in 1988, only to plunge again in 1990–1991 with the events surrounding the First **Gulf War** that found them on opposite sides.

Relations between the Nasser regime and South Yemen were less complicated or intense. President Nasser, with thousands of his forces in the YAR, campaigned against the continued British presence in South Yemen and then stepped up efforts to control the course of events after Britain announced in 1966 that it intended to quit Aden and the **Aden Protectorates**. Indeed, his decision not to pull out of the YAR in 1966 was influenced by Britain's decision, since the latter raised the possibility of another foothold on the Arabian Peninsula from which to pursue his long conflict with **Saudi Arabia**. Unfortunately for the Egyptians, they chose the **Front for the Liberation of Occupied South Yemen** (FLOSY) over the **National Liberation Front** (NLF); the NLF then defeated FLOSY in the fight to succeed the British and bury the stillborn **Federation of South Arabia**. As a result, relations between the Nasser regime and the NLF were neither good nor frequent after the latter took over in Aden in late 1967. Relations did not improve in the 1970s as the PDRY veered toward Marxism–Leninism and the socialist camp and Egypt moved under President Anwar Sadat toward the West and a mixed **economy**—and toward Camp David and peace with Israel.

Since the early 1990s, after the First Gulf War became less salient, relations between Egypt and the ROY have improved, and have been generally good. Presidents Mubarak and Salih have developed a good working relationship—the former having been in office since 1981 and the latter since 1978.

EIGHTEEN POINTS, YSP'S. *See* DOCUMENT OF PLEDGE AND ACCORD (AL-WATHIQA).

ELECTIONS, PDRY. Far more so than in either the YAR or the ROY, elections in the PDRY were more about legitimizing the regime and spreading a message than about choosing representatives, this being a consequence of the role of the **Yemeni Socialist Party** (YSP) and its immediate predecessors as a "vanguard party." As prescribed in the **1970 State Constitution**, the **People's Supreme Council** (PSC) was the elective legislature that, in theory, was the source of sovereign authority in independent South Yemen. It was an appointed PSC that met beginning in 1971, and the first elections for the 111-member PSC were not held until 1978. The next PSC elections were held eight years later, in 1986, after a three-year postponement caused by political convulsions inside the ruling YSP. In both cases, the elections were structured so as to militate against the representation of **tribes** and regions—as opposed to the nation—as well as to ensure the election of some political independents and **women**. Upon **unification** in 1990, the PSC merged with the YAR's **Consultative Council** to form the transitional **Council of Deputies** of the new ROY.

ELECTIONS, ROY. Since Yemeni **unification** in 1990, the politics of the ROY have been punctuated and influenced to some degree by three parliamentary elections, two popular presidential elections, and two **local council** elections. The first elections for the 301-member **Chamber of Deputies** were held in April 1993, nearly three years into the transition period, and were marked by open and vigorous multiparty competition and the participation of **women**, a rarity for the Arabian Peninsula. Despite a controversial postponement of several months, the elections served to legitimate Yemeni unification and the unification regime at home and abroad. No players of consequence boycotted the elections, and the notable losers accepted the results after only the briefest grumbling and cries of fraud. Despite their skepticism regarding the winners' commitment to democracy, the losers seemed prepared to assume the role of opposition. Perhaps relieved that this first electoral effort took place with relatively little chaos and violence, the local and international monitors cut the regime some slack on the question of the degree to which the process was "free and fair."

President **Salih** and his centrist **General People's Congress** (GPC) were the big winners, as expected. The other half of the unification regime, the **Yemeni Socialist Party** (YSP), while much diminished, survived in good order. Finally—and very important—the regime's **tribal** and **political Islamist** critics, represented by **Islah**, the Reform Grouping, made a good showing. The GPC won 40 percent of the seats, and the YSP and Islah each won roughly 20 percent. Most of the remaining 20 percent were won by "independents," with the **Baath Party** winning several. These results facilitated the formation of a broad coalition government ranging from center-left to center-right—the "big tent" favored by President Salih. Interestingly, this 2:1:1 ratio of GPC to YSP to Islah translated roughly into a 3:2:1 ratio in positions in the new cabinet, suggesting that Islah's strength relative to that of the YSP was more apparent than real. The considerable leverage that the YSP enjoyed was largely a result of a clean sweep of nearly all the seats in the former South Yemen. Indicative of his ambiguous role as both an old ally of President Salih and head of Islah, Shaykh Abdullah ibn Husayn **al-Ahmar** was named speaker of the council, arguably the third most important office in the ROY.

Despite initial hopes that this coalition government would stay together and address some of the ROY's pressing problems, 1993 ended with the government virtually immobilized by a prolonged, escalating political conflict between the GPC and the YSP. The YSP-led **War of Secession** in mid-1994 registered the failure of Yemen's politicians to translate the election results into a workable pattern of politics and governance.

The April 1997 parliamentary elections, coming nearly three years after the War of Secession, occurred under very different circumstances and with very different results and consequences. Demoralized and in disarray, the YSP boycotted the election and ceased to have a significant presence in the Council of Deputies. The GPC, with 225 (75 percent) of the seats, chose to rule alone and not go into coalition with Islah, which had won 62 (21 percent) of the seats. Local and international monitors, less forgiving than in 1993, marshaled much evidence challenging the freeness and fairness of the electoral process.

Although Islah became the core of the opposition in the chamber of deputies, one Islah member was named to the cabinet and, again, Shaykh al-Ahmar was named speaker. The size of the GPC majority, the ambivalence of Islah as opposition and the further consolidation of power in the president's hands caused the council both to command less public interest and to be less a shaper of public opinion than it had been after the 1993 elections.

The first popular presidential election in the ROY was held on 23 September, 1999. This potentially historic event became something of a non-event in the absence of a credible opponent to President Salih. At the last minute, the GPC reneged on its promise to deliver the constitutionally required 10 percent vote of the Chamber of Deputies needed to secure approval of the candidacy of the head of the YSP, Ali Salih **Obad**. Faced with the prospect of no opponent to President Salih, the GPC majority in the Chamber then approved the candidacy of another GPC member, Najib al-Shaabi, the little-known son of South Yemen's first president, Qahtan **al-Shaabi**. Needless to say, the campaign and President Salih's sweeping victory—he garnered 96.3 percent of the votes—were predictably anti-climactic.

The first local council elections took place, after a long delay and much controversy, in February 2001. These administratively complex elections were hastily thrown together and poorly conducted, and some claim that the regime only held them when it did in order to get a bigger turnout for the referendum extending the terms of the president and the parliament, which was held on the same date. More than two dozen people died in violent incidents on or before the day of the elections. The coalition of opposition parties formed to challenge the GPC rejected the preliminary results as fraudulent—charging media bias and misuse of public funds, in addition to chicanery at the ballot box—and called for new elections. As something of a rejoinder, Prime Minister Abd al-Qadr Bajammal announced that the government might abolish three-fourths of the councils, claiming that the elected councilors lacked the needed education and expertise.

In early March, the Supreme Election Committee finally reported that the preliminary results had the GPC winning comfortably with 60 percent of the votes and 61 percent of the governorate- and district-level council seats. For many, the bigger news was Islah getting 24 percent of the votes and a somewhat smaller percentage of the seats. More specifically, the GPC won 69 percent and 56 percent of the governorate- and district-level seats, respectively, whereas Islah won 19.5 percent and 21.3 percent of the governorate- and district-level seats, respectively. The YSP did poorly, taking only 4 percent and 3.2 percent of the governorate- and district-level seats. The comparable figures for independents were 7.5 percent and 11.1 percent. The other parties did even worse. Again, notable was the showing by Islah, especially on the district level—something attributed to its grassroots organization and support.

The ROY's third parliamentary elections, coming 10 years after the first, took place in April 2003. Aware of how self-defeating its 1997 boycott was, the YSP participated this time, restoring a bit of its credibility. Still, it won only 8 of 301 seats (2.7 percent of the seats). The GPC was again the overwhelming winner, with 226 (75 percent of the seats), one more seat than in 1997. Islah reconfirmed its place as the leading opposition party, taking 48 (16 percent) of the seats, a third less than in 1977. The minor parties—the Nasirites, Baath, Union of Popular Forces, and Al-Haqq—won only five seats.

The second popular presidential election and the second local council elections were held on the same day, 20 September 2006. The most notable difference from the first presidential election in 1999 was a credible opposition candidate, Faysal **Bin Shamlan**, a political independent chosen by the new opposition coalition, the **Joint Meeting Parties** (JMP). Much of the drama turned on whether the coalition could agree on a candidate and, if so, whether it could stay together and support that candidate throughout the campaign. It did both. The question of whether President Salih would reverse his nearly year-old declaration that he would not be the GPC's candidate provided far less drama. Most assumed that he would—and he did.

Predictable as the results were, Bin Shamlan and the JMP made a respectable showing, getting 21.82 percent of the vote to President Salih's 77.17 percent. The JMP claimed electoral fraud but then pulled back and accepted the results. The **European Union** and many of the other monitors, local and international, judged the campaign to be biased in favor of the ruling GPC and the reasonably well-administered balloting to be tainted by fraud and irregularities—but not by enough to affect the outcome.

Some thought that the strong grassroots base of Islah and the vestiges of loyalty to the YSP in the south, as well as the unimpressive showing of the GPC in 2001, made it likely that the parties in the JMP would do better against the GPC in the local council elections than in the presidential race. They were to be disappointed by results that had the GPC winning 73.75 percent and 74.12 percent of the district- and governorate-level seats, respectively. Rather than go silent or resort to whining, the JMP vowed to learn from its electoral Parliamentary mistakes, to hold the GPC accountable, and to win the next round of elections in 2009.

Beginning in the second half of 2008, several months of acrimonious negotiations between the GPC and the JMP failed to produce agreement on electorial reform and other issues. As a result, the elections scheduled for April 2009 were postponed for two years until 2011.

ELECTIONS, YAR. The **1970 Constitution** placed legislative power in the mostly elective Majlis al-Shura, the **Consultative Council** (CC), and over the life of the YAR only two national elections were held, in 1971 and 1988. The North Yemenis experienced their first national elections when they went in to the polls March 1971 to elect members of the 179-member CC in 159 constituencies (the remaining 20 were appointed by President Abd al-Rahman **al-Iryani**), and these elections were nominally non-partisan. The CC that convened in April 1971 was essentially an assembly of notables, not unlike early British parliaments. In the absence of explicit party organization and ideology, the members were grouped into shifting factions and only tenuously linked to one another and to their constituents. As a result of fraud and a districting system skewed toward rural and **tribal** areas, the majority of the members of the CC were tribal chiefs or other notables with conservative orientations or connections. This bias was reinforced by the selection of Shaykh Abdullah ibn Husayn **al-Ahmar** as speaker.

The constitution and CC were suspended by President Ibrahim **al-Hamdi** in 1974, and were restored by President Ali Abdullah

Salih only in 1988, about a decade into his long tenure. The restored constitution called for a 159-member CC, of which 128 were to be elected from single-member constituencies and and 31 appointed by President Salih. Held in July 1988, nearly 15 years after President al-Hamdi suspended the first CC, the elections caught the Salih regime quite by surprise when Islamist candidates swept **Sanaa**, winning six of seven seats. Throughout the country, most of the winning candidates had not been members of the new CC's immediate predecessor, the fully appointed **People's Constituent Assembly**. Choosing among 1,293 candidates, the people indicated that they wanted change and—at least in Sanaa—that they thought that the Islamists seemed most likely to provide it. As in 1971, the elections were nominally non-partisan, a fiction difficult to maintain given the open identification of many candidates with the president's umbrella "political institution"—the **General People's Congress**—and the **Muslim Brotherhood**. It was this reconstituted CC that combined with the PDRY's **People's Supreme Council** to form the **Council of Deputies** (Majlis al-Nuwab) on the occasion of **unification** and the creation of the ROY in May 1990.

In terms of growing electoral experience and expectations in the YAR, the series of **local development association** (LDA) elections that began in 1976 were every bit as important as the parliamentary elections. Sponsored by President al-Hamdi, the first of these non-partisan but hotly contested popular elections were held for council seats on more than 75 LDAs across the country. The members of the new councils then chose provincial- and national-level councils, the last being the ruling body of the **Confederation of Yemeni Development Associations** (CYDA). In the late 1970s, and soon after President Salih assumed power, a second round of LDA elections was held in 187 districts and towns. In the mid-1980s, in an effort to end the ambiguous relationship between the YAR's local district governing bodies and the LDAs, which, in theory, were semi-autonomous and outside the state, the two were merged throughout the country into **Local Councils for Cooperative Development** (LCCDs). LCCD elections were held in the second half of the 1980s, but by this time the spirit and substance of the LDA movement were dead.

ELECTRICITY. *See* INFRASTRUCTURE DEVELOPMENT.

EMERGING DEMOCRACIES CONFERENCE, 1999. The successful conference in Sanaa in July 1999 that was held with the help of the United States' National Democratic Institute primarily to highlight the ROY's political stability and progress towards democracy. Indeed, the ROY had held its second round of parliamentary **elections** in 1997 and was planning to hold its first direct popular presidential election later in 1999. Bringing together representatives from ten "emerging democracies," Yemeni and non-Yemeni non-governmental organizations in the new democratization business, and other guests the conference consisted of three days of panels, workshops, addresses, and other opportunities to share successes and ongoing problems—and to cast the ROY in a flattering light.

EMIGRATION. For a millennium or two, and perhaps longer, climate, geography, human biology, and culture have often combined to produce more Yemenis than the land could support, and then to pump many of them out of Yemen to all corners of the known world to earn livings, to simply stay alive, and, often, to send money home. For this reason, emigration and emigrants—and their impact upon economic, sociocultural, and even political life—have long been important facets of the history of Yemen and its people.

Located just south of Mecca and Medina in the **Hijaz**, North Yemenis converted early to Islam and were many of the soldier–settlers who spread Islam across North Africa and into Spain in the eighth and ninth centuries A.D. Far to the east in **Wadi Hadhramawt**, Sayyid Ahmad Ibn Isa settled in about the 10th century, and his offspring multiplied and came to influence—if not dominate—the area as a spiritual and learned aristocracy. Unable to support their number in the Wadi, they started the tradition centuries ago of seeking their fame, fortune, and spiritual fulfillment abroad—in East Africa and the East Indies, especially in Indonesia and Malaysia. Many of them were successful as merchants and traders, some fabulously so, and the money they sent home supported their families and retainers as well as a large learned religious community. They started families in the Wadi, frequently went abroad for a generation, often beginning new families there, and often then returned to the Wadi to spend their old age with their original family.

Since the early decades of the 20th century, economics and hopes of finding a better livelihood were forces that pushed and pulled a growing stream of North Yemenis to go abroad as sailors, unskilled workers, and small shopkeepers and traders. Most returned to Yemen after having earned a modest living and saved a small amount; many repeated this process several times in the course of their lifetimes. In the second half of the century, an increasing number stayed abroad, often coming "home" for short periods. A small number became wealthy as merchants and businessmen; many became shopkeepers and factory and agricultural workers. Often the first male to go abroad was soon followed by his brothers, sons, and other male relatives; sometimes, wives and daughters joined them.

Over the middle decades of the 20th century, nearly all of the emigrants were **Shafiis** from the southern uplands of North Yemen, the **Tihama, Aden** and its environs, and Wadi Hadhramawt. These Yemenis went in large numbers to **Great Britain** and the **United States,** as well as to East Asia, South Asia, East Africa, **Ethiopia,** and the **Sudan.** World War II disrupted and sharply lessened new emigration, especially of the Hadhramis to Japanese-occupied Southeast Asia.

After the war, emigration again picked up and, in the 1960s, became generalized, growing to include the **Zaydis** of the long-insular northern highlands of North Yemen. By this time, moreover, the emigrant workers from both Yemens were increasingly going to **Saudi Arabia** and the new Arab **Gulf** states as rapidly increasing **oil** revenues created the jobs needed to build the infrastructure of these places. To Saudi Arabia from Wadi Hadhramawt came one of several families that in a couple of decades became fabulously rich and successful: the **bin Ladens.** The upward spike in oil prices in 1973 and 1979 transformed this outflow of Yemenis into a flood. The Saudis especially needed Yemeni workers and allowed them to enter without the permits or sponsors required of others. The republican–royalist **reconciliation** that ended the **Yemeni Civil War** in 1970 facilitated the flow from the YAR; despite its embrace of a militant Marxism, and with it the goal of self-sufficiency and a ban on emigration, the PDRY also experienced a surge in emigration. In about 1980, at the peak of emigration, an estimated 800,000 North Yemenis were abroad in Saudi Arabia and the other Arab Gulf states; for South Yemen, with one-fourth the population of North Yemen, an estimated 200,000 were abroad.

Labor migration was the subversive force that began to end the isolation of North Yemen from the outside world, from the 20th century. Emigration also contributed greatly to Aden's and Wadi Hadhramawt's very different versions of cosmopolitanism. More generally, moreover, the common experience of emigration, cutting across religious and regional differences in Yemen, probably added to a sense of common identity among Yemenis. The loneliness, alienation and existential experience of emigrants became an early theme of Yemenis exploring modern modes of poetry and prose—for instance, Muhammad Anaam **Ghaleb's** *Strangers on the Road.*

Arguably, the biggest impact of emigration on the two Yemens from the 1960s through the 1980s came from the **remittances** sent or brought back by Yemenis working overseas. By the early 1980s, remittances were contributing as much as 40–50 percent of the GDPs of the YAR and the PDRY—indeed, the YAR fit well the model of the "**remittance economy**." The remittances brought unprecedented prosperity and a vast array of foreign consumer and capital goods, especially to North Yemen. Although they largely bypassed the state, the remittances bought time for both regimes. At the same time, however, the remittances made the regimes and populations of both Yemens very vulnerable and dependent, especially on Saudi Arabia. This became painfully clear only a few months after Yemeni **unification** in 1990, when nearly all Yemenis working in Saudi Arabia were expelled as a result of the ROY's stand on what became the First **Gulf War** in 1991. The ROY suddenly found itself faced with a precipitous drop in remittances and a huge, increasingly impoverished, unemployed population.

Another kind of emigration had begun in the 1940s: that of students from Aden and long-insulated North Yemen who went abroad to Cairo and beyond for modern educations. Starting as a trickle, most notably in North Yemen with the **Famous Forty**, the flow of educational emigrants abroad became a stream in the 1950s and then a mighty torrent after the **1962 Revolution** in North Yemen and the creation of an independent South Yemen in 1967. When the first-generation educational emigrants returned home in the 1960s after their long odyssey—as nearly all of them did—they brought big or small bits of the modern world home with them. Often lumped together by their defining experience as "the graduates," these returnees became the **modernists** and modernizers of the two late-modernizing

Yemens. Beginning in the 1960s, they provided an increasing share of the cabinet ministers and top civil servants in both Yemens.

EMPTY QUARTER. The vast and forbidding, almost impenetrable desert area of **Saudi Arabia**, lying to the northeast and east-northeast of the ROY, that serves as a natural barrier between Yemen and Saudi Arabia. More correctly, the intersection of Saudi Arabia and what used to be the two Yemens is in the **Ramlat al-Sabatayn** desert, the western arm of the much larger Empty Quarter.

ENGLAND. *See* GREAT BRITAIN.

ERITREA. Independent only since 1993, this very poor, small country of 5 million people, because of its proximity across the **Red Sea**, has had a close but volatile relationship with the YAR and now the ROY. Ruled by Italy for 51 years, largely Muslim Eritrea was swallowed up with no superpower protest by **Ethiopia** in 1962, the year the YAR was created. The YAR and the PDRY supported "the struggle" for independence led by the Eritrean Liberation Front (ELF) for all three decades of that effort, an effort that became something of an Arab–Islamic cause. Indeed, over the years the YAR's beaches provided haven for hospitals and R&R facilities run by the ELF. The newly created ROY welcomed newly independent Eritrea in 1993, as did the rest of the Arab world. The culturally diverse Eritreans, united by the long struggle, were hopeful about the future.

Two years later, in 1995, Eritrea and the ROY stumbled into a very brief military fight over possession of the Hanish Islands, an archipelago of several small islands in the Red Sea between the two countries. Although the two former allies quickly pulled back and had the conflict over possession of the islands settled by international arbitration, largely in the ROY's favor, relations thereafter tended to swing between warm and cool. Recurring tensions usually involved territorial waters and fishing rights.

In 1998, three years after the fight with the ROY and five years after independence, Eritrea and Ethiopia went into what amounted to a second round of warfare, this time a senseless bit of trench warfare over a bit of borderland and the town of Badme. Two years later, after the death of thousands, a truce was brokered with the help of the

United States. A **United Nations** commission then awarded Badme to Eritrea, but Ethiopia ignored the ruling, with the result that the 21st century contains the threat of a new war between the two states.

By 2002, after **9/11**, the conflict between Eritrea and Ethiopia and just about everything else on the **Horn of Africa** was reinterpreted in terms of the United States' **War on Terror**. The **Sanaa Forum** for Cooperation in 2003, bringing together the presidents of the ROY, Ethiopia, and **Sudan** in the first of what became annual meetings, was motivated by a desire to exercise some regional control over this new issue, as well as to address its members' individual issues with Eritrea. Eritrea interpreted the Sanaa Forum as a "ganging up" against it and its interests, and after U.S.-backed Ethiopia intervened in **Somalia** against the Islamist regime based in Mogadishu in 2006, Eritrea supported both the Islamists in Somalia and the revived rebellion in **Ogadan** as ways of confronting Ethiopia. In 2007, the United States put its gloss on this by threatening to add Eritrea to its list of countries supporting terrorism.

ETHIOPIA. Opposite Yemen at the southern end of the **Red Sea**, and towering over the rest of the **Horn of Africa**, Ethiopia (in earlier times called Abyssinia) is Yemen's nearest sizable non-Arab neighbor, and one that has had an important impact on Yemen over the ages, particularly in the distant past and again in the 20th century. The culture and pigmentation of the people of the **Tihama** is testimony to the closeness of Ethiopia and Yemen both geographically and historically. Their closeness is also expressed in national myth and lore: both claim to be home to the biblical **Queen of Sheba**, and both claim to be the source of two items they both cherish highly, **coffee** and **qat**. (There is in Yemen a region named al-Udayn, the "two sticks"—i.e., coffee tree and qat bush.)

The bad treatment of the lowly dark-skinned **akhdam** caste has been rationalized by some Yemenis as the eternal punishment of the remnants of Ethiopians who invaded and occupied Yemen not long before the rise of Islam. Indeed, Christian Ethiopia, then known as Aksum, had emerged as a strong rival to Yemen's **Himyarite** Kingdom for control of the incense trade and had conquered Yemen twice over three centuries. Thereafter, with the Islamization of Yemen and the decline of the South Arabian **trading kingdoms**, Ethiopia and Yemen ceased to be salient to each other for many centuries.

In the middle third of the 20th century, the long reign of Ethiopia's Emperor Haile Selassie, interrupted for several years by his exile and replacement by the occupation regime of Mussolini's fascist Italy, intersected on several occasions with the reigns of North Yemen's Imams **Yahya** and **Ahmad**. Imam Yahya first had good relations with Emperor Haile Selassie and then had diplomatic relations with Italy in the 1930s and early 1940s, long before contacts with other European states. The warm relations with the occupiers of Ethiopia derived from Italy's opposition to the British occupiers of South Yemen.

Beginning in the late 1960s, the recently created YAR and PDRY tried with difficulty to balance relations with the restored Haile Selassie against their support for the **Eritrean** Rebellion, a cause that had taken on Arab–Islamic overtones. The final overthrow of the emperor in 1974 and his replacement by the Marxist regime headed by Mengistu Haile Mariam made Ethiopia more salient to the two Yemens in terms of their ongoing inter-Yemeni troubles, **Red Sea** security, and, more generally, the political future of the Arabian Peninsula. These years saw the continuation of the Eritrean Rebellion, the **Ogadan War** between **Somalia** and Ethiopia, and the increased presence of the **Cold War** on the Horn of Africa. The **Soviet Union** and the **United States** upped their involvement and suddenly changed partners, the former becoming the patron of Ethiopia and the latter the patron of Somalia. Marxist PDRY moved toward Ethiopia, a tendency that culminated in the inconsequential **Tripartite Agreement** among Ethiopia, the PDRY, and **Libya** in 1981. The YAR tried with difficulty to balance correct relations with the Mengistu regime with continued support for the Eritreans.

In the second half of the 1980s, the YAR significantly improved relations with both the PDRY and Ethiopia. Yemeni **unification** in 1990 and the overthrow of the Mengistu regime the next year rendered moot these shifts. Thereafter, the ROY adjusted to a non-Marxist Ethiopia and an independent Eritrea. Dramatic though they were, the events in Ethiopia and Eritrea during these years were less salient to Yemen than they had been in the turbulent 1970s.

The ROY did not get deeply involved in the border fighting between Ethiopia and independent Eritrea that broke out in 1998, ended in 2000, and threatened to erupt again a few years later. In part, this was because of the ROY's own strained relations with Eritrea that began with the dispute over the Hanish Islands in 1995. When

President Salih launched the Sanaa Forum in 2003 to promote peace and development on the Horn of Africa, its members included the ROY, Ethiopia, and, later, Somalia—but not Eritrea. *See also* RED SEA AND HORN OF AFRICA SECURITY.

EUROPEAN UNION (EU). This rapidly spreading and deepening economic and political union of European nation-states, now consisting of 27 members, continues with increasing success to exert economic as well as diplo-political influence over the non-European world, the ROY included. Those European countries with long-standing and major bilateral relations with Yemen—i.e., Germany, the Netherlands, Great Britain, France, and Italy—are increasingly pooling their efforts through the EU to trade their collective support and aid for the ROY for economic reforms and steps towards good governance.

Bilateral relations between the ascendant EU and a struggling YAR were established in the basis of the Cooperative Agreement of 28 November 1987, the terms of which were extended to the ROY upon **unification** in 1990. These relations initially focused on trade and aid. With its common currency and trade rules and regulations, the EU has become the ROY's major trading partner, ranking first in exports to Yemen and eighth in imports from Yemen in 2003. Over the years, the aid component became considerable and served to both supplement and substitute for that of the individual European countries. In recent years, a major emphasis of EU aid to Yemen has focused on poverty reduction—for example, an effort to develop a sustainable fishery sector. Also new is an effort to help the ROY conserve Socotra Island's environment—its unique and fragile flora and fauna—as it works to develop its potential for tourism. In mid-2007, a visiting EU commissioner pledged at least 60 million euros in aid for 2007–2010—this on top of the sizable amount pledged by EU to Yemen at the London donors' conference in 2006.

The European Commission opened a permanent mission in the ROY in late 2003, about the time that the two sides began a "political dialogue" with a focus on democracy, human rights, non-proliferation, and the effort against global terror. The EU strategy for 2005–2006 called for a strengthening of pluralism, democracy, and human rights by encouraging a partnership between Yemen's government and its non-governmental organizations. The EU's Election Observation Mission took the leading role in monitoring the 2006 presidential and local council **elections**.

EXCHANGE RATES. *See* MONEY, CURRENCY, AND FOREIGN EXCHANGE.

EXPORTS. *See* IMPORTS AND EXPORTS

EXXON CORPORATION. Spurred by the discovery in 1984 of commercial amounts of **oil** in the Marib/al-Jawf basin by the **Yemen Hunt Oil Co.** (YHOC), in 1985 the Exxon Corporation made its second bid for a piece of the action in North Yemen by buying a 49 percent stake in YHOC's share in its production-sharing agreement (PSA) for the Marib/al-Jawf basin. It also gave up on its earlier separate effort to find oil in the area in the northern highlands, in **Dhamar** province, covered by its own PSA with the YAR. In exchange for access to a known supply of oil, Exxon agreed to provide YHOC with several hundred million dollars in 1986–1987 for the rapid development of the basin. This big infusion of needed capital made it possible for the export of oil to begin in late 1987—and for Exxon to profit from this.

Exxon was also a partner in another consortium with YHOC that in the late 1980s secured the concession for what was then the "neutral zone" between the two Yemens. The search for oil in this area began in the early 1990s, and the **Jannah** field began producing modest amounts of oil before the decade's end. Exxon (by then ExxonMobil) continued to have this stake in the Jannah field in 2008.

In 2003, ExxonMobil was a party to YHOC's agreement with the ROY to a five-year extension of the expiring 20-year production-sharing agreement for the Marib/al-Jawf Basin. In early 2005, the ROY abruptly scrapped this new agreement, leading ExxonMobil and Hunt Oil to file for arbitration before the Paris-based International Chamber of Commerce (ICC) in November, charging the ROY with expropriating YHOC's holding in Yemen—but in August 2008, the ICC ruled against ExxonMobil and Hunt.

In the late 1990s, ExxonMobil was also a partner in plans with **Total** and Hunt Oil for the development of an LNG project for the considerable gas reserves in the Marib/al-Jawf basin. However, after repeated delays in finding the needed customers and financing, ExxonMobil chose to pull out of this project in 2002.

– F –

FADHLI SULTANATE OF SHUQRA. The Fadhli sultanate was seated on the coast of South Yemen in the fishing and fish-marketing town of Shuqra, northeast of Aden and **Zinjibar**, and its territory extended inland to include a portion of the agriculturally productive **Abyan** region. The sultanate, thanks to cotton production in Abyan, was to become—after **Lahej**—the most prosperous member of the Western **Aden Protectorate**. It had been one of the nine states in Aden's hinterland that Britain originally put under "protection" in the 19th century, and it was one of the six states in 1959 to initiate the **Federation of Arab Amirates of the South**, the predecessor to the **Federation of South Arabia**. Sultan Ahmad bin Abdullah al-Fadhli was active in the politics of planning South Arabia's future during this period, but he found the plans for a federation headed by traditional leaders overtaken by the more radical alternatives that became popular by the mid-1960s. As with the other traditional states and rulers, the Fadhli sultanate was abolished and the ruling family, including **Tarik al-Fahdli**, forced into exile at the time of independence.

AL-FADHLI, TARIK. The son of the last ruler of the Sultanate of Shuqra in Abyan who joined the jihad against the **Soviet Union** in **Afghanistan** in the 1980s and returned to Yemen as an "Afghani Arab" only to be co-opted in the early 1990s by the ROY's President Ali Adullah **Salih**. Upon his return from Afghanistan, al-Fadhli formed the Yemeni Islamic Jihad (YIJ) in order to drive Marxism from South Yemen and destroy the PDRY. In the early 1990s, and after Yemeni **unification** resulted in the PDRY's absorption in the ROY, the YIJ set about to assassinate **Yemeni Socialist Party** leaders who had driven the al-Fadhli and other ruling families in South Yemen into exile more than 20 years earlier.

At the end of 1992, members of the YIJ bombed the **Goldmur Hotel** in Aden and attempted to do the same to the city's biggest hotel. Al-Fadhli was sought, besieged in a mountain redoubt and arrested by the authorities, only soon to "escape" and thereafter align himself and some of his followers with the **Salih regime**. By contrast, other members of YIJ went on to form the **Aden–Abyan Islamic Army** and continued their armed struggle. Al-Fadhli's sister married President Salih's relative and colleague, **Ali Muhsin**. Already a member of the permanent committee of the ruling **General People's Congress**, Al-Fadhli was appointed to the new **Shura Council** in 1997. However, al-Fadhli broke with the regime in mid-2009 returned to the seat of the old Fadhli sul-tanate, and cast his lot with the new and growing secessionist movement in the south.

FAHD IBN ABD AL-AZIZ, KING. *See* AL-SAUD (BAYT SAUD).

FAMOUS FORTY. The first sizable group of young men from North Yemen to be sent abroad for education—first to Lebanon, in late 1947, for more than a year; to Egypt for several years; and then—about a third of them—to West Europe and the United States in the late 1950s. Sent out by a somewhat reluctant Imam **Yahya**, nearly three quarters of the Famous Forty were **Zaydis**, and almost all of them came from humble backgrounds, not from families that might pose a threat to the **imamate**. Nearly all of them returned to Yemen, most with university degrees. They were an important part of Yemen's first generation of **modernists** and educational emigrants. They and their cohorts blazed the trail soon taken by thousands of other North Yemenis. For these boys, the move from Yemen to Cairo and beyond was something like going from the 16th to the 20th century.

Most of the Famous Forty returned just before or just after the **1962 Revolution**, and all of them opposed the **royalists** in the **Yemeni Civil War** that quickly followed the revolution. Indeed, the group included several of the military officers who plotted and carried out that revolution. Most of the others served the republic in one capacity or another for their entire careers, some as politicians and technocrats who held ministerial and other high offices from 1962 to the 1990s—and even beyond.

FATAT AL-JAZIRAH (YOUTH OF THE PENINSULA). *See* LUQMAN FAMILY AND MUHAMMAD ALI LUQMAN.

FATIMIDS. *See* ISMAILIS IN YEMEN.

FAYSAL IBN ABD AL-AZIZ, KING. *See* AL-SAUD (BAYT SAUD).

FEDERALIS. The name used by the British for the rulers and high officials of the states of the Western **Aden Protectorate** who in the 1950s and 1960s favored the creation of an independent federation of South Arabian states, first without and later including **Aden** Colony.

FEDERATION OF ARAB AMIRATES OF THE SOUTH (FAAS). The federation of 6 (later 10) states of the Western **Aden Protectorate** that was created with the encouragement and protection of **Great Britain** in 1959 and that, on the occasion of the merger of Aden with the states in its hinterland in January 1963, was transformed into the **Federation of South Arabia** (FSA). The FAAS founded a new capital at **al-Ittihad**, just outside **Aden Colony**, and started from scratch, with British help, establishing the institutional framework and patterns of behavior of a modern state. In existence for less than four years, the FAAS did not really have the time needed to get up and running and to use experience to reach a balance between self-rule on the one hand and its continuing treaty ties to Britain in such areas as external relations, security, and development on the other. The same can be said of its short-lived successor, the FSA.

FEDERATION OF SOUTH ARABIA (FSA). The federation created in January 1963 out of the merger of **Aden** with the 10 Western **Aden Protectorate** states that comprised the less-than-four-year-old **Federation of Arab Amirates of the South.** One of the big problems in this combination, one barely papered over in the negotiations, was how to give relatively modern, densely populated Aden enough power—but not too much power—in relationship to the large number of far more traditional and conservative states in the hinterland. This effort to combine an apple with oranges soon proved moot. Opposed by many political Adenis and created shortly after the **National Liberation Front** (NLF) came onto the scene with the "up-country" **Radfan Rebellion,** the FSA was almost immediately overtaken by fast-moving, radicalizing events. It was relegated to the status of a historical curiosity by a struggle that saw the NLF take power from the British in 1967.

A number of Adeni politicians tied their careers to the creation of the FSA. It was Hasan Ali Bayoomi, an Arab native of **Crater** and from a family that long ago came to Aden from Egypt, who in early 1963 led an increasingly divided, polarized Aden into merger with the protectorate states. He became Aden's first chief minister under constitutional changes that went into effect with the merger but then died very suddenly in the middle of that year. Bayoomi had been the archrival of Abdullah **al-Asnag** for leadership in Aden after the mid-1950s in a rivalry that was sharpened by his sponsorship, as Aden's minister of labor, of legislation designed to make political strike action by al-Asnag's **Aden Trade Union Congress** more difficult.

Sayyid Zayd Baharun, a leading Adeni merchant, succeeded Bayoomi in 1963 as chief minister of Aden at a time of accelerating political change. Alongside the Radfan Rebellion, the polarization and radicalization of politics inside the FSA soon rendered impossible the political cooperation required to make the federation work. Baharun resigned in 1965 in a dispute between the Aden government and the protectorate politicians—the **Federalis**—over the possible place of the **Hadhramawt** in the FSA.

Husayn Ali Bayoomi, the brother of Hasan and the FSA's minister of information, failed in a desperate effort in mid-1967 to form a moderate government for the FSA that included leading Adeni nationalists. This failure doomed the FSA and opened the way to victory by the militant NLF later that year.

FINANCE, MINISTRY OF. Formally created in 1974, the Finance Ministry evolved out of the antiquated Treasury Ministry, one of the few republican institutions with roots in the **imamate**. The process was midwifed by a new Budget Office staffed by young Yemeni graduates and a team of foreign experts funded by the International Monetary Fund, the **IMF**. This effort to use the Budget Office to create a ministry that would be able to exert some real control over government expenditures is associated with Muhammad Ahmad **al-Junayd**, who had become treasury minister in 1973. Al-Junayd had the Budget Office prepare a trial budget for fiscal 1973–1974; the next year, he had a budget prepared for actual application and persuaded the rest of the government and the IMF that enough progress had been made to go ahead and merge the Budget Office and salvageable elements from the Treasury Ministry into a new Finance Ministry. This was done, and he became minister of finance, a post in which he remained for many years. Some observers say that the move was premature and hastily executed and that at, the expense of the goal of sound public finance, too many ideas and practices of the old ministry survived in the new.

Criticism of the Finance Ministry from the late 1990s through most of the next decade shifted and focused on its alleged role as the chief instrument through which the **Salih regime** concentrated and maintained political control—and facilitated **corruption** and siphoned off much of Yemen's wealth. Indeed, some accused the regime and the pyramid of patronage on which it sat as depending as much upon the Finance Ministry as upon the security forces or the military. Furthermore, proponents of decentralization viewed its financial control over other ministries and agencies of the central government, as well as over government at the governorate and locals levels, as the chief institutional barrier to decentralization as well as to other measures of good governance and economic reforms

FINANCIAL CRISIS OF 1968–1971, YAR'S. A period of great economic and financial disarray in the YAR that was marked by runaway inflation, the collapse of the Yemeni riyal, and staggering budget and balance-of-payments deficits. A number of factors combined to create a situation beyond the capacities of the weak state: the sharp drop in the inflow of outside funds that had artificially fueled the **economy** during the **Yemeni Civil War**; the long **drought** that crippled the once self-sufficient agricultural system; and the opening of the country to an uncontrolled flood of foreign goods. The crisis slowly receded reached its dramatic high point with the sudden resignation of Prime Minister Ahmad Muhammad **Numan** after only a few months in office in mid-1971. In retrospect, this period was a trough between the era of the civil war and a period of fairly rapid growth and development that was to be fueled by matters tied to the end of that long conflict: subsidies and other financial aid from **Saudi Arabia** and development aid from the West and international aid organizations. Most important, however, was the explosion of

remittances from the rapidly growing number of Yemenis working abroad, mostly in Saudi Arabia. *See also* ECONOMY AND POLITICAL ECONOMY.

FIRST GULF WAR, 1991. *See* GULF WAR (1991), FIRST.

FISHING AND FISHERIES. South Yemen's **economy** has long been highly dependent on fish for protein and livelihoods, continues to have potential access to vast fish resources, and made considerable progress in the 1970s and 1980s toward the development of a modern fishing industry able to realize just such a potential. Several economic and technical assistance projects after independence in 1967 focused on fishing **cooperatives** and on efforts to increase their efficiency and capacity to satisfy domestic and export markets.

Compared with South Yemen and the **Tihama** of North Yemen, is populous highlands have never not always been dependent on fish for protein. Indeed, fish have become widely available and acceptable as food on the highlands only since the mid-1970s—and that only with refrigeration. Vast fish resources are also available to North Yemen, and some progress in developing a larger and more modern fishing industry on the **Tihama** was made after the 1960s. The capacity for further development of the fisheries and fishing industry—for moving from subsistence fishing to fishing for the local and world markets—is great in both parts of Yemen, and this was made a priority after **unification** in 1990. External aid and some Yemeni investment focused on modern fishing technology and on modern processing. At the same time, the ROY concerned itself both with protecting the small fisherman and with protecting the local fisheries from larger and more efficient foreign fishing fleets. The latter remained largely a losing battle through the first decade of the 21st century.

FLAG. The flag of the ROY is simply three equal horizontal stripes: from top to bottom, red, white, and black. The YAR's flag was the same, but with a single green star in the middle of the white stripe. A bit more elaborate, the PDRY's flag had the same three stripes but a red star in a sky-blue triangle next to the hoist end. The republican flags of Egypt, Syria, and Iraq are based on the same red, white, and black stripes.

FLOSY. *See* FRONT FOR THE LIBERATION OF OCCUPIED SOUTH YEMEN (FLOSY).

FOREIGN AID. *See* AID, FOREIGN.

FOREIGN INVESTMENT LAWS. *See* INVESTMENT LAWS.

FOREIGN POLICY. *See* AFGHANISTAN; ARAB COOPERATION COUNCIL (ACC); ARAB–ISRAELI CONFLICT; ARMS AND MILITARY AID; BORDERS; CHINA, COLD WAR; CUBA; EGYPT, ERITREA; EUROPEAN UNION (EU); GERMANY; GREAT BRITAIN; GULF COOPERATION COUNCIL (GCC); GULF WAR (1991), FIRST; IRAN (PERSIA); IRAQ; ISRAEL; JORDAN, KUWAIT; LIBYA; NETHERLANDS; OMAN, SULTANATE OF; OTTOMAN TURKS; PALESTINE; RED SEA AND HORN OF AFRICA SECURITY ISSUES; SAUDI ARABIA, SOVIET UNION; SYRIA; UNITED ARAB EMIRATES (UAE); UNITED NATIONS (UN); UNITED STATES; WAR ON TERROR; WORLD WARS.

FORSSKAL, PETER. *See* TRAVELERS.

"FORWARD POLICY." Beginning slowly in the 1930s, and coming to prevail during the decade after World War II, **Great Britain**'s "forward policy" involved a shift on the part of the **colonial administration** in South Yemen toward a more intrusive, interventionist approach to governance and government-fostered socioeconomic development activities in the **Aden Protectorates**. This was in marked contrast to many decades of "indirect rule," and beginning in the late 1930s, the replacement of treaties of protection with advisory treaties marks this shift. For the most part, however, the flurry of modest government reforms and development projects that followed primarily drew attention to the fact of rule by outsiders and alien practices in an increasingly anti-colonial age. The subsequent shift in policy in the late 1950s that again put government in the hands of the traditional rulers of the protectorate states spelled the abandonment of the "forward policy" and led to the induced birth of the ill-fated **Federation of South Arabia**.

4 MAY AGREEMENTS. The set of agreements reached at summits in Taiz and Sanaa, in mid-April and early May 1988, respectively, which together ended more than two years of dangerously strained inter-Yemeni relations and put future relations back on the firm foundations laid down during the several years before the PDRY's leadership crisis in 1986, the **13 January events.** The agreements were reached by YAR President **Salih** and Yemeni Socialist Party Secretary General **al-Baydh.** One called for restoration of the **Supreme Yemeni Council** and the lesser organs that had functioned from mid-1982 until the leadership crisis, preparation of a new timetable for adoption of the draft constitution for a united Yemen, and establishment of the **Joint Committee on a Unified Political Organization.** Another agreement provided for the free movement of Yemenis between the two parts of Yemen, an arrangement that was to be implemented over two months and that would involve new joint border posts and the use of nothing more than identity cards.

Last was the several-part agreement that resolved the potentially explosive dispute over the border area between **Marib** and **Shabwa,** a dispute made salient by the strong possibility of **oil** reserves in that area. The agreement called for demilitarization of an 850-square-mile neutral zone, establishment of a joint corporation to explore for oil and minerals in that area, and authorization of the oil ministers of the two Yemens to launch this project.

14 OCTOBER REVOLUTION. *See* RADFAN AND THE RADFAN REBELLION.

FRANKINCENSE AND FRANKINCENCE TRAIL. *See* INCENSE AND OTHER FRAGRANCES; TRADE ROUTES, ANCIENT; TRADING KINGDOMS, SOUTH ARABIAN.

FREE OFFICERS ASSOCIATION. The 15 or so junior officers who were at the center of the planning and execution of the **1962 Revolution** in North Yemen that overthrew the **imamate** and replaced it with the YAR. The group, which included a few of the **Famous Forty** who had studied in Egypt from the late 1940s to the mid-1950s, was inspired by the 1952 Egyptian Revolution and **Nasserism.** The Free

Officers recruited Abdullah **al-Sallal** and the other prominent senior officers as participants in the revolt, only to be largely upstaged or shunted aside by these older figures in the sharp political struggles that followed.

FREE YEMENI PARTY. Founded in Aden in 1944 by such fathers of the modern Yemeni nation-state as Muhammad Mahmud **al-Zubayri**, Ahmad Muhammad **Numan** and Ahmad M. **al-Shami**, the Free Yemeni Party (al-Ahrar) was the first major modern expression by North Yemenis for constitutional reform and political opposition to the **Hamid al-Din imamate.** In 1946, with funds from **Shafii** merchants from the north, the Free Yemenis founded a newspaper, *Sawt al-Yaman*, to voice their case and demands for reform in imamate Yemen. The paper ceased after some months, only to be revived by Numan in Cairo in 1955 as an organ for the **Yemeni Union.**

Although it existed as an organization for only a few years in the 1940s, the Free Yemeni Party had a major role to play in the events that led to the failed **1948 Revolution**—and in laying the foundations for the successful **1962 Revolution** years later. However, far from being radical political modernists, the Free Yemenis started out as the mid-20th-century equivalents of the Turkish reformers of the **Ottoman** Empire during the Tanzimat period of the 19th century. They quickly evolved from reformism and a constitutional imamate to new political ideas and the means of expressing them—i.e., the ideas of republicanism and revolution, and the Yemeni Union. Indeed, a fairly straight line goes from the short-lived Free Yemeni Party to the 1962 Revolution.

FREE ZONE, ADEN. *See* ADEN CONTAINER PORT AND FREE ZONE.

FRONT FOR THE LIBERATION OF OCCUPIED SOUTH YEMEN (FLOSY). The South Yemeni independence movement that was forged under heavy Egyptian pressure in early 1966 out of a combination of the **National Liberation Front** (NLF) and the **Organization for the Liberation of the Occupied South** (OLOS), when the NLF quickly backed out, Flosy became nothing more than a renamed OLOS, the political property of Abdullah **al-Asnag** and Abd al-Qawi **Makkawi**—and the political opponent that the NLF would fight and defeat in its successful effort to succeed **Great Britain** in South Yemen in 1967. FLOSY then became a vehicle for opposition from abroad to the NLF-dominated PDRY, especially for Makkawi, and it remained so, but with decreasing relevance after the late 1960s.

FUNDAMENTALISM, ISLAMIC. *See* POLITICAL ISLAM, MODERN.

– G –

AL-GAMISH, GHALIB. *See* SECURITY SERVICES.

GARBAGE AND WASTE DISPOSAL. *See* INFRASTRUCTURE DEVELOPMENT.

GAS. *See* OIL AND GAS EXPLORATION AND PRODUCTION.

GENDER AND GENDER POLITICS. *See* WOMEN, RIGHTS AND POSITION OF.

GENERAL INVESTMENT AUTHORITY (GIA). The much-heralded organization called for in the Investment Law of 1991 for the purpose of attracting to the ROY capital from overseas Yemeni, other Arabs, and non-Arab sources by providing "one-stop shopping" and guidance on a simplified set of foreign investment steps and requirements. As in the case of previous efforts to attract investments, the success of this one has depended less on the concept than it has on actual organization, administration, and personnel—and the record of the GIA over its first 15 years was spotty at best, and slow to improve. Most of the investments it facilitated have been modest in size, and the total number has been disappointing.

In all fairness, however, the lasting effects of the First **Gulf War** in 1991, the **War of Secession** in 1994, and the **War on Terror** since 2001 did nothing to create an economic environment conducive to the work of the GIA. Nevertheless, growing concern in the donor community and among some key Yemeni political actors over the need for poverty reduction and the imminence of a post-oil economy did lead to an effort in 2007 to give the GIA an enhanced role.

GENERAL PEOPLE'S CONGRESS (GPC). The umbrella political party created in the YAR by the **Salih regime** in 1982 that remained the dominant political organization during the last years of the YAR and, except for the years of power sharing during the transition period after **unification** in 1990, during the life of the ROY. After its initial task of meeting to revise and adopt the **National Pact**, the GPC was transformed into a permanent body charged with articulating national goals, in accordance with that pact, and with organizing political life toward the achievement of those goals.

The **1970 Constitution** prohibited political parties, and President Salih initially claimed that it was a "political institution," not a party. However, the GPC quickly articulated most of the features of a modern party, such as a permanent secretariat, political cadres and cadres training, popular political education programs, and its own mass media organs. President Salih has been president of the GPC since its creation, and Dr. Abd al-Karim **al-Iryani** was secretary general from 1995 to 2005, yielding that office to then-Prime Minister Abd al-Qadr **Bajammal** in late 2005.

The nature and function of the GPC reflect President Salih's notion of it as an umbrella party or movement—a "big tent" for all people. Positively, for the Salih regime, this has made it possible for the GPC to accommodate a broad spectrum of political views and interests and, in the process, to co-opt members of other parties, sapping those parties of their strength. On the negative side, by almost replicating Yemeni society, by being all things to all people, the GPC has meant little for many people. At its worst, it has become the party for government workers and others dependent on the regime—a party for careerists.

With Yemen unification in 1990, the big task for the GPC as a ruling party was to adjust to the new multi-party environment and to extend itself into South Yemen. The learning curve was steep during the period of joint rule and power sharing with the **Yemeni Socialist Party** (YSP) and then in coalition governments with the YSP and/or **Islah** after parliamentary **elections** in 1993. Since its big victory in the next elections in 1997, the GPC has chosen to form governments without any partners.

As to the GPC's internal governance, 700 of the congress's 1,000 members are elected (the balance are appointed), and popular participation in these internal elections was expanded and further institutionalized in 1985. The congress is selected for four-year terms, meets biennially, and is represented between sessions by a prestigious 75-member Standing Committee headed by the president of the GPC.

GEOGRAPHY AND CLIMATE. The ROY is located on the southwest corner of the **Arabian Peninsula**. Bounded on one side by the **Red Sea** and on the other by the **Gulf of Aden** and the **Arabian Sea**, this corner of the peninsula is pointed toward the African continent and is separated from **Ethiopia** and **Djibouti**—and, more generally, the rest of the **Horn of Africa**—by only the narrow **Bab al-Mandab Straits**. To the north and northeast lies **Saudi Arabia** and to the east is **Oman**, the ROY's only contiguous neighbors. The country is relatively small in area, its estimated 182,278 square miles making it somewhat smaller than California and Oregon combined, and considerably smaller than France. Although the country itself is dwarfed by Saudi Arabia, which has four-and-a-half times its area and occupies most of the Arabian Peninsula, the ROY's population of about 24,000,000 may be as much as twice that of the indigenous Saudi population and is certainly more than half that of the entire peninsula.

Yemen and its people were largely shaped by the geography of the place. Geologically, much of Yemen is the upturned corner of the rectangular plate that defines the Arabian Peninsula. The upturned edge takes the form of a steep, jagged mountain range—in places, an escarpment—that forms the western and southern edge of a high plateau, the Yemeni highlands, that descends gradually east and north from these mountains until it is lost in the desert interior on the edge of the vast **Empty Quarter**.

About 25 miles inland from the Red Sea and originating in **Asir**, the Sarat mountains rises abruptly from a low, flat coastal desert plain, the **Tihama**. These mountains parallel the sea, running north to south the length of North Yemen, and then abruptly turn east near **Turba** and the old border between the two Yemens. They then run east, parallel to the Gulf of Aden, for part of the length of South Yemen and slowly but greatly diminish in height. The mountains average several thousand feet in North Yemen, and at one point rise to the highest point on the Arabian Peninsula at about 12,300 feet—at Jabal Nabi Shuayb—some 20 miles west of Sanaa, just north of the main road from Sanaa down to the coast via **Manakha**. An easy hike to the top, it affords a fine view in all directions, especially north to **Shibam–Kawkaban**.

The Yemeni highlands have a generally semi-arid, but otherwise temperate climate, despite being located well south of the Tropic of Cancer. The temperature rarely drops to freezing, and snow is extremely rare. By contrast, the Tihama coast is hot and humid much of the year, and at times extremely so, as are Aden and the coasts of the Gulf of Aden and Arabian Sea.

Thanks to the annual **monsoon** winds that blow inland after crossing the water, picking up moisture, the mountains mean seasonal rainfall; they cause the warm air to rise, cool, and drop its moisture. It is this considerable, albeit erratic, annual rainfall that accounts for intensive cultivation, much of it in stream bottoms—wadis—and on steep, terraced hillsides, and for the relatively dense sedentary agricultural population that has resided in Yemen for millennia. Over these centuries, Yemen had a largely self-sufficient **economy** based mostly on subsistence **agriculture**.

The highlands are loftier and more prevalent in the former YAR than in the former PDRY, hence the former's generally less hot and arid climate, greater rainfall, more intensive and extensive agriculture and considerably larger population. Indeed, the eastern two-thirds of the old South Yemen are all but uninhabitable, except for coastal oases, fishing villages, the port of **Mukalla**, and, deep in the interior, the large, densely populated Wadi **Hadhramawt**. Half again larger in area than the former North Yemen, the former South Yemen has less than one-third as many people—in 2004, roughly 5 million compared to 17 million. Nearly all of the north's population is sedentary, something that is only somewhat less the case in the south. What nomadic pastoralists there are can be found in and on the edge of the desert near the eastern border with Saudi Arabia. Life in most of Yemen, north or south, is constrained severely by the shortage of water, and the water table in many areas—most notably, the Sanaa basin—is now falling at an alarming rate.

The ROY has at least eight distinct regions: the northern highlands that include much of the upper half of old North Yemen and that are bounded on the west by the mountains; the southern uplands that consist of the lower half of North Yemen and include the regions of **Taiz** and **Ibb**, Yemen's breadbasket; the Tihama, the narrow coastal desert that runs the length of North Yemen between the Red Sea and the mountains; the arid east, on the edge of the desert, consisting of the remote regions of **Marib, al-Jawf,** and **Shabwa**; far to the south, **Aden** and its hinterland, running from the Arabian Sea up to the mountains between the two Yemens; far to the east, Wadi Hadhramawt, an isolated island of dense habitation enclosed by the hills and cliffs of the large, arid Hadhramawt region; even farther to the east, along the Arabian Sea and bordering on Oman, the culturally distinct **Mahra** region; and the magical, otherworldly **Socotra** Island, in the Gulf of Aden, well off the coast of South Yemen.

The ROY has four major cities: **Sanaa** (the capital), Aden, al-Hudayda, and Taiz. Aden and al-Hudayda are the major ports, the former being one of the greatest and best-protected natural harbors in the world. There are several large towns: **Saada**, far to the north; **Dhamar, Yarim**, and Ibb, in the middle region; Mukalla, on the southern coast; and, in Wadi Hadhramawt, the trio of **Shibam, Seiyun**, and **Tarim**. The population of the former PDRY is highly concentrated in a few places—in Mukalla and the towns of Wadi Hadhramawt, in the highlands north and east of Aden, and, above all, in Aden proper and its environs. By contrast, the far larger population of the former YAR is much more widely scattered over a great many towns, villages, and hamlets, this despite the huge growth of Sanaa and the considerable growth of al-Hudayda, Taiz, and the other cities and large towns in recent decades. Thus, the combined populations of Sana, Taiz and al-Hudayda make up roughly only 20 percent of North Yemen's total.

GERMANY. Partly a reflection of the **Cold War**, the Federal Republic of Germany (FRG), West Germany, became a major patron of the YAR, and the German Democratic Republic (GDR), East Germany, became a major patron of the PDRY in the 1970s and 1980s. West Germany in 1969 was the first western country to establish diplomatic relations and extend aid to the politically isolated YAR near the end of the **Yemen Civil War**, and this involved a major *quid pro quo*: West Germany provided the YAR with the opening to the West and western aid that, out of deference to **Saudi Arabia**, had been denied to the YAR during the civil war, and the YAR broke the boycott imposed on West Germany by the Arab states for its having provided military aid to Israel in the mid-1960s. For years thereafter, West Germany was the biggest and perhaps most successful donor of aid to the YAR, something partly traceable to advantages inherent to its role as provider, beginning in the mid-1970s, of institutional support for the **Central Planning Organization**. Thereafter, relations between the two countries flourished, this despite the fact that the YAR also maintained very good relations with East Germany.

By contrast, West Germany suspended diplomatic relations with South Yemen when the latter recognized East Germany in 1969. Although relations were restored in 1974, this did not result in aid or very friendly ties between the PDRY and the FRG. By contrast, South Yemen and East Germany established and maintained good relations, and the latter provided over many years institutional support for the organization and operation of the former's intelligence and security services. Many young South Yemenis went to the GDR for technical training and higher education, and in late 1979 the two countries signed a 20-year treaty of friendship and cooperation.

Yemeni **unification** preceded by a matter of months the unification of the two Germanys in 1990. When a German reporter covering the ROY's creation noted the pending German event, ROY's President Ali Abdullah **Salih**, perhaps tongue-in-cheek and mindful of the much aid given by the two Germanys to the two Yemens, offered Yemeni assistance to the Germans for their unification. Unification behind both of them, the ROY and Germany continued to maintain good relations, and considerable German aid continued to come to the ROY. Although relations were strained in 2004 when Germany extradited a prominent Yemeni cleric to the United States, relations and aid levels got boosts with President Salih's visit to Germany late that year and the high-profile visit of Prime Minister Gerhard Schroeder to the ROY in early 2005.

AL-GHADIR, NAJI IBN ALI. The **Bakil** chief from the **Khawlan al-Tiyal** who, more than most Yemeni **tribal** leaders, became rich, powerful, and independent during the long **Yemen Civil War** by playing the **royalists** and republicans against each other and by taking money, arms, and other gratuities from both sides. His place in history, however, is based on a consequence of his also profiting by helping the Saudis aid the cross-border guerrilla activities of South Yemeni opponents of the revolutionary PDRY regime. In early 1972, in a spectacular deception, the PDRY lured al-Ghadir and dozens of his lesser shaykhs over the border for talks and then blew them all up in a booby-trapped banquet tent, an event that enraged other North Yemeni tribal leaders and made them prime actors in the bellicose talk and action that escalated into the **border war** between the two Yemens later that year.

GHALEB, MUHAMMAD ANAAM (*CA.* 1933–2009). The **Hujari-yya**-born and Aden-, Cairo-, and United States-trained first-generation Yemeni **modernist**, poet-intellectual, and nationalist who, after returning from exile to the YAR in 1968 and serving as minister of economics and in other posts, spent most of his career in public service as the first dean of the National Institute for Public Administration (NIPA), a post he held until the early 1990s. He was appointed to the new **Shura Council** in 1997.

Muhammad Anaam was a both a modernist and a man with a love of Yemen's long history. He often said that Ahmad M. **Numan**—known widely as al-Ustaz (the professor)—was his teacher, and that he in turn was al-Ustaz for the next generation. Also a poet, he was one of the first Yemenis writing in Arabic on modern themes and in western poetic forms. Much of his poetry, especially in his volume *Strangers on the Road*, is reminiscent of Albert Camus and expresses achingly the existential alienation and doubts about the identity of the Yemeni **emigrant** in the modern world.

Going to Cairo in 1949, Muhammad Anaam completed his law degree in the mid-1950s and then went to the United States as one of the first four Yemenis to receive a Point IV scholarship. He studied economics at the University of Texas between 1958 and 1960. Back in Aden at the time of the **1962 Revolution**, he went north and became minister of education in 1963. He went into exile later that year and spent much of the time until late 1968 teaching in Aden at the **Bilqis** Preparatory College.

His career in government in the YAR revived in 1968, during the **al-Iryani** era, when, in addition to serving again as minister of economics, he founded the Technical Office in 1968, precursor to the **Central Planning Office**. He recruited a team of young, able Yemeni graduates and foreign experts and set them to collecting the data and doing the analyses he felt were needed for the YAR's development; they prepared the YAR's first statistical yearbook and did initial studies toward the first national census.

Headed by Muhammad Anaam, NIPA was created in 1974 for the purpose of training civil servants and otherwise upgrading public administration. Preceded by a small clerical and secretarial institute founded only months after the 1962 Revolution, over the years NIPA received considerable support from the United Nations and other donors.

GHAMDAN PALACE. Fabled royal palace built in **Sanaa** a few centuries before the rise of Islam by the rulers of the dual kingdom of **Saba** and **Himyar**, a palace that Yemeni legend says was a 20-story tower roofed with translucent alabaster, allowing those within to see the forms of birds flying overhead, and guarded at its four corners by hollow statues of lions fashioned so that they roared when the wind blew. Residents of Sanaa today can point out the mound that is the alleged site of the palace. They claim that the palace served as model and inspiration for "skyscraper" houses that grace and distinguish Sanaa even today.

AL-GHASHMI, AHMAD HUSAYN (*CA.* 1923–1978). A career soldier of limited education and strong **tribal** connections, al-Ghashmi provided crucial support to President Ibrahim **al-Hamdi** in his struggle to consolidate power in the YAR after the 1974 coup. Commander of armored forces at the time of the coup, he occupied the number-two post as **armed forces** chief of staff for the next three years. Al-Ghashmi was involved directly in the assassination of al-Hamdi in October 1977, succeeded Al-Hamdi as president, and then was assassinated in June 1978—after only eight months in office. He was killed in his office by a briefcase bomb carried by an emissary from the PDRY. His demise had little or nothing to do with YAR politics and much to do with the epic power struggle going on in the PDRY at the time.

Born in Dhula, an area just northwest of Sanaa, Al-Ghashmi's older brother was the paramount shaykh of the strategically located, but otherwise not very important or powerful, **Hamdan** tribe. Fears of his **modernist** critics notwithstanding, al-Ghashmi during his short tenure seemed inclined to protect the weak Yemeni state from its **tribal** challengers and from **Saudi Arabia**.

AL-GHAYDA. *See* MAHRA PROVINCE AND SULTANATE.

GLOBAL REVOLUTIONARY ISLAM, MODERN. *See* POLITICAL ISLAM, MODERN.

GOLDMUR HOTEL BOMBING, 1992. *See* AL-FADHLI, TARIK.

GOVERNORATES (MUHAFAZAH). The largest territorial units into which the two Yemeni states were divided, comparable to the provinces of France and other modern unitary states. South Yemen, in an effort to transcend "reactionary" regional and tribal identifications, created seven governorates and then labeled them numerically, "One" to "Seven." In fact, the seven did roughly correspond to historic regions or areas, and in 1980 six of the seven were given place names and the seventh, **Thamoud**, was merged into the **Hadhramawt**. The six are **Aden** (formerly First); **Lahej** (Second); **Abyan** (Third); **Shabwa** (Fourth); Hadhramawt (Fifth); and **Mahra** (Sixth).

The YAR had 11 governorates in the 1980s, having added **al-Mahwit** in the mid-1970s and **al-Jawf** in 1980. The 11, listed roughly from highest to lowest in population size, are **Taiz, Ibb, Sanaa, al-Hudayda, Dhamar, Hajja, al-Baydha, al-Mahwit, Saada, Marib,** and **al-Jawf**. It was announced shortly after Yemeni **unification** in 1990 that the governorates abutting the old border between the two Yemens would be reconfigured so as to erase this old border. In fact, little was done in this regard. The governorates of **Dhala** and **Rayma** were subsequently carved out of existing territorial units, bringing the total to 19.

Talk about governorates in an essentially unitary political system is almost inseparable from the issues of decentralization, autonomy, and local self-rule. And talk about decentralization, a major issue in the political crisis that resulted in the **War of Secession** in 1994, has since 1994 focused on the issue of the powers of district- and governorate-level **local councils**.

GREAT BRITAIN. Britain began to make itself felt in South Arabia in the 17th century, countering **Portuguese** and **Ottoman** Turkish thrusts into the area. The East India Company, the English trading company chartered in 1600, became involved in its first years in the growing **coffee** trade in Yemen at **al-Mukha**. Two hundred years later, as a result of the activities of Napoleon in **Egypt** and **Muhammad Ali** on the Arabian Peninsula, the company became interested in **Aden** as a possible coaling station and, more ambitiously, as a base to secure strategically the western approaches to British possessions in India.

British **colonial administration** both came relatively late to South Yemen and and stayed there until the sunset of the empire. Sir Robert Grant was the British Governor of Bombay in the late 1830s and, unlike his superior, the Governor General of India, was a staunch believer in seizing Aden and adding it to the empire. It was he who dispatched Commander A.B. **Haines** of the Bombay Marines to seize Aden in 1839. Lord Gladstone, the foreign secretary at the time of the seizure, favored the move and the activist imperial policy of his Whig government. This controversial policy regarding Aden prevailed, only to be followed shortly both by the end of the threat posed to British access to India by Muhammad Ali's push down the coast of Arabia to Yemen and by the formation of a more cautious government in London.

The second Otoman occupation of North Yemen, beginning in 1849, meant decades of confrontation between the two imperial powers in Yemen. Early in World War I, this confrontation ended in something of a Gilbert and Sullivan imperial moment. Sent with reinforcements from Egypt on the dire report that "the Turks are on the golf course" outside Aden, General Sir George Younghusband succeeded in stopping the enemy. This led to a more than three-year standoff with both sides dug in at **Shaykh Othman**—a standoff that ended only with the end of the war and Turkish forces embarking from Aden amidst pomp and circumstance.

In an effort to protect its growing interests, in the 1920s and 1930s Britain gradually extended its influence over the territories to the north and east of the port and garrison of Aden, eventually organizing them into the Western **Aden Protectorate** and the Eastern Aden Protectorate. As had been the case with the Ottomans, these efforts brought Britain into periods of intense diplomatic and military contact with the expansive **Hamid al-Din** imamate that succeeded the Turks and, then, the YAR that replaced the **imamate** after the **1962 Revolution**. Months later, Tory Prime Minister Harold Macmillan decided to withhold diplomatic recognition from the new Egyptian-dominated YAR. The reports of MP and adventurer Col. "Billy" McLean, based on his wide travels in the eastern part of North Yemen after the revolution, helped convince the government and public opinion that the new YAR should not be granted diplomatic recognition. He argued that the little-known country was in the throes of the **Yemeni Civil War**, in which the **royalists** controlled most of the country and the republicans survived only through Egypt's big military intervention. Macmillan also pushed for a merger between Aden and the new **Federation of Arab Amirates of the South**, hoping that such a merger would contain the rising nationalism and political turmoil in Aden. The **Federation of South Arabia** (FSA) was the result.

After World War II, Britain had greatly increased its presence in Aden and the protectorates, making them the heart of its "East of Suez" policy. With the Suez Crisis of 1956, a milestone in **Arab–Israeli** conflict, Britain became increasingly preoccupied with the status and governance of these possessions. The Conservative government's Defense White Paper of 1957 concluded that meeting Britain's security responsibilities in the Far East and Australasia would require a base "East of Suez." It was believed that hostile Arab countries, able to refuse access to airspace, could act as a barrier between British forces in the Mediterranean and vital areas east of Suez. This decision led to the fourfold increase in military personnel in Aden in three years, with dramatic effect on the society and economy of that city. However, actions taken on these perceived defense needs ran head-on into rising anti-colonialism in Aden, making for the worst possible timing for these changes.

Tory Prime Minister Sir Alec Douglas Hume was in office when the politics of Aden and the protectorates changed radically during the first half of the 1960s. Those changes, and especially the emergence of the **National Liberation Front** (NLF) and "armed struggle," largely determined when and how Britain would depart and who would be left in charge. The thoughts and actions of the conservative government during this period involved a reluctant but steady retreat from the old assumption that Aden, almost like Gibraltar, was British and would remain so forever. This was paralleled from the late 1950s through the mid-1960s by the complex rise and then sudden demise of the FSA.

It was, however, the coming to power of the Labour Party and Prime Minister Harold Wilson in 1964 that decided Britain's quick exodus and the transfer of authority to the NLF in 1967. The Defense White Paper of 1966 declared that South Arabia would become independent by 31 December 1968 and that all British forces would be withdrawn at that time. Prompted by budgetary reasons, this action reversed the Defense White Paper of 1957. It rendered moot the Hone–Bell Report of only months earlier that had laid out a framework for a sovereign federation—the FSA—as a means of squaring the interests of more modern Aden with those of the traditional protectorate states. It also pulled the rug from under those Adenis and the **Federalis** who had staked their political futures on an FSA that both included Aden and was tied to Britain by a defense treaty and a continuing British military presence. Finally, it also caused Egypt's President Gamal Abdul **Nasser** to decide to maintain a large military presence in the north in the ongoing Yemeni Civil War in order to be better positioned to influence and take advantage of the course of events in South Yemen before and after Britain's withdrawal. Britain's departure from Aden and the creation of an independent South Yemen in 1967 was the end of an era.

GREATER YEMEN. "Natural," "historic," or "cultural" Yemen— "bilaad al-yaman"—has been differently defined by Yemenis and non-Yemenis over the centuries. Perhaps the designation most widely shared among Yemenis since the early 20th century has had Yemen going from Hali on the **Red Sea** in the north to the Kuria–Muria Islands in the **Arabian Sea** in the east, and including the vast land of mountains, high plateau, and coastal and eastern interior desert between those places. This definition cut deeply into the territories of both modern **Saudi Arabia** and modern **Oman**. This was not a burning issue for many Yemenis in the second half of the 20th century, preoccupied as they were with gaining control of one or the other of the two Yemens as defined by international law in the 20th century, and then with the question of Yemeni **unification**. In any case, expansive views of a Greater Yemen were pretty much put to rest by final **border agreements** with Oman and Saudi Arabia in 1991 and 2000, respectively.

GULF, THE. The Persian (or Arab) Gulf is the long, narrow body of water with **Iraq** at it northern end, **Iran** on its north side, and all the Arab states of the **Arabian Peninsula** (except Yemen)—**Saudi Arabia**, **Kuwait**, Bahrayn, the **United Arab Emirates**, **Qatar**, and **Oman**—on its southern and its mouth. Although on the other side of the peninsula from the two Yemens, and separated from them by vast deserts, the Gulf states have had a big impact on the Yemens, especially the YAR (since the early 1970s) and the ROY (since Yemen **unification** in 1990).

Significant during the Age of Imperialism for its strategic location, and since the mid-20th century for its huge reserves of **oil** and gas, the gulf has meant for the YAR since about 1970—and for the ROY since 1990—jobs and aid but also political problems. The YAR, in particular, was dangerously dependent upon the Gulf states for aid and **remittances**. The YAR's attempt to use aid and support from Kuwait and then Iraq as counterweights to an overbearing Saudi Arabia ended suddenly in 1990 in the events surrounding the First **Gulf War**. Since then, the ROY has devoted much effort to mend relations and secure aid from the Arab Gulf states that make up the **Gulf Cooperation Council**.

GULF COOPERATION COUNCIL (GCC). The regional alliance of six mostly oil-rich but otherwise weak and vulnerable Arab **Gulf** states that was formed in 1981 for the purpose of advancing and defending the mutual interests of those states—**Saudi Arabia, Kuwait**, Bahrayn, the **United Arab Emirates**, **Qatar**, and **Oman**. The major events in the regional environment that prompted the creation of the GCC were the **Iranian** Islamic Revolution and the **Iraq–Iran War**, and it was hegemonic Saudi Arabia that led, and that has subsequently dominated, this Gulf initiative. The YAR was conspicuously absent from the GCC, and the PDRY (or at least the militant PDRY of the late 1960s and the 1970s) was clearly a hypothetical opponent. Although greeted by much of the rest of the world with more than a little skepticism during most of its first decade, the GCC kept itself very busy with meetings, studies, decisions, and a not inconsiderable number of concrete joint actions.

The **Arab Cooperation Council** (ACC), created in 1988 and consisting of Iraq, Egypt, Jordan, and the YAR, was designed in part as a counter to the GCC. The GCC took on a greatly increased significance two years later with the Iraqi invasion of member Kuwait and the ensuing First **Gulf War**. The GCC and its member states, especially Saudi Arabia and Kuwait, harshly punished the newly created ROY for, in effect, siding with Iraq. Most of the members cut ties and aid, and Saudi Arabia expelled several hundred thousand Yemeni workers.

The ROY devoted much effort in the second half of the 1990s to repairing relations with—and regaining aid from—Saudi Arabia and the other GCC states, and much of that effort focused on the effort to gain membership in the GCC. The ROY first applied for membership at the end of 1996 and was denied membership on that occasion, but was admitted several years later to GCC ministerial councils on education, health, social affairs, and sports. GCC aid and support to the ROY did increase considerably, often in the name of getting Yemen up to some vague standards required for future membership. Privately, many GCC leaders remain skeptical of ROY as a member and see increased aid primarily as lessening the likelihood of a politically unstable and dangerous Yemen on the Arabian Peninsula.

GULF OF ADEN. The narrow arm of water connecting the **Red Sea**, via the **Bab al-Mandab Straits**, to the **Arabian Sea** and Indian Ocean, bounded on the north by Yemen and on the south by **Djibouti** and **Somalia**. This configuration of land and sea, funneling sea traffic from the Indian Ocean, enhanced the ability of anyone in command of air and naval forces in Aden to control access to the Red Sea and this major sea lane.

GULF WAR (1991), FIRST. The explosive international crisis that began on 2 August 1990 with **Iraq**'s invasion and occupation of **Kuwait**, precipitating the mobilization led by the **United States** and **Saudi Arabia** against Iraq and ending with the massive U.S.-led military campaign, Operation Desert Storm, that expelled Iraqi forces from Kuwait in early 1991. Coming just a little more than two months after formal Yemeni **unification**, the occupation of Kuwait blindsided Yemenis elated by and preoccupied with the ROY. Close regional ties with Iraq, strong personal ties between Saddam Husayn and President **Salih**, and the desire to assert its independence from **Saudi Arabia** caused the ROY to favor an Arab diplo-political solution at variance with the U.S.- and Saudi-led effort.

As chance had it, the ROY was also a member of the UN Security Council at this time. As the crisis unfolded in the fall of 1990, it abstained from or voted against several resolutions favored by the United States and, most important, joined **Cuba** in November in voting against the resolution authorizing the possible use of force against Iraq. After the vote, a top U.S. official rhetorically asked the ROY ambassador to the UN whether he realized that this vote was probably the most expensive vote he would ever cast. The United States, Saudi Arabia, and the other Arab Gulf states immediately cut off relations and economic aid to the ROY. Most important, the Saudis expelled several hundred thousand Yemeni workers and many small businessmen—more than 5 percent of Yemen's population—virtually destroying the **remittance economy** upon which Yemen depended.

The economic hardship and social dislocation caused by the loss of aid and the remittances and by the influx of unemployed returnees added greatly to the inevitable difficulties involved in unification. Arguably, the unification regime headed by President Salih initially gained more support than it lost, able as it was to blame others for the hard times and to play upon deep-seated anti-Saudi feelings to rally the nation. Thereafter, however, the growing ranks of opponents to the Salih regime used its stand on the Gulf crisis to attack unification itself, thereby adding to the political crisis that resulted in the **War of Secession** in 1994. It would be several years before the ROY overcame most of the effects of its stand on the Gulf War—and, late in the first decade of the 21st century, it had not yet overcome the effects of the end of the remittance system.

– H –

HABASH, GEORGE. *See* ARAB NATIONALIST MOVEMENT (ANM); PALESTINE AND THE PALESTINE QUESTION.

HADDA. Hadda village, road, and urban western enclave has come to epitomize **Sanaa**'s transformation over the generation from the early 1970s into the 21st century. In the mid-1970s, the paved portion of Hadda Road ended only several blocks south of downtown Sanaa, and the dirt road then ran maybe three miles past the Hadda Ramada Hotel and the oil and soap factory before reaching the low hills around the village of Hadda. Nearby were the imam's well-watered gardens with the big orchards of almond and apricot trees, a place where Sanaani families loved to come and picnic on Thursdays or Fridays. By 1990, Hadda Road was paved out to and far beyond the now indiscernible village and gardens; the springs had dried up, the flowering fruit trees had died, and no one picnicked there. From downtown Sanaa to the "village," both sides of the road were now filled chock-a-block with embassies, foreign residential compounds, hotels, upscale stores, restaurants, and Sanaa's largest supermarket. The change was and is breathtaking—and, not unquestionably, progressively so. Still, Hadda Road is to the Sanaa of 2005 what Hamra Street was to the Beirut of 1970.

HADHRAMAWT AND WADI HADHRAMAWT. The largest, mostly inhospitable region of Yemen that begins nearly 200 miles east northeast of **Aden** and is largely defined by the Wadi Hadhramawt, with its huge watercourse and drainage basin, and the land that lies between it and the **Empty Quarter** of **Saudi Arabia**, to the north, and the land between it and the seacoast, to the south. The long, wide, and deep wadi and its many lesser tributaries, the repositories of the groundwater that supports a relatively large population and considerable agriculture, constitute one of the largest and most distinctive geographic and sociopolitical subregions in Yemen. Among the major regions of South Yemen, it ranks second in population size only to Aden and its environs. To the north and south of the wadi is the barren, virtually uninhabitable, high limestone plateau called the **Jol**. Bunched-together in the wadi are three large and strikingly different towns—**Shibam**, **Seiyun**, and **Tarim**—and to the south, and in the shadow of the Jol, is the busy seaport **Mukalla** now connected to Seiyun by a modern highway. In the past, Wadi Duan, a long, narrow wadi that bends south to north into the larger wadi near Shibam, was the main overland route between Mukalla on the coast and the interior. Wadi Duan is famed for its honey, dates, beautiful villages, rich families, and palatial homes—and as the ancestral home of the **bin Laden** family.

In ancient, pre-Islamic times, the Hadhramawt **trading kingdom** was strong and renowned. For much of the past millennium, and down to recent decades, the Hadhramawt has been tied together by complex patterns of emigration and remittances with Southeast Asia, the Indian subcontinent, and East Africa, making it quite dependent on distant places to the east and south—and quite independent of relatively nearby Aden to the west. Through much of the 19th and early 20th centuries, the Hadhramis was preoccupied with the **Quaiti** and **Kathiri** sultanates, the Quaiti–Kathiri War and **Great Britain's** gradual assertion of control over the region.

Many Hadhramis do not look and behave like most other Yemenis, the result of a cultural blend, broad horizons, and intermarriage with non-Yemenis. One of the major concerns of the regime in the PDRY after independence in 1967 was tying the Hadhramawt firmly to Aden and its environs, a concern shared by the **Salih regime** after Yemeni **unification** in 1990. Providing material support for this concern was the discovery in **Masila** just before unification of Yemen's largest reserves of **oil**.

Indeed, since the early 1990s, many Hadhramis have come to question whether they are Yemenis, or even want to be Yemenis. What started out in the **War of Secession** in 1994 as an attempt to reestablish the South Yemen of 1967–1990 quickly devolved into an attempt by Ali Salim **al-Baydh** to create an oil-rich mini-state of the

Hadhramawt, an outcome that Saudi Arabia welcomed and actively supported. Nevertheless, with the survival of the ROY assured in 1994, many affluent Hadhramis in Yemen and in the Gulf and beyond were caught up by the idea of investing in their homeland. This faded in the second half of the 1990s as they found their wealth at the mercy of corrupt and greedy North Yemeni politicians and military officers bent on reaping the spoils of war. Prominent Hadhramis soured on the ROY to the point that by the middle of the first decade of the 21st century many of them admitted that they were just waiting to seize any opportunity to have the Hadhramawt go its own way. Knowledge of these sentiments made the Salih regime suspicious of calls for decentralization and regional autonomy. *See also* HYDERABAD.

AL-HADI ILA AL-HAQQ YAHYA IBN HUSAYN. *See* ZAYDI SHI-ISM IN YEMEN.

HAINES, COMMANDER A. B. The British commander of the Bombay Marines who from the mid-1830s advocated the establishment of a British base at **Aden**, led the forces that actually occupied Aden peninsula in 1839, and then served there as political agent until 1854. Haines had a grand vision of Aden as a port, commercial center, and military base, and he used his almost unlimited powers during these years to realize his vision for that tiny, almost abandoned coastal fishing town. Nevertheless, he was recalled to Bombay in 1854 under a cloud of charges of financial irregularities, and, although acquitted of charges, spent all but the last days of the last six years of his life in a debtor's prison.

HAJJA. The province and provincial capital high in the rugged Yemeni highlands west-northwest of Sanaa. Quite remote and parochial, like **al-Mahwit** directly to the south, Hajja was reached by paved road only at the beginning of the 1980s. It opened up, joined the rest of the country, and has benefited from considerable development since that time. The Hajja region had been a stronghold of the **Zaydi** imamate, and Hajja town is the site of the infamous prison in which so many of the famous Yemenis involved in the failed **1948 Revolution** were kept for several years. North of Hajja is Shahara, a center of learning and another stronghold in which harried **imams** from time to time took refuge—for example, during the first decades of the **Ottoman** Turkish reoccupation of North Yemen after 1850. Shahara is best known today for its old, beautiful, gravity-defying stone bridge.

AL-HAJRI, QADI ABDULLAH. The very religious and traditional **qadi** who, after loyally serving the imams and siding with the **royalists** in the Yemeni Civil War, helped pave the way for the republican–royalist **reconciliation** by switching sides and working to give the **al-Iryani** regime a more pronounced conservative cast to its republicanism. He used his year as prime minister in 1973 to secure from his Saudi friends large amounts of state-to-state aid on a regular, annual basis. To secure that aid, however, he renewed suspension of Yemen's claim to regions to the north controlled by **Saudi Arabia** under the 1934 **Taif Treaty**, and was harshly criticized for this by Yemeni nationalists. He also cracked down harshly on leftists in general, and North Yemeni friends of the PDRY regime in particular. In the mid-1970s, al-Hajri acted as a fatherly adviser to the much younger, and much less conservative, President **al-Hamdi**. He was assassinated in London in early 1977, possibly on the orders of al-Hamdi, who may have feared that al-Hajri and the Saudis were plotting to replace him with a more conservative and submissive client.

The al-Hajri family remained well-connected and quite prominent. President Ali Abdullah **Salih** subsequently married one of Qadi Abdullah's daughters. One son was longtime governor of Taiz Governorate and another was longtime ambassador to the United States.

HALEVY, JOSEPH. *See* TRAVELERS.

AL-HAMDANI, HASAN BIN AHMAD. The great Yemeni poet and historian–genealogist who lived in the 10th century A.D. and whose writings provide a fairly detailed picture of life and times in the Yemeni highlands, especially for the **Hashid** and **Bakil** tribes, in the first half of that century. The content of his geographical and genealogical works provide many benchmarks for students of modern Yemen who, more often than not, are struck by the persistence of customs and practices as well as tribal names and the relationships of tribes to one another and to place.

HAMDAN TRIBES AND REGION. An ancient and important tribal grouping in the northern highlands of North Yemen around **Sanaa** that, in its broadest definition, includes both the **Hashid and Bakil** tribal confederations, or, defined more narrowly, only those two branches of the Hashid confederation that use the word "Hamdan" in their tribal names. The Hamdan tribes, as broadly defined, were allegedly converted to Islam during Muhammad's life by the Prophet's cousin and son-in-law, Ali, and consequently throughout the following centuries have tended to embrace and defend **Shii** Islam in general and **Zaydism** and the Zaydi **imamate** in particular.

The Hatim Sultans of Hamdan, leaders of the Yam tribe, a section of the Hamdan, acquired control of Sanaa and much of the north with the loosening of the grip of the **Sulayhids** at the end of the 11th century A.D. The 12th century witnessed much competition, from intrigue to wars, as well as truces and alliances, between the Hatim Sultans in Sanaa and the relatively new Zaydi imams based in the north in **Saada**. Previously adherents of the **Ismaili** faith of the Sulayhids, the Hatim sultans and most of their followers gradually shifted from opposition to Zaydism and the imamate to acceptance. Despite the ebb and flow of the imams' power over the subsequent centuries, Zaydism from this time forward was firmly established in the Sanaa region and the northern highlands of Yemen. However, the earlier Ismaili period helps explains how President Ahmad Husayn **al-Ghashmi**, of a Hamdan tribal family, based just outside of Sanaa, could be Ismaili.

AL-HAMDI, PRESIDENT IBRAHIM MUHAMMAD (1943–1977). The young, charismatic, and very popular soldier who, after becoming YAR head of state in a bloodless coup on 13 June 1974, expelled the strongest tribal leaders from the state, sought to make a strengthened state an instrument of modernization, and then began to assert a measure of independence for the YAR from **Saudi Arabia.** Al-Hamdi was killed by a group of his fellow officers in October 1977, after little more than three years in office.

The tribal and other conservative friends of Saudi Arabia who helped make the takeover by the **armed forces** possible were more interested in getting President **al-Iryani** out than with getting al-Hamdi in. Shaykh Ali al-Matari, his high-mountain domain strategically astride the highway between Sanaa and **al-Hudayda**, was one of the leaders against whom President al-Hamdi moved quickly in 1975 in his effort to lessen the ability of the tribal leaders to control and contain the state. The astute al-Matari had earlier warned his fellow shaykhs that al-Hamdi was using divide-and-conquer tactics against them, but his warnings had by then gone too long unheeded.

Seizing power in the name of the **13 June Correction Movement**, Al-Hamdi suspended the **1970 Constitution** and its legislative and executive organs and placed supreme power in a small council of officers chaired by him: the Military Command Council. Within a year, and after a couple civilians had been added to it, the council ceased to be the real center of collective leadership as al-Hamdi incrementally concentrated power in his own hands. He increasingly surrounded himself with cronies by whom he was often ill-advised—such as Ahmad Damaj, the leader of his revived Correction Movement—and cut himself off from wise and powerful political and military figures. As important, the seemingly suspicious and distrustful al-Hamdi created a climate of fear and distrust. After growing uneasy, many of his army colleagues apparently decided to get him before he got them.

Perhaps because of his distrustfulness, al-Hamdi made only half-hearted tries to organize politics to support his statist and modernist goals after he reined in the tribal leaders in 1975. In this regard, then, he was more politically destructive than constructive during his short time in office. For example, despite being a founder of the **local development association** (LDA) movement, he pulled back from his apparent plan to make the LDAs the basis of a grassroots political organization. Similarly, he revived his 13 June Correction Movement in 1976, only to pull back quickly from a reform effort that had the potential to galvanize and organize political life.

Provocatively, in an effort to free himself from a demanding Saudi patron and from the tribalists and other conservatives, al-Hamdi attempted with some success to improve relations with North Yemen's dissident leftists, as well as with the PDRY and the other Red Sea countries. In an effort to counter pressure from **Saudi Arabia**, he hosted in 1977 the Taiz Summit on **Red Sea Security**, attended by the presidents of **Sudan**, **Somalia**, and the PDRY. By this time, the Saudis feared that al-Hamdi had become a "little Nasser."

It is rumored that some in the Saudi royal family were privy to the plot against him, if not more directly involved, and that they had applauded the deed after the fact.

As with John F. Kennedy, opinion about what might have been has necessarily colored assessments of al-Hamdi. Clearly, he was the YAR's first populist leader, and he did serve as a symbol of modern Yemeni nationalism and as a popularizer of the idea of development. The nation truly grieved on the occasion of his assassination. To some degree, his legacy survived him into the 1980s in the **13 June Movement** and the **Nasirites**.

The son of a **qadi**, al-Hamdi studied for and began this same career, only to shift to the military at the time of the **1962 Revolution**. He advanced quickly, serving as commander of the **Reserves**, an elite unit, and as deputy commander in chief. His civilian posts included that of deputy prime minister in 1972 and president of the LDA movement. Al-Hamdi was only in his mid-thirties when he became the YAR's third head of state. Col. Abdullah al-Hamdi, Ibrahim's older brother, was commander of the elite, nontribal Giants (Amaliqa) Brigade who used his position to help his brother gain and maintain control. Abdullah was a very tough, coarse man, feared and disliked by many, and he may have caused his brother more harm than good between 1974 and when the two al-Hamdi brothers were assassinated together.

AL-HAMDI REGIME. *See* AL-IRYANI AND AL-HAMDI REGIMES AND TRANSITION PERIOD.

HAMID AL-DIN FAMILY AND IMAMATE. The **sayyid** family that provided the last dynasty of **Zaydi** imams, a late, brilliant flowering of the traditional authoritarian, pre-democratic political institutions that had been an important part of North Yemen's politics for more than a millennium. **Al-Mansur Muhammad** Hamid al-Din claimed and won the Zaydi **imamate** in 1891. Thereafter, he both laid the groundwork for the establishment of a family dynasty and led the renewed revolt against the **Ottoman** Turkish occupiers, thereby identifying the family and the imamate with the early stirrings of a vague sense of modern Yemeni nationalism.

The Hamid al-Din dynasty was consolidated and reached its zenith during the long reign of al-Mansur's son, **Yahya bin Husayn** bin

Muhammad, a reign that began in 1904 and ended with his assassination in old age in 1948. Imam Yahya early on took the title al-Mutawakkil (the Relier), and the regime headed by his family was known thereafter as the Mutawakkilite Kingdom (Imamate) of Yemen. Crown Prince **Amad bin Yahya** quickly ousted those who had murdered his father and undid the short-lived **1948 Revolution**. While he refined further the institutions and practices of his father from then until his death in 1962, Imam Ahmad's reign was both much shorter and far more troubled by intrusions of the outside world and modernity than his father's had been.

Crown Prince Muhammad **al-Badr** succeeded his father only to be overthrown a week later by the **1962 Revolution** that ended the imamate and created the YAR. After leading the losing royalists against the **republicans** during most of the eight-year **Yemen Civil War**, al-Badr went into permanent exile in London, where he died in 1996. Imam Yahya may have undermined the imamate by going against an anti-dynastic tradition by naming a crown prince, something that Ahmad did in turn.

HANISH ISLANDS. *See* ERITREA.

AL-HAQQ PARTY. The Truth Party is the very small conservative political party of **Zaydis** from **sayyid** families that was formed at the time of Yemeni **unification** in 1990. It was a party of the formerly privileged who were as much nostalgic for the good-old pre-republican days as they were concerned about possible consequences of union with a South Yemen led by a Marxist party. Al-Haqq was one of the five parties in the opposition coalition, the **Joint Meeting Parties**, which took form after 2000 and which became the main opposition to the **Salih regime** by the middle of the decade.

HARAD CONFERENCE. *See* YEMENI CIVIL WAR

HARAZ REGION. *See* ISMAILIS IN YEMEN.

HARIB AND WADI HARIB. The town and region that in ancient times comprised part of Qataban, one of the **trading kingdoms** on the frankincense trail, and that today comprises one of the easternmost settlement areas in the former YAR, one close to the old undemarcated border with the PDRY. Long a backwater on the periphery, Harib took on some new significance in the 1980s because of its proximity to the newly developed oil fields in the **Marib** region. Earlier, in 1905, **Great Britain** and the **Ottomans** agreed to a border that began in the west near **Bab al-Mandab** and ended to the northeast near Harib. Later, shortly before the demise of the Ottoman Empire, the same two parties drew a straight boundary line from this point near Harib northeast across Arabia to a point near **Qatar**.

AL-HARITHI, ALI QAID SINAN. The reputed **al-Qaida** leader in Yemen, a leader in the plot that resulted in the suicide bombing of the U.S.S. *Cole* in October 2000, and the target in late 2002 of a Hellfire missile fired from an unmanned Predator drone controlled by **United States** forces in **Djibouti**. The missile killed him and four others in a car near **Marib**. Some months earlier, anxious after **9/11** to show the United States that it was willing and able to deal with terrorists in Yemen, the **Salih** regime had suffered a costly military defeat when it sent forces to get al-Harithi, who was under tribal protection near Marib. Al-Harithi's killing and the ongoing intrusive FBI inquiry in Yemen into the *Cole* bombing marked the increasingly salient and strained relationship between the United States and the ROY in the **War on Terror**.

HASAN BIN YAHYA, SAYF AL-ISLAM. The able, highly regarded son of Imam **Yahya** and brother of Imam **Ahmad** who both served his father and brother well as a soldier and administrator and posed a threat as a credible alternative to Ahmad's choice of his successor, his son, Crown Prince Muhammad **al-Badr**. Prince Hasan helped save the imamate for his brother and the **Hamid al-Din** family by quickly rallying the northern tribes after the **1948 Revolution**. Later sent by his brother to New York as ambassador to the United Nations, a venue posing less of a threat to al-Badr, he quickly returned to Yemen on the occasion of the **1962 Revolution**, rallied royalist forces against the newly proclaimed YAR, and placed himself at the service of Imam al-Badr in the losing effort that was the **Yemeni Civil War**.

AL-HASANI, ALI NASIR MUHAMMAD. *See* ALI NASIR MUHAMMAD AL-HASANI.

HASHID AND BAKIL TRIBES AND CONFEDERATIONS. Most of the **tribes** of the northern highlands of North Yemen, around and mostly to the north of Sanaa, have been for the past millennium grouped loosely into two fairly stable alliances or confederations, the Hashid and the Bakil. Estimated to be more than a million—or more than 5 percent of the total population of Yemen—the highland's tribal population is divided rather unevenly among some 7 major Hashid tribes and about 15 from Bakil. The 7 major tribes in the Hashid confederation are the al-Usaymat, Idhar, Kharif, Bani Suraym, **Sanhan**, Bilad al-Rus, and **Hamdan**. Among the Bakil tribes are the Dhu Muhammad, Dhu Husayn, **Arhab**, Sufyan, Nihm, Murhibah, Iyal Yazid, Iyal Surayh, Bani Matar, Bani Hushaysh, Khawlan al-Aliyah, Khawlan al-Tiyal, Khawlan Saada, al-Ammar, al-Salim, al-Amalisah, Bani Nawf, and Wailah. Two of the largest of the widely scattered Bakil tribes, Dhu Muhammad and Dhu Husayn, had roots in Jabal Barat, a rugged mountainous area in the far northeast, but also migrated south and established themselves in Ibb province. The Nihm, in a resource-poor, thinly populated region located 30 to 40 miles northeast of Sanaa, was best known in the 20 years after the **1962 Revolution** as the tribe to which Sinan **abu Luhum** and the other important members of the Luhumi clan belonged.

In the 20th century, the less scattered Hashid tribes have been more united and better organized and led—and thus stronger—than the Bakil tribes. Shaykh Abdullah ibn Husayn **al-Ahmar**, shaykh of al-Usaymat and paramount shaykh of the Hashid confederation since just before the **1962 Revolution**, was the most powerful and important tribal leader in North Yemen throughout the republican era until his death in 2007. No shaykh of the Bakil has matched his influence and prodigious staying power, these due only in part to his ability to call up a large and loyal following.

Hashid tribes have often been in conflict with Bakil tribes, and on occasion, the tribes of one confederation have been mobilized in opposition to the tribes of the other. At other times, however, they have stood together against outside tribes or non-tribal forces. Early converts to **Zaydi** Islam, the Hashid and Bakil have tended over the centuries to be providers of support and arms for the Zaydi **imamate**—indeed, the two confederations were long called "the wings of the imamate." In fact, however, they were more like difficult allies than loyal subjects of the imams, and the price that they exacted for their support was the autonomy of their tribal domains. At times, either or both confederations, or parts thereof, broke with and even turned on the imamate when they felt wronged or threatened. For example, Shaykh Abdullah withdrew Hashid support from Imam **Ahmad** on the eve of the 1962 Revolution after the latter ordered the shaykh's father and older brother slain during protected talks, a serious break with custom. As a result, the **republicans** prevailed over the royalists in the long **Yemeni Civil War** after the revolution, in part because most of the Hashid gave their support to the republic. Similarly, some of the Bakilis sided with the republicans against the royalists during the civil war. Indeed, the Luhumi clan of the **Nihm** tribe became very influential in republican politics from the mid-1960s into the mid-1970s, and the then head of the clan, Sinan **Abu Luhum,** came to be known as a maker and breaker of governments.

The **Salih regime** that seized power in 1978 came to be seen as dominated by and favoring the interests of the Sanhanis and other Hashidis, the president and much of his coterie being from Sanhan and closely allied to Shaykh Abdullah. Accordingly, many Bakilis came to feel left out of a largely tribalized regime, and some of them drifted into the opposition. Indeed, as Yemeni **unification** unraveled and resulted in the **War of Secession** in the mid-1990s, some Bakilis supported the secessionists.

HATIM SULTANS OF HAMDAN. *See* HAMDAN TRIBES AND REGION.

HAWATMAH, NAYIF. *See* PALESTINE AND THE PALESTINE QUESTION.

HAWSHABI TRIBE, REGION AND STATE. Located just north of **Lahej** and south of **Dhala**, Hawshabi was one of the tribes and mini-states in Aden's immediate hinterland that was in the sphere of influence of the stronger, more prosperous British-dominated **Abdali** sultanate. Like its neighbors, Hawshabi was indirectly influenced, if not ruled, by **Great Britain** in Aden through the Abdalis down to the 1930s. By the time that it joined in the formation of the **Federation of South Arabia** in the early 1960s, Hawshabi had been very much absorbed and diluted by the modern economics of the Lahej and Aden region.

HAWTA. *See HIJRA.*

HAYFAN. A town and district southeast of **Taiz** in the **Hugariyya** region of North Yemen that, because of proximity to the main track connecting Taiz and **Aden**, was both the place in North Yemen most exposed in the first six decades of the 20th century to the outside world and the birthplace of many of the leading first-generation **modernists** and politicians from North Yemen and even some leaders from South Yemen. For example, Hayfan in the birthplace of both the U.S.-educated, longtime YAR prime minister, **Abd al-Aziz** Abd al-Ghani, and the ex-party chief and head of state of the PDRY, **Abd al-Fattah** Ismail. In the 1950s, Hayfan was the site of perhaps the first of North Yemen's local self-help associations, which used **remittances** sent or brought home by overseas workers to build schools, cisterns, and village access tracks. Possibly more than any other specific place in the country, Hayfan exemplified the hunger of the majority but subordinate **Shafii** for modern **education** and its openness to modern economic, social, and political ideas.

HAYL SAID (SAEED) ANAAM (?–1990). The North Yemeni of modest origins from the **Hugariyya** region who, with business savvy and hard work as a dock worker, shopkeeper, and import–export merchant in **Aden** from the 1930s into the 1960s, went on to help finance the nationalist struggle in North Yemen and to become a multimillionaire capitalist and the scion of the richest and most powerful trading, banking, and industrial combine in the YAR. Even socialists held him up to merchants as a member of the "national bourgeoisie," a model capitalist prepared to invest in the development of a backward **economy** and the future of the country.

An old-fashioned Yemeni, a devout Muslim, somewhat retiring and Gandhi-like in appearance, Hayl Said insisted that his grandsons and others in high positions in his modern economic empire have business degrees and apply modern management practices. His aromatic biscuit factory north of Taiz on the road to Sanaa stood, depending on one's disposition, as a symbol of hope or despair for modernists in the 1970s.

The Hayl Said Group, still an economic giant among the several major **Shafii** business combines in Yemen, has had to exert its economic power cautiously since the early 1980s and the **Salih regime**'s concerns about the loyalty of the Shafii majority and its attempt to advance northern **Zaydi** business groups by "affirmative action."

HAYTHAM, MUHAMMAD ALI (?–1993). The moderate **National Liberation Front** (NLF) leader in South Yemen whose support of the NLF's left wing during the **22 June Corrective Movement** in 1969 made possible the ouster of President Qahtan **al-Shaabi** and his rightist colleagues. Haytham had placed his support in the army and among the tribes at the disposal of the left because of personal, not ideological, differences with Qahtan. He became prime minister, but in August 1971, his own removal in a reshuffle signaled the complete triumph of the NLF's left under the uneasy co-leadership of **Abd al-Fattah** Ismail and Salim **Rabiyya Ali**. He then went into exile in Cairo, where—although for the most part retired from politics—he was the object of two assassination attempts in the mid-1970s. In a bit of a comeback, after Yemeni **unification**, he was given a minor cabinet post in the new government of the ROY after the 1993 **elections**, only to die of natural causes only months later.

HICKINBOTHAM. *See* COLONIAL ADMINISTRATION AND ADMINISTRATORS.

HIJAZ, THE. The province and region of **Saudi Arabia** on the western side of the Arabian Peninsula, bordering on the **Red Sea** north of Yemen, that contains Islam's holiest places, Mecca and Medina. It also contains the port city of Jidda, Saudi Arabia's largest city and commercial center and, paradoxically, both that long isolated country's window on the outside world and the Islamic world's gateway for the pilgrimage to the holy cities.

Yemen was one of the first regions to convert to Islam in the seventh century, and from time to time over the centuries strong Yemeni rulers marched north and conquered and ruled part or all of the Hijaz. The Hijaz became a part of the soon to-be Kingdom of Saudi Arabia in the mid-1920s, after **Ibn Saud** defeated the forces of the Hashimite ruler of the Hijaz and Guardian of the Holy Places Sharif Husayn. In what was the last major step in the expansion of his domain, Ibn Suad's forces marched south from the Hijaz and defeated Imam **Yahya**'s forces in the **Saudi–Yemeni War of 1934**, thereby securing physical control of the contested regions of **Asir**, **Najran** and **Jizan**.

HIJRA. Towns, markets, and other places that are accorded protected status and to which others can flee and find safety. Dating from long before the rise of Islam, this institution remained a feature of Yemen and other parts of Arabia under Islam. It came to be associated with the **sayyid** caste and the mediation of conflict, and continued to provide an element of stability to a potentially disordered and volatile tribal environment. In the southern and eastern parts of Yemen, sacred enclaves called *hawta* provided the same safety and place for arbitration, and were often associated with saints or holy families.

HIMYARITE KINGDOM. The last of the several great indigenous pre-Islamic kingdoms in Yemen, it emerged in the second century B.C., established and maintained its rule to varying degrees for several centuries over much of Yemen to and including the **Hadhramawt** kingdom to the east. It declined as a political force over the several generations of economic crisis, religious upheaval, and invasions by **Ethiopia** and **Persia** that occurred before the rise and spread to Yemen of Islam in the seventh century A.D. The decline was marked by the reign of **Dhu Nuwas**, a convert to Judeaism from the late fifth to the early sixth century A.D. The Himyarite Kingdom had its capital in Zafar (Dhu Raydan), in the highlands, on a hill near modern **Yarim**, where its ruins can still be seen to this day. The only great pre-Islamic kingdom to be centered in the Yemeni highlands rather than in the east astride the **trade route** on the edge of the desert, the Himyaris were also able to exercise control over the increasingly important ports on Yemen's **Red Sea** coast.

Yemenis today—modern or traditional, educated or not—are aware of their Himyari past, and it is an important foundation of modern Yemeni national identity. Many have collapsed their pre-Islamic past, the histories of the several **trading kingdoms**, into the one term "Himyar." The expression "hatha himyari"—i.e., this is something made by or pertaining to the Himyarites—is used proudly by many common folk of North Yemen to categorize ruins or art objects that appear old, be they pre-Islamic, Islamic, or even 19th-century Ottoman.

AL-HIRSI, BADR. The British-born, -raised, and -educated Yemeni who wrote and directed *New Day in Old Sanaa*, the first Yemeni-made feature film and the recipient of, among other awards, designation as the best Arab film in the 29th International Cairo Film Festival in 2005. In this ambitious, lengthy movie, Sanaa's Old City is very much a lead character in this romantic tale of love, duty, and mistaken identity. A few years earlier, al-Hirsi wrote and directed the more modest, but insightful and very funny, *The English Shaykh and the Yemeni Gentleman*. It starred him as the thoroughly Anglicized Yemeni gentleman being introduced to his native Yemen by the English shaykh Tim Mackintosh Smith, an Arabist, travel writer, and 25-year resident of Yemen.

AL-HITAR, HAMOUD. The somewhat charismatic judge and expert on sharia who developed the **"dialogue process"** and presided over the Religious Dialogue Council beginning in 2002 and who was then appointed minister of religious endowments and guidance in the 2007 cabinet reshuffle. Suddenly something of a celebrity, al-Hitar traveled to Europe on more than one occasion to explain and promote the process of "reprogramming" and release of jailed **political Islamists**, a few of whom later turned up in Iraq. Skeptical of the dialogue process from the start, the **United States** was not happy.

As minister, one of his first tasks in 2007, and this was in the context of the ongoing **al-Houthi Rebellion**, was to admonish clerics and warn them against preaching a partisan or militant line. Another immediate task was to decide whether the dialogue process used in the recent past to rehabilitate militants of the **al-Qaida** variety could be applied to the **sayyids** and other **Shii** who had joined the al-Houthi cause.

HODEIDA. *See* AL-HUDAYDA (HODEIDA).

HORN OF AFRICA SECURITY ISSUES. *See* RED SEA AND HORN OF AFRICA SECURITY ISSUES.

HOSTAGE-TAKING AND THE HOSTAGE SYSTEM. Hostage-taking and the billeting and levying of soldiers were key methods by which the **Hamid al-Din** imams exerted some control over—and at times punished—the tribes that lived in territory which the **imamate** presumed to be part of its domain. As a sort of insurance, a **tribal** chief who pledged his allegiance to the imam were often forced to surrender hostages, often his own sons and nephews. Depending on how the shaykh in question behaved, the young hostage or hostages might live in relative comfort, often virtually as part of the imam's family, or end up in a dark, dank dungeon. It is estimated that this hostage system involved a few thousand hostages at its height in the 1950s.

With the tables somewhat turned, hostage-taking assumed a different form and function after the **1962 Revolution**, and especially after Yemeni **unification** in 1990. Most often, tribes took hostages, usually foreigners, as leverage in their effort to get the state either to do or to cease doing something—e.g., to provide a social or economic benefit or to release tribal members jailed for alleged crimes. More often than not, this hostage-taking reflected the weakness or marginality of the shaykhs and their tribes in the modern political process. It was a crude way of trying to secure promised pumps, schools, clinics and roads, or to secure redress of a grievance against the state or another tribe.

Hostage-taking took on epidemic proportions after 1990—rising, falling, and then rising again. While the surge of kidnappings in the 1990s was the biggest, there were, by one count, 47 kidnappings of foreigners in the period 2001–2006, involving some 114 tourists and 43 resident expatriates—often oil workers. In both periods, the hostage-taking paralleled and compromised the ROY's efforts to attract desperately needed foreign investment and **tourism**. In the 1990s, the kidnapping took on regional import because leaders in the ROY came to suspect that **Saudi Arabia** was urging tribal clients it funded to engage in the practice as a means of embarrassing and weakening the ROY. Indeed, the ROY eventually made kidnapping punishable by death, something that turned out to be an empty threat.

HOUSE OF REPRESENTATIVES. *See* COUNCIL OF DEPUTIES (MAJLIS AL-NUWAB).

AL-HOUTHI (AL-HUTHI) REBELLION. The large, protracted military–political conflict, waged primarily in **Saada** province and in waves from mid-2004 through 2008, that pitted the **Salih regime** against a **sayyid** minority of **Zaydis** inspired and led by members of the al-Houthi family—a movement that evolved from modest, obscure beginnings into a direct challenge to the legitimacy and existence of the regime, even of republicanism itself. The movement was founded in the late 1990s by Husayn Badruddin al-Houthi, a former member of parliament and a founder of the **al-Haqq** party, and its initial membership included an organization created by him in 1997, the "Believing Youth," and its offshoot, the "Slogan Movement." Although al-Houthi's message and mission quickly became more extreme, the Salih regime had supported his initially moderate teachings and his schools as a needed antidote to militant **Salafis** in the **Sunni** community.

In terms of issues and actions, the conflict went from youthful Friday mosque demonstrations in Sanaa in 2000 calling for "death to America, death to Israel" to, by the middle of the decade, vicious and bloody battles and calls for an end to the republic and the restoration of the Zaidi **imamate**. What started out as a clash between al-Houthi's immediate followers and the police and military evolved into a much wider conflict. Involved were tribal elements on both sides, political opponents of the Salih regime in general, residents of Saada province standing up to the central authorities, and Sunni **salafists** opposed to Zaydism.

Triggered by attempts by the regime to rein in the movement, the first round of fighting erupted in Saada province in June 2004 and ended in September with the death of Husayn al-Houthi—and at the cost of the lives of more than 400 insurgents and government troops, and with great property damage. With Husayn's death, the leadership of the movement passed to his father, the Shiite cleric Badruddin al-Houthi. Fighting broke out again in Saada in mid-2005, and over the next several months some 525 troops and hundreds of rebels were killed in this second round of fierce fighting. In May 2006, after especially intense fighting in April, the Salih regime announced an amnesty for al-Huthis and his followers, freeing some 600 prisoners. Despite this move, the conflict refused to die, and the third round erupted at the beginning of 2007, this time with Abd al-Malik,

Husayn's younger brother, in command of the "houthis." President Salih issued an ultimatum: surrender or death. When they refused his call, he unleashed the full force of the military and its heaviest weapons, as well as tribal irregulars and salafis—and the houthis replied in kind. Fierce fighting from February through May took a heavy toll on both sides as well as on the civilian population of Saada province.

By this time, Yahya al-Houthi, another brother and a member of parliament in exile in Germany, was taking the message to the regional level. Officials in Sanaa were talking about outsiders'—i.e., Qaddafi's **Libya** and the Islamic Republic of **Iran**—supporting the rebellion. Indeed, the ROY recalled its ambassadors from Libya and Iran in May. Even the attention of **Israel** and the **United States** was attracted when some 45 of the few remaining Jews in Saada were threatened and displaced from their homes in early 2007. The mood was grim, and despair widespread, as the rebellion came to dominate politics in 2007, just when the recently reelected President Salih sought to put the focus on reform in exchange for foreign aid and investments. The opposition, especially the **Joint Meeting Parties**, particularly condemned the regime for its resort to unbridled violence, and the regime increasingly accused the opposition of supporting the rebellion. Talk of "sectarian war" became common, and connections were even made between the conflict in Saada and the regional Sunni–Shii conflict triggered by the conflict in Iraq. Uncertainty about what was really going on was compounded by the fact that the regime had cut off media access to Saada in February, allowing rumors on all sides to flourish.

In May 2007, the ruler of **Qatar**, Emir Hamad bin Khalifa al-Thani, intervened in the political stalemate and in June brokered a nine-provision agreement to end the fighting. The houthis were to come down from their fortified mountain bases and surrender their heavy armaments, and their top leaders were to go into temporary exile in Doha, Qatar; the regime was to withdraw its forces from the countryside, declare an amnesty and release all prisoners, permit the houthis to form a political party, and compensate the people of Saada province for the widespread death and destruction. Under the supervision of a parliamentary committee, the agreement was implemented fitfully, and only partially, over the following months. Threats and accusations from all sides filled the air through fall 2007, and sporadic fighting renewed at the beginning of 2008—as did the peace efforts of Qatar and a new presidential committee. In early August 2008, the two sides seemed exhausted and ready to end the fighting. The much-anticipated "Sixth war," one in which the regime unleashed all it's fire-power, erupted in August 2009 and continued through the fall.

AL-HUBAYSHI, HUSAYN ALI (*CA. 1929– *). Aden-born and -raised son of a family from North Yemen's **Hugariyya** region, al-Hubayshi became the founding principal of **Bilqis Preparatory College** in Aden in the early 1960s and then came north to serve the YAR after the ouster of President **al-Sallal** in 1967. He put his rare expertise in western law to use as founding head of the Legal Office and as legal adviser to YAR and ROY presidents until the end of the 20th century. Leaving Aden with three colleagues in early 1948, just months after the **Famous Forty** had left for Lebanon, al-Habayshi by the end of the 1950s had earned a law degree in Cairo and a degree in international law at the University of London. His very long marriage to an English woman is one of the few lasting unions based in Yemen between a member of his generation and a western woman.

AL-HUDAYDA (HODEIDA). Located in the **Tihama** on the **Red Sea** west-southwest of Sanaa, it was the YAR's major port and second largest city. The result of increasing commerce and port-inspired development activity, it grew rapidly in the 1960s, passing Taiz in population by the end of the 1970s. Its population had nearly reached a half-million even before the sudden infusion of Yemeni workers expelled from **Saudi Arabia** in late 1990.

By the mid-20th century, Al-Hudayda still lacked any deep-water berthing facilities; ships anchored offshore and goods and people were brought ashore on barges and small boats. Modernized and expanded by the **Soviet Union** from the early 1960s onward, its port facilities grew in importance when persistent hostility between the two Yemens cut North Yemen almost completely off from the port at **Aden** after the mid-1960s. After Yemeni **unification** in 1990, al-Hudayda continued as the primary port for the northern highlands and southern uplands of old North Yemen.

Influenced in so many ways by the sea, by the Tihama's merciless summer heat and humidity, and by African influences on the culture and racial makeup of the population, al-Hudayda is quite unlike North Yemen's other major cities, Sanaa and Taiz. It is an ugly place not graced by a noteworthy setting or great buildings. Indeed, it is flat as can be; the last of the handsome shore-front Ottoman buildings have collapsed or have been torn down. Still, al-Hudayda has its charms, especially in the souk at night—and, above all, in the fish souk.

AL-HUDAYDA INCIDENT OF 1968. The brief fight in March 1968 at the port of **al-Hudayda** between conservative and progressive republican forces over whether a newly arrived shipment of arms from the **Soviet Union** should go to tribal elements or to the more professional units in the regular army. It was the conservatives allied to General Hasan **al-Amri** who won the day—and the tribalists who got the arms. This was a preview to the defeat of the Yemeni left and its purge from the YAR armed forces—and, largely, from YAR political life in general—several months later with the suppression of the **Sanaa Mutiny**. Ali Abdullah **Salih**, a very junior officer who played a role in the al-Hudayda incident, was rewarded by superiors whose attention he caught and began his sharp rise to power.

AL-HUD, PROPHET. As recorded in the Quran and Yemeni mythology, the great-grandson of Sam and the father of **Qahtan**, the figure from whom allegedly sprang all South Yemeni tribes. The tomb of al-Hud, east of **Tarim** in **Wadi Hadhramawt**, may be the holiest spot and the most popular pilgrimage site in Yemen. Below the white buildings surrounding the tomb spreads a town totally empty except when temporarily filled by thousands for a few days during the annual pilgrimage. *See also* RELIGION AND RELIGIOUS GROUPS IN YEMEN.

HUGARIYYA REGION. The area that fans out in a rough half-circle over the uplands from **Taiz** south to the edge of the high escarpment that overlooks **Aden** and the western tip of South Yemen. The Hugariyya region is the well-populated sociocultural heartland of the **Shafii** portion of North Yemen and the longtime incubator of Yemeni **emigrants** from which many of the Arab residents of Aden and a very large percentage of North Yemen's first-generation **modernists** (with or without much formal education) hail. **Al-Turba**, due south of Taiz, and **Hayfan**, to the east on Taiz, are the main towns of the Hugariyya.

HUNT OIL CO. *See* YEMEN HUNT OIL CO. (YHOC).

HUSAYN, KING OF THE HIJAZ. *See* HIJAZ, THE.

HUSSAINOUN, SALEH ABU-BAKR BIN (?–1994). The young technocrat of **Hadhramawt** origins who, in the wake of the leadership struggle surrounding the **13 January events** in the PDRY in 1986, rose to deputy prime minister and minister of minerals and energy. After Yemeni **unification** in 1990, he occupied the same ministerial position in the ROY. Over these years he oversaw the initial development of the **oil** discovered in **Shabwa** and **Masila**. Bin Hussainounin sided with his southern colleagues before and during the **War of Secession** in 1994. He was killed at a checkpoint as he fled east from Aden to **al-Mukala** in the last days of that short war.

AL-HUTHI REBELLION. *See* AL-HOUTHI.

HYDERABAD. The princely state in old India wherein members of certain **Hadhramawt** families originally from **Yafi** served the local rulers as mercenaries, reaching positions of some influence and considerable wealth. Many of them then proceeded to use these newfound gains to advance their political and social ambitions back home in the Hadhramawt. For example, the leaders of both the **Quaitis** and the **Kathiris**, who competed over the second half of the 19th century for control of the Hadhramawt, had been in the service of the ruling Nizam of Hyderabad, the Quaiti leader being no less than the Nizam's chief of security forces. This link between wealth and power in Hyderabad and the same at home in the Hadhramawt lasted for generations, and affords a good example of the region's historic dependence on a complex pattern of **emigration** and **remittances**—and, through this, of its independence of Aden.

– I –

IBADIYA (IBADIS). The more moderate of the two branches of the separatist Kharijite movement that in the late seventh century refused allegiance to either of the warring wings of Islam, the **Sunni** and the Shii. In the eighth century, the Ibadis were the basis of a failed attempt launched from the **Hadhramawt** to overthrow the Damascus-based **Umayyads** and though put down, remained an influence in the Hadhramawt for several centuries. The Ibadis survived in modern times mainly in mountainous inner **Oman**, from which their imam waged an episodic revolt until put down by Oman in the 1950s. Small groups of Ibadis exist in Libya, Tunisia, Algeria, and Tanzania.

IBB CITY AND PROVINCE. The largest inland city after **Taiz** in the **Shafii** southern highlands of North Yemen, located about 45 miles north of Taiz on the road to **Sanaa**, Ibb is a thriving commercial and marketing center and the capital of Ibb province, the well-watered "green province," which has the largest and densest population in the country. The population of the southern uplands—Ibb and Taiz provinces—has been based over the centuries upon a relatively rich **agriculture**, and this, in turn, has depended upon the seasonal **monsoon** rains. In times past, at times of drought and other hardships in the northern highlands, tribes would sweep down into this region and seize land and crops.

Although tribal ties exist in Ibb and Taiz provinces, the social fabric there is often described as peasant-based and is defined in terms of land and place. Since the 1940s, both provinces have been sources of many migrants who went to Europe and the United States for study and work, sent home **remittances**, and brought back modern ideas and experiences.

IBN ALWAN AHMAD. The son of a scribe at the 13th century **Rasulid** court in **Taiz** who became a **sufi** and who, after missionary work in Africa, founded a mosque and **madrasa** at Yufrus. Located at the base of the western side of Jabal **Sabr**, on the road between **Taiz** and **Turba**, this lovely large, white place of study and worship remains a major pilgrimage site. An ascetic who gave up the life of the court, ibn Alwan is said to have used **qat** in his prayers, meditations, and efforts to reach religious ecstasy. *See also* RELIGION AND RELIGIOUS GROUPS IN YEMEN.

IBN HUSAYN, MUHAMMAD. *See* YEMENI CIVIL WAR.

IBN ISA, SAYYID AHMAD. See EMIGRATION.

"IBN SAUD," KING. *See* AL-SAUD (BAYT SAUD).

IBN ZIYAD, MUHAMMAD. *See* ZIYADI STATE AND DYNASTY.

IBRAHIM BIN YAHYA HAMID AL-DIN, PRINCE. The son of Yemen's Imam **Yahya** who joined the opposition **Free Yemenis** in **Aden** in 1946 and then, in the wake of his father's assassination, joined the group that made the failed **1948 Revolution**. He was executed on the orders of his brother, Imam **Ahmad**, when that revolution was quickly put down in the spring of 1948.

IDEOLOGY AND POLITICAL IDEAS, MODERN. Modern political ideologies came late to the two Yemens, save for **Aden**, and even Aden was about half a century behind more cosmopolitan Cairo, Beirut, and Damascus. For this reason, ideology in the Yemens has been especially derivative, and its sources and evolution rather easily traced. The initial political ideas of the first major group of modern dissidents in **imamate** Yemen—e.g., the **Free Yemenis** of the mid-1940s—made them sound like mid-20th century equivalents of the Turkish reformers of the **Ottoman** Empire during the Tanzimat period of the mid-19th century. They wanted a reformed imamate to end "backwardness," and they evolved only slowly from favoring a constitutional imamate to favoring a republic—and had a sketchy and dated conception of republicanism.

In a marked change, many young Yemenis came to modern styles of political thinking in Cairo and Aden in the late 1940s and early 1950s by way of the **Muslim Brotherhood**, a movement whose call for the use of modern means to achieve traditional Islamic goals at least had something in common with their traditional upbringing in Yemen. Indeed, as one from the **Famous Forty** put it: "We went abroad as innocents in 1947, knowing of only Allah and the Imam."

While a few of these young Yemenis stayed with the thought of the Brotherhood or other variants of **political Islam**, most of them moved on to the competing secular pan-Arab **nationalisms** that swept the Arab world in the 1950s: **Baathism**, the thought of the **Arab Nationalist Movement** (ANM), and the ideas associated with Gamal Abdel **Nasser**, Nasserism. As fervent Yemeni nationalists, though, few of these young men were captive to the pan-Arabism of these ideologies. Instead, most of them were drawn to these ideologies by their goals of national strength and development, and by the strong state as the means to achieve those goals. In short, they were statist ideologies, and most of the young Yemenis became statists.

Each of these modern Arab ideologies also came to espouse a one-party party state and some sort of socialism or state capitalism. Whereas Baathism started with socialism as a main pillar, Nasserism later added "Arab socialism" to its initial nationalism, and a main strand of ANM thought morphed into a radical Third World Marxism. Given this heady ideological environment, it is perhaps not surprising that few Yemenis at this time were drawn to, or even extensively exposed to, liberal political and economic thought. Fewer still, it seems, were drawn to orthodox communist parties and their dogma—or, for that matter, to Islamic fundamentalism.

It was this body of thought, variously expressed, that informed the **republicanism** that shaped the **1962 Revolution** in North Yemen. This republicanism was to varying degrees, populist; it was broad enough to embrace both Yemeni Marxists and President Abd al-Rahman al-**Iryani**, the transitional figure dubbed by some "the republican imam." Yemeni republicanism is statist and embraces the need to create and maintain a strong central authority, a sovereign. Furthermore, it was the statist inclinations of Yemeni conservatives and traditionalists, including some who had served the imamate, that enabled many of them to embrace the Yemeni brand of republicanism. For their part, the **modernists** and modern nationalists virtually equated republicanism with statism. In a place often marked by the absence of even a minimalist state, the need to choose among liberal democracy, capitalism, and socialism seemed untimely and irrelevant—a matter for the future. These choices became more relevant with Yemeni **unification** in 1990, but even then the choosing of democracy and multi-party politics was quite pragmatic and non-ideological.

Improbably, the PDRY had the only Marxist regime in the Arab world in the 1970s and 1980s, and its Marxism owed much to the ideas of Palestinian George **Habash**, whose changing thought shaped the old ANM and, later—since the mid-1960s—the **Popular Front for the Liberation of Palestine**. Many members of the Yemeni branch of the ANM (from both Yemens) found their way into the **National Liberation Front** (NLF), the revolutionary Yemeni movement that reflected Habash's new thought. In 1963, the NLF launched the rebellion against the British imperialists and the Yemeni "feudalists." The NLF and its successor, the **Yemeni Socialist Party** (YSP), opted in stages over several years for a radical socialist path and for internationalism over either pan-Arabism or positive neutralism. Maturing late in the short history of an independent Third World, the "scientific socialism" of the NLF and then the YSP was less Soviet or Maoist—or even a blend of the two—than it was a version of the neo-Marxist theory of dependence and underdevelopment that attracted worldwide attention in the 1970s. This theory, with its emphasis on the distorting effects of imperialism on the nature and functioning of peripheral states, seemed to describe and explain the sociopolitical setting to which the NLF and YSP fell heir. The goal was greater independence and shared prosperity, and the means was a party–state guided by "scientific socialism." By the time of Yemeni unification in 1990, however, the ideological fire had pretty much gone out of the leaders of the YSP, and a united Yemen segued quite easily into a less ideological, more capitalist and liberal democratic post-**Cold War** world. However, waiting in the wings or already on stage were moderate and virulent strains of political Islam. *See also* IMPERIALISM AND COLONIALISM; NATIONAL IDENTITY, TRADITIONAL.

IDRISIS AND SAYYID MUHAMMAD ALI AL-IDRISI. The **sayyid** clan in **Asir** which, due to the collapse of **Ottoman** Turkish authority in Arabia and the political skill and energy of its leader, Sayyid Muhammad Ali al-Idrisi, was able to turn its vague spiritual overlordship into a rough approximation of an organized, independent state in Asir during the first quarter of the 20th century. The

British tried to use al-Idrisi in their jostlings with both the Turks and Imam **Yahya** during **World War I**, encouraged him to extend his domain through **tribal** subsidies, and called the ephemeral results of his efforts, perhaps wishfully, "the Confederacy." After the war, Great Britain's doubts about its ability to work with imam Yahya led it to allow the Idrisis to take over the northern **Tihama** and **al-Hudayda**. The British realized that this was possible when Imam Yahya appeared to be too weak to secure the release of Colonel H. F. Jacob, a colonial officer held for four months in 1919 by a Tihama tribe. Jacob had been on his way from just-occupied al-Hudayda to Sanaa to meet with Imam Yahya.

By 1920, the Idrisis occupation of **al-Hudayda** had made irreconcilable the conflict between the Idrisid state and the Yemeni **imamate**. With the death of the wily Sayyid Muhammad Ali in 1923, however, the Idrisid state collapsed under the weight of internal quarrels and armed fights, and Imam Yahya was able to occupy al-Hudayda and the Tihama up to **Midi** by early 1925. At the same time, the new and expansive Kingdom of **Saudi Arabia** occupied much of the territory in Asir previously ruled by the Idrisis. This set the stage for the short **Saudi–Yemeni War of 1934** that would result in the **Taif Treaty** and the start of the demarcation of the border between Yemen and Saudi Arabia, a process not completed until the year 2000.

AL-IKHWAN AL-MUSLIMAN. *See* POLITICAL ISLAM, MODERN.

IMAMATE AND IMAM, ZAYDI. The state and political system founded by al-Hadi ila al-Haqq Yahya ibn Husayn in the highlands of North Yemen in the late ninth century in order to defend and advance **Zaydi Shiism** and its believers. The Zaydi imamate was to persist with numerous changes of fortune and breaks in continuity until the establishment of the YAR on the occasion of the **1962 Revolution**, all the while maintaining many of the features that al-Hadi and his immediate successors had decreed for it. Over the centuries, the Zaydi imamate patronized learning, culture, and the arts, albeit to a modest degree.

The strong imams of the first six decades of the 20th century, Imam **Yahya** and his son, Imam **Ahmad**, served as the spiritual leaders and temporal rulers and defenders of the community of Islam much as had their predecessors a millennium earlier. They worked hard, and with considerable success, to isolate and insulate traditional Yemen from the outside world, the modern world, during these crucial decades. Dormant since the final defeat of the royalists in the **Yemeni Civil War** in 1970, the effort to restore the imamate resurfaced after a generation in the **al-Houthi Rebellion** in 2004.

IMF/WORLD BANK AID (1970–1990). The International Monetary Fund (IMF) and the International Bank for Reconstruction and Development (the World Bank), both Washington-based, were the two major global organizations created shortly after World War II both to rebuild the international financial and economic order destroyed in the war and the Great Depression and to prevent a recurrence of financial and economic collapse. With the rapid completion of postwar reconstruction, the World Bank focused its attention primarily on the economic development of the countries of Latin America, the Middle East and the rest of Asia and Africa. The IMF, often working closely with the World Bank, also came to direct most of its attention to these areas and their fiscal and monetary needs, problems, and crises. While not agencies of the United Nations, the IMF and World Bank often coordinated their efforts with UN agencies.

Both Yemens joined the IMF and World Bank in 1969, and each of them received significant assistance from both organizations over the subsequent decades. For the YAR, membership was one of its earliest and most important steps in the sought-for opening to the West and western aid sources at the end of both the **al-Sallal** era and the **Yemeni Civil War.** For its part, South Yemen had just gained independence followed by over a year of political infighting and turmoil and needed all the external assistance it could get.

Both the IMF and the World Bank provided foreign experts and conducted studies for each of the Yemens in the 1970s and 1980s. In addition, the IMF helped the PDRY address short-term balance-of-payments problems over this period and helped the YAR deal with its severe budget and payments difficulties in the early 1980s. Each of the Yemens also received significant economic and technical assistance from the World Bank, mostly via its soft-loan arm, the International Development Agency (IDA). In particular, the IDA funded major infrastructure and agricultural projects in both Yemens. Despite its anti-dependency rhetoric, the PDRY received aid—and respect—from the World Bank and IDA on the basis of its honesty and careful use of aid. These bodies were perhaps even more responsive to the development needs of the YAR.

IMF/WORLD BANK REFORMS (1995–PRESENT). With Yemeni **unification** in 1990, and despite the immediate need to turn to the International Monetary Fund (IMF) for help in rescheduling its foreign debt and addressing its payments problems, the ROY was upbeat if not euphoric about an economic future fueled by recently found **oil**. Most of this optimism quickly evaporated when the Gulf states cut off aid and, most important, Saudi Arabia expelled several hundred thousand Yemeni workers as punishment for the ROY's stand in the First **Gulf War**, thereby cutting off the flow of **remittances** and creating massive unemployment. The near destruction of Yemen's remittance system, combined with the high costs of both unification and the **War of Secession** in 1994, meant that by the end of that year the ROY's economy was in free fall. As then structured, it was well on its way to nonviability, this despite the steady rise of modest oil revenues. Indeed, the gross domestic product for 1995 was reduced to less that half its 1990 size and the value of the Yemeni riyal plummeted, raising the cost of goods, especially needed imports. Because of the unemployment and loss of remittances, inequality and abject poverty increased at alarming rates throughout Yemen. In short, it would be hard to exaggerate the grimness of Yemen's situation and prospects in the mid-1990s.

At this point, Yemen and the Yemenis became dependent on the IMF and World Bank as never before. The country in 1995 provided a textbook case of an economic crisis requiring immediate triage and then a regimen of long-term reform. In mid-year, the Salih regime agreed with the IMF and the World Bank that the economy required stabilization measures and a multifaceted program of structural reforms. The premise was that significant IMF/World Bank aid, and the program of stabilization and reforms upon which that aid was conditioned, would begin to turn the Yemeni economy around. The promise was that sacrifices required of the Yemeni people would soon yield an economic environment that would attract from abroad needed investment.

The sequence of events after mid-1995 regarding Yemen's collaboration with the IMF/World Bank on domestic reform followed closely the script of the best-case scenario. Indeed, the major events through the first half of 1997 seemed orchestrated by the Salih regime, the IMF/World Bank, the **European Union (EU)** and Japan to portray Yemen in the best possible light. From the outset, the relationship between the regime and the two international bodies was collaborative and non-adversarial. The regime, for the most part, stuck to its agreements, and those bodies provided promised aid and were understanding of Yemen's political problems and need for social "safety-net" projects for those least able to bear the pain of the reforms.

Specifically, the Salih regime in late 1995 and 1996 put in place the stabilization measures and the initial set of structural reforms designed, among other things, to bring inflation under control. The several exchange rates for the Yemeni riyal were unified and allowed to float. The budget deficit was narrowed through a combination of spending restraints and increased oil revenues; imports were suppressed, with the results that the current accounts situation improved and foreign exchange reserves rose considerably. Then, in late 1996, the regime took a cautious first step toward lifting state subsidies of essential goods; it took further steps to cut these subsidies in 1997 and 1998. In return, the IMF and World Bank lent the ROY roughly $1 billion to support reform projects over these years. In addition, they were among the sponsors and organizers of two donors' conferences that yielded pledges of another $2 billion in aid. The IMF pledge of financial support also paved the way for a big reduction of Yemen's foreign debt by the Paris Club of creditor nations.

The IMF/World Bank structural reform program faltered in late 1997. Political problems and the sharp decline in oil revenues were major culprits. The government became hopelessly deadlocked in late 1997 and resigned in early 1998. In mid-1998, its successor ran into serious resistance in its effort at reform. Oil prices, which had held fairly steady at about $20/barrel for some years, plunged in 1998 to $10/barrel. The decline in revenues greatly limited the government's ability to soften the painful effects of the reforms through development and social spending—and this caused widespread unrest.

The new IMF/World Bank agreement negotiated in 2000 was demanding, and called for the broadening and deepening of reforms in exchange for new credits worth hundreds of millions of dollars. It required the complete lifting of subsidies for essential goods. Moreover, the required downsizing of the civil service and the privatizing of bloated public corporations meant the loss of existing jobs for many Yemenis.

Perhaps more important, the new reforms reached beyond the poor and the working class and directly touched some of the prerogatives and benefits of the privileged and highly placed. Among them were measures designed to fight **corruption**, increase transparency in government, make the courts fairer and more efficient, and reform the banking and financial sectors. For many of the well off, the reforms were getting too close for comfort; many lost whatever appetite they had had for reform.

After the good start from 1995 through 1997, the program of structural reforms was virtually abandoned by 2001. Most of the measures in the agreement of 2000 were not implemented or were done so partially and half-heartedly. Reforms of the judiciary and the civil service lagged, and the rampant corruption in the public and private sectors was barely addressed, except verbally. Although the bombing of the U.S.S. *Cole* and the **9/11** events in 2000 and 2001, respectively, caused the reforms to be upstaged by the **War on Terror**, the reform program had already virtually collapsed by then.

The Salih regime seems by that time to have had a failure of will and a decline in its capacity to effect structural reform, and thereafter it resisted IMF/World Bank pressure to revive the process. In February 2004, these bodies expressed publicly their growing impatience and displeasure with Yemen, particularly regarding failure to complete the lifting of subsidies on petroleum products and to implement civil service reforms designed to address corruption and inefficiency. The petroleum subsidies were seen as hugely limiting revenues available for poverty reduction and safety-net programs especially since a big part of the subsidized products were smuggled abroad and sold at considerable profit. These criticisms were accompanied by not-so-veiled warnings that continued aid to Yemen remained contingent on Yemen keeping its part of the old aid-for-reform bargain. A few months later, in announcing a delay on lifting subsidies, President

Salih put himself between the people and the IMF and World Bank and said that, while he hoped those two bodies would understand, this "is still a sovereign issue in our hands."

To some degree, revival of the IMF–World Bank reform program became captive to the 2003 parliamentary **elections** and the 2006 presidential elections. In the case of the latter, the campaign of the coalition of parties opposed to President Salih's reelection, the **Joint Meeting Parties**, cut both ways: it railed against both the effect of corruption and inefficiency on development and the toll of the early stages of reform on the average Yemeni. The words and deeds of the reelected Salih regime led the IMF and World Bank to give the ROY another chance, at least to a degree. New aid was committed to Yemen at the London donors' conference in late 2006, and the World Bank played a key role in the success of the conference. By 2008, relation between the Salib regime and the international bodies had again become strained.

IMMIGRATION. *See* EMIGRATION.

IMPERIALISM AND COLONIALISM. North Yemen experienced imperialism in the form of conquest and occupation by the **Ottoman** Turks on two occasions, the 16th century and the 19th century, and neither episode was very long or profound in its influence. Unlike most of the rest of the Arab world, North Yemen was not subjected to a period of western imperial rule. Whatever benefits were to be gained from the latter, such as modern modes of thought, organization, and technology, North Yemen missed out on these. On the other hand, it also avoided on the negative effects: the intense love–hate feeling toward the West, the confused sense of superiority–inferiority and the master–servant relationship that came with the colonial experience. In short, North Yemenis were never Franz Fanon's "wretched of the earth," manifesting a "colonial mentality."

By contrast, a key link on the trade route from **Great Britain** to its Asian and East African possessions, Aden Colony was by the early 20th century both a cosmopolitan imperial outpost and a claustrophobic colonial hothouse, the inescapable recipient of the good and bad of **colonial administration**. However, given that the **Aden Protectorates** were administered separately from Aden, and much more indirectly even with Britain's **"forward policy"** of the last decades, the impact of colonialism and the British presence on them was much less than on Aden. *See also* IDEOLOGY AND POLITICAL IDEAS, MODERN.

IMPORTS AND EXPORTS. Imamate Yemen rested upon a primitive **economy** that was largely self-contained and self-sufficient, one that imported and exported very little. Although this situation ended abruptly with the **1962 Revolution**, the economics of the long **Yemeni Civil War** that followed prevented the new imbalance between growing dependence on imports and almost no exports from having a major impact until the end of the 1960s. At that time, the trade imbalance and budget deficits served to produce the **financial crisis of 1968–1971**. By the mid-1970s, however, this crisis was eased by increasing external aid and, more importantly, by a massive inflow of **remittances** from several hundred thousand Yemenis working in oil-rich **Saudi Arabia** and, to a lesser extent, in the other oil-rich Gulf states. The remittances, most of which never passed through the banks, and a full range of goods smuggled across the border from Saudi Arabia served to create an economy that was not reflected in the annual balances of trade and payments figures. The effort in 1980 to encourage agricultural production, reduce imports and to impose duties on imports and license importers had positive effects but also led to a new level of corruption and increased smuggling.

In the second half of the 19th century, the economy of Aden and its environs was gradually plugged into that of the British imperial system. To the east, Wadi **Hadhramawt** and Mukalla, with trade links to Southeast Asia and East Africa, had their own little niche in an earlier age of globalization. Independence in 1967, followed by the rapid and drastic effort to lay the basis of a socialist system, produced a situation in which the dependence on imports and lack of exports were largely masked by widely shared scarcity and much aid from the Soviet Union and its allies. The PDRY, too, benefited from emigration and an inflow of remittances.

Remittances and foreign assistance carried the YAR and the PDRY well into the 1980s, but by late in the decade it became clear that time was running out for each of the Yemens, but for different reasons. Remittances to the YAR fell off in the second half of the 1980s, just as the PDRY felt the effect of the Soviet Union and its bloc drifting towards insolvency and collapse in the late 1980s. A few months after Yemeni **unification** in 1990, the Saudis harshly punished the just-created ROY for its stand during events leading up to the First **Gulf War** by expelling virtually all Yemeni workers—causing remittances to plunge.

Foreign **oil** companies struck significant amounts of oil in the YAR in the mid-1980s and in the PDRY at the end of the decade, and this began to generate a balance-of-trade surplus at the time of unification, this despite the loss of remittances. For the next 15 years, the surplus was a function of rising oil production and, with declining production since 2006, soaring oil prices. Natural gas production, coming online in 2009, should maintain the trade surplus for the next couple of decades. Unfortunately, efforts to ensure a trade surplus in a post-hydrocarbon Yemen by diversifying the economy have lagged. Projects to develop and exploit Yemen's mineral resources and **fisheries**, and to realize the promise of the **Aden container port** and free zone, have moved forward slowly. If these and other opportunities are not exploited in the near future, then the imbalance between Yemen's needed imports and available exports will again reassert itself.

INCENSE AND OTHER FRAGRANCES. Frankincense and myrrh were the two aromatic resins, highly prized by the advanced civilizations of the Mediterranean basin during the classical age, which were main sources of the considerable wealth of South Arabia during the first two millennia B.C. and through the first several centuries A.D. The **trading kingdoms** sat astride and benefited from the **trade route**, the Frankincense Trail. Frankincense, used in burnt offerings and on funeral pyres, comes from trees that grow in **Dhufar** and **Somalia**, small trees that have stiff low branches, sparse foliage, and red flowers. Myrrh resin, used in cosmetics in classical times, comes from trees that resemble low, spreading cedars and grow in western Somalia and over much of South Yemen east to Wadi **Hadhramawt**.

INDIA AND INDIAN SUBCONTINENT. The historic links between the former South Yemen and the Indian subcontinent are strong and varied. For nearly a century, **Great Britain** ruled **Aden** Colony and its hinterland from Bombay through its Government of India, and the common framework provided by the British Empire made it possible for many Hindus and Muslims from the subcontinent to come to Aden as merchants, clerical workers, and civil servants. Some of them stayed for generations, and the subcontinent's cultural influence persists, long after most of these people have left. In a separate development, many residents of the **Hadhramawt** migrated decades ago to India, where they served in the employ of the local rulers— e.g., the Nizam of **Hyderabad**—often as mercenaries. By contrast, the link between the former North Yemen and the Indian subcontinent is pretty much limited to the past emigration of many members of the **Ismaili** Muslim community in Yemen to the Indian subcontinent, and, beginning in the 1980s, to the visits and relocation of increasing numbers of these persons back to Ismaili pilgrimage sites in the Haraz region of Yemen near **Manakha**.

INDIAN OCEAN. The vast body of water to the south and southeast of South Arabia, running into the Arabian Sea and Gulf of Aden. This ocean for millennia provided the wind-borne moisture that falls as rain and supports life in Yemen and the sea routes that allowed Arab sailors and traders to use their sailing ships propelled by the **monsoon** winds to connect South Arabia, East Africa, the Indian subcontinent, and points farther east. From the beginnings of the Age of Imperialism in the 16th century, the Indian Ocean made South Arabia an object of interest and concern to expansive European states.

INDONESIA. See HADHRAMAWT AND WADI HADHRAMAWT; IRSHAD SOCIETY.

INFRASTRUCTURE DEVELOPMENT. The **1962 Revolution** found North Yemen virtually without any components of a modern infrastructure. The country was without electricity and systems of piped water; there were no local telephone systems, much less a national one. There were virtually no paved roads. Although work was progressing on the motorable highway that would enclose the triangle formed by **Sanaa**, **Taiz**, and **al-Hudayda**, the three cities were still connected only by unpaved roads and tracks—and by the telegraph line left from **Ottoman** Turkish days. There was no regular air service and no modern airport, and the construction of modern port facilities at al-Hudayda was just beginning.

The situation in South Yemen at independence in 1967 was different. Aden had a modern, well-equipped port and the makings of a modern international airport were available at the British airbase at **Khormaksar**. Generally, Aden had most of the modern amenities, albeit in short supply and antiquated versions thereof. But Aden was an island of modernity in South Yemen, and that was the problem. Not much modern infrastructure was to be found beyond the environs of Aden—and, more important, that modern port city was not connected to the rest of the country by modern means of transport and communications. The infrastructure connecting the major settlement areas consisted of dirt tracks, unpaved roads, small airstrips, and wireless and telegraph communications. Indeed, one profound, unintended effect of Great Britain's policy of **air control** of the **Aden Protectorates** was that the country that the British left in 1967 was one held together tenuously by a network of small airstrips and small planes rather than one of motorable roads and lorries.

As a consequence, infrastructure development was a top priority for the YAR after the 1962 Revolution and for the PDRY after independence in 1967. Both of them made considerable progress in this regard in the 1970s and 1980s. If the YAR made more progress than South Yemen, it is primarily because it was the recipient of far more external development aid, both during and after the **Yemeni Civil War** of 1962–1970. One of the YAR's major achievements was its new network of roads, and the development and integration of the country is captured in space and time by road building: first, the paved outline of the triangle connecting Sanaa, Taiz, and al-Hudayda; then the paved ribbons going from the triangle north to **Saada**, south to **Turba** and **Mawiyah**, east to **Marib** and **al-Baydha**, and west to **Hajja** and **al-Mahwit**; next the paved roads inside the triangle; and finally—and perhaps most important—the hundreds of unpaved tracks blasted and bulldozed to connect thousands of villages and hamlets to the main roads and the cities and big towns. These tracks were largely the results of ad hoc, semiprivate and locally based efforts, the fortuitous mix of a burgeoning **Local Development Association** movement and the inflow of vast amounts of workers' **remittances**. The latter also made possible the thousands of four-wheel drive Toyotas to ply these roads and tracks.

By contrast, road building in South Yemen was less well funded, controlled by the state at the center, and less extensive—and the autos available to use the roads were far fewer. Still, the PDRY also made significant progress on this score. The paved coast road connected Aden to **Mukalla** and points farther to the east; two paved roads made Wadi **Hadhramawt** accessible to the rest of the country; and paved roads also gave access to the highlands north and east of Aden. Finally, a paved road went to the border with North Yemen and met a paved road coming South to the border from Taiz.

With Yemeni **unification** in 1990, the roads connecting the two parts of Yemen took on new significance. A paved road connected Sanaa to Wadi Hadhramawt by way of Marib. In addition, roads are being paved that connect the ROY to **Oman** through **Mahra** and to connect the ROY to **Saudi Arabia** on the **Tihama**.

Domestic air transport developed slowly in both Yemens, but perhaps more slowly in the YAR than in the PDRY. With unification, however, a strong network has emerged that connects Sanaa, Aden, al-Hudaida, Taiz, Mukalla, **Seiyun**—and even **Socotra**. The railroad never came to the Yemens, although there is talk in the 21st century of a line from the **Gulf** via **Oman**.

Both Yemens built modern international airports, in Sanaa and Aden (Khormaksar), which they continued to enlarge and improve in the 1980s. Rehabilitation of the Aden airport, damaged during the **War of Secession** in 1994, was completed in mid-2001 and included a new runway able to handle large, long-haul aircraft. Hopes that the Aden airport could become a regional cargo hub were set back, at least temporarily, when the plans to build an "air cargo village" ran afoul of corruption involved in the second phase of the Aden Free Zone project. Yemen also has major airports at al-Hudayda, Taiz and Riyan (Mukalla).

In the days before modern air travel, access to and from Yemen was largely by sea and through its ports. The main ports of Yemen today are al-Hudayda, Aden, Mukalla, and al-Mukha. In the 1960s, al-Hudayda was transformed by the **Soviet Union** from a shallow, unprotected harbor into a modern port. It has gone through successive upgradings and expansions and remains the main port of entry for Sanaa and most of North Yemen. By the 1950s, Aden's magnificent harbor had grown into one of the busiest in the entire world, only to go into sharp decline after independence in 1967. Since the mid-1990s, however, the run-down, out-of-date port facilities have been repaired, modernized, and expanded. Although getting off to a slow start due to corruption, mismanagement and security concerns after **9/11** and the U.S.S. *Cole* and *Limburg* bombings, the **Aden Container Terminal** and the Aden Free Zone promise to restore Aden's stature as a port. **Mukalla** is the main port of entry to Wadi Hadhramawt, and a revived **al-Mukha** helps serve the needs of North Yemen's southern uplands. Bir Ali, just to the west of Mukallah, is a terminal for oil exports, as is Ras Isa on the Red Sea.

As with the various avenues and means of transportation, the spread of electricity traced the development and integration of each of the Yemens. The government of each brought unreliable supplies of electricity to its cities and major towns in the 1970s and then started to create countrywide power grids in the 1980s. Work in the late 1980s to connect the power grids of Taiz in the YAR with Aden in the PDRY for the purpose of power sharing anticipated the political unification that came in 1990. Especially in the YAR, the small locally and often privately owned generator for village or household picked up in many places where the state system ended. Electricity also meant radio networks, extended by portable radios. And with electricity came television, beginning in 1975 in the YAR.

Despite a major effort to meet the ROY's growing energy needs, demand has outstripped supply, and in 2009 there were few place in the ROY not faced with frequent, and often prolonged, blackouts and brownouts. The generation of electricity in Yemen has depended upon ample supplies of relatively cheap oil, and Yemen's rapidly dwindling oil supplies have become a source of concern. Plans now have Yemen converting from oil to gas as its primary fuel for power generation, a process that began in 2007. A gas-fueled electricity plant with a first-phase output of 341 megawatts, and funded at $159 by the Saudi Fund for Development (SFD), the Arab Fund for Economic and Social Development and the Yemeni government is being built near Marib. It was due to be completed by in 2009, and a second phase is planned for completion in the near future.

Telephone communications within the two Yemens developed in a similar manner in the 1970s and 1980s, as it did between the two parts of Yemen, especially after unification. By 2000, moreover, the cell phone network had leapfrogged over the old communications technology. Each of the Yemens, and especially the YAR, improved its telephone communications with the outside world beginning in the mid-1970s, and the telegraph and telex were soon largely discarded. Not long after unification, the Internet and e-mail came to Yemen, and Internet cafés began springing up after 2000, connecting people in a new way both within Yemen and with the outside world.

Both Yemens provided their major cities with modern water systems, but these have not kept up with population growth and have spread slowly. Modern water systems came to the large towns only in the 1990s, and crude piped-water systems have become common in villages and small towns only since the mid-1990s. As the population grows and urbanization spreads, Yemen remains plagued by the lack of abundant, readily available supplies of clean water. The big towns and even some of the cities, especially Taiz, are subject to water shortages and rationing.

The two Yemens, but especially the YAR, were generating large and growing amounts of garbage and other waste at an alarming rate by the 1980s, a problem theretofore unknown in what had been a culture of scarcity. Cities, towns and roadsides were increasingly festooned with, among other things, plastic bags of many colors and empty plastic water bottles. This problem remains generally unsolved, save for a few successful waste-collection schemes—e.g., Sanaa's surprising success in this area since 1999 with a horde of diligent men in orange and women in blue and a system based on cost recovery, decentralization, and private contracting.

The problem of collecting and treating of human waste and other liquids largely remains pressing and unsolved, especially outside the several largest cities. Even Sanaa has a big problem. Its incomplete, defective sewage treatment facility, which is located close by Sanaa International Airport, has been dubbed the "Sanaa Perfume Factory."

INGRAMS, HAROLD AND DOREEN. The British colonial officer who as the first resident adviser to the **Quaiti** sultanate in **Mukalla** organized the government of the newly created Eastern **Aden Protectorate** in the late 1930s and who in 1936 had overseen the grand truce that brought the **Hadhramawt** out of a long period of anarchy and fighting. The truce, the result of long and difficult negotiations and allegedly the signatures of more than 1,400 major and minor tribal figures, came to be known as "the Peace of Ingrams." It was a remarkable and lasting achievement, the credit for which Ingrams properly shared with Sayyid abu Bakr ibn Shaykh **al-Kaf**, the revered head of a great **sayyid** family.

Ingrams was a skilled Arabist and student of Arabia in the classic British imperial mold, almost the last of his kind. He was the author of such books of lasting value as *Arabia and the Isles* (London, 1942) and *The Yemen: Imams, Rulers and Revolutions* (London, 1963). The former is a detailed narrative of his experiences in South Arabia, and the latter is an insightful comparison of the two Yemens on the occasion of the **1962 Revolution** and the creation of the YAR—and half a decade before Great Britain's departure from Aden. The third edition of *Arabia and the Isles,* published in 1966, the year before Britain's exit, contains a long introduction in which Ingrams argues with himself, T. E. Lawrence, his friend Sir Charles **Johnston**, and others over Arab political realities and possibilities and the proper role of British **colonialism** in light of them. Doreen Ingram, the colonial officer's wife and true partner, authored books, articles, and reports on their experiences and social conditions in the Hadhramawt. *See also* COLONIAL ADMINISTRATION AND ADMINISTRATORS.

INTEREST (PRESSURE) GROUPS. Notwithstanding much talk in and about Yemen since the mid-1990s regarding non-governmental organizations (NGOs) and civil society organizations, the network of organizations standing between Yemeni individuals and groups on the one hand and the state and its institutions on the other remained relatively weak through the first decade of the 21st century. These intermediaries had exploded in number and had become very assertive in the heady pluralist setting that prevailed from just before Yemeni **unification** in 1990 through the mid-1990s, only to be systematically reined in by the **Salih regime** in the years after the **War of Secession** in 1994. Since about 2000, however, there have been a number of instances of interest groups or NGOs trying to reassert the independence needed to represent and defend their members in relation to other groups and especially the state.

In South Yemen, during the period of Great Britain's rule, interest groups had represented Yemeni and other interests. There were the

Aden Trade Union Congress and various merchant and trade associations After 1967, these were destroyed or absorbed by a regime that envisioned a socialist regime and society led by a vanguard party. The ideology of the **Yemeni Socialist Party** (YSP) did call for mass membership organizations. In the 1970s and 1980s, mass organizations linked, with varying degrees of success, the people to the PDRY's party–state by performing the functions of policy transmission and feedback, advocacy, socialization, and recruitment. Among them were the General Union of Workers, the Democratic Yemen Peasant's Union, the Democratic Yemen Youth Organization, the General Union of Yemeni Women, the General Union of Yemeni Students, and a number of professional groups. These groups and others were harnessed to the task of socialist construction, leaving them little freedom to represent the interests of their members to the party–state.

In the YAR after the **1962 Revolution**, there were no comparable organizations that allowed the regime to mobilize and organize the "masses." In part, this was because there were few masses—i.e., few large economic institutions in which a large number of people worked. In the few situations where interest groups with large memberships did appear, those groups, while possibly more autonomous and representative than their counterparts in the PDRY, were generally weak and ineffectual. Perhaps indicative of the situation in the YAR, one of the most assertive organizations in the 1970s and 1980s was the taxi drivers union.

With unification in 1990, many of PDRY's mass organizations merged with their comparable interest groups in the YAR—e.g., the umbrella **labor and trade unions** merged and became the General Federation of Yemeni Labor Unions. The merged organizations were somewhat Janus-faced, sometimes representing their members but more often acting on behalf of the state. Since 2000, however, some of these interest groups in the ROY have begun to reassert themselves and have begun to push back against the Salih regime's pushback of a half-decade earlier. The chambers of commerce and industry and the syndicates representing teachers, professors, doctors, lawyers, and workers in other professions have spoken out and taken to the street in response to growing hardships. By contrast— except for the bigger farmers, who rely heavily on subsidized diesel fuel—Yemen's largely impoverished agricultural majority has not effectively asserted itself.

Institutional advocacy for **women** provides a special case. With unification, the General Union of Yemeni Women, which had vigorously and successfully defended the rights, status, training, and employment of women in the PDRY after 1968, merged with the smaller, weaker women's organization in the YAR to form a single organization, the Yemeni Women's Union (YWU). After a decade's effort to reconcile the very different political cultures of the two groups, the YWU began to assert itself forcefully on the political stage after 2000.

Perhaps the model NGO fighting for the rights of its members and rights in general since 2000 has been the Yemeni Journalists Syndicate (YJS). The YJS, though originally serving primarily to enable the Salih regime to manage and discipline the journalists, increasingly evolved into a organization ready to defend and fight for freedom of the press and the rights of journalists. *See also* LABOR UNIONS.

INTERNAL SECURITY. *See* SECURITY SERVICES.

INTERNATIONAL BANK FOR RECONSTRUCTION AND DEVELOPMENT. *See* IMF/WORLD BANK.

INTERNATIONAL MONETARY FUND. *See* IMF/WORLD BANK.

INVESTMENT LAWS. The 1991 investment law for the ROY, in a bid to attract overseas Yemeni, other Arab, and non-Arab foreign capital to Yemen, claimed to create "one-stop shopping" by concentrating an allegedly simplified set of investment procedures in a newly created **General Investment Authority** (GIA). Included also were substantial import duty and profit tax exemptions and new inducements for investments in certain geographic areas of the country.

The YAR had adopted its first foreign investment law in 1975, but that law did not lead to a significant increase in the inflow of private foreign capital. The PDRY, after adopting laws in 1971 and 1972 that severely restricted foreign investment in order to prevent distortion of its socialist revolution, reversed course and adopted the

Investment Promotion Law in 1981, a law that offered guarantees and tax concessions to foreign investors. It, too, had only a modest effect, and that mostly on investment by expatriate Yemenis. Efforts in each of the Yemens to implement revisions of their foreign investment laws were overtaken by **unification** in 1990—and thus the new law of 1991. The results of the new law and the GIA were to prove to be modest.

IRAN (PERSIA). The large non-Arab Muslim country, formerly called Persia, that faces the **Arabian Peninsula** from the other side of the **Gulf**, lying far to the northeast of the Yemens. In response to a call for help from **Himyarite** aristocrats, the Sassanid king of ancient Persia, Chosroes I, in A.D. 575 sent to Yemen an army that ousted the Christian ruler **Abraha** and then made South Arabia a province of an expanding Persian Empire. With the rise of Islam about a half century later in the nearby **Hijaz**, the Persian governor of Yemen and most Yemenis became early converts, and Yemen became a part of the new Arab–Islamic polity based in Mecca and Medina.

Thereafter, Persia had little impact on Yemen for more than a millennium, largely due to Yemen's isolation and parochialism. In addition, Persia was not Arab, and its brand of **Shii** Islam was quite unlike the **Zaydi** Shiism in North Yemen. In modern times, the Shah of Iran's support of **Oman** against the PDRY-supported **Dhufar Rebellion** made it relevant to South Yemen. The creation of the Islamic Republic of Iran in 1979, the militancy and inspirational effect of Ayatollah Khomeini, and the regional political impact of the **Iraq–Iran War** made Iran more salient in the 1980s to both Yemens. Hewing a line close to that of the Arab mainstream, the YAR worked for years to end the Iraq–Iran War on terms more favorable to **Iraq** than Iran. By contrast, and in tune with its old antagonistic relationship with the **Baath Party** regime in Iraq, the PDRY joined Syria in tilting toward Iran in the Iraq–Iran War.

Since Yemeni **unification** in 1990, the ROY has maintained good relations with Iran. In the middle of the first decade of the 21st century, the ROY did not seem overly concerned about Iran's alleged hegemonic ambitions in the Gulf region or talk of its leadership of a Shii bloc in the Middle East. Talk in Yemen about the latter possibility became more frequent with Iran's alleged support of the Shii in the growing Sunni–Shia sectarian conflict in Iraq in the gears after the United States invasion in 2003. It became louder with Iran's support for Hizbullah in Lebanon before, during, and after its short war with Israel in 2006 and during sectarian political conflict in Lebanon in 2007. Charges by some Yemenis that Iran was supporting the Shii militants fighting the ROY in the **al-Houthi Rebellion** strained relations briefly in 2007. Through it all, however, the ROY frequently expressed its support for Iran's right to develop nuclear power, a position most strongly challenged by the United States.

IRAQ. Probably the most consequential act for North Yemen in its relations with Iraq in the mid-20th century occurred during the reign of Imam **Yahya**. The treaty of 1931 led to the training in Iraq of several of Yemeni army officers who, years later, would play key roles in the **1962 Revolution,** including president-to-be Abdullah **al-Sallal**.

Iraq had it revolution in 1958 and, after a decade of instability and turmoil, the Iraqi **Baath Party** began nearly a generation of rule in 1968, most of it under Saddam Husayn. Despite occasional high hopes, relations between the YAR and Iraq—and, after 1990, between the ROY and Iraq—usually proved to have greater costs than they had benefits. Iraq's role in pressing for the **Kuwait Agreement** in 1979 did help prevent a decisive defeat of YAR forces in that year's **border war** with the PDRY. Thereafter, however, the hoped-for aid from oil-rich Iraq, as well as the hoped-for role it might play as a counterweight to **Saudi Arabia**, were not forthcoming, for Saddam Husayn soon got bogged down in the long, costly **Iraq–Iran War**. Nevertheless, Iraq did provide Yemen some aid, and the increasingly warm relations between Iraq and the YAR helped pave the way for their joining together in the **Arab Cooperation Council** in 1988.

Relations between the PDRY and Iraq from the late 1960s and 1990 were less dramatic and salient than in the case of the YAR. They got off on a bad footing in the mid-1960s when the Baath regime in Baghdad favored the **Front for the Liberation of Occupied South Yemen** and suspected the politics of the new **National Liberation Front**. By the mid-1970s, their increasingly hostile relationship seemed driven mostly by the fact that they were two "revolutionary" regimes driven by different **ideological** perspectives, Iraq sticking to its Baathism while the PDRY moved from pan-Arab socialism to a version of George **Habash**'s Marxist internationalism. Relations probably hit their nadir in 1980 when the PDRY recalled its ambassador after Iraqi agents killed an Iraqi exile in Aden. Iraq then began championing exiles opposed to the PDRY's **Yemeni Socialist Party** regime and the PDRY did not back Iraq in the long Iraq–Iran War. At the same time, both regimes did share close ties with the **Soviet Union**, supported the **Palestinian** cause, and feared the perceived hegemonic ambitions of Saudi Arabia.

Iraq invaded Kuwait in 1990, only a few months after Yemeni **unification**, triggering the events that led to the First **Gulf War**. The close the strong personal ties between Saddam Husayn and President **Salih**, and the desire of Yemens to assert their independence from Saudi Arabia caused the ROY to favor an Arab diplo-political solution at odds with the U.S.- and Saudi-led effort against Iraq. This position brought no benefits but rather staggering costs to the ROY, most notably the expulsion of Yemeni workers from Saudi Arabia, the loss of a huge amount of **remittances**, massive unemployment, and the loss of most foreign aid. Even by 2009, the ROY had yet to recover from this.

IRAQ–IRAN WAR. This long, costly war between **Iraq** and **Iran** from 1980 to 1988 had several, albeit minor, effects on both Yemens: it diverted the attentions of **Saudi Arabia** toward the **Gulf** and away from the Yemens, giving them some breathing room; it placed some strain on what had been improving relations between the two Yemens; it helped give the YAR a more important role to play in the Arab mainstream; and it served to isolate further the PDRY from most of the Arab world. The two Yemens tilted in opposite directions in the Iraq–Iran War, the YAR tilting toward Iraq and the PDRY toward Iran. Paradoxically, although the war made still stronger the ties between the YAR and Iraq that had become very strong at the end of the 1970s, the great financial cost of the war precluded the major financial aid hoped for by the YAR and promised by Iraq. The PDRY's stance on the war was close to that of Syria, the only major Arab state to side with Iran, and this served further to make the PDRY an odd man out in the Arab world. By contrast, the YAR took an active part in efforts to get the warring parties to accept a United Nations–mediated truce, a path favored by most of the Arab world and seen as advantageous to Iraq.

IRSHAD SOCIETY. The political organization, formed in 1915 by aspiring, well-to-do non-sayyids from Wadi **Hadhramawt**, which sought to challenge and reduce the **sayyid** families' privileged position and influence. The "Irshadi" engaged in a bitter struggle with the sayyids in Wadi Hadhramawt and especially in Indonesia and other places overseas where emigrants from the wadi had established communities over the centuries. Although the serious fighting ended in 1920, the struggle became a part of the political lore of South Yemen and, years later, the **National Liberation Front** interpreted it as the beginning of the "class struggle" and claimed the "Irshadi" to be political forebears.

AL-IRYANI AND AL-HAMDI REGIMES AND TRANSITION PERIOD. The regimes of presidents Abd al-Rahman **al-Iryani** and Ibrahim **al-Hamdi** constitute a decade-long transition period, 1967–1977, between the chaos of the **Yemeni Civil War** and Ali Abdullah Salih's long presidency of the YAR and then the ROY.

In retrospect, a turning point in this transition period was the **financial crisis of 1968–1971.** Beginning in 1970, significant state building took place under President al-Iryani, including the republican–royalist **reconciliation**, adoption of the **1970 Constitution**, and the holding of the 1971 **elections**. At the same time, some of the ministries and other agencies erected after the **1962 Revolution** were strengthened, among them the **Yemen Bank for Reconstruction and Development** and the Treasury Ministry, renamed the Ministry of **Finance**. The **Central Bank of Yemen** (CBY) was established, making possible the start of a commercial banking system, and the **Central Planning Organization** (CPO) was founded, creating a needed interface between Yemen's needs and external donors. As these efforts suggest, economic needs as well as political constraints caused Yemeni leaders during the al-Iryani era to focus on financial and economic institutions rather than on the military or the state bureaucracy. Only halting first steps were taken toward creating a modern civil service and toward the reform and reequipment of the **armed forces**—matters of great political sensitivity.

President Ibrahim al-Hamdi, who forced President al-Iryani into exile in 1974, believed in the modern state and worked to realize it during his three-and-a-half years in office. He promoted efforts to create or reform state institutions at the center, initiated the first major reequipment and reorganization of the armed forces, and fostered at the popular level an **ideology** of development and the idea of exchanging the benefits of state-sponsored modernization for allegiance to the state.

The YAR's northern border with **Saudi Arabia** was reaffirmed in 1973 when the al-Iryani regime acknowledged provisions of the **Taif Treaty** of 1934. Thereafter, President al-Hamdi tried to assert greater control over the Yemeni side of this border. Independence for South Yemen in 1967 and the final end of the civil war in the YAR in 1970 soon exposed the contradiction between the popular notion of one Yemen and the fact of two Yemeni states. The previous support of each of the Yemens for the other's national struggle gave way to strained relations and border incidents by the decade's end and, finally, a **border** war in 1972. Although this war ended, oddly enough, in an agreement for Yemeni **unification**, relations between the two Yemens remained strained through the last two years of al-Iryani's tenure. Relations did improve under al-Hamdi, but the agreement to unify was put on hold.

The results of efforts by the al-Iryani and al-Hamdi regimes at political construction in the YAR were far more modest. One aspect of the republican–royalist reconciliation was the granting of high office and influence in the state to leading **tribal** shaykhs in exchange for their allegiance to the republic. Although this incorporation of the tribalists nominally strengthened the state, the power of the al-Iryani regime was more apparent than real in the tribal heartland in the north and east. The influence of the shaykhs in the central government and over the fragmented, "tribalized" army enabled them to block further efforts to strengthen the state in relationship to the tribes.

In addition, reconciliation had been purchased at the price of expulsion of the **modernist** left from the military and the body politic after the **Sanaa Mutiny** in 1968. This weakened the position of other advocates of a strong state and undermined the loyalty of the more modern **Shafii** population in those provinces. Specifically, it led to the forced disbanding of the **Popular Resistance Forces** throughout the YAR and to the suppression of the new **peasant leagues** in the southern provinces. By 1970, it had ignited a low-level rebellion in the borderland next to the newly independent PDRY, one that became more explosive in the late 1970s. More broadly, the result was the narrowly based right-of-center republican regime that, with changes—real and cosmetic—persisted from the late 1960s into the 21st century.

The little political construction that took place during the al-Iryani era revolved primarily around the 179-member legislature, the **Consultative Council** (CC), which first convened after the 1971 elections. The CC replaced the National Council, the appointed 45-member quasi-legislature created in 1969. Political parties were banned outright by the 1970 Constitution, however, and in the absence of explicit organizational and ideological ties, the council functioned as an assembly of notables, oligarchs grouped into small shifting factions and only tenuously linked to one another and to their constituents. The barely clandestine parties that persisted were small and inconsequential, and the one half-hearted attempt by the al-Iryani regime to create a national political party in 1973—the **National Yemeni Union**—was stillborn.

After assuming office, President al-Hamdi soon came to personify the Yemeni nation and advanced this nationalism at the expense of narrow sectarian identities. This notwithstanding, al-Hamdi was unable to strengthen his position by translating his unprecedented popularity—and his charisma—into political organization. Indeed, his major political achievement inadvertently narrowed his regime's political base and shortened the state's reach at the same time that it consolidated the state at the center. Aware that the big shaykhs were using their new positions to protect the tribal system, al-Hamdi moved swiftly in 1974 to drive them from the state; to this end, he dissolved the legislature and suspended the constitution. The tribes replied with virtual rebellion, and the long standoff that ensued had the effect of extending the area of *de facto* tribal autonomy.

President Al-Hamdi's efforts to make up for this loss of support for the state and himself by reincorporating the modernist left seemed hesitant. In addition to maintaining old personal ties with a few key leftists, his attempt to create a more broadly based center-left coalition involved three initiatives: the **local development association** (LDA) movement, the **Correction Movement**, and a general people's congress. The LDA movement, launched formally in 1974, held out the promise of a grassroots organization nationwide; the Correction Movement, revived in 1975, offered a means to train and

place political cadres at all levels of the state. Despite these initiatives' initial promise, al-Hamdi seems to have had second thoughts
and to have pulled back from efforts to use these two initiatives as
bases for a broad, popular political movement. His subsequent plans
for a general people's congress were overtaken by his assassination in
1977. Frustrated by al-Hamdi's failure to grant them reentry into the
polity, several leftist groups created the **National Democratic Front**
(NDF) in 1976, which, in turn, became the basis of the **NDF rebel-**
lion that challenged the YAR regime a few years later.

The civil war finally behind it, the YAR of the 1970s underwent
significant socioeconomic development based upon the rapid creation of a modest capacity to absorb economic and technical aid, the
quite generous provision of this aid by the outside world, and—most
important—the massive inflow of workers' **remittances** that fostered
widespread and unprecedented consumption and prosperity. The
modest increase in state capacity was critical to Yemen's ability to
absorb significantly increased foreign aid. At the start of the decade,
the establishment of the CBY, and the creation of the CPO were
keys to this increase in capacity. By the late 1970s, work on an array
of state-sponsored, foreign-assisted infrastructure, agricultural, and
human resource development projects existed side by side with high
levels of remittance-fueled consumption, business and development
activity in the private sector. However, since they mostly passed
directly to the people without passing through the banks or other state
institutions, the remittances did more to buy time for a weak state
than to contribute directly to the state's capacity.

AL-IRYANI, DR. ABD AL-KARIM (1933–). The U.S.-educated
member of a great **qadi** family of North Yemen who, after returning
to the YAR in 1967 with a PhD in biology from Yale, served in key
positions for 40 years. He was founding director of the **Wadi Zabid**
project (1968–1972), founding chairman of the **Central Planning**
Organization and minister of development (1973–1976), and minister of education and president of Sanaa University, 1976–1978.

During a 1978–1980 hiatus from government, Dr. al-Iryani held
a high post in the **Kuwait Fund**, thereby strengthening his already
close ties with the Arab and international development communities.
Thereafter, he was prime minister twice (1980–1983 and 1998–2001)

and deputy prime minister and foreign minister nearly continuously from the mid-1980s through the mid-1990s. In addition, he was secretary general of the **General People's Congress** (1995–2005) and, most recently, adviser to the president (from 2002 to the present).

Dr Abd al-Karim was chief architect of the multi-staged process in the early 1980s that led to the **National Pact** and then the General People's Congress, the package of ideas and the political organization needed so badly by the still-fragile **Salih regime**. In addition, he was an architect of the YAR's hard line and then improved relations with the PDRY in the 1980s. Thereafter, he was an architect—perhaps the chief architect—of the **unification** of the two Yemens in 1988–1990. In 1994, shuttling between the **United Nations** in New York and Washington, D.C., he played a leading political role in preventing the undoing of the ROY during the **War of Secession**.

The nephew of Qadi Abd al-Rahman **al-Iryani**, the YAR's second head of state, he is arguably the best-educated, ablest, and most influential of the YAR's first-generation **modernists**. To many foreigners and Yemenis alike, he has been Yemen's "Mr. Development," the initiator of development planning in the YAR and a chief designer of the exploitation of its **oil** resources.

Despite dissembling claims in the 1970s to being a nonpolitical technocrat, Dr. Abd al-Karim proved to be a keen student of politics, unafraid of hard, fierce political combat. He served as informal political adviser to his uncle when he was head of state and has been an architect of domestic politics and foreign relations during the long tenure of President **Salih**. Indeed, critics have accused him of being too accommodating to—even an apologist for—the Salih regime.

Switching late in his youth from traditional qadi training, he received his modern secondary education in Aden and Cairo in the 1950s. As one of the first four Yemenis chosen for training in the United States' Point IV aid program, he began his 10-year educational odyssey in the United States in 1958, one that took him to universities in Texas, Oklahoma, Georgia, and Connecticut.

AL-IRYANI, QADI ABD AL-RAHMAN (1909–1998). The head of state of the YAR from late 1967 until mid-1974, his seven-year tenure was most notable for the republican–royalist **reconciliation** that ended the **Yemen Civil War** in 1970, holding of drafting and adoption of the **1970 Constitution** and the first parliamentary **elections** in 1971. President al-Iryani's tenure marked the transition from concern for the sheer survival of the republic to the beginnings of an effort, albeit fitful and unfocused, at political construction and socioeconomic development. Although his regime depended upon and was finally undone by the military, it was to be the YAR's only civilian regime.

Born in the Iryan region of North Yemen, al-Iryani was in the second half of the 20th century the head of an esteemed family of Sunni judges and teachers, followers of Qadi Muhammad Ali **al-Shawkani**. He ranks as a father of the Yemeni republic for his pre-1962 political efforts, alongside Muhammad **al-Zubayri** and Ahmad Muhammad **al-Numan**. A traditionally trained qadi who held to some modern ideas, he served as a bridge between the old **imamate** Yemen and the new republic. Indeed, some called him the "republican imam" and claimed that this was key to the successful transition. Most Yemenis referred to him as "al-Qadi."

President al-Iryani was placed in office with the ouster of the **Sallal** regime and remained there until the bloodless coup led by Ibrahim **al-Hamdi** in mid-1974. Col. Husayn Maswari, a relative of President al-Iryani with close ties to **Saudi Arabia**, was head of the **armed forces** during the al-Iryani era. With Prime Minister Abdullah al-**Hajri**, he secured major aid from the Saudis and conducted a purg of leftist politians and military officers in 1973. He was ousted in the al-Hamdi coup the following year.

President al-Iryani spent his exile after 1974 in Syria, was officially invited to return to Yemen in 1982, and thereafter made annual visits to his homeland. Upon his death in 1998, he was returned to Yemen for a hero's burial.

ISLAH (YEMENI REFORM GATHERING). This political party created shortly after Yemeni **unification** in 1990 and with the support of **Saudi Arabia**, combined politically strange bedfellows skeptical of, if not opposed to, the merger of the YAR with the Marxist PDRY: the **political Islamists**, especially the Muslim Brotherhood and its offshoots; the northern tribal shaykhs, especially those in or allied to the **Hashid** confederation; and some other conservative elements. The symbolic and often actual leaders of Islah were, on the tribal side, Shaykh Abdullah ibn Husayn **al-Ahmar**, the paramount shaykh of the Hashids, and Abd al-Majid **al-Zindani**, one-time head of the Yemeni branch of the Brotherhood and a leading Yemeni **salafi**. Conflicting interests and tensions between the tribes—who often take their Islam lightly—and the Islamists was evident virtually from the outset. In addition, the Islamists in Islah ranged from salafists led by al-Zindani, who became chairman of its Shura Council (Political Bureau) to moderate Islamic reformers such as Abd al-Wahab al-Anisi, its first secretary general.

Islah has proven to be both the most formidable challenger to the **Salih** regime and the party with the most ambiguous relationship to that regime and its **General People's Congress** (GPC). Regarding the ambiguity—when not in the government—has often acted, and been treated, as if it were; and, when in the government, Islah it has often behaved as if in the opposition. In short, it has often been difficult to describe Islah's behavior as oppositional, even when it was formally in opposition. This, in turn, is related to the ambiguous relationship between the president and his tribal ties with the Hashids led by Shaykh al-Ahmar; the shaykh is the president's shaykh, and the regime relies heavily on Hashid tribal ties. Manifestations of this ambiguity are Shaykh al-Ahmar's having remained speaker of the **Chamber of Deputies** after Islah went into opposition after the 1997 **elections** and Islah's having supported President Salih's reelection in 1999 while still in the opposition.

Islah's formidable nature is a function of its organization and dedicated cadres, grassroots support, and its network of educational, medical and other social services. It is a party that has a message and services—and a capacity to deliver both. On the tribal side, the shaykhs still command the respect and support of their followers and are able to deliver voters as well as fighters. Given these features, Islah quickly proved to be the largest and most formidable opponent of the unification regime headed by the GPC and the **Yemeni Socialist Party** (YSP) during the 30-month transition period after formal unification in 1990. It focused its attack on the new constitution's insufficiently Islamic character—boycotting the 1991 referendum on it—and on the ROY's stand on the First **Gulf War** in that same year. Islah did well in the April 1993 elections—way behind the GPC but on a par with the YSP—entered a three-party grand coalition government with these two parties and reaped some cabinet and other posts. Nevertheless, Islah remained largely marginalized until 1994 and the YSP's almost successful attempt at committing political suicide. The **War of Secession** that year ended the GPC–YSP partnership and forced the exile of most YSP leaders. Thereafter, the new government formed by the GPC and Islah provided the latter with additional cabinet posts, patronage, and increased political strength.

In the 1997 **elections**, having made a slightly poorer showing than in 1993, Islah went into the opposition. After the 2003 elections, it continued to play the role of opposition to the GPC government, increasingly as a leader of a coalition formed in 2002, the **Joint Meeting Parties** (JMP); Muhammad Qahtan of Islah became the JMP's official spokesman. The coalition was able to select a credible candidate for the 2006 presidential election and waged a respectable campaign against President Salih. Between its creation in 1990 and the 2006 election, Islah had evolved from being something of an uncertain, ambiguous appendage of President Salih to being part of an increasingly credible and formidable opposition.

This evolution is paralleled by an evolution within Islah itself. Since the mid-1990s, there have been the conflicting interests and tensions between experienced, pragmatic, moderate political Islamists—especially Muhammad al-Yadumi, Abd al-Aziz al-Anisi, and Muhammad Qahtan—on the one hand, who want to play, and benefit from, parliamentary politics, and both the strong tribal elements and the fringe of militant Islamists on the other hand. The pragmatists and moderates have been and continue to be in high-ranking party positions: Qahtan was a founding member of Islah in 1991 and is now head of its political office and a member of its Shura Council; al-Yadumi was founding editor in 1985 of *al-Sahwa*, the paper close to the Muslim Brotherhood that is now the voice of Islah, and secretary general of Islah in the 2000s to early 2007; and, finally, al-Anisi was Islah's first secretary general in 1991. The party conference in early 2007 registered the further ascendance, if not the triumph, of the younger wing of the party. True, Shaykh Abdullah was for the fourth time elected president of Islah—and this despite the party's three-term limit and his being in his seventies and in very bad health. However, while remaining a member of Islah's Shura Council, the militant al-Zindani was replaced as its chairman by Muhammad Ali Ajilan, a member of parliament. Yassin Abd al-Aziz al-Qubati, who now represents the moderate Muslim Brotherhood current of the party, was elected to Islah's Central Committee. Al-Yadumi was elected party vice president and Abd al-Wahab al-Anisi was again elected secretary general. The moderates, for the most part, had prevailed.

ISLAH PASS. The mountain pass about 30 miles south of Sanaa that separates the Sanaa region—its narrow plateau bounded by rugged mountains—from the long and wide plain of **Dhamar** to the south. Because it cradles the only easy route to the highlands from the southern part of North Yemen, as well as South Yemen, it has provided for millennia both a channel for goods, people, and ideas and a formidable line of defense for those from the north.

ISLAMIC FRONT. The political–military organization formed in the YAR in 1979 by leading tribalists and other conservatives with the encouragement and material support of **Saudi Arabia** for the purpose of opposing the insurgent **National Democratic Front** (NDF) and its "communist" PDRY allies. This was the time of the 1979 **Border War**, when the resolve and strength of the new **Salih regime** seemed suspect. From its birth until the virtual end of the **NDF rebellion** in 1982, the front occasionally contributed tribal forces to the anti-guerrilla fight, propagandized against the NDF and the PDRY, and put political pressure on the Salih regime not to accept a compromise short of suppression of the rebellion.

ISLAMIC JIHAD, YEMENI. See ADEN–ABYAN ISLAMIC ARMY (AAIA); AL-FADHLI; POLITICAL ISLAM, MODERN.

ISLAM IN YEMEN. See ISMAILIS IN YEMEN; POLITICAL ISLAM, MODERN; RELIGION AND RELIGIOUS GROUPS IN YEMEN; ZAYDIS AND SHAFIIS IN POLITICS AND SOCIETY.

ISLAMISTS AND ISLAMIC FUNDAMENTALISM. See POLITICAL ISLAM, MODERN.

ISMAIL, ABD AL-FATTAH. See ABD AL-FATTAH ISMAIL.

ISMAILIS IN YEMEN. These are members of an early esoteric, secretive, conspiratorial and eminently political sect of **Shii** Islam who, then as now, preferred to be called "Fatimids"—followers of Fatima, the Prophet's daughter, and her husband, Ali—but were called by their foes "Ismailis," an epithet that stuck. The Ismailis attempted without lasting success in the late ninth and early 10th centuries to establish a political base in remote, distant Yemen from which to challenge openly the orthodox **Sunnis** of the Abbasid Empire in Baghdad. This failed attempt had involved the efforts of secret "missionary" groups headed by ibn Hawshab Mansur al-Yeman and Ali ibn al-Fadl.

Changing their strategy, the Ismailis successfully established an independent political entity in North Africa that in the second half of the 10th century took the form of the Cairo-based Fatimid Caliphate. From this base, they finally succeeded in extending their rule over all of Yemen from the mid-10th to the mid-11th centuries under the local **Sulayhid** dynasty. With the demise of the Sulayhids after the rule of Queen **Arwa**, however, the Ismailis ceased to be a political force in Yemen. Indeed, they dwindled in number and became a much- and long-persecuted minority, their main and most persistent persecutors in Yemen being their fellow Shii Muslims, the **Zaydis**.

Harassed by the two strong Zaydi imams who ruled Yemen during the first half of the 20th century, the Ismailis who did not emigrate concentrated in only the tens of thousands in the mountainous Haraz region, below and east of Manakha, about halfway between Sanaa and al-Hudayda. With an increase in tolerance after the **1962 Revolution**, the Ismailis began to return to Yemen and, beginning in the late 1970s, many non-Yemeni Ismailis from the Indian subcontinent and farther east began to make pilgrimages to their important holy sites in Haraz—and some stayed. This process has continued in the new millennium. *See also* RELIGION AND RELIGIOUS GROUPS IN YEMEN.

ISRAEL. Israel's modest interest in the Yemens has been based primarily on the **Arab–Israeli conflict** and the possibility that, singly or together, they might allow their strategic location to be used to deny Israel access to and from the **Red Sea** via the **Bab al-Mandab Straits**. From time to time, there have been rumors of an Israeli surveillance presence on one or another island in the lower Red Sea. Israel also established some ties with **Eritrea** after the latter's independence in 1993 and about the time of the latter's conflict with the ROY over the Hanish Islands in 1995. In addition, Israel was concerned about the alleged role of the PDRY in the 1970s as a haven and training site for Palestinian fighters. When the **Palestine** Liberation Organization was forced to leave Lebanon in 1983, some of its forces were relocated to camps in the Yemens, remaining there until the Oslo peace process allowed them to be moved to Palestine in the mid-1990s.

Finally, Israel and many Israelis have always been interested in Yemen as the place from which many thousands of new Israeli citizens came shortly after independence in 1948—most by way of Operation Flying Carpet—and as the place in which a few thousand Yemeni Jews stayed but in diminishing numbers into the 21st century. Over the years, discrete contacts between Israel and the ROY have facilitated this trickling exodus of Yemeni Jews. After 2000, a small number of Israelis were allowed to visit Yemen, and rumors spread about the possible establishment of diplomatic relations—rumors that worsening relations between Israel and the Palestinians soon put an end to. Some of the remaining Jews were harrassed and forced from their homes in 2008 during the *al-Houthi Rebellion.*

AL-ITTAHAD. *See* MADINAT AL-SHAAB.

– J –

JABAL NABI SHUAYB. *See* NABI SHUAYB, JABAL.

JABAL NUQUM. *See* Sanaa.

AL-JAMAI FAMILY. *See* AL-UDAYN REGION.

JAMIL, JAMAL. This Iraqi army officer came to Yemen in 1940 as an instructor on a training mission, remained in Yemen in the service of the **imamate** after the mission ended in 1942, and inspired with his modern political ideas many of the young Yemeni officers who were beginning to think that the imamate stood in the way of national progress and other goals. He rose to the rank of colonel in Imam Yahya's army and by 1948 had become the director of public security for the Sanaa district. He took an active part in the military aspect of the **1948 Revolution** after the assassination of Imam **Yahya** and paid for this involvement with his life when the coup was quickly undone. Jamil had had a role in the Bakr Sidqi coup in Iraq in 1936 and may have stayed in Yemen in 1942 because he could not go home.

After the **1962 Revolution**, Jamal Jamil was made a Yemeni national hero by the men who carried out the revolution. Among the latter were President **al-Sallal** and General Hasan **al-Amri** who, as young soldiers, had been sent by Imam Yahya to Iraq in the mid-1930s for training, had been trained by Jamil in Iraq in the mid-1930s, and had come under his influence again in Yemen in the 1940s. On Tahrir Square in Sanaa, a school remains named in his honor.

JANAD. The site of possibly the second oldest mosque in Yemen, one allegedly built during the life of the Prophet. Janad is located not far south of **Ibb** and not far north of **Taiz**, just to the east of the main road from Taiz to Sanaa.

JAPAN. Japan's presence diplomatically and as a source of economic and technical assistance in Yemen, while increasing dramatically in the 1980s and since, has lagged behind its sometimes dominant commercial presence, most evident in consumer electronics, construction equipment, and the various models of four-wheel drive Toyotas, long the vehicle of choice of Yemenis since the mid-1970s. The cement factory in **Amran**, a major turnkey and management-support project, completed in the early 1980s, provided a good indication of Japan's growing presence.

JARULLAH UMAR (1942–2002). The politically astute and pragmatic politician and political thinker who, at the time of his assassination in 28 December, 2002, was deputy secretary general of the **Yemeni Socialist Party** (YSP) and the chief architect of the then half-formed **Joint Meeting Parties** (JMP). The JMP is significant as the first successful attempt to forge a coalition of parties in opposition to President **Salih** and his **General People's Congress** (GPC). Jarullah was killed just after delivering a speech before a conference held by **Islah**, the YSP's chief partner in the JMP. He was killed by a militant **political Islamist** and, two days later, his assassin's colleague killed three staff members of the American Baptist hospital in **Jibla**.

The leader of the **Revolutionary Democratic Party**, Jarullah in 1979 became the head of the **People's Party for Yemeni Unity**, the single Marxist party formed out of a merger of several opposition parties, and a leader of the more diverse and fluid **National Democratic Front** (NDF). In these capacities, he was deeply involved as a guerrilla leader in the **NDF rebellion** waged from the late 1970s to 1982. Unlike most of the NDF leaders who went north after the rebellion was put down, Jarullah chose to stay in Aden and continue opposition to the **Salih regime**. As NDF leader and as a member of the YSP politburo, he and his fighters played a key role in the YSP's intra-party bloodbath in Aden, in 1986, the **13 January events**.

With Yemeni **unification** in 1990, Jarullah came north and assumed an active political role as a leader of the YSP and as minister of culture in the GPC–YSP transitional government. Opposed to the path that took his party into the **War of Secession**, he went into exile in Egypt in 1994. He returned in the ROY in 1996 and set about to create a new YSP. His experience in the PDRY in 1986 and in the unification process in the first half of the 1990s had made Jarullah a fervent believer and eloquent advocate of pluralism and multiparty democracy—and in the rights associated with liberal democracy. He became equally sure of the need to create the broad opposition coalition—the JMP—capable of defeating the Salih regime.

From the province of Ibb in North Yemen, Jarullah studied Islamic jurisprudence as a youth and later trained at the police academy in Sanaa. In jail after the **Sanaa Mutiny** in 1968, he evolved from being a nationalist in the **Arab Nationalist Movement** to being a socialist and a lifelong opponent of the conservative republicanism that came to prevail in the YAR in the 1970s.

His assassination and his loss to Yemeni politics were lamented generally by supporters as well as opponents of the regime. However, his untimely death probably strengthened the resolve of the parties in the JMP to overcome obstacles to building a strong opposition coalition, perhaps making this his greatest legacy.

AL-JAWF AND WADI JAWF. The province and large geographic region northeast of Sanaa in North Yemen that fans out from near **Amran** east to the desert and the border with **Saudi Arabia**, embracing the vast drainage area that feeds Wadi Jawf. Although rainfall is modest at the head of this drainage area, its sheer size gathers a considerable reserve of groundwater, the potential of which for irrigated agriculture was only beginning to be tapped by the mid-1980s. Al-Jawf province was created after 1980, and the **tribal**, thinly populated, and quite inaccessible region was the last large area of the YAR to come under more than nominal state control, this taking place gradually in the 1980s.

Known in ancient times for the rich **trade route** that traversed it, al-Jawf became important in the 1980s for its sharing in the YAR's earliest-discovered sizable oil and gas reserves in the **Marib/al-Jawf basin**. In addition came a growing realization of its considerable agricultural potential. Since the new millennium and its emphasis on the **War on Terror** this still-weakly controlled province has provided sanctuary to militant **political Islamists**, and its long, porous border with Saudi Arabia has provided a path for the flow of arms and militants between Yemen and its neighbor.

AL-JAWI, UMAR (1938–1997). The independent socialist intellectual who at the time of Yemeni **unification** in 1990 founded the Yemeni Unionist Gathering (Tajammu Wahdawi), sought to save the ROY through the **Document of Pledge and Accord**, declared Tajammu's opposition to secession on the eve of the **War of Secession** in 1994 and thereafter led Tajammu in opposition to what it regarded as the corrupt and anti-democratic practices of the **Salih regime**. Al-Jawi and Tajammu joined with the **Yemeni Socialist Party** and other opposition parties to boycott the 1997 parliamentary **elections**. Tajammu, the talkative, loosely knit group of mostly **Adenis**, called by poet Abdullah Baradduni "the party of intellectuals," continued to oppose the Salih regime after al-Jawi's 1997 death in its weekly discussion meetings and its newspaper, *Al-Tajammuaa.*

A native of **Lahej**, Umar al-Jawi went to Cairo in the early 1950s for prep school, started university only to be expelled from Egypt for political activities in 1958, and went to Moscow, where he earned a

B.A. and an M.A. by 1966. Al-Jawi was one of the southerners who came north in late 1967 to help keep Sanaa in republican hands during the 70-day **Siege of Sanaa**. In the wake of the **Sanaa Mutiny** in 1968, he was involved in the creation of the Laborers and Farmers Party in 1969. Back in Aden, he worked to create the Yemeni Authors and Writers Union in early 1970 and edited its magazine. In 1989, he founded and became president of the Yemeni Council for Professional and Intellectual Authorities. Al-Jawi authored a number of books, mostly political in content and significance.

JEWS AND JUDAISM IN YEMEN. *See* ISRAEL; RELIGION AND RELIGIOUS GROUPS IN YEMEN.

JIBLA (DHU JIBLA). The beautiful hillside town several miles southwest of **Ibb** that Queen **Arwa** made her new capital and embellished with fine mosques, palaces, and other public buildings in the late 11th and early 12th centuries. Jibla thereafter served for centuries as a center of Islamic teaching and scholarship in Yemen. Largely bypassed by the main highway and modern Yemen, Jibla has since the 1960s been home to a small but highly regarded American Baptist hospital. At the end of 2002, the hospital was witness to the killing of three American health workers by a Muslim militant, an associate of the killer, two days earlier, of **Yemeni Socialist Party** leader **Jarullah** Omar.

JIDDA. In the **Hijaz** and more than 450 miles north of the border with Yemen, Jidda is Saudi Arabia's major city and port on the **Red Sea** and, as such, has for many centuries been the historic gateway to Mecca and Medina for Muslim pilgrims from throughout the world. Long the most "modern," socially tolerant city in—and window on the world for—the long-isolated expanse that become the Kingdom of Saudi Arabia in the 1920s, Jidda now has a modern commercial center, port, and modern international air terminus and is the nearest major Saudi city to the ROY.

JIDDA AGREEMENT, 1965. *See* YEMENI CIVIL WAR.

JIDDA AGREEMENT, 2000. *See* BORDERS.

AL-JIFRI, ABD AL-RAHMAN ALI (1943–). The member of the aristocratic and well-to-do **sayyid** family in **Lahej** prior to independence in 1967 who, as head of the League of the Sons of Yemen (Rabita or RAY) and later the National Association of Opposition Groupings (MAWJ), was a key Yemeni front man for **Saudi Arabia**'s opposition to the PDRY and then the ROY. Rabita had its roots in the **South Arabian League**, an early political organization founded in 1951 by Muhammad al-Jifri. Abd al-Rahman created Rabita years after he was forced into exile in the late 1960. After three decades, by then a Saudi citizen, he returned to Yemen at the time of Yemeni **unification** in 1990 and positioned himself and his party in the opposition during the transition period, the 1993 **elections** and the year of turmoil that followed. He aligned himself with the mostly southern secessionists in the **War of Secession** in 1994 and became vice president in the short-lived **Democratic Republic of Yemen**.

Again in exile in 1994, al-Jifri created MAWJ and used it to wage an unremitting public relations campaign against the **Salih regime** in the United States, Europe, and, especially, Great Britain in the second half of the 1990s. With the conclusion of the **Saudi–Yemeni Border Agreement** in 2000, the Saudis quickly and quietly put al-Jifri and MAWJ on the shelf. He returned to Yemen shortly before the 2006 presidential elections, with the blessings of his old opponent, President Ali Abdullah **Salih**, and announced plans to work for political reforms. No one paid much attention.

JIHADISM. *See* POLITICAL ISLAM, MODERN.

JIHAF, JABAL. The nearly 8,000 foot mountain that looms over **Dhala** in the mountainous area north of Aden not far from the border with North Yemen which, because of its strategic location, figured in conflict between the **Great Britain** in the south and either the **Ottoman** Turki or the Zaydi **imamate** in the north. Later, after 1967, Turks it figured in conflict between the YAR and both the PDRY and the PDRY-supported **National Democratic Front** rebels.

JIZAN. The small port and region on the **Red Sea** in **Saudi Arabia**, about 50 miles north of the border with Yemen, that has long served much of the **Asir** region. Part of the area claimed as Yemeni by many

Yemenis, Jizan was occupied by Saudi Arabia in the brief **Saudi–Yemeni War of 1934**. Imam **Yahya** suspended Yemen's claim to Jizan—and to **Najran** and Asir—in that same year in the **Treaty of Taif**. Many Yemenis continued to claim Jizan, and the claim was not given up formally and finally until the **Saudi–Yemeni Border Agreement** of 2000.

JOHNSTON, SIR CHARLES H. *See* COLONIAL ADMINISTRATION AND ADMINISTRATORS.

JOINT COMMITTEE ON A UNIFIED POLITICAL ORGANIZATION. The joint YAR–PDRY committee that, although called for in the original 1972 **unification agreement**, met for the first time in late October 1989, signaled the political breakthrough that led to the **30 November Agreement** on Yemeni **unification**, and thereafter led the way in talks and decisions on the organization of political life in unified Yemen. It was this six-man committee, co-chaired by YAR Foreign Minister Abd al-Karim **al-Iryani** and PDRY leader **Salim Salih** Muhammad, which proposed and then helped implement a multiparty system for the ROY—instead of a "unified political organization" combining the ruling parties of the two Yemens.

JOINT MEETING PARTIES (JMP). The coalition of opposition parties that began to take form after 2000 and by the middle of the decade consisted of five parties: **Islah**, the **Yemeni Socialist Party** (YSP), the **Popular Nasirist Unity Organization**, the **Union of Popular Forces** and **al-Haqq**. Largely the result of the vision and persistence of YSP leader **Jarullah** Umar, the JMP formed shortly after Jarullah's assassination at the end of 2002. The coalition has been dominated by the YSP and even more so by the more politically formidable Islah. The predecessor to the JMP, the Higher Coordination Council for the Opposition (HCCO), was formed to contest the **General People's Congress** (GPC) in parliamentary elections in 1977 and in the presidential and local council elections in 1999 and 2001, respectively. The HCCO had included the YSP and some of the small parties—but not Islah. Getting Islah on board was the work of Jarullah, Muhammad Abd al-Malik **al-Mutawakkil**, and leaders of the moderate wing of the party.

The JMP was created to present a united opposition to the GPC in the 2003 parliamentary **elections**, and in December 2002 they agreed on a policy of "coordination" in the upcoming voting. Despite strong efforts by the **Salih regime** to lure away either or both Islah and the YSP, the JMP grew in strength and confidence. The JMP's presence was felt only modestly in the 2003 elections, and its first big test as a credible and formidable opposition were the 2006 presidential and local council **elections**. In late 2005, the JMP adopted a program of reforms that focused on the economic and political needs of Yemen and the failings of the regime. With voting set for September, the JMP selected a credible presidential candidate, the political "independent" Faisal **bin Shamlan**, and with him waged a vigorous presidential campaign. Under the circumstances, bin Shamlan's 22 percent, against President Salih's 77 percent, was judged respectable, although the poor showing of the JMP's member parties in the local council elections was disappointing to many in the opposition. The JMP took heart from the results and remained intact in the subsequent years. It analyzed the results and its performance, declared its intention to closely monitor and critique the Salih regime, and began planning for the parliamentary elections in 2009 elections that were subsequently postponed for two years. Sometimes without unity and inconsistent in its message and actions, the JMP has disappointed some of the harshest critics of the Salih regime.

JOINT MILITARY COMMISSION. *See* WAR OF SECESSION.

JOINT UNIFICATION COMMITTEES. The joint YAR–PDRY specialized technical committees that were set up in 1972 to facilitate Yemeni unification under the **Cairo Agreement** and the **Tripoli Summit Agreements**. Each committee had a task: the constitution; foreign affairs and diplomatic representation; military affairs; economics and finance; legislative and judicial affairs; health; and education, culture, and information. The committees soon became moribund, only to be revived as politics suggested or required in the mid-1970s, 1979, and the mid-1980s. Paradoxically, the work of these committees both served as a substitute for concrete steps toward **unification** that either or both sides were unwilling to take at the time and, by producing key reports, studies and other products, facilitated the unification process when its time came so unexpectedly in 1990.

JOL. The arid and generally forbidding and uninhabitable high limestone plateau that stands between the coast of South Yemen and southern edge Wadi **Hadhramawt** and between the northern edge of the wadi and the **Empty Quarter** of Saudi Arabia. The southern Jol is almost waterless and rises to several thousand feet in places. It has served both to separate the well-watered and populated wadi from Aden and much of the rest of South Yemen and to keep the wadi's secrets from all but a small number of western **travelers** until the middle decades of the 20th century. Although modern means of transport have overridden this barrier in recent times, its effects are still apparent in the persistent cultural and sociopolitical separateness of the society and people of Wadi Hadhramawt.

JORDAN, HASHIMITE KINGDOM OF. Both poor and quite dependent on **Saudi Arabia** and the other oil-rich Arab Gulf states for aid in the 1970s and 1980s, Jordan and the YAR have been each other's good, but not-too-important, moderate, centrist Arab friend since the mid-1970s. After the 1960s and the **Yemeni Civil War** in which King Husayn sided with the Saudis against the YAR and Egypt's intervention in Yemen, Jordan began providing the YAR with modest amounts of military training assistance and other forms of technical aid. These two countries were, along with **Iraq** and **Egypt**, members of the short-lived **Arab Cooperation Council** in 1989. By contrast, except for the mid-1970s, when King Hussein provided some military aid to **Oman** against the PDRY-backed **Dhufar rebellion**, Jordan's relations with the PDRY were inconsequential over these decades.

During the crisis that resulted in the First **Gulf War** in 1991, Jordan and the just-created ROY were the two key Arab countries which refused to endorse the plan of the U.S.- and Saudi-led international coalition to use force to expel **Iraq** from **Kuwait**, a position for which they both were punished by the Saudis and the Gulf states in the early 1990s. If anything, this strengthened the ties between Jordan and the ROY. The former made a serious effort to mediate in the political conflict between President **Salih** and the leaders of the **Yemeni Socialist Party** in 1993 and 1994 and favored the maintenance of the

ROY and opposed the **War of Secession** in mid-1994. King Abdullah's accession to the throne after the death of King Husayn did not noticeably affect the good relations between Jordan and the ROY, which have remained steady in the first decade of the 21st century.

JOURDAIN, JOHN. *See* TRAVELERS.

JOURNALISTS SYNDICATE, YEMENI. *See* INTEREST (PRESSURE) GROUPS.

JUBAN. The North Yemeni border town and military garrison that, lost after a heavy siege and then retaken, became the site of some of the sharply escalating fighting between the YAR- and PDRY-supported **National Democratic Front** (NDF) forces in early 1982. This fighting led into the major YAR offensive that broke the back of the NDF rebellion by the middle of that year.

JUGHMAN, YAHYA. A member of the **Famous Forty**, a man known for his eloquence in spoken Arabic and English, who, after studying in France and the United States, served the YAR after 1962 as ambassador to the United Nations, minister of foreign affairs, deputy prime minister for foreign affairs, and adviser to the president at various times in the 1960s and 1970s. He was known as a friend of the United States and an enemy of the "communism" that gained a foothold in South Yemen by the late 1960s. As such, he was most prominent in the late 1960s and early 1970s, when the YAR was trying to build links to the West and was sliding into hostility with the radical regime in Aden.

AL-JUNAYD, MUHAMMAD AHMAD. One of North Yemen's first three civil engineers and a member of a learned and esteemed family of religious leaders from the **Tihama** near al-Hudayda who, after receiving a modern education in Aden and England between the late 1940s and the early 1960s, returned to the new YAR about a year after the **1962 Revolution** and began a long and continuous career in government service. His career probably reached a high point in the 1970s when he served as founding minister of finance, 1974–1978, and as deputy prime minister for economic and financial affairs,

1977–1980. He had served previously as minister of agriculture and served subsequently as minister of power, water, and sewage, minister of development, chairman of the **Central Planning Organization**, and governor of the **Central Bank of Yemen** (CBY). Upon Yemeni **unification** in 1990, he again became governor of the CBY. He was again minister of finance from 1994 to 1997, and then minister of civil service from 1997 to 2001.

Al-Junayd always appeared very English—almost "tweedy"—and is one of the few first-generation modernists to be long married to a western woman, a Spaniard. He was a self-confident and ambitious technocrat who proved over the years to be very sensitive to shifting political winds. However, his administrative and leadership skills came to be questioned late in his career.

JUNE 1980 AGREEMENT. The secret agreement concluded by YAR President Ali Abdullah **Salih** and PDRY President **Ali Nasir Muhammad** at their summit in Sanaa in mid-1980, under which each pledged not to support military, political, or propaganda activity directed against the other regime. The agreement, if implemented, had obvious implications for the future of the PDRY-supported **National Democratic Front** (NDF) and its rebellion against the Salih regime. Not honored by militants in the PDRY regime, the pledge was repeated by the two presidents at a second summit in Kuwait in November 1981. Not honored again, the pledge was repeated again in the agreements between the presidents at the 5 May 1982 summit in Taiz that finally ended the **NDF rebellion** and set a pattern for improved relations between the two Yemens. The June 1980 summit had also yielded agreements for joint companies for tourism and sea and overland transport.

JUZAYLAN, ABDULLAH. One of the soldiers in the **Famous Forty** who returned to Yemen in the mid-1950s and went on to become a player in the **1962 Revolution** and a top military officer in the **Yemeni Civil War**. Strongly pro-Egyptian, with close ties to Egyptian security, his career ended abruptly with the withdrawal of the Egyptian forces and the ouster of President **al-Sallal**. His memoirs consist largely of his account of the revolution and civil war—and his role in both dramas.

– K –

AL-KAF CLAN. The great **sayyid** clan of **Tarim** and **Seiyun** in Wadi **Hadhramawt** that, renowned equally for its learned men and its businessmen, wielded considerable power and influence over the politics and social life of the Hadhramawt for generations before independence and the emergence of the PDRY. Members of the family became rich in major ventures in Indonesia and elsewhere. Sayyid abu Bakr al-Kaf, the head of the clan in the first half of the 20th century, joined with Harold **Ingrams** in the late 1930s to knit together the many intertribal truces and agreements required to bring a good measure of peace—the "Peace of Ingrams"—to the strife-torn wadi. World War II, which cut the clan in the wadi off from it main source of wealth in Indonesia, and the revolutionary social changes initiated in South Yemen after 1967, took tolls on the wealth and position of the clan, although much of its vast property holdings in the wadi remained intact and financial losses were recouped in the **Gulf** states and elsewhere.

KAMARAN ISLAND. About 200 miles up the **Red Sea** coast from **Bab al-Mandab** and only 1 mile across the water from the small North Yemeni port of **Salif**, Kamaran is the large, flat desert island that South Yemen inherited from **Great Britain** at independence and that the YAR then seized during the 1972 **border war**. Although this "unbrotherly" seizure was decried in times of inter-Yemeni conflict in the 1970s and early 1980s, the PDRY informally acceded to YAR possession in the mid-1980s, probably because of improving inter-Yemeni relations as well as Marxist PDRY's difficulty at making a claim based on British imperialism. The issue was rendered moot by Yemeni **unification** in 1990.

During their tenure, the British had used Kamaran as a quarantine center for Muslim pilgrims to Mecca and Medina from East Africa, the Indian subcontinent, and points east. The flat, largely barren, and waterless island is of grayish-pink coral broken here and there by a mangrove swamp or a poor fishing village. After 1972, the YAR limited access to and maintained a military presence on the island. This presence became more important with the location of the YAR's oil export terminus at **Ras Isa**, near Salif, in 1987.

Stark Kamaran does have potential for **tourism**, and an enterprising Yemeni built a small seaside resort and diving center there in the late 1990s, slowly expanding it over the years. Since 2005, there has been talk of foreign investment in a resort complex on the island, possibly accessible by air.

KATHIRIS AND KATHIRI SULTANATE. Traditional rulers of Wadi **Hadhramawt** who from their capital in **Seiyun** competed in the 19th century with their **Quaiti** rivals for control of the Hadhramawt region, most notably in the **Quaiti–Kathiri War**. In the last decades of that century, the Kathiris found themselves confined by their own weakness and **Great Britain**'s intervention to nominal rule of only the interior of the wadi eastward from **Shibam**. The British maintained a largely nominal division of authority between the Kathiris and the Quaitis territories that remained in place until the British withdrew and South Yemen became independent in 1967. This was in marked contrast to the situation in the 16th and 17th centuries when the Kathiri sultanate had been a force to be reckoned with in the region. *See also* HYDERABAD.

KAWKABAN. *See* SHIBAM-KAWKABAM.

KAWR (KOR),THE. The main range of mountains in South Yemen that runs parallel to the coast of the **Arabian Sea** and that is an extension of and at right angles to the larger range that runs north to south, parallel to the **Red Sea**, the full length of North Yemen and into South Yemen. Running east into the **Hadhramawt**, the Kawr becomes the **Jol**. Over the centuries, the Kawr, with many peaks of well over several thousand feet, has allowed the small fighting tribes that dwell there to resist effective control by governments based in Aden, Sanaa, and elsewhere. Indeed, in modern times, this area may have been freer of outside control for longer periods than any other area in either of the Yemens—often beyond the reach of **Great Britain** to the south, the **Ottoman** Turks or the **imamate** to the north, and even the PDRY and the ROY.

KENNEDY, PRESIDENT JOHN F. (1918–1963). Elected in 1960, and popular around the world, U.S. President John F. Kennedy granted full diplomatic recognition to the YAR in December 1962, less than three months after the **1962 Revolution** ousted the imamate. This quick response was apparently designed to let the Third World know that the "New Frontier" was open to populistic reformist regimes and not wedded to the defense of reactionary, status quo regimes. Arguably, it was an attempt at a modest Arab-world equivalent of Kennedy's Alliance for Progress for Latin America. In any case, he was severely criticized at the time, especially by Great Britain and France, for recognizing a regime that was already massively dependent on **Egypt**'s military and that was on a collision course with a major ally of the West, **Saudi Arabia**—and not yet in control of the country. Not surprisingly, Kennedy's endorsement was appreciated by the **Sallal** regime and the republicans who were fighting for their lives against the **royalists** in the **Yemeni Civil War**. Assassinated in 1993, President Kennedy did not live to see U.S. relations on the Arabian Peninsula become really complicated. Built during the short Kennedy era, the then-modern, U.S.-funded water system in **Taiz** is still called the John F. Kennedy Water Works.

KENYA. The East African country to which a considerable number of Yemenis migrated over the decades, especially **Ismailis** persecuted or at least discriminated against by the Zaydi **imamate** in North Yemen prior to the **1962 Revolution**. In a preview of **9/11**, the suicide bombing of the U.S. Embassy in Nairobi in 1998 served to link Kenya to the **Horn of Africa** and Yemen in what was to become the United States' **War on Terror**.

KHALID BIN ABD AL-AZIZ, KING. *See* AL-SAUD (BAYT SAUD).

KHAMIR (KHAMR). North of Sanaa, a large provincial town just west of the main road to **Saada**—a bit closer to the former than to the latter—and long the home of the family of Shaykh Abdullah ibn Husayn **al-Ahmar**, the paramount shaykh of the **Hashid** Confederation. Khamir was the scene of two important but unsuccessful tribal conferences, in 1965 and 1975. The first, called by Shaykh al-Ahmar, sought a truce in the **Yemeni Civil War** and the withdrawal of Egyptian forces; the second, also called by al-Ahmar, sought to challenge

President **al-Hamdi**'s effort to rein in the power of the tribes over the state.

KHAMIS, LT. COL. MUHAMMAD (?–1981). The powerful and much-feared YAR security officer who was appointed by President **al-Hamdi** in 1975 as head of the enlarged and modernized Central Organization for National Security, a post he continued to occupy through the short tenure of President **al-Ghashmi** and more than two years into the **Salih** regime. Khamis, who had made many enemies over the years, apparently lost control of the security apparatus in the government reshuffle in 1979 and was assassinated under mysterious circumstances at the checkpoint near **al-Manakha** in early 1981. His tenure marked the permanent rise to prominence of the **security services** in governance in the YAR—and subsequently in the ROY. Khamis, who came from a village west of Sanaa, between **Shibam–Kawkaban** and **Thula**, was reputed to have had close ties with leaders in **Saudi Arabia**.

KHANFAR DEVELOPMENT BOARD. *See* ABYAN.

KHARIJITE MOVEMENT. *See* IBADIYA (IBADIS).

KHARTOUM CONFERENCE AND AGREEMENT. *See* YEMENI CIVIL WAR.

KHAT. *See* QAT (CATHA EDULIS FORSSKAL).

KHAWLAN TRIBES. Two widely separated and only distantly related tribal groupings in North Yemen. The one, Khawlan al-Sham, is located in the far northwest of the country and is part of the **Bakil** tribal confederation. The other, Khawlan al-Tiyal, is located in the area known as "the Khawlan," between Sanaa and Marib, and is also part of the Bakil.

KHORMAKSAR. The area with the major cluster of military facilities in the old **Aden** Colony, especially the military airport, located on the isthmus at the start of the Aden peninsula about halfway between **Crater** and **Shaykh Othman**. In the last major step in the military upgrading of Aden, in the early 1960s, these facilities were modernized and enlarged after **Great Britain** moved its Middle East Command to Aden from an increasingly inhospitable Kenya, which had previously replaced the inhospitable **Suez Canal** Zone. Aden's modern international airport is now located in Khormaksar.

KIDNAPPINGS. *See* HOSTAGE-TAKING AND THE HOSTAGE SYSTEM.

KINGDON OF SAUDI ARABIA. *See* SAUDI ARABIA, KINGDOM OF.

AL-KIPSI, SAYYID HUSAYN (?–1948). A member of a great **sayyid** family and a personal adviser to Imam **Yahya** who, as one of a very few frequent emissaries abroad, came to realize the backwardness of North Yemen, grew to favor reform of the **imamate**, and joined the **Wazir** regime as foreign minister in the ill-fated **1948 Revolution**. He was executed late that year, after the revolution failed.

KISSINGER, DR. HENRY. The forceful, intellectual national security adviser and secretary of state who dominated **United States** foreign policy during the administrations of President Richard Nixon and President Gerald Ford, 1969–1976, a time in which the long-lasting patterns of conflict between the United States and Marxist South Yemen and of Saudi-mediated friendship between the United States and the YAR first emerged. It was during this period that diplomatic relations were reestablished between the United States and the YAR and that those between the United States and the PDRY were severed. The key place that **Saudi Arabia** occupied in Kissinger's strategic thinking about the Middle East—and in the thinking of his successors—made it almost inevitable that the PDRY would be cast in the role of a pariah and client of the Soviet Union and that U.S.–YAR relations would be strained and conditioned by the United States' tendency to defer to Saudi interests on issues pertaining to the YAR. *See also* COLD WAR.

"KULAKS" AND "FEUDALISTS." The pejorative labels applied in political discourse in the PDRY in the 1970s and 1980s to small bourgeois property owners and larger landowners, groups reviled by those intent upon effecting social revolution in the countryside through state farms and cooperatives. The use of the terms is indicative of the degree to which the left wing of the **National Liberation Front**, triumphant over the Arab nationalist right wing in 1969, applied to the Yemeni context the social categories and analyses of Marxist–Leninist ideology, calling it "scientific socialism."

KURIA MURIA ISLANDS. Islands off the southern coast of the Sultanate of **Oman**, about 150 miles east of al-Salala, that, although nominally under the authority of the governor of Aden, were administered during the last years of the British colonial era by the political resident in the Persian Gulf. The islands were ceded to the Sultan of Oman only days before South Yemen became independent in late 1967, an act protested by the **National Liberation Front** immediately after it assumed authority in Aden. Although the PDRY continued to press its claim to the islands as a part of its territorial dispute with Oman throughout the 1970s, it ceased to do so after the two countries agreed in 1982 to establish diplomatic relations.

AL-KURSHUMI, ABDULLAH (*CA.* 1930–). The oldest member of the **Famous Forty** and an Egyptian-trained civil engineer who, after returning to North Yemen as one of the country's first engineers more than two years before the **1962 Revolution**, filled a number of high posts in the YAR before making the Ministry of Public Works his fiefdom by serving as its minister continuously from 1975 into the mid-1990s. During the period before 1975, he served briefly as minister of public works as well as minister of communications and founding head of the Highway Authority. He also served as prime minister for a politically stormy few months from late 1969 to early 1970. A student leader and ardent nationalist in his student days in Cairo, he chose not to become a partisan political leader during his decades of service in the YAR. He was a brusque, outspoken man, regarded as more hardworking and decent than thoughtful or visionary. Originally from the village of Bayt Bawz, just south of Sanaa, he lived there in virtual seclusion after retiring from public service.

KUWAIT. The oil-rich Arab **Gulf** state, at the head of the Gulf and wedged between **Iraq** and **Saudi Arabia**, that was the oldest and most continuous Arab donor of development aid to both Yemens as well as a major mediator in inter-Yemeni conflict and a facilitator of Yemeni **unification**. Behind Kuwait's generous, friendly policy in these areas was its interest in strong, independent Yemens—or one united Yemen—as counterweights to a Saudi Arabia seemingly intent on establishing its hegemony over Kuwait and all of the Arabian Peninsula. Kuwait's main vehicle for its economic diplomacy was the Kuwait Fund for Arab Economic Development. The Kuwait Hospital and Sanaa University stand as testaments to this aid.

Given this pattern of friendship and aid, the events just before the First **Gulf War** in 1991 were ripe with irony. While opposed to Iraq's invasion and annexation of Kuwait in 1990, the newly created ROY sought to straddle the fence between Iraq and Saudi Arabia and to assert a degree of independence of the Saudis. To this end, the ROY proposed an Arab diplo-political solution that would include the withdrawal of Iraq from Kuwait and the withdrawal from Saudi Arabia of foreign forces aimed at Iraq—and voted in the United Nations Security Council against the United States-crafted "all necessary means" resolution. This was to place the ROY, along with Jordan, the PLO, and Iraq, in the opposition to Saudi Arabia, the United States, the rest of the international coalition—and Kuwait. Feeling stabbed in the back by its Yemeni client, Kuwait severed relations with the ROY and cut off all aid. After 1991, the Kuwait Hospital and the Kuwait-funded Sanaa University, both starved for operating funds, stood as stark reminders of a patron–client relationship gone bad.

Kuwait resisted efforts by the ROY to restore relations in the mid-1990s and supported the southern leaders whose effort to withdraw from the ROY ended in the **War of Secession** in mid-1994. Finally, after major Yemeni efforts, Kuwait agreed to reestablish full relations in 2000—and Kuwaiti aid gradually began to flow again. *See also* ARAB REGIONAL FUNDS.

KUWAIT AGREEMENT OF 1979. The agreement reached at the Reconciliation Summit in Kuwait in March 1979, just after the second Yemeni **border war**, in which the heads of state of the two Yemens reaffirmed the goal and process of Yemeni **unification** as spelled out in the **Cairo Agreements** of 1972—or, in other words, agreed, for the second time in seven years, to end a border war by agreeing to unify. The agreement was the result of the mediation and pressure of the Arab League and certain of its members—particularly Kuwait, Iraq, and Syria—which argued for a united Arab world to face the challenge of events after **Camp David** and in **Afghanistan** and **Iran**. Although joint work on a draft constitution for a united Yemen did proceed over the next two years, most efforts to implement the letter and spirit of the Kuwait agreement were put on hold until the PDRY-supported **National Democratic Front rebellion** against the YAR ended in 1982.

– L –

LABOR PARTY, YEMEN. Founded in the YAR in 1969, the small independent Marxist–Leninist party that included some former **Nasirites** and **Baathists**. In 1976, it joined with most of YAR's other leftist parties to create the **National Democratic Front**.

LABOR UNIONS. *See* TRADE AND LABOR UNIONS.

LAHEJ. The large oasis town and area in South Yemen roughly 20 miles north-northwest of **Aden** that owed its importance in recent generations to its proximity to that expanding port city and its location at the junction of the two main routes from Aden to North Yemen. The growing locally based prosperity of Lahej after the 1940s resulted from a scheme of cotton cultivation based on pumped irrigation, but this also resulted in growing land inequality and inequality in general in the area. The prominence of Lahej in the Western **Aden Protectorate** was also a function of its being the seat of the well-to-do and powerful **Abdali** sultanate in the decades before the creation of the republic in 1967, and, since that event, the seat of provincial government offices. Given the close political and economic links forged between Aden and Lahej over the colonial era, it is perhaps not surprising that a Lahej-based group, the **South Arabian League**, would be the first to advocate a South Arabian state that included Aden.

LAND REFORM AND LAND TENURE. *See* AGRICULTURE.

LDA MOVEMENT. *See* LOCAL DEVELOPMENT ASSOCIATIONS AND THE LDA MOVEMENT.

LEAGUE OF THE SONS OF THE ARAB SOUTH. *See* SOUTH ARABIAN LEAGUE (SAL).

LEAGUE OF THE SONS OF YEMEN (RABITA OR RAY). *See* AL-JIFRI, ABD AL-RAHMAN ALI.

LEBANON. Called "the Switzerland of the Middle East," with its capital, Beirut, "the Paris of the Middle East," Lebanon epitomized the modern Arab World when poor, parochial, and "backward" North Yemen and the hinterland of South Yemen were exposed widely to the modern world for the first time in the 1960s. Beirut and Lebanon were like cosmopolitan Aden, but with more than two decades of national independence and a reputation for being the most open, pluralist, quasi-democratic place in the Arab world.

By contrast, with the start of its long, brutal civil war in 1975, multi-sectarian Lebanon became a metaphor to many North Yemeni **modernists** for the ethno-religious and regional strife and fragmentation that they feared and hoped to avoid by creating a strong Yemeni state and national identity. Particularly during the **al-Hamdi** era in the mid-1970s, the politicians who seemed to be playing to either the **Zaydi** or the **Shafii** community fell into disfavor and were admonished for being "partisan" and for risking "the Lebanese model" in Yemen. The two Yemens did experience the Lebanese Civil War first-hand when they contributed troops to the ill-fated Arab League peacekeeping force in Lebanon in 1976 and when they later helped the **Palestine Liberation Organization** evacuate its forces from Beirut after the **Israeli** invasion in 1982.

In the 1950s and 1960s, the Lebanese had little interest in or knowledge of Yemen and the Yemenis, and only a handful of Yemenis knew Beirut as a place for study, business, pleasure, intrigue, and exile. Among those few were the **Famous Forty,** the first big group of North Yemenis to study abroad; they experienced their first bit of the modern world in Lebanon from 1947 to 1949. In the mid-1960s, a number of political refugees from the **Yemeni Civil War**, especially members of the **Third Force**, found a haven and an operational base in Beirut. At about this time, a handful of younger North Yemeni began their studies at the American University of Beirut, a few of them coming under the spell of George **Habash** and his radical political ideas. On the eve of the Lebanese Civil War, in the mid-1970s, Beirut was witness to the unsolved murder of a prominent **Taiz** businessman and the assassination of the YAR's former foreign minister and deputy prime minister, Muhammad Ahmad **Numan**. By the late 1970s, however, all but a few of the many Yemeni students studying in Beirut were forced by the civil war to leave Beirut and go elsewhere, many to the United States.

LEGISLATIVE COUNCIL, ADEN. The first legislative body in **Aden Colony**, created in 1947 with all members nominated by the governor, and chaired by him as well. It was reformed in 1955 to include a small minority of elected members; in 1958, it was reformed again to include a majority of elected members under the chairmanship of an independent speaker, not the governor. These constitutional changes were soon made irrelevant by politics outside the council. There was the conflict over the merger of Aden and the states of the Western **Aden Protectorate** to form the **Federation of South Arabia** in early 1963 and then the armed struggle begun by the **National Liberation Front** and others that same year.

LEGISLATURES. *See* CONSULTATIVE COUNCIL (MAJLIS AL-SHURA); COUNCIL OF DEPUTIES (MAJLIS AL-NUWAB); PEOPLE'S CONSTITUENT ASSEMBLY (PCA); SHURA COUNCIL; SUPREME PEOPLE'S COUNCIL.

LIBERATION ARMY AND PEOPLE'S MILITIA. *See* ARMED FORCES.

LIBERATION STRUGGLE, SOUTH YEMEN'S. *See* FRONT FOR THE LIBERATION OF OCCUPIED SOUTH YEMEN (FLOSY); NATIONAL LIBERATION FRONT (NLF); ORGANIZATION FOR THE LIBERATION OF THE OCCUPIED SOUTH (OLOS); RADFAN AND THE RADFAN REBELLION.

LIBYA AND MUAMMAR QADHAFI. The considerable involvement of Libya and its head of state, Muammar Qadhafi, in the affairs of the Yemens in general and the politics of Yemeni **unification** in particular in the 1970s is largely traceable to the fact that the first serious conflict between the two Yemens began in 1969, at about the same time that Qadhafi overthrew the Libyan monarch and soon came to see himself as heir-apparent to **Egypt's** President Gamal Abdul **Nasser** and the cause of Arab unity. The 1972 Yemeni **border war** offered Qadhafi an early opportunity to assume the mantle of **Nasserism**, and he threw himself into Yemeni politics. Promising both Yemens much-needed financial aid, he pressured them to end their fight by agreeing to unify, a quickly ignored decision ratified at the **Tripoli summit** held under Qadhafi's auspices in 1972.

Qadhafi took other chances to become involved in Yemeni politics since the mid-1970s. A major intervention occurred in 1978 when he provided funds and encouragement for the thwarted **October Coup** attempt by the **Nasirites** against the then new **Salih regime**. Thereafter, Qadhafi joined Libya with the PDRY and newly Marxist **Ethiopia** to form the **Tripartite Alliance** of 1981, a radical regrouping that really never got off the ground.

LIMBURG **SUPERTANKER BOMBING.** The suicide bombing of the French-flagged oil super-tanker *Limburg* off the coast of Yemen in October 2002, two years after the suicide bombing of the U.S.S. *Cole* in the port of Aden and one year after **9/11**. The event both tied Yemen more closely to the United States' **War on Terror** and compromised the ROY's top-priority effort to expand and promote the new **Aden Container Port and Free Zone** by driving maritime insurance rate through the roof. The ship was struck by Islamic militants in the Arabian Sea not far from a terminal near **Mukalla**. The *Limburag* did not sink, and the oil spillage and loss of life were relatively modest, but the political fallout from the bombing was critical, raising questions about the ROY's reliability in President George W. Bush's War on Terror. After confusion and delays, the alleged perpetrators were tried and convicted in a trial that paralleled that of the U.S.S. *Cole* suspects. Confusion continued over sentencing, sentence changes, and the escape of some of those sentenced.

LIQUEFIED NATURAL GAS (LNG) PROJECT. *See* OIL AND GAS EXPLORATION AND PRODUCTION.

LOCAL COUNCILS, ROY. With **unification** and the adoption of the **1990 Constitution**, all of united Yemen was to be blanketed with a network of local councils (LCs) in order to bring power over local affairs to the local level. The calls for autonomy and decentralization and for local council elections were key issues in the political conflict that resulted in the **War of Secession** in 1994. After years of discussion, controversy, and acrimony, a local authorities law was passed in early 2000, and **elections** for governorate- and district-level LCs were held nationwide in 2001. LC elections were held again in 2006, this time along with the presidential elections.

The bigger, ongoing controversy focused on the budgetary and programmatic powers of the LCs as well as on the election (versus appointment) of chairmen of the governorate- and district-level LCs. Responding to the demands of the opposition during the 2006 elections, President Salih pledged to hold elections for these chairmen. When these elections were held in 2008—and the opposition boycotted over electoral procedures—the president's **General Peoples' Congress** won a sweeping victory.

LOCAL DEVELOPMENT ASSOCIATIONS AND THE LDA MOVEMENT. Due probably to the absence of supportive ideas or ideology, as well as small production units and limited organizational capacity, production and marketing cooperatives did not cover the rural and urban landscape in the YAR the way they did in the PDRY. By contrast, however, the YAR had notable success in the 1970s with the widespread use of cooperative-like organizations to address the growing demand for basic infrastructure, such as feeder roads, village water systems and cisterns, small-scale electricity generators, and one- and two-room schools and clinics. The vehicles for this were the local development associations (LDAs).

The LDA movement was a response to the dilemma caused by the great **infrastructure** needs in the countryside and by the severely limited capacity of the government in Sanaa to meet them. It was facilitated by a tradition of local self-help in the **Hugariyya,** where villagers who worked in Aden created "village associations" for this purpose beginning in the 1940s. Although there were urban antecedents in **al-Hudayda** and **Taiz** in the early 1960s, the movement first spread slowly on the countryside in the southern part of the YAR in the early 1970s—e.g., in **Turba**—and grew exponentially and northward throughout the 1970s. It achieved a remarkably large number of small successes during this period, acquired a national organization based in Sanaa, and reached its apogee in the early 1980s. With only nominal help from the central government, some 200 towns and districts all over North Yemen were by the late 1970s organizing their own LDAs, planning projects to meet locally defined needs, and then proceeding to carry out those projects with considerable success. In so doing, the LDAs helped to sustain a fragile YAR by meeting local demands at a time when the central government lacked the capacity to reach into the countryside for this purpose.

The LDAs' good results were made possible by the low level of technical and administrative demands of the projects and, most important, by the abundance of funds to pay for them. In the 1970s, people in the rural areas of Yemen wanted basic low-tech infrastructure that could be provided with a minimum of "modern" expertise—an unpaved feeder road and three hours of electricity per day—and the countryside was awash with **remittance** money sent home by locals working abroad.

Obvious basic needs, unprecedented amounts of available money, and the leadership and organization provided by the LDAs fit together perfectly at this time. Indeed, a number of Yemeni politicians saw the political as well as the economic development potential of the LDAs, and in 1973 the **Confederation of Yemeni Development Associations** (CYDA) was created with Ibrahim **al-Hamdi** as its first head, a year before the coup that made him YAR head of state. CYDA was supposed to promote and tangibly support the LDAs as well as regulate them, and for some years the benefits of this promotion and support outweighed the dead hand of regulation from the center, a center that eventually ensnared LDA activities in a bureaucratic thicket and in high and low politics. Furthermore, by the mid-1980s, the flow of remittance money began to slow at the same time that the projects needed in the countryside required increasing technical, administrative, and financial support—support that proved to be beyond CYDA's capacities, much less the capacities of the individual LDA.

Although identified with the assassinated President al-Hamdi, the LDA movement and CYDA had the support of President Ali Abdullah **Salih** after he assumed power in 1978. Al-Hamdi had held LDA elections for all of the LDA in 1976, and President Salih repeated this process in the winter of 1978–1979. In 1985, however, he initiated a major change by holding popular elections throughout the country for a vast network of local councils for cooperative development (LCCDs). The LCCDs were the product of merging the old LDAs and the local district-level administrative units and the local organs of the ruling party, the **General People's Congress** (GPC). The LCCDs were more tightly integrated into the state structure than the LDAs had been and were charged with other local political–administrative tasks as well as with the development activities of the LDAs. With the creation of the LCCDs, CYDA was transformed into the LCCD Federation. The LCCDs were also used to greatly expand participation in the GPC's internal elections; 17,500 LCCD members were elected locally in 1985, and these LCCD members in turn served as electors of most of the 1,000 members of the new GPC that met in 1986. The LCCDs receded in significance after **Yemeni unification** in 1990; since 2000, most their state functions have been taken over by the new system of **local councils**.

LOCAL PEOPLE'S COUNCILS. Governing bodies on the provincial and district levels in the PDRY that were to be elected for two-and-a-half year terms to manage economic, social, and cultural affairs on the local level under the supervision of the central government and in cooperation with the mass organizations and the state farms. Concerned about the many great inequalities between the center and the periphery in South Yemen, the leaders of the **National Liberation Front** saw the councils as a way of organizing and giving weight to the periphery. Although the councils did increase participation and some accountability on the local level, the effort to translate the notion of "democratic centralism" into practice often found the regime sacrificing grassroots democracy for centralized decision-making and control. Elections to the councils were held in 1977, in 1983, and again after the **13 January events** in 1986.

LOWER YEMEN. *See* UPPER, MIDDLE, AND LOWER YEMEN.

LUCE, SIR WILLIAM. *See* COLONIAL ADMINISTRATION AND ADMINISTRATORS.

LUHUMIS. *See* ABU LUHUM, SINAN.

LUQMAN FAMILY AND MUHAMMAD ALI LUQMAN. A leader of Aden's first generation of modern Arab politicians and a member of the family of Adeni intellectuals that owned and edited a number of newspapers; Muhammad Ali Luqman from the mid-1940s advocated an independent Aden and, fearful of modern Aden being swallowed up by the backward states of the **Aden Protectorates**, remained opposed to the merger of Aden into the **Federation of South Arabia** that occurred from the late 1950s through the mid-1960s. The **Aden Association**, led by the Luqmans from the early 1950s, favored a sort of Singapore-like city–state solution, an independent Aden within the British Commonwealth. Earlier, in the mid-1940s, Luqman's newspaper, *Youth of the Peninsula (Fatat al-Jazirah)*, had provided an outlet for the ideas of the **Free Yemenis** from the north and for the idea of a **"greater Yemen,"** uniting north and south. Luqman was also headmaster of the first Arab secondary school in Aden.

– M –

MAABAR. The market and farming town located about 40 miles south of Sanaa on the north end of the **Dhamar** plain and at the intersection of the only inland north–south highway and the old track down to the **Tihama** that was restored and paved in the mid-1980s. The pipeline from the oil fields in **Marib/al-Jawf** down to the terminus at **Ras Isa** on the Red Sea crosses the north–south highway at right angles near Maabar.

MAAZIBA TRIBE. *See* ZARANIQ TRIBE.

MADHHIJ TRIBAL CONFEDERATION. The third major **tribal confederation** in Yemen, smaller and weaker than either the **Hashid** or **Bakil** in part because its constituent tribes were divided into two groups by the boundary line drawn by **Great Britain** and the **Ottoman** Turks in the early 20th century. In the mid-1960s, that line became the boundary between two states, the YAR and the PDRY. Since the 1990 **unification** that erased this boundary, the Madhhij confederation seems to have revived and become stronger.

The Madhhij are **Shafi**, and among its constituent tribes are the Murad, Ans, al-Hada, and Qayfah. Occupying the area between **Harib** and Juba, south of **Marib**, the Murad enjoyed nearly complete autonomy until the forces of Imam **Yahya**, campaigning to expand and consolidate the Yemeni **imamate**, defeated them in battles in the second half of the 1920s. Harboring grievances, it was the leader of Murad, Shaykh Ali Nasir al-Qurdai, who assassinated Imam Yahya at the outset of the **1948 Revolution**.

MADINAT AL-SHAAB. The new, only partly built town, originally named al-Ittahad (the Union), which served between the late 1950s and 1967 as the capital of the **Federation of the Arab Amirates of the South** and then the **Federation of South Arabia** (FSA). It became Madinat al-Shaab (City of the People) after the **National Liberation Front** triumphed and scuttled the FSA in 1967. The new town was built on the site of a tiny village in **Lahej** just over the border from the narrow arc of coast that connects **Aden** and Little Aden. The rather forlorn, faded, sun-drenched place now houses much of Aden University as well as some other public institutions.

AL-MAFRAQ. The shop-filled and bustling but sun-baked and ugly market at the intersection of the Taiz–Hudayda highway and the paved spur road to the port of **al-Mukha** on the **Red Sea**, a common rendezvous for smugglers and purchasers of alcoholic beverages. The place took on new prominence with the completion nearby of the Japanese-financed (and Japanese-built) al-Burh cement works and with the modernization and expansion of al-Mukha's port.

MAHFOUZ, KHALID BIN. *See* BIN MAHFOUZ.

MAHMOUD, ABDUL-WAHAB. The old-time, still active **Baathi** and an economist who served in the YAR as minister of economics in the early 1970s and again in the **al-Aini** government in 1974, only to fall out of favor and be dropped from YAR governments during the **al-Hamdi** and **Salih** regimes. After Yemeni **unification** in 1990, Mahmoud was elected to the **Council of Deputies**; in 1993, he became deputy speaker. He has also been minister of agriculture and minister of water and electricity, as well as ambassador to Kuwait and Morocco.

MAHRA PROVINCE AND SULTANATE. The PDRY's easternmost, most isolated, poorest and least populated province, named the "Sixth Province" under the anti-regionalist renaming after independence. The native language of the Mahris is not Arabic, and some maintain that Mahra's 80,000 residents are not Arabs. Many Mahris live in the coastal towns of Sayhut, Qishn, and al-Ghayda. Al-Ghayda, near the border with **Oman**, is the provincial capital. Sayhut, east of **Mukallah**, lies at the point where the Wadi al-Masila extention of Wadi al-Hadhrmawt ends; it is the site of the **Nexen's** terminus for the oil for export from its **Masila** oil field.

Before and during the British colonial era, this land was at least nominally the domain of the Mahra Sultanate of Qishn and Socotra. The sultan, who resided some distance away on the island of **Socotra**, did not have effective control over his mainland territory in the last decades of British colonial rule, although he did seek, without success, to reassert control with British help in the 1960s when he saw advantage in granting the **Pan-American Oil Company** permission to search for oil in his domain—and needed to be able to guarantee security for this purpose.

Because of its location, Mahra was from the late 1960s through the mid-1970s the focus of much of the aid from the PDRY and others to the **Dhufar Rebellion** against Oman. Years later, in the early 1990s, the ROY and Oman negotiated and signed an agreement demarcating their border. Since then, good relations, trade agreements, and a new highway to the border have increased the integration of Mahra into the rest of Yemen and made it a new link between Yemen and the prosperous Arab Gulf states.

AL-MAHWIT. The province and provincial capital located in the rugged mountains 75 miles west of Sanaa and north of the highway between Sanaa and **al-Hudayda**. Created only in the 1970s, and then the smallest of the YAR's provinces in terms of area, al-Mahwit was until at least the late 1970s extremely isolated and barely affected by the modernization and development taking place in much of the rest of the country. The provincial capital, al-Mahwit, was a town of less than 10,000 in the early 1980s, still without piped water, a sewage system, and daytime electricity. Central government services were virtually nonexistent, despite the growing number of central government offices. These conditions, and the quality of life generally, changed for the better in al-Mahwit town in the late 1980s; some modern **infrastructure**, government services, and paved roads connecting al-Mahwit to the rest of the country have made a big difference. Throughout most of the mountainous province, a moderate amount of rainfall supports a sizable population and **agriculture**—most notably the terraced cultivation of some **coffee** and considerable amounts of **sorghum** and **qat**.

MAIN (MINEAN) STATE. *See* TRADING KINGDOMS, SOUTH ARABIAN.

MAJLIS AL-NUWAB. *See* COUNCIL OF DEPUTIES (MAJLIS AL-NUWAB).

MAJLIS AL-SHURA. *See* CONSULTATIVE COUNCIL (MAJLIS AL-SHURA).

MAKKAWI, ABD AL-QAWI (1918–1998). The anti-British nationalist politician in Aden in the 1960s whose career was ended by the triumph of the **National Liberation Front** (NLF) as successor to **Great Britain** in South Yemen and who was thereafter relegated to increasing irrelevance and rhetorical outbursts from exile in Egypt from the late 1960s through the 1990s. Opponents of the regime in the PDRY and, more recently, of the ROY would parade an eager Makkawi out at opportune times. In the mid-1990s, he joined with Abd al-Rahman **al-Jifri** in opposing the ROY. He joined the mixed bag of southern leaders who in 1994, sought to restore an independent South Yemen and was named a member of the five-member

Presidential Council in the short-lived **Democratic Republic of Yemen**.

In the mid-1960s, the British high commissioner appointed Makkawi chief minister of the Aden government, a position from which he increasingly criticized British efforts to make a viable successor to colonial rule out of the merger of Aden with the **Federation of South Arabia**. Along with the **Luqmans**, he favored "Aden for the Adenis," self-rule within the British Commonwealth. Makkawi was soon dismissed as chief minister for failing to publicly condemn terrorist acts. Running to keep up with the militant NLF and the recently created **Organization for the Liberation of the Occupied South** (OLOS), Makkawi in 1966 became the head of the stillborn **Front for the Liberation of Occupied South Yemen** (FLOSY), the Egyptian-inspired effort to amalgamate the NLF and OLOS. When the NLF quickly pulled out of FLOSY, Makkawi's political fate was sealed, and soon after he went into exile in Egypt.

MAKKI, DR. HASAN MUHAMMAD (*CA*. 1935–). The Egyptian- and Italian-educated North Yemeni politician from a prominent **al-Hudayda** family, a first-generation **modernist** and member of the **Famous Forty** who, despite his "European" leftist political ideas and posture, managed to occupy high government office much of the time in each of the regimes since the **1962 Revolution**. Dr. Makki was a youthful foreign minister for a time under President **al-Sallal** in the mid-1960s. Thereafter, he was foreign minister from 1967 to 1968, deputy prime minister from 1972 to 1974, and, in 1974, the last prime minister under President **al-Iryani**. During the short **al-Hamdi** era, he was deputy prime minister from 1974 to 1975 and president of **Sanaa University** from 1975 to 1976.

Dr. Makki was again deputy prime minister for all but a short interval of time under President **Salih** from 1979 until Yemeni **unification** in 1990. After unification, he continued in this post until he became acting prime minister during a short, tumultuous period just before, during, and just after the **War of Secession** in 1994. Since then, he has served as adviser to the president and as a member of the **Shura Council**.

Hasan Makki's family had migrated to al-Hudayda from the northern **Tihama** shortly before his birth in 1935. He stood out in the

Famous Forty by virtue of his family's prominence and his Tihama origins. Because he was considered worldly, his youthful colleagues from the interior deferred to him on things modern. Years later, his years in Italy—first as a student studying for his bachelor and advanced degrees between the mid-1950s and early 1960s and then as YAR ambassador to Italy from 1976 to 1979—gave Dr. Makki a sophisticated, urbane demeanor more typical of Europe or the Mediterranean than of Yemen. He took pride in being an intellectual with advanced "socialist" ideas and a Third World politician—both probably more negative than positive in the context of Yemeni politics in the late 1960s and afterward.

Above all, however, Dr. Makki was a Yemeni nationalist. He is credited with acting with courage as a leader and a mediator during the **Siege of Sanaa** and the **Sanaa Mutiny** in 1967 and 1968, at a time when most of the other civilian politicians had fled the city, and he was forced into temporary exile for his bravery. He was seriously wounded during his mediation effort in 1968, and again in an act of political vengeance in the tumultuous spring of 1994. Continuing to work, he has often been in ill health since the mid-1990s.

AL-MAKTARI, DR. ABDULLAH. *See* EDUCATION.

MAMLUKS. Circassian rulers of Egypt who, in 1515, alarmed by the appearance of the **Portuguese** off **Aden** and in the **Red Sea**, conquered the **Tihama** coast and southern uplands of Yemen. The Mamluks introduced firearms to the Arabian Peninsula and, in effect, served as an advance party for the first occupation of Yemen by the **Ottoman** Turks, who overran Egypt only two years after the Mamluks came to Yemen. Qansuh al-Ghuri was the Mamluk sultan who launched the campaign in Yemen in 1515 to check the Portuguese. Two years later, he was defeated and slain by the Ottoman forces near Aleppo.

MANAKHA AND MANAKHA PASS. The small, dusty, bustling commercial town high in the mountains west of **Sanaa** at the pass where the main highway between Sanaa and **al-Hudayda** begins its precipitous plunge down to the **Tihama**. The gateway to the northern highlands, the pass's strategic location made it militarily significant for centuries, and a key **infrastructure** link in the 20th century. It has always been vital to the defense and control of the Yemeni highlands. The age of the telegraph gave the town and pass significance for communications, and completion of the paved highway in the 1960s increased its significance for transportation.

MANID DYNASTY. *See* SULAYHID DYNASTY AND ALI BIN HASAN AL-SULAYHI.

MANSOUR HADI, ABD AL-RABO. *See* ABD AL-RABO MANSOUR HADI.

AL-MANSUR MUHAMMAD HAMID AL-DIN. *See* HAMID AL-DIN FAMILY AND IMAMATE.

AL-MAQALIH, ABD AL-AZIZ (1939–). A major Yemeni poet and perhaps the one best known in the Arab World in the last decades of the 20th century and thereafter. A fervent Yemeni and Arab nationalist, much of his poetry reflects the tumultuous events of the second half of the century in Yemen and the greater Arab World. While a student in Cairo before Yemen's **1962 Revolution**, he came under the influence of the **Free Yemenis**. He came home on the eve of the revolution and broadcast for Sanaa Radio after the revolution and during the **Yemeni Civil War** until 1967. He then spent a decade in Cairo earning his BA, MA, and PhD After returning home again, he joined the faculty of **Sanaa University** and served as its president for nearly two decades, 1982–2001. During much of this period, continuing to the close of the first decade of the new century, he was also president of the Yemeni Center for Study and Research—and always continued to write his poetry.

Born in the town of al-Nadirah in Ibb governorate, Dr. Maqalih is a longtime resident of Sanaa, and much of his poetry reflects his love for this city. One of his earliest collections is entitled *Sanaa— There Is No Escaping Her*, and one of his most recent is *The Book of Sanaa*.

MARIA THERESA THALLER. *See* MONEY, CURRENCY, AND FOREIGN EXCHANGE.

MARIB/AL-JAWF BASIN. *See* AL-JAWF; OIL; YEMEN HUNT OIL.

MARIB PROVINCE, TOWN, AND DAM. Located about 100 miles east of Sanaa on the edge of the **Ramlat al-Sabatayn** desert, Marib until in recent decades was the small, sleepy, uninviting provincial capital and garrison of the large, sparsely populated Marib region and province. The town is close by the site of the fabled Marib dam—rather, the Arim Dam at Marib—and was for centuries before the Common Era the capital of the rich and powerful kingdom of **Saba**, allegedly once ruled by Bilqis, the Queen of Sheba (Saba).

Since the mid-1980s, the town has undergone a major revival as the center closest to the **oil** and natural gas operations in the Marib/al-Jawf basin. The new military significance of Marib province increased further when the PDRY in 1986 discovered oil directly to the east in **Shabwa**, on the other side of the then-undemarcated border between the two Yemens. With Yemeni **unification** in 1990, the potential danger of inter-Yemeni conflict based on a mixture of oil and disputed territory was eliminated. However, territory claimed by **Saudi Arabia** encroached on both Marib and Shabwa provinces, and the potential for conflict between the ROY and the Saudis in this region remained high until the **Saudi–Yemeni Border Agreement** was signed in 2000. Finally, and especially since **9/11**, Marib province, with its large areas beyond effective government control and its long, porous border with Saudi Arabia, has figured in the U.S.-led **War on Terror**.

Marib town is located at the mouth of Wadi Adhana, which drains a portion of the eastern slopes of the **Sarat** mountains. The Marib Dam spanned the mouth of the wadi, and the monumental remains of the dam as well as those of the vast irrigation system it supplied are still much in evidence. The abandonment of the dam and irrigation works over the early centuries of the Common Era forced the **emigration** of most of the area's then sizable population. Because the tribe of the rulers of **Abu Dhabi** were allegedly part of this emigration, Shaykh Zayed bin Sultan al-Nahayan, the ruler of that oil-rich emirate, chose to finance the construction of a new dam at Marib in the 1980s. This made possible a significant revival of irrigated agriculture in the area. Completed in the 1990s, the project then entered a second phase, an expansion, again funded by Abu Dhabi. Overall, however, Marib province remains a harsh setting, and much of its small, widely scattered population lives in poverty.

MARXISM. *See* IDEOLOGY AND POLITICAL IDEAS, MODERN.

MASAKIN (S. MASKIN). *See* SOCIAL SYSTEM AND STRUCTURE.

MASHAYIKH (S. SHAYKH). *See* SOCIAL SYSTEM AND STRUCTURE; TRIBES AND THE TRIBAL SYSTEM.

MASILA REGION. The region located between and to the east of **Mukalla** and **Seiyun** in the **Hadhramawt**, where the Canadian Occidental Oil Company, renamed **Nexen**, struck **oil** in commercial quantities in late 1990. It soon became clear that Block 16 in Masila contained by far the greatest reserves in the just-created ROY. This fact was to be a major factor contributing to the decline in enthusiasm for Yemeni **unification** on the part of most southern politicians and subsequently to the **War of Secession** in 1994. True to predictions, the Masila field and Nexen soon overtook and passed the Marib/al-Jawf basin and the **Yemen Hunt Oil Company** in the oil sweepstakes in Yemen. Output reached 180,000 barrels/day in 2005—about 45 percent of the country's total and more than twice that of Marib/al-Jawf's Block 18. On the downside, it was predicted that the Masila reserves would be exhausted by about 2015.

MASS MEDIA. Given a culture with a strong oral tradition and still limited literacy, even in the more literate PDRY, it is not surprising that a leapfrogging modern technology—phone, radio, and TV—has given the spoken word the edge over the written word in Yemen. (Then, again, the latter are returning to significance with e-mailing, text messaging, and the Internet.) In the 1970s, the battery-run radio/cassette player was the modern possession found in practically every home, even the poorest. Since then, VCRs and video-cassettes have long been available and ubiquitous—mostly pirated and beyond all effective control.

Broadcast radio and television—the latter introduced in the mid-1970s—has become more available with the spread of electricity to the countryside. By the turn of the century, most people had access to a standard radio and a television set—in the village café if not at home—even if powered, as in the most remote areas, by village or household generators. Despite rising demand in 2005 and thereafter for competition and private ownership, radio and television in the ROY are state-owned and-managed, state monopolies. In recent years, however, the satellite disc has made regional and international TV available to affluent Yemenis.

Newspapers and magazines are not unimportant in Yemen. A press that offered little choice and that operated under tight government control in both Yemens became more varied, open, and assertive with Yemeni **unification** in 1990. *Al-Thawra* was the major daily newspaper in North Yemen and is still published in Sanaa, whereas *14th October* was and still is the daily in Aden. *Al-Thawri* and *Al-Mithaq*, both weeklies, are the organs of the **Yemeni Socialist Party** and the **General People's Congress**, respectively. *Al-Sahwa*, also a weekly, is the organ of **Islah**. *September 26* is the mouthpiece of the Ministry of Defense.

Although most of them were short-lived, the dozens of privately owned and edited newspapers, magazines, and journals that sprang up after unification were more politically varied, outspoken, and assertive than any of the official organs. Two of the private newspapers that survived are Abd al-Aziz **al-Saqqaf**'s *Yemen Times* and Faris Abdullah al-Sanabani's *Yemen Observer*. Al-Sanabani is also spokesman and advisor to President **Salih,** an example of the extent to which the line between state and print media remains blurred.

Since the mid-1990s, the Salih regime has with considerable success reined in the independent print media that remain by its control of newsprint and licensing and its power to punish owners, publishers, and journalists in a variety of ways. However, since 2003, the publishers and journalists have closed ranks and pushed back, often behind a newly courageous Yemeni Journalists Syndicate (YJS). No longer a vehicle through which the state controls the press, the YJS has increasingly challenged the state and defended its own members and their rights. On the other side, the Ministry of Information has scoffed at calls for its abolition and pushed a new press law anathema to the YJS. Indeed, during these years, the fight for press freedom has been at the forefront of the effort to expand democracy, transparency, and freedoms in general. As of 2008, gains had been made despite the fining and jailing of journalists and publishers and the suspension and cancelation of the right to publish or to work in the profession. *See also* INTEREST (PRESSURE) GROUPS.

MASS ORGANIZATIONS, PDRY. *See* INTEREST (PRESSURE) GROUPS.

MASWARI, COL. HUSAYN. *See* AL-HAJRI, QADI ABDULLAH; AL-IRYANI, QADI ABD AL-RAHMAN.

AL-MATARI, ALI AHMAD. *See* AL-HAMDI, PRESIDENT IBRA-HIM MUHAMMAD.

MAWIYAH. *See* RAHIDA.

MAWJ. *See* AL-JIFRI, ABD AL-RAHMAN ALI.

MAWR, WADI. The largest and northernmost **wadi** of the several wadis in North Yemen that carry surface and groundwater from the western slopes of the mountains across the **Tihama** toward the Red Sea, and the one with the greatest potential for development by means of irrigated agriculture. The wadi drains the well-watered slopes of the mountains from **Hajja** to al-Mahabisha and courses toward the coastal town of al-Luhayya. The **Tihama Development Authority** launched the Wadi Mawr project in the 1980s, and considerable agricultural development has been a result. But since Wadi Mawr is distinguished from most of the other wadis by large landholdings, and now landless tenants, the new prosperity has been very unequally shared.

MECCA AND MEDINA. Located close to each other in Saudi Arabia in the **Hijaz** region north of Yemen, these two ancient commercial towns close to the northern end of the ancient **trade route** are the two holiest sites in the Islamic world, and the subject of the pilgrimage, or the Hajj. (Mecca, in fact, has been a pilgrimage site from pre-Islamic times.) Because of their importance and proximity, these two cities have often figured in the political and military plans of strong and ambitious rulers in Yemen in both pre-Islamic and Islamic times.

MERCHANTS. *See* SOCIAL SYSTEM AND STRUCTURE.

MIDDLE YEMEN. *See* UPPER, MIDDLE, AND LOWER YEMEN.

MIGRATION. *See* EMIGRATION.

MILITARY AND MILITARY AID. *See* ARMED FORCES; ARMS.

MILITARY COMMAND COUNCIL. *See* AL-HAMDI, PRESIDENT IBRAHIM MUHAMMAD.

MILITARY ECONOMIC CORPORATION (MECO). The state institution created in 1975 by the **al-Hamdi** regime as a way to provide poorly paid soldiers with inexpensive boots, uniforms, canned goods, and bread that grew and spread like a cancer to most sectors of the economy, selectively stifled private-sector business, and—most important—became a key institution in the military–tribal–(northern) business complex that crystallized in the 1980s and contributed so much under the **Salih regime** to the patronage system and the inequality and **corruption** that came with it. Using its connections and other anti-competitive means, MECO ended up with big stakes in sectors as far from the military as agriculture, land speculation, construction, and—with unfair access to import licenses—the importing of goods ranging from wheat to furniture and household furnishings. Military officers were rewarded with MECO positions that served as profit centers, and many of them then retired to the private sector, where they added to their newfound wealth.

MECO remained a dominant force after the **War of Secession** in 1994, which served only to increase the disproportionate benefits reaped by northerners from Yemeni **unification**. Given the shift that came with the **IMF–WB reforms** in 1995–1996, the oligarchs chose to "privatize" MECO, and changed its name to the Yemen Economic Corporation (YEMCO). The new YEMCO continued to blur the lines between public and private, military and civilian.

AL-MITHAQ AL-WATANI. *See* NATIONAL PACT (AL-MITHAQ AL-WATANI).

AL-MOAYYAD, MUHAMMAD ALI HASSAN. *See* WAR ON TERROR.

MOCHA. *See* AL-MUKHA.

MODERNISTS, MODERNIZATION AND MODERN SECTOR. Those people in late-developing countries who desire and possess some of the skills needed to promote, among other goals, nation-state building and socioeconomic development are often labeled modernists. Most of them become technocrats or administrators in the modern institutions in the expanding modern sector of society, and a small number of them make up the group of modernist politicians. The two Yemens were not exceptions to this. The fact that the term "the graduates" was often used as a synonym for "modernists" in both places indicates the important role of education and of the educational **emigrants** in each Yemen.

This said, the appearance and spread of modernists and modern sectors was very different in the two Yemens. In South Yemen, the modernists and modern sector of the early 20th century were concentrated in **Aden** Colony, making it the bustling island of modernity in South Arabia, a byproduct of the colonial regime and maritime trade. Modernists and their ideas and goals spread only slowly in the 1930s to the major towns and government centers of the much larger, more remote, more traditional **Aden Protectorates**. Not surprisingly, a major goal of the PDRY in the years after independence in 1967 was to end this dichotomy by spreading modernity over the country, creating modernists, and expanding the modern sector. In grander terms, the goal was national strength and development—and with a socialist face. The leaders in this were the early modernists, nearly all of whom had gone abroad to study.

By contrast, one has to look hard for traces of modernists and a modern sector inside insulated, isolated, traditional North Yemen prior to the **1962 Revolution**. There were a few of them in **Taiz**, perhaps in **al-Hudayda**, and among the handful of students who had recently returned to **imamate** Yemen after studying abroad. With the establishment of the YAR in 1962, modernity spread quite rapidly, with a growing number of students with modern educations returning home and an even greater number going out to study. Still, the distribution of modernists and the modern sector remained concentrated in the growing nodes along the roads that trace the triangle formed by **Sanaa**, Taiz, and al-Hudayda.

The recent and abrupt beginnings of the transition to modernity in North Yemen was largely the work of a cohort of a few hundred first-generation Yemeni educational emigrants and modernists who were to play a major role in government and politics as well as in the cultural and economic life of the YAR. This generation begins with the **Famous Forty** and their colleagues, who emigrated for education in the late 1940s, and ends, arguably, with the 1958 departure for the United States of a group that included Abd al-Karim **al-Iryani** and Abd al-Aziz **Abd al-Ghani**. Most of them completed university educations abroad, nearly all of them returned to Yemen between 1960 and 1968, some helped create the 1962 Revolution (a few very directly), and a large number of them occupied top- and middle-level posts in the government and its bureaucracy from the 1960s into the 1990s. Many of them continued to hold prominent positions in the ROY after Yemeni **unification** in 1990.

In short, this was a generation of truly extraordinary Yemenis. By contrast, the second-generation modernists are far more numerous and less distinguishable (or distinguished). By the late 1970s, moreover, their numbers were being diluted by an increasing number of graduates of Sanaa University and other Yemeni institutions. Modernists were becoming more the norm—and more ordinary.

MONEY, CURRENCY, AND FOREIGN EXCHANGE. The economies of the two Yemens were widely monetized only recently, quite differently, and largely in step with their incorporation into the regional and international economic systems. In South Yemen, the main impetus for monetization was the British occupation of Aden in 1839 and the gradual incorporation of its growing port and commerce into the international economy and the British Empire. This process spread as **Great Britain** became increasingly interested in Aden's hinterland in the last decades of the 19th century and, especially, after World War II. After independence in 1967, establishing the Adeni dinar throughout the country was a basic part of efforts by the new Yemeni regime to create a national as well as a socialist economy.

To the extent that North Yemen in the time of the **imamate** needed money—poor, isolated, largely self-sufficient, and based primarily on subsistence agriculture as it was—this need was oddly met largely by modern mintages of the Maria Theresa thaler (dollar), a very large, heavy, silver coin minted in Europe and bearing the dour profile of the 18th-century European empress. The thaler was at the mercy of a silver price set far from Yemen's shores and made exchanges of any consequence quite ponderous. Robert Stookey tells of Imam Ahmad's onetime need to buy from the U.S. Embassy a U.S.-treasury check for $38,000: "An exchange rate was agreed upon without haggling, and shortly a palace jeep arrived at the legation groaning under the weight of about one and one-half tons of Maria Theresa thalers sewn into burlap bags of one thousand." Perhaps not surprisingly, although the need was not widespread, there was a chronic shortage of money in imamate days, a cause of major complaints among the merchant families of **Taiz** with commercial ties to Aden.

With the coming of the **1962 Revolution** and the sudden opening of North Yemen to the outside world, the quaint old ways of exchange had to change. In 1964, the new Yemeni riyal first appeared as paper money, thereafter contributing further to the growth of a market economy and a system of cash exchange. Exchange controls were removed in 1971, and the riyal was pegged to the U.S. dollar throughout the 1970s and into the 1980s. As late as the 1980s, the wide acceptance of the riyal in Yemen notwithstanding, there were markets in the north and east of the country—near the border with **Saudi Arabia**—where the Saudi riyal was more common and welcome than the Yemeni riyal.

Lacking goods to exchange for hard currency, both Yemeni republics were plagued more or less continuously by shortages of foreign exchange, and both were beset from time to time by severe bouts of inflation. These problems and the related balance-of-payments problem were made more manageable in the 1970s and early 1980s by the increasing inflow of hard-currency **remittances** from the vast number of Yemenis working abroad, especially in the case of the

YAR. Unfortunately, remittances dropped off in the 1980s and then plummeted with the crisis that resulted in the First **Gulf War**, only months after Yemeni **unification** and plans to adopt a new common currency in mid-1990. This made all the more important the discovery of oil in both Yemens in the mid-1980s, making it possible for the needs of unified Yemen for foreign exchange in the 1990s and beyond to be met largely by oil revenues. The ROY's adoption in 1995 of the **IMF/World Bank** package of stabilization measures and structural reforms, designed to reverse the implosion of the Yemeni economy in the wake of **War of Secession** in 1994, allowed the common riyal to float freely and at a single exchange rate.

MONSOONS AND WATER RESOURCES. The monsoon is the seasonal wind over the **Indian Ocean** that, by reversing direction each year, both brings rainfall to the higher elevations of Yemen and provides the wind power that for millennia has pushed—and still pushes—Arab dhows, single-masted ships with a lateen sail, sharp prow, deep forefoot, and raised deck at the stern, back and forth from the southern coast of Yemen and East Africa, the Indian subcontinent, and beyond. The monsoon regularly blows from the southwest from April to October and from the northeast during the rest of the year. During the long age of sail power, the predictable annual rhythm of the monsoon made possible the Indian Ocean trade route that skirted **South Arabia**, pushing ships east from spring through summer and back the other way from fall through winter.

More important for Yemen, especially today, the warm monsoon out of the southwest picks up moisture as it crosses the open sea and carries that moisture to Yemen, where it falls as rainfall when the airflow is forced by the mountains to rise, cool, drop its moisture. All other things being equal, the higher the elevation and the closer to the coast, the greater the amount of annual rainfall across Yemen—hence the relatively abundant rainfall (and intensive agriculture and high population density) on the western slope of the mountains running the full length of North Yemen, in **Taiz** and **Ibb** provinces especially, and in the adjacent highlands of South Yemen. In those parts of Yemen favored by significant rainfall, there is a small rainy season in the spring and a bigger one in mid-summer. Even in these areas, the rains vary greatly from year to year, and sometimes do not come at all, a hostage to the variable strength of the monsoon.

The monsoon is the principal source of Yemen's ground water as well as its seasonal surface runoff. To the extent that Yemen's aquifers are recharged over time, it is the erratic annual monsoon that does it. Unfortunately for Yemen, its ancient aquifers are being depleted at a far faster rate than they are being recharged by new rainfall. As a result, the water table in settled and farmed parts of Yemen is dropping rapidly. Thus, Yemen, with its rapidly growing population—now at about 24 million—is faced with the prospect of "running out of water." The situation is most acute in the Sanaa basin, and some say that a significant percentage of its burgeoning population will have to be relocated in the near future.

MOSER, CHARLES. See TRAVELERS.

AL-MUAYYAD MUHAMMAD BIN QASIM, IMAM. *See* QASIMI IMAMATE.

MUHAMMAD ALI PASHA OF EGYPT. The dynamic ruler of Egypt whose assertive, expansionist activities in the **Hijaz** as well as in Syria and Palestine in the early decades of the 19th century caused both **Great Britain** and the **Ottoman** Turks to attend with greater concern to their separate and potentially conflicting interests in the **Red Sea** and **South Arabia**. This contributed directly to Britain's decision to occupy **Aden** in 1839 and to that of the Turks to occupy **al-Hudayda** in 1849. Muhammad Ali had occupied the Hijaz in 1812 and then seized the **Tihama** south to **al-Mukha** in the 1830s, positions he was forced to give up after 1840.

MUHAMMAD ALI UTHMAN. *See* UTHMAN, SHAYKH MUHAMMAD ALI.

MUHAMMAD SAID ABDULLA ("MUHSIN"). *See* "MUHSIN."

MUHAMMAD, SALIM SALIH. *See* SALIM SALIH MUHAMMAD.

AL-MUHANI, AHMAD ALI (*CA*. 1935–). A North Yemeni from Sanaa, a member of the "**Famous Forty**," and one of North Yemen's first technocrats who, after higher education in the United States at Lafayette College and Tulane University, returned to Yemen to work as a water engineer just before and after the **1962 Revolution**. He then went abroad for a nearly 15-year career with the United Nations in Vienna. Al-Muhani returned to Yemen in the late 1970s to serve as YAR minister of municipalities, ambassador to Saudi Arabia, and, from 1985 to 1990, minister of petroleum and mineral resources. In this office, al-Muhani played a direct role in the development of the oil resources first found in 1984 and in the search for additional oil. Criticized for a lack of vision and leadership as well as for his alleged mishandling of natural gas negotiations, he was not offered a ministerial post on the occasion of Yemeni **unification** in 1990, but he was appointed chairman of the Yemen Bank for Reconstruction and Development in early 1991, and remained in that post for some years until he retired. Well connected, al-Muhani is the brother-in-law of Muhammad Ahmad al-Jubari, a leading businessman with close ties to Kuwaiti investors. *See also* BANKS.

"MUHSIN," MUHAMMAD SAID ABDULLAH. The PDRY politician of North Yemeni origins whose long tenure in the 1970s as the feared, powerful minister of state security earned him the title of "the butcher." His dismissal in 1979 was a major step toward the overthrow of **Abd al-Fattah** Ismail by **Ali Nasir** Muhammad al-Hasani. Muhsin's return from exile in 1984 was an early event in the chain that led to the overthrow of Ali Nasir in the **13 January events** in 1986, the bloody intraparty fight that led to formation of a new government in which he assumed a key **Yemeni Socialist Party** (YSP) post and became minister of construction and housing.

Although a leader of the hard-liners on inter-Yemeni affairs in the late 1980s, Muhsin was awarded the politically sensitive post of minister of local government affairs in the new government after Yemeni **unification** in 1990. This post placed him in charge of—among other things—the **local councils of cooperative development**. In 1993, he became minister of housing and urban planning. Muhsin chose to follow the YSP leadership when it opted for secession in 1994 and headed the same ministry in the newly formed **Democratic Republic** of Yemen (DRY). The DRY met with defeat in the **War of Secession** in July 1994, ending his career in politics and government.

MUJAHID. *See* ABU SHUWARIB, MUJAHID.

MUJAWAR, ALI MUHAMMAD. The technocrat who was appointed prime minister of the ROY at the end of March 2007, apparently in part to convince Yemeni critics and the skeptical and crucial international donor community that the **Salih regime** was truly serious about launching economic and political reforms and especially fighting widespread corruption. An economist trained in France, his actions as minister of electricity in the previous government—when, for example, he allegedly cut off the power to an office of the ruling **General People's Congress** that refused to pay its bills—suggested that Mr. Mujawar was prepared to fight **corruption**. Although the 33-member cabinet he headed contained only 11 new faces, it was maintained that he would soon appoint younger technocrats to the cabinet. By late 2008, his efforts to effect change were complicated by plunging **oil** revenues and other effects of the global recession.

Faced at the outset with the ongoing **al-Houthi rebellion**, Prime Minister Mujawar was confronted in 2008 with both renewed violence involving **al-Qaida** in Sanaa and the **Hadhramawt** and angry demonstrations by disillusioned southerners in **Aden** and nearby regions. He is himself a southerner from **Shabwa**.

MUKALLA. South Yemen's second most important port, far smaller and without the protection of the great natural harbor at **Aden**, 300 miles to the west. Situated on the **Arabian Sea**, Mukalla historically served as the port of the **Hadhramawt** and the seat of both the **Quaiti** sultanate and Great Britain's **colonial administration** in the Eastern **Aden Protectorate**. Crammed as it is between sea and the sheer, high cliffs of the **Jol**, it remains a visually arresting place of concentrated urban and waterfront activity. Mukalla is the port from which Hadhramis have for hundreds of years embarked, and thus is a cosmopolitan place with important trading links with **Oman**, ports in the Persian Gulf, and points far to the east and south. It was a key element in South Yemen's expanding **fishing** industry and remains so in the ROY. The discovery of **oil** at **Masila** in 1990 and the construction of oil and gas terminals and a gas liquefaction plant nearby guarantee Mukalla an important place in Yemen's future. Indeed, it enjoyed a building boom—one that got somewhat ahead of itself—beginning in the mid-1990s. Mukalla is served by the airport at **Riyan**, located just to the east.

AL-MUKARRAM AHMAD AL-SULAYHI. *See* SULAYHID DYNASTY AND ALI BIN HASAN AL-SULAYHI.

MUKEIRAS. The small market town and military outpost in South Yemen on the more than 6,000-foot-high plateau north of the **Awdhali** escarpment and just across the border from the North Yemeni town of **al-Baydha**. Through the centuries it benefited from its location on an ancient **trade route** between the coast and the interior of Yemen. In the 20th century, the British in Aden valued it for its relatively pleasant climate and for the airfield that played a key role in **Great Britain**'s policy of **air control** of South Yemen's up-country and its efforts to fend off the Yemeni **imamate**.

AL-MUKHA (MOCHA). The small, largely silted-in and sand-covered port west-southwest of **Taiz** on the southern end of the **Tihama** that from the mid-16th to the late 18th centuries—with its warehouses and offices of European and American merchants—thrived as an international hub for the export of the newly prized, highly priced Yemeni **coffee** beans. The port's name remains an English slang term for coffee.

Al-Mukha lost its place as a great coffee port when Yemeni coffee lost out to the coffee grown in the great plantations of Indonesia and Brazil. Superseded by British Aden and then al-Hudayda, it became a tiny, sleepy fishing and smuggling village set amid great sand-covered ruins. Construction began in the early 1980s to convert al-Mukha into a small, modern deepwater port. Yemeni **unification** in 1990, and new emphasis on the ports of Aden and al-Hudayda, has probably placed new limits on the revival of al-Mukha. Nearby is thought to be the site of the lost port of Muza, prominent for centuries in the trade between the Mediterranean and points eastward, especially during the **Himyarite** kingdom early in the Common Era.

MUKHTAR PASHA, AHMAD. *See* OTTOMAN TURKS IN YEMEN.

MUNASSAR, QASIM. *See* YEMENI CIVIL WAR.

MURAD TRIBE. *See* MADHHIJ TRIBAL CONFEDERATION.

MUSLIM BROTHERHOOD. *See* POLITICAL ISLAM, MODERN.

MUTAWAKKILITE KINGDOM (IMAMATE). *See* HAMID AL-DIN FAMILY AND IMAMATE.

AL-MUTAWAKKIL, MUHAMMAD ABD AL-MALIK (1942–). The professor of political theory at Sanaa University and deputy secretary general of the **Union of Popular Forces** (UPF) who for more than two decades has used his version of liberal democracy to harshly and daringly critique the **Salih regime.** Since the mid-1990s, he worked to get **Islah** and the **Yemeni Socialist Party** (YSP) to dialogue toward the creation of a united opposition to that regime, working on this project with **Jarullah** Umar, the chief architect of the **Joint Meeting Parties** (JMP), created in 2002. He drafted much of the program adopted by the JMP in late 2005 in anticipation of the 2006 presidential **elections.** The key feature of that program was the call for the replacement of the ROY's current presidential system with a parliamentary one, and al-Mutawakkal has tirelessly promoted this form of democracy and argued for this major bit of constitutional engineering.

Al-Mutawakkil pursued his graduate studies in political theory in the United States. He is from a great family of **sayyids,** and the political party of which he is an officer, the UPF, is the small liberal **Zaydi** party created decades ago by the al-Wazirs, another great sayyid family now based mainly in the United States. Everpresent at political gatherings, his actions and appearance resemble those of a guru or a saint.

AL-MUTAWAKKIL, YAHYA MUHAMMAD (1943–2003). The quite charismatic, politically skillful, and ambitious North Yemeni leader who occupied important military, government, diplomatic, and political posts in the YAR and then the ROY from 1962 until his death in an auto accident in 2003. He participated in the **1962 Revolution**, fought as an officer in the **Yemeni Civil War**, took part in 1967 in the coup that replaced the **al-Sallal regime** with that of Qadi Abd al-Rahman **al-Iryani**, and then worked with President al-Iryani to realize republican–royalist **reconciliation** in 1970. He was a member of the Military Command Council after the **al-Hamdi** coup in 1974 and served as interior minister in the al-Hamdi regime. In the **Salih regime**, he was governor of Ibb province in the late-1980s and became interior minister again in the mid-1990s. Al-Mutawakkil played a key role in the efforts to achieve Yemeni **unification** in 1990 and then to resolve the political crisis that ended in the **War of Secession** in 1994. He served as assistant secretary general of the ruling **General Peoples' Party** (GPC) in the mid-1990s and, finally, from 1997 until his death, as a member of the **Shura Council** and adviser to the president.

Yahya al-Mutawakkil was born in **Shahara**, the son of a judge and a descendent of a famous 17th century imam. He went to Sanaa as a young man in 1956, entered the Air Force Academy, and then, in 1961, became an instructor at the Military College. By this time, he had joined the **Free Officers Association** committed to overthrowing the imamate. Wounded early in the civil war, he went to the Soviet Union for further military education and then, back in Sanaa in 1965, was put in charge of military training.

Al-Mutawakkil became associated with liberal republicans opposed to Egypt's "occupation" of the YAR and to President al-Sallal's pro-Egyptian stance and then spent more than a year in jail in Cairo. It was as deputy commander of the **armed forces** that Brigadier-General al-Mutawakkil worked for reconciliation between republicans and royalists. A longtime member of the **Baath Party** until the 1980s, al-Mutawakkil served the GPC well even as he maintained good relations with the weakened opposition party, the **Yemeni Socialist Party**.

Al-Mutawakkil's interludes abroad over much of the 1970s as YAR ambassador to Egypt and then to the United States and France can be explained partly in terms of the chemistry between his known aspirations to high office and his family name and origins. His political ambitions allegedly contributed to al-Hamdi's sending him off early to Washington. He held high posts throughout his career despite the fact that he came from a great **sayyid** family closely associated with the **imamate** and the old **Zaydi** establishment. Still, many non-sayyad republicans were not comfortable with his background and political ties. Fairly or unfairly, his name continued to be associated with those who favored a constitutional imamate and more recently advocated a moderate Islamic republic.

MUTI, MUHAMMAD SALIH YAFI (?–1981). The old **National Liberation Front** leader and high-level PDRY government and political figure in the late 1960s and the 1970s who had backed **Ali Nasir Muhammad** al-Hasani in his takeover and consolidation of power in early 1980 and who, only several months later, was quietly arrested and then shot and killed "while trying to escape" in early 1981. Muti had served as interior minister after the **22 June Corrective Move** in 1969 and as foreign minister from mid-1973 to mid-1979. Until his arrest a year later, he was regarded as one of the most powerful survivors of the factional strife that had resulted in the demise of Salim **Rabiyya Ali** in 1978 and **Abd al-Fattah** Ismail in 1980.

MUZA. *See* AL-MUKHA.

MUZAYYIN CLASS. *See* SOCIAL SYSTEM AND STRUCTURE.

– N –

NABI SHUAYB, JABAL. At about 12,300 feet, the highest mountain on the **Arabian Peninsula**, located roughly 20 miles west of Sanaa, just to the north of the main road from Sanaa down to the coast via **Manakha**. Accessible by an easy, gradual hike to the top, it affords a fine view in all directions, especially north to **Shibam–Kawkaban**.

NAJRAN. The oasis town and region in the southwest corner of **Saudi Arabia** that, though long regarded by many Yemenis as part of cultural and geographical Yemen, has been firmly under Saudi control ever since the forces of **Ibn Saud** defeated those of Imam

Yahya in the **Saudi–Yemeni war in 1934**. The war's result was conditionally registered in the **Taif Treaty**. The region formally and finally became a part of Saudi Arabia under the terms of the **Saudi–Yemeni Border Agreement** of 2000. Najran's fame in ancient times turned on its being the northernmost point on the **trade route**, a gateway to the great and rich civilizations of the Mediterranean basin.

NASIRITES AND NASIRITE PARTIES. The vaguely defined and diverse political groups in the YAR in the 1970s and 1980s that identified with Egypt's Gamal Abdul **Nasser** and Nasserism. The Yemeni Corrective Organization (Tashih) was the party of that faction of the Nasirites that perceived his legacy as carried on by President Ibrahim **al-Hamdi** and aligned itself with al-Hamdi and his program in the mid-1970s. Because its members were thought to be merely political careerists or stalking-horses for al-Hamdi, the Tashih was refused entry by the several opposition groups on the Yemeni left when they formed the **National Democratic Front** in 1976.

Nasirites, with the moral and material support of **Libya**'s Muammar **Qadhafi**, were at the center of the failed **October 1978 coup** attempt, which occurred a year after al-Hamdi's assassination and a few months after Ali Abdullah **Salih** had become president. Although top leaders were executed and others were jailed in the wake of this attempt, the Nasirites survived this setback and went on to make modest showings in the three parliamentary elections since Yemeni **unification** in 1990. The Popular Nasirite Unity Organization is one of the five parties that in 2002 created the **Joint Meeting Parties**, the opposition coalition. By themselves, however, the Nasirites are, as they always have been, a small group of educated Yemenis with little organization and no mass base.

NASSER (NASIR), GAMAL ABDUL (1918–1970). The president of **Egypt** and leader of Arab nationalism whose person, words, and deeds from the mid-1950s to the early 1970s dominated the politics of the Arab world, perhaps especially and differently in the two Yemens, which came so lately to modern nationalism. Almost exactly a decade after the 1952 Egyptian Revolution, the

YAR regime that grew out of the **1962 Revolution** modeled itself on Nasser's United Arab Republic (UAR). The UAR's intervention in the **Yemeni Civil War** in the 1960s both saved the YAR and distorted its development. Similarly, Nasser and his local supporters greatly influenced the national struggle in **Aden** and the **Aden Protectorates** from the late 1950s on, a struggle that pitted the nationalist groups against each other as much as against **Great Britain**. Nasser's involvement regionalized and then internationalized both the Yemeni Civil War in North Yemen and the independence struggle in South Yemen. The stunning and total defeat of Egypt in 1967 in that key round of **Arab–Israeli conflict**, the Six-Day War, precipitated the decline of Nasser, who died in 1970, and of his **ideology**, Nasserism.

Nasserism, although sometimes vague and constantly evolving, was the touchstone for other variants of revolutionary Arab nationalism from the mid-1950s to at least 1970. In its first phase, it was a confrontational anti-imperialist, pan-Arab nationalism and, in its second phase, beginning in 1961, it was all that plus a version of non-Marxist socialism or socialism without class warfare— i.e., Arab Socialism. Nasserism was a powerful weapon in the struggle against the ideologically less articulate conservatives and monarchists in the Arab world. But it competed most fiercely with the ideologies closest to it, **Baathism** and the thought of the left wing of the **Arab Nationalist Movement**. Nasserism and these other ideologies found their way into the nationalist discourse and struggle in the two Yemens. Learning and deriving much from Nasserism early in the course of their own national development, each of the Yemens later reacted against Nasserism, the YAR tending toward a Yemeni nationalism (or a Yemeni Arab nationalism) and the PDRY opting for "scientific socialism" (its take on Marxism) and internationalism. *See also* NASIRITES AND NASIRITE PARTIES.

NATIONAL ASSOCIATION OF OPPOSITION GROUPINGS (MAWJ). *See* AL-JIFRI, ABD AL-RAHMAN ALI.

NATIONAL BANK OF YEMEN, PDRY'S. *See* BANKS.

NATIONAL DEMOCRATIC FRONT (NDF) AND NDF REBEL-LION. The several-member leftist opposition organization created in 1976 in the YAR that, unable to gain political access, launched an armed revolt—the NDF rebellion—from the late 1970s to the early 1980s against the regime of President Ali Abdullah **Salih.**

The NDF largely traces its roots to the expulsion of the left from the YAR polity following the **Sanaa mutiny** in 1968. This was followed by leftist protest, sometimes violent and often in the countryside, which sputtered on for several years. Anxious to become players and to have their concerns and goals in the mix, the leaders of the several groups acted singly and together to find a place in the regime after the mid-1974 **al-Hamdi** coup that replaced the conservative republican **al-Iryani** regime. Repeatedly rebuffed, they closed ranks and formed the NDF in 1976.

The NDF originally had six members: the **Revolutionary Democratic Party**, the **Organization of Yemeni Resisters**, the **Labor Party**, the **Popular Democratic Union**, the **Vanguard** (the pro-Syrian wing of the **Baath Party**), and the pro-Iraqi wing of the Baath Party. The last of these chose to quit the NDF in 1978. Along with political ambitions and a mixed bag of socialist reforms, the NDF sought to unite the YAR with the new revolutionary South Yemen, end dependency upon **Saudi Arabia**, curb the power of tribal leaders, and open the political system to popular participation.

The NDF continued to be denied by the embattled al-Hamdi into 1977 and became increasingly militant in the bitter political climate after his assassination by conservative, pro-Saudi elements in October of that year. After a tumultuous year during which al-Hamdi's successor, Ahmad **al-Ghashmi**, was also killed, the NDF in 1978 launched its armed revolt against the **Salih regime** and with the active support of the Marxist PDRY in Aden.

After successes that at times sorely challenged the Salih regime, the NDF rebellion petered out in spring 1982. It was beaten in battle by a revitalized military and the tribal **Islamic Front** and was politically weakened as a result of the 1979 **border war** between the YAR and the PDRY and thereafter, accession of the less militant **Ali Nasir** Muhammad in the PDRY. Its demise allowed the YAR to establish for the first time its presence in the area along the demarcated portion of the border between the Yemens.

At this point, most NDF leaders and fighters accepted the regime's reconciliation terms and went north, effectively ending the NDF as an organized force in YAR politics. Sayyid Yahya al-Shami, an old Baathi and NDF leader, played a key role in the negotiations but did not finally come to terms with the Salih regime until Yemeni **unification** in 1990. Some NDF members had become closely involved in the PDRY's ruling **Yemeni Socialist Party** in the late 1970s. Indicative of these links, NDF fighters who remained in Aden, led by **Jarullah** Umar, played a key role in the bloody **13 January events** in the PDRY in 1986.

Al-Shami did take a post in the government after unification. Other NDF leaders, such as Jarullah Umar and Sultan Ahmad Omar, also reconciled on the occasion of unification. They and other former NDF leaders ended up playing important roles in the ROY—most in the opposition, but some in the ruling **General Peoples' Congress**. In the **War of Secession** in 1994, the NDF played no role as an organization.

NATIONAL DIALOGUE AND NATIONAL DIALOGUE COMMITTEE (1981–1982). The elaborate process of structured nationwide discussion throughout which the **Salih regime** attempted in the early 1980s, with considerable success, both to foster and shape political discourse in the YAR and to generate support and legitimacy for itself. The process involved hundreds if not thousands of gatherings large and small, all orchestrated by the National Dialogue Committee (NDC) and its many local subsidiaries. The discussions at these gatherings focused on explication and elaboration of the **National Pact** (al-Mithaq al-Watani) and were a prelude to the **General People's Congress** (GPC), a gathering in 1982 that became a permanent political organization that from the outset had all the attributes of a national political party except the label.

Despite fits, starts, and more than a little confusion, President Salih and the NDC worked hard at these initial tasks. They surprised skeptics and critics with a sustained effort that had a cumulative, positive effect on the organization of political life in the YAR, and thereby on the staying power and prospects of the **Salih regime**. This sequence of steps, conceived largely by Dr. Abd al-Karim **al-Iryani**, amounts to the most ambitious and important act of political construction during the life of the YAR.

NATIONAL DIALOGUE COMMITTEE OF POLITICAL FORCES (1993–1994). The ad hoc, extra-constitutional, multi-party body set up by Sinan **abu Luhum,** Mujahid **abu Shuwarib** and other notables in November 1993 to find a political and constitutional solution to the deepening crisis that threatened Yemeni **unification,** an attempt that produced the **Document of Pledge and Accord** (al-Wathiqa) in mid-January 1994. The National Dialogue Committee consisted of about 25 members drawn from the three parties in the ruling coalition, the lesser parties and other groups. It worked almost continuously from December 1993 through February 1994 to draft, adopt, and promote a document that represented a broad consensus and an amalgam of earlier reform proposals.

The widespread popular support for its efforts enabled the National Dialogue Committee to pressure the leaders of the three parties in the fractured ruling coalition to accept and sign the document in Amman, Jordan, on 20 February, 1994. Nonetheless, the efforts of the committee failed, and in March the fighting began that soon led to the **War of Secession.** The National Dialogue Committee disintegrated, and both abu Luhum and abu Shuwarib went into exile in protest.

NATIONAL FRONT. *See* NATIONAL LIBERATION FRONT (NLF).

NATIONAL IDENTITY, TRADITIONAL. Modern Yemeni nationalism and identity are rooted in the pre-Islamic past, have an Islamic dimension, and fit quite closely the territory and people embraced by the polity created through **unification** in 1990: the ROY. The notions of a single place called "al-Yaman" and of one Yemeni people are old ones. This notion of place embraces at least all of what was called North Yemen and a larger swath of land to the south and east, including Aden, the place known in literature as "the eye of Yemen."

In addition, Yemenis have a sense of a shared history and are inclined to define themselves in terms of a vaguely recollected past greatness. As often as not, an illiterate peasant will point to an old and imposing pile of rubble and proudly proclaim "hatha himyari," identifying the rubble and himself with the great pre-Islamic **Himyarite** kingdom—even if the rubble, in fact, dates back only a few hundred years. At the same time, most Yemenis equate being Yemeni with being Muslim. The Islamic nature of Yemen and Yemenis is implicit and is assumed to be in the nature of things. In North Yemen, traditional Yemeni nationalism was identified in part with the **imamate** and strengthened by the struggle led by the imams to end two occupations of Yemen by the **Ottoman** Turks, first in the 17th century and again in the late 19th to early 20th centuries. *See also* GREATER YEMEN; IDEOLOGY AND POLITICAL IDEAS, MODERN.

NATIONALISM, YEMENI. *See* IDEOLOGY AND POLITICAL IDEAS, MODERN; NATIONAL IDENTITY, TRADITIONAL.

NATIONAL LIBERATION FRONT (NLF). The political formation in South Yemen that, shortly after its creation in 1973 out of the Aden branch of the **Arab Nationalist Movement** and several other radical groups, launched the **Radfan Rebellion** and then went on to win the fierce struggle to succeed the departing British in late 1967. The NLF's opponents in Radfan were both the colonial power and the traditional up-country rulers and notables, the "feudalists." The opponents it defeated in the succession struggle were proponents of and participants in the **Federation of South Arabia** and the more radical **Front for the Liberation of Occupied South Yemen** (FLOSY). After independence, the NDF—or National Front (NF), as it called itself after assuming power—went on to dominate the ruling coalition that it fashioned with the pro-Syrian **Baath Party** (the **Vanguard**) and the **People's Democratic Union** in the early and mid-1970s. It then merged with these two to create and dominate the ruling **Yemeni Socialist Party** (YSP) in 1978.

The NLF went through a rapid succession of changes in terms of orientation, leadership and homogeneity, and these changes were recorded in three congresses. The Fourth Congress of the NLF, held in March 1968, provided the first public display of the internal struggle being waged inside the NLF between the right wing, led by President Qahtan **al-Shaabi**, and the left wing, led by **Abd al-Fattah** Ismail and Salim **Rabiyya Ali**. It resulted in the adoption of resolutions and a program that amounted to a total victory by the left wing. President Qahtan's refusal to implement the congress's revolutionary decisions led to a leftist uprising, the victory of leftist forces over the "regular army," and, in mid-1969, the forced resignation of President Qahtan and Prime Minister Faisal **al-Shaabi** in what the victors came to call the **22 June Corrective Move**. The now more homogeneous regime used the next 18 months to introduce socialist measures and to consolidate its position by purging institutions and such remaining non-leftist NLF leaders as Prime Minister Muhammad Ali **Haytham**.

The Fifth Congress was held in March 1972, exactly four years later, and it registered the earlier, complete victory of the left and projected the image of a revolutionary regime firmly in control and facing all sorts of domestic and external enemies and adversities with optimism and fervor. Discourse took place within the terms of "scientific socialism," and the congress reaffirmed the NLF's **ideology,** commitment to its revolutionary program of building socialism at home and its solidarity with national liberation movements abroad. As further steps toward the building of a proper vanguard party, the NLF changed its name to the **National Front Political Organization** (NFPO) and pledged to continue negotiations with its two major radical allies, the People's Democratic Union and the Vanguard.

In March 1975, the Sixth Congress decided to unite the NFPO with these two parties to form the **Unified Political Organization, National Front** (UPONF) and to commit it to the comprehensive and detailed development and application to Yemen of "the theory of scientific socialism." The Unification Congress of the three parties endorsed this decision in October, thereby paving the way for the final stage in political construction, the creation three years later of a true Soviet-style Marxist–Leninist ruling party, the **Yemeni Socialist Party**. This occurred against a background of growing conflict between the "Stalinist" Abd al-Fattah and the "Maoist" Rabiyya Ali—and in the mock trial and execution of the latter.

NATIONAL PACT (AL-MITHAQ AL-WATANI). The guide for and principles of national political action that were drafted in the YAR in early 1980, that the centerpiece of the extensive **National Dialogue** conducted throughout the country in 1980–1982, adopted as amended during the sessions of the **General People's Congress**

(GPC) in August 1982, and used thereafter by the **Salih regime** as the touchstone for political discourse and education. Criticized by some for its conservatively Islamic content, the National Pact was vague and general enough to accommodate a broad array of political perspectives, thereby making it a useful tool for both building a political consensus and deflecting **ideological** attacks. As President Salih was wont to say, the pact provided the ideas and the GPC the organization for the successful effort at national political development in the 1980s. Together, they were important parts of much-needed political construction.

NATIONAL SECURITY. *See* SECURITY SERVICES.

NATIONAL YEMENI UNION (NYU). The stillborn official political organization created in the YAR in 1973 by the **al-Iryani** regime, and the last modest attempt by that regime at needed political construction. Despite the constitutional ban on political parties and President al-Iryani's distrust of them, the NYU was proclaimed the political body for all Yemenis, with an ample budget and a blue-ribbon political bureau headed by the president himself. In fact, however, the NYU was never developed to the point of having any lasting impact on politics. It never launched organizing and promotional campaigns, and it did not even open itself for membership until the spring of 1974. In retrospect, it appears that it was less an expression of a new commitment to political organization than a hastily designed attempt by the regime to preempt the political arena during the period of uncertainty after the two Yemens had agreed in 1972 to end their **border war** and unite. As the prospect for unification with the PDRY quickly faded, the YAR leaders just as quickly lost interest in the NYU, and no one mourned its passing when it was abolished after the **al-Hamdi** coup in 1974.

NATURAL DISASTERS. Nature can be harsh in Yemen, and much of that harshness has to do with limited rainfall and, just as important, the variability of that rainfall from season to season. The culprit is the unreliable **monsoon** winds. When the winds fail, as has happened many times in the past—sometimes for several years—the result is drought and famine. On the other hand, when the rain comes it sometimes takes the form of downpours producing flash floods that erode land, destroy crops, and take lives.

Apart from the fact that a failed rainy season is generally a good predictor of political unrest, some of the natural disasters in Yemen in recent decades have resonated with special force through the body politic. The exigencies of World War II and drought throughout South Yemen in the mid-1940s led **Great Britain** to start several ambitious irrigation projects, making the regime's invasive **"forward policy"** in the **Aden Protectorates** almost inevitable. In North Yemen, the devastating socioeconomic effects of the **Yemeni Civil War** were compounded by the prolonged drought and famine that ravaged much of the country from the late 1960s through the early 1970s, aggravating already huge political problems.

In the spring of 1982, the PDRY experienced heavy rains and flooding, and the costs and crippling effects of these disasters figured in the regime's decision to honor recent agreements with the YAR and to end support for the **National Democratic Front Rebellion**. Later that same year, North Yemen's **Dhamar** province was wracked by an earthquake that took 1,500 lives, leveled whole villages, and left 400,000 homeless. This disaster both added to the dilemmas of a government and society under economic duress and served to rally and unify the Yemeni nation. On the other hand, severe flooding in the PDRY some months after the **13 January events** in 1986 only aided the forces that were conspiring to make the PDRY unviable.

NATURAL GAS. *See* OIL AND GAS EXPLORATION AND PRODUCTION.

NDF REBELLION. See NATIONAL DEMOCRATIC FRONT (NDF) AND NDF REBELLION

NETHERLANDS. Dutch traders arrived off the coasts of **Aden** and **al-Mukha** in the early 17th century and were active in the lively Yemeni **coffee** trade for several decades, by which time they had smuggled coffee plant cuttings and started coffee plantations far to the east on the island of Java. The American slang for coffee, "mocha-java," is a legacy of this bit of history. In modern times, the Dutch government began giving a considerable amount of bilateral economic and technical aid to the YAR in the mid-1970s, and has continued to do so regularly since the creation of the ROY in 1990. Indeed, this small but rich country remains one of Yemen's chief donors, and in this capacity has, since 1995, joined forces with other major donors and the **IMF/World Bank** in trying to make generous amounts of aid to Yemen conditional on economic and political reforms.

NEUTRAL ZONE. *See* 4 MAY AGREEMENTS.

NEWSPAPERS AND MAGAZINES. *See* MASS MEDIA.

NEXEN. The **oil** company, formerly named Canadian Occidental Petroleum Co. (CanOxy), that discovered oil in Block 14 in the **Masila** region in the **Hadhramawt** in 1990, that began producing in late 1993, and that went on quickly to become the leading oil producer in Yemen. Spurred by the find, a pipeline was completed down to the Arabian Sea coast at **Shihr**, east of **Mukalla**, by the fall of 1993. By 2005, Nexen production from Block 14 had reached nearly 180,000 b/d, more than twice that of the nearly depleted field exploited by the **Yemen Hunt Oil Co.**, the first and formerly biggest producer in Yemen. Fairly or unfairly, Nexen came to be compared very favorably to Yemen Hunt as a good foreign corporate citizen.

NGO. *See* INTEREST (PRESSURE) GROUPS.

NIEBUHR, CARSTEN. *See* TRAVELERS.

NIHM TRIBE AND REGION. *See* HASHID AND BAKIL TRIBES AND CONFEDERATIONS.

NIMR PETROLEUM CO. *See* BIN MAHFOUZ; OIL.

9/11. Popular shorthand for the remarkably well-executed, devastating suicide attacks by members of Usama **bin Laden's** al-Qaida on the Twin Towers in downtown Manhattan and the Pentagon just outside Washington, D.C., on 11 September 2001. These events quickly defined the then largely undefined foreign policy of the George W. **Bush** administration in terms of a **War on Terror**. The latter quickly metastasized, shaping—and, some say, distorting—the **United States'** relations with a host of states, much as the United States' struggle against communism in the **Cold War** did for a generation after 1945. The ROY quickly found its relations with the United States redefined primarily by the preoccupation of the latter with the War on Terror.

1948 REVOLUTION. The revolution—or, perhaps more correctly, the coup—in which an odd assortment of allies plotted the overthrow of the **Hamid al-Din imamate**, assassinated the aged Imam **Yahya**, had the Abdullah bin Ahmad **al-Wazir** proclaimed imam, and established a new government and a professedly constitutional imamate. The entire enterprise collapsed and its leaders were summarily executed, jailed, or forced to flee in only a few weeks when Crown Prince **Ahmad** successfully rallied the tribes and others, and marched on Sanaa. Support for the al-Wazir imamate evaporated or failed to materialize when it became clear to the **tribal** shaykhs, various notables, and the ruling family in neighboring **Saudi Arabia** that the coup leaders then calling for pledges of loyalty had had a hand in the plot to assassinate Imam Yahya. Ali Nasir al-Qurdai, a poet and shaykh of Murad in the **Madhhid** confederation, was recruited to ambush and kill Imam Yahya. He did this out of vengeance, having had a long, stormy personal relationship with the imam that grew out of the perceived impact upon the tribes of efforts to extend the sway of the imamate.

The plotters and supporters of the coup included, in addition to a few true revolutionaries, members of other disgruntled, rival imamate families, other **sayyid** and **qadi** families, the leaders of the **Free Yemenis** and **Yemeni Unionists**, the **Muslim Brotherhood**, and assorted army officers and tribal leaders. Exposed by the failed coup attempt, the execution, imprisonment, or exile of these varied opponents gave the Hamid al-Din imamate under the harsh Imam Ahmad a new lease on life and deferred important political change in North Yemen for nearly the 15 years until the successful **1962 Revolution**.

1955 COUP ATTEMPT. The quickly aborted, possibly unplanned, and narrowly focused attempt by a senior army officer and a brother of Imam **Ahmad** to depose him in 1955. Lt. Col. Ahmad Yahya al-Thalaya, inspector general of the army, took strong issue with Imam Ahmad over his handling of an incident between soldiers and villagers near **Taiz**. Having gotten no satisfaction, he besieged the imam in his palace in Taiz and extracted from him a letter of abdication in favor of his brother, Prince **Abdullah bin Yahya**. With unseemly, perhaps suspicious, haste, Prince Abdullah proclaimed himself imam, appointed Prince Abbas, his brother, prime minister, and called for the loyalty of all officials in Sanaa and the provinces. Some religious leaders and some of the other notables pledged allegiance to him, but many others chose not to violate their oaths of loyalty to Ahmad quite so quickly. Moreover, Abdullah and al-Thalaya did not move against the besieged Ahmad, remembering well how the assassination of Imam **Yahya** had turned many key elements against the **1948 Revolution** and doomed it to failure. This gave the wily and courageous Ahmad the time he needed to intimidate or win back the loyalty and support of the ordinary soldiers who were holding him in the palace. Meanwhile, Crown Prince Muhammad **al-Badr**, Ahmad's son, had rallied northern tribal forces and was hastening with them to Taiz. In less than a week, Imam Ahmad was again in complete control and the coup leaders, brothers Abdullah and Abbas among them, were summarily executed. *See also* ARMED FORCES.

1962 REVOLUTION. Known as the "26 September Revolution" to most Yemenis, this was the momentous event that one night in Sanaa ousted the Zaydi **imamate**, created the YAR, and abolished the **sayyid** caste's ascriptive right to rule. Most important of all, it opened North Yemen to the modern world and the irreversible rush of political, cultural, and sociopolitical change for the first time. Compared with this opening, such major circumstances as the long **Yemeni Civil War** that followed in the wake of the revolution, the intervention by **Egypt** that both saved and deformed the revolution, and the erratic, sometimes bizarre course of the regime of President Abdullah **al-Sallal** pale in significance.

Most of the **Septembrists** who made the 1962 Revolution were young, Egyptian-trained army officers, some of them from the **Famous Forty**, who at the last moment recruited the older al-Sallal as its nominal head. Al-Sallal and his friends soon took charge; they, too, were committed to national change and were inclined to model the YAR after the Egyptian Revolution and Gamal Abdul **Nasser**'s Arab Socialism. Interrupted by the long **Yemeni Civil War**, the 1962 Revolution changed course and picked up momentum only after al-Sallal was ousted in 1967.

1970 CONSTITUTION, YAR'S. The constitution that, probably because it was identified with the respected President Abd al-Rahman **al-Iryani** and, in a peculiar way, with the movement forward of the Yemeni nation and the republic, had the staying power to survive the political turmoil of the 1970s and 1980s, serving during that period as something of a beacon or standard of political life in Yemen. Its adoption after **Egypt**'s withdrawal and at the end of the **Yemeni Civil War** made it a marker on the way to national **reconciliation** and the resumption of Yemen's destiny by Yemenis.

Liberal democratic in form, with deference paid to Islam, the 1970 Constitution has its share of escape clauses and silences and was from the outset often honored in the breach. At its center was the legislature, the mostly elected Consultative Council (CC). Accountable to the CC, the Republican Council (RC) was the three-member—later, for a time, the five-member—executive. Chairmanship of the RC was supposed to rotate among its members but never rotated past "President" al-Iryani.

The constitution was suspended outright by President **al-Hamdi** when he seized power in 1974 and was then mostly, and confusingly, reinstated by President **al-Ghashmi** in 1978 without its centerpiece, the CC, and with an amendment that replaced the plural executive with a single president. During the 1980s, President **Salih** repeatedly promised new elections to a restored CC—and almost as frequently put them off. In July 1988, however, a new CC was finally chosen in accordance with the 1970 Constitution, and the council both elected President Salih to another five-year term and voted approval of the composition and program of the new government that the president had asked the outgoing prime minister to form. As a consequence, for the first time since the al-Iryani regime was ousted by al-Hamdi in 1974, the head of state and government of the YAR were elected in accordance with the 1970 Constitution: namely, by a properly selected legislature. The amended 1970 Constitution was again fully in place. Less than two years later, on the occasion of Yemeni

unification, it was replaced by the **1990 Constitution** of the ROY, which was very similar to its predecessor.

1970 STATE CONSTITUTION, PDRY'S. The constitution adopted in South Yemen that reflected the 1969 triumph of the left wing of the **National Liberation Front** and its **22 June Corrective Move**. It embodied the increasingly radical regime's commitment to a future based on its **ideology** "scientific socialism." On this occasion, the name of the state was changed from the **People's Republic of South Yemen** to the **People's Democratic Republic of Yemen**, the PDRY.

1972 AND 1979 BORDER WARS AND UNIFICATION AGREE-MENTS. *See* BORDERS; CAIRO AGREEMENTS ON UNIFICA-TION; KUWAIT AGREEMENT OF 1979; TRIPOLI SUMMIT.

1990 CONSTITUTION, ROY'S. The formally liberal democratic fundamental law of the ROY, a mix of presidential and parliamentary elements, that featured a fully elective legislature—the **Council of Deputies** (Majlis al-Nuwab)—a five-member **Presidential Council** elected by the Council of Deputies, and a president and vice president chosen from its midst by the Presidential Council. Constitution was referred to the legislatures of the two parts of Yemen by the two governments in the **30 November Agreement** in 1989, approved by the two legislatures meeting separately on 21 May 1990, and declared in force on the following day on the occasion of Yemeni **unification** and the creation of the ROY. The constitution is a slightly revised version of the draft unity constitution submitted by the joint Yemeni constitutional committee in December 1981—the draft that then gathered dust on a shelf for most of the next decade.

Although endorsed overwhelmingly by the people in a referendum in the fall of 1991, the constitution was used by the enemies of unification from the outset, both within and without Yemen. Critics asserted that the new basic law, unlike the YAR's **1970 Constitution**, which banned all "partisanship" and declared the Islamic **sharia** to be "the source of all law," sanctioned political parties and partisanship and reduced the sharia to merely "the main source" of the law. These important differences aside, the new constitution was very similar to the YAR's first non-controversial, consensus-building constitution.

In the fall of 1994, after the ROY survived the **War of Secession**, the constitution was amended in major ways. The Presidential Council was abolished and replaced by a single president; the election of the president and vice president became the responsibility of the Council of Deputies. In addition, the status of the sharia as the source of law was enhanced, and provision was made for some future decentralization to the provincial and local level.

In mid-1997, after the parliamentary elections, a second chamber was authorized. This chamber, the **Shura Council**, was to consist of 59 members, all appointed by the president, and was to have only limited advisory powers. In addition, it was decided at the time that the president would be chosen in 1999 by direct popular vote, rather than by a vote of the Council of Deputies.

In 2001, constitutional changes extended the presidential term from five to seven years and set a two-term limit on the office. At the same time, the term of the Council of Deputies was extended from four to six years. In addition, the size of the appointive Shura Council was increased to 111, and its duties were somewhat increased.

NON-GOVERNMENTAL ORGANIZATIONS. *See* INTEREST (PRESSURE) GROUPS.

NUMAN, DR. YASSIN SAID (1946–). The technocrat and **Yemeni Socialist Party** (YSP) member who, after being PDRY prime minister from 1986 to 1990 and parliamentary speaker in the ROY after Yemeni **unification** from 1990 to 1994, became secretary general of the YSP in mid-2005 and head of the Supreme Coordinating Council of the opposition **Joint Meeting Parties** (JMP) in early 2007.

Dr. Numan, an economist by training, was minister of fisheries in the PDRY in the 1980s, and it was the bloodbath marking the **13 January events** in 1986 that made possible his becoming prime minister in a government of survivors. As luck would have it, he had been abroad when these events occurred.

Parliamentary speaker after Yemeni **unification** in 1990, Dr. Numan was forced into exile by the political crisis that led to the **War of Secession** in 1994. Later tried and convicted of treason, but then granted amnesty, he returned to the ROY from the United Arab

Emirates in 2003 and resumed a leadership role in the YSP and the general opposition to the **Salih regime**. In this capacity, Dr. Numan worked to revive and reposition the YSP in the ROY's multiparty system, one dominated by the ruling **General People's Congress**. He has tried to do this by making the YSP a force in the JMP, and of all the YSP leaders he has proven to be the one able to appeal to and gain the trust of all sides of that five-party opposition coalition. In his capacity as head of the JMP's Supreme Coordinating Council, he became perhaps the most often heard and respected voice of the opposition during the period leading up to and following the 2006 presidential **elections**, **Islah's** greater weight in the JMP notwithstanding. Dr. Numan proved to be a popular political figure in the ROY both before the war in 1994 and has continued to be so since his return to Yemen.

NUMAN FAMILY. The powerful landowning family in the **Hugari-yyah** which held sway and thrived under Shaykh Abd al-Wahhab Numan during the rule of both the **Ottoman** Turks and Imam **Yahya**, from the late 19th through the early decades of the 20th century. The Numans were **Shafiis** and resided in a great stone compound north of **al-Turba**. From the 1940s, and for decades thereafter, political and intellectual leadership of the family fell to Abd al-Wahhab's nephew, Ahmad Muhammad **Numan**.

In turn, the highly regarded heir apparent to Ahmad Muhammad was his eldest son, Muhammad Ahmad Numan, who, in his early twenties in the 1950s, probably nudged his father in a more modern and radical political direction. After serving the YAR as roving ambassador on several occasions and as deputy prime minister and foreign minister in 1973, Muhammad Ahmad was assassinated at about age 40 in Beirut in 1974. Some say that political elements had conspired to keep him out of the YAR for years out of fear of his skills as a Shafii political leader—and that this may also account for his death. Forced to pass up higher education in order to take over leadership of the family during his father's political exile, he became quite learned through self-study. Allegedly, he admired Henry **Kissinger's** thinking, trying to view Yemen's political future in broad conceptual terms. His loss from Yemeni politics is still regretted by aging first-generation **modernists**.

Muhammad Ahmad's younger brother, Abd al-Rahman, set up the first **local development association** (LDA) in al-Turba, a town in rural Yemen, and was the first to seek foreign donor support for an LDA. In the early 1970s, he began to act on the idea of creating a national network of LDAs as a vehicle for development and as a nationwide grassroots political base. Unfortunately for him, a young army officer, Ibrahim **al-Hamdi**, seized upon this idea and took over the movement in 1973.

NUMAN, SHAYKH AHMAD MUHAMMAD (1907–1996). The revered head of the then-powerful Numan family of the **Hugariyya** in North Yemen who is regarded as one of the fathers of the modern Yemeni nationalism, a man who worked from the beginning of the 1940s to the mid-1970s to find a political way out of Yemen's backwardness, ignorance, and oppression. He is perhaps best known as having been a founder of the **Free Yemenis** in Aden in 1944 and, several years later, as a promoter of the **Yemeni Unionists** in Cairo. The next generation of Yemenis affectionately called him "al-Ustaz"—"the professor"—partly because of his lead in founding **Bilqis Preparatory College** in Aden, a school created to meet the need to prepare Yemenis from North Yemen and the **Aden Protectorates** for the modern world and the tasks facing Yemen.

Numan served as YAR prime minister twice—once for a few months in mid-1965, and again for a few months in mid-1971—and he served the republic in other important ways during these years. However, despite his role as a major force and symbol of a new Yemeni nationalism, Numan never seemed to realize his political potential during the republican era, on at least two occasions withdrawing from the political fray rather than fighting on. In this regard, he is sometimes contrasted to that other founding father, President Abd al-Rahman **al-Iryani**. His virtually complete withdrawal is traced largely to grief over the assassination in 1974 of his beloved son and colleague, Muhammad Ahmad Numan. From this time on and until his death, he preferred to live abroad, in Saudi Arabia or Cairo.

Numan had received a traditional **Shafii** education in **Zabid** and then set up North Yemen's first school offering a "modern" curriculum in a town just south of **Taiz**. He went to Cairo in 1937, where he was exposed for the first time to modern political ideas, and studied at al-Azhar University. Back in Taiz, under the wing of Imam **Ahmad,** he and his colleague, Muhammad **al-Zubayri,** fled to Aden in 1944 when the imam lashed out at the **"modernists"**—and then founded the Free Yemenis. From this time until the **1962 Revolution**, Numan chose or was forced to live in exile.

– O –

OBAD ("AL-MUQBIL"), ALI SALIH. The relatively minor leader of the **Yemeni Socialist Party** (YSP) who became secretary general when virtually all of its top leaders were forced into exile in 1994 in the wake of defeat in the **War of Secession.** A member of the "old guard," Obad's efforts to revive and redirect the YSP were mixed. He led it in its wrongheaded boycott of the 1997 parliamentary **elections,** organized the protests in **Mukalla** that same year, was denied by parliament the right to run for president in the 1999 presidential elections, and led the party back to participate in the 2003 parliamentary elections. Things did take a step forward when he chaired the YSP party congress in late 1998—the first since the mid-1980s—and he was also involved, after 2000, in the incubation of the **Joint Meeting Parties**, the new opposition coalition. Despite ill health, Obad remained head of the YSP until Dr. Yassin Said **Numan** took over in 2005.

OCTOBER 1978 COUP. The major, nearly successful attempt by the Yemeni **Nasirites** to overthrow—with support from **Libya**—the new and still shaky regime of President Ali Abdullah **Salih.** The armed attempt involved some high-ranking government officials and military commanders and was put down violently only after it was already well in motion. Although exposing the precariousness of the Salih regime, it served the regime well in the longer run by flushing out many opponents and intimidating many others. A large number of persons were arrested, and the coup leaders were tried and executed in a matter of days. In this action against President Salih, the Nasirites were probably as much motivated by the urge to avenge the assassination of President Ibrahim **al-Hamdi,** with whom they had worked and had identified closely, as by other political impulses. As

Nasirites, they apparently had the material—but not moral—support of Col. Muammar **Qaddafi**'s regime.

OIL AND GAS EXPLORATION AND PRODUCTION. Unlike most countries in Middle East by the mid-1970s, the two Yemens and then the ROY relied from the outset on foreign oil companies—albeit rarely major multinationals—with which they reached production-sharing agreements. The Age of Oil came late but suddenly to the YAR in 1984 when the **United States'** Hunt Oil Company of Dallas, Texas, struck oil in commercial quantities with the first well it drilled in the Alif field far to the east on the edge of the desert near **Marib**. Good fortune seemed also to befall the PDRY only two years later, when the **Soviet Union**'s Technoexport struck oil in the Iyad in Block 4, in **Shabwa** and not far to the east of Marib. Pessimists were quick to note that, as Yemeni luck would have it, both finds were close to the intersection of the undemarcated borders of the YAR, the PDRY, and **Saudi Arabia**.

These two oil strikes in the 1980s had been preceded by several cursory searches for oil over the six decades that began when engineer Karl Twitchell predicted the likelihood of oil in the east, near Marib. Twitchell's services over several years in the 1920s were a gift to the imam from Charles **Crane**. Thereafter, rumors of oil seepages and shales went essentially unchecked in a remote, forbidding interior known for its harsh desert climate and terrain, fiercely independent tribes, and undemarcated borders. Western oil companies were deterred by a suspicious Imam **Yahya's** refusal to grant concessions to foreigners for oil exploration and, later, by an apparently willing Imam **Ahmad** who was known for capriciousness.

In South Yemen, ruled by **Great Britain**, the **Quaiti** and **Kathiri** sultanates signed an agreement in late 1961 with the Pan-American International Oil Co., a subsidiary of the Standard Oil of Indiana, for a concession to drill for oil in the desert strip north of Wadi **Hadhramawt** east of Swabwa. The subsequent search was unfruitful, but the hopes for oil wealth that it engendered help explain why the major sultanates of the Eastern **Aden Protectorate** were not interested in joining with the poor members of the Western Aden Protectorate in the creation of the short-lived **Federation of South Arabia**. At about this time, Pan American was also granted permission to search for oil in his domain by the sultan of the **Mahra** Sultanate of Qishn and Socotra.

The 1960s and 1970s, the early republican years, did not prove more receptive to oil exploration, what with the **Yemeni Civil War**, socialist upheaval and transformation in South Yemen, and then two **border wars** between the two Yemens. Efforts to find oil did pick up in the early 1980s, however. In addition to the beginning of Hunt Oil's activity in the YAR, a small offshore strike by the Italians near **Mukalla** in 1982 and the positive results of extensive seismic surveys of the country raised hopes by the mid-1980s of an imminent commercial oil strike in the PDRY.

The **Yemen Hunt Oil Company** (YHOC), the partnership formed in 1984 by the Hunt Oil Company, the Exxon Corporation and a Korean firm, with Hunt as operator, quickly developed the Alif field and built a pipeline down to Ras Isa, near **Salif** on the Red Sea. Oil was flowing to this terminus for export by the end of 1987. A small oil refinery with a capacity of 10,000 barrels/day (b/d) for domestic use had already opened near Marib in early 1986. Over the next few years, several other fields were discovered and developed in the Marib/al-Jawf basin.

In the PDRY, although several thousand b/d were being trucked from Shabwa's Block 4 to the **Aden refinery** by the late 1980s, financial and technical problems delayed Technoport's completion of a pipeline from Shabwa to the Gulf of Aden until 1991. The pipeline terminated at Bir Ali, then a small, poor fishing village on a stretch of beautiful white sand beach about 35 miles west of **Mukalla**. Shortly thereafter, further activity in the three fields in Shabwa passed from the Soviets to the Nimr Petroleum Company owned by **bin Mahfouz** of Saudi Arabia.

In the late 1980s, and prior to Yemeni **unification** in 1990, the two Yemens jointly signed an exploration and production-sharing agreement with a consortium of France's Total and Yemen Hunt for the formerly disputed "neutral zone" between Marib and Shabwa. Exploration activities in this area by Hunt went forward in 1990 and over the next few years resulted in strikes of commercial quantity in the Jannah field.

Canadian Occidental Petroleum, soon renamed **Nexen**, made a major commercial oil strike at the end of 1990 much farther to the east in the Hadhramawt, in **Masila** (Block 14), northeast of Mukalla and not far from the coast. Quantities initially estimated to be comparable to those in the Marib/al-Jawf basin proved to be greater. A pipeline to the coast was quickly built and put into operation by the fall of 1993, and within a few years Masila's production was exceeding that in Marib/al-Jawf.

The Masila strike transformed already keen petroleum industry interest in Yemen into a feeding frenzy in the early 1990s, everybody wanting—and willing to pay a lot for—a piece of the action. By 1992, the still-new ROY had exploration and production-sharing agreements for different blocks with about 20 oil companies or consortia of companies, and prospects for new strikes in new areas seemed very good. This enthusiasm was fed by Yemen's rapidly rising oil production, which reached 340,000 b/d in late 1993. Of this, 200,000 b/d were being produced by YHOC in Marib/al-Jawf and 135,000 b/d by Nexen in Masila. Projections of 1,000,000 b/d by the year 2000 seemed within the realm of the possible.

These projections were to prove wildly optimistic. The oil bubble gradually deflated, and the limited nature of Yemen oil bounty became the dominant theme in the late 1990s. Political and armed conflict—from the **War of Secession** in 1994 to the **al-Houthi Rebellion** in 2004–2007, as well as events related to the **War on Terror** after **9/11** in 2001—raised questions about Yemen as an environment in which foreign oil companies could safely operate. More important, those companies that did persist did not come up with much new oil. As a result, the rapidly declining production in and then Malisa Marib/al-Jawf was not being fully offset by production from the several new small oil fields that came online since 2000.

Starting at 10,000 b/d in 1987, Yemen's oil production peaked at 465,000 b/d in 2003 and dropped to 420,000 in 2005 and 310,000 b/d in 2008. Oil revenues decreased from $4.1 billion in 2006 to $3.3 billion in 2007. Reserves are now estimated to be around 3 billion barrels, and it is not thought that new exploration offshore or in territory made safe by the **border agreement** with Saudi Arabia in 2000 will add dramatically to these reserves. Studies by the **IMF** and the World Bank project the depletion of the ROY's reserves by 2020. Even the usually upbeat President Salih, in arguing the need for reforms at mid-decade, warned that Yemen's oil would be gone in a decade.

Just as oil was oversold in the 1980s as the panacea for solving Yemen's economic ills and needs, so, too, was natural gas and its liquefaction for export in the mid-1990s and beyond. In the early 1990s, the ROY reached an agreement with YHOC to study the development of the sizable natural gas reserves in the Marib/al-Jawf basin. Murky politics in 1993 led to an agreement between the ROY and the United States' Enron Corporation for a $3.3 billion project to develop these gas resources and produce liquefied natural gas (LNG) for export over the next 30 years. YHOC and some of its Yemeni allies challenged the deal with Enron as a violation of the 1984 agreement giving it rights to Block 18. The agreement was scrapped—and, in any case, Enron soon became history.

In 1997, a new group, Yemen Liquified Natural Gas (Yemen-LNG) was formed, with Total of France taking the largest stake (39.6 percent) and joined by Hunt Oil, ExxonMobil, a South Korean company, and the Yemeni government. The agreement called for a pipeline from the gas reserves in Marib down to a two-train liquefaction facility and export terminus in Balhaf, a town on the Arabian Sea near Bir Ali and west of Mukalla. Production was due to begin in 2001.

The project was beset by problems, setbacks and delays almost from the outset. The U.S.S. *Cole* bombing and events after **9/11** raised new questions about security that made it difficult to find financiers and the long-term customers upon which the up-front financing of $3.5 billion was contingent. In addition, a worldwide oversupply drove LNG prices down. ExxonMobil, with a 14.5 percent stake, had second thoughts and pulled out of the project in 2002. Then, in 2005, the year that construction began, the reliability of the gas supply came into question: The ROY canceled the new oil agreement for Block 18 with YHOC and gave it to Safir Exploration and Production Company, leading Hunt Oil and ExxonMobil to charge the ROY with breach of contract and to seek redress through arbitration. That same year, however, the parliament gave its approval—but only after challenging the LNG sales agreements as too favorable to the buyers and insisting on a significant set-aside of gas for domestic use over a 20-year period.

By 2007, the project was again largely on track, its cost estimated to be about $4 billion. YemenLNG was reconstituted, another Korean partner was added, and Safir committed itself to providing sufficient gas to meet YemenLNG's needs, beginning in late 2008. Enough customers had signed 20-year purchase agreements to provide LNG to U.S. and Korean markets and financing was progressing adequately, with four export credit rating agencies providing coverage for a $2.8 billion debt page. Work on the pipeline and first train of the two-train project on the coast at Balhaf went forward. The first train came on stream by the end of 2008 and the second train was scheduled for completion by late-2009. The first LNG shipments going to Korea were scheduled for the end of that year.

When both trains are fully on stream in 2010, YLNG will produce for export 6.2 million tons/year of LNG. Given that Yemen estimate natural gas reserves are 17.1 trillion cubic feet, YLNG should be able to produce at this level for 25 years. In light of current estimates regarding the depletion of Yemen's oil reserves—and oil revenues—this is good news. LNG production at 6.2 million tons/year is equivalent to about 175,000 b/d of oil in volume term—well over half of Yemen's current oil production. In addition, it was reported in late 2007 that the Arab Yemeni–Libyan Holding Co. and the Indian TATA Group were planning to build a $1.5 billion petrochemical industries plant in Balhaf. Promising additional revenue.

OMAN, SULTANATE OF. The small, thinly populated and, until recently, poor and backward country that wraps around the southeast corner of the Arabian Peninsula and abuts the eastern end of the ROY. Much smaller in population and covering half the area, Oman is the country of the **Arabian Peninsula** that most resembles Yemen in terms of climate, geography, history, settlement pattern, and social organization. In the distant past, the country was known for **incense** from **Dhufar**—i.e., for frankincense—and for its Arab sailors, dhows, the port of Muscat, and the tales of Sinbad. In modern times, it has been known especially for its strategic location at the southern end of the **Gulf** and across from **Iran** at the Straits of Hormuz.

The political system of Oman, formerly known as the Sultanate of Muscat and Oman, is authoritarian and headed by a rather enlightened, Western-trained ruler, Sultan Qaboos Ibn Said. After deposing his father, Oman's long-ruling tyrant, in 1970, Qaboos went on in the first half of the decade to successfully put down the

PDRY-supported **Dhufar Rebellion**—this with help from conservative neighbors and **Great Britain**. He then successfully opened the country to the outside world in a controlled manner and initiated the gradual, oil-fueled development and modernization of Oman that has continued since that time. The law and order of Qaboos's Oman has often been contrasted to the relative absence of both in YAR and now the ROY.

In the 1980s, relations with Oman provided a good barometer of the PDRY's fitful drift toward moderation and improved relations with its conservative and mostly oil-rich Gulf neighbors. After the Dhufar Rebellion petered out in the late 1970s, there remained the questions of diplomatic relations and the long-standing **border dispute** between the two countries. Formal ties had been restored and agreement on the border almost completed when Yemeni **unification** came in 1990.

What had acted for some years as a drag on truly good relations between the PDRY and Oman was Oman's active role in the **Gulf Cooperation Council** and its security arrangements with the **United States**. The drag increased shortly after unification, when events leading up to the First **Gulf War** in 1991 found the new ROY at odds with the anti-Iraq international coalition of which Oman was a part. Despite this, the two sides did come to terms: and signed a final border agreement in late 1992, an act of diplomacy with implications for the ongoing border dispute between the ROY and **Saudi Arabia**.

Sultan Qaboos paid a state visit to unified Yemen in October 1993, signifying closer ties, and tried hard to mediate the worsening political crisis in the ROY in early 1994, both singly as well as jointly with King Husayn of **Jordan**. However, the meeting he hosted between the two opposing Yemeni leaders in early April failed to prevent the **War of Secession** in mid-1994.

Plans for a major road link to facilitate the movement of goods and people between the two countries, begun in 1993, resumed after the war. In 1996, the two countries signed the road deal and agreed to establish a free-trade zone near the border. They also signed an air services accord. Since then, high-level diplomatic contacts have increased and other key bilateral agreements have been reached.

OMAR, SULTAN AHMAD. *See* NATIONAL DEMOCRATIC FRONT (NDF) AND NDF REBELLION; REVOLUTIONARY DEMOCRATIC PARTY.

ORGANIZATION FOR THE LIBERATION OF THE OCCUPIED SOUTH (OLOS). The independence movement created by Abdullah **al-Asnag** in 1965, which, in contrast to the **National Liberation Front** (NLF) and its reliance on armed struggle, believed in the timely achievement of independence for all of South Yemen by political means—yet without ruling out the need for violence. Formed in Taiz with the blessings of President Gamal Abdul **Nasser**'s representatives in the YAR, the short-lived OLOS was an amalgamation of the old **South Arabian League** and al-Asnag's **People's Socialist Party**. It was essentially a party of the educated Adeni bourgeoisie with some leftover North Yemeni workers whom al-Asnag had recruited into the Aden Trade Union Congress, and it had virtually no links to the people and problems of the **Aden Protectorates**. As politics polarized in Aden in the mid-1960s, such obviously bourgeois figures as Abd al-Qawi **Makkawi** joined the ranks of the OLOS. Under Egyptian pressure, OLOS and the NLF united in 1966 to form the **Front for the Liberation of Occupied South Yemen** (FLOSY), from which the NLF almost immediately withdrew.

ORGANIZATION OF YEMENI REVOLUTIONARY RESISTERS. *See* RESISTERS.

OTHMAN, ABDU ALI. *See* EDUCATION.

OTTOMAN TURKS IN YEMEN. The Ottoman Turks invaded and occupied North Yemen, incorporating it into the Ottoman Empire, during two relatively short periods separated by two centuries: 1538–1636 and 1849–1918. The first occupation took place during the reign of Sulayman the Magnificent, the great sultan who ruled between 1520 and 1566, and was a time of major expansion of the empire. Saana, as the center of imperial rule in both cases, reflected currents of the day in Istanbul. Indeed, in the late 19th century, European visitors to Sanaa found it a surprisingly vibrant, urbane place—perhaps more so than it was during the first half of the 20th century.

On neither occasion did the Turks really establish their rule over the **Zaydi** northern highlands. Moreover, the occupations fostered a traditional variant of Yemeni nationalism, one associated with the Zaydi **imamate**, which on both instances took the lead in fighting to free Yemen and the Yemeni people from the Turks. Ahmad Faizi Pasha, the tough pasha of Yemen, could only fight to a draw the Yemen revolt led by the **Hamad al-Din** imams in the first decade of the 20th century. Although neither period of occupation profoundly imprinted itself on Yemen and the Yemenis, the imamate's rudimentary army, state bureaucracy, and territorial organization after 1918 all reflected Ottoman practices to some degree. This was true in part because Imam **Yahya** retained a number of Turkish army officers and bureaucrats after the second occupation ended.

The second Ottoman occupation had conspired with the occupation of **Aden** by **Great Britain** in the mid-19th century to gradually divide Yemen into two distinct territorial–political units—perhaps the Turks' most important legacy. Governor Ahmad Mukhtar Pasha's policy of expanding Turkish authority southward from Sanaa to the **Hujariyya** and beyond caused Britain to begin the process of organizing Aden's hinterland into the **Aden protectorates**. These reciprocal actions in the early 1870s precipitated the **Anglo–Ottoman clash** of 1873. This, in turn, led to the demarcated **Anglo–Ottoman line** of 1904, a boundary between the two Yemens that would persist until **unification** in 1990. As a consequence, two Yemeni national struggles unfolded from the late 19th to the late 20th centuries, producing the two different political cultures and the two different sets of sociopolitical institutions and practices that marked the YAR and PDRY—and that made the building of the ROY all the harder.

The Ottomans did not stay to see much of this 20th-century drama. Accomplished at soldiering and diplomacy, Ali Said Pasha commanded the forces that confronted those of the British outside Aden—on the edge of the golf course, it was reported—for the whole of World War I. He withdrew those forces ceremoniously via Aden some weeks after the Ottomans signed an armistice with the victorious Allied Forces.

– P –

PALESTINE AND THE PALESTINE QUESTION. Palestine and
the Palestinians are not as far from the two Yemens as geography
might suggest. After 90 years of colonialism, Aden was witness
to its first serious protest against British rule in 1947, a three-day
general strike against what was seen as Britain's pro-Zionist policy
in Palestine. In 1980, in a remote town in the YAR, an angry local
elder could cut short an American with: "If you gave us just the price
of one of the Phantom jets you give to Israel, al-Mahwit could have
the water system it needs." More than most Arab countries, the two
Yemen republics came of age with the Palestine question, particularly
the new phase ushered in by the greatest **Arab–Israeli** event—the
Six-Day War—and the rise of the Palestine Liberation Organization
(PLO). Both became strong supporters of the PLO, as did the ROY.

The moderate YAR was most comfortable with Chairman Yasir
Arafat and the PLO mainstream led by his organization, Fatah,
whereas the more radical PDRY tended to identify with the often
mutually antagonistic Popular Front for the Liberation of Palestine
(PFLP) and Democratic Front for the Liberation of Palestine (DFLP)
and their respective leaders, George Habash and Nayif Hawatmah.
The PDRY's links to these two groups and leaders were direct. In
the mid-1960s, what became the ruling **National Liberation Front**
(NLF) in South Yemen grew out of the Yemeni branch of the **Arab
Nationalist Movement** (ANM), and Habash was the founder of the
ANM. As Habash evolved from Arab nationalism to the Marxist
internationalism of his PFLP, so too did the left wing of the NLF.
When Nayif Hawatmah and his DFLP split off from the PFLP and
moved farther left, they maintained close ties and a sense of solidarity
with elements of the ruling NLF in Aden—indeed, Hawatmah even
wrote a study of the NLF's move to the left.

Over the years, the two Yemens have given what little support they
could to the PLO and its main factions, most notably when the PLO
needed havens for the forces evacuated from Beirut in 1982. In return,
Palestinian leaders—especially Arafat, Habash, and Hawatmah—
have frequently mediated conflicts within as well as between the two
Yemens. For this and other reasons, visits by one or another Palestinian leader to either or both Yemens became regular occurrences. The

ROY stood by Arafat during and since the Oslo peace process of the 1990s and since 2004 has backed Mahmoud Abbas, Arafat's successor as head of Fatih and chairman of the Palestinian Authority.

PEASANT LEAGUES. The short-lived popular organizations set up in the late 1960s in the countryside in the southeastern borderlands of North Yemen with the help of old **Arab Nationalist Movement** members and the new **National Liberation Front** regime in Aden. The purpose was to bring the revolution to the countryside or, more modestly, check the power of the local tribal shaykhs and landowners. The peasant leagues were suppressed after the **Sanaa Mutiny** was put down in August 1968. *See also* AL-IRYANI, QADI ABD AL-RAHMAN.

PEOPLE'S CONSTITUENT ASSEMBLY (PCA). The appointed interim legislature created by President **al-Ghashmi** in 1978 that began to assume an air of permanence in the years after President **Salih** increased its size and duties in 1979. It was finally replaced in 1988 by the long-promised, largely elected **Consultative Council**, the legislature called for in the **1970 Constitution** that had been permanently adjourned after the **al-Hamdi** coup in 1974. As long as the PCA, and not the constitutionally prescribed council remained in place, questions were raised about the legitimacy of the **Salih regime** and the process by which he was elected and reelected in the first decade of his tenure.

PEOPLE'S DEFENSE FORCE. *See* ARMED FORCES.

PEOPLE'S DEMOCRATIC REPUBLIC OF YEMEN (PDRY). The South Yemeni state that prevailed from late 1970, when the name **"People's Republic of South Yemen"** was dropped and a new constitution adopted, until Yemeni **unification** in 1990—and the birth of the ROY. South Yemen became independent on 30 November 1967, when the victorious **National Liberation Front** (NLF) assumed power on the occasion of **Great Britain**'s departure from **Aden** and the Aden **Protectorates**.

Britain had first occupied Aden in 1839, and the key facts for the next century were its preoccupation with the port of Aden and its benign neglect of the dozen or so small states in the hinterland with which it signed treaties of protection only in the late 19th century. As a consequence, no single political entity in modern times embraced even most of what was to become South Yemen in 1967, except for the stillborn **Federation of South Arabia** of the mid-1960s. Instead, what existed was the 75-square-mile Aden Colony—a city–state, a partly modern urban enclave, and, by some measures, the world's second- or third-busiest port in the late 1950s—and a vast, mostly distant, politically fragmented hinterland that was, for the most part, based on subsistence agriculture and traditional sociocultural institutions. Neither the British administrators nor the nationalists who first stirred in Aden in the 1940s had much knowledge of, interest in, or impact on this hinterland, even with Britain's adoption of a new **"forward policy"** during the last decades of imperial rule. As a result, the people of Aden were closer, in more ways than just geographically, to the city of **Taiz** in North Yemen than to the **Hadhramawt**, which lay far to the east of Aden and had its strongest business and familial ties with people in the **Gulf**, India, Indonesia, and East Africa.

The **infrastructure** barely holding together the major settlement areas of South Yemen at independence in 1967 consisted of dirt tracks, unpaved roads, a number of airstrips, and the telegraph. The country consisted of many micro-economies, each largely self-sufficient. For example, isolated Wadi Hadhramawt was dependent upon emigration to and remittances from the Gulf and Southeast Asia. What little market economy existed during the British period mostly centered on the port of Aden and its environs, and this area, in turn, was plugged less into its hinterland than into the international economic system via its sea lanes. This fragile modern sector was dealt a devastating blow within a few months prior to independence in 1967 when port activities were brought nearly to a halt for years with the blocking of the **Suez Canal** that occurred when the **Arab–Israeli conflict** erupted into the Six-Day War. At virtually the same time, Britain's rapid withdrawal ended both subsidies from London and the significant economic activity tied to the large British presence.

The history of South Yemen since independence is distinguished by five major periods: (1) the period of political takeover and consolidation (1967–1969), the initial phase during which the NLF established control in Aden and over the hinterland at the same time that the balance of power within the ruling NLF passed from the nationalists led by Qahtan **al-Shaabi** to the party's left wing, (2) the long period of uneasy leftist co-leadership of Salim **Rubiyya Ali** and **Abd al-Fattah** Ismail from 1969 to 1978, distinguished by the efforts of these two rivals both to organize the country in terms of their differing versions of Marxist–Leninist **"scientific socialism"** and to align the country with the **Soviet Union**, the socialist camp, and national liberation movements around the world, (3) the Abd al-Fattah Ismail interlude (1978–1980), a period that began with the violent elimination of Salim Rubay Ali by Abd al-Fattah and that was notable for the firm entrenchment of **Yemeni Socialist Party** (YSP) rule and bitter conflict between a militant PDRY and the YAR, the other Yemen, (4) the era of **Ali Nasir Muhammad** al-Hasani, from 1980 to 1985, the period during which the consolidation of power in this single leader was paralleled by increasing moderation in both domestic affairs and external relations, especially with the YAR, (5) and the final period of collective leadership and political weakness (1985–1990), the period that began in early 1986 with the intraparty bloodbath that ousted Ali Nasir and otherwise decapitated the YSP—the **13 January events**—and ended with Yemeni **unification** and the creation of the ROY. During the transition period that followed formal unification in May 1990, the YSP shared power with the ruling party of the YAR, the **General People's Congress**, under their respective leaders, Ali Salim **al-Baydh** and Ali Abdullah **Salih**: the "two Alis."

Despite this pattern of bitter and sometimes lethal intraparty conflict, the PDRY regime over the more than two decades from 1967 to 1990 did maintain its rule and order throughout the country, made progress in bridging the gap between Aden and the rest of the country, pursued with some success a number of admirable social goals, and made good use of extremely limited resources in efforts to develop a very poor country. Despite pressures toward fragmentation, perhaps especially in the case of the Hadhramawt, South Yemen held together during difficult political and economic times. This was largely the result of political will, agitation, and organization. The gap between city and countryside remained a top concern of the leadership, and real progress was made in extending **education**, medical care, and other social services beyond Aden and the large towns. Indeed, a major campaign was waged to extend **women**'s rights and other progressive ideas and institutions to the countryside. Great differences in wealth and property were narrowed, and the **economy** was organized along socialist lines, most notably in terms of a variety of **agricultural** and **fishing** collectives and cooperatives.

Modeled after revolutionary **Cuba**, the popular defense committees were an institutional expression of these concerns. Local neighborhood committees established in the mid-1970s throughout the PDRY were designed to engage and mobilize the people and to perform educational and other revolutionary tasks as well as simple problem-solving, administrative, control, and security activities. Admirable in theory, the committees did not live up to hopes, largely because of low popular participation and the emphasis on security and control at the expense of educational and other social tasks.

In the end, however, the socialist experiment, short on time as well as money, failed; the discovery of **oil**, in 1986, simply came several years too late. In addition, the modern ideas and institutions had neither the time nor the funds needed to reach far and deep into the countryside, where entrenched tradition prevailed. Nevertheless, the experiment was a good try, and the regime that tried it remained surprisingly committed, egalitarian, and free of corruption over nearly a quarter century.

In many ways, the PDRY of the 1970s and 1980s was a lesser Cuba, and, like Cuba, it became both heavily dependent upon, and a great burden to, the Soviet Union. The sudden collapse of the latter and its socialist bloc in the late 1980s left the PDRY weak and in isolation, shorn of fraternal and material support. This, as much as the bloodbath that decapitated the YSP in early 1986, left South Yemen unable to resist the YAR's call for unification in late 1989.

The **1970 Constitution** specified a 111-member elective Supreme People's Council (SPC), the seat of popular sovereignty that , in turn, elected from its members a Presidium of from 11–17 members. The SPC had sole law-making power, elected the prime minister, and voted on cabinet members, judges, and other high officials. Due to organizational problems on the local level, the SPC formed in 1971 was appointed, not elected; national elections were first held in 1978. Although candidates were screened, they were not required to be members of the ruling YSP—indeed, 40 of the 111 elected 1978 were not YSP members. Given that the PDRY had quickly evolved into a socialist system led by a vanguard party, the SPC was never the object of much attention—or of much hope, or despair.

Selected by the Presidium, the PDRY's plural executive was meant to embody a new collective leadership after the ouster of President al-Shaabi in 1968, and its chairman acted as head of state. The Presidium and its chairmanship *per se* declined in importance over the years as the ruling party, the YSP, took command. Salim **Rabiyya Ali** was Presidium chairman for nearly a decade, followed by **Abd al-Fattah** Ismail, **Ali Nasir Muhammad** al-Hasani, and, finally, Haidar abu Bakr **al-Attas**.

PEOPLE'S DEMOCRATIC UNION (PDU). The first communist party in Yemen, it was formed in Aden by Abdullah Abd al-Razzak **Badhib** in 1961 and quickly spread to North Yemen, especially to **Taiz**. In 1976, more than a decade after the **1962 Revolution**, the PDU became one of the six parties that formed the leftist **National Democratic Front** that went on to wage a guerrilla war for nearly a decade against three successive regimes in the YAR. Meanwhile, in the PDRY, the PDU and the **Baathists** (the **Vanguard Party**) joined with the majority **National Liberation Front** to form the ruling coalition. In 1978, these three parties merged into the ruling **Yemeni Socialist Party**. Although very small in both Yemens, the communist party had far greater influence than its numbers suggest, especially in the PDRY, which was tied much more closely to the **Soviet Union**. However, the influence of the party declined in the 1980s and, after 1990, far more so with the collapse of the Soviet Union and Yemeni **unification**.

PEOPLE'S MILITIA. *See* ARMED FORCES.

PEOPLE'S PARTY FOR YEMENI UNITY. The single Marxist party that was created for North Yemen in 1979 by the partial merger of five of the six opposition parties that had joined forces against the regime in the YAR in the mid-1970s. The party was based in Aden, and its first secretary was **Jarullah** Umar, a leader of the **Revolutionary Democratic Party** (RDP). In addition to the RDP, the merger included the **People's Democratic Union**, the **Organization of Yemeni Resisters**, the **Vanguard**, and the **Labor Party**. Despite the merger, these old opposition parties maintained their places in the more diverse and fluid **National Democratic Front** (NDF) and were important elements in the NDF Rebellion.

PEOPLE'S REPUBLIC OF SOUTH YEMEN. The original name of the regime that was established in South Yemen upon independence on 30 November 1967, only to be changed to the "People's Democratic Republic of Yemen"—the PDRY—on the occasion of the republic's third anniversary and the promulgation of a new constitution. The name change marked the beginning of the worsening of relations between the two newly independent Yemens. It angered leaders of the YAR because the dropping of the "South" seemed to imply that the renamed regime was the legitimate one for all Yemen—and the "Democratic" one, as well.

PEOPLE'S SOCIALIST PARTY (PSP). The political party founded by Abdullah **al-Asnag** in 1962 as the political arm of the **Aden Trade Union Congress** for the stated purpose of fighting the impending merger of Aden with the conservative **protectorate** states to form the **Federation of South Arabia**. The PSP quickly became the nationalist political voice of many Adeni workers. Galvanized by both events in Aden and North Yemen's **1962 Revolution**, it called increasingly loudly and clearly for independence from **Great Britain**, withdrawal of all British armed forces, and unity with the YAR in the north. With ties to the British Labour Party and hopes that a Labour electoral victory in Britain would ease the way to independence, the PSP started out committed to political and diplomatic means and opposed to armed struggle, unlike its new rival, the **National Liberation Front** (NLF).

In 1965, the PSP and the **South Arabian League** (SAL) joined in coalition to form the **Organization for the Liberation of the Occupied South** (OLOS), which announced its willingness to resort to armed conflict. Very quickly, the SAL lost interest in the OLOS, allowing the latter to become increasingly dominated by al-Asnag and Abd al-Qawi **Makkawi**. The next year, 1966, the OLOS was transformed into the **Front for the Liberation of Occupied South Yemen** (FLOSY), but it soon became apparent that FLOSY and the large PSP element it contained were about to be swept aside by the tide of revolution—and by the NLF.

PERIM ISLAND. The small, barren, crescent-shaped volcanic island with a well-protected harbor in the **Bab al-Mandab Straits**, close to the point where the two Yemens meet and to **Djibouti** on the coast of Africa. Perim Island was seized by **Great Britain** in Aden in 1857 and became a part of the PDRY upon independence in 1967, and of the ROY with **unification** in 1990. Although eyed by the French in the 19th century and used as a coaling station by British interests in competition with other British interests in Aden from the 1880s to the 1930s, the island had no real strategic or economic significance in the second half of the 20th century. It now serves as little more than a huge base for a small lighthouse in the straits. A poor fishing village exists side by side with the rusting, collapsing remnants of its glory days as a coaling station.

PERIPLUS OF THE ERYTHRAEAN SEAS. A book written by an unknown Greek from Alexandria at the beginning of the Common Era that provides a vivid account of the activities of Yemeni sailors and traders from Cana and other ports involved in the **incense** trade, as well as of trade down the east coast of Africa as far as the island of **Zanzibar**. These activities, it can be inferred from his text, went back as long ago as seven centuries B.C. The book provides the first and very detailed set of sailing directions to the **Indian Ocean**. The author's first-hand familiarity with the subject matter suggests that he was a merchant or a sea captain and that he had made many voyages and often visited many of the ports he mentioned. He records that the commerce of the Zanzibar coast was in the hands of men from **al-Mukha** who "know the whole coast and understand the language" and "who send thither many large ships using Arab captains," and that Aden had "convenient anchorages and watering places, sweeter and better than those at Ocelis, opposite **Perim**." *See also* TRAVELERS.

PHILBY, H. ST. JOHN. See TRAVELERS.

PLANS AND PLANNING, ECONOMIC. Both Yemens expressed early a commitment to comprehensive development planning, and after initial periods of political turmoil and consolidation, both tried to act on that commitment. Beginning in 1971 and 1973–1974, respectively, the PDRY and the YAR implemented rudimentary three-year development efforts. Thereafter, each regime went through three five-year planning cycles, albeit with slippage, revisions, and varying degrees of success. The YAR's Third Five-Year Plan (1987–1991) was the first to factor in **oil** revenues.

The planning function in the PDRY resided in the Ministry of Planning, created in 1973, whereas in the YAR it resided in the **Central Planning Organization** (CPO), created in 1972, and in the Ministry of Development. If the PDRY was more effective than the YAR in planning and plan implementation—and it probably was—this was possibly a function of both ideological commitment to planning as a matter of faith and the more controllable nature of its largely nationalized **economy**. In both Yemens, the things that were planned for were almost wholly those things for which outside funding could be secured. Especially in the case of the YAR, the plan was something of a wish list, and plan preparation and promotion largely involved the effort to match desired projects with the interests of donors. Given the level of development in both Yemens, the plans necessarily focused on the provision of basic infrastructure—e.g., roads, electrification, and water resources.

With Yemeni **unification** in 1990, responsibility for planning was located in the new Ministry of Planning and Development. It was assumed that the merged planning process would address the development problems and prospects posed by unification itself and the expectation of a major increase in oil revenues. However, the sure-to-be challenging planning process for the ROY was thrown into turmoil over the next four years by the economic and political consequences of both the ROY's stance on events leading up to the First **Gulf War** and the escalating political conflict over unification that resulted in the **War of Secession** in 1994. There were false starts at planning from 1990 to 1992, and for 1993 and 1994 there was no annual budget, much less planning and a plan.

It was announced in mid-1995 that the ROY was preparing a five-year plan for development that would be keyed to phases of the new **IMF/World Bank** structural reform package for Yemen. Adopted in late 1996, the First Five-Year Plan (1996–2000) proved relatively successful, focusing as it did on inflation and deficit reduction and an annual GDP growth rate of about 7 percent. With the less successful

Second Five-Year Plan (2001–2006), the plans and planning process seemed increasingly conflated with, and even overshadowed by, the IMF's Poverty Reduction Strategy and Growth Facility, the United Nations' Millennium Development Goals, and even the United States' Millennium Challenge Corporation. Indeed, the strategies and goals of these three programs were more or less incorporated into the Third Five-Year Plan (2006–2010), renamed the Development Plan for Poverty Reduction. Stated goals included reducing poverty by one-half by 2015, a sustained and real GDP growth rate of over 7 percent, and movement of Yemen from the low Human Development Group into the middle group. The Ministry of Planning and Development was renamed the Ministry of Planning and International Cooperation, thereby acknowledging the dependence of Yemen's development upon external aid. It was announced in 2008 that work was to begin soon on the again-renamed Fourth Economic and Social Development Plan (2011–2015).

POLICE. *See* SECURITY SERVICES.

POLITICAL CONSTRUCTION AND DEVELOPMENT. *See* AL-IRYANI AND AL-HAMDI REGIMES AND TRANSITION PERIOD; ECONOMY AND POLITICAL ECONOMY; SALIH REGIME AND ERA; SALLAL ERA; UNIFICATION AND UNIFICATION PROCESS, YEMENI.

POLITICAL ECONOMY. *See* ECONOMY AND POLITICAL ECONOMY.

POLITICAL ISLAM, MODERN. Those forms of present-day Islam that embrace all recent Islamic thought and action in which control and use of the state is central to the goal of maintaining the Islamic status quo in society or to subjecting society to reform or revolutionary transformation according to an Islamic model or ideal. To the extent that it uses, or accepts the use of, the state to achieve its goals, what is loosely called "Islamic activist" is political and can be politically conservative, reformist, or revolutionary.

The two forms of reformist and revolutionary political Islam most relevant to modern Yemen, each a variant of **Sunnism**, are the

Wahhabism of Saudi Arabia and the ideology of the Egyptian Muslim Brotherhood (al-Ikhwan al-Musliman). In competition with one another in the Arab world since the mid-20th century, the similarities between Wahhabism and Brotherhood thought are greater than often realized, especially when considering the most virulent form of each. Transplanted to and nurtured in Yemen, the thought and action of the Brotherhood from a more modern and politically advanced Egypt and the Wahhabism of the much less politically developed Saudi Arabia produced almost indistinguishable variants of revolutionary political Islam.

Wahhabism is the Saudi variant of salafism, the puritanical movement in Sunni Islam based on a return to fundamentals and a literal reading of the Quran and sunnah. It derives from the teachings of the 18th century thinker, Shaykh Muhammad ibn al-Wahhab. The Wahhabi religious establishment became the partner of **al-Saud** (the House of Saud) and, in three waves of conquest and rule of Arabia since the 18th century, traded protection by the Saudi rulers for the legitimization of those rulers. The latest was initiated by Abd al-Aziz bin Abd al-Rahman al-Saud ("Ibn Saud") at the start of the 20th century and continues to this day—since the mid-1920s, in the form of the Kingdom of **Saudi Arabia**.

North Yemen, inspired by the **Zaydi** variant of **Shii** Islam and led by Imam **Yahya**, and Saudia Arabia, driven by Wahhabism under Ibn Saud, collided in the short, decisive **Saudi–Yemeni War of 1934**. Although Saudi Arabia and North Yemen—first the Zaydi **imamate** and then, after 1962, the YAR—were frequently in conflict since the 1930s, the conflicts have rarely been matters of Wahhabism versus Zaydism—or, for that matter, Wahhabism versus the **Shafii** variant of Sunnism shared by most Yemenis, north and south. To the extent that conflict between Saudi Arabia and the Yemens—the YAR, PDRY, or ROY—was tinged by religion, it was mostly a matter of the Wahhabism of Saudi Arabia versus secular trends in the Yemens.

Although Wahhabism and the Wahhabis were tamed and made instruments of the *status quo* by Ibn Saud in the course of consolidating his rule over most of the Arabian Peninsula in the 1920s—i.e., were fashioned into a variant of conservative political Islam—the puritanical and literal back-to-fundamentals nature of Wahhabism left it with the potential to mutate again into a revolutionary variant of political Islam. This radical potential of Wahhabism was realized in the last third of the 20th century when Saudi Arabia, in an effort to defend itself and extend its influence in the Arab world and beyond, used the spread of Wahhabi teaching and institutions as a key instrument of foreign policy. Inadvertently, its export gave birth—or, rather, rebirth—to an untamed, wild variant of Wahhabism.

In particular, beginning in the early 1970s, the Saudis used the fostering and funding of Wahhabism as a major means of moderating, if not controlling, its "dangerous" republican neighbor, the YAR. As a result, Yemen became something of a center of Wahhabism and other variants of salafism at the same time that the greater Arab world and the rest of the Islamic world was experiencing the eruption and consequences of militant, revolutionary Islam. By the 1980s, this variant of political Islam was suddenly in vogue, and many of the growing number of salafis began waging holy struggle—jihad—in word and in deed across the Islamic world.

The other major source of modern political Islam, the Muslim Brotherhood, was a popular religious movement founded in Egypt by Hasan al-Banna in 1928. Wedding modern political party methods and organization to a puritanical and revolutionary message, the Brotherhood spread to most Arab countries from the 1930s through the 1950s and has remained a political presence and force, whether openly or clandestinely, in most of these countries into the 21st century.

North Yemen is a case in point. Given the deeply Islamic nature of isolated **imamate** Yemen, it is not surprising that the first Yemenis who went abroad for education in the late 1940s—most often to Egypt—found the Brotherhood to be a comfortable, almost familiar introduction to the drama of modern politics. Although most of the young Yemenis graduated to secular political parties in the 1950s and thereafter, some stayed with the Brotherhood, and a few worked to enlist the politically uncommitted in a still very traditional Yemen. Modern political Islam had already come to North Yemen when, in 1947, an agent of the Brotherhood, al-Fudayl **al-Wartalani**, arrived to spread the faith and was soon caught up in advising and advancing the ill-fated attempt to wrest the imamate from Imam Yahya's family, the **1948 Revolution**. By the 1970s, after the successful **1962 Revolution**, the Brotherhood grew in North Yemen both because

Saudi Arabia chose to influence Yemeni politics indirectly through it and because so many of the thousands of teachers from Egypt and other Arab countries in Yemen were its members, if not its agents. At about the same time, the Brotherhood established itself in Aden as South Yemen fought for and achieved independence from Great Britain.

In the YAR, the secular and nationalist politicians were very wary of the Brotherhood because of its message, organization, and grass-roots support. Indeed, it proved to be a big vote-getter in the various **elections** held in the 1970s and 1980s—this despite the constitutional ban on all parties. During the 1970s, and especially the mid-1970s, the most prominent Islamic political figure was Abd al-Majid **al-Zindani**, the head of the Brotherhood in North Yemen and a client of Saudi Arabia. Indeed, to rein in al-Zindani, the **al-Hamdi** regime made him head of the agency responsible for moral guidance in 1975. Politics inside the Brotherhood led to the ouster of al-Zindani and his replacement by Yassin Abd al-Aziz al-Qubati in 1978, and the latter remained head of the Brotherhood for decades.

As in the case of Wahhabism, the Brotherhood also generated its own militant, revolutionary variants. Beginning in the 1960s, al-Sayyid Qutb and his successors provided the ideological bases of a movement committed to the creation of an Islamic state through jihad against Israel, the West, and the Soviet Union, as well as the secular regimes in Muslim countries. As part of the Brotherhood moved toward mainstream politics in the 1970s and 1980s, this militant part developed, mutated, and split into numerous groups, largely beneath the surface of public politics.

The incubator that fostered the rapid growth of the global revolutionary Islam beginning in 1980 was the Saudi- and Central Intelligence Agency–organized and -funded jihad against the Soviet forces that had entered **Afghanistan** in 1979 to put down a nationalist uprising inspired partly by Islam. The result was an explosive blending of the militant strands of Wahhabism, the Brotherhood, and other salafi groups. Deeply Muslim and next door to Saudi Arabia, Yemen was an ideal recruiting ground for a disproportionate number of recruits who went to Pakistan to train and to Afghanistan to fight. A key figure in this recruitment in the 1980s, moving back and forth among Yemen, Saudi Arabia, and the war zone, was the self-same al-Zindani who, ousted as head of the Brotherhood in the YAR by 1980, had spent most of the 1980s in Saudi Arabia. Usama **bin Laden**, a rich young Saudi who had studied with al-Zindani and then joined the jihad in Afghanistan was at this time a young adult.

The experiences of these mostly young men in the Islamic schools (madrasas), training camps, and combat zones made many of them skilled fighters as well as more militantly devout and members of a single movement that transcended any country of origin. The role of the struggle in Afghanistan in the 1980s—and again with the rise of the Taliban in the mid-1990s—in forging global revolutionary Islam can best be compared to the role of the Spanish Civil War in forging the Socialist Internationale in the 1930s.

With the winding-down of fighting at the end of the 1980s, the chickens came home to roost—and wage jihad—in Egypt, Algeria, Bosnia, Chechnya, Yemen, and elsewhere. Many of these **"Afghani Arabs,"** both Yemeni and non-Yemeni, drifted or slipped into Yemen, facilitated by porous borders and large areas beyond the reach of the state.

Some of the returning Yemenis saw the Marxist PDRY as their next target. However, with Yemeni **unification** in 1990 and the end of the PDRY, the Yemeni "Afghani Arabs" sought new enemies. Shadowy cells targeted leaders of the former PDRY for assassination during the first years of unification. In the many returnees came under the protection of **Ali Muhsin** Salih, a powerful soldier, colleague, and relative of President Ali Abdullah **Salih**. They were folded into North Yemeni army units and then fought on the president's side in the **War of Secession** in 1994, making the victorious regime indebted to them.

In addition, with the U.S.- and Saudi-led **Gulf War** on 1991, many of the returnees came to see the United States and Saudi Arabia as the real enemies of Islam. Yemeni Islamic Jihad, a group headed by Tariq **al-Fadhli**, veteran of Afghanistan and the son of the former ruler of one of the sultanate abolished in 1967, bombed one hotel in Aden and tried to bomb another in late 1992, places where American servicemen involved in nearby **Somalia** were staying. After al-Fadhli's quick arrest and co-optation by President Salih, remnants of Islamic Jihad morphed into the **Aden–Abyan Islamic Army** (AAIA) a group that was to engage in many acts of armed struggle and violence over much of the next 15 years.

With unification and multiparty politics in 1990, it soon became apparent that moderate political Islam in general—and especially the Brotherhood—was to be a presence and force in the southern as well as the northern part of the ROY. From the outset, the Brotherhood and its leaders—and al-Zindani, who was to make a big comeback in the ROY—played a dominant role in the Reform Grouping (**Islah**), the party of Islamic and tribal elements created in 1990. Islah placed second to the ruling **General People's Congress** (GPC) in the 1993 elections and joined the GPC in governments from 1993 to 1997. Thereafter, Islah became and has remained the major opposition party. More diverse than Islah's tribal side, its Islamist side ranged from a large pragmatic, moderate, "democratic" faction led by Abd al-Wahhab al-Anisi, Muhammad al-Yadumi and Muhammad Qahtan, to more militant elements ranging up to and including jihadists—and the spiritual leader of most of these militants was, again, al-Zindani.

After the mid-1990s, the moderates in Islah, interested in achieving Islamic goals through the democratic process—and coming to enjoy the perks of politics—grew in number and power relative to the militants. As a result, by the beginning of the new century, Islah and two tiny conservative Zaydi parties, **al-Haqq** and the **Union of Popular Forces**, were the major expressions of reformist political Islam in the ROY. In 2002, these three parties joined with the **Yemeni Socialist Party** and the small **Nasirite** Party to create the **Joint Meeting Parties** (JMP), the five-party opposition coalition. Thereafter, Islah and the YSP shared leadership of the JMP.

During the second half of the 1990s, in addition to the AAIA and other Yemen-specific groups, Usama bin Laden and the organization he came to lead and symbolize, al-Qaida, established a presence and following in Yemen. In particular, the re-location of al-Qaida and its leaders to Afghanistan where they identified with the new Taliban regime and al-Qaida's bombing of the U.S. embassies in Kenya and Tanzania served to foster al-Qaida in Yemen.

Closer to home, the suicide bombings of the U.S.S. *Cole* in Aden and the French tanker *Limburg* just off the southern coast in 2000 and 2002, respectively, focused attention on the "Afghani Arabs" and other militants in Yemen. However, it was **9/11** and the launching of President George W. Bush's the **"War on Terror"** in 2001 that changed Yemen's relationship to global political Islam—and to the United States. From that time forward, President Salih and patrons of the "Afghani Arabs" within the regime found themselves caught between a rock and a hard place. On the one hand, there were the growing realities of domestic politics, going all the way from strong Yemeni nationalism to increasing support for the Islamic militants, the latter being fed by anti-Israeli and anti-U.S. sentiment that, in turn, was being fed by events in Palestine, Afghanistan, and Iraq. On the other hand, there was the demand that the **Salih regime** be one with the United States in the War on Terror, in word and deed, and the implicit threat that the United States would punish or even bring that war to Yemen if the ROY did not fall into line.

Indeed, the United States did put al-Zindani on an official list of those supporting terrorism and did fire a missile from a drone in Yemeni airspace that killed an al-Qaida figure, Qais Salim **al-Harithi**—events that greatly embarrassed the Salih regime. In addition, the United States sent scores of Yemenis, mostly captured in Afghanistan, to Guantanamo, and it arrested a number of prominent Yemenis in Europe. For its part, the Salih regime tried its best to maneuver between Washington and the realities of Yemen's domestic politics. Along with strong statements of support for the War on Terror, arrests were made, and trials were held. One means of trying to square the circle was the dubious effort to rehabilitate militant Islamists through the **"dialogue process"** in the middle years of the first decade of the new 21st century.

The view that revolutionary political Islam in Yemen since the 1970s was strictly a Sunni affair ended with the emergence of "the Believing Youth" in the late 1990s and the outbreak in 2004 of the **Al-Houthi Rebellion** in the far north, in Saada governorate. Founded by Husayn al-Houthi and carried forward by other family members after his violent death in 2004, the movement challenged the regime with the assertion that it was in the service of Israel and the United States, both mortal enemies of Islam. More serious, some of the "Houthis" also came to openly question the legitimacy of the Salih regime—even of the republic itself. They based this last on Zaydi doctrine that dictates that the Muslim community must be led by a Zaydi sayyid, and called for restoration of the imamate. The rebellion burst out in 2004, was suppressed, and erupted again in mid-2005, early 2007, 2003 and again in mid-2009.

POLITICAL OFFICER. The title of the career colonial officers who were posted to the **Aden Protectorates** and assigned the task of representing **Great Britain** as well as advising (and pressuring) the local rulers with whom Britain had advisory treaties. Often "up-country" and on their own, they were faced with daunting tasks, ones that required great political as well as sociocultural sensitivity, nerve, power of persuasion, and a good measure of trust and respect. The last flowering of British colonialism, these officers were, on average, quite remarkable. *See also* COLONIAL ADMINISTRATION AND ADMINISTRATORS.

POLITICAL PARTIES, MAJOR. *See* BAATH PARTY (ARAB SOCIALIST RENAISSANCE PARTY); COMMUNIST PARTY; GENERAL PEOPLE'S CONGRESS (GPC); ISLAH (YEMENI REFORM GATHERING); JOINT MEETING PARTIES (JMP); NATIONAL DEMOCRATIC FRONT (NDF) AND NDF REBEL-LION; NATIONAL LIBERATION FRONT (NLF); YEMENI SOCIALIST PARTY (YSP).

POPULAR DEFENSE FORCES. *See* ARMED FORCES.

POPULAR DEMOCRATIC UNION. *See* COMMUNIST PARTY.

POPULAR FRONT FOR THE LIBERATION OF OMAN AND THE ARAB GULF. *See* DHUFAR REBELLION.

POPULAR FRONT FOR THE LIBERATION OF OMAN (PFLO). *See* DHUFAR REBELLION.

POPULAR FRONT FOR THE LIBERATION OF PALESTINE (PFLP). *See* ARAB NATIONALIST MOVEMENT (ANM); PAL-ESTINE AND THE PALESTINE QUESTION.

POPULAR NASIRITE UNITY ORGANIZATION. *See* NASIR-ITES AND NASIRITE PARTIES.

POPULAR RESISTANCE FORCES (PRF). The citizens militias organized and armed by the Yemeni in Sanaa, Taiz, al-Hudayda, and the large towns of the YAR for the purpose of defending the republic against the royalist offensive in the **Yemeni Civil War** after the withdrawal of Egyptian forces from Yemen in 1967. The PRF were tied to the Yemeni branch of the **Arab Nationalist Movement** and received fighters and other support from the newly triumphant **National Liberation Front** in Aden. Their forced disbanding after the **Sanaa Mutiny** in 1968 was part of the process by which the center-right **al-Iryani** regime consolidated its position by expelling the left from the polity. Some PRF members then helped create the **Organization of Yemeni Resisters** and later took part in the guerrilla war phase of the **border war** fought by the two Yemens in 1972 and in the more serious **National Democratic Front Rebellion** from the late 1978 to 1982.

POPULAR REVOLUTIONARY ORGANIZATION. *See* AL-SAL-LAL REGIME.

PORTUGAL. The country whose penetration of the **Indian Ocean** via the Cape of Good Hope in 1498 and whose appearance with armed forces at the southern end of the **Red Sea** early in the next century marked a temporary end to Yemen's long isolation and anonymity. It also marked the start of the first extended period of European and **Ottoman Turkish** interest in Yemen.

Portugal's interests were vigorously advanced during the first two decades of the century by Alphonso de Albuquerque, a great strategist of imperial expansion, and forts were planted on the east coast of Africa, on the Strait of Hormuz at Muscat, in India, and elsewhere. Still, Portuguese interests and power in the Indian Ocean region went into steep decline after a couple of generations, and it was the Ottomans who within a generation had occupied and established control over much of Yemen—this in the name of Sulayman the Magnificent, who ruled from 1520 to 1566.

PRESIDENTIAL COUNCIL. The five-member plural executive that, under the terms of the ROY's **1990 Constitution**, was elected by the legislature—the **Council of Deputies**—and that, in turn, selects from its five members the president and vice president of the ROY. In May 1990, President Ali Abdullah **Salih** and Vice President Ali Salim

al-Baydh were the first to be elected in this manner. After the **War of Succession** in 1994, the constitution was amended to eliminate the Presidential Council and replace it with a singular presidency elected first by the Council of Deputies, and since 1999, by direct popular election.

PRESS. *See* MASS MEDIA.

PRESSURE GROUPS. *See* INTEREST (PRESSURE) GROUPS.

PROTECTORATES. *See* ADEN PROTECTORATES.

PROVINCES. *See* GOVERNORATES (MUHAFAZAH).

– Q –

QAA AL-YAHUD (AL-QAA). *See* SANAA.

QABUS (QABOOS) IBN SAID, SULTAN (1940–). *See* OMAN, SULTANATE OF.

QADHAFI, MUAMMAR (1942–). *See* LIBYA AND MUAMMAR QADHAFI.

QADI CLASS. *See* SOCIAL SYSTEM AND STRUCTURE.

QAHTAN AL-SHAABI. *See* AL-SHAABI FAMILY.

QAHTANIS AND ADNANIS. Qahtan is the mythical ancestor from whom South Arabians, and especially the indigenous South Arabian tribesmen, proudly claim descent. (Qahtan is the Joktan of the Book of Genesis, great-great-great grandson of Noah.) The Qahtanis distinguish themselves from the North Arabians or Adnanis, the descendants of Adnan, many of whom migrated south after the rise of Islam. The Adnanis both became a distinct religious and scholarly class outside the tribal system and added the **sayyid** caste to the social system in South Arabia. On occasion, even today, the term "adnani" is used negatively to mean "foreigner" or "outsider" (in contrast to "qahtani," or "native"). For example, this was the case in some of the heated exchanges between sayyids and non-sayyids during the **al-Houthi Rebellion.**

QAHTAN, MUHAMMAD. *See* ISLAH (YEMENI REFORM GATHERING).

AL-QAIDA. *See* BIN LADIN FAMILY AND USAMA BIN LADEN.

QANA. *See* TRADING KINGDOMS, SOUTH ARABIAN; TRADE ROUTES, ANCIENT.

QARNAW. *See* TRADING KINGDOMS, SOUTH ARABIAN.

QASIMI IMAMATE. Al-Mansur Billah Qasim bin Muhammad declared himself **imam** in 1598, and between that date and 1635 he and his son and successor, al-Muayyid bin Qasim, strove to drive the occupying **Ottoman** Turks from Yemen and paved the way for the establishment by their successors of a **Zaydi** imamate state that held sway over Yemen from **Asir** in the north to **Dhufar** in the east during the middle decades of the 17th century. Thereafter, a fragmented and greatly weakened imamate was at least nominally headed by members of the Qasimi dynasty into the 19th century. This much-diminished Qasimi imamate was still in place when the Ottomans began to reoccupy Yemen in 1849.

QASIM, SALIH MUSLIH (?–1986). PDRY minister of defense in the mid-1980s who cast his lot with **Ali** Nasser **al-Antar** against President **Ali Nasir Muhammad** al-Hasani and who, like Ali al-Antar, paid for it with his life in the **13 January events** of 1986, the events that within days forced Ali Nasir to flee north and into exile. Earlier, in 1981, Salih Muslih had sided with Ali Nasir against Ali al-Antar, replacing the latter as defense minister. This illustrates well the game of shifting alliances played in the PDRY from the late 1970s to the early 1980s, a game that became lethal in 1978—and wildly so in 1986.

QASSIM MUNASSER. *See* YEMENI CIVIL WAR.

QASSIM SALAM. *See* BAATH PARTY (ARAB SOCIALIST RENAISSANCE PARTY).

QAT (CATHA EDULIS FORSSKAL). The shiny-leaved, privet-like shrub of various shapes and sizes that is cultivated extensively in the highlands of Yemen and **Ethiopia** (and to a lesser extent in Kenya and Somalia) for its tender young leaves, which, when chewed and stored in the cheek, produce a mildly stimulating effect. The result is less euphoria than it is simply a general sense of well being. Probably a majority of adults in North Yemen, especially males, chew qat at least once a week, and many do so on a daily basis. The afternoon qat session, or "qat chew," usually lasting from early afternoon until early evening, is certainly the most distinctive, and possibly the most important, of Yemen's social and cultural institutions. Although "qat" is the most common spelling today, it is sometimes spelled "khat," "ghat," and "gat."

The kinds of qat, and the array of words used to describe and classify it, attest to its sociocultural significance—it is to Yemen what wine is to France. Since most qat is consumed in the afternoon of the day on which it is picked, the transportation and marketing of qat is a major undertaking and achievement, although these tasks have been made easier in recent years by new roads and fast Toyota pickups. For some Yemenis, especially heavy chewers among the traditionally privileged, life seems to be organized around the qat chew, and for most others it is a cherished time of rest and relaxation as well as a time when a lot of important work gets done. The chew binds people together and provides focus for the various elements of Yemeni society. It is where contacts are made and renewed, opinions exchanged, issues discussed, decisions taken, deals struck, and disputes heard and settled. It is also a place where Yemeni history and culture are shared and transmitted from the older to the younger generation, partially through traditional Yemeni stories, poetry, and music.

Taxi drivers, artisans, and shopkeepers do their work and ply their trade, and students cram for exams, while chewing, and with no apparent impairment. If qat is psychologically addictive, it is so for only a small minority of the heavy chewers. Hundreds of thousands of Yemeni qat chewers have gone abroad to work for many months or years at a stretch, leaving their qat habit behind apparently without serious problems. Its negative health effects—and there are some, such as constipation, insomnia, loss of appetite, and, according to some women, sexual disinterest or impotence for males—seem minor compared with those of cigarettes and alcohol. Though it does detract and subtract in various ways from some of the socioeconomic development activities desperately needed in Yemen, it is just about Yemen's only widely shared extravagance. Clearly on the negative side, the lower and middle classes allocate too much of their modest incomes to buying qat, and this undoubtedly means that many children and women go without the food, clothes, health care, and education that they might otherwise get. Finally, its production consumes a disproportionate share of Yemen's scarce and shrinking water supply—and this is the biggest negative.

On the positive side, qat culture has made it economically possible for a significant proportion of Yemen's population to stay on the land in the countryside, rather than become part of the growing population of urban unemployed or under employed. Many people live off of the production, transport, and marketing of qat. In addition, the value of qat as a cash crop has led to the maintenance of the ancient and magnificent terraces that distinguish the rural highlands of Yemen. While it is true that qat and **coffee** grow best at about the same altitude and under the same conditions, it does not seem to be the case that the decline of coffee as a cash and export crop in recent centuries was a function of the rise of qat cultivation.

An attempt by the state to limit the production and consumption of qat helped bring about the fall of Prime Minister Muhsin **al-Aini** in the 1970s. The attempt by President **Salih** to set an example by giving up qat for "exercise and learning the computer" near the dawn of the new millennium was a failure for Yemen, and for him. An unsuccessful effort was made in early 2007 to pass legislation designed to gradually woo Yemenis from the production and marketing—and chewing—of qat.

QATABA. The border town in North Yemen just north of the old **Anglo–Ottoman line** that was the object of bombing and occupation on various occasions in the course of conflict, first between **Great**

Britain and the Yemeni **imamate**, and later between the PDRY and the YAR during the 1979 **border war**. On the road from Yarim to Aden, Qataba and the nearby towns of **Juban** and Damt are in the area in which the **National Democratic Front Rebellion** flourished until 1982. Interestingly, this old hotbed of radicalism is also the area where many Yemenis live off of Social Security checks from the United States and **remittances** sent back by Yemenis still working and living in the United States.

QATABAN. *See* TRADING KINGDOMS, SOUTH ARABIAN.

QATAR. The tiny, thinly populated and fabulously gas-rich Arab **Gulf** state that, because of a history of border and other conflicts with its often-overbearing neighbor, **Saudi Arabia**, has for over 30 years made a point of maintaining good relations with—and providing economic aid and political support to—the YAR and then the ROY. This was especially important during the several years after the First **Gulf War** in 1991, when Saudi Arabia, **Kuwait**, and other Arab Gulf states chose to punish Yemen economically and politically for its failure to join the United States– and Saudi-led coalition against the occupation of Kuwait by **Iraq** in 1990. Qatar is probably the Gulf state most open to the idea of the ROY becoming a full member of the **Gulf Cooperation Council** (GCC), and it has argued the ROY's case before its more reluctant GCC partners. In 2007, the Emir of Qatar came forward and brokered an agreement temporarily ending the **al-Houthi Rebellion**, a lethal, struggle between the **Salih** regime and militant Islamists in **Saada** Province.

AL-QIRBI, ABU BAKR. The British-trained pathologist who, after practicing medicine for some years, served as foreign minister beginning in 2002 in both **Bajammal** governments and in the **al-Mujawar** government that followed them in early 2007. Prior to this, in his first major public position, he served as vice rector of Sanaa University. On the basis of his well-regarded performance in this post, he was appointed minister of education. His active involvement in the ruling party, the **General People's Congress**, helped pave the way for his appointment as foreign minister, this despite no prior experience in international relations. Aligned with Bajammal, he allegedly advanced

Bajammal's people in the ministry sometimes at the expense of more experienced and qualified members of the diplomatic team created by longtime foreign minister, Dr. Abd al-Karim **al-Iryani**.

QISHN. *See* MAHRA PROVINCE AND SULTANATE.

QUAITI–KATHIRI WAR. The long and chaotic struggle in the second half of the 19th century for control of the **Hadhramawt** between the long-ruling but declining **Kathiri** sultanate and the **Quaiti** sultanate. The struggle ended with Britain imposing a more or less lasting *modus vivendi* under which the Quaitis were conceded nominal rule over the coast and the western approaches to Wadi Hadhramawt and the Kathiris nominally controlled the interior of the wadi eastward from **Shibam**.

QUAITIS AND QUAITI SULTANATE. With its capital in **Mukalla** on the coast of the **Arabian Sea**, the Quaiti sultanate was far more populous than the **Kathiri Sultanate** with which it nominally shared authority over the **Hadhramawt** from the last decades of the 19th century to the independence of South Yemen in 1967. Wadi Amd, the westernmost major tributary of Wadi Hadhramawt, was the heart of the sultanate. Originally from the mountainous **Yafi** tribal area to the west, the Quaiti ruling family and its followers settled in the Hadhramawt. They emigrated to **Hyderabad** in India to make their fortune as mercenaries and then returned to Mukalla and launched a campaign to gain control of the relatively rich wadi in the second half of the 19th century.

Great Britain, the colonial power, saw fit to impose an end to the **Quaiti–Kathiri War**. Because of their access to the Quaiti rulers in Mukalla, it was relatively easy for the British to deal with and have an impact on them, as well as to initiate some modest government reforms and development activities. Indeed, it was with the Quaiti sultanate that Britain signed in 1937 the first of its several intrusive advisory treaties with states in what became the Eastern **Aden Protectorate**. Along with the rulers of the other states, the Quaiti sultanate disappeared when independence came in 1967.

AL-QUBATI, ABD AL-AZIZ. *See* POLITICAL ISLAM, MODERN.

QUEEN OF SHEBA. *See* SABA (SHEBA) AND SABEAN KINGDOM.

AL-QUHALI, MAJOR MUJAHID. The YAR army officer—a shaykh of the Iyal Yazid of the **Bakil** confederation as well as a **Nasirite** and strong **al-Hamdi** loyalist—who, after forming the **13 June Movement** and leading his garrison in mutiny in early 1978 against those who succeeded the slain al-Hamdi, went into exile in the PDRY and became active in the **National Democratic Front** and its militant opposition to the **Salih** regime in the late 1970s and early 1980s. Al-Quhali came north with Yemeni **unification** in 1990, was elected to the parliament in 1993, and soon joined with the **Yemeni Socialist Party** (YSP) and others demanding major political reforms of the ROY. As the political conflict worsened in early 1994, al-Quhali organized a large tribal gathering in Bakil country just north of Sanaa that reiterated the call for major reforms to save Yemeni unity. After fierce fighting in **Amran** in late April, the big prelude to the **War of Secession**, al-Quhali and his Bakil colleagues facilitated the retreat south of the southern forces.

AL-QURDAI, SHAYKH ALI NASIR. *See* MADHHIJ TRIBAL CONFEDERATION; 1948 REVOLUTION

QUTAYBI TRIBE. *See* DHALA (DHALIA) TOWN, REGION, TRIBES, AND EMIRATE.

– R –

RABITA (RAY). *See* AL-JIFRI, ABD AL-RAHMAN ALI.

RABIYYA ALI, SALIM. *See* RUBAYA ALI.

RADA. A large town in **Dhamar** province, east of Dhamar town, on the east–west road between it and the town of **al-Baydha**. An important marketplace and administrative center, it is a very unattractive, plastic bag– and bottle-covered place. It does contain a gem, however: the Amiriya, a large six-domed palace, mosque, and school dating from the 16th century. It was expertly restored over two decades by Dr. Selma al-Radi, which helps make up for all the plastic trash.

RADFAN AND THE RADFAN REBELLION. The poor region of high, jagged mountain peaks and deep, steep-sided, rock-strewn ravines in South Yemen where in October 1963 the **National Liberation Front** (NLF) translated tribal dissidence into the start of its guerrilla war against **Great Britain**. In turn, the British responded with a major counterinsurgency campaign in the region over the first several months of 1964. In retrospect, the Radfan Rebellion and efforts to put it down were of relatively little military import but of great symbolic political significance. It was seen as the beginning of the armed struggle of the NLF against the British imperialists and the traditional "feudal" rulers in South Yemen, the 14 October Revolution. In the south, Revolution Day is celebrated on this date; Independence Day comes on 30 November, marking the day in 1967 when the British turned authority over to the NLF.

The Radfan region lies close to the border with North Yemen, well to the north of **Aden** and **Lahej** and east of the main route between Aden and major population centers in North Yemen. Though nominally subjects of the **Dhala** amirate, the several small, fractious, scrappy tribes of the region have rarely been subjected to any central government over the centuries.

RADIO AND TELEVISION. *See* MASS MEDIA.

RAGHIB BEY, MUHAMMAD. The **Ottoman** diplomat and governor of al-Hudayda, a Turk from Cyprus who returned to Yemen a few years after the Ottoman Turkish withdrawal at the end of World War I and entered the service of Imam **Yahya** as his "foreign minister." Although Raghib Bey's influence and status waxed and waned more than once between the mid-1920s and the late 1940s, he remained the imam's principal adviser on an increasingly intrusive outside world as well as on "modern" Ottoman government forms and practices. Increasingly unhappy with Yemen and his lot therein, feeling used and abused by Imam **Ahmad** and members of his coterie, and belatedly nostalgic for the good old Ottoman diplomatic days in Europe, Raghib Bey died in obscurity in Yemen in the late 1950s.

RAHIDA. East of Taiz and northwest of Aden, the North Yemeni town on the main route between those two cities that, along with the town of Mawiya, has served for generations as a major crossing point between the two Yemens. Although little crossing took place in the 1970s and 1980s, the great increase in trade and traffic shortly before and since Yemeni **unification** in 1990 has increased the importance and prosperity of this old "frontier" town, one now well within the borders of the ROY.

RAINFALL. *See* MONSOONS AND WATER RESOURCES.

RAMLAT AL-SABATAYN. The inhospitable expanse of sandy desert in the interior of the southwest corner of the **Arabian Peninsula**, just south and west of (and barely separated from) region much larger and more forbidding **Empty Quarter**. It was in this the that the two Yemens found oil in the 1980s, and here that the undemarcated borders of the YAR and the PDRY intersected with those of **Saudi Arabia**. The forces of the two Yemens confronted each other on two occasions in this newly oil-important region in the 1980s, and after **unification** in 1990, much of the increased conflict between Saudi Arabia and the ROY occurred in and over this area. The Saudi–Yemeni **border agreement** of 2000 largely removed this source of conflict between the two neighbors.

RASULID STATE AND DYNASTY. The state and dynasty that, founded by Nur al-Din Umar bin Ali al-Rasul in 1232 and based in **Zabid** and **Taiz**, was to rule over a large part of Yemen for more than 200 years, competing with the Zaydi **imamate** for predominance in Yemen and firmly establishing **Shafii** Sunnism as the dominant branch of Islam in South Yemen and the southern half of North Yemen for future centuries. The Rasulids assumed rule peacefully from the Cairo-based **Ayyubids**, and under their rule this large part of Yemen probably achieved its highest level of civilization and prosperity.

REBELLION AND GUERRILLA WARFARE. At least six major rebellions or guerrilla wars have had significant impact on the Yemens in the 20th and early 21st centuries. Beginning in the late 19th century and continuing through the first decade of the next, the **Zaydi** imamate-led rebellion against the **Ottoman** Turks strengthened traditional Yemeni nationalism and identified the Zaydi **imamate** with that nationalism. Arguably, it made the 20th century imamate possible.

The **Radfan Rebellion**, launched against **Great Britain** and Yemeni "feudalists" in 1963, led the way to the creation of an independent South Yemen under the leadership of the **National Liberation Front** (NLF) in 1967. The **Dhufar Rebellion**, waged against **Oman** from the mid-1960s to the mid-1970s, and strongly supported by the NLF regime, both pushed the PDRY further to the left and isolated it from the oil-rich states of the **Arabian Peninsula**, as well as from other moderate, nonrevolutionary countries. The NDF rebellion, waged with PDRY support by the **National Democratic Front** against the YAR regime from the late 1970s until 1982, drained the resources of the YAR and added to the already severely strained relations between the two Yemens.

In mid-2004, and again on six occasions between early 2005 and 2009, the **al-Houthi Rebellion** pitted the **Salih regime** against a Zaydi **sayyid** movement centered in **Saada** Governorate in the north. The rebellion expressed the profound alienation of some Zaydis from the republic and renewed the call for a Zaydi-led religious state— for some, a restored imamate. Finally, from 2007 through 2009, a revised secessionist movement brought protest and violence to much of South Yemen.

RECONCILIATION AGREEMENT, 1994. *See* DOCUMENT OF PLEDGE AND ACCORD (AL-WATHIQA).

RECONCILIATION OF 1970, REPUBLICAN–ROYALIST. The long-sought, elusive agreement reached in March 1970 under which the **Yemeni Civil War** between the republicans and the **royalists** came to an end, and nearly all of the latter, the main exception being the exiled **Hamid al-Din** family, were allowed to return to Yemen to take up their property and place in society in exchange for their acceptance of the republic. It was Prime Minister Muhsin **al-Aini** who in April 1970, on the occasion of the Islamic foreign ministers' meeting in **Saudi Arabia**, got the Saudis to pressure its divided royalist clients and then negotiated the final peace that most wanted so desperately.

In May 1970, the first royalists flew to Sanaa from Saudi Arabia. Their property was restored, and many of them resumed positions of social prominence in the cities, towns, and countryside. Although no longer able to claim governance as a birthright, and although denied access to the most politically sensitive offices, many ex-royalists, **sayyids** included, were given posts in the republican state and participated actively, albeit discreetly, in politics. Indeed, five of the returnees received ministerial posts, and a sixth—Ahmad **al-Shami**, the former royalist foreign minister—joined President al-Iryani on the multimember executive, the Republican Council. In time, many of the great sayyid families reemerged as forces in Yemeni politics. For their part, the tribal leaders who had sided with the royalists remained in place in their historic domains or assumed places in the republican regime in Sanaa.

The reconciliation, desired by all but those on the extreme right and left, ensured that the republic that prevailed would be a conservative republic—and it served to push the center-right **al-Iryani** regime a bit farther to the right. The reconciliation also opened the way to a major amount of financial aid from Saudi Arabia to the YAR—and to the YAR's growing dependence on the Saudis—as well as to relations with, and aid from, the industrial West.

RED SEA. The long, narrow, shallow, and rather treacherous sea that bounds the ROY on the west from Midi, near the border with Saudi Arabia, south to the **Bab al-Mandab Straits** and the old border with South Yemen. The Red Sea is connected with the Mediterranean Sea by the **Suez Canal** and with the Indian Ocean by Bab al-Mandab and the **Gulf of Aden** and the **Arabian Sea**. An avenue of waterborne commerce for millennia, it became the lifeline of the British Empire, especially after the opening of the Suez Canal in 1869. This fact alone goes most of the way toward explaining **Great Britain**'s occupation of **Aden** in 1839 and the one-and-a-quarter-century British rule that followed. In addition, from the early 1950s through the 1960s, most of the increasingly important oil from the Gulf came north and west via the Red Sea and Suez Canal. Just as the canal explains the growth, wealth, and importance of Aden, the canal's blockage for a decade after the **Arab–Israeli** war in 1967, the very year that South Yemen became independent, goes a long way towards explaining the decline and impoverishment of Aden during that decade. Egypt's Sumed Pipeline between the Red Sea and the Mediterranean did win back some of the oil traffic for the service facilities at Aden that was lost when the oil industry shifted to the deep draft supertankers after the canal's closure in 1967.

The heavy traffic up and down the Red Sea since the opening of the canal in 1869 makes it all the more surprising that North Yemen could remain so isolated and unknown to the modern world until the mid-20th century. The country's wide, inhospitable coastal desert, the **Tihama**, with its hazy, humid, and cloudy atmosphere during much of the year, helps explain this.

The Red Sea is a major source of dietary protein, and **fishing** and related activities have largely defined the hard life and culture of the Tihama. The sea's narrowness has made easy the carrying east of the goods, people, and culture of **Ethiopia** and the rest of the **Horn of Africa**.

RED SEA AND HORN OF AFRICA SECURITY ISSUES. The **Red Sea** security issue has long been rooted in its importance to international trade and commerce and the movement of naval forces and in the fact that its two ends, the **Suez Canal** and the **Bab al-Mandab Straits**, constitute what geopoliticians call strategic choke points. After World War II, this was magnified by the onset of the **Cold War**, the growing importance of Middle East oil to the West, and the rise of nationalism and anti-imperialism in the Third World. To the YAR, the issue of Red Sea security really had to do with whether it could or should be an "Arab" sea—i.e., one not controlled by **Ethiopia**, or even **Israel**—and whether it could be kept free of the meddling of Cold War superpowers. The YAR's "Arab" focus and the PDRY's socialist "internationalism" at times caused the two Yemens to view Red Sea security in different terms.

The Taiz Summit on Red Sea Security in March 1977 was a tangible expressions of concern over this issue. The summit, hosted by YAR President **al-Hamdi**, brought together the presidents of the two Yemens, **Sudan**, and **Somalia** in **Taiz** for the purpose of finding a regional solution to threats to the peace and security of the area. Al-Hamdi's hidden agenda, however, involved his desire to enhance his stature at home and in the region, thereby gaining a little leverage in his dealings with his increasingly demanding neighbor, **Saudi Arabia**. Although the summit did focus some attention for a short time on al-Hamdi and the YAR, it was doomed to come to naught because of hostility between newly revolutionary Ethiopia and Somalia. Indeed, it almost failed to take place in the first place. Ethiopia refused to attend, and soon after, it and Somalia fought each other in the Ogadan Rebellion.

As the Taiz Summit's complications suggested, the question of Red Sea security often merged or at least overlapped with that of the Horn of Africa. The long-running **Eritrean** Rebellion against Ethiopian rule, the rise of a would-be Marxist Ethiopia in 1974, and the fighting between Somalia and Ethiopia over Ogadan made this apparent. For the two Yemens, however, the security questions regarding the Red Sea, and especially the Horn of Africa, in the 1970s and 1980s had less to do with this sea and those countries than with relations between the two Yemens and, secondarily, their relations, singly or together, with Saudi Arabia. In other words, the very salient relationships among the three neighbors on the southern corner of the Arabian Peninsula sometimes gave meaning to and were expressed in terms of these more remote regional security questions.

The salience of the Horn of Africa to the security concerns of the two Yemens declined in the 1980s, despite revival of the Cold War and talk of an "arc of revolution" including conflict between the two Yemens. This decline continued with the end of the Cold War and as Yemenis focused their attention on Yemeni **unification** in 1990, the **War of Secession** in 1994, and the effort to restore relations with Saudi Arabia that finally bore fruit with the **border** agreement in 2000.

Then came **9/11** and the **War on Terror**—and the abrupt increase of the Horn of Africa's importance for the ROY. Indeed, in late 2002, the **United States** fired a missile over Yemeni airspace from a drone launched and controlled from its small special operations base in **Djibouti**, killing al-Qaida leader **al-Harithi**. President Salih's Horn of Africa initiative in 2003, including the presidents of Sudan and Ethiopia in meetings in Sanaa, was designed to address both the regional significance of the escalating War on Terror and regional development and conflict in the region.

This first meeting quickly evolved into annual summits of the Sanaa Forum for Cooperation. Eritrea has been conspicuously absent from these summits. Since independence in 1993, Eritrea has been fighting an on-and-off border war with Ethiopia and in 1995 engaged in armed conflict with the ROY over a small archipelago. Not surprisingly, the Eritreans suspected that the Sanaa Forum was really directed against them.

Somalia's hard-to-find transitional government joined the Sanaa Forum in mid-decade, but in late 2006 Ethiopian forces entered Somalia with U.S. intelligence and air support to back the transitional government in its struggle to oust forces of the Islamic Courts. Only months earlier, the Islamic Courts had assumed control of Mogadishu and southern Somalia. To complicate matters further, after slumbering for years, the Ogadan rebellion revived in 2007 allegedly with Eritrean help; Eritrea was also accused of helping the Islamic Courts in their effort to defeat the transitional government and drive the Ethiopian forces from Somalia.

The Sanaa Forum's meeting in Khartoum in December 2008, with the presidents of Sudan, Yemen, Ethiopia, Somalia, and Djibouti in attendance, had a lot on its plate. After pledging support for the Sudan in its dispute with the United Nations over Darfur, it had to add to its agenda the tragic flood of refugees to Yemen from Somalia and, to a lesser extent, Ethiopia and the issue of growing Somali piracy in the Gulf of Aden. Clearly, the Sanaa Forum had been overtaken by events beyond its limited capacities and the limited mutual interests of its members—and by the magnitude of the tasks of dealing with regional conflicts and containing the regional fallout from the escalating War on Terror.

REFINERIES, OIL. The ROY has very limited oil refining capacity and, despite sharply rising crude **oil production** since the late 1980s, has to import most of the refined products upon which it increasingly depends. The Aden refinery, the ROY's oldest and largest facility, was completed by **British Petroleum** (BP) in 1952, became a major feature of the growing, dynamic **Aden Colony** of the 1950s and 1960s, and then went into decline after independence in 1967. Its construction and operation in Little Aden, just across the bay from **Aden** proper, contributed much to the modernization of Aden and generated thousands of jobs directly or in the hundreds of small factories and workshops that served its needs.

Despite its growing obsolescence, the Aden Refinery continued to dominate the PDRY's tiny modern industrial sector in the 1970s and 1980—indeed, it remained that country's biggest industrial enterprise. The increasingly outmoded and underused refinery escaped the wave of nationalization in 1969; a decade later, in 1979, it was handed over by BP to the PDRY in an agreement under which BP continued operations. Discovery of its own oil in the mid-1980s led the PDRY to plan to modernize the refinery, which had declined in capacity to about 100,000 barrels per day (b/d) and which was also able to produce only a limited number of needed petroleum products.

In the later-developing YAR, and after the discovery of oil in 1984, the **Yemen Hunt Oil Company** built the country's first oil refinery in 1987: a small, prefabricated unit with a 10,000 b/d capacity, located close to **Marib** and the oil in the Marib/al-Jawf basin. Conceived as a stopgap measure, it was assumed to be able to meet only a small and diminishing part of the country's daily needs for petroleum products.

With Yemeni **unification** in 1990 and the discovery of oil in commercial quantities in other areas of Yemen, planning for increased refining capacity focused on a major upgrading and expansion of the Aden Refinery, a modest expansion of the Marib facility, and a new refinery at a coastal location. The upgrading and expansion of the Aden Refinery was advanced as part of the effort to make Aden the "economic capital" of the ROY. Instead, the **War of Secession** in 1994 and a series of controversies thereafter—e.g., northern vs. southern priorities and continued state ownership vs. privatization— intervened and held back major efforts for 15 years. Finally, in 2007, the Ministry of Oil and Mineral Resources unveiled its plan to modernize the refinery.

At the same time, the ministry announced plans to expand, at the cost of $100 million, the refinery in Marib from a capacity of 10,000 b/d to 25,000 b/d; the expanded capacity was expected to come on stream in 2011. Finally, the ministry also announced plans to construct three more refineries: two at Ras Isa, on the Red Sea coast just north of al-Hudayda, and one in **Mukalla**, in the Hadhramawt on the Arabian Sea. If all of these projects were to come to pass, they would more than double the ROY's output of refined products, adding about 150,000 b/d to the country's production (in 2007, just 110,000 b/d).

REFORM GATHERING. *See* ISLAH (YEMENI REFORM GATHERING).

REILLY, COL. SIR CHARLES. *See* COLONIAL ADMINISTRATION AND ADMINISTRATORS.

RELIGION AND RELIGIOUS GROUPS IN YEMEN. Yemen entered the new millennium in 2000 still a largely traditional, non-secular country, this despite almost a half-century's infusion of secular ideas in both Yemens and more than 20 years of a Marxist regime in South Yemen. Except for several hundred Jews in villages north of Sanaa, and a similarly small number of Hindus in Aden and other coastal towns in South Yemen, virtually all the citizens and other permanent residents of Yemen embrace Islam as their religion—and, of these, nearly all are **Shafii** Sunnis or **Zaydi** Shii. (There are some non-Shafii Sunnis: for example, the followers of Qadi Muhammad **al-Shawkani**.) The various Christian groups that lived in parts of Yemen at various times before the rise of Islam in the seventh century have long since disappeared. Most of the sizable population of Hindus who came to Aden with its absorption into the British colonial system in the 19th century left South Yemen after its independence in 1967.

The Jewish community maintained a continuous presence in Yemen for two millennia and numbered some tens of thousands in the middle of the 20th century, living mostly in **Sanaa**, **Aden**, and the other cities and large towns. **Sanaa**'s old Jewish quarter, Qaa al-Yahud, located half a mile from the high-walled Islamic city, was a large, self-contained town. Despite being second-class citizens, the Jews of Yemen nonetheless had a defined and protected place in Yemeni society; they were perhaps most famous as Yemen's most accomplished artisans, especially as makers of finely detailed silver jewelry and windows of alabaster or colored glass framed in sculpted plaster. Nearly all of Yemen's Jews left *en masse* shortly after the creation of modern **Israel** in the Zionist-organized "Operation Flying Carpet" around 1950. Their departure left an empty space in Yemeni life and society, one recognized and missed by many older Yemenis.

Yemen's onetime large and prominent **Ismaili** Shii minority dwindled over recent centuries, mostly the result of persecution at the hands of the Zaydi **imamate**. The weak, marginal group of some tens of thousands of remaining Ismailis were concentrated high in the mountains between Sanaa and the Red Sea coast, in Haraz. The Ismaili population in this and other areas of North Yemen has grown in recent years as a result of their return since the **1962 Revolution** and the overthrow of the imamate.

Despite Zaydi dominance and alleged numerical parity, Shafii Muslims considerably outnumbered the Zaydis in North Yemen in the mid-20th century. The Zaydis were and still are found in the sparsely populated northern highlands, whereas the much more numerous Shafii are found in the southern uplands, especially the densely populated **Taiz** and **Ibb** governorates as well as on the **Tihama** coast. In South Yemen, nearly the entire population is Shafii. As a consequence, the population of the unified ROY is probably 80 percent Shafii. One leitmotif of North Yemeni history since at least the mid-20th century has been Zaydi fears of being deposed or overwhelmed by the Shafiis, along with Shafii demands for a fair share of power, status, and well-being. The doubts and concerns of some Zaydis about Yemeni **unification** in 1990 turned on this same consideration.

Sufi orders and the tombs of saints are common in the Shafii regions of North Yemen and in South Yemen. Perhaps the most notable are the beautiful tomb and mosque of **Ibn Alwan** in the **Hugariyya** south of Taiz and the tomb of the Prophet **al-Hud** in **Wadi Hadhramawt**, east of **Tarim**. The rise of the Wahhabi variant of militant **political Islam** in Yemen has resulted in attempts to destroy the tombs of Sufi saints, most notably in South Yemen during the **War of Secession** in 1994.

Modern **political Islam** first found expression among Shafiis in Yemen in the Muslim Brotherhood. Other, more militant or revolutionary strains of Islam were not much in evidence in Yemen through the 1970s, and even the Muslim Brotherhood there seemed more moderate and inclined to join mainstream politics than its counterpart in other Arab countries. Yemen during this period may have largely been immune to revolutionary political Islam because of—rather than in spite of—the degree to which most Yemenis remain so implicitly and unself-consciously Muslim.

This changed in the 1980s and thereafter, especially with the return of the "Afghani Arabs," the veterans of the struggle against the jihad the Soviet invaders in **Afghanistan**. Since then, political Islam in

Yemen has been best described in terms of Wahhabis, salafis, and jihadis, militant groups that have had an impact on Yemeni society and that have deeply penetrated the **Salih regime**. Events before and since **9/11** have focused attention on al-Qaida, Islamic Jihad, and the **"War on Terror"** in Yemen.

Beginning in 2004, Islamic militancy among some Zaydi **sayyids** in Yemen found expression in the form of the protracted **al-Houthi Rebellion** against the Salih regime and, for some, the republican form of government. The rise of the "houthis" was partly a response to the growing power of the salafis, and salafi elements have been involved in the extremely harsh response to the rebellion. *See also* ZAYDIS AND SHAFIIS IN POLITICS AND SOCIETY.

REMITTANCES AND REMITTANCE ECONOMY. Yemen has depended more than most countries upon remittances sent home to their families by **emigrant** laborers, sailors, shopkeepers, and merchants. In particular, life as lived in Wadi **Hadhramawt** in South Yemen has been made possible over recent centuries by the flow of remittances. The same has been true in at least the last half of the 20th century in North Yemen for the **Shafiis** along the arc connecting **Yarim, Ibb, Taiz**, the **Hugariyya**, and **Aden**. In the 1970s, this also became true of the **Zaydis** of the northern highlands of North Yemen. Beginning in the early 1970s, the two Yemens, and especially North Yemen, became very dependent on, as well as beneficiaries of, the oil-based boom in **Saudi Arabia** and the other Arab **Gulf** oil-states. The boom meant jobs for a large percentage of working-age Yemeni males, who then remitted what amounted to a very large percentage of the gross domestic products of each of the Yemens.

Spread rather evenly over all parts of the country, the flow of remittances into the YAR both blunted the inequality that usually accompanies the early stages of development and bought needed time for the YAR. It was not until many years after the **1962 Revolution** that the state acquired some capacity for development, found external aid donors, and then struck its own **oil**. In the PDRY, remittances probably carried the impoverished socialist regime from the late 1970s through the 1980s as much as did aid from the **Soviet** bloc and international organizations.

The amount of the remittances to the Yemens roughly quadrupled over the 1970s, contributing vitally to the GDP of both the YAR and the PDRY. They began to fall in the mid-1980s as the oil-fueled boom in Saudi Arabia and the Gulf faltered, and this downward trend continued gradually until the end of the decade. And then, in late 1990, the still-substantial remittances plummeted as a result of the mass expulsion of Yemeni workers from Saudi Arabia in the course of the crisis that resulted in the First **Gulf War**. The drop in remittances and the dramatic rise in unemployment were disastrous, presenting Yemeni **unification** with a major setback and challenge. Still, remittances have continued to make an important contribution to the ROY's **economy** into the new millennum.

In the 1970s and 1980s, remittances were not much talked about in the PDRY, given the socialist regime's commitment to self-sufficiency and ban on emigration. In the YAR, by contrast, their importance was acknowledged. Indeed, many North Yemenis regard the period from the mid-1970s through the 1980s as the halcyon years, the best of times in living memory. Remittance money was flooding into the country from Yemenis working abroad—more than 800,000 of them, mostly in Saudi Arabia. Because of this emigration, nearly anyone who remained in Yemen could find relatively good-paying jobs, and wages in the cities and the countryside were pushed up by the labor shortage. The remittances were distributed widely—as if sprinkled from above—with some going directly or indirectly to nearly all families in all parts of the country; only a little of this money passed through the hands of gatekeepers in the state or the banks. In the 1970s, for the first time people had the money for consumer products new to Yemen, and such products poured in. Thermos jugs and portable radios and cassette players were everywhere; the main streets of villages were nearly paved with crushed Chinese juice cans. Many Yemenis had the capital to add a second story to their modest homes, to open and stock a new store or shop, or to buy a big Toyota—a *tota habbatayn*—to use as a taxi. Mixing remittances with other funds, the **local development associations** that coincidentally sprouted up in the 1970s built thousands of feeder roads, schools, clinics and cisterns on the countryside.

REPUBLICAN COUNCIL. *See* 1970 CONSTITUTION.

REPUBLICAN–ROYALIST RECONCILIATION, 1970. *See* REC-ONCILIATION OF 1970, REPUBLICAN–ROYALIST.

REPUBLICANS AND ROYALISTS. *See* ROYALISTS AND REPUBLICANS.

REPUBLIC OF YEMEN (ROY). The territorial state and polity created on 22 May 1990 as a result of the **unification** of the YAR and the PDRY, making it the only extant case of the merger of two Arab countries. Although Aden was declared the "economic capital" upon the ROY's creation, Sanaa quickly became in all respects the capital. The ROY survived the **War of Secession** in 1994, the event that sorely tested it and marked the end of the battle for dominance between the **General People's Party** (GPC), (the party of President Ali Abdullah **Salih**), and the **Yemeni Socialist Party** (YSP), (the ruling party of the former PDRY). This event was followed by the reconsolidation of a **Salih regime** that was to remain in power through the first decade of the 21st century, bringing republican Yemen an unprecedented period of political stability. That stability was sorely tested in the second half of this decade by a resurgence of discontent and anger in the south, the **al-Houthi** rebellion in the Zaydi north and an upsurge of al-Qaida and related salafi groups in the center and the east.

The ROY's life spans the development and exhaustion of Yemen's **oil** resources, the largely failed attempt to restore the viability of the post-**remittance** economy through the package of **IMF/World Bank reforms**, and the very flawed attempt at democratization over the course of a series of **elections** beginning in 1993.

The birth of the ROY occurred at the end of the **Cold War** and its concomitant international patron–client relations. A decade later, in 2001, **9/11** and the George W. Bush administration's **War on Terror** served to reorder both the ROY's external relations as well as some of its domestic politics. The change in relations with the United States had become apparent in the wake of the bombing of the U.S.S. *Cole* in 2000. Revolutionary **political Islam** came to reorder and redefine relations among the ROY, the United States, Saudi Arabia, and Afghanistan. *See also* ECONOMY AND POLITICAL ECONOMY.

RESISTERS. The progressive, largely **Shafii** political movement created in the waning days of the **Yemeni Civil War** by members of the banned **Popular Resistance Forces** and soldiers purged from the army after the **Sanaa Mutiny** in 1968. The Resisters (the Organization of Yemeni Revolutionary Resisters) proceeded to wage guerrilla war before, during, and after the 1972 **border war** and then became a component of the leftist oppositional **National Democratic Front** (NDF) created in 1970. It operated in the rural areas of the southern uplands—in much of **Ibb** and Taiz governorate—and, in the name of the people and peasants, directed its efforts against the YAR regime, the shaykhs and other landowning feudalists and lackeys of **Saudi Arabia**, and the imperialists. Later, as part of the NDF, the Resisters participated in the NDF Rebellion from the late 1970s to the early 1980s.

REVENUE AND TAXES. Like most pre-modern polities in the early stages of state-building, **imamate** Yemen lacked much capacity to extract resources from society to establish control, maintain order and secure borders, much less to take the lead in social and economic development. Much of what little revenue there was came in the form of *zakat* (the traditional Islamic tax collected by tax farmers in the cities and on the countryside) and import duties and license fees. Allegedly, Imam **Ahmad** personally telegraphed his tax agent in the port of **al-Hudayda** every day to find out the day's take. The imamate's limited revenues were matched by the limited state functions to which funds were applied. For example, the standing army was virtually non-existent. By contrast, in South Yemen under **Great Britain**'s rule, state functions grew in the 20th century and were largely covered by taxes, duties, and fees levied on the growing commercial activities of the port of Aden and its growing environs.

With the **1962 Revolution** in North Yemen and independence from the British for South Yemen in 1967, the felt need for both state-building and the growth of state functions presented the two regimes with the need for revenues. As independent South Yemen quickly evolved into the PDRY and its project of building socialism, the one-party state learned how to efficiently extract what revenue it could from its essentially poor society. Further revenue came in the form of aid from international organizations and—especially—assistance from the Soviet Bloc. By the 1980s, **remittances** from citizens abroad, most which bypassed the state treasury, also eased the austerity.

The YAR's weak and unstable governments after the **Yemeni Civil War** failed to significantly increase a capacity to extract revenue from society. Indeed, the YAR faced a revenue crisis in the late 1960s and early 1970s. While the capacity to extract revenue did increase incrementally over the 1970s and 1980s, what really did the most to bring a measure of prosperity to many North Yemenis during this period were increased external aid and, far more important, the massive inflow of remittances. In the mid-1980s, as the amount of the remittances declined, the state became the recipient of significant new revenue from the exploration, development, and sale of newly found **oil**.

With Yemeni **unification** in 1990, and the further development of oil resources in the north and, more important, the discovery and development of major oil reserves far to the east in South Yemen, the ROY became an oil-based polity with an oil-based economy. Among other things, this lessened the necessity to develop the state's capacity to extract revenue from other sources. By the mid-1990s, oil revenues averaged about 75 percent of total state revenues. However, what distinguished the ROY from Saudi Arabia and the other oil-rich Gulf states after 2000 was a growing awareness that Yemen's oil reserve were dwindling rapidly, and that this source of revenue would quickly cease to exist. Thereafter, and under pressure from the IMF and others, the ROY placed greater emphasis on developing its capacity to extract revenue from other sources, including, for example, the unsuccessful effort to impose a general sales tax in the middle of the decade and the beginning of a serious effort to address the effects of widespread corruption on the state's ability to increase its revenue.

REVOLUTIONARY DEMOCRATIC PARTY. The political party formed in 1968 by North Yemeni leftists, mostly **Shafii** and mostly former members of the **Arab Nationalist Movement**. Driven underground by the purge of the left that followed the **Sanaa Mutiny** in 1968 and then by the ban on parties in the **1970 Constitution**, the party became a major component of the **National Democratic Front** (NDF) created by the excluded YAR left in 1976. The original head of the party, and at that time a leader in the NDF, was the Beirut-trained Sultan Ahmad Omar; another leader of both parties was **Jarullah** Umar, soon to be a leader in the ROY.

REVOLUTIONS OF 1948 AND 1962. *See* 1948 REVOLUTION and 1962 REVOLUTION.

RIHANI, AMIN (1876–1940). *See* TRAVELERS.

RIYAN. The town on the South Yemeni coast, east of **Mukalla** and about halfway between it and **Shihr**, that is an important provincial transportation hub, both as the terminus of the primary road between the coast and the major towns of Wadi **Hadhramawt** and as the site of the main airport serving Mukalla and all of **Mahra** province stretching east to the border with **Oman**.

ROADS AND HIGHWAYS. *See* INFRASTRUCTURE DEVELOPMENT.

ROYAL AIR FORCE (RAF). The then still-inchoate theory of air power and the RAF figured prominently in the defense of **Aden** and the **Aden Protectorates** from external threats and in the maintenance of internal order within the Protectorates after 1918. The RAF was used regularly thereafter in efforts to thwart Imam **Yahya's** expansionist actions in the borderlands and to get him to suspend these actions and sign the **Treaty of Sanaa** in 1934. For **Great Britain**, and beginning in about 1930, the RAF had a key role in the **"forward policy"** in the Protectorates. Instead of ground forces garrisoned in remote bases, the RAF was given responsibility for internal order and security in the more remote areas. The doctrine of **air control**, devised to this end, called for the maintenance of control through the threat, and use, of aerial bombing and strafing from strategically placed and secured air bases. For example, the air base at **Mukeiras** was crucial to the execution of this policy.

The RAF's presence in South Yemen increased rapidly in the second half of the 1950s and early 1960s with the decision to make Aden the center of defense "east of Suez." That presence declined just as quickly only a few years later with the decisions to give up on basing east of Suez and to withdraw from Aden and South Arabia.

ROYALISTS AND REPUBLICANS. Most specifically, the republicans and royalists (monarchists, or "malakis") were the two opposing groups during the **Yemeni Civil War** in the 1960s, the former consisting of those who favored maintaining republicanism as embodied in the YAR and the latter consisting of those supporting restoration of the **imamate**. Save for diehards in the imamate family and some other **sayyids** who continued to favor a restored **Zaydi** imamate— including, surprisingly, some leaders of the **al-Houthi** Rebellion in 2004 and thereafter—the royalists ceased to exist after the republican–royalist **reconciliation** in 1970. By contrast, the republicans survived and were from the outset more varied, ranging from the Marxist left to some conservative, traditional elements that were more anti-imamate than pro-republican. Most of the republicans tended to be nationalists and statists, more inclined toward some sort of socialism than liberal democracy. Having come to associate the imamate with Yemen's "backwardness," they equated the republic with progress and development. The radical minority among them placed their emphasis on "the people" and "democracy."

The republicanism that prevailed for a generation after the civil war was a conservative republicanism. Some of the conservative republicans gravitated to it by way of earlier belief in a reformed or constitutional imamate. President **al-Iryani**, an example of this, was called, and only half in jest, the "republican imam." For their part, the several major **tribal** leaders who did support the YAR during and after the civil war were dubbed "republican tribalists" and were primarily opposed to the **Hamid al-Din** imamate family. *See also* IDEOLOGY AND POLITICAL IDEAS, MODERN.

AL-RUB AL-KHALI. *See* EMPTY QUARTER.

RUBAYA ALI (SALMAYN), SALIM (*CA.* 1935–1978). Co-ruler of the PDRY with his rival **Abd al-Fattah** Ismail from mid-1969 until his execution in 1978, the popular Rubaya Ali, nicknamed Salmayn (or Salamayn), served throughout this period as the PDRY's head of state. He came to be identified with state institutions as well as popular organizations, in contrast to the offices and cadres of the ruling party, the **Yemeni Socialist Party**. The latter were Abd al-Fattah's turf, and the conflict between the two leaders was often cast in terms of Rubaya Ali's "Maoist approach" versus Abd al-Fattah's "Stalinist approach." However, this oversimplified their policy differences and ignored the elements of ambition and growing personal dislike.

The intraparty struggle between these two strong-willed men for control of the revolution intensified and in mid-1978 erupted into armed conflict triggered by Rubaya Ali's efforts to improve formerly hostile relations with the YAR, Saudi Arabia, and the other Arab Gulf states and, more immediately, by mutual accusations about responsibility for the assassination of YAR President Ahmad Husayn **al-Ghashmi**. Forces loyal to Rubaya Ali lost the fight, and he and two of his colleagues were summarily tried and executed.

The tragic final chapter of their relationship notwithstanding, Rubaya Ali and Abd al-Fattah were among the founders of the **National Liberation Front** (NLF), were early leaders of the NLF's left wing, and allied with each other to decisively rout the right wing in 1969. Rubaya Ali came from the interior northeast of Aden, and he made his name fighting up-country in the **Radfan Rebellion** in the mid-1970s.

RUSSIA. *See* SOVIET UNION.

RUWAYSHAN FAMILY AND KHALID AL-RUWAYSHAN. A family of shaykhs from the **Khawlan** that built on merchant activities since the 1960s and went on to became one of the several richest and most important families in Sanaa. The Ruwayshans are an example of the results of the "affirmative action" beginning in the 1980s that added northern businessmen to the military–tribal oligarchy that got most of what there was to get in the YAR and the ROY from the 1980s on into the 21st century. Khalid Ruwayshan, the leader of the family, was minister of culture from 2001 to early 2007.

– S –

SAADA (SADAH). The northernmost province and city of Yemen, a rather parochial, inward-looking place, the antithesis of Taiz and

Aden in the south in the 1970s and 1980s. Located about 150 miles north of Sanaa and 50 miles from the border with **Saudi Arabia**, the town is known for its strong identification with **Zaydism**—it is the birthplace of the sect and is its **imamate** in Yemen. The graves of imamate founder **al-Hadi** and other early imams are located just outside the walls. Saada is also famous for its graceful layered mud multistoried buildings and its sensuously serpentine outer wall of layered mud. Unfortunately, much of the wall and many of the homes have fallen victim to the forces of growth and "development."

During most of the **Yemeni Civil War** in the 1960s, the town and its immediate environs were an island of **republicanism**, kept largely by force of arms in the face of the royalist inclinations of many. Since then, rare rumors of tribal revolt, Zaydi separatism, and revival of the imamate have often focused on Saada. Rumor suddenly became reality when the **al-Houthi Rebellion** erupted unexpectedly in 2004. The area's frontier status, as well as suspicions of its loyalties, were reinforced by the huge, sprawling smugglers' bazaar not many miles from the city, a major, open-air exchange for arms, autos and other goods brought in illegally from Saudi Arabia.

SAAR TRIBE. *See* TRIBES AND THE TRIBAL SYSTEM.

SABA (SHEBA) AND SABEAN KINGDOM. One of the pre-Islamic **trading states** of South Arabia, based in **Marib** and astride the **incense** and spice trail on the edge of the desert a short distance after it turns north toward **Najran** and the rich markets of the ancient world. The great prosperity and strength of Saba, which probably reached its peak between 500 and 200 B.C., was based on its control of the passage of trade and on its extensive system of irrigated agriculture, which in turn was based upon the fabled **Marib** dam. Although **Ethiopia** disputes this, Saba is almost certainly biblical Sheba, the fabled queen of which was Bilqis. If Bilqis is the "Queen of Sheba," she did much more than just woo and win Solomon. The Sabean leaders were vigorously expansionist, and the five major Yemeni trading states were united under a single Sabean regime for about a century around 400 B.C. Karib il-Watar was one of the Sabean kings who maintained hegemony over these states during this era.

SABR, JABAL. *See* TAIZ, CITY AND PROVINCE OF.

SADAT, ANWAR (1918–1981). The president of **Egypt** from President Gamal Abdul **Nasser**'s death in 1970 until his assassination in 1981, who, as a member of the Revolutionary Command Council under Nasser, was the Egyptian official immediately responsible for Yemen and for Egypt's disastrous involvement in the **Yemeni Civil War** from 1962 to 1967. Sadat was related by marriage to Dr. Abdul Rahman **Beidani**, the controversial part-Yemeni raised in Egypt who led Egypt's propaganda attack on the Yemeni **imamate** during its last months and then served briefly as Egypt's man in Yemen during the first few months after the **1962 Revolution**.

Probably because it began only a few years after Egypt withdrew from Yemen to the great relief of Egyptians and Yemenis alike, the Sadat presidency was marked by relations between Egypt and the YAR that, while mostly good, were neither intense nor very important for either party. Regard for Sadat and Egypt increased in both Yemens with the October War in 1973, a major **Arab–Israeli** event, but it plummeted when the Camp David peace process led to a separate peace between Egypt and Israel.

SAFER EXPLORATION AND PRODUCTION CO. *See* YEMEN HUNT OIL.

SAID, AHMAD ABDU. A prominent North Yemeni first-generation **modernist** who, after earning a BA at Cornell and a MA in economics at the University of Chicago, returned to Yemen just before the **1962 Revolution** and then went on to serve as minister in 10 of the roughly 14 YAR governments between 1962 and about 1975, usually as minister of the treasury, minister of economics, minister of state, or deputy prime minister for financial and economic affairs. An energetic, hard-working top bureaucrat, Said was complimented by President **al-Iryani**, as "my ant." He will be remembered less for his career in Sanaa, which ended abruptly during the **al-Hamdi** era, than as the founder in **Taiz** of the prototypical **local development association** and as the founder and guiding spirit of the Muhammad Ali Uthman School, also in Taiz. He modeled the private K–12 school after the International College in Beirut, the school that he credited for having prepared him for higher education in the English-speaking world.

From **Hayfan**, Said was a **Shafii**, like the vast majority of the early modernists. Not part of one of the many organized student groups, he went off to Beirut and to the United States on his own, with funds provided by a private Yemeni patron. He died in the late 1980s, while still in his fifties.

SAID PASHA, ALI. *See* OTTOMAN TURKS IN YEMEN.

SAIHUT (SAYHUT). *See* MAHRA.

SALADIN (SALIH AL-DIN) BIN AYYUB. *See* AYYUBIDS.

SALAFISM AND SALAFIS. *See* POLITICAL ISLAM, MODERN.

AL-SALAMI, ALAWI SALIH (1945–). Longtime minister of **finance** who came to personify the key role that the Finance Ministry played in the steep-sided pyramid of control, patronage, and corruption that increasingly marked the **Salih regime** beginning in the mid-1980s. The regime used the ministry's control of funds at the center to frustrate efforts to decentralize and to give ministries and local government greater autonomy. Al-Salami was minister of finance in the 1980s, from 1993 to 1994, and again from 1997 to 2006. He was also deputy prime minister from 2004 to 2006 but was dropped along with Ahmad Muhammad **Sufan** in the donor-induced cabinet reshuffle in early 2006. Before his stint as minister of finance, al-Salami had been governor of the **Central Bank of Yemen**.

SALIF. The small port and fishing town on the **Red Sea** north of **al-Hudayda**, opposite **Kamaran** Island, that is close by vast salt deposits and, since 1987, the terminus at Ras Isa of the **oil** pipeline from the oil field in **Marib**. Although Salif was the site of salt mines for centuries, efforts began only in the 1970s to mine and export salt on a modern, large-scale basis.

SALIH, ALI ABDULLAH (1942–), AND THE SALIH FAMILY. The poorly educated career soldier of humble tribal origins who rose through YAR army ranks, became president in mid-1978, went on to enjoy the longest tenure of any of the YAR's five heads of state, and then led the way to Yemeni **unification** and the creation of the ROY. When reelected president of ROY for a new seven-year term in 2006, he had been in that office in the YAR and the ROY for 28 years; if he completes this term, he will have been in office for 35 years. His tenure was marked by increasing political stability, considerable state-building, and, most notably, unification. By the late 1980s, however, his record was also marred by deep-seated corruption, great inequality, and uneven socioeconomic growth and development. Still, the Central Intelligence Agency's station-chief at the **United States** Embassy in Sanaa was taking bets in late 1978 on this ill-prepared young soldier not surviving the spring of 1979.

As a junior officer, Ali Abdullah caught his superiors' attention for his role in an incident in 1968 in which he acted to ensure that a shipment of arms went to army units supported by major tribal shaykhs and not those allied to radical nationalists. He was rewarded with command of a tank unit and a headquarters assignment. In the mid-1970s, he became military commander of Taiz with a big assist from Lt. Col. Ahmad Husayn **al-Ghashmi** during the **al-Hamdi** presidency. He allegedly participated in the latter's assassination in 1977 and then succeeded President al-Ghashmi when he, too, was killed in 1978.

In the 1980s, President Salih presided over a major effort at political construction, marked most notably by the creation and elaboration of the **General People's Congress** (GPC) and the holding in 1988 of long-promised **elections** to the legislature, the **Consultative Council**. As important, he also presided over the defeat of the PDRY-backed **National Democratic Front** rebellion, worked to improve inter-Yemeni relations, and then led the way to unification in 1990. He become the first president of the ROY and was reelected by the parliament in the fall of 1994, shortly after leading forces loyal to the ROY to victory in the southern-led **War of Secession**.

President Salih was only in his mid-thirties when he first took office. Well advised and willing to take advice, he surprised many people by seeming to grow to fit the office. In the early 1980s, people contrasted him and his style to the suspiciousness and growing isolation of al-Hamdi, who had seemed increasingly unable to reach beyond a narrowing inner circle and build political relationships and institutions. President Salih became, among other things, a master of co-optation, and he began to look at-ease and very presidential.

By the late 1990s and the new millennium, however, the long time in office seemed to be taking its toll. Increasingly, President Salih came to rely on his own narrowing circle of military associates, especially members of his extended family. Subject to increasing pressure and criticism, he seemed more inclined to hunker down and lash out at his enemies. Indeed, some began to see similarities between his behavior and al-Hamdi's behavior in 1977. After the 2006 elections, however, he seemed to be reaching out and seeking dialogue with his opponents—and thinking about his legacy.

President Salih comes from the **Sanhan** tribe, a minor member of the **Hashid** confederation located in the Sanhan region south-southeast of Sanaa. The Salih family and other Sanhani families related to it by marriage, especially Bayt Ismail and Bayt al-Qadi, have had a disproportionately large presence in the political oligarchy and steep pyramid of patronage that came to distinguish the Salih regime, especially since the War of Secession in 1994. Because his hold on power at the outset in the late 1970s was tenuous, he placed close relatives whom he trusted into key military positions. From the outset, he relied heavily on his half-brother, Ali Salih, who was first charged with securing the Sanhan and then made head of the Republican Guard. Muhammad Abdullah Salih, the president's older full brother, soon became chief of Central Security. **Ali Muhsin** Salih, also from Sanhan village, and the cousin of his half-brother, became commander of the 1st Armored Brigade, the first of the many key military posts he occupied over a three-decade period.

Muhammad Ahmad Ismail, uncle of the president, commanded forces in **Shabwa** and the **Hadhramawt** after the War of Secession in 1994, only to die in a helicopter crash in 2001. Muhammad Ali Muhsin, another uncle, commanded the southern **Tihama**, the **southern uplands** and the area around **Lahj**, **Abyan**, and the rest of the hinterland of Aden after the 1994 war. He also took over the command of Shabwa and the Hadhramawt upon the death of Muhammad Ahmad Ismail.

The Salih family has not been a political monolith. Ali Muhsin Salih has been described as both President Salih's major supporter and most likely challenger. The alleged agreement that Ali Muhsin was eventually to succeed President Salih was thrown into question by the election of the president's oldest son, Ahmad Ali Abdullah, to the legislature in 1997 and by speculation that Ahmad was being groomed to succeed his father. Rumors of strained relations between Ali Muhsin and the president circulated when Ahmad was made commander of Special Forces in 1999 and the Presidential Guards in 2000. But Ali Muhsin continued to be in charge of the northern and eastern military zone.

SALIH MUSLIH QASIM. *See* QASIM, SALIH MUSLIH.

SALIH REGIME AND ERA. The long era that includes the increasingly confident and assertive YAR regime headed by President Ali Abdullah **Salih** from mid-1978 until Yemeni **unification** in 1990, the tumultuous interlude ending with the **War of Secession** in 1994, and then the long period of relative political stability and order down to and since his victory in the 2006 presidential **elections**. If President Salih completes his current term in 2013, he will have been in office for 35 years—fully two-thirds of the combined lifetimes of the YAR and the ROY. The Salih era began after the eight-month tenure of Ahmad **al-Ghashmi**, who, like his predecessor Ibrahim **al-Hamdi**, died at the hands of assassins.

Positive steps for which the Salih regime will be remembered include restoration of the **1970 Constitution** in 1987 and elections to a new, mostly elected **Consultative Council** (CC) in 1988—and cessation of the 10-year-old interim **People's Constituent Assembly**. As a result, for the first time since **al-Iryani**'s ouster in 1974, the head of state and the government were chosen by a properly chosen CC. Earlier, and equally memorable were a set of sequential acts of political construction by a regime that in late 1978 had little domestic political support outside the military. These acts began in early 1980 with the drafting of the **National Pact**, the widespread dialogue on this pact as orchestrated by the **National Dialogue Committee**, and then, in 1982, the holding of the elected, 1,000-member **General People's Congress** (GPC) at which the pact was discussed, revised, and adopted. This done, the GPC declared itself a permanent "political organization" that would be selected every four years, meet biennially, and be led between sessions by a 75-member Standing Committee headed by President Salih. The GPC was to become the YAR's broadly based ruling political party.

By design and a bit of luck, moreover, this sustained initiative did more to strengthen the regime than merely organize its center-right base of support. It also provided a political process, largely controlled by the regime, into which elements of the Yemeni left could be safely incorporated when, in 1982, the **National Democratic Front (NDF) Rebellion** was defeated and many of the NDF leaders and followers "came home." Two dialogues, one between the Salih regime and the NDF and a more public one involving the regime and the rest of the nation, converged finally in a structure that facilitated a second national reconciliation.

This three-year effort to organize politics did not end with the closing gavel of the GPC in 1982. The new Standing Committee met on a regular basis, and the second biennial session of the GPC met in 1984. This session adopted a plan to greatly expand participation in GPC elections by having 17,500 elected members of **local councils for cooperative development** (LCCDs) serve as electors of most of the 1,000 members of the new GPC that was to meet the following year. The LCCDs did this in mid-1986, and the new GPC held its first session in August.

The politics of the GPC and the opening to the left were not the only ways—although they were the most important ones—by which President Salih sought to organize politics so as to generate support and legitimacy. The creation of a 15-member Presidential Advisory Council gave him an opportunity to invite an array of leaders back into the fold, notably many of the tribal leaders who had been on the outside since al-Hamdi put them there in 1975. Ex-presidents al-Sallal and al-Iryani accepted invitations to come home from exile in 1982. Political returnees between 1979 and the mid-1980s included many leading modernists and technocrats, and many of them became members of the three governments formed between 1980 and 1988. Increasing the Presidential Advisory Council to 25 members in 1988 afforded additional posts to allocate to a broad array of groups and tendencies. Later, in 1997, the 59-member appointed **Shura Council** was created, and in 2001 it grew to include 111 members. Few leaders had not been co-opted by President Salih in one way or another by this time.

Most certainly, however, the events for which the Salih regime will be most remembered by Yemenis are the unification of Yemen and the preservation of the ROY through victory in the War of Secession in 1994. The **Council of Deputies**, the ROY's parliament, reelected President Salih to a new term in late 1994, and in 1999 he won Yemen's first direct popular presidential **election**. The GPC, the president's party, dominated the parliamentary elections in 1993, 1997, and 2003. During this decade, the ruling party in the old PDRY and the partner in the unification regime from 1990 to 1994, the **Yemeni Socialist Party** (YSP), ceased to be a political force of consequence. Indeed, the only real opposition to the GPC after 1997 was **Islah**, a party combining **tribal** and **political Islamist** elements that had initially feared unification and the power of the YSP.

These domestic changes during the Salih era were paralleled by a changing pattern of regional and international politics. Relative to the 1960s and 1970s, the YAR under President Salih rose in stature and acceptance regionally and internationally throughout the 1980s. This trend was abruptly broken when, in 1990, just after unification, the ROY was regionally and internationally ostracized and materially punished for failing to join the coalition against Iraq that resulted in the First **Gulf War** in 1991. Hundreds of thousands of workers were expelled from **Saudi Arabia**, cutting off most of the **remittances** that had fueled the Yemeni **economy** for two decades, and the flow of external aid that had grown in the 1980s was virtually cut off. The second half of the 1990s was devoted largely to attempts to restore relations with key sources of aid, especially Saudi Arabia, and the other members of the **Gulf Cooperation Council** (GCC). A milestone of this effort was the Saudi–Yemeni **border agreement** in mid-2000. Restoration of good relations with—and aid from—the **United States** and Europe was also pursued, with success.

The promise of these later developments was complicated and compromised by **9/11** and the almost equally strong pressures for and against joining fully in the United States' **War on Terror**. The conflicting imperatives of domestic politics and international relations became increasingly apparent at this juncture. These cross-pressures had been evident just after the bombing of the U.S.S. *Cole* in 2000, and they increased through the decade. The Salih regime often had to choose between the wishes and demands of the United States and those of the large minority of Yemenis and of elites close to, or even in, the regime, who identified with or had ties to militant political Islam.

Economically and socially, it was apparent after the War of Secession in 1994 that the loss of remittances and external aid had had a devastating impact on Yemen. It was equally clear that the oil revenues that had begun to flow in the late 1980s could not replace the growth and welfare provided by the old remittance economy. Also apparent were both the urgent need for major economic and political reforms to address this situation and, at least by 2000, the Salih regime's lack of the will and capacity to adopt these reforms. Specifically, after a good start through 1997, the regime failed to implement much of the **IMF/World Bank** package of structural reforms adopted in 1995 and designed to attract the aid and investment needed to replace the remittances of the 1970s and 1980s.

The effects of the regime's failure were evident by 2005. The Yemeni economy, then so dependent on the state, modest oil revenues, and outside donors, was not creating enough jobs and income to keep up with one of the highest birth rates in the world. As a result, the alarming levels of unemployment, poverty and malnutrition were as high or higher than they had been a decade earlier. The once-promising middle class had been pauperized and had shrunk, and the gap between the few rich and the many poor had grown much wider and more visibly so. Finally, the education, health, and other social service systems were worse than they had been, qualitatively and quantitatively, and were now close to being dysfunctional. Longer-term, and more intractable, Yemen's small, finite reserves of oil and water were rapidly being depleted. Aquifers in densely populated regions were being tapped faster than they could be recharged, and forecasts expected known oil reserves to be exhausted by 2015.

The Salih regime's lack of the will and capacity needed to do what had to be done was a function of its composition and the nature of the state. The trappings and beginnings of democracy notwithstanding, the ROY was an example of rule by the few—an oligarchy. Most of the relatively small number of persons and families who were getting the most of what there was to get—be it political power, economic well-being, good health, or high social status—came from the northern highlands of old North Yemen. They had either (or both) strong

tribal and military (or security) connections; indeed, many were officers from the president's **Sanhan** tribe in the **Hashid** confederation. After 1980, to the military–tribal complex of the late 1960s and 1970s was added a northern commercial–business element, the result of an "affirmative action" program toward this end. Political power was increasingly concentrated in the hands of these elites in the 1980s, and this trend, somewhat suspended at unification, accelerated after the War of Secession eliminated or weakened politicians from the old PDRY and the YSP.

With the start of oil revenues in the mid-1980s, as well as increased external aid, the Yemeni state quickly, and for the first time, had become a principal source of wealth and private gain for the well-placed and fortunate few. As a result, the Salih regime evolved after 1994 into a special variant of oligarchy, a kleptocracy. The occupants of key government posts and offices through which flowed revenues and development aid were able to enrich themselves, usually at the expense of development and other policy goals. They used their positions in the state—their "profit centers"—to extract a price for rendering services or granting permission, thereby increasing the cost of government and development. The associates, friends, and relatives of occupants of key posts and offices were also enriched in this manner, with the reaping of riches being a matter of connection as well as location.

The degree of corruption, not just the fact of it, was key to understanding the Salih regime after the War of Succession. Graft, bribery, and other forms of thievery pervaded the system at all levels of a steep-sided pyramid of patronage. At the broad base of this pyramid were the hundreds of thousands of employees of the government and the military, who were paid extremely low salaries and who were thus forced to take petty bribes—had to "eat money"—in order to barely make ends meet. Perhaps the most visible measures of this corruption higher up the pyramid were the growing number of high-end SUVs and new villas—some virtual castles—on the outskirts of Sanaa, most of which were owned by high-ranking government officials receiving modest salaries.

The YAR and then the ROY also suffered from arrested statehood, a legacy of North Yemen's modern political history. The Yemeni **imamate**, occupied by the **Hamid al-Dins** from the early 20th century until the **1962 Revolution**, did not have a monopoly on the legitimate use of violence in its territory, whether for the purpose of maintaining internal order and providing defense or for the purpose of realizing other goals. Nor did it have instruments of coercion—army and police—that were subservient to it and readily available for use in its pursuit of order, defense, and other goals. In this regard, the old description of the Hashid and **Bakil** tribal confederations as "the wings of the imamate" is suggestive. The major tribes and their leaders conceived of themselves, and were conceived by others, as outside and not in or under the imamate, not subject to or "subjects" of it. They often acted accordingly and were thus able to use their armed tribesmen sometimes to support and protect the imamate and sometimes to contain or oppose it in defense of their perceived tribal interests.

North Yemen's first-generation **modernists** were prevented by events after the 1962 Revolution from creating the modern state to which they aspired. The **Yemeni Civil War** in the 1960s diverted the modernists from the task of state building, and the republican–royalist **reconciliation** in 1970 determined that the republic that survived would be a conservative one. It would preserve much of the traditional order, political as well as socio-cultural; in particular, it would assure a prominent role for the tribal leaders and the tribal system. The Salih regime continued to reflect this history. As a result, the state remained severely limited in terms of what it had the power and authority to do and where it could do it. Indeed, in vital ways, the ROY in 2005 resembled the old imamate more than it did a modern state.

Given these features of the Salih regime and the Yemeni state, it was clear by the middle of the first decade of the 21st century that the regime had to be quickly reoriented, reconstituted, or replaced in order to effect the socioeconomic reforms so urgently needed. Unable to deliver on popular wants and needs, the regime had markedly lost legitimacy and support by the late 1990s. As a result, by 2005, Yemen already had already become a failing state, one that risked becoming a failed state in the near future. If the state did fail, then the country could slide into anarchy (Somalia) or civil war (Lebanon). Under these circumstances, Yemen risked becoming an arena in which militant political Islam would be a serious contender for power, as was the Taliban in Afghanistan in 1994, and again a decade later.

The presidential and local council **elections** in September 2006 shed initial light on whether the Salih regime could and would meet the deepening crisis with needed reforms. President Salih, who in 2005 had declared that he would not be a candidate, reversed himself in mid-2006. It was assumed by all that he would again win and, barring a most unlikely coup or death, would remain in office until 2013.

It was assumed that after the 2006 elections the Yemeni state would effect the necessary reforms by, say, 2010, only if the Salih regime were pressured by or partnered with a strong, credible opposition. In 2005, the organized opposition consisted of only the **Joint Meeting Parties** (JMP), the loose coalition of five parties dominated by Islah and by the revived YSP. Accordingly, most proponents of change in 2005 reasoned that the performance of the JMP in the 2006 **elections** and the 2009 parliamentary election, as well as during the more than two years between them, would determine whether the Salih regime could be persuaded or pressured to adopt needed reforms. It was reasoned that the better the JMP did in the elections in 2006, the better it would be positioned to begin the long march to a strong, convincing show of strength in the parliamentary elections in 2009. If the 2006 and 2009 elections convincingly demonstrated the JMP to be a credible and formidable opponent—and possible partner—of the present regime, then the likelihood of the adoption of needed reforms would be increased. Slightly farther out, and perhaps just over the survival horizon, were the next presidential and local council elections in 2013.

The tasks before the JMP were daunting in 2006. At the end of 2005, it adopted a program that was strong, relevant and very critical of the Salih regime. Thereafter, it resisted efforts by the GPC to divide it or to boycott the elections and selected a worthy presidential candidate, Faisal **bin Shamlan**, a political "independent" from the south, the Hadhramawt. Bin Shamlan and JMP waged a strong, focused campaign. Even though its candidate won only 25 percent of the vote, the JMP did come out of the elections as an increasingly credible and formidable opposition, a force to be reckoned with. The results made it unlikely, if not impossible, for President Salih or the GPC to dictate the choice of the president's son—or anyone else—as the next president in 2013.

Concerned about his legacy, and aware of Yemen's dependence on increasingly demanding international donors, President Salih reiterated his campaign pledges to fight corruption, create jobs, and end poverty when he was sworn in for his new term in late September 2006. On its side, the JMP pledged to closely monitor the Salih regime and said that its immediate goals were electoral reform, freedom of the press, and the fight against corruption.

In 2007 and 2008, both the Salih regime and the JMP tried, with some success, to act on their pledges. Increasingly, however, the international and domestic political environments distracted both sides and limited their abilities to act on these efforts. The generous $4.7 billion pledged at the donors' conference in London in November 2006 came with demanding conditions to which the donors seemed determined to hold the Yemenis. Many of these conditions would be painful, and they would be demanded of a population that had already suffered greatly and was calling for relief. For both sides, the temptation was to play politics with this situation at the risk of losing much of the promised aid and falling short on the needed reforms. In addition, the War on Terror and U.S. demands that Yemen act clearly on the right side placed further strain on cooperation within and between the Salih regime and the JMP.

Domestically, the militant **Zaydi**-based **al-Houthi rebellion** in **Saada** in the far north, which had begun in 2004, reerupted in 2007, and again in 2008. Some of the most disaffected Zaydi **sayyids** questioned the legitimacy of the Salih regime and even of the republic itself. Meanwhile, from mid-2007 through 2008, there occurred in many locations in the south protests and demonstrations by former members of the PDRY's military and civil service, and then by southerners in general; these actions often ending in violence and repression by the security forces. What started as demands for jobs, pensions, and other economic opportunities soon morphed into assertions that unification had turned out to be the north's "occupation" and exploitation of the south. Finally, a succession of violent incidents pointed to a revitalized al-Qaida in Yemen. Most notable were the suicide bombing of eight Spanish tourists in **Marib** in August 2007, several acts of violence in the **Hadhramawt** in 2008, and the deadly attack on the U.S. Embassy in Sanaa in September of that year. In combination, these events revealed a Salih regime under attack from nearly all areas—north, south, east, and center.

In August 2009, the often-predicted "sixth round" the al-Houthi rebellion erupted. It proved to be the most violent, in part because the Salih regime unleashed all it's fire power in an effort to finally put an end to it. And, after a couple of month of relative quiet, the southern secessionist movement and it's regime attempt to crush it broke out again in September.

The varied domestic conflict and violence served to complicate and heat up the political climate in which the Salih regime and the JMP in 2008 increasingly turned their attentions to the parliamentary elections scheduled for April 2009. The JMP threatened to boycott the elections if the composition and rules of the Supreme Committee for Elections and Referendums (SCER) were not changed to its satisfaction. In early 2009, the government and opposition continued to clash, sometimes violently, over the electoral law and the composition and powers of the SCER.

In the last half of January, with the southern protest simmering and the al-Houthi rebellion threatening to erupt again, a new organization, al-Qaida on the Arabia Peninsula, was proclaimed, and often-violent conflict escalated between the Salih regime and the Islamic militants. In this context, the GPC and JMP on 25 February gave up and agreed to both a two-year postponement of the April elections and a set of electoral and constitutional changes; the Chamber of Deputies endorsed this two days later.

In March, the conflict between the Salih regime and both the "houthis" and al-Qaida escalated. By late March, however, these conflicts were dwarfed by the conflict between the regime and the southern protesters. On 2 April, southerner **Tarik al-Fadhli** broke with the President Salih and declared that the northern regime had used unity to occupy and plunder the south; two weeks later, he announced that he had joined the Southern Mobilization Movement and shared its goal of full independence. On 25 April, President Salih delivered a stark warning to a gathering of leaders that any division of Yemen would lead to many states, not just two. In late April and the beginning of May, as the southern protest movement grew bigger and more violent, many civilians and police or soldiers were killed or injured in a rash of incidents across the south. The first half of May also witnessed an upsurge of conflict between the regime and the "houthis," with judicial action against the latter. On 13 May, the leader of al-Qaida on the Arabian Peninsula declared its support for the southern secessionist revolt against the Salih regime. On 21 May, the 19th anniversary of unification, President Salih declared at a celebration in Sanaa that unity would prevail and, in Aden, the breakup of a counter-demonstration left three dead and 25 wounded. Also on 21 May, Ali Salim al-Baydh, the ex-vice president of the ROY, vowed from exile to return to politics to lead the new secession effort.

SALIM RUBAYA ALI. *See* RUBAYA ALI (SALMAYN), SALIM.

SALIM SALIH MUHAMMAD (1947–). The second-tier leader in the PDRY who lost his post as foreign minister in 1982, reemerged as the deputy secretary general of the **Yemeni Socialist Party** (YSP) in the regime of survivors of the **13 January events** in 1986, and then played an important role on the PDRY side in the **unification** negotiations in 1989–1990. Salim Salih co-chaired the key **Joint Committee on a Unified Political Organization** and joined the five-member **Presidential Council** when the ROY was proclaimed in 1990, retaining that position after the April 1993 **elections**.

Although Salim Salih did not clearly align himself with his fellow southerners during the **War of Secession** in 1994, he nevertheless did go into exile at that time. In 2002, he was escorted home from exile by President **Salih**, and in 2003 he was appointed to the ROY's **Shura Council** and to the post of special adviser to the president on counter-terrorism. Salim Salih is originally from **Yafa** in South Yemen.

AL-SALLAL, PRESIDENT ABDULLAH (1919–1994). The older soldier and political dissident who, brought in as president by the younger officers who made the **1962 Revolution**, quickly sidelined most of these officers and made the revolution his own, only to become dependent on the **Egyptian** patrons who had intervened to save the YAR from the **royalists** in the **Yemeni Civil War**. Increasingly opposed by most republicans and others who yearned for an end to the civil war and a Yemen for the Yemenis, President al-Sallal was ousted while abroad in the fall of 1967, only several weeks after Egyptian forces had withdrawn in the wake of defeat in the latest **Arab–Israeli conflict**, the Six-Day War.

Al-Sallal was one of the 13 young men sent by Imam **Yahya** to **Iraq** for training in the mid-1930s, the very first such group to be sent abroad. From that time forward he intermittently conspired and acted in the army to bring about reform and change. Up from the *muzayyan* class, al-Sallal was coarse in appearance and manner, and of limited imagination and intelligence. His attempt to emulate his patron, Egypt's President Gamal Abdul **Nasser**, was woefully bad. When Nikita Khrushchev berated Nasser for bringing al-Sallal along on a Black Sea cruise, Nasser allegedly replied: "I just wanted you to see what I have to put up with."

Upon invitation, Al-Sallal returned from exile to his homeland in 1982. Thereafter he often sat with old **Septembrists** and young Yemenis wanting to know of the YAR's early years, served as something of an elder statesman and symbol of republican unity and, most publicly, led pro-Iraq, anti-coalition demonstrations before and during the First **Gulf War** in 1991. Upon his death in 1994, aged seventy-four, he was eulogized as a national hero.

AL-SALLAL REGIME AND ERA. The period of YAR history that started with its birth in the **1962 Revolution** and that ended with the overthrow of President Abdullah **al-Sallal** in 1967. It was marked by the long and painful **Yemeni Civil War**, the **Egyptian** intervention in that costly and painful event, the uneven beginnings of state-building and modernization in North Yemen, and—above all—the rapid and irreversible opening of that country to a seductive and unforgiving modern world.

Given the isolation and the decentralized nature of North Yemen's traditional sociopolitical order, it is not surprising that the al-Sallal regime was preoccupied from the outset with what A. F. K. Organski called "the politics of primitive unification." In this first stage of political development a state seeks to establish sovereignty over a territory and its people and to achieve the capacity to maintain public order and provide a minimal level of services. The long civil war that came on the heels of the revolution both increased these needs and interfered with their being met. Although Egyptian advisers helped to erect quickly a panoply of state institutions after the overthrow of the **imamate**, many of them were or soon became empty shells, existing in name only. Many of these institutions were very pale carbon copies of their Egyptian counterparts, and many ot them were largely controlled and staffed by Egyptians. Oddly, the YAR did not even get much of a modern military out of the civil war, for it was fought mostly by Egyptian forces that had almost exclusive use of the modern weaponry they had brought to Yemen.

The balance of power between the tribal periphery and the state at the center tipped back toward the **tribes** during the civil war. The territory of imamate Yemen was quickly divided among the republicans, the **royalists**, and the tribes that secured subsidies and autonomy by playing the two competitors for the state off against each other. As a consequence, and despite aspirations to modern statehood, the reach of the new YAR in 1967 barely extended beyond the towns on the sides of the triangle in the southern half of the country that was traced by the main roads linking the cities of **Sanaa, Taiz,** and **al-Hudayda**. Even many areas in the interior of this triangle were beyond the reach of the republican state. The occupation of territory by the Saudi-backed royalists and tribes rendered moot the question of the northern and northeastern borders with Saudi Arabia, and the just-beginning nationalist struggle against **Great Britain**'s rule in South Yemen left the southern border open to both friends and foes of the new YAR.

The YAR created in 1962 lacked both political institutions and an organized base of support. The civil war and Egyptian intervention quickly arrested and deformed the politics of the new republic. The intervention quickly evolved into what amounted to Egyptian occupation and administration of Yemen, leaving little room for Yemeni national politics and politicians to develop. Instead, Yemeni republicans ended up conspiring with or against the Egyptians and fighting among themselves often along **Zaydi–Shafii** sectarian lines.

The one feeble attempt by President al-Sallal to create a broad political party or movement in 1965 was the Popular Revolutionary Organization. It was not launched until 1965, held its first congress at the beginning of 1967, and quickly passed into history with the overthrow of the regime later that year.

As with other late-developing countries, the pressing tasks of state-building in the new YAR went beyond the maintenance of order and security to include the creation of a capacity to monitor and influence, if not control, the rate and direction of socioeconomic development. The weighty events that from the outset buffeted the country—among them the economic dislocation and decline that resulted from the civil war, the drought-induced malnutrition and starvation, and the unregulated inflow of foreign goods and practices—made it obvious that state-building, in all of its aspects, was sorely needed. When the al-Sallal era ended in 1967, these needs had barely begun to be met.

SANAA, CITY AND PROVINCE OF. One of the world's oldest continuously inhabited urban sites, Sanaa was the capital of the YAR from 1962 to 1990, when Yemeni **unification** made it the political capital of the ROY. In earlier times, it had been the capital and chief city of a succession of political entities: the **Hamid al-Din** Zaydi imamate from the end of World War I to 1962, the two **Ottoman** Turkish occupation regimes during the 16th and then the 19th centuries, earlier Zaydi **imamates** before and after the first Ottoman occupation, and an assortment of other regimes major and minor, indigenous and foreign. Regardless of the ruler of the day, Sanaa was for centuries the great **Zaydi** urban center in the highlands of North Yemen, surrounded by tribes that accepted and defended Zaydism. The city has been Islamic since the earliest days of Islam, and the Great Mosque of today is said to be built on the ruins of a mosque built before the death of the Prophet Muhammad. In recent decades, the city has been the stage for much of Yemen's highest political drama: the sacking of Sanaa by the northern tribes as punishment for its role in the aborted **1948 Revolution** and the heroics of its citizens and republican defenders during the 70-day **Siege of Sanaa** in late 1967 and early 1968.

Sanaa is located on a mountain-rimmed plateau at about 7,500 feet in the geographical middle of modern North Yemen, making it one of the highest capitals in the world. One goes "up" to Sanaa from **al-Hudayda** on the coast or from **Taiz** in the southern uplands. Although its sprawling modern sector now hides this, Sanaa was once an austere, almost monastic place in a rather barren setting. It is a place blessed by a year-round dry high-altitude temperate climate, marred only by short seasons of lip-cracking dryness and dusty winds. Wells and erratic rains in the spring and late summer allow for both irrigated and dry farming as well as animal husbandry in the region around the city. Sanaa is not a green place, particularly since the 1970s, when people and commerce began to win out decisively over trees, plants, and flowers in the competition for water. Indeed, Sanaa and the large basin in which it is located are facing in the new millennium a calamitous water crisis as the water table drops at an alarming rate.

The fortressed-topped Jabal Nuqum, a large upthrust of rock, guards Sanaa and towers over it. It was integral to the city's defense for centuries and remains for many Yemenis a symbol and a reminder of the heroic defense of Sanaa and the republic during the dire Siege of Sanaa. It abuts Sanaa's eastern flank, severely limiting growth in that direction. Instead, the city stretches to the west, north, south, across a wide plain. Pre–**1962 Revolution** Sanaa was shaped like a figure-eight or hourglass, with the **Jewish** quarter (Qaa al-Yahud) to the west, separated by a half-mile of gardens and the usually dry watercourse from the much larger, wall-encircled Islamic city at the foot of Jabal Nuqum. This configuration was largely erased by the unplanned growth of the 1960s and 1970s, and more so by the urban sprawl that began in the 1980s and that continues relentlessly today. The new city, epitomized by **Hadda** Street, is undistinguished, full of garish, ugly embassies and residential or commercial buildings. Marking the spread of the jarringly unattractive new city are two concentric roads that encircle it, the Ring Road and Outer Ring Road.

Still, the Old City remains one of the urban treasures of the world. It was declared a World Heritage Site by UNESCO in the early 1980s and since then has been the object of a major preservation and restoration campaign. It is distinguished by Bab al-Yemen and restored portions of its high outer wall, dozens of slender minarets, and, above all, its many whimsically whitewash-trimmed, stained-glass-windowed, mud-brown "skyscraper" houses of cut stone and baked or sun-dried bricks, many of them several stories tall.

The Old City is a living old city. It has ancient, still-thriving souks, the most famous one at its very center. In addition to shops selling all sorts of things from all over the world, this souk is also home to the workplaces and shops of artisans and traditional manufacturers. In recent years, the rapidly growing new city and its outskirts have become the locale for modern stores, even shopping centers, showrooms, shops and light industry. Still, the Old City souks thrive.

During the 1960s and 1970s, Sanaa was known for its fine stone public buildings, old and new, as well as for many mosques, schools, and old, magical skyscraper houses. By contrast, **Taiz** was then the commercial and business center of North Yemen and claimed to be the more modern city, more open to the ideas and practices of the outside world. By the 1980s, however, with a population of more than 500,000 and growing at a breathtaking pace, Sanaa had emerged as the undisputed center of economic as well as political and cultural life in North Yemen. It also became a city of schools—most notably Sanaa University.

With Yemeni unification in 1990 and the flood of government officials and supplicants from **Aden** to Sanaa, the preeminence of Sanaa became even more apparent. It remains to be seen what ranking and division of labor eventually prevails between Sanaa and Aden, the designated economic capital of the ROY. The cities are wildly different in appearance and lifestyle, making them neatly complementary. As they grow, both must cope with traffic congestion, water and electricity shortages, inadequate sewage facilities, housing needs, and the inadequacies of other urban services. The great challenges of becoming a livable modern city in a poor, developing country were compounded for Sanaa after 1990 by the deluge of unemployed workers expelled from **Saudi Arabia** just before and after the First **Gulf War** in 1991. By 2004, Sanaa's population was nearly a one-and-a-half million. Now rimmed by slums and replete with beggars, Sanaa is nonetheless beginning to meet some of these challenges—at the last, trash collection. Indeed, the Old City looked its best in 2004 when, its watercourse paved and many of its tall houses given a white-trimmed facelift, it proudly served as the Arab League's Capital of Arab Culture. *See also* SANAA MUTINY.

SANAA FORUM. *See* RED SEA AND HORN OF AFRICA.

SANAA MUTINY. The bloody three-day battle in Sanaa in August 1968 that, sparked by the seemingly arbitrary replacement of a handful of progressive **Shafii** army officers, resulted in the triumph of army and tribal elements loyal to General Hasan **al-Amri** and other conservative leaders over what they perceived to be a challenge by Shafii elements inspired by the old **Arab Nationalist Movement** and the **National Liberation Front** which had just taken over from the British in Aden. In the next several months the conservatives consolidated their position by purging the **armed forces**, banning both the **trade unions** and the new **Revolutionary Democratic Party**, and dissolving recently created **peasant leagues** and the **Popular Resistance Forces**. This swift excision of the weak, ill-fitting left made the year-old **al-Iryani** regime more homogeneous and shifted its center of gravity in a more conservative and traditionalist center-right direction. Conservative republicanism had prevailed.

SANAA, TREATY OF. The treaty signed in 1934 between the Yemeni **imamate** and **Great Britain** that temporarily ended the ongoing conflict between the two parties and provided for the withdrawal of the imam's forces to north of the **Anglo–Ottoman line** of 1904. The treaty was negotiated on the eve of the **Saudi–Yemeni War** of 1934, a prospect not unrelated to Imam **Yahya's** desire to lessen conflict on his southern border. The treaty also included British recognition of the imam as ruler of North Yemen, set up procedures for handling border incidents, provided for British responsibility for the security on the roads between North Yemen and the Port of **Aden**, and led the imam to lift an embargo on trade with Aden and the **Aden Protectorates**.

The treaty did not end conflict between the signatories, however. Its consultative procedures worked only on occasion, and its ambiguities were cause and excuse for conflict. The imamate did not renounce claims to sovereignty over the vast territory to the south and southeast and, for the next 25 years, it interpreted security and other changes by the British in the Protectorates as violations of the letter and the spirit of the treaty and its presumed endorsement of the *status quo*. The treaty did have an important, enduring effect, however: it firmed up the border later inherited by the two Yemeni republics, the YAR and the PDRY—a border drawn by non-Yemeni imperial powers.

SANAA UNIVERSITY. *See* EDUCATION.

SANABANI, FARIS. *See* MASS MEDIA.

SANHAN TRIBE AND REGION. The tribe and poor tribal area south-southeast of Sanaa and east of the **Islah pass** from which President Ali Abdullah **Salih** and many of his colleagues come. A minor tribe in the **Hashid** confederation, the Sanhan contributed a large number of soldiers to the service of the imams and then to the republic. But it was the Salih presidency after 1978 that brought the Sanhan tribe and "Sanhanis" a truly disproportionate share of power in the YAR. This soon produced grumbling among Yemenis in general—and members of the rival **Bakil** tribal confederation, in particular—about the influence and position of Sanhanis (and other Hashidis) in the state, the military and, later, commerce and business. Indeed, the term "Sanhani" in Yemen became equivalent to "Tikriti" in Saddam Hussein's Iraq—shorthand for being connected—and was applied both positively and negatively.

In addition to the president's extended family, a few other families and villages in the Sanhan, linked to his family by marriage, figure prominently in the patronage network that distinguishes the **Salih regime**. To cite but a few of many examples, members of Bayt Ismail have figured prominently in the military; one member of Bayt al-Qadi acquired control of the public pharmaceutical company, and another became head of the national airline.

AL-SAQQAF, ABD AL-AZIZ (1951–1999). The economist and professor who in his capacity as founding owner–editor of the *Yemen Times* served as a tireless, ever-present, often overbearing commentator and critic—one who was at various times punished, tolerated, or even co-opted—of the politics and policies of the **Salih regime** in the 1990s until his death at an early age in 1999. During this first decade of the ROY, Dr. al-Saqqaf contributed as much as, if not more than, anyone else to beginning to build an independent print media willing and able to speak truth to power. He died when struck by an automobile; circumstances suggest his death to have been a very unfortunate accident, but nothing more. *See also* MASS MEDIA.

SARAT MOUNTAINS. *See* GEOGRAPHY AND CLIMATE.

AL-SAUD (BAYT SAUD). Bayt Saud, commonly referred to as "Al-Saud," has been prominent in the politics of the **Arabian Peninsula** for centuries. It has had a profound impact on its Yemeni neighbors at least since the first quarter of the 20th century. Abd al-Aziz Bin Abd al-Rahman al-Saud, known as "Ibn Saud," was the extraordinary head of the household who, beginning shortly after 1900, forged by conquest, diplomacy, and marriage the Kingdom of **Saudi Arabia**, a premodern state that by the mid-1930s covered about four-fifths of the Arabian Peninsula and shared borders with each of the several smaller political units on the periphery of the peninsula, including those that became the two Yemens. Ibn Saud fought and won the **Saudi–Yemeni War of 1934** with Imam **Yahya**. This secured the southwest corner of his domain, territory regarded as part of Yemen by many Yemenis even through the 1990s. Nevertheless, when Imam Yahya was assassinated during the **1948 Revolution**, Ibn Saud provided crucial moral support for the claim to the Yemeni imamate by Crown Prince **Ahmad**.

Under Ibn Saud, his family for the third time in about 150 years joined forces with the spiritual leaders and followers of **Wahhabism**, the teachings of 18th-century Islamic scholar Muhammad ibn Abd al-Wahhab, to unite most of Arabia. Returning to Najd in 1901 from exile in **Kuwait**, he soon established himself as sultan of Najd. From this base, he proceeded to use the zealous Wahhabi fighters, the Ikhwan, to extend his domain, only to have to rein them in during the mid-1920s as Saudi Arabia approached its present size and pushed up against territory protected by **Great Britain**.

It was Ibn Saud who, desperate for revenue for his vast but impoverished kingdom in the 1930s, opened his arid, barren domain to oil exploration by the West and forged close relations with the **United States** in particular. He lived to see his kingdom begin to experience the curses as well as the blessings of oil wealth. By virtue of his many marriages, which produced more than 40 sons, he left behind a huge, exponentially growing royal family.

Ibn Saud was succeeded upon his death in 1953 by Saud Ibn Abd al-Aziz, his eldest surviving son, a lesser man and ruler. King Saud lost the support of his family and was replaced by his brother, Crown Prince Faysal, in 1964; he chose to go into exile and died abroad in 1969. His decade of rule was one of newly found oil wealth and profligate living by the Saudi royal family and of bitter conflict between the conservative Arab monarchies and the revolutionary Arab nationalism personified by **Egypt**'s Gamal Abdul **Nasser**. This conflict brought Egypt and Saudi Arabia close to war as chief patrons of the opposing sides of the **Yemeni Civil War** that started just after the **1962 Revolution** and the creation of the YAR.

The able, broadly experienced Faysal Bin Abd al-Aziz ruled until his assassination by a nephew in 1975. During a decade of rule marked by the great surge in the price of oil, King Faysal oversaw the transformation of Saudi Arabia from a still-impoverished tribal kingdom into an oil-rich, partly modern state. He also oversaw the regularization of the patron–client relationship through which the Saudis hoped to use their wealth to dominate a dependent YAR in the years after the Yemeni Civil War. Prince Faysal had been viceroy of the **Hijaz** during the war with imamate Yemen in 1934, and he allegedly remained concerned throughout his life about the potential threat that an ascendant North Yemen, especially if allied or united with South Yemen, posed for the Saudi kingdom. Faysal served as foreign minister virtually the entire period from the creation of the Foreign Ministry in 1930 until his death in 1975, including the decade of his own kingship.

Khalid Bin Abd al-Aziz ruled in poor health and a rather disinterested manner from 1975 until he died of a heart attack in 1982. Crown Prince Fahd, who succeeded him in 1982, largely ran the day-to-day operations of the Saudi state during his brother's reign, a period in which surging oil prices gave the Saudis incredible wealth and considerable economic power—power that they used to try both to get the YAR to do their bidding and to prevent close ties between the two Yemens. During Khalid's reign, both Yemens experienced violent regime changes over issues partly related and of interest to their Saudi neighbors.

Spanning the long period 1982–2005, the reign of Fahd Ibn Abd al-Aziz was witness to improving relations between and then **unification** of the two Yemens, something long opposed by, or at least worrisome to, the Saudis. He also oversaw the severe economic punishment of the new ROY by Saudi Arabia for its failure to join the United States– and Saudi-led coalition against **Iraq** in the First **Gulf War** of 1991. Under King Fahd, Saudi Arabia supported the breakup of the ROY and, in 1994, the **War of Secession**; thereafter, and throughout most of the rest of the 1990s, it maintained very cool, if not hostile, relations toward the ROY. During Fahd rule, subject to growing internal demands for social and political change, the Saudi regime initiated some political reforms and successfully contained other reform efforts. It also weathered the collapses in oil prices in both the late 1980s and late 1990s.

Formally becoming king in 2005 at age 80, Abdullah Bin Abd al-Aziz had dominated and run the day-to-day affairs of state for much of the last decade of the reign of his half brother, King Fahd. Previously, he had been crown prince and head of the important National Guards. Taking over in the post–**Cold War** decade, he has been less inclined to be broadly and automatically pro-American in his international orientation. He is also alleged to be more pan-Arab and Islamic in perspective and orientation. It was largely he who, on the Saudi side, made possible both the **Saudi–Yemeni Border Agreement** in 2000 and the improvement in Saudi–Yemeni relations in general.

Sultan ibn Abd al-Aziz has been crown prince since the accession of his half-brother, Abdullah. For more than four decades, since 1962, he has been minister of defense and the member of the royal family with primary responsibility for shaping and executing policy toward the Yemens. In 1975, he was the first senior member of the family to make a state visit to the YAR. Some Yemenis point to this bit of the defense minister's job description as evidence that the royal family views the Yemens, singly and together, primarily in military terms.

If Crown Prince Sultan survives King Abdullah and accedes to the throne, the list of the sons of Ibn Saud of kingly stature will have been exhausted, opening the way to competition among the huge number of princes that make up the next generation of Al-Saud.

SAUDI ARABIA, KINGDOM OF. The large, thinly populated, fabulously oil-rich desert kingdom that was created in the first quarter of the 20th century and occupies all but the periphery of the **Arabian Peninsula**. It has been the only geographical neighbor of both Yemens and the country with the greatest continuous influence on them as patron or antagonist. From the 1960s to the year 2000, its foreign policy has been driven as much by fear of the Yemens as by fear of any other state or set of states.

Saudi Arabia sided with the royalists against the **republicans** and the YAR in the **Yemeni Civil War** in the 1960s. With the end of the Civil War and the independence of South Yemen in the late 1960s, what developed was a South Arabian triangle consisting of Saudi Arabia and the two Yemens. Saudi Arabia sought to establish its hegemony by keeping the YAR weak and dependent, by undermining or overthrowing the Marxist PDRY, by using the YAR as its surrogate in this latter effort and, above all, by preventing the unification of the two Yemens. With the Yemeni **unification** that the Saudis feared, the triad became a more simplified dyad in 1990. Moreover, the discovery of commercial amounts of **oil** in the YAR and the PDRY in the middle and late 1980s, respectively, added a new dimension, extending the possibility of a stronger Yemen, one less dependent on Saudi Arabia.

Caught up in the unification process, the ROY was blindsided by **Iraq**'s unexpected invasion of **Kuwait** in 1990. Refusing repeatedly to endorse the decision by the **United States**– and Saudi-led coalition to expel Iraq by armed force, Yemen soon found itself bereft of most development aid as well as budgetary and balance-of-payments support from Saudi Arabia. Far more important was the loss of the substantial **remittances** of the several hundred thousand Yemeni workers and many merchants who were forced by the Saudis to return to Yemen and likely unemployment.

During 1990 and 1991, the exchange of public accusations and criticism between the ROY and Saudi Arabia rose to a level not seen since the Yemeni Civil War. Much of the rhetoric focused on their longtime **border disputes**. The ROY expressed its eagerness for a dialogue with Saudi Arabia to resolve these disputes. Often in the same breath, however, it asserted that the cruel and unjust expulsion of Yemenis amounted to an abrogation of the 1934 **Taif Treaty**, calling into question Saudi rule over **Asir**, **Najran**, and **Jizan**. For its part, Saudi Arabia expressed surprise at President Salih's siding with Saddam Husayn against Yemen's friends and benefactors, ignored Yemeni calls for border talks, and announced plans in the spring of 1991 for oil exploration in an area near their unmarked border.

The strained relations after the events in 1990–1991 went beyond mere talk. The Saudis sought to weaken the ROY and then, in 1994, went on to encourage and materially support the southerners in the **War of Secession**. In the second half of the 1990s, their relations consisted mostly of border incidents and provocations and on intermittent efforts to settle their border disputes. Finally, with the **Saudi–Yemeni Border Agreement** in 2000, relations improved significantly, some aid resumed, and a small number of Yemeni workers were readmitted to Saudi Arabia. Saudi Arabia originally strongly opposed the ROY's request to join the **Gulf Cooperation Council**, though its opposition gradually softened after 2000.

With **9/11** and the **War on Terror** in 2001, however, a whole new dimension was added to Saudi–Yemeni relations. Through it all, the Saudi royal family, **Al-Saud**, remains conscious that the ROY is a still-poor republic with a population of 24 million that is very nationally conscious and larger than its own. The fact remains that Saudi Arabia's own population of nearly 25 million includes about 7 million foreigners, nearly all guest workers.

SAUDI–YEMENI BORDER DISPUTES AND THE BORDER AGREEMENT OF 2000. *See* BORDERS.

SAUDI–YEMENI JOINT COORDINATING COUNCIL. Created in 1973, the joint body that met more or less on an annual basis to assess the YAR's aid needs and to negotiate the level and form of **Saudi Arabia**'s efforts to meet those needs. The importance over time of the council was indicative of the importance of Saudi aid to the YAR—and of YAR dependence on the Saudis—and its meetings were charged with politics. The meetings were a good barometer of the changing state of Saudi–YAR relations. With the creation of the ROY and the First **Gulf War** in 1991, relations between the Saudis and the Yemenis turned cold, Saudi aid stopped, and the council became far less important—only to take on some of its old importance after the **Saudi–Yemeni Border Agreement** of 2000. *See also* ARAB REGIONAL FUNDS.

SAUDI–YEMENI WAR OF 1934. *See* BORDERS; AL-SAUD (BAYT SAUD).

SAWT AL-YAMAN. *See* FREE YEMENI PARTY.

SAYHUT. *See* MAHRA PROVINCE AND SULTANATE.

SAYYID CASTE. *See* SOCIAL SYSTEM AND STRUCTURE.

SAYYUN (SEIYUN). The vibrant, bustling city in the heart of Wadi **Hadhramawt** that served as the seat of the **Kathiri** sultanate until its abolition in 1967. Flanked by the towns of **Shibam** to the west and **Tarim** to the east, Sayyun is the wadi's largest urban center and its major center of government, commerce, and communications. It is linked to **Mukalla** on the coast by the main road over the **Jol**, and its small airport connects it with **Aden** as well as Mukalla. An unattractive place, Sayyun does have the large Kathiri palace, now a museum—and it does dramatically back up against the towering wall of rock that defines the southern side of Wadi Hadhramawt.

SCIENTIFIC SOCIALISM. *See* IDEOLOGY AND POLITICAL IDEAS, MODERN.

SCOTT, HUGH. *See* TRAVELERS TO YEMEN.

SECURITY SERVICES. In both the YAR and the PDRY, regular police functions were performed by Public Security, a large uniformed force, located in the respective Ministry of the Interior. National security ("secret police") functions, those concerned with protecting the state from internal as well as external enemies, were performed since the mid-1970s in both Yemens by organizations that more or less combined the functions of the **United States'** Federal Bureau of Investigation and their Central Intelligence Agency: the Ministry of State Security in the PDRY and, in the YAR, the Central Organization for National Security, nominally under the minister of the interior. These agencies grew in importance in both Yemens in the late 1970s and 1980s, and both Yemens took on aspects of the *mukhabarat* (national security) state that came to plague much of the Arab world.

Created in 1975 during the **al-Hamdi** regime, the Central Organization for National Security evolved by the modernization, enlargement, and reorganization of existing agencies into the YAR's major and most feared instrument of state surveillance, control, and coercion from the mid-1970s through the 1980s. The first head of the Central Organization for National Security was Lt. Col. Muhammad **Khamis**, and the security forces were "modernized" with aid from the West. Khamis, who served until he was eased out in a government shake-up in 1979, was assassinated at the **Manakha** checkpoint in 1981. The national security organization underwent further enlargement and upgrading in the 1980s under the direction of Ghalib al-Gamish.

Created in 1974, the Ministry of State Security housed the Revolutionary Security Service, the PDRY's major security and intelligence agency. The security forces reached a peak of brutal efficiency under Muhammad Said Abdullah **"Muhsin"** after he became head of the new ministry in 1974. It was during his tenure that the anti-fraternization laws were issued, along with specific rules as to what could and could not be discussed by students and civil servants with foreign teachers or foreign technical experts, respectively. Dissent was harshly put down, and many dissidents and critics of the regime were jailed under oppressive conditions and often tortured; many simply disappeared or died under strange circumstances, even some in exile abroad. Much of this was made possible by the "modernization" of the PDRY's security apparatus, the result of technical assistance provided by East **Germany**'s secret police agency, Stasi. By the late 1970s, "Muhsin" had so alarmed and frightened his colleagues that they ousted him from office and created a high-level committee to oversee internal security affairs.

Amidst the euphoria of Yemeni **unification** and the dawning of a new age of freedom, the old national security apparatus of the YAR and PDRY were abolished by degree. Ghalib Al-Gamish became minister of the interior, and the new regime soon announced that the merged security apparatus would be reduced in size and significance. Despite the maintenance of two of the old security organizations and the creation of a new one, the **Political Security Organization** (PSO), the people sensed they had, and to some degree did have, more freedom from 1990 to 1994. Many openly expressed their distaste for the old security system and security officers.

In the wake of the political crisis and 1994 **War of Secession**, however, the security agencies were gradually reconstituted, and the PSO assumed a high profile and an important place in the **Salih regime**. Perhaps because of the memory of their fall from power and prestige after unification, the security forces reasserted themselves with a vengeance and were allowed to largely rebuild the *mukhabarat* state of the 1980s. Increasingly, people talked of the penetration and compromise by security of many institutions and organizations, for example, **Sanaa University**. Al-Gamish, a loyal and nonthreatening figure, remained head of security throughout its revival. In mid-2002, the National Security Organization (NSO) was created, reporting directly to the president and responsible for ferreting out and thwarting foreign threats to national security. The differences in tasks of the new NSO and the old PSO are unclear.

SEPTEMBRISTS. The vaguely defined group of young men, mostly junior army officers, who more than any other group launched the **1962 Revolution**, only in most cases to be shunted aside or at least denied much access to the corridors of power by the older President **al-Sallal** and his close friends in the mid-1960s—and again and even more so by President **al-Hamdi** in the mid-1970s. Disgruntled or embittered, some of the Septembrists withdrew from public service. A few even joined the **National Democratic Front** in the late 1970s, usually only to be won back with good positions, respect, and recognition by the **Salih regime** in the early 1980s and later. Most of the Septembrists were among the first Yemenis to receive military training in **Egypt** from the late 1940s through the 1950s, and a few of the most notable were from the **Famous Forty**.

SERJEANT, ROBERT. *See* SOUTH ARABIA.

AL-SHAABI FAMILY. Qahtan al-Shaabi was the Arab nationalist and early member of the **National Liberation Front** (NLF) who, supported by the nationalist, nonsocialist right wing of the NLF, became its secretary general and then the first president of independent South Yemen in late 1967. After a year and a half of bitter conflict with the Front's rising left wing, Qahtan was forced from office and jailed in the **22 June Corrective Move** in 1969; he was released from house arrest in the 1970s and was recognized for his service by the PDRY upon his death in 1981.

Qahtan had started out in the **South Arabian League** and was much more at home with **Nasserism** than with the Marxist **ideology** of the left wing of the NLF. An agricultural officer from a modest clan in **Lahej**, he had fled to Cairo in 1958; in 1962, the **Egyptians** announced the formation of a National Liberation Army to free the South—and with Qahtan as its head. Then, meeting in **Taiz** in 1963, the **Aden** branch of the **Arab Nationalist Movement** (ANM) announced the formation of the NLF with him as its head. The facts that he was the best known of the NLF leaders and the only one more than 40 years old probably bolstered his claim to the post of head of state in 1967. Decades later, in 1999, Qahtan's son, Najib al-Shaabi, a political unknown and a member of the ROY's ruling **General People's Congress** (GPC), ran feebly for president against President Ali Abdullah **Salih**.

Faysal Abd al-Latif al-Shaabi, a cousin of Qahtan, was a founder, with Qahtan, of the Yemen's ANM and an early leader of the NLF.

He served in the earliest governments of the republic, first as minister of economy and foreign trade, and then, in early 1969, as prime minister, only to be purged along with his cousin and the rest of the Front's right wing in 1969. He had been a civil servant in Aden before and during the early days of the NLF in the mid-1960s.

SHABWA. A town and province northeast of **Aden** and west of Wadi **Hadhramawt**. The province runs from the edge of the **Ramlat al-Sabatayn** desert down to the **Arabian Sea**; most of it is arid and quite remote. Shabwa town attained importance in ancient times as the market for the fabled nearby salt mines, a depot on the inland **trade route**, the Frankincense Trail, and the sometime capital of the Hadhramawt state. Then, after centuries as a backwater, the province attracted attention in the mid-1980s as the locale of the first of South Yemen's newly found **oil** fields. Shabwa is still very much a rough-and-ready frontier town, but it and its poor province are a focus of increased aid efforts in the new millennium. Balhaf, a town on the coast, is the site of the pipeline terminus and LNG plant for natural gas from the **Marib/al-Jawf** basin; it is also the proposed site of a large petrochemical plant.

SHAFII (SHAFAI) SUNNISM. One of the four great doctrinal schools of orthodox Sunni Islam, Shafism is the school that was permanently established by the end of the 13th century during the **Rasulid** dynasty as the dominant school in the southern uplands of North Yemen, the **Tihama** coast, and virtually all of South Yemen. The "Shafii south" of North Yemen begins at **Samara Pass**, where one drops down from the northern highlands to **Ibb** and **Taiz** provinces.

The Shafiis have more often been the ruled rather than the rulers, and Shafii Sunnism in Yemen has lacked a political culture and theory of rulership comparable to **Zaydi Shiism** and its **imamate**. In addition, the Shafiis of Yemen in recent centuries have not had the means and opportunity to support and develop law, literature, and the arts, at least as compared to the Zaydis. On the other hand, Shafii Sunnism in Yemen is rich in many forms of popular Islam, notable as it is for the worship of Sufi saints and for many pilgrimage sites. It has long been less austere and more tolerant than its Zaydi counterpart and, since the 1940s, more open to the outside world and its ideas and opportunities. In recent decades, however, Shafiis in Yemen have proven vulnerable to the Muslim Brotherhood, as well as to Wahabbism and other militant forms of **political Islam**. *See also* RELIGION AND RELIGIOUS GROUPS IN YEMEN; ZAYDIS AND SHAFIIS IN POLITICS AND SOCIETY.

SHAHARA. *See* HAJJA.

AL-SHAMI, AHMAD MUHAMMAD (1924–2005). A leader of a large **sayyid** family who, despite being part of the movement to reform the **imamate** in the 1940s, chose to cast his lot with Imam **al-Badr** after the **1962 Revolution**, served as **royalist** foreign minister during the long **Yemeni Civil War**, and finally led moderate royalists into the republican–royalist **reconciliation** in 1970. He returned to **Sanaa** that year and joined his old friend, Abd al-Rahman **al-Iryani**, and three others on the YAR's plural executive, the **Republican Council**. He left Yemen in the early 1970s, served briefly as ambassador to France and **Great Britain**, and retired from public life in 1974. He lived in England for the next three decades, seriously incapacitated by illness during his last years.

A friend and colleague of Ahmad Muhammad **Numan** and Muhammad **al-Zubayri**, Al-Shami fled with them from **Taiz** to **Aden** in 1944 and with them founded the **Free Yemenis**. Four years later he was one of a number of prominent opponents of the imamate to be imprisoned in **Hajja** for their roles in the failed **1948 Revolution**. After his friend Crown Prince al-Badr secured his release from prison in 1952, he did serve Imam **Ahmad** in Taiz in the years before the 1962 Revolution. He worked for republican–royalist reconciliation in the 1960s and was less committed to the imamate and the royalist cause than he was opposed to **Egyptian** intervention in the civil war and to some of the leaders and policies of the YAR.

AL-SHAMI, MUHAMMAD ABDULLAH (*CA.* 1890–*CA.* 1964). Head-quartered in the border town of **al-Baydha**, he was Imams **Yahya** and **Ahmad**'s wily and energetic frontier officer in the 1940s and 1950s, their counterpart to **Great Britain**'s Basil **Seager**. This was a time when the British were pushing north from **Aden**, and the Yemeni **imamate** was resisting that push—or pushing south. Qadi al-Shami repeatedly negotiated with Seager and just as repeatedly used money and arms to induce the tribes on either side of the ill-defined border to act against the British. From a prominent **Zaydi** family in **Kawkaban**, near **Sanaa**, Qadi al-Shami's career of loyal service to the imamate also included top posts in **Zabid**, **Rada** and, at the time of the **1962 Revolution**, Sanaa. In the wake of the revolution, he was put in prison, tried, and convicted; released after some months, he retired to Kawkaban, where he spent his last couple of years.

AL-SHAMI, YAHYA. *See* NATIONAL DEMOCRATIC FRONT (NDF) AND NDF REBELLION.

SHAMLAN, FAISAL BIN. *See* BIN SHAMLAN, FAYSAL UTHMAN.

SHARAF AL-DIN FAMILY AND IMAMATE. The **imamate** family based in the **Zaydi** stronghold of **Kawkaban** and **Thula**, a bit to the west of **Sanaa**, that occupied the imamate and led the intermittent (and unsuccessful) fights against the **Ottoman Turks** during the first half of their occupation of Yemen in the middle decades of the 16th century and against the only-decades-earlier occupations by the **Tahirids** and the Circassian **Mamluks**. The family persisted, and a Sharaf al-Din eventually became imam in the late 19th century—and another was regarded as a claimant to the imamate in the last days of Imam **Yahya**'s rule in the mid-20th century.

SHAWKANI, QADI MUHAMMAD ALI (?–1834). A senior judge and the influential Islamic reformer of the late 18th and the early 19th centuries who, while serving under the **Qasimi** imamate, argued in his writings for a rejection of the four main schools of **Sunni** Islam and the adoption of a generic, "non-sectarian" Sunni Islam closer to the original message of Islam. Although he was head judge in the service of the **Zaydi imam**, a main component of Shawkani's thought was what amounts to a Sunni theory of the state, one at variance with Zaydi political theory. Many Yemenis, especially "liberal" and modernist ones, today regard themselves as "followers of Shawkani," among them members of the prominent **al-Iryani** family.

AL-SHAYIF FAMILY. A leading family of Dhu Husayn, a great tribe in the **Bakil** confederation, which long has had its base in the mountainous Barat region in the far northeast but also has land in the southern uplands. Despite serious issues with the imams in the 20th century, the al-Shayifs and Dhu Husayn came down on the royalist side during the long **Yemeni Civil War** in the 1960s.

Shaykh Naji abd al-Aziz al-Shayif, the leader of the family, has been one of the strongest, if not the strongest, shaykh of the divided, loosely organized Bakil confederation since the 1970s, and the family has benefited from its relationship to President Ali Abdullah **Salih** in recent decades. The family sided with President Salih during the political crisis that ended in the **War of Secession** in 1994. Critics of the Salih regime point to an event in 1994 as epitomizing the tribal basis and mentality of the regime—and the importance of the al-Shayif family. After a mutually insulting shouting match between Shaykh Muhammad Naji al-Shayif and Acting Prime Minister Hasan **Makki**, the urbane modernist, in revenge al-Shayif's men gravely wounded Makki and killed his guards; only days later, the shaykh and the president were seen hand in hand at a public ceremony. By contrast Makki and nontribalists in the regime had to accept a traditional tribal apology, President Salih continued to support and get support from. Shaykh al-Shayif who was appointed to the **Shura Council** in 1997 and remained active in politics through the next decade. In early 2008, he led a group of parliamentarians who opposed the recent peace agreement between the Salih regime and the **al-Houthi rebels** and instead favored a military solution.

SHAYKH. *See* SOCIAL SYSTEM AND STRUCTURE; TRIBES AND THE TRIBAL SYSTEM.

SHAYKH OTHMAN. *See* ADEN.

SHEBA AND THE QUEEN OF SHEBA. *See* SABA (SHEBA) AND SABEAN KINGDOM.

SHIBAM. The improbable and architecturally breathtaking town of 6- to 10-story mud brick "skyscrapers" built on a low rectangular platform on the very edge of the watercourse in Wadi **Hadhramawt**

in South Yemen, close by and to the west of **Sayyun** and **Tarim**. This small, densely packed urban enclave had for centuries been a major center of business and commerce in the wadi. In recent decades, despite its still being densely populated, it has conveyed a sense of lifelessness, seeming more like a museum than a living city. It was declared a UNESCO International Heritage Site, and attention is being given to its preservation and restoration.

SHIBAM-KAWKABAN. Historic, picturesque twin towns 20 miles west-northwest of **Sanaa**. It is comprised of Shibam, a bustling, rough-and-tumble market town at the foot of a high plateau and on the edge of a large cultivated plain, and Kawkaban, the historic home of great **Zaydi sayyid** families and a fortified town of lavish, multistoried houses that command the plain from atop that plateau. The **Sharaf al-Din** imamate family is the most illustrious of the families of Kawkaban, which was a bastion from which the imamate defended itself against the **Ottoman Turks** in 16th century and against the Yemeni republic and the **Egyptians** during the **Yemeni Civil War** in the 1960s. Since the 1960s, it has been almost empty of the great families, which now live in Sanaa; it is quite empty generally. Kawkaban is also famous for its musicians—its singer-poets—and their distinct style.

SHIHR. The small, unprotected port on the South Arabian coast roughly 20 miles east of **Mukalla** through which, over the centuries, have passed many of the learned men and merchants of Wadi **Hadhramawt** going abroad to teach or do business and make their often considerable fortunes in East Africa, the **Hijaz**, **India**, and the East Indies. With the building of the main road between the wadi, **Rayyan**, and Mukalla in the second half of the 20th century, Shihr became much less important. However, after 1990, Shihr became the site of **Nexen**'s terminus for the important **Masila** oil field.

SHII ISLAM IN YEMEN. *See* ISMAILIS IN YEMEN; RELIGION AND RELIGIOUS GROUPS IN YEMEN; ZAYDI SHIISM IN YEMEN; ZAYDIS AND SHAFIIS IN POLITICS AND SOCIETY.

SHUQRA. *See* FADHLI SULTANATE OF SHUQRA.

SHURA COUNCIL. The second legislative chamber in the ROY, appointed by the president, that is basically a body of notables with little more than review and advisory functions. Created in 1997 by amendment to the constitution, this 59-member body has served both as a vehicle through which President **Salih** co-opted allies and potential enemies and as a repository for aging politicians, soldiers, shaykhs, senior functionaries, and prominent businessmen. From the outset, the speaker of the Shura Council has been Abd al-Aziz **Abd al-Ghani**, the longtime prime minister. In 2001, another constitutional amendment approved by referendum increased the size of this appointive body to 111 and gave it the power, when asked by the president, to vote jointly on legislation with the elected 301-member **Majlis al-Nawab.** Some constitutional reformers hope to create a true bicameral legislature by making the Shura Council elective and giving it full lawmaking powers, a change that seemed increasingly likely in 2009. (Note: the Shura Council of the ROY is not to be confused with the Majlis al-Shura, the **Consultative Council**, the legislature in the YAR, 1971–74 and, again, 1988–90.)

SIEGE OF SANAA. The 70-day siege of **Sanaa** by the **royalists** and their **tribal** allies from late 1967 through February 1968, and perhaps the republic's finest, most heroic hour during the long **Yemeni Civil War.** The resurgent royalists surrounded and cut off Sanaa after the **Egyptian** forces withdrew from Yemen earlier in 1967, leaving the unprepared **republicans** on their own. Despite great privation, the regular and irregular republican forces made their stand and then broke the siege, ending the royalists' last chance to bring down the republic. The siege was followed in a few months by another event of almost equal importance, the **Sanaa Mutiny**.

SINAN ABU LUHUM. *See* ABU LUHUM.

SIRWAH. *See* TRADING KINGDOMS, SOUTH ARABIAN.

SIYALI, SALIH MUNASSIR. The radical Hadhrami who, as governor of the **Hadhramawt** in the early and mid-1970s, waged a murderous campaign against the "feudalists" on behalf of the **National Liberation Front** regime in the new PDRY. One of those who survived and benefited from the **13 January events** that decapitated the ruling **Yemeni Socialist Party** in 1986, Siyali became interior minister and then, with **unification** in 1990, became defense minister in the ROY. As the political crisis unfolded in the early 1990s, he sided with President **Salih**. However, in the course of the **War of Secession** in 1994, he disappeared, allegedly with a large amount of money.

SMUGGLING. The smuggling of goods into the YAR was a major feature of that country's economic life since at least the early 1970s, be it over the northern and northeastern border with **Saudi Arabia** or across the **Red Sea** from **Djibouti** to **al-Mukha**. To a much lesser extent, goods were smuggled over the southern border to and from South Yemen, but the regime in **Aden** from the late 1960s through the 1980s, the PDRY, had little tolerance for this activity. By contrast, an amazing amount and variety of goods came into the YAR across the porous Saudi border—Toyotas by the tens of thousands, an endless flow of tank trucks of oil and gasoline, TVs, weapons of all sorts, steel pipe, construction materials, etc.—and much of it was on display for sale in many open-air markets outside **Saada**, **Sanaa**, and elsewhere. Alcoholic beverages of all sorts were and still are ferried across the Red Sea to al-Mukha, and foodstuffs and other goods subsidized by the PDRY found their way north to the YAR. The smuggling was indicative of the extent to which the YAR state was riddled with corruption and, in any case, unable to control its periphery and borders.

In the 1980s and since Yemeni **unification** in 1990, persistent smuggling has compromised if not thwarted efforts by the YAR and the ROY both to increase revenues through import taxes and to regulate the level of imports and consumption. Attempts by the state to end this activity have been largely unsuccessful and occasionally the source of serious strife; at times the state has found it advantageous tacitly to accept if not encourage an activity that got goods into the hands of people who wanted them. Powerful figures in Saudi Arabia as well as tribal leaders, officials, and military officers in the Yemens have had big stakes in smuggling, thereby further complicating efforts to bring it under control.

Since the mid-1990s and continuing into the new millennium, the biggest problem was the smuggling of subsidized goods—in particular petroleum products—out of Yemen to **Somalia**, Saudi Arabia, and elsewhere. The ROY allocated a huge part of annual expenditures to subsidize basic goods needed by the poor and almost poor, a large percentage of which then were smuggled out of the country at a huge profit. A major part of the package of **IMF/World Bank reforms** adopted in 1995 and fitfully implemented thereafter was designed to take the profit out of smuggling by ending the subsidies—and make the funds budgeted for subsidies available for health, education, and other needed services. Progress in this effort was limited, at best.

SOCIAL DEVELOPMENT FUND (SDF). Established with World Bank funds in 1997, the SDF was created to provide social safety nets and other measures to alleviate and compensate for the dislocations and hardships accompanying the **IMF/World Bank reforms** adopted by the ROY in 1995. To this end, the SDF was envisioned as raising living standards by promoting income-earning opportunities through community development, capacity building, and micro-financing projects. Under the leadership of the very able and honest Abd al-Karim **al-Arhabi**, the SDF came to be regarded as possibly the best run and least corrupt of the ROY's institutions from the late 1990s to late in the first decade of the 21st century.

SOCIALISM. *See* IDEOLOGY AND POLITICAL IDEAS, MODERN.

SOCIAL SYSTEM AND STRUCTURE. The traditional social structure of Yemen has made room for the class, status, and occupational distinctions common to the modern world in South Yemen and, since the **1962 Revolution**, in North Yemen. The small industrial working class and the larger new middle class of civil servants, teachers, technicians, and other professionals have been growing and will continue to grow.

In both parts of Yemen, the *ulama* and other religious figures with knowledge of Islamic law, theology, and tradition have had over the centuries an important role in shaping and protecting culture and in the selection and legitimization of local and central rulers. Since the start of the republican era, moreover, the political leaders of the YAR and the PDRY, secular as well as non-secular, have been careful to secure the endorsement of the *ulama* for their rule and policies whenever possible. Most recently, they went to great effort to get such an endorsement for the **1990 Constitution** of the ROY.

However, without much hierarchical organization, the Shii and Sunni *ulama* have rarely acted as a strong, independent political force over the centuries in Yemen and usually have been beholden to the rulers and submissive to their wishes. For example, the **Zaydi** branch of Shii Islam in Yemen in past centuries did not produce the strong religious organization and leadership that another branch of Shii Islam produced in Iran, most recently with creation of the Islamic Republic in 1979.

That said, modern **political Islam** has mobilized and made a political force of some of the *ulama* in Yemen in recent decades, initially through the Muslim Brotherhood. Since the mid-1970s, moreover, a number of them espousing **Wahhabism**, Salafism, or some other variant of militant Islam have become political forces in their own right. The **al-Houthi Rebellion** that erupted in 2004 was largely led by Shii *ulama* and their close associates, an occurrence not typical of Zaydi Islam.

Today, most Yemenis still live and work in the countryside in tiny villages, small towns, and provincial capitals. Rooted largely in pre-Islamic and early Islamic times, the traditional social system remains vital and continues to make itself felt even in the newest, most advanced parts of the modern sector of Yemeni society. It is complex, varying from one part of Yemen to another, and composed of two distinguishable but interdependent and even overlapping subsystems, tribal and nontribal, that meet primarily but not only in the marketplace (the *souk*)—whether at the *souk* in a town or city or the weekly *souk* at a rural crossroads.

There is also a long history both of Yemeni **tribes** sacking the cities and towns of the northern highlands and of tribal forays—even large-scale, permanent migrations—into richer agricultural areas to the south and west. The northern tribes pillaged **Sanaa** as recently as 1948, an event still fresh in the memories of both tribal and nontribal people. The tribes called the people living in the cities and towns *masakin* or *duafa*, the weak people; worse, they sometimes dismissed them as the "*souk* rats." At the same time, certain towns, market-places, and even some family compounds were accorded the status of sanctuary—places where tribesmen could safely interact and deal with other tribesmen or with nontribal persons. In North Yemen, such a place was called a ***hijra*** (in South Yemen, a *hawta*).

The cities and large towns of Yemen, the foci of commerce, the state, and Islamic law and learning, are and always have been largely nontribal and, in some ways, anti-tribal. These urban settings, even those in strongly tribal areas, consist mostly of nontribal or detrib-alized people, those for whom tribal ties have been replaced or at least diluted over the generations by other ties. Sanaa, though in the northern highlands and surrounded by tribes and tribal lands, is largely nontribal—and this is far more the case with **Taiz, al-Hudayda, Aden**, and the big towns of Wadi **Hadhramawt**. The "banyans," merchants and traders from the Indian subcontinent who came in growing numbers to Aden and **Mukalla** in the wake of the British due to the new opportunities afforded them by colonial rule, composed a distinct and important non-tribal social and economic segment of society.

For well over a millennium, much of the history of North Yemen has been one of tension if not conflict between the tribes, in their tribal lands under their customary law, and the urban centers. In the latter, the **imamate** or its equivalent resided and served to protect and promote Islamic law, morals, and faith. In much of South Yemen, the state-like ***dawla*** performed this same function. Although virtually all tribesmen in Yemen profess to be Muslim, their Islam tends to make big concessions to tribal law and custom, much of it pre-Islamic, a matter of concern over the centuries to the nontribal guardians of Islamic law and morals.

The traditional social order in Sanaa, as well as in the other urban centers of the northern highlands, the **Tihama**, the southern uplands, Aden and its environs, and Wadi Hadhramawt, existed alongside the tribal system. With variations from place to place, it consisted of a sharply stratified class system bounded on the top and bottom by castes. Still firmly in place in the 1950s, this system has changed only in part in the decades since. At the bottom of the heap are the *akhdam* (the servants) or, in parts of South Yemen, the *hujur*—a caste consist-ing of black descendants of **Ethiopians** or other Africans who toiled as street sweepers, popular musicians, unskilled manual workers, and other menials. Long concentrated in the Tihama, in recent decades they have spread around the country following available work. In South Yemen, alongside if not slightly below the *akhdam* were the *subyan* (s. *sabi*: houseboy), whose role was confined to personal service to and waiting upon the members of well-to-do families.

In contrast to efforts in socialist South Yemen after independence in 1967, little was done in the north after the 1962 Revolution to raise the status of the *akhdam* or to eliminate the barriers that prevent them from exiting this ascriptive group and its lot. Yemeni lore has the *akhdam* as descendants of the Ethiopian Christians who invaded Yemen shortly before the rise of Islam, suggesting that their present fate is a justifiable form of punishment. In any case, the *akhdam* provide a visual reminder of black Africa's closeness to and influence on Arab Yemen.

At the top of the traditional social pyramid was another caste, the **sayyids** (*sayyid*/p. *sada*), descendents of the Prophet Muhammad who, in the case of the Zaydi Shiis in North Yemen, traced this descent through Fatima and Ali, the Prophet's daughter and nephew and son-in-law. Zaydi law and political theory prescribed that all candidates for the imamate be Zaydi sayyids, and most of the imams had been drawn over the centuries from several great sayyid families. The sayyid caste in North Yemen also provided many of the small number of administrators and judges who served the imamate as well as many of the larger number of religious leaders, teachers, and scholars of Islamic law and theology. Some sayyid families were relatively well off, but many were quite poor.

In South Yemen, the **Shafii** Sunni descendants of the Prophet, also sayyids, occupied these same roles—those appropriate for persons with a monopoly of formal education and specialized knowledge. Many of them from Wadi Hadhramawt emigrated for a time to South Asia, Indonesia, East Africa, and elsewhere, sometimes becoming rich and famous as merchants and spiritual leaders, as well as gaining the political experience needed to increase their influence when they returned home. Whether comfortable or poor, and many were poor, the sayyids made up the aristocracy of Yemen, protected by the tribes and often used by them to mediate disputes and to issue judgments on legal and religious matters. In parts of Yemen, sayyids were known as "sharafs," another honorific title for a descendant of the Prophet.

In North Yemen, just below the sayyid caste was the qadi (*qadi*/p. *qudat*) class, a privileged group of "commoners" who occupied often very high and sensitive positions as judges, administrators, and advisers to the imam. The qadis were not eligible by reason of non-sayyid lineage to be imam and, as a consequence, the imams used members of the qadi class to protect themselves from and to make themselves less dependent upon strong sayyid pretenders to the imamate. Perhaps the best example of an able, powerful, and loyal qadi coupled to a strong imam is Qadi Abdullah **al-Amri**, Imam **Yahya**'s longtime "prime minister." In theory open to all who were schooled and became learned in Islamic law and theology, the qadi class tended over the centuries to be the preserver of an only slowly changing group of great qadi families, for example, the **al-Iryani** family in the 19th and 20th centuries.

Well below the qadi class in North Yemen and the sayyids in both Yemens came the nontribal peasants—small landowners, sharecroppers, or both—as well as the artisans, skilled workers, merchants, small traders, and shopkeepers. Often organized into guilds, this very heterogeneous group of "market (*souk*) people" was not closed and allowed for some upward and downward movement. Some families, through hard work, connections, and luck, went from rags to relative riches and even (but rarely) could rise into the qadi class. In the mid-20th century, most of the small number of "big" merchant and business families were Shafiis from the southern uplands of North Yemen—especially from Taiz—from Aden, or from Wadi Hadhramawt. Only in the 1980s did big merchant and business families come from the Zaydis in the northern highlands, and especially Sanaa.

Finally, just above the *akhdam* caste was the hard-to-escape *muzayyin* class, which consisted of families of butchers, barbers, bath attendants, messengers and, in some areas, growers of vegetables—occupations defined by the culture as dirty or otherwise demeaning. With the 1962 Revolution and the social change and turmoil that followed it, the chance of "unknown persons" rising to high posts from the *muzayyin* class, often via the military, increased, a most notable example being the YAR's first president, Abdullah **al-Sallal**.

The *muzayyin* as well as the *souk* people were especially looked upon with scorn or pity by the proud, independent, and armed tribesmen.

The hierarchical differences that existed in traditional Yemeni society were more matters of status and role than of wealth. For nearly all of recorded history, Yemen has been a very poor country in which the economy generated very little of the surplus required for great differences in wealth. There was more than a little substance to the egalitarian ethos of the tribes, and the economically poor tribal areas imposed an austere lifestyle on shaykh and follower alike. Just as the tribesmen had easy physical and social access to their shaykhs, ordinary folk in the cities and towns had ready access to the imam, sultan, governor, or other notables. The imam lived better than most other notables in the north—sayyids and qadis—and the latter groups lived better than the lower classes, but the differences were surprisingly small by modern standards. For proof, one has only to visit Imam **Ahmad**'s "palace" in Taiz, now a museum.

There was (and still are) a small number of great landowners in North Yemen, especially on the southern uplands and the northern Tihama, but they were often land poor. More typically, most peasants in most parts of the country had ownership or other rights to a parcel of land and often a water source. The exception that proves the rule of limited inequality is provided by the rich, landed sayyids and others of Wadi Hadhramawt who repatriated the fortunes they made in business abroad, built great houses, and lived conspicuously well.

SOCOTRA. Part of an archipelago in the Arabian Sea, Yemen's largest island is distinguished by its rugged beauty, biodiversity, and great number of endemic fauna and especially flora species. Indeed, Socotra is sometimes referred to as the Galapagos Island of the **Indian Ocean**, and its favored symbol is the unique, improbable-looking Dragon's Blood tree. This tree and many other trees, plants, and flowers—and an often stark, hostile, moon-like topography—give socotra an appearance both magical and otherworldly. Since ancient times, it was known for its prized frankincense, the red resin of the Dragon's Blood tree, and the medicinal sap of the Socotran Aloe.

Many of Socotra's unique features are attributed to its isolation and inaccessibility caused by seasonally violent seas, heavy winds and rain, dense mist, and the absence of any natural harbors. It is located east-southeast of **Mukalla** and about four times closer to the eastern tip of **Somalia** than to the coast of Yemen—indeed, it is geologically an extension of the **Horn of Africa**, the result of the drifting apart of the African and Asian landmasses. It is a long, narrow island of about 1,200 square miles, 238 miles long, with narrow coastal deserts, sandy beaches and coves, a partially verdant interior, and a mountainous granite spine consisting of the Haggier Mountains, which rise to 5,000 feet. The island is sparsely populated—about 50,000 inhabitants—and most of its people engage in farming, herding, and fishing. The physical features and skin color of Socotrans are more African than Arabian. Their language is unique and shared with the people of **Mahra**, the easternmost region of mainland Yemen.

The ruler of the Mahra Sultanate of Qishn and Socotra ruled from and resided on the island under British rule from the mid-19th to the mid-20th century. The island became a part of South Yemen when the British withdrew in 1967 and, with Yemeni **unification** in 1990, it became a part of the ROY. At different times over recent centuries, Socotra has been thought to be of strategic significance in terms of controlling access to the **Red Sea** and to the east coast of Africa. The **Portuguese** had a brief presence there in the early 16th century. During the latter half of the **Cold War**, its minor importance turned on the limited naval and air facilities that the PDRY made available to the **Soviet Union** and on the perceived significance of these facilities to a Soviet presence in the Indian Ocean and Africa. During the late 1990s, there were rumors about a deal between the **United States** and the ROY over military facilities on the island, but the nationalist outcry they produced and the fallout from the U.S.S. *Cole* **bombing** in 2000 squelched this talk.

In mid-1999, a new airport opened Socotra year-round to the outside world by way of **Sanaa** and **Aden**. Since then, the considerably increased talk and activity regarding Socotra have focused on its development as a major **tourist** destination featuring—and somehow protecting—its environment and unique biodiversity. One can only hope. As of 2008, facilities consisted of modest guesthouses in the town (and capital) of Hadibo and a number of well-located campsites. There is talk of major hotel construction, a source of anxiety among environmentalists. Ongoing highway construction with little regard to the environment is also a source of anxiety.

SOMALIA AND SOMALIS. The poor, thinly populated country that bounds the **Horn of Africa** south of and across the **Gulf of Aden** from the ROY and the southern entrance to the **Red Sea**. In colonial times, part of it was British Somaliland and the source of emigrants and livestock for a fast-growing **Aden Colony**. The British favored English-speaking Somalis for their reliability but, as with immigrants from India, they fared badly when South Yemen became independent in 1967.

Independent Somalia figured centrally in the overlapping regional and superpower competition to which the two Yemens were also subjected. In the **Cold War** game of musical chairs on the Horn in the second half of the 1970s, Somalia, headed by President Siad Barre, switched patrons from the **Soviet Union** to the **United States**, as the newly revolutionary **Ethiopia** did just the opposite. Somalia and Ethiopia then engaged in a short war, the **Ogadan Rebellion**. American strategists saw a connection between these conflicts involving Somalia and the **border war** between the two Yemens in 1979, seeing them as links in the revived Cold War's "arc of revolution."

Unification in 1990 corresponded to the overthrow of the Barre regime in Somalia and the start of nearly two decades of statelessness and intermittent civil war. For the ROY, this meant an increasing flow of Somalis fleeing the conflict and landing on its southern shores. Desperate Somali refugees saw Yemen as the first step to a future in the Gulf or in Europe, but only a minority of them made it beyond Yemen. The flood of refugees increased in years of the new millennium, the some washing up dead on the beaches and many more ending up in refugee camps or elsewhere in Yemen. In 2008, some 50,000 crossed the Gulf of Aden to Yemen, twice the number of in 2007; the pattern persisted in 2009.

Traveling in the opposite direction, arms, petroleum products, and other goods moved in the opposite direction, smuggled by persons who often had connections to the government or military in the ROY. In addition, Somalia's unending chaos, conflict, and poverty bred a new occupation on the Gulf of Aden: piracy. With the new century, pirates based in Somalia began preying upon the commercial traffic that entered the Gulf of Aden and moved to and from the Red Sea. This reached epidemic proportions in 2008 and 2009, attracting the world's attention and regional and international efforts to curtail it.

In addition, with **9/11** and the **War on Terror**, the situation in stateless Somalia took on new significance, especially to the United States, which believed, among other things, that al-Qaida members involved in the U.S. embassy bombings in Kenya and Tanzania in 1998 enjoyed sanctuary in Somalia. In 2006 and 2007, the rise and then ouster of the Islamic Courts Union (ICU) from Mogadishu and southern Somalia—the latter with a big assist from invading Ethiopian forces backed by the material support of the United States—served to regionalize the conflict. Late 2007 saw the revival of the ICU, the rise of the more militant al-Shabab group, and a renewal of fighting among Somali factions. The withdrawal of Ethiopian forces in early 2009 did not fundamentally change this situation. Although Ethiopia, **Eritrea**, and many of the Somali groups continued to view this as a regional conflict, the United States tended to cast it in terms of the War on Terror and to act accordingly. *See also* RED SEA AND HORN OF AFRICA SECURITY.

SOUTH ARABIA. A vague geographic designation that has been defined largely according to western academic conventions. "South Arabian studies," which emerged as a discipline in the 20th century, was confined largely to the languages, history, and artifacts of the people of the several pre-Islamic trading kingdoms that occupied what was in recent years the two Yemens, **Asir**, and **Oman**'s **Dhufar** province. Robert Serjeant was the British scholar who did as much as, if not more than, anyone else to define and advance South Arabian studies, as well as the study of modern Yemen, through his teaching and publications over the four decades following World War II.

Those forced to deal with the politics and the political geography of the 20th century—such as British colonial officers, political analysts, and academics—tended to distinguish among "Yemen," "**Aden**," and "South Arabia." The last of these was usually equated with the **Aden Protectorates**, allowing for a distinction between them and both Aden proper and **imamate** Yemen (and, later, the YAR). However, the term has also been used to encompass the territories of both modern Yemeni states, as has the term "Southwest Arabia."

SOUTH ARABIAN LEAGUE (SAL). Formed in 1951, and one of the first modern political groups in South Yemen, the SAL advocated the union between **Aden Colony** and the **Aden Protectorates** to create a single South Arabian state independent from **Great Britain**, one that at some future date could unite with North Yemen. First known formally as the League of the Sons of South Arabia, the SAL was led by the head of the prominent **al-Jifri** family of **sayyids** from **Lahej**, Sayyid Muhammad al-Jifri, and by Sheikhan al-Habshi from the **Hadhramawt**. Its principal backer was the young sultan of Lahej, Ali ibn Abd al-Karim **al-Abdali**, who aspired to be the ruler of the proposed state.

The call for an inclusive independent South Arabian state, and the suggestion of union with North Yemen, made the SAL anathema to the British in **Aden** and London, especially after Sultan Ali fell under the spell of **Egypt**'s President Gamal Abdul **Nasser** and his radical brand of Arab nationalism. Actually quite conservative, the SAL was equally anathema both to the other traditional rulers of the major protectorate states and to the more modern urban politicians of Aden, both of whom recoiled at the idea of a South Yemen led by the **Abdali** rulers of Lahej. Very much at the center of political talk and action in South Arabia in the 1950s, the SAL was marginalized politically by the end of the decade. Its leadership was forced into exile in Cairo and soon came under the material support and patronage of a **Saudi Arabia** worried about developments in South Yemen. In 1990, the aristocratic and well-to-do al-Jifri family and its organization, renamed the **League of the Sons of Yemen** and led by Abd al-Rahman Ali al-Jifri, climbed out of the dustbin of political history and involved itself in the newly formed ROY.

SOVIET UNION. The only non-regional country to have a major impact on both Yemens, the Soviet Union was the cautious, even reluctant, patron upon which the PDRY became almost totally dependent in the 1970s and 1980s, as well as a major provider of economic and military assistance to the YAR from shortly after the **1962 Revolution** through the 1980s. This Soviet involvement helped to focus the attention of the **United States** on the Yemens and to make them a minor theater of the global **Cold War**. The collapse of the Soviet Union at the end of the 1980s, causing the PDRY to lose its patron, was one of the two or three most important changes that made Yemeni **unification** possible in 1990.

STARK, FREYA. *See* TRAVELERS TO YEMEN.

STATE-BUILDING AND STATE–SOCIETY RELATIONS. *See* ECONOMY AND POLITICAL ECONOMY; AL-IRYANI AND AL-HAMDI REGIMES AND TRANSITION PERIOD; SALIH REGIME AND ERA; AL-SALLAL REGIME AND ERA.

STATISM AND STATIST IDEOLOGIES. *See* IDEOLOGY AND POLITICAL IDEAS, MODERN.

STOOKEY, ROBERT. The **United States** foreign service officer who, after serving as charge d'affaires in North Yemen before and during the first several months of the **1962 Revolution**, gave up a diplomatic career for a scholarly one and went on to write the first—and still best (in English, at least)—political history of North Yemen from early pre-Islamic times to the mid-1970s, as well as a number of other works on the Yemens and other states of the **Arabian Peninsula**.

SUBAYHI TRIBE AND REGION. The relatively small and very highly fragmented tribal grouping living in the small desert region, the Subayhi, at the westernmost tip of South Yemen between **Bab al-Mandab** and **Lahej**. The resource-poor area lacked the wherewithal to support its own *dawla*, with the result that the Subayhi tribes were usually forced into the orbit of the **Abdali** sultanate of Lahej.

SUBSIDIES. *See* SMUGGLING; IMF/WORLD BANK REFORMS.

SUDAN. Across the **Red Sea** on the **Horn of Africa**, the Sudan is Yemen's nearest non-peninsular Arab neighbor and has been tied to the YAR, PDRY, and now the ROY by regional strategic interests since the mid-1970s. In 1977, President Ibrahim **al-Hamdi** hosted the **Taiz Summit** on Red Sea Security, bringing together the presidents of Sudan, **Somalia**, and the PDRY. This proved something of a non-starter and, in any case, al-Hamdi was assassinated that same year. During the 1990s, the **Salih regime** went out of its way to show support for the al-Bashir regime when it was under international pressure over the civil war in the south. The ROY supported the regime in the mid-1990s when it was under the influence of militant Islamic cleric

Hasan al-Turabi and provided a sanctuary for Usama **bin Laden,** then a refugee from **Saudi Arabia** and in the process of creating al-Qaida.

Early in the new millennium, more than a quarter century later, President Ali Abdullah Salih initiated the **Sanaa Forum for Cooperation,** which brought together annually the presidents of Ethiopia, Sudan and, more recently, Somalia, for the purpose of addressing **Red Sea and Horn of Africa strategic issues.** The forum gave qualified support to the Sudan and President Omar Bashir as the Darfur issue heated up between 2007 and 2009.

In the 1970s and 1980s, the Sudan played a largely non-political role in the development of the less-developed North Yemen, providing many teachers, legal experts, and economists. Many Yemenis claimed that they and the Sudanese liked each other and worked especially well together. This may be because both peoples were near the bottom of an old Arab sociocultural pecking order and because both countries were relatively poor, underdeveloped, and on the periphery of the Arab world.

SUEZ CANAL. The man-made waterway in **Egypt** that connects the **Red Sea** to the Mediterranean Sea. Its opening in 1869 transformed **Aden** from a minor regional port and military outpost in the British Empire into a major strategic link and one of the busiest and most important ports in world trade and commerce. Moreover, in the second half of the 1950s, Aden was greatly expanded when it was chosen to serve as **Great Britain**'s major defense outpost "East of Suez." Egyptian president Gamal Abdul **Nasser** had nationalized the canal and forced Britain to give up its military facilities in the Canal Zone. In the mid-1960s, with effects just as dramatic for Aden, budgetary constraints caused Britain to decide against maintaining its forward position there and, indeed, to end its long presence in South Yemen.

The **Arab–Israeli conflict** played a big part in the Suez Canal's impact on Aden in the second half of the 20th century. There was the blockage and closure of the canal to traffic during the Suez War in 1956. Far more consequential, the blockage and much longer closure as a result of the Six-Day War in 1967—the year South Yemen became independent—largely ended Aden's role as a major world port and caused great economic difficulties for South Yemen and its new regime.

By contrast, the Suez Canal's first century had little impact on insular, isolated North Yemen, this despite the great increase in traffic up and down the Red Sea shipping lanes along the full length of its desert coast. However, the canal did figure significantly in the development, growth, and increased activity of **al-Hudayda** as a regional port after the **1962 Revolution**. Al-Hudayda was a major beneficiary of the reopening of the Suez Canal after the Camp David peace accord between Egypt and Israel in 1979.

SUFAN, AHMAD MUHAMMAD. Minister of planning and international cooperation in the **al-Iryani** government (1998–2001) and in both **Bajammal** governments beginning in 2001. In addition, beginning in 2003, he was deputy prime minister. He had been minister of industry from early 1996 to 1998. Sufan became known as a man who could seize opportunities and get things done, and in the middle of the first decade of the 21st century he was picked by some to be the next prime minister. However, in early 2006, he was among several senior ministers purged in a major cabinet reshuffle, in his case amid rumors of serious corruption. In late 2006 and early 2007, after the 2006 presidential **elections**, Sufan's name again came up as the possible head of a new government, but he did not get the call.

Sufan is from one of **Sanaa**'s wealthiest **Zaydi** families. His father prospered as customs collector at the **Rahida** border crossing with South Yemen in the time of the imamate; after the **1962 revolution**, he acquired great wealth through property in expanding Sanaa and its growing suburbs. Sufan studied economics at Leeds University in **Great Britain**, 1976–1981, and later in the **United States**.

SUFI ISLAM AND SUFIS. *See* RELIGION AND RELIGIOUS GROUPS IN YEMEN.

SULAYHID DYNASTY AND ALI BIN HASAN AL-SULAYHI. The **Ismailis** dynasty that ruled virtually all of Yemen in the name of the **Fatimid** Caliphate in Cairo for more than a century, from about 1040 to about 1150. The dynasty was founded by Ali bin Hasan al-Sulayhi, a very able ruler with great military and diplomatic skills, who conquered and governed Yemen over three decades, firmly establishing Ismaili rule in Yemen. He killed the **Zaydi imam** and stopped the Zaydis and their previously ascendant movement for a century.

Murdered in 1067, he was succeeded by his able son, al-Makarram, who expanded the kingdom to its maximum geographic extent, from the **Hijaz** in the north to **Dhufar** in the east. After only several years of vigorous rule, al-Makarram retired from public life and left the day-to-day running of affairs to his extraordinary wife, Queen **Arwa**, who ruled for another half century. The Sulayhid dynasty disintegrated rapidly just before and after her death in 1137. Despite the overlordship of the Sulayhids to the north, the Manid dynasty, based in **Aden**, had prospered and enjoyed Queen Arawa's considerable autonomy during reign.

SULTANATE OF MUSCAT AND OMAN. *See* OMAN, SULTANATE OF.

SULTAN IBN ABD AL-AZIZ, PRINCE. *See* AL-SAUD (BAYT SAUD).

SUMARA PASS. Halfway between **Sanaa** and **Taiz**, the main pass that one crosses when going from the northern highlands to the southern uplands of North Yemen. Featuring a precipitous descent and breathtaking views, the pass marks the great climatic, geographical, and cultural divide between "upper Yemen" and "lower Yemen"—the arid, austere, closed, and parochial highlands of the **Zaydi** tribal north and the humid, green, warmer, socially more open **Shafii** peasant south. This caricature notwithstanding, the changes are palpable and enliven the senses as you drive south from **Yarim**, cross the pass, and drop down into **Ibb** province, the "green province." The view down and south is always worth the trip.

SUNNI ISLAM IN YEMEN. *See* RELIGION AND RELIGIOUS GROUPS IN YEMEN; SHAFII (SHAFAI) SUNNISM; ZAYDIS AND SHAFIIS IN POLITICS AND SOCIETY.

SUPREME PEOPLE'S COUNCIL. *See* PEOPLE'S DEMOCRATIC REPUBLIC OF YEMEN (PDRY).

SUPREME YEMENI COUNCIL (SYC). The main institutional embodiment of the revived Yemeni **unification** process in the 1980s, the SYC was formed by the heads of state of the two Yemens at the **Aden** summit in late 1982. It served thereafter as the vehicle for the fruitful, nearly semiannual summits of YAR president Ali Abdullah **Salih** and PDRY chairman **Ali Nasir** Muhammad al-Hasani until the overthrow of the latter after the **13 January events** in 1986. The SYC and its activities were made possible by the ending early in 1982 of the PDRY-supported **National Democratic Front rebellion** against the YAR. In addition to the two heads of state, the SYC consisted of a Joint Ministerial Committee and a Secretariat. Although the SYC was charged with developing and implementing specific steps toward unification, its efforts to normalize and strengthen inter-Yemeni relations were seen by some as actually an alternative to—rather than a means to—the risky, highly unlikely, and even undesired goal of Yemeni unification. Suspended in early 1986, efforts by the SYC to improve inter-Yemeni relations or achieve unification were not revived until 1988 after another summit and the **4 May agreements** a little more than a year before the definitive step toward unification was taken in the fall of 1989.

AL-SUSWA, AMAT AL-ALIM (1958–). Appointed in 2003 to the ROY's new post-election government, she became the second **woman** to be a minister in the ROY and the first minister of the newly created Ministry of Human Rights. Al-Suswa previously attracted attention when she became ROY ambassador to the Netherlands. Active, visible, and respected as minister over the next three years, she was appointed at the end of 2005 as director of the United Nations Development Program's Arab Program and as assistant to UN Secretary General Kofi Anan. Born in **Taiz** and married with two children, Al-Suswa earned a BA and an MA in communications in Cairo and the **United States**, respectively.

SYRIA. Usually to the left of the Arab mainstream under **Baath Party** rule since the mid-1960s, Syria was more the natural ally of the PDRY than of the YAR. Their shared refusal to compromise on issues of Zionism and Western imperialism usually overrode differences caused by the pan-Arabism of the Baath Party and the internationalism of the PDRY's **ideology** of scientific socialism. In addition, they were united in the 1970s and 1980s by their antipathy for the Baath regime of **Iraq**, a matter that led both of them to lean toward **Iran** in the **Iraq–Iran War**. For their part, the YAR and Syria have managed to maintain fairly good relations since the late 1960s despite their different degrees of militancy and the close ties between the YAR and Iraq since 1979. Since Yemeni **unification** in 1990, Syria and the ROY have been on very good terms. Still, neither is all that important to the other.

– T –

TAHIRIDS. The dynasty of Yemeni notables from the Banu Tahir, which usurped power from the long-reigning **Rasulids** and then held sway from **Aden** over most of South Yemen and much of North Yemen from the mid-15th century until the second decade of the 16th century. Its forces were then defeated in rapid succession by the **Mamluks** of **Egypt** and the ascendant **Ottoman Turks**. Al-Zafir Amir bin Tahir was the first Tahirid sultan and the founder of the dynasty; al-Zafir Amir bin Abd al-Wahhab, defeated by both the Mamluks and the Ottomans, was the last.

TAIF, TREATY OF. The peace treaty of mid-1934 ending the war between Imam **Yahya**'s Yemen and **Ibn Saud**'s Kingdom of **Saudi Arabia** that required the defeated imam to suspend for 40 years claims to **Asir**, **Najran**, and **Jizan**. In return, the advancing Saudi forces withdrew from **al-Hudayda** and other towns and positions on the **Tihama** south of Jizan. The treaty led to the demarcation of the **Saudi–Yemeni border** from just north of Midi on the **Red Sea** coast eastward to a point just south of the oasis of Najran. The suspension of Yemen's claims was renewed at the Saudis' insistence by Prime Minister Abdullah **al-Hajri** in 1973, opening the way to sizable Saudi aid and to the Saudi–Yemeni patron–client relationship—and to protests by Yemeni nationalists against al-Hajri's action. The treaty's suspension of claims, rather than their total renunciation, provided for some Yemenis a legal basis for continuing to claim the region north of the present border, the "three lost northern provinces."

These claims were put to rest with the Saudi–Yemeni **Border Agreement of 2000**, the western portion of the border closely following the line drawn in the 1930s.

TAIZ, CITY AND PROVINCE OF. Taiz province, embracing the **Hujariyya** region is, with **Ibb** province, the heart of the **Shafii** south of North Yemen, and the city of Taiz is its soul. The southern uplands of Taiz province, at a few thousand feet, have a more temperate climate and more rainfall than do the northern highlands, and agriculture in the province supports a much larger, denser population than in the highlands.

In the past, the city of Taiz was an important center of political power in Yemen, especially under the **Rasulids** from the mid-13th to the mid-15th century and, more recently, when Imam **Ahmad** chose to base the **imamate** there between 1948 and 1962. Linked since the early 20th century by an increasing flow of workers, merchants, and students to a growing **Aden**, and then through Aden to the outside world, Taiz was far more a part of world commerce and in touch with the modern world and its ideas than was **Sanaa**. By the 1940s, it had become the hotbed of modernist, republican, and even revolutionary views in the Yemen ruled by Imams **Yahya** and Ahmad.

Through the 1970s, Taiz was compared favorably to Sanaa in importance, especially by "patriotic" Shafiis from Taiz and its region. By the 1980s, however, it was clearly outstripped in size and political importance by Sanaa and in commercial importance by both Sanaa and **al-Hudayda**; with Yemeni **unification** in 1990, it was further challenged in importance by Aden. As part of this process, its basic **infrastructure**—roads, water, and electricity— was allowed to degrade. Still, in 2005, Taiz remained a major center of business and light industry. Its links to Aden, and Aden's revival as an economic center, may enhance its position in the ROY. Just as easily, however, it may be bypassed by a new al-Hudayda–Sanaa– Aden axis.

In any case, the Taiz of old is no more. Within defining walls and highlighted by great whitewashed mosque minarets and domes, its back pressed against **Jabal Sabr**, Taiz was a jewel of a small Arab Islamic city. Today, its old boundaries breached; it is an ugly sprawl. But it still has Jabal Sabr, the well-watered, cloud-topped mountain that towers over the city and protects it from the south, rising abruptly several thousand feet to a height of nearly 10,000 feet. It is perhaps best known for its outspoken and independent-minded, as well as beautiful, colorfully clothed, and unveiled **women**—the Jabal Sabr women—who come down the mountain each day to sell **qat** and other goods. Made accessible almost to its top by a new paved road, the mountain with its breathtaking views, especially north and down to the city below, became a place for recreation and relaxation after 2000 for **tourists** as well as Yemenis.

TAIZ SUMMIT, 1977. *See* RED SEA AND HORN OF AFRICA SECURITY ISSUES.

TAJAMMU WAHDAWI. *See* AL-JAWI, UMAR.

AL-TALIA. *See* VANGUARD PARTY (AL-TALIA).

TALIBAN. *See* AFGHANISTAN AND "AFGHANI ARABS."

TARIM. The large town in Wadi **Hadhramawt** to the east of **Sayyun** in which many of the holiest and wealthiest **sayyids** in the wadi lived, among them the **al-Kaf** clan and its most prominent 20th-century leader, Abu Bakr ibn Shaykh al-Kaf. Very dependent on the remittances of sayyid fathers and sons in business in such places as Singapore and Malaysia, Tarim fell on hard times during and after World War II, only to recover somewhat when its greater and lesser families redeployed their forces to the increasingly oil-rich Gulf.

Blessed with rich patrons, Tarim became famous for its buildings and builders—and for its great library of old books and manuscripts and its main mosque and minaret. At first glance, the massive, boxy, richly detailed Italianate-looking palaces of the al-Kafs and other great families appear to be mirages in this mostly austere setting. Some of these mud masterpieces are being restored and opened to the public, adding to Tarim's **tourist** appeal. It also remains a center of Islamic learning and instruction.

TASHIH. *See* NASIRITES AND NASIRITE PARTIES.

TAXES. *See* REVENUE AND TAXES.

TECHNOEXPORT. *See* OIL AND GAS EXPLORATION AND PRODUCTION.

TELEPHONE AND TELEGRAPH. *See* INFRASTRUCTURE DEVELOPMENT.

TERRORISM, ISLAMIC. *See* POLITICAL ISLAM, MODERN; WAR ON TERROR.

AL-THALAYA, LT. COL. AHMAD YAHYA. *See* 1955 COUP ATTEMPT.

THAMOUD. The small region, spartan trading center, and military outpost near the edge of the **Empty Quarter** in the **Jol** to the north of Wadi **Hadhramawt**. Still serving the needs of a scattered bedouin population, as it has since long in the past, the town became the focus of the unsuccessful search for oil in the Hadhramawt after World War II and before independence in 1967. Petroleum industry interest in the area around Thamoud revived in the late 1980s and the 1990s—and with the **border** agreement with **Saudi Arabia** in 2000—but with little to show for it in the new millennium.

AL-THAWR, ALI LUTF. A **Zaydi** from the northern highlands who was in government from the mid-1970s to the mid-1980s, usually as minister of economics. In that capacity, he fought for the establishment of an oil and soap factory in the **Hadda** suburb of **Sanaa**, justifying it as the northern equivalent to the **Hayl Saeed** oil and soap plant in **Taiz**. Some mark this as the beginning of the regime's successful "affirmative action" program for northern Zaydi businessmen long overshadowed by their southern **Shafii** counterparts. Al-Thawr subsequently joined the International Bank of Yemen and joined the expanded **Shura Council** in 2001.

THIRD FORCE, YEMENI. *See* YEMENI CIVIL WAR.

13 JANUARY EVENTS. The intraparty bloodbath beginning on 13 January 1986 in **Aden** in which the largely successful attempt by head of state **Ali Nasir** Muhammad al-Hasani to assassinate all his leading opponents before they got to him backfired terribly. The events resulted in the virtual decapitation of the ruling **Yemeni Socialist Party** (YSP), the flight into exile by Ali Nasir and his colleagues, and the assumption of power in Aden by a generally younger, lower-level group of YSP leaders. In addition, the escalation of the bloodbath to near civil war proportions over a 10-day period caused a great loss of life and property in and around Aden, the disruption of the PDRY's economy and development, and severely strained relations with the YAR. The steps toward good inter-Yemeni relations and even **unification**, which distinguished the brief Ali Nasir Muhammad era, were put on hold. In retrospect, however, the 13 January events did facilitate unification by weakening the PDRY and by eliminating from its top leadership all who could claim to be the equal of YAR president Ali Abdullah **Salih**—soon to be president of the ROY.

13 JUNE CORRECTION MOVEMENT. The PDRY and the YAR have each used variations of this term to denote a period of reform or renovation in the "revolutionary process"—in practice, a mid-course correction. The label "13 June Correction Movement" was used by Lt. Col. Ibrahim **al-Hamdi** and his colleagues to describe the coup that firmly but respectfully deposed Qadi Abd al-Rahman **al-Iryani** as YAR head of state on 13 June 1974. The label quickly fell into disuse, only to be revived with much fanfare by al-Hamdi exactly one year later, in 1975, to characterize the program that he had launched to force government and other key institutions to be less corrupt and more efficient and responsive to the needs of the people.

The new Higher Correction Committee was chaired by Ahmad Damash, a friend and political confidant of al-Hamdi, and was charged with creating and supervising a system of lower-level correction committees. Committees were set up in each of the provinces, and each of these, in turn, appointed many committees to study, evaluate, and recommend reform in the organization, staffing, and operations of every organization in the province. The Correction Movement was very active and visible in its first year, challenging and criticizing many individuals and groups, and held its first national conference in **Sanaa** at the end of that year, in June 1976. Its stated purpose was to decide the directions and methods of the movement and to instruct and generate enthusiasm among its new cadres.

Although the Correction Movement in the YAR did focus some attention on procedures and performance, it lacked the programmatic content of South Yemen's **22 June Corrective Move** of 1961, and it seemed to be losing steam well before the assassination of al-Hamdi in October 1977. Some thought that al-Hamdi's hidden agenda in reviving the movement was to build the infrastructure of a new political movement in support of his regime, but this remains a matter of conjecture. The movement did trigger a couple of self-serving, self-righteous witch-hunts and purges, and it did invite the question among cynics of, "who will correct the correctors?"

13 JUNE MOVEMENT. The small, non-Marxist reformist political grouping formed in 1978 by colleagues and followers of the assassinated YAR head of state, Ibrahim **al-Hamdi**, for the purpose of avenging his death and toppling the regime of his assassins. In the months after the failed **October 1978 coup attempt**, which involved some of its members, the 13 June Movement became part of the two-year-old **National Democratic Front**. Colonels Abdullah **Abd al-Alim** and Mujahid **al-Quhali** were among the movement's most prominent members.

30 NOVEMBER (ADEN) AGREEMENT. The agreement reached in **Aden** in late 1989 by YAR President Ali Abdullah **Salih** and PDRY leader Ali Salim **al-Baydh** under which the leadership of the two Yemens agreed to political **unification** over the next year. The agreement prescribed that the December 1981 draft unity constitution, pretty much left on the shelf since its completion eight years earlier, would be submitted to ratification by the legislatures and then to popular referenda in the two parts of Yemen. This was to take place within two successive six-month periods and be completed by the end of November 1990. If the new constitution was approved, then the "Republic of Yemen" would be proclaimed, the constitution declared in force, and a transitional government put in place in the new capital, **Sanaa**. This government was to remain in place only until early elections for an all-Yemen legislature were conducted, a president selected, and a regular government formed. Finally, the **Joint Committee on a Unified Political Organization** was charged with the task of coming up with a proposal for the organization of political life in a united Yemen. The announcement of the 30 November Agreement electrified the two parts of Yemen and surprised most non-Yemenis who thought they knew Yemen—leaving some in disbelief.

TIHAMA AND THE TIHAMA DEVELOPMENT AUTHORITY. The Tihama is the long, narrow, and flat coastal desert between the **Red Sea** and the foothills of North Yemen's abruptly rising mountains, 20 to 40 miles wide and running from well north of ROY's border with **Saudi Arabia** south to **Bab al-Mandab**. Near sea level, it constitutes a distinct region of Yemen—one distinguished by its hot, humid, almost rainless climate and by a variant of Yemeni culture and society greatly influenced by nearby black Africa. **Al-Hudayda** and all of the other ports of North Yemen are on the Tihama, and the region depends heavily upon fishing, shipping, and other maritime activities. The Yemeni highlands have usually dominated and ruled the Tihama over the centuries, and the people of the highlands have tended to regard themselves as superior to the Tihamis, in part, it seems, on racial grounds and even to the point of questioning their identity as "true Yemenis." In South Yemen, the littoral running east from Bab al-Mandab the full length of the country is essentially a much narrower extension of the Tihama.

Most of the Tihama is inhospitable, even uninhabitable. Life is highly concentrated on the margins, at the base of the foothills and on the banks of the stream beds—the **wadis**, where agriculture is possible—and on the coast in ports and fishing villages reached by groundwater that also supports palm groves. Nevertheless, vast, mountain-fed aquifers and surface runoff from the mountains during the rainy seasons historically have made the Tihama the area of greatest agricultural potential in Yemen. This bounty was contingent upon building and operating extensive systems of dams, canals, and pumps. This has been the central task of the Tihama Development Authority (TDA), the umbrella organization created in the early 1970s with international financial and technical support to plan and supervise the integrated agricultural development of the several major wadis on the Tihama. Beginning with the Wadi **Zabid** project, which began before the TDA's creation, the TDA exhibited over the decades a degree of continuity not common to development activities in Yemen and has learned from past successes and failures.

TIMNA. *See* TRADING KINGDOMS, SOUTH ARABIAN.

TOTAL OIL COMPANY. Present in Yemen for more than 20 years, the Total Oil Company of France became, mostly by virtue of its 39.6 percent stake in the big liquefied natural gas project, the leading foreign investor in Yemen by 2007. Total is the operator of YemenLNG and shares ownership with the **Hunt Oil Company**, two Korean companies, and the Yemeni government. (ExxonMobil, an original participant in 1997, dropped out in 2002.) Exports of gas began in late 2009. Total is also involved in about 12 percent of Yemen's **oil** output. It is the operator of a producing block in **Masila** and is a partner in the Jannah Block in **Marib**, in which Hunt Oil is the operator.

TOURISM. Yemen's great potential for wealth and renown through tourism has been matched by the barriers and frustrated efforts to realize that potential during the last quarter of the 20th century and the first decade of the 21st century. The potential was multiplied by Yemeni **unification** in 1990. Among the attractions is the surprising natural beauty of this rugged desert- and sea-bounded corner of the **Arabian Peninsula**. Added to this is the human imprint, including the still-maintained green hillside terraces, the otherworldly flora and fauna of **Socotra**, the architectural legacy of the past millennium, and archaeological evidence of earlier millennia. Perhaps above all are Yemen's magnificent and varied urban settings: **Sanaa, Saada, Aden, Taiz,** the tri-cities of Wadi **Hadhramawt**—**Shibam, Sayyun,** and **Tarim**—and even the ports of **al-Hudayda, al-Mukha,** and **Mukalla.**

Given its emphasis on building socialism, and without the help of the imperialist West, tourism and its promotion was not a priority for the PDRY in the 1970s and 1980s. By contrast, the YAR saw value in tourism and sought to promote it in the mid-1970s and thereafter. Both the amateurish effort at promotion and the inadequate **infrastructure** for tourism—from hotels to tourist agencies—was symbolized by the historic but broken-down Ministry of Tourism on the western extension of Tahrir Square. Those who ventured to Yemen were mostly those seeking adventure and a new frontier of tourism.

With Yemeni **unification** in 1990, national pride and economic needs led to a new emphasis on tourism. Efforts in the last decade of the 20th century and thereafter to devote thought, effort, and funds to a major expansion of tourism were severely compromised by a series of formidable obstacles: the **War of Secession** in 1994, the epidemic of **hostage-taking** by the **tribes** throughout the 1990s and beyond, the killing of tourists by Islamic militants in 1998 and on a few occasions in the next decade, the episodic **al-Houthi Rebellion** between 2004 and 2009, and, renewed southern secessionist and violence from 2007 through 2009. Still, the belief persists that tourism will one day become a major—perhaps *the* major—source of wealth for Yemen.

TRADE. *See* ECONOMY AND POLITICAL ECONOMY; IMPORTS AND EXPORTS.

TRADE AND LABOR UNIONS. Trade unionism began in **Aden** in the early 1950s, especially with the Aden Trade Union Congress (ATUC), an umbrella organization for the city's growing body of organized workers, which was founded with a strong assist from Britain's Trade Union Congress and Labour Party. Under the leadership of Abdullah **al-Asnag**, the ATUC quickly showed its strong interest in politics by boycotting the 1959 elections to the newly created **Legislative Council**. In the 1960s, the ATUC was used by al-Asnag and his mostly Adeni allies in the struggle against both the British rulers and the rival **National Liberation Front** (NLF). When independence came in 1967, the victorious NLF took over the ATUC from rival nationalists and gradually extended it beyond Aden, renamed it the General Union of Workers, and transformed it into an instrument of what became the PDRY party–state, rather than an independent representative of labor.

Trade unionism began from scratch in North Yemen in **Taiz** after the **1962 Revolution**, and one of the first of the few groups to organize and make demands were the "modern" taxi drivers who motored within and among the growing urban centers of **Sanaa**, Taiz, and **al-Hudayda**. The nationwide organization that evolved over the next two decades, the General Federation of Trade Unions, never became an important instrument of either labor or state power.

With Yemeni **unification** in 1990, the trade unions of the two Yemens merged to form the General Federation of Yemeni Labor Unions. The federation flexed its muscles in the ROY's new pluralist setting by calling for a one-day general strike on 1 March 1992 to protest inflation and corruption. The general strike, the first in either Yemen's history, was widely supported, especially in the former PDRY. It had its most notable effect in disrupting the banks, airports, ports, and the petroleum industry. This sign of union strength and assertiveness in the early days of the ROY notwithstanding, the union movement did not play an increasingly prominent, decisive role in Yemeni politics and social action in subsequent years. This is a function of both the growing limits on open, pluralist politics after the **War of Secession** in 1994 and the lack of significant growth in the industrial sector of the economy in the years after unification. *See also* INTEREST (PRESSURE) GROUPS.

TRADE ROUTES, ANCIENT. The prominence of the sailors and merchants of **South Arabia** over past millennia is a function of a geographic location that made it possible for them to sweep east and west as well as north and south overland and by sea. Primitive sail technology and knowledge of the obliging **monsoon** winds in the **Indian Ocean** allowed them to sail east in one season and west in another—from East Africa and **Zanzibar** all the way to Indonesia. Indeed, the island and sultanate of Zanzibar attest to the pervasive cultural, socioeconomic, and political influence of the sailors, traders, merchants, and rulers of South Arabia over two millennia on East Africa. This activity was first recorded early in the Christian era in the book by an unknown mariner, *Periplus of the Erythraean Seas*.

Regarding overland trade, domestication of the camel and the culture of the desert made it possible for merchants to travel north and south on the caravan route between the ports of South Arabia and the rich markets of the Nile, the Mediterranean basin, and Mesopotamia. This east–west and north–south flow accounted for much of the world's commerce in **incense**, spice, and other luxury goods, especially from about 1500 B.C. to A.D. 500. The "Frankincense Trail" started from **Dhufar** and the port of Qana on the **Arabian Sea** near Bir Ali and arced west and north to Wadi **Hadhramawt** and then along the edge of the desert across South Arabia to **Najran**, Petra, and prosperous points north, west, and east. Among the most valued goods carried over this caravan route were the myrrh of South Yemen and the frankincense of Dhufar and **Somalia**. Like gems on a necklace, astride and in control of the route were the prosperous **trading states**: Awsan, Main, **Saba**, Qataban, and Hadhramawt.

However, **Rome** absorbed **Egypt** in the middle of the first century B.C., and within a century the Romans were making use of the ports and sea lanes of the **Red Sea**. They soon learned the secret of the monsoon winds and used this knowledge to meet their demand for luxury goods on their own by sea, thereby causing the caravan routes and trading states of South Arabia to be bypassed and to decline.

TRADING KINGDOMS, SOUTH ARABIAN. The several states that controlled and thrived on the main overland **trade route**, the Frankincense Trail, that linked the coast of **South Arabia** to **Egypt**, the Fertile Crescent, and the Mediterranean world. They flourished in pre-Islamic times, from about 1500 B.C. to A.D. 500.

Awsan was the earliest of these states, and it extended from the edge of the desert in the interior, across the highlands, and south to the coast and **Aden**. Unlike the states that followed it, Awsan was oriented both toward the sea and maritime destinations and toward the overland route north to the Mediterranean basin. It reached its apex in about the seventh century B.C. The fact that the **Zanzibar** coast at the time of Christ was known in the north as the Ausanitic (Awsanitic) coast attests to its power and importance in trade centuries earlier. Awsan was swallowed up by Qataban, which was centered in Wadi **Bayhan** and Wadi **Harib** and ruled from the city of Timna. The state of Qataban owed its prosperity, in addition to its location on the Frankincense Trail, to its highly developed system of spate irrigation. It rose and fell in power and reach, and did so more than once, between several centuries BC and about AD 400.

Saba (the Sabean Kingdom) was located in **Marib** on the edge of the desert and astride the Frankincense Trail a short distance after it turns north toward **Najran** and points north. Second only to Marib, the capital, **Sirwah** was another Sabean urban center. To the west of Marib, just off the road west to **Sanaa**, Sirwah today is a dramatic archaeological site that, located in a volatile tribal area, has neither been greatly studied nor become readily accessible to visitors.

The great prosperity and strength of Saba, which probably reached its peak between 500 and 200 BC, was based on its control of the passage of trade and on its extensive system of spate agriculture, which in turn depended upon the huge and fabled Marib dam. The Sabean leaders were vigorous expansionists, and the five major Yemeni trading states were united under a single Sabean regime for about a century around 400 BC

Main was the northernmost of the ancient pre-Islamic trading states of South Arabia, located in Wadi **al-Jawf** north-northwest of Marib on the Frankincense Trail and the edge of the desert. Its capital was Qarnaw, also called Main. It flourished from about 350–100 BC and, unlike the hegemons of neighboring Saba, the leaders of Main focused almost totally on the development and protection of the trade routes.

The prominence of the **Hadhramawt** state, the easternmost of the states, was based upon its spate irrigation agriculture and, more important, the abundance of locally available myrrh shrubs and some frankincense trees, as well as its proximity to frankincense-rich **Dhufar** and points east. Frankincense and other products were brought by boat to the Hadhrami port of Qana on the Arabian Sea near Bir Ali and then taken by caravan through Wadi Hadhramawt to **Shabwa** and points west and north.

TRANSPORTATION. *See* INFRASTRUCTURE DEVELOPMENT.

TRAVELERS TO YEMEN. Yemen, largely unknown and hard to visit, especially its northern interior, has attracted only a small number of travelers over the centuries. Perhaps because of the difficulties, many in this small band are fascinating and bigger than life. The unknown author of *Periplus of the Erythraean Seas*, a Greek from Alexandria, visited **Aden, al-Mukha**, and other Yemeni ports at the beginning of the Common Era. Most certainly a merchant or ship's captain who made many trips to and from these ports, he provides a vivid account of the activities of Yemeni sailors and traders during his era as well as over the previous several centuries. He talks about men from al-Mukha "who send thither many large ships using Arab captains," and notes that Aden had "convenient anchorages and watering places."

Coming forward to the first half of the 16th century, an Italian from Bologna, Ludovico de Varthema, traveled to North Yemen before the first **Ottoman** occupation and became the first European to describe **Sanaa**; he portrayed the state and society there as rich and well run. The first Britain to travel in Yemen was John Jourdain, an officer on a ship of the East India Company who was taken from Aden to Sanaa in 1609 and left in his journals a picture of Yemen during the first period of Ottoman Turkish rule.

The modern man who first gave the world a detailed description of much of Yemen in the 18th century was Carsten Niebuhr, the German surveyor and sole survivor of a several-member scientific expedition sent by the king of Denmark to Arabia in 1762. Traveling in Yemen from December 1762 until August 1763, Niebuhr and his ill-fated colleagues were the first Europeans to visit unknown Yemen for scholarly rather than commercial reasons. Losing colleagues to malaria along the way, he traveled down the **Tihama** to al-Mukha, across the Tihama and up to **Taiz**, and then on up to Sanaa, where he had an audience with the **imam**—and then finally back down to the **Red Sea** coast. Niebuhr had the account of his expedition published as *Travels through Arabia and Other Countries in the East* and then went on to live a long, unexceptional life in quiet obscurity. He was accompanied by a botanist, Peter Forsskal, who died and was buried in **Yarim**, one of the very few non-Muslims to be buried in North Yemen since the rise of Islam. Niebuhr later edited and had published Forsskal's detailed biological observations.

More than a century later, in 1868, the French epigrapher Joseph Halevy, visited **Sanaa** in 1868 and reported on the sad state of the city, the countryside, and the **Zaydi imamate** during the time just before the Ottoman Turks reoccupied Sanaa in 1871; he then exited Yemen by traveling north to **Najran**. Samuel M. Zwemer, a missionary from the Arabian Mission of the Dutch Reformed Church of America became the first American to visit the Yemeni highlands and Sanaa, in 1891 and again in 1894. The object of his trip had been Sanaa's **Jewish** community, which he reckoned to number 20,000 out of a total population of only 50,000. By this time, Sanaa and much of North Yemen were subject to the second Ottoman occupation. Visiting just 25 years after Halevy, the widely traveled Zwemer regarded Sanaa as the most flourishing city after Baghdad in all Arabia. Returning to his home in rural Pennsylvania, he wrote of Yemen and his visits.

In 1910, Charles Moser, the American consul in Aden, became the fourth American to penetrate the North Yemeni highlands. He had traveled north to investigate the violent death in **Manakha** of Charles F. Camp, a missionary who had settled there with his wife five years earlier, thereby becoming the second and third Americans to visit the highlands and the first two to reside there. Through his contacts and at least one *National Geographic* article, Moser went on to spread the word about Yemen's wonders to, among others, Charles R. Crane.

Heir to a bathroom-fixtures fortune, Crane is best known as co-leader of the King–Crane Commission, the mission sent by President Woodrow Wilson to former Ottoman possessions to gather the facts needed to apply his principle of self-determination at the Paris Peace Conference. In 1926, Crane, an enthusiast of exotic places and their rulers, visited North Yemen, struck up a friendship with Imam **Yahya**, and then hired Karl S. Twitchell, a mining engineer, and made a gift of his services to the imam. Twitchell, an American who had been working in Ethiopia, conducted six expeditions to Yemen between 1926 and 1932. He undertook a range of projects that included searches for mineral wealth, distribution of gifts of farming and industrial machinery, and assistance in the building of roads, experimental farms, and the **Arabian Peninsula**'s first steel truss bridge. Prophetically, he reported to Imam Yahya the possibility of oil under the desert east of Sanaa near **Marib**, a possibility that the imam refused to pursue out of fear that this would only bring western imperialism to Yemen.

Bringing a very different sensibility, Amin Rihani, the well-known Lebanese American writer, traveled to Yemen in the late 1920s and wrote evocatively about what he experienced on his way to and from Sanaa and about his encounters with Imam Yahya and other Yemenis. His *Arabian Peak and Desert* is marred somewhat by passages of purple prose and his sense of "mission" and condescension as an Arab, perhaps especially a Lebanese Arab, encountering "backward" Yemen and Yemenis.

Wyman Bury was a British political officer who, disguised and going by the name of Abdullah Mansur, traveled among the tribes and the statelets in the western interior of South Yemen—**Yafa,**

Fadhli, **Dhala**, and **Lahej**—in the first decade of the 20th century. He left one of the few written accounts of these places, their people, and their rulers—often uncomplimentary—during this decade.

In the mid-19th century, Baron Adolf von Wrede became the first European to explore the area from **Mukalla** to Wadi **Duan**, but this only took him about 50 miles from the coast and well short of the much larger Wadi **Hadhramawt**. Not until nearly 50 years later, in 1893, did Leo Hirsch become the first European to penetrate Wadi Hadhramawt and see its three big towns. In **Shibam** he was surprised by the wealth and by products from Italy, France, and Holland in the *souk*; in **Sayyun**, he met with a courteous, well-educated ruler; but in **Tarim**, the center of religious learning, he was hounded by a mob calling for his blood. Only months later, Theodore and Mabel Bent were the next two Europeans to visit the Wadi and to be surprised by the East Asian–based wealth, culture, and awareness of the outside world they found in this unlikely corner of Arabia. The Bents then traveled west through Fadhli and Yafa. In 1900, the book they published on their travels provided Europeans the first readily available account of the Wadi.

It was Freya Stark, the famous traveler and travel writer, who really made South Yemen and especially Wadi Hadhramawt available to a large readership. Beginning in the mid-1930s, she frequently visited North Yemen, as well as South Yemen and the Wadi. She often traveled unaccompanied and, in the case of the Wadi, was the first western woman to go there alone. She wrote much and with eloquence—accompanied by wonderful photos—of her experiences and of the places and people she visited. Published in 1936, *The Southern Gates of Arabia: A Journey in the Hadhramaut* is a classic of the genre. Among other books, she also wrote *A Winter in Arabia*. She died in 1993 at age 100.

H. St. John Philby, the British Arabist and explorer, traveled in the interior of South Yemen in the first half of the 20th century and wrote extensively about ancient and modern **South Arabia**. A resident for much of his life in **Jidda**, Saudi Arabia, it was Philby who in the mid-1930s introduced Charles Crane to another exotic person, Abd al-Aziz ibn **Saud**, the then quite poor ruler of the newly formed Kingdom of Saudi Arabia. In turn, Crane again hired Karl Twitchell and put him in the service of this new friend, Ibn Saud. Twitchell's survey and positive assessment of the oil prospects of Hasa province opposite Bahrayn were the first steps toward the momentous discovery later in the 1930s of what proved to be Saudi Arabia's fabulous oil reserves.

Hugh Scott, a scientist and traveler to North Yemen via Aden in the late 1930s, stayed for several months. His book *In the High Yemen*, published in 1942, and his other writings provide one of the most vivid and insightful pictures of political, economic, and social life in the latter years of Imam Yahya's long reign. The book also provides a scientist's careful, detailed description of the geology, geography, flora, and fauna of Yemen.

TREATY ARRANGEMENTS, PROTECTORATE. During the century after 1840, **Great Britain** concluded three types of formal treaties with the roughly two dozen states of **South Arabia** that came to be known as the **Aden Protectorate** states: treaties of friendship, treaties of protection, and advisory treaties. The first two types were concluded in the 19th century and differed primarily in the degree to which the later treaties of protection entailed somewhat greater British involvement in the affairs of a state's hinterland, usually on matters of security and the settlement of local disputes. This difference aside, these treaties were similar in that both provided for very little British involvement and exemplified the notion of indirect rule.

The first of the formal treaties of protection was the 1886 Treaty of Protection with the **Mahra** Sultanate of Qishn and Socotra. That was followed over the next several years by similar treaties with the rulers of the other statelets along the **Arabian Peninsula**'s southern coast, as well as with the major shaykhs of the tribal regions in the interior to the west. The latter were deemed crucial to the security and commerce of **Aden**. Designed to counter growing threats posed by the **Ottoman Turks** in North Yemen and by the other European imperial powers, these treaties, under which control of foreign policy was traded for British protection and modest subsidies, constituted a major step toward both the creation of the Aden Protectorates and the binding of Aden to its hinterland. Between 1886 and 1895, Britain signed treaties of protection with the **Aqrabis**, Lower **Awlaqis**, **Fadhlis**, **Hawshabis**, **Alawis**, Lower **Yafis**, and some of the **Wahidis**.

Most of these initial treaties were converted into the more intrusive advisory treaties beginning in the late 1930s. The latter involved the British much more deeply in the governance, socioeconomic development, and domestic affairs of the states, albeit in theory in an "advisory" role. These treaties fit and reflected the Colonial Office's new **"forward policy,"** a policy that called for the colonial power's very active role in the states. The first of these advisory treaties was signed in 1937 with the **Quaiti** ruler, Sultan Salih.

TREVASKI, SIR KENNEDY. *See* COLONIAL ADMINISTRATION AND ADMINISTRATORS.

TREVELYAN, SIR HUMPHREY. *See* COLONIAL ADMINISTRATION AND ADMINISTRATORS.

TRIBES AND THE TRIBAL SYSTEM. In Yemen, especially the former North Yemen, tribes and tribalism, rather than being mere vestiges of the past, are vital parts of the **social system** and continue to play determinant roles in the political as well as in the social and cultural spheres. The major spatial domains of the tribal system in Yemen are the hamlets and towns of the northern highlands of North Yemen and the mountainous knot north of **Aden** in South Yemen, although tribes are also evident on the maritime **Tihama**, on the **Jol** in the **Hadhramawt**, and in the arid eastern reaches of North Yemen.

Indeed, despite the tendency to characterize the highlands of North Yemen as "tribal" and the southern part of North Yemen and most of South Yemen as "peasant," tribes and tribalism are part of the cultural, social, and political landscape of nearly all regions of Yemen. However, what for centuries has distinguished the northern highlands from the other regions of the country is the importance, almost to the exclusion of anything else, of the tribe as a unit of identification and action and the great extent to which tribes can be mobilized and organized into larger tribal units when the interests of the tribal system or its constituent parts are at stake. By contrast, many residents of the southern uplands of **Ibb** and **Taiz** provinces or the Hadhramawt may claim a tribal lineage, but this often seems to be less important as a basis of personal identity than family, place of origin—a village, valley, or region—or some other attribute.

The tribal system is made up of a large number of greater or lesser units, each consisting of a tribal leader (a *shaykh*) and his tribal followers. Some units stand alone as separate tribes, but often several units are grouped together as the "sections" of a tribe headed by a "bigger" shaykh. In turn, a number of tribes and their shaykhs can be grouped together in a tribal confederation headed by a paramount shaykh or shaykh of shaykhs (*shaykh al-mashayikh.*) For example, most of the tribes of the northern highlands of North Yemen are grouped into two great tribal confederations, the **Hashid** and the **Bakil**, the former composed of some 7 tribes and the latter of perhaps 14, some quite small. Although varying over time in terms of internal cohesiveness and unity, the two groupings and their constituent parts have persisted in the same places for over a millennium.

Yemeni shaykhs, greater and lesser, have been preoccupied over the centuries with defending both the autonomy of the tribes in relation to nontribal authorities and the rights of their tribe within the tribal system. Often serious and prolonged, conflict between Yemeni tribes has been common, but tribes have not often conquered and occupied the lands of neighboring tribes, much less destroyed those tribes.

The shaykh represents and protects the members of his tribe in their dealings with other tribes and with the nontribal system. In the past, the tribesman could hardly think of being or acting outside his tribal unit, and this sense of dependence on tribe and shaykh has long been a key to tribal solidarity and the power of the shaykh. This way of thinking—and the strength of the tribes and their shaykhs—has declined to a considerable degree since the mid-20th century

Most tribesmen in most parts of Yemen are sedentary farmers, not camel-herding nomads. However, the sparsely populated, arid land on the edge of the **Empty Quarter** in South Yemen and the **Ramlat al-Sabatayn** shared by both Yemens is home to nomadic tribes principally engaged in animal husbandry. The Saar tribe is a major bedouin tribe in the northern reaches of the Hadhramawt, as are the Manahil and Bayt Kathir tribes. These nomadic tribes have declined in size and importance in recent years, in part because they were forced to give up their traditional roles as guardians and pillagers of trade routes, and they now constitute a tiny portion of the total population of unified Yemen.

TRIPARTITE ALLIANCE OF 1981. The stillborn treaty initiated by Muammar Qadhafi that included the PDRY, **Ethiopia**, and **Libya**, a banding together of disparate regional radicals. The alliance envisioned Libyan financial aid for its poor allies and military assistance from the other two if one of them were attacked. The alliance seemed to be a delayed response to the attempt in the late 1970s of conservative states such as **Saudi Arabia** and **Egypt** to dominate the **Red Sea**, and these states were quick to criticize the alliance. Oddly, the alliance was made at about the time that the PDRY under President **Ali Nasir** Muhammad al-Hasani was beginning to relax its confrontational posture toward the conservative and moderate states of the region.

TRIPOLI SUMMIT AND AGREEMENT, 1972. The summit meeting in late 1972 between YAR president Abd Al-Rahman **al-Iryani** and PDRY head of state Salim **Rabbiya Ali**, chaired by Col. Muammar Qaddafi, that reaffirmed the recent **Cairo agreements** and produced a more detailed agreement on the **unification** process and the desired final result. The agreement had a more radical flavor than the Cairo agreements and probably reflected Col. Qaddafi's input. The future ROY, with **Sanaa** as capital and Islam as state religion, would seek to achieve socialism and to create a national democratic government based on a "unified political organization," one modeled on **Libya**'s Arab Socialist Union. Procedurally, the agreement fleshed out the decision in Cairo to create several specialized **joint unification committees**. However, the Tripoli agreement was less specific than the Cairo one on timing, urging only that the joint constitutional committee report "as soon as possible" instead of requiring preparation of the new constitution within the next year. The Tripoli and Cairo agreements were the improbable "solution" to the 1972 **border war**.

TRUCIAL STATES. *See* UNITED ARAB EMIRATES (UAE).

TUBAN, WADI. Running north to south from near Mawiyah in North Yemen to **Lahej** in South Yemen, the **wadi** that provided the easiest and most direct route via **Rahida** between the port of **Aden** and **Taiz** and the rest of the interior of North Yemen. Use, control, and protection of the wadi route were matters of great concern over the centuries. Agriculture in the wadi was the source of much of the wealth that allowed the

Abdali sultanate of Lahej to exercise influence over Aden's hinterland out of all proportion to the size of the population under its control.

TURBA. The largest town and a district in North Yemen's **Hugariyya** region, due south of **Taiz** and perched on the edge of the great escarpment just before the land plunges a couple of thousand feet and then slopes down southeast to **Aden** and southwest to **Bab al-Mandab**. On clear nights from hilltops and the towers of fortress towns around Turba one can see both the glow of the lights of Aden and the flash of the beacon at Bab al-Mandab guiding ships to and from the **Red Sea**. The **Numan** family, a force in the politics of the Hugariyya for decades and into the 1970s, was based near Turba.

TURKS AND TURKEY. *See* OTTOMAN TURKS IN YEMEN.

TURNBULL, SIR RICHARD. *See* COLONIAL ADMINISTRATION AND ADMINISTRATORS.

26 SEPTEMBER REVOLUTION. *See* 1962 REVOLUTION.

22 JUNE CORRECTIVE MOVE. The label "22 June Corrective Move" was used by the left wing of the **National Liberation Front** (NLF) to describe its ouster of the head of state Qahtan **al-Shaabi** and the rest of the front's right wing in June 1969, an action that paved the way for implementation and elaboration of the revolutionary program adopted a year earlier in March 1968 by the Fourth Congress of the NLF. In fact, however, the NLF left was not in complete control, and discourse and debate over variations on the theme of **scientific socialism** raged until the ouster of moderate prime minister Muhammad Ali **Haytham** in August 1971. Thereafter, the regime was more completely subject to the uneasy co-leadership of Salim **Rabbiya Ali** and **Abd al-Fattah** Ismail. In terms of program, the 22 June Corrective Move called for a new phase of "popular democratic liberation." This involved a purge of suspect government and military apparatuses, land reform that included the seizure of land on the countryside owned by religious endowments and **"kulaks,"** or "feudalists," nationalization of residential property in the towns, and the extension of state control over all sectors of the economy.

TWITCHELL, KARL S. *See* TRAVELERS TO YEMEN.

– U –

UAE. *See* UNITED ARAB EMIRATES (UAE).

UBAR. The long-lost, fabled caravan city inland in **Dhufar** at the beginning of the Frankincense Trail not far from the source of that once-prized resin in the Qara Mountains, the location of which was probably discovered by an American-British-Omani expedition in 1991. The site suggested that something, possibly an earthquake, caused the city to collapse into vast limestone caverns, confirming ancient accounts. Ubar likely reached its apex early in the Common Era, in Roman times. In 1992, the same team uncovered another site that it thinks is Saffara Metropolis, an ancient trading center even closer to the valued **incense** and only seven miles inland from the ancient seaport of Moscha, discovered and excavated in the 1950s. If these are the sites of Ubar and Saffara Metropolis, then it would seem that archaeology has finally found the southeastern terminus of the ancient overland **trade route**. Moscha is only 15 miles east of the modern port of Salalah.

AL-UDAYN REGION. A town and a quite well-watered part of the southern uplands of North Yemen to the west of **Ibb** and north of **Taiz**. The name means "two sticks," and legend has it that al-Udayn is the place where both **coffee** and **qat** were first found in the wild and then cultivated by locals who came to enjoy their effects. The al-Jamai family, a **Shafii** family of shaykhs, has been a force in the region at least from late **Ottoman** times; its leaders included Ali Muhsin Pasha, Muhammad Ali Pasha, and Sadiq Ali Muhsin.

ULAMA **AND RELIGIOUS LEADERS.** *See* SOCIAL SYSTEM AND STRUCTURE.

UMAR, JARULLAH. *See* JARULLAH UMAR.

UMAYYADS. *See* ABBASIDS AND UMAYYADS.

UN. *See* UNITED NATIONS (UN).

UNIFICATION AGREEMENTS, 1972 AND 1979. *See* BORDERS; CAIRO AGREEMENTS ON UNIFICATION; KUWAIT AGREE-MENT OF 1979; TRIPOLI SUMMIT AND AGREEMENT, 1972.

UNIFICATION AND UNIFICATION PROCESS, YEMENI. In 1987, the YAR and the PDRY celebrated their 25th and 20th anni-versaries, respectively. On 22 May, 1990, roughly two and one-half years later, they ceased to exist as independent states when they merged into one, the ROY. *Wahida* unity had triumphed. The **1990 Constitution** was declared in force, a large transitional government was appointed, and the YAR's Ali Abdullah **Salih** and the PDRY's Ali Salim **al-Baydh** were elected president and vice president, respectively, by the transitional **Council of Deputies** just then con-stituted by merging the legislatures of the two Yemens. Even most of those Yemeni leaders who favored and expected Yemeni unification were surprised by this turn of events, having come by the late 1980s to assume a long time frame and an incremental process.

The unification process—and it was more this than a matter of reunification—was confounded by a contradictory political legacy: the ancient ideas of "the Yemen" (*al-yaman*) as a place and of being "Yemeni"—ideas shared by Yemenis and non-Yemenis alike—on the one hand, and two distinct modern histories, national political struggles, and resultant territorial states in the 20th century, on the other. Yemen had constituted a single political entity for only short periods over the past two millennia, the last occasion coming after the end of the first period of **Ottoman Turkish** rule in the 17th century. In these rare moments of unity, moreover, it was a matter of the sub-jugation and domination of one part of Yemen over the rest. Instead, for most centuries, Yemenis were divided among a few or many dif-ferent political units, much like the Germans and the Italians in the years before the creation of the German and Italian nation-states in the 19th century.

The goal of Yemeni unification was espoused by two strong imams in the 20th century and by most modern nationalists in both Yemens since the middle of that century. Moreover, during the second third of the 20th century, increased trade and labor migration between **Aden**

Colony, with its increasingly active port, and the southern part of North Yemen—**Taiz** and **Ibb** provinces, in particular—added substance to the old idea of one Yemen. They provided the buckle that increasingly joined together major parts of the two Yemens.

Diametrically opposed to this trend, however, the bisecting of Yemen by the **Anglo–Ottoman Line of 1904** served to foster the division of Yemen and the Yemeni people into what became two very different polities and two different political cultures, each with different political interests and preoccupations. This process actually began in earnest in the mid-19th century with the second Ottoman occupation of part of North Yemen and **Great Britain**'s seizure of Aden. On the one hand, the creation of a united and independent South Yemen in 1967 was the cumulative result of subsequent interactions between the British colonial rulers and both the Adenis and the notables of what came to be the **Aden Protectorates**. On the other hand, the creation of North Yemen resulted from the struggle until early in the 20th century between the Ottoman occupiers and a resurgent **Zaydi imamate**, the latter's efforts to extend its rule over all of Yemen through the 1950s, and the political fight to reform or abolish the imamate that began in the 1940s and ended with the **1962 Revolution**.

Although the struggles against the imams in the north and the British in the south seemed to many in the late 1940s to be two sides of the same Yemeni political coin, the YAR and the PDRY were destined to emerge out of what were mostly separate and qualitatively different political struggles. The attentions of the southerners focused on Aden and the British, whereas those of northerners focused on **Sanaa**, the Ottomans, and then the Zaydi imamate. Out of these histories emerged the ideas and realities of a North Yemen and a South Yemen—of the YAR and the PDRY. After their creation, moreover, each polity turned inward and followed a different political path. The result, rapidly achieved, was considerable political and socioeconomic differentiation. There evolved in the north a moderate if not conservative republicanism, whereas in the south there tumbled onto the scene the only avowedly Marxist–Leninist regime in the Arab world.

This tangle of cross-pressures fostered a confusing, shifting pattern of inter-Yemeni relations. Confounded from the start by the bad fit between state and nation, relations between the two Yemens swung wildly between conflict—even war, at the one extreme—and agreements for Yemeni unification at the other. Indeed, the 15 years that followed the creation of the PDRY in 1967 contained two major **border wars**, in 1972 and 1979, as well as the PDRY-backed **National Democratic Front (NDF) rebellion**, begun in the late 1970s against the Salih regime in the YAR. Both border wars ended improbably in agreements to unify. In each instance, the bid for unification proved to be a disguise that was quickly shed when it ceased to be useful to either or both sides.

The modern Yemeni unification process arguably begins with the 1972 border war, which ended with the **Cairo agreements on unification** and the **Tripoli summit and agreement**. These back-to-back agreements formally committed the YAR and the PDRY to the goal of unification and specified procedures to be followed. Thereafter, the **Kuwait agreement of 1979**, at the end of second border war, essentially restated the goal and spelled out the work of several joint unification committees and the approval process. Despite this last agreement, the NDF rebellion continued. Suppression of the rebellion by the Salih regime in 1982 and the ending of related conflict between the two Yemens ushered in a new era of improved inter-Yemeni relations. A major step taken at a summit in Aden in late 1982 was the creation of the **Supreme Yemeni Council** and its subsidiaries, the Joint Ministerial Committee and the Secretariat. These new institutions met and acted with vigor over the next three years. More important, however, this era was marked by practical, discrete steps toward greater economic and social cooperation and by close ties between the YAR's President Salih and the PDRY's President **Ali Nasir** Muhammad.

Given these personal ties, it was inevitable that inter-Yemeni relations would be strained by the **13 January events** in Aden in 1986, the bloodbath inside the ruling **Yemeni Socialist Party** (YSP) that caused President Ali Nasir and his followers to flee north to safety in the YAR. For two years after these events, the new leaders of the PDRY wrapped themselves in the legitimizing rhetoric of Yemeni unification, and the YAR just as adamantly refused to reciprocate in both word and deed—for example, refusing to revive the moribund Supreme Yemeni Council. For their part, the weak leaders in Aden refused to reconcile with Ali Nasir's followers and thereby ease the burden of the new refugees on the YAR.

A crisis erupted in late 1987 when this refugee problem combined with new tensions along the undemarcated border separating the YAR's oil field in the **Marib** region, discovered only in 1984, from the one found even more recently in the PDRY's **Shabwa** region. Amid reports that oil exploration teams were surveying in the disputed borderland, the dispute took a turn for the worse with both Yemens massing **armed forces** in the area in March 1988. In mid-April, a summit meeting was held between President Salih and the new secretary general of the YSP, Ali Salim al-Baydh. On 4 May, after another summit, the two leaders signed major inter-Yemeni agreements.

One of the **4 May Agreements** defused conflict over the borderland. It called for demilitarization of an 850-square-mile "neutral zone" between Marib and Shabwa, precise demarcation of the zone, and creation of a joint oil and mineral exploration and development company for the zone. Another agreement provided for the free movement of Yemenis between the two Yemens, a plan that was to involve joint border posts and require only a domestic identity card to cross the border in either direction. Finally, there was the agreement to revive the Supreme Yemeni Council, set a new timetable for the draft unity constitution, and form for the first time a body called for in the original 1972 unification agreement, the **Joint Committee for a Unified Political Organization**.

As in the past, the two Yemens in May 1988 used the sweeping rhetoric of, and small steps toward, unification to camouflage an exercise in crisis management and problem solving. The real achievement was the defusing of a border dispute that had threatened to escalate into serious fighting. Only days after the agreements, opposing forces were withdrawn, and the tensions of the previous months quickly subsided. The oil ministers promptly met to create the joint company that was to operate in the neutral zone. Plans were quickly prepared to open the common border. This program went into effect on schedule in July, and it proved immensely popular with the people of both Yemens.

Subsequent events emphasized further the revival of the inter-Yemeni cooperation that had begun in 1982. The two Yemens agreed in late 1988 on a major project to construct a Taiz–Aden link between their electrical power grids. The new joint venture for the neutral zone, named the Yemen Company for Investment in Oil and Mineral Resources, began operations swiftly in early 1989; within a few months, it was in advanced negotiations with a consortium for a concession to explore in the zone. In spring 1989, the Secretariat of the Supreme Yemeni Council met for the first time since the bloodbath in Aden in 1986; the PDRY also announced plans to release many of those convicted for involvement in that episode, a move hailed by the YAR. There was even talk about the possibility of using the excess capacity of the Aden refinery to process crude from the YAR, talk that assumed the likelihood of friendly ties over the long run.

The reestablished pattern of improving inter-Yemeni relations was transformed dramatically—and, to most observers, unexpectedly—into the politics of Yemeni unification in late 1989. This activity began at the end of October with the first-ever meeting of the Joint Committee for a Unified Political Organization. During a much-publicized summit in Aden only four weeks later, President Salih and Secretary-General al-Baydh committed "the two parts of Yemen" to a series of steps designed to result in unification in roughly one year. The **30 November Agreement** prescribed that the draft constitution, shelved since completion in late 1981, would be submitted to ratification by the legislatures of the two Yemens and then to popular referenda within two successive six-month periods—that is, by the end of November 1990. If the new constitution was approved in this two-step sequence, then the "Republic of Yemen" was to be proclaimed, the new constitution declared in force, and a transitional government established in Sanaa, the new capital. This government was to remain in place only until early elections for an all-Yemen legislature, which would then select a president and vote approval of a regular government.

The several months after the 30 November Agreement were witness to an explosion of meetings in Sanaa and Aden, including three joint cabinet meetings, the focus of which was the merging of institutions, policies, and procedures. During this period, very hard bargaining at two summits between President Salih and Secretary-General al-Baydh and at meetings of the Joint Committee for a Unified Political Organization produced major changes in the form, stages, and timing of Yemeni unification. Despite talk about one or another type of federation or even confederation, it was decided to merge the two parts of Yemen into a unitary system. The date for proclaiming the ROY was advanced six months from November to May 1990, and a 30-month transition period was added in order to allow time to merge state institutions and reorganize political life.

In what was perhaps the major change, the popular referenda were canceled, and the new national legislative elections were deferred until the end of the transition period—that is, November 1992. During the transition, the ROY was to be governed by a five-member **Presidential Council** (which would select the president and vice president from its membership), an expanded 39-member cabinet consisting of most of the current ministers of the two Yemens, and a 301-member Council of Deputies (Majlis al-Nuwab) made up of the 159 members of the YAR's **Consultative Council**, the 111 members of the PDRY's **Supreme People's Council**, and 31 new presidential appointees. As in the case of cabinet and other senior posts, lesser positions in the government and bureaucracy were to be allocated equally between the two parts of Yemen for the duration of the transition period.

Belying its name, the Joint Committee for a Unified Political Organization opted for a multiparty system in its meetings after the 30 November Agreement. The top leaders of the two Yemens accepted its proposal and then charged the renamed committee with the task of conducting a dialogue with all political parties to arrive at an acceptable multiparty organization of political life. The leadership justified the new system in terms of democracy and pluralism and declared that the rights to speak, meet, and organize were its requisites.

The draft constitution, as revised over previous months, was adopted by the two Yemeni legislatures meeting separately on 21 May 1990, and on the following day President Salih proclaimed from Aden the birth of the ROY. He and Secretary-General al-Baydh were named president and vice president, respectively. The cabinet, drawn about equally from Salih's **General Peoples' Congress** (GPC) and al-Baydh's YSP, was announced. The ex-president of the PDRY, Haidar Abu Bakr **al-Attas**, was named prime minister. The two legislatures were merged and supplemented to create the Council of Deputies, and Dr. Yasin Said **Numan**, the ex–prime minister of the PDRY, was elected its first speaker.

Even before the proclamation, the armed forces of the two parts of Yemen had withdrawn from the old border, and military units of the one part had taken up positions in the other part. The process of constituting the new state and polity proceeded at a frenetic pace through the summer, suggesting that the long transition period would be hectic from beginning to end. Much of it was exhilarating and much mundane and prosaic, marked as it was by countless trips back and forth, meetings, discussions, deals, decisions, memos, studies, and reports. Some 30 political parties sprouted like mushrooms in the new pluralist environment. The same was true of the print media and non-governmental organizations representing all sorts of interests.

Newly unified Yemen, self-absorbed and caught up in the unification process, was blindsided on 2 August 1990 by **Iraq**'s invasion of **Kuwait**, only a little more than two months after the ROY was proclaimed. Events leading up to and following the First **Gulf War** in 1991 both diverted the attentions of Yemenis from unification and placed great burdens on that process. Refusing to endorse the decision by the coalition led by the **United States** and **Saudi Arabia** to expel Iraq by armed force, Yemen soon found itself bereft of most development aid as well as budgetary and balance-of-payments support from the Saudis and the other Arab Gulf states. Far more important was the loss of the **remittances** of the several hundred thousand Yemeni workers and many merchants who were forced by the Saudis to return to Yemen and likely unemployment. Strained relations with Saudi Arabia and some of the Gulf states were to persist for the rest of the decade. The ROY's relations with the United States also suffered. United States aid for 1990–1991 was cut practically to nothing; thereafter, its restoration was limited and conditional. In short, regional events in those two years created a largely hostile regional and international environment for the newborn ROY.

The referendum on the new constitution was held in mid-May 1991, a few days before the ROY's first anniversary. Although the great majority of those voting approved the constitution, less than half of the eligible voters voted, in part because of a boycott called by those who demanded changes in a constitution that they regarded as insufficiently Islamic. This criticism of the constitution, and of unification itself, had emerged in the months before unification, peaked around referendum time, and continued thereafter at a lower level. Demands for constitutional changes tended to go hand in hand with criticism of the regime's stand on the Gulf crisis. This opposition found institutional expression in a new political party, **Islah** (the Reform Grouping), headed by the tribal leader Shaykh Abdullah ibn Husayn **al-Ahmar** and Yemen's leading **political Islamist**, Shaykh Abd al-Majid **al-Zindani.**

Equal partners in the unification regime, the GPC and the YSP competed against each other at the same time that they joined forces against the several other major parties, new and old, during the transition period. Increasingly, however, worsening economic conditions as well as problems with the effort to merge the two states and to reorganize their politics heightened competition and strained cooperation between the two coalition partners. The huge number of unemployed, expelled workers and the sharp drop in remittance income and aid caused economic hardship throughout Yemen. This both distracted the government from the unification process and poisoned the political atmosphere. Beginning in late 1991, day-to-day politics was increasingly marked by acrimony, popular protests, strikes, riots, and even bombings. In addition, the kidnapping of foreigners—often oil company workers—became epidemic. Most notable was the growing number of unsolved assassinations and attempted assassinations of persons high in the YSP of the old PDRY.

All this placed the unification regime under great strain. Late in the summer of 1992, Vice President al-Baydh withdrew to Aden and began a long boycott of the government. The legislative elections, originally scheduled for November 1992, were postponed until early 1993, further adding to the acrimony. Things came to a head in late 1992 with the violent suppression of widespread price riots in cities in North Yemen and a series of terrorist acts in South Yemen, apparently by Islamic militants.

These events had a sobering effect on the two parties in the regime and its moderate opponents, and this led to a closing of ranks and an easing of the political crisis. This trend was facilitated by a number of **conferences** held by tribal, political party, and Islamic elements outside the regime that all sought to pressure it to adopt reforms thought necessary to redirect and save unification. Holding the postponed elections for the Council of Deputies in April 1993 served to legitimate anew Yemeni unification and the regime at home and abroad.

No major Yemeni players boycotted the balloting, and the losers accepted the results after only brief grumbling and cries of fraud. The losers seemed willing to assume the role of opposition.

The elections produced a coalition government that seemed potentially able both to stay together and to address at least some of Yemen's pressing problems. President Salih and the GPC were the big winners, as expected. The other half of the unification regime, the YSP, while much diminished, survived in fairly good order. Just as important, the regime's tribal and moderate Islamic critics, represented by Islah, made a strong showing, but not overly so. Specifically, the GPC won 40 percent of the seats, and the YSP and Islah each won roughly 20 percent. The remaining seats went to independents and the minor parties. These results facilitated the formation of a broad tripartite coalition government ranging from center-left to center-right, from the YSP to the GPC to Islah—the "big tent" favored by President Salih.

During its first months, the new government emphasized new beginnings and, in particular, launched a concerted effort to restore good relations with Saudi Arabia, Kuwait, and the other Arab Gulf states. However, popular demonstrations and strikes during the summer and fall that occurred to protest inflation and the late payment of salaries and wages made it clear that the government was under the gun to deliver on campaign pledges to ease the "pains" of unification and hard times in urban areas. Vehicle thefts and kidnappings by the tribes resumed, causing chagrin to the regime that had made the end of "lawlessness" a campaign promise and had hoped to attract foreign investors. Most worrisome, sporadic political violence resumed, including assassination attempts.

It was soon apparent that the elections had not provided passage to a more comprehensive, more permanent stage of unification—or to more effective government. Formed with difficulty, the tripartite coalition government gave early evidence of serious strain and discord. The armed forces' chief of staff (a northerner) resigned over the failure of the minister of defense (a southerner) to proceed with the long-delayed merger of the armed forces, another top electoral promise. Rumor had some YSP leaders urging the party to join the opposition rather than continue as junior partner in a coalition dominated by a suspected alliance between the GPC and Islah, the two "northern" parties.

In August 1993, about 10 weeks after the new government was formed, Vice President al-Baydh resumed his boycott in Aden—and signaled the start of a second full-blown political crisis. He left behind a list of 18 conditions for his return, a full plate of administrative, economic, political, and military reforms. Efforts to mediate by Arab friends and statements of concern by the United States, the Russian Federation, and others were of no avail. As a result, the political climate near the end of 1993 was as bad if not worse than a year earlier. Moreover, unlike during the crisis of 1992 that preceded the elections, the combatants inside the ruling tripartite coalition did not close ranks, put aside differences, and take joint action to save both the coalition and unification when warning bells sounded in late 1993 and 1994.

Al-Baydh's refusal to come north and be inaugurated as vice president in October 1993, nearly six months after the elections, was indicative of the continuing stalemate. Thereafter, the attempt by the religious leadership to bring al-Baydh and Salih—"the two Alis"—together near Taiz in early January 1994 failed when at the last minute al-Baydh declined to attend. By this time, moreover, most of the other YSP leaders in the regime had quietly left Sanaa and joined al-Baydh in Aden, adding further to the *de facto* creation of a separate government in the old capital of the PDRY. By this time, the southern leaders were openly calling for federation, and their northern counterparts were interpreting this to be a call for the end of unification. Each side was accusing the other of resupplying and redeploying their military units along the former border.

The failed effort by the religious leaders was followed by an effort by King Husayn of Jordan, which led to the Amman meeting of the two Alis on 20 February. There they signed the **Document of Pledge and Accord**, an agreement on reforms and reconciliation hammered out over two months by an unofficial **Political Forces Dialogue Committee** that was set up in late 1993 to meet the crisis. After the signing, Vice President al-Baydh declined to return to Sanaa with President Salih, instead choosing to go straight to Saudi Arabia. With this, the two leaders launched what amounted to separate, opposing diplomatic initiatives in the Arab world.

On the day after the signing, fighting broke out between army units of the north and south stationed in South Yemen's **Abyan** province, compromising implementation of the agreement. In early April, hastily arranged talks between the two Alis in **Oman**, under sponsorship of Sultan Qaboos, failed to get reconciliation back on course. Shortly after this new setback, a serious incident involving a southern army unit occurred in **Dhamar**, in the north. By this time, as the fiction of unity gave way to clear physical division, the wagers of the war of words dropped the euphemisms of the recent past: al-Baydh accused Salih and his cronies of abandoning unification for "annexation" and of conspiring to "marginalize" the YSP, and Salih charged al-Baydh and his greedy "secessionist" friends with forsaking the unity of Yemen and the Yemeni people and seeking to rule over "a mini oil-state."

Then, on 27 April, the first anniversary of the elections, a bloody, four-day battle between northern and southern armored units erupted in a camp in **Amran**, north of Sanaa. Continuous fighting began on 4 May—the **War of Secession** had begun. After 10 weeks of fighting, the forces aligned with President Salih won and the ROY survived, at least as a territorial state. The ROY was quickly to become dominated by the northern oligarchy headed by Salih regime, and many southerners came to see Yemeni unification as nothing more than invasion and occupation by the north.

How and why did Yemeni unification come when it did? Despite the prominent place of unification in public discourse, good inter-Yemeni relations were being touted by many as the preferred alternative to formal unification. Many regarded the latter as too unlikely, difficult, and even dangerous; to try seriously to unify, they reasoned, would be to overreach—and to put improving inter-Yemeni relations in jeopardy. To these people, the rhetoric and theatrics of the unification merely provided cover for the "real" news, concrete steps toward close, mutually beneficial ties between the two Yemens.

Initiated in this setting, the process that led in 1990 to unification was neither inevitable nor the next step in a logical, incremental series. Instead, the process that was revived in the fall of 1989 involved a big, abrupt change or, as systems theorists say, a step-level change. The change between the fall of 1989 and just months earlier was at least as much qualitative as quantitative. Specifically, it involved a shift in goals from just improved relations to the merger of the two Yemens. Unlike past unification flurries, this one was not meant to mask a pragmatic effort at conflict resolution or another prosaic, practical advance in inter-Yemeni relations. Nor was it designed by either or both Yemens primarily as a device to build domestic political support or as a weapon for use against the other Yemen. In the fall of 1989, the bid for unification was, for the most part, real.

The YAR was the initiator of this sudden change, and this in itself was part of the difference between this attempt and other ones. In the past, it had usually been the PDRY that seized the initiative on the issue of unification, from time to time acting on it and forcing the YAR to react. In 1989, however, the roles of pursuer and pursued were reversed and stayed that way during the negotiations leading to formal unification.

Why did the YAR suddenly opt for unification then—and not before or later? In part it was an act of human will, most certainly a matter of willfulness on the part of President Salih. This political animal had a string of recent successes behind him, starting with the celebration of the YAR's 25th anniversary and the export of its first oil in 1987. Then there were the long-awaited elections of a new Consultative Council and his selection for a third five-year term in mid-1988. He then hosted in Sanaa both an Islamic summit and, in September 1989, a summit meeting of the **Arab Cooperation Council**. It appears that at about this time he was faced with the question, what next? Apparently, the answer was a serious bid for Yemeni unification.

Changed conditions caused President Salih and his advisers to perceive such a bid as worth making and attainable. For one thing, over the 1980s, the balance of power had gradually, but decisively, shifted in favor of the YAR over the PDRY. Important political construction—especially creation of the GPC and the holding of elections—significantly increased the strength and legitimacy of the Salih regime. This allowed certain latent YAR advantages to assert themselves: a much larger population; a greater development potential, especially in agriculture; and a much larger, albeit declining, inflow of workers' remittances and development aid. The clincher was the discovery and rapid, almost textbook-perfect development of the YAR's oil reserves after 1984. Although the YAR did experience serious economic problems in the late 1980s, its prospects for the future looked fairly bright, and this bred new optimism and confidence.

By contrast, the already sad state of the PDRY's economy had worsened decidedly since the mid-1980s, and the likely benefits from its newly discovered oil seemed less certain and farther in the future than in the YAR's case. Of greater importance, the PDRY had suffered a number of staggering political setbacks just as the YAR was getting on its feet politically. Arguably, the regimes headed by Ali Nasir Muhammad and Ali Abdullah Salih were of roughly equal weight in the mid-1980s, and a serious attempt at unity at this time would have had to contend with the presence of two strong-willed candidates for the top post in a unified Yemen.

But parity ended abruptly when the YSP decapitated itself in the 13 January events of 1986. In the course of only a few days, President Muhammad was forced to flee the country, and nearly all of the other top YSP leaders were killed, jailed, or in exile. As a consequence, President Salih stood alone atop an all-Yemeni leadership pyramid, his stature unequaled by that of YSP Secretary-General al-Baydh or any other YSP leader. Moreover, despite efforts to repair the damage through economic and political reforms and a clear victory for Secretary-General al-Baydh and the moderates in mid-1989, the YSP remained weakened and discredited in South Yemen—and was perceived as such by politicians in the YAR.

Probably as important to the undermining of the PDRY regime as the YSP's intraparty leadership fight were the sudden withdrawal of Soviet Union support and the rapid crumbling of the socialist camp in the late 1980s. Moscow informed the regime in Aden in early 1989 that it could no longer grant the PDRY preferential economic and political treatment. This sharp cutback in global commitments by the Soviet Union and East Bloc caused the PDRY's leaders to feel isolated and without support, moral or material. The loss of important Soviet and East Bloc aid made it seem impossible for the PDRY to survive the wait for oil export **revenues**—unless it was prepared to risk dependence on Saudi Arabia.

This window of opportunity opened in the late 1980s just as political leaders in Sanaa became increasingly concerned about the need to lessen the likelihood of events that might compromise or threaten plans to capitalize on the YAR's new oil wealth. To this end, unification was perceived as serving to "domesticate" the question of access to, and the sharing of, the oil resources of the two Yemens. Recent history suggested that the neutral zone between Marib and Shabwa could again become a disputed borderland as long as the two Yemens existed side by side. Containing this potentially explosive issue within a unified Yemen, while not eliminating the issue *per se*, would eliminate the chance of it again becoming a matter of state against state, army against army.

The same logic for this domestication through unification applied to other issues that could either pit the two parts of Yemen against each other or involve one of the Yemens in the affairs of the other with unpredictable results. For example, mindful of the turmoil of the 13 January events, some leaders in the north in 1989 feared that the regime in Aden was on the verge of total collapse. They saw the risks of unification as less than those involved in this almost certain collapse and the necessity then for the YAR to intervene militarily to prevent the domestic strife—even civil war—and outside meddling that could easily spill over the border from the faltering PDRY into the YAR.

Finally, a measure of opportunism on both sides helps to explain the decision to unify. The relative strength of the YAR and its leadership in 1989 made its unification initiative a win-win situation: If the effort was successful, the leaders of the YAR could take most of the credit and set most of the terms. If it failed, they could take credit for trying and place blame on their old enemies in the PDRY. For their part, the YSP and its leaders were so weakened and discredited that they could not afford to say no to a call for unification; they had little choice but to buy time by committing themselves now to this goal, hoping that with time their political fortunes would improve, permitting them to prosper in the union or to slip out before it became final.

Accordingly, the YAR forced the issue of merger during the summit meeting in late November 1989, and its position in the hard negotiations thereafter was for complete merger—and the sooner the better. For its part, the PDRY favored commitment to unification now and implementation the later the better. Knowing that the weakened PDRY leadership had already tried to use the unification cause only to strengthen itself after the 13 January events, President Salih and his advisers refused to give Secretary-General al-Baydh and his colleagues a free ride politically; in part, their insistence on moving up the unification date to May in exchange for the long transition period reflected this. In the end, however, the leaders of both Yemens got so swept up in their joint effort to unify that their initial opportunism probably counted for little.

The dynamics of the transition period were interesting. Negotiations and collateral events over the several months after the 30 November Agreement provided the leadership of both parts of Yemen with a heavy dose of practical in-service training in the unfamiliar arts of unifying and pluralizing. In the course of their jockeying for position, the leaders of the GPC and the YSP converged in their acceptance of the "unify now, go to the people later" formula. By advancing the date, they presented internal and external enemies of unification with a *fait accompli* and, by putting off national parliamentary elections for 30 months, they gave themselves time to work out the bugs and to show the benefits of unification. Most of them realized that the economies of both parts of Yemen were in bad shape, would get worse before they got better, and that some of the worsening would be caused by the hard choices, confusion, and mistakes that would inevitably accompany the attempt to implement unification. They were also aware that unification placed demands on the state and raised popular expectations regarding it, at the very time that the many inevitable defects in the merger process were sure initially to weaken, if not immobilize, the state.

The leadership had reason for feeling cursed as well as blessed by the initial popularity of unification. The likelihood that it would later be judged a success was made problematic by the unrealistically high expectations it raised in many Yemenis. Some thought that unification itself would solve economic ills and bring good times. They believed that a stable, peaceful, larger ROY would act as a magnet for foreign investors as well as wealthy Yemenis with funds abroad; in particular, they made much of the untapped potential of Aden, the "economic capital" of the ROY, as a transit port and industrial zone. Similarly, many younger, idealistic North Yemenis embraced unification as the vehicle for ending the corruption, favoritism, disorder, and lack of organization that they deemed of crisis proportions in the YAR; the infusion of southerners, reputedly untainted on these counts, would help the northerners effect the needed reforms that they could not effect alone. These expectations were wildly inflated, and the near certainty that they would go largely unmet made it likely that many would judge unification a failure and the regime identified with it as illegitimate and unworthy of support.

These concerns notwithstanding, most of the political leaders, north and south, became increasingly confident in mid-1990 that the unification process could be brought to a successful conclusion and that they individually stood good chances of being among its political beneficiaries. Most of them had been surprised by the great popularity of the border opening in 1988—by the citizens of both parts voting for one Yemen with their feet—and were keenly aware of the apparent upsurge in their own popularity in the months after the 30 November Agreement. Noted especially were both the new near-hero status accorded President Salih in the south as well as in the north and the rapid revival of the all-but-spent political fortunes of Vice President al-Baydh and his southern colleagues.

These optimistic conclusions, only wishful thinking on the part of some, were the result of cold calculation by other Yemeni leaders. Although mindful that hard times and economic grievances placed heavy burdens on the unification process, the latter were convinced that most of the populace would give them until the end of the transition period in late 1992 to show the positive effects of unification. They thought that this 30-month grace period would be sufficient to effect the merger of state institutions and the reorganization of political life, and that the revenue from as much as a doubling of oil output in the two parts of Yemen to about four hundred thousand barrels per day would begin to revive the economy by the eve of their first electoral test as the leaders of the ROY. These optimists held to an economic scenario that had the rising curve of oil revenues intersecting the virtually flat trend of remittances and external aid before the end of the transition period and projected that improved economic conditions would take hold broadly by that time. Aware that this would be cutting it close, most of them thought nonetheless that they had a better-than-even chance that their moment of truth at the polls would take place in a setting marked by signs of new prosperity and improved prospects.

Questions about the possible impact of unification on the organization of political life were the most worrisome and least answerable ones for the leaders of the two Yemens after November 1989. The futures of the GPC and the YSP were thrown into question by Yemeni unification. Would the fragile, gossamer umbrella organization that the Salih regime had used with some success to contain politics in the YAR remain a dominant force in the enlarged and more challenging environment created by the ROY? Of only limited political relevance even in its own time and place—the 1980s and the north—could the GPC be made to have as much or more relevance in the 1990s in a setting that included the southern part of Yemen and politically advanced Aden? Would the YSP, largely discredited in Aden and the rest of the old PDRY, revive and survive in a unified Yemen? Would the socialist conceit of the inevitable triumph of superior ideology and organization over a leader and mere numbers, reminiscent of the optimism of the Syrian **Baath Party** in the **United Arab Republic** in the late 1950s, prove valid in the ROY? What would be the relationship between these two "ruling parties"—would they, as some suggested, join forces formally or informally in a new, broader umbrella political organization? What would their relationship be, singly or together, to the many old and new political parties—more than 30 by some counts—that had already surfaced by early 1990? Would the two compete with each other for power and somehow at the same time conspire together to exclude others from sharing significantly in power?

That the leaders of the two Yemens were aware that they were heading into the politically unknown, full of uncertainties, is evident in two of the most important changes they made in the unification process during the months between the 30 November Agreement and the declaration of unity in May 1990: the deferral for many months of recourse to the people through elections or referenda, and the shelving of the idea of a "unified political organization" in favor of a multiparty system. The leaders had been uncomfortable with the prospect of letting the people decide on important matters in the very near future. If elections were held as early as originally planned or, so dark humor in Sanaa had had it, Vice President al-Baydh would win in the north and get voted out in the south, while President Salih and the GPC would take the south and lose the north. Similarly, realization that the political configuration of united Yemen was uncharted—and likely to change rapidly for some time to come—led the leadership to conclude that the vagaries of an untried multiparty system were in all likelihood safer than the consequences of a probably futile attempt to contain politics in a "unified political organization," however open and broad in theory.

Yemeni politicians, north and south, were neither versed nor experienced in multiparty politics and, for various reasons, were unsure and uncomfortable with this abstraction. While most of them were convinced nearly from the outset that political change toward a more open, "pluralist" system was unavoidable and even desirable, they had a more difficult time even sketching the broad outlines (much less the details) of this emerging political order and the path to it. They wondered among themselves where the balance between unity and diversity (or multiplicity) should be struck and, as important, how it could be maintained and institutionalized. The leaders of the GPC and the YSP did a lot of wishful thinking in late 1989. For example, they believed they could, in effect, "federalize" politics so that each of the two parties could continue to enjoy a virtual political monopoly in its part of Yemen, at least through a transition. They quickly went from this to a frantic effort to keep up with a fast-changing (fast-"pluralizing") political reality in which both new and old parties were popping up all over the political map.

The alternatives proposed by those in the two ruling parties all tried, implicitly or explicitly, to reserve some special position or advantage for both the GPC and the YSP. They ranged from a broad national front or umbrella organization into which at least these two parties would largely merge—a super-GPC, or something like the three-party coalition that had ruled in the PDRY in the mid-1970s—to a system of many separate, independent parties over which an official gatekeeper would still have considerable say concerning which parties qualified for inclusion. The ruling parties were soon under great pressure from the other parties to give up the former for the latter alternative. Some of the new and previously illegal old parties were even objecting to a gatekeeper or anything else that might favor the *status quo ante*—i.e., the GPC and the YSP. Indeed, in early 1990, the ruling parties were accused by the revived **Nasirites** and the **Union of Popular Forces** of "coordinating" their affairs so as to monopolize political life. At mid-year they were still trying to fashion a political party law with registration criteria that would both seem neutral and actually serve to exclude or cripple certain parties—for example, any party claiming to be *the* Islamic party, or parties having foreign connections.

In the several months after the 30 November Agreement, opposition to the particular terms of unification or to unification in general was predictable. The militant left, mostly in the south, protested that unification was going to be achieved at the expense of past gains and future goals, secular and socialist; some wondered, for example, whether the south's more liberated **women** would have to pay a big price for unity. The Islamic fundamentalists and other conservatives, mostly in the north, focused on the draft constitution and judged it wanting for its failure to make the *sharia* the sole source of legislation—rather than merely "the main source" (Article 3)—and for its approval of parties in an Islamic society (Article 39). Understandably, much of the initial opposition in the north turned on calculations of winners and losers, present and future. Some northerners objected to the parity formula for the allocation of top positions during the transition period only to be told by its defenders that, in exchange for some ministries and offices, the north was really getting the south. At the same time, many of those who realized the stronger and more populous north was absorbing the south also realized that the minorities that had defined and dominated the north for centuries—the Zaydis and the tribes—were going to be overwhelmed numerically by **Shafiis** and nontribesmen in this process. For the most part, however, the critics of unification and its alleged consequences were on the defensive at this time, forced to mute their criticisms because of the great popularity of the ideas of unity and democracy.

Largely in response to this quite inchoate and fast-changing political environment, the ad hoc coalition of ruling parties that negotiated and effected formal unity between late 1989 and mid-1990 rapidly evolved into a unification regime. The competition and antagonism between the GPC and the YSP, the two halves of this unification regime, while not expunged, were increasingly overridden by their shared interest in surviving the growing challenge of a host of other old and new political players. Leaders who did not like or respect—and often did not really know—one another learned to work together for this purpose.

The swift and easy appointment of ministers, their deputies, and other top officials in the first weeks after unification masked problems and concerns that were out in the open in a few months. The assurances that during the transition period jobs would be distributed equally between northerners and southerners caused some to fear that a pernicious Lebanese-style quota system would persist beyond the transition. Similar assurances that during this period no one would be dismissed as redundant caused some to conclude that the choice being deferred until after the transition was between a bloated public bureaucracy and a period of bitter job competition and wholesale dismissals. By late fall of 1990, the talk was of unfilled posts at the level of department head and below, confusion over chains of command, disputes about duties and procedures, and preoccupation with job security and jockeying for position. The capacity of the state to make and implement public policy in the socioeconomic sphere, after having improved in both Yemens in recent years, suffered a setback. Routine government operations were reduced to a snail's pace, if not a standstill. Were it not for the fact that Yemen was still at a level of development where the lives of most citizens were not closely dependent on the quality and quantity of government, the situation would have been a disaster.

Yemen's stand on the Gulf War proved very costly in socioeconomic terms, multiplying the problems caused by the unification process. The impact, cushioned for a time by the hard currency and possessions brought back by the workers and businessmen forced to leave Saudi Arabia and the other Gulf states, included serious strains, dislocations, and deprivations. Because few of the workers went to their villages or found work in the cities, the most notable new problems were the great increase in unemployment and the growth of shantytowns on the outskirts of Sanaa and **al-Hudayda**. The virtual end of remittances and the cutoff of most development funds and other financial aid soon produced a severe shortage of hard currency, and this then caused inflation to soar as the Yemeni rial plummeted in value. Much of the declining hard currency had to go for increased food imports to feed the returnees, leaving little for production and development activities that depended on hard currency for imports. Many projects, public and private, had to be put on hold for want of financing, thereby costing additional jobs. Essential services also had to be cut for want of funds, and a minimal system of relief and humanitarian aid was stretched to its limits by the growing demand.

These acute problems and the unification regime's attempt to cope with them produced popular discontent and public protests. Bread-and-butter issues took their place beside speculative and ideological ones and were pressed vigorously. Taxi owners protested steep rises in gasoline prices, and work stoppages occurred in the oil fields and at the oil refinery. In early 1992, unified Yemen's main trade union group successfully held a 24-hour general strike to protest the government's failure to deal with widespread corruption, soaring prices, and other problems.

The ROY's refusal to join the United States– and Saudi-led coalition against Iraq played into the hands of enemies of unification in Yemen. After 2 August 1990, many of the naysayers who had protested that unified Yemen and its new constitution were not sufficiently "Islamic" added to their litany the failure of the unification regime to take sides with Saudi Arabia, Kuwait, and the other Gulf states against Iraq; they blamed this failure for the hard economic times. Shaykh Abdullah ibn Husayn al-Ahmar, after denouncing multipartism in principle, announced in late 1990 the organization of his new party, Islah, around the issue of the Islamic nature of the Yemeni polity. Islah coupled its dissent on unification with harsh criticism of the regime for its Gulf stand and the domestic effects of that stand. In mid-1991, Islah joined with Abd al-Rahman **al-Jifri** and his **League of the Sons of Yemen** and several other smaller opposition parties to fight against the constitutional referendum as well as the regime's Gulf stance. Earlier, these and other pro-Saudi elements had formed a Committee for the Defense of the Rights of Kuwait.

Still, the Gulf crisis may have initially generated as much support for unification and the unification regime as it later eroded. The quick and undisguised punishing of Yemen by the Saudis and Americans enabled President Salih and his colleagues to sound a call to all to rally and close ranks against a real challenge to the Yemeni people. The latent anti-Saudi sentiment of many Yemenis became manifest, and the regime turned it to its domestic political advantage. Although disavowed by the regime, the scores of demonstrations and other forms of protest against the United States– and Saudi-led coalition throughout Yemen during the crisis channeled much anger and frustration harmlessly away from the regime. Moreover, the economic hardships and austerity that increased after unification could now be partly blamed on or masked by the Gulf crisis and its effects on Yemen.

In part because of the Gulf crisis, the united front formed by the two halves of the unification regime was maintained through 1991 in the face of problems and discontents that could have divided them. There were rumors of differences and rifts between the leaders of the GPC and the YSP, but these were denied. In early 1992, moreover, a leader in the regime said that the GPC and the YSP had decided to maintain their alliance after the upcoming legislative election and to invite other parties to join them.

UNIFIED POLITICAL ORGANIZATION, NATIONAL FRONT (UPONF). *See* NATIONAL LIBERATION FRONT (NLF).

UNIONIST GATHERING, YEMENI. *See* AL-JAWI, UMAR.

UNION OF POPULAR FORCES (UPF). The small, nostalgic party of **Zaydis**, mostly from **sayyid** families, which was founded by the **al-Wazir** family after the **1962 Revolution**. The party was originally dedicated to the restoration of the old ruling caste's political rights and even the restoration of the imamate, albeit a constitutional imamate. Still dominated by the al-Wazirs based largely in the United States, the current incarnation of the UPF is a liberal Zaydi party, one of the five parties that comprise the **Joint Meeting Parties**, the opposition coalition founded in 2002. *Al-Shura* is its respected newspaper.

UNITED ARAB EMIRATES (UAE). The federation of seven Gulf shaykhdoms—called the Trucial States during a century of British protection—that was created in 1971 as **Great Britain** exited from the Gulf region. Abu Dhabi, by far the richest, biggest, and most powerful of the seven, has been since the early 1970s a major Arab benefactor of the YAR and, to a lesser extent, the PDRY, largely through an **Arab regional fund**, the Abu Dhabi Fund. Shaykh Zayid bin Sultan al-Nahayan, traditional leader of Abu Dhabi and president of the UAE, showed special interest in and generously funded the reconstruction of the Marib Dam. He did so in part because tradition has his tribe migrating across the **Arabian Peninsula** to the Gulf from the **Marib** area sometime after the failure of the original dam.

Abu Dhabi and the UAE have few people and, except for vast amounts of oil, almost no resources. Although the UAE is a member of the **Gulf Cooperation Council** and, as such, an ally of **Saudi Arabia**, the UAE has a history of trying to maintain a degree of autonomy from this larger hegemonic neighbor, which helps explain its generosity toward the two Yemens. Born at about the same time and at opposite ends of the political spectrum, the UAE and the radical regime in **Aden** had little else to bring them together.

After Abu Dhabi, the next most important UAE state is **Dubai** which, since its meteoric rise beginning in the 1980s, has become a major commercial and shipping hub as well as a tourist and shopping destination. Dubai's relationship to **Aden** became somewhat adversarial in the 1990s because the to-be-expanded **Aden container port** was much touted by the ROY as a future competitor of Dubai. This was not to be and, in 2007, Dubai Ports World, the operator of Dubai's facilities, signed an agreement to finance and operate Aden's troubled facilities. Yemeni politicians expressed fears of an inherent conflict of interest, but to no avail.

UNITED ARAB REPUBLIC (UAR). The political system created in 1958 out of the merger of Gamal Abdul **Nasser**'s **Egypt** and a **Syria** led by the **Baath Party**, surely the single greatest event of 20th-century pan-Arabism and one billed as the first step toward the unification of the entire Arab nation. It carried Arab nationalists from the heights of elation and brotherhood to the depths of despair and acrimony when the UAR fell apart in 1961. Latecomers to modern nationalism, many Yemenis were affected and moved by these events in profound ways, among them the first-generation **modernists** studying in **Aden**, Cairo, and elsewhere outside Yemen. For one thing, the rise and fall of the UAR was seen as a cautionary tale for those increasingly concerned about Yemeni **unification**. The even shorter history of the **United Arab States** loosely and opportunistically tied **imamate** Yemen to the radical republican UAR.

UNITED ARAB STATES (UAS). The loose association between the **United Arab Republic** (UAR) and the Yemeni **imamate**, created at the request of Imam **Ahmad**. Given his call for others to join the march to Arab unity, **Egypt**'s President Gamal Abdul **Nasser**

could hardly deny the imam. Far from having been swept away by Nasser's call, Imam Ahmad saw this new arm's length association with Nasser and the Syrians as a way of coping with the dangers of revolutionary Arab nationalism and to blunt the calls of his growing domestic opposition for change. President Nasser dissolved the UAS shortly after the collapse of the UAR, but not until Imam Ahmad had presented his famously scandalous poem in which he condemned **Nasserism** as incompatible with Islam. These bizarre events illustrate how hard the politics of the modern world, especially those of the Arab region, were pressing in on isolated, traditional Yemen, despite the protective efforts of the imamate.

UNITED NATIONAL FRONT (UNF). The most radical of the early political groups that emerged in **Aden** in the mid-1950s, the UNF called for no less than the formation of a republic embracing Aden, the **Aden Protectorates**, North Yemen, and **Oman**. The UNF drew most of its support from workers and **trade union** officials who were from and usually still closely tied to places in North Yemen. From its start in 1955, it was closely associated with the **Aden Trade Union Congress** (ATUC); indeed, a year later it was absorbed by the ATUC.

Although not long on the scene, the UNF was led by men who in the following decade were to fight to drive **Great Britain** from South Yemen and then to fight among themselves to succeed the British. Although its secretary general was Abdullah Muhammad Abdu **Numan**, a **Free Yemeni** from North Yemen, two of its most prominent members were Abdullah **al-Asnag**, the founder and head of the ATUC, and Abdullah **Badheeb**, Yemen's first communist.

UNITED NATIONS (UN). The UN has had a vital role to play in the politics and development of the YAR and the PDRY from the mid-1960s through the 1980s and, to a lesser but still important degree, in the politics and development of the ROY since 1990. **Imamate** Yemen had joined the UN with **United States** sponsorship in 1947, and South Yemen joined after independence in 1967. As with many small, poor, and weak Third World states, both the YAR and the PDRY used their UN membership as a relatively cost-effective way of establishing and maintaining contact with the outside world.

The UN had a visible but ultimately unproductive role to play during the early days of the YAR. In 1963, the year after the **1962 Revolution**, Secretary-General U Thant, aided by the mediation of Undersecretary Ralph Bunche and U.S. envoy Elsworth Bunker, secured agreement from **Egypt** and **Saudi Arabia** to end material support for their respective republican and **royalist** clients in the only-months-old **Yemeni Civil War**. The agreement called for a supervised cease-fire, and this led to the formation of the 200-man United Nations Yemen Observation Mission (UNYOM) under the command of Arab–Israeli truce supervision veteran General Carl von Horn. The agreement, never accepted by the royalists, came undone at once, the UNYOM was disbanded after a year, and the civil war dragged on for several more years.

In the mid-1960s, the UN was also drawn into the politics—and the debates, missions, and studies—of the struggle between **Great Britain** and various political elements in South Yemen during the very last years of colonial rule. For example, the UN's Special Committee on Colonialism, taking interest in South Arabia on the occasion of the **Radfan Rebellion** and the merger of **Aden** with the **Federation of South Arabia** in 1963, carried out a fact-finding trip to the area and passed resolutions hostile to Britain's last-ditch actions.

But with independence for South Yemen in 1967 and an end to the civil war in the north not long afterward, the Yemens ceased to be very salient politically to the UN, and vice versa. This was to remain so until 1990 and the events leading up and including the First **Gulf War** in 1991. Only months after Yemeni **unification** and with the bad luck of being on the Security Council, the ROY attracted much unwanted attention when it joined Cuba in voting against the resolution threatening **Iraq** with "all possible means" if it failed to withdraw from **Kuwait**. The ROY was duly punished by many members of the UN, most notably the United States and Saudi Arabia.

During the **War of Secession** in 1994, the UN and the ROY again became salient to each other. The UN Security Council resolution passed on 1 June 1994 called for an immediate cease-fire to the fighting between the **Salih regime** and southerners, resumption of negotiations between the two sides, the halt of arms shipments to both sides, and the dispatch of a UN fact-finding mission to Yemen. The resolution, embraced enthusiastically by the secessionists, was accepted reluctantly and belatedly by the Salih regime, which feared this "internationalization" of what it viewed as an internal uprising. The real fear was that an early cease-fire and pullback of forces would lead to the *de facto* dissolution of the ROY. Shuttling back and forth between the UN in New York and Washington, D.C., Dr. Abd Karim **al-Iryani** was able to stonewall the diplomatic process until the secessionists were defeated in early July, rendering moot the cease-fire efforts of the fact-finding mission and others.

Less dramatic but much more important than the UN's involvement in the politics of the two Yemens and the ROY was its role in providing economic aid and technical assistance. Each of the Yemens, but especially the YAR, received considerable help from the UN and its specialized agencies over the years. In the mid-1970s, the YAR sought increased help just at the time that the United Nations Development Programme (UNDP) devised the category of "less developed countries (LDCs)" eligible for special attention. The YAR embraced this designation with enthusiasm and, viewed by the UNDP as something of a model and test case for the program, was soon the recipient of a relatively generous package of projects, including institutional support for a number of ministries and other agencies. By contrast, the proudly socialist PDRY shunned the designation until well into the 1980s, only to find the UNDP very short of funds for the LDCs by that time.

Apart from the UNDP, other UN agencies have been active in the PDRY as well as the YAR. The United Nations Children's Fund (UNICEF) had a big program in each of the Yemens, as did the United Nations Educational, Scientific, and Cultural Organization (UNESCO). The latter has been, among other things, assisting in the architectural preservation and restoration of the Old City of **Sanaa** and the "skyscraper" city of **Shibam** in Wadi **Hadhramawt**. The World Food Organization had a major presence in the two Yemens, and now the ROY. Since the ROY's economic and financial crisis in the mid-1990s, the UNDP and other UN aid agencies seem to have endeavored to coordinate their effort with the substantial **IMF/World Bank reforms** adopted initially in 1995. On the downside for the ROY, UN aid agencies joined forces with the International Monetary Fund and World Bank in the first decade of the 21st century to pressure it to implement needed reforms.

UNITED STATES. Relations between the United States and each of the Yemens were very different and, in both instances, shaped by the **Cold War** from the 1950s through the 1980s. The United States had diplomatic relations with, and provided economic aid to, **imamate** Yemen during its last years. It recognized the YAR shortly after the **1962 Revolution**, broke relations in 1967, and reestablished them in 1972. Thereafter, it maintained a sizable economic aid and technical assistance program and, beginning in the mid-1970s, a military assistance program. Despite U.S. aid and the moderation of the YAR, efforts to establish very close ties and understanding between the two countries were limited due to Washington's "special relationship" with **Saudi Arabia**, the oil-rich neighbor most feared by, and fearful of, the Yemenis. Almost always, the United States deferred to the wishes of the Saudis on matters pertaining to the YAR—and the Yemenis resented this.

By contrast, the United States and South Yemen broke off relations in 1969, not long after the latter gained independence. For the next 20 years, the United States treated the PDRY as a pariah state—a supporter of revolution and terrorism and a client of the **Soviet Union**, among other things—and the PDRY condemned the United States as the leader of a doomed capitalist and imperialist world order. In the 1970s, the United States perceived the PDRY as a haven for European Marxist terrorist groups and the Popular Front for the Liberation of **Palestine**. With the revival of the Cold War in the late 1970s, the inter-Yemeni **border war** in 1979 was viewed by U.S. strategists as one point on the Soviet-nurtured "arc of revolution," and this led to a major increase in U.S. military aid to the YAR.

The United States restored diplomatic relations with the PDRY on the eve of Yemeni **unification** in 1990. With unification in May 1990, relations between the United States and the ROY got off to a good start, with the United States viewing this as a victory over the Soviet Union in the fading Cold War and Yemen viewing it as a means to less dependence on an overbearing Saudi Arabia.

These relations were soon and suddenly derailed by **Iraq's** occupation of **Kuwait** less than three months later, in August 1990, and the failure of the ROY to join the United States– and Saudi-led coalition against Iraq, which resulted in the First **Gulf War** in early 1991. Despite the near break in relations that followed, the

United States went against Saudi wishes and, after some wavering, opted for the maintenance of Yemeni unity during the **War of Secession** in 1994. In 1995, moreover, the United States chastised Saudi Arabia for threatening international oil companies with deals with the ROY in territory along the disputed Saudi–Yemeni border. Thereafter, relations between the United States and the ROY improved and grew significantly. They became both more important and far more complicated in 2000 with the bombing in **Aden** of the U.S.S. Cole and, in 2001, with **9/11**—and the United States' **War on Terror**.

UPPER, MIDDLE, AND LOWER YEMEN. In Yemeni usage, Upper Yemen roughly refers to the northern highlands of North Yemen and Lower Yemen to the southern uplands that descend to the lowlands of South Yemen. The sharpest and most dramatic dividing line between Upper and Lower Yemen is the **Sumara Pass** on the main north–south inland road about 95 miles south of **Sanaa**, distinguished as it is by breathtaking views of the south and by an equally breathtaking descent to **Ibb** province and the southern part of North Yemen. The secondary road from **Yarim** to Wadi **Bana** also drops from Upper to Lower Yemen, albeit less abruptly. Middle Yemen or the Central Region (*mantaga wasta*) is the relatively small area just before the sharp descent from Upper to Lower Yemen, and it includes the regions of **Dhamar**, Yarim, and the Iryan.

AL-USAYMAT TRIBE. *See* HASHID.

U.S.S. *COLE*. *See COLE* BOMBING, U.S.S.

USSR. *See* SOVIET UNION.

UTHMAN, SHAYKH MUHAMMAD ALI (*CA.* 1908–1973). A Yemeni nationalist and republican who was a strong supporter of both the **1962 Revolution** and the 1967 coup that replaced the **al-Sallal** regime with that of Qadi Abd al-Rahman **al-Iryani**. He then served on the **Republican Council**, the new plural executive, until his assassination in 1973. His killing, the result of a local dispute, was wrongly attributed at the time to PDRY-supported leftist dissidents and contributed to the worsening of inter-Yemeni relations that shortly before had led to the 1972 **border war**. A traditional local notable and landowner, Shaykh Uthman was a **Shafii** leader with much influence on **Jabal Sabr** and the lower elevations south of the city of **Taiz**, in the **Hugariyya**. What was then the best modern school in the YAR, an English-language preparatory school in Taiz, was renamed in his honor after his death.

– V –

VANGUARD PARTY (AL-TALIA). *See* BAATH PARTY (ARAB SOCIALIST RENAISSANCE PARTY).

VARTHEMA, LUDOVICO DE. *See* TRAVELERS TO YEMEN.

VIETNAM WAR. The two Yemens took form in the shadow of the Vietnam War, a global event that much affected political thinking and action from the mid-1960s through the mid-1970s, even on this far corner of Arabia. The **Cold War**, quite warm worldwide over much of this period, was waged within and between the two Yemens, and the fact that there was a divided Yemen, north and south, as well as a divided Korea and Vietnam, was not lost on the Yemenis. The radical heirs to the **British** in South Yemen, the leaders of the **National Liberation Front**, identified with Ho Chi Minh and the Vietnamese as much as with **Castro** and the Cubans—and with them loathed the **United States** and the forces of imperialism and reaction. In the YAR, the long Vietnam War was fought during the long **Yemeni Civil War** and the republican–royalist **reconciliation** and consolidation that followed. The **Egyptians**, whose forces fought in Yemen with the YAR against the **royalists**, came to refer in despair to the Yemeni Civil War as "our Vietnam." Indeed, the first decade of the two Yemens' existence was the decade of the Vietnam War.

VILLAGE ASSOCIATIONS. *See* LOCAL DEVELOPMENT ASSOCIATIONS AND THE LDA MOVEMENT.

– W –

WADI. A large riverbed or watercourse, usually free of all or almost all surface flow between rainy seasons. Wadis often meet the water needs of major settlement areas in the two Yemens as well as elsewhere in the water-poor Middle East. They usually support intensive agriculture, the water being provided by either wells or spate irrigation (or both). Even when bone-dry on the surface, wadis usually trace significant flows of groundwater, and the watersheds of wadis often charge major aquifers. In many cases, especially before motorable roads, they have also served as avenues for the flow of people, goods, and ideas. Due to sparse vegetation, erosion, and steep descents, wadis are often transformed into raging torrents and the scenes of flash floods during the rainy season.

Given the elemental relationship among water, agriculture, and human settlement, wadis are where life and society exist in large parts of the two Yemens. In North Yemen, life and livelihood on the **Tihama** are largely defined by several major wadis, such as Wadi **Mawr** and Wadi **Zabid**, which run west from the foothills all the way to the fishing villages on the **Red Sea**. Similarly, in the arid eastern North Yemen are Wadi **al-Jawf** and the wadi that opens up at **Marib**. More dramatically, Wadi **Hadhramawt** and the lesser wadis that feed into it sharply define life and livelihood in the eastern reaches of South Yemen. The two parts of Yemen share only a few north–south wadis, but the most important, Wadi **Bana**, has long provided a well-trodden route from one Yemen to the other.

WADIAH. The desert town and region seized from newly independent South Yemen by **Saudi Arabia** in late 1969. The Saudis built a road to Wadiah and garrisoned troops there, thereby incorporating it into the kingdom. Wadiah remained a bone of contention between the PDRY and the Saudis for three decades, and it was only with the **Saudi–Yemeni Border Agreement** of 2000 that possession by Saudi Arabia was finally affirmed.

WADI HADHRAMAWT. *See* HADHRAMAWT AND WADI HADHRAMAWT.

WADI ZABID PROJECT. *See* ZABID AND WADI ZABID.

WAHHABISM AND WAHHABIS. *See* POLITICAL ISLAM, MODERN.

WAHIDI TRIBES AND SULTANATE. The smallest and westernmost of the territorial units and tribal groupings that in 1937 became the Eastern **Aden Protectorate**, and the only one of those units to opt to join the **Federation of South Arabia** in 1962. The Wahidi are located on the margins between the rugged uplands of South Yemen's west and the more open, expansive **Hadhramawt** and other areas to the east.

WAILAH TRIBE. The tribe straddling the northwest border between Yemen and **Saudi Arabia**, whose seasonal migrations were accommodated in the open border provision of the **Taif Treaty** of 1934. That treaty assigned the Wailah to Yemen and the **Yam tribe** to Saudi Arabia. In 2006, protest by the Wailah tribe temporarily held off the final signing on the final demarcation of the border called for in the **Saudi–Yemeni Border Agreement** of 2000.

AL-WAJIH, MUHAMMAD KHADIM GHALIB (*CA.* 1932–). A member of a prominent family from the **Tihama** in North Yemen who, after studying abroad in **Egypt** and England for long periods between the late 1940s and early 1960s, returned and held a number of ministerial posts in the YAR. He was minister of agriculture from 1975 to 1978, minister of education from 1978 to 1980, and minister of finance from the mid- to late 1980s. He became minister of civil service and administrative reform in the first government after Yemeni **unification** in 1990 and then served as minister of petroleum and mineral affairs in two successive governments from 1997 through 2001. Al-Wajih is regarded as a very religious man, honest and hardworking. His father, a Tihama notable with extensive merchant and landowning interests, was executed after the abortive **1948 Revolution**, causing the family's fortune to decline.

WAQF (pl. AWQAF). Pious endowments used in Yemen and throughout the Islamic world over the centuries to support religious activities in particular and to fund public institutions in general, such as mosques, schools, libraries, fountains, and orphanages. A main attraction of the device has been that it allows accumulators of wealth and property to keep their acquisitions intact and to minimize the fragmenting effects of Islamic inheritance laws. The facts that Yemeni governments always include a minister of waqfs and that the Ministry of Awqaf is important are indicative of the continuing magnitude and significance of these endowments.

WAR OF SECESSION, 1994. The 10-week armed conflict from late April to early July 1994 between the **Salih regime** and its forces and mostly **Yemeni Socialist Party** (YSP) leaders and southern forces—the former seeking to preserve Yemeni **unification** and the latter seeking to redefine if not reverse it. The conflict ended with the defeat of the secessionists and the survival of the ROY. Coming four years after unification and at the end of two years of increasingly bitter political conflict, the short but intense war also resulted in the increased dominance over the political system by President Salih as well as increased power for the **General People's Congress** (GPC), the surviving military-security apparatus, the tribes, and northern business interests. Also among the winners were the southern allies of ex-PDRY President **Ali Nasir** Muhammad, among them **Abd al-Rabo** Mansour Hadi, the military commander who then had a long tenure as vice president after 1994. The northern and southern Islamic militants, especially the **"Afghani Arabs,"** who supported and fought on President Salih's side, also benefitted. A long-term product of the war was the tendency for many southerners to come to view unification as occupation.

A skirmish between northern and southern army units in **Abyan** in February 1994 led to the creation of a Joint Military Commission for the purpose of defusing the conflict and seeking a lasting resolution. Composed of Jordanian, Omani, and North and South Yemeni military officers, as well as the **United States** and French military attachés, the commission only bought a little time. After a couple of other incidents, in **Dhamar** most notably, the war really began in late April with a bizarre and horrific battle in **Amran**, north of **Sanaa**, on a base shared by northern and southern armored units. With tensions high on both sides, the confrontation quickly turned into a full-scale battle in which tanks and artillery pieces fired at each other at extremely close range; the casualties, civilian as well as military, were high. Despite efforts to contain the conflict, fighting again broke out in Dhamar in early May, just days after Amran.

The fighting escalated and spread down the center of the country, turning into full-scale, army-to-army engagements. Southern **armed forces** in the north were quickly encircled or scattered, and northern forces went on the offensive and entered the south. Major battles were fought in **Lahej** and Abyan. After the fall of the strategic southern base of al-Anad, on the road to **Aden**, northern forces laid siege to Aden and cut it off from the **Hadhramawt**. After about two weeks of fighting, Ali Salim **al-Baydh**, secretary general of the YSP and vice president of the ROY, publicly sought outside mediation and urged an immediate cease-fire and separation of forces. For his part, President Salih opposed efforts to "internationalize" what he claimed to be an "internal conflict" and demanded surrender of the "secessionists" and the trial of 15 top "rebels," al-Baydh included. On 21 May, with Aden and its environs largely cut off from the rest of the south, al-Baydh formally announced the creation of a separate **Democratic Republic of Yemen** (DRY); Salih replied with a pledge to crush the new state and to restore unity. The next day was the ROY's fourth anniversary.

The secessionists had the political and material support of the Saudis, who wooed the United States and other key external actors—but hesitantly, ineptly, and with little success. The United Nations Security Council resolution passed on 1 June 1994 called for an immediate cease-fire, resumption of negotiations between the two Yemeni sides, the halt of all arms shipments, and the dispatch of a UN fact-finding mission. Embraced by the secessionists, the resolution was accepted reluctantly by the north, which feared that the implementation of this resolution would lead to a pullback of forces and the *de facto* dissolution of the ROY. The ROY's former foreign minister, Dr. Abd al-Karim **al-Iryani**, shuttled between Washington, D.C., and UN headquarters in New York in an effort to delay the cease-fire until after forces on the ground thwarted the effort to re-divide Yemen—and he succeeded.

On 7 July, besieged Aden fell and was sacked by soldiers and tribesmen; Islamic militants bulldozed saints' tombs and, alas, torched the sole brewery in Yemen. **Mukalla** fell a couple of days later, bringing the fighting and the secession to an end. By this time, the leaders of the newly created DRY, who had fled from Aden to Mukalla, fled Mukalla into exile in **Oman, Saudi Arabia**, and elsewhere in the Gulf. The 16 top leaders of the DRY were charged with treason, tried *in absentia*, and sentenced in early 1998. Five of them were sentenced to death. In a bid for reconciliation, the soldiers and other supporters of the DRY were quickly granted amnesty, and those who had fled abroad were urged to return. The sentences of all the leaders were subsequently commuted.

The damage had been done, however. Aden had been devastated, and the Adenis traumatized by the siege and the looting. In Aden and elsewhere, property was seized by northern military figures and by southerners claiming it to be theirs pre-PDRY. Aden's economy and society were in shambles and remained so for a long time. Life returned to that great port city only slowly.

WAR ON TERROR. The political and military campaign single-mindedly, if not obsessively, pursued by President George W. **Bush**'s administration in the wake of **9/11**. The War on Terror came to define the **United States**' response to the perceived threat of global revolutionary **political Islam** as exemplified by Usama **bin Laden** and al-Qaida. The response was overwhelmingly understood by the Bush administration in military terms, emphasizing direct and major military operations instead of the intelligence and police actions favored by many others.

The Bush administration seems to have consciously perceived the War on Terror as equivalent to the **Cold War** during which the United States had divided the world into the Communists and the people of the Free World—into children of darkness and children of light. After 9/11, relevant players were expected to choose between the proponents of freedom and those who adhered to the ideas and practices of global revolutionary Islam. In the United States' Manichean view, these countries were expected to be either "with us or against us."

This new perspective quickly and dramatically affected the United States' relations with a host of countries, perhaps especially the ROY. The suicide bombing of the U.S.S. *Cole* in **Aden** harbor by Yemeni al-Qaida operatives had preceded 9/11 by nearly a year, in October

2000, and that event and the investigation of it had already begun to reorder relations between the two countries. After the United States' attack on Afghanistan to get bin Laden and bring down the **Taliban** just weeks after 9/11, many of those asking "who's next?" said "Yemen." This probably helped President Ali Abdullah **Salih** decide to go with haste to Washington to see President Bush and to pledge Yemen's full support in the War on Terror.

The pattern of high U.S. expectations and demands, on the one hand, and President Salih's attempt to maneuver between those demands and the demands of his domestic political friends and enemies, on the other, had begun with the Cole bombing. It became more pronounced over the rest of the decade, and the bombing of the French tanker *Limburg* and the killing of three American medical missionaries in **Jibla** in 2002 reinforced this pattern. The problem was, in part, strong nationalist, Islamic, and anti-American feelings in Yemen. More important were the facts that there were many militant Islamists there and that some of them were associated with the Salih regime, some even in high places in the regime.

As U.S. demands and expectations increasingly posed political problems for the ROY, relations were strained and even threatened. Perhaps the first public example of this was in 2002 when the United States, operating from **Djibouti**, used a Hellfire missile fired from a Predator drone deep in Yemeni airspace to kill the leader of al-Qaida in Yemen at the time of the *Cole* bombing, Ali Qaid Sinan **al-Harithi**. The United States quickly and publicly congratulated itself, and the ROY, while publicly saying that it was coordinating all anti-terrorist activities with Washington, was embarrassed and angered by the United States' announcement and the action's likely impact on the domestic politic of Yemen.

Thereafter, this pattern was repeated in a number of high-profile cases. In early 2003, Imam Muhammad Ali Hassan al-Moayyad was lured to Frankfurt and arrested in an elaborate Federal Bureau of Investigation "sting" operation that allegedly caught him negotiating to channel funds to al-Qaida. Al-Moayyad was well-known and well-regarded in **Sanaa**—he ran a charity providing aid to Sanaa's poor and was the imam of a mosque in Sanaa and a custodian of all of Yemen's mosques, as well as a member of **Islah** party's consultative council. Al-Moayyad's arrest was greeted with disbelief and protest throughout Yemen, but especially in Sanaa. The United States sought his extradition from Germany, and in 2005 both the ROY minister of justice and President Ali Abdullah **Salih** traveled to Germany in unsuccessful efforts to secure his release into Yemeni custody. Al-Moayyad was extradited to the United States, tried, convicted, and sentenced to 75 years. Protests continued in Sanaa, and in mid-2007, during a visit to the United States, President Salih repeated to no avail his country's request that the physically ill imam be repatriated to Yemen. He was a last, sent home in 2009.

Even more high profile was the case of Shaykh Abd al-Majid **al-Zindani**, perhaps the figure who, over the decades, best personified political Islam in Yemen. He had been head of the Muslim Brotherhood in Yemen in the 1970s, a cofounder of Islah, the Islamist party in 1991 (and the head of its Political Bureau), and he was the founding head of al-Iman University. In 2004, the U.S. treasury placed al-Zindani on its list of persons providing financial support to terrorists and, in 2006, President Bush asked President Salih to arrest al-Zindani for the same reason. Al-Zindani publicly refuted the United States' charges, and President Salih and many others were quick to come to his defense. While al-Zindani's old links to **Afghanistan** and current links to **"Afghani Arabs"** and other militants in Yemen was a source of embarrassment for President Salih, he was even more embarrassed and angered by the Bush administration's demands.

Relations were increasingly strained by what some called President Salih's "catch-and-release" approach to those suspected and even convicted of terrorism. Centerpiece of this was the **"dialogue process"** launched by Judge Hamoud **al-Hitar** in 2003 to rehabilitate militants through "re-education" in the true meaning of Islam. Several hundred men in custody "successfully" went through this process between 2003 and 2006. The United States was skeptical and suspicious of this from the start and became even more so after some of the rehabilitated militants later turned up as jihadis in **Iraq**. Its alarm and anger grew as it learned that many of these militants had been freed largely on the basis of a pledge that they would not engage in violent acts in Yemen, with the understanding that the pledge did not extend to actions outside Yemen.

Two high-profile cases not falling under the "dialogue process" framework especially failed to meet U.S. demands for a no-nonsense crackdown on terrorists. Jamal al-Badawi, a key member of al-Qaida in Yemen and the alleged mastermind of the *Cole* bombing, was tried and sentenced to death in 2003 for that and for his involvement in the attack on the *Limburg*. His sentence was reduced to 15 years, much to the irritation of the United States, which then tried without success to get him extradited for trial there. Its irritation was fed by the fact that al-Badawi had escaped twice, in 2003 with 9 others from a prison in Aden and, notoriously and very suspiciously, in 2006 with 22 others from the main security prison in Sanaa. The United States responded by putting a $5 million bounty on his head. In the fall of 2007, as the police were about to capture him, al-Badawi surrendered. Then, in mid-October, possibly in an effort by the regime to repair ties with local Salafi groups in the face of serious political unrest in South Yemen, the regime placed him under very loose house arrest. Furious, the United States suspended an that very week agreement to reinstate the ROY to the Millennium Challenge Corporation program and the generous aid it promised. Amid confusion and uncertainty, the ROY then claimed to re-arrest al-Badawi, and the United States said it would reconsider its suspension.

More bizarre, another case involved Jabr al-Banna, a Yemeni American and former resident of Lackawanna, New York, who, as an older associate of the "Lackawanna Six," had gone with them to Afghanistan for jihadist training in the spring of 2001, several months before 9/11. In 2003, al-Banna was charged *in absentia* in the United States with conspiring with the "Lackawanna Six." When he was later arrested in Yemen in 2004, the ROY did not extradite him. Tried and sentenced by the ROY for involvement in the *Limburg* bombing, al-Banna was one of the 23 who, along with Jamal al-Badawi, escaped from prison in Sanaa in early 2006; as in the case of al-Badawi, the United States then put a $5 million price on his head. In mid-2007, after 15 months on the run, al-Banna surrendered and, despite an ongoing trial for his involvement in the abortive attacks on two oil installations in September 2006, was allowed to stay at home after pledging not to carry out terrorism in Yemen. Sentenced to 10 years in prison in late 2007, he continued to stay at home under loose house arrest. In an act of inexplicable bravado, he appeared at an appeals hearing in late February 2008, stated who he was, declared his innocence, and walked out with his four personal guards. In early

March, he again appeared before the court and this time was released on bail. The United States was dismayed.

Acutely aware that the United States wanted actions as well as words, the ROY had made much of the arrest of Muhammad Hamdi al-Ahdal by security forces in a sting operation in Sanaa in late 2003. Al-Ahdal, from **Saudi Arabia**, was the putative successor of al-Harithi as head of al-Qaida in Yemen and allegedly a veteran of jihad in Afghanistan, Chechnya, and Bosnia. This operation was held up by the regime as evidence that it was a willing and able partner of the United States in the War on Terror. Charged with financing and facilitating terrorist acts, al-Ahdal was finally tried in early 2006, found guilty, and given a short sentence—three years with the possibility of it being reduced to one year. In his defense, he claimed that he had merely raised money for the families of martyred jihadis.

United States and the ROY disagreed—and increasingly so—over the treatment and continued holding of the many Yemenis in prisons at Guantanamo. Repeated calls and demands for the release of the upward of one hundred Yemeni prisoners came from the public, their families and lawyers, parliament, and even President Salih. Indignation increased as many prisoners from Saudi Arabia and Afghanistan were released to their governments, making the Yemeni contingent all the more conspicuous. The United States was quite explicit in indicating that its lack of trust that the ROY would act seriously on charges against the Yemeni prisoners—and indeed, would simply turn them loose—was behind its reluctance to turn them over to the ROY. Faced with President Barak Obama's declaration that he would close Guantanamo in a year, the ROY announced that it would build a high-end "reorientation" facility for these returnees and their families. The two allies argued heatedly over the issue through 2009.

AL-WARTALANI, AL-FUDAYL. The French-educated Algerian member of the Muslim Brotherhood who brought modern **political Islam** to North Yemen. He befriended some young, reform-minded Yemeni students in Cairo before World War II, visited Yemen in 1947 to establish the Brotherhood, publicly advocated there the cause of Islamic political reform, and secretly advised the group of conspirators who planned and carried out the **1948 Revolution**. Allegedly, he even advocated the assassination of Imam **Yahya**, which did occur.

Al-Wartalani survived the quick suppression of the revolution by being out of Yemen on a failed mission with Qadi Muhammad **al-Zubari** to secure the support of **Saudi Arabia**'s ruler for the new Yemeni regime. Victorious Imam **Ahmad** made al-Wartalani the foreign scapegoat, the outside agitator, in his father's assassination. Al-Wartalani took refuge in Beirut and, after the Egyptian Revolution of 1952, in Cairo.

WATER RESOURCES. *See* MONSOONS AND WATER RESOURCES.

WATER, SEWAGE, AND WASTE DISPOSAL SYSTEMS. *See* INFRASTRUCTURE DEVELOPMENT.

AL-WAZIR, ABDULLAH BIN AHMAD, AND THE WAZIRS. Abdullah bin Ahmad (?–1948), a leader of a prominent **sayyid** and **Zaydi** family who, seeking to realize a long-held goal of replacing Yemen's **Hamid al-Din** rulers, conspired with other makers of the **1948 Revolution** to have Imam **Yahya** assassinated on 17 February of that year and then, a week later, had himself proclaimed imam. Two weeks later, the al-Wazir **imamate** collapsed. Less than a month later, Abdullah bin Ahmad was summarily tried and executed. He had earlier served Imam Yahya in high posts—e.g., as governor of **al-Hudayda** and as a member of Yahya's "inner cabinet"—and had married Yahya's daughter. Although shunted aside later in favor of the imam's sons, he had remained a regular attendant at the court and was among those who pledged to support the eventual succession of Crown Prince **Ahmad**. Ambition and discontent got the best of him and led him to join with those seeking a reformed imamate and an end to Yemen's "backwardness."

The large, well-to-do al-Wazir family, descended from a 19th-century imam, had regarded itself as a strong, rightful claimant to the imamate and, as such, had posed a threat to the continued tenure and dynastic aspirations of the Hamid al-Din family in the second quarter of the 20th century. The leader of the family, Sayyid Ali bin Ahmad al-Wazir, had led Imam **Yahya**'s forces in battle in the years following World War I and had served as governor of **Taiz** from 1920 to 1938.

A decade later, the quick defeat and overthrow of the al-Wazir greatly diminished the place of that family in Yemeni politics, and this condition persisted after the **1962 Revolution** and the creation of the YAR. In exile in Beirut during the **Yemeni Civil War** in the 1960s, Sayyid Ibrahim Ali al-Wazir led the **Union of Popular Forces**, a segment of the **Yemeni Third Force** that, with **Saudi Arabia**'s blessings, sought to find an alternative to both the **Egyptian-**dominated republic and a restored imamate.

Perhaps because they were regarded as too close to both the imamate and the ruler of Saudi Arabia, the al-Wazirs did not return to political prominence after the republican–royalist **reconciliation** in 1970. However, the Union of Popular Forces, largely supported and led by family members who went into exile in the **United States** after the civil war, reemerged as a minor Zaydi sayyid party after Yemeni **unification** in 1990. It became a minor part of the **Joint Meeting Parties**, the opposition coalition formed in 2002 to challenge the **Salih regime**.

WESTERN ADEN PROTECTORATE. *See* ADEN PROTECTORATES.

WEST GERMANY. *See* GERMANY.

WILSON, HAROLD. *See* BRITAIN.

WOMEN, RIGHTS AND POSITION OF. Casting a pall for some over **unification** in May 1990 was the question of whether the women of the PDRY would be forced to give up more in terms of freedom and equality than their more numerous YAR sisters would gain. As it turned out, they did give up more, in part because of the north's existing socioreligious conservatism and in part because unification occurred coincidentally with the growing strength of conservative Islam throughout both Yemens and the rest of the Islamic world.

After independence in 1967, the PDRY took seriously its commitment to equal rights for women, and this was plainly evident in education and employment, as well as in dress code and social relations. The General Union of Yemeni Women (GUYW), founded in the PDRY in 1968, vigorously concerned itself with the rights, status, training, and employment of women. Indeed, the Marxist regime in

Aden treated its skilled, trained women as valuable resources that had to be fully utilized in the effort to build socialism. Women's equality was most closely approximated in Aden, its immediate environs, and **Mukalla**; it was realized less in the smaller cities and towns and almost not at all in many of the villages and hamlets in rural areas, where patrimonial ideas and practices were more prevalent. But on the streets of the cities, in the universities and in public life, the liberated woman was much in evidence—and promoted as the model for the rest of society.

By contrast, in North Yemen, the ending of the theocratic **imamate** and a quarter century of republicanism were witness to a spread of women's veiling and seclusion in the more urban areas. This was partly the result of a growing middle class emulating the traditional upper class and partly the result of the fact that veiling was an urban phenomenon and that the YAR's cities were growing rapidly. Mostly, however, it was a function of the persistence of conservative, traditional thought and of the strength of the groups that continued to promote this thought. In any case, when out of the home, women increasingly wore the *sharshaf,* covering themselves from head to foot in black.

This was the pattern in cities and big towns in the YAR, but less so in **Taiz, Ibb,** and on the **Tihama. Sanaa University** and most other universities, which were coeducational, were exceptions to the rule of segregation by gender in public places. Only a minority of girls went to secondary school, much less the university. Especially in the countryside, where the majority lived, the ability to read the Quran and to make simple calculations was thought sufficient for most girls.

Similarly, few young women were found in "modern" jobs, since it was thought shameful for women to work outside the home in markets, factories, and offices; those who did wore the *sharshaf.* By contrast, in the countryside, where life revolved around family, farming, and the fields, the practices of veiling, separation, and seclusion were much less prevalent.

In theory, relatively liberal social legislation in the YAR provided such rights for women as pregnancy leave, voting, driving, travel, running for office, and property ownership. In fact, however, only a small minority took—were able to take—advantage of these laws. In the public sphere, there were no women ministers or parliamentarians, and only a handful held high administrative positions. Those who did enter government service other than as secretaries and other clerical workers were often isolated—and treated somewhat like strange, exotic creatures. Females were legally authorized to run in the 1988 parliamentary elections, but they were actively discouraged from doing so.

With unification in 1990, the PDRY's GUYW and the smaller, weaker women's organization in the YAR were merged into a single **interest group**, the Yemeni Women's Union (YWU). The merger was made difficult because of a split among women's activists over the personal status law of 1992, which many northerners saw as properly Islamic and most southerners saw as revoking or limiting rights to divorce, child custody, and housing enjoyed in the old PDRY. Since then, however, the YWU has overcome some of these differences and proven to be the women's organization most able to work closely with the government and other civil society organizations. The National Women's Committee has also become an outspoken women's advocacy group.

Despite the efforts and protests of religious conservatives, women in the ROY have managed to hang on to most of the legal rights and opportunities enjoyed under either of the previous regimes. Several thousand female professionals, still a small minority of the total, are in positions in communications, health, education, law, and business. The universities remain coeducational, despite becoming a main target of religious conservatives and militants. In one bizarre incident after the start of the new millennium, Sanaa University's Women's Study Center was temporarily shut, and its confrontational director, Dr. Raufa Hassan, went into exile temporarily after a conservative campaign against its scandalous focus on "gender studies."

In the political sphere, the results have been mixed and modest. Women have registered and voted in large numbers, but holding elective office has been another matter. In 1990, televised sessions of the merged transitional parliament pictured 10 females from the former PDRY interacting with their male counterparts, a matter of great interest to many northerners. In the 1993 elections, however, only 2 of the 50 women who ran won parliamentary seats; most of these candidates and both of the winners were from the south. In

1977, 23 women ran and, again, only 2 won seats, both in southern constituencies. Finally, in the 2003 elections, only a single woman won one of 301 seats. Although all major parties except Islah have declared that women should be in parliament, the parties have proved reluctant to run women against men because of the belief that the voters would chose men over women on election day. Since about 2000, there has been serious talk by the parties about reserving 15–20 percent of the seats for women, but agreement on a plan to implement this had not been agreed upon in the months leading up to the soon-to-be canceled 2009 parliamentary elections.

The new government in 2003 included a woman minister—Amat **al-Suswa**, former ambassador to the Netherlands—and there were two women in the government formed in 2007. There were about a dozen female judges in the late 1990s and, while this number has grown, most have been appointed to jurisdictions in South Yemen and to family or juvenile courts. Women have been moving into senior government posts, but it is estimated that only about 225 women occupy such posts as compared to more than 7,000 men. As of 2009, Yemen's women still had a long way to go.

WORLD BANK. *See* IMF/WORLD BANK REFORMS.

WORLD WARS. The two Yemens were removed from, yet profoundly affected by, the two world wars in the 20th century. The defeat of the **Ottoman Turks** in World War I ended the Ottoman occupation of North Yemen and set the stage for the last flowering of the **Zaydi imamate**. Except for a flirtation between Imam **Yahya** and Benito Mussolini's Italy—the legacy of which are a couple of rusting airplanes outside of **Taiz**—World War II had little effect on North Yemen. By contrast, that war profoundly exhausted **Great Britain** and paved the way for the end of the British Empire—and for the emergence of an independent South Yemen. **Aden** was rapidly and massively built up as a vital link in Britain's war effort and then, right after the war, as the vital link "east of Suez" in the rapidly retreating British Empire. In broad terms, an independent North Yemen was a product of World War I, just as an independent South Yemen was a product of World War II.

– X, Y –

AL-YADUMI, MUHAMMAD ABDULLAH. *See* ISLAH (YEMENI REFORM GATHERING).

YAFI TRIBES AND REGION. An important tribal grouping and region in the South Yemeni highlands, beginning about 50 miles northeast of Aden and extending to the border not far from the North Yemeni town of **al-Baydha.** Usually beyond the reach of any higher authority, the tribes of Upper Yafa tended to enjoy greater autonomy than those of Lower Yafa, who lived in a lower-elevation area slightly to the south and closer to the coast—and much more accessible. Willing fighters, the Yafi were often available for hire as mercenaries, and one group hired in this capacity settled in the **Hadhramawt** generations ago and became a permanent factor in struggles for control of Wadi Hadhramawt and the adjacent coast. In the second half of the 19th century, under the **Quaiti** sultanate, these Yafi came to share in the governance of the coast and the western approaches to the wadi. In addition, some Yafi from the Hadhramawt went to **Hyderabad** in India and served the local ruler as mercenaries; some became quite wealthy and used their wealth to enhance the position of their families back home.

YAHYA, ANIS HASAN. The South Yemeni **Baathi** who led the (Vanguard Party) a coalition partner in the **Unified Political Organization, National Front** in 1975 and then, three years later, merged it with the other coalition partners to form the **Yemeni Socialist Party** (YSP). Yahya served as economics minister in the PDRY in the first half of the 1970s and then moved on to a high post in the YSP as **Abd al-Fattah** Ismail tightened his grip on the party in the late 1970s. Soon an ally of **Ali Nasir** Muhammad al-Hasani in his intraparty struggle with Ismail and his allies in the 1980s, he was finally on the losing side in the **13 January events** that caused the overthrow of Ali Nasser in 1986.

YAHYA BIN HUSAYN BIN MUHADDAD HAMID AL-DIN, IMAM (?–1948). The imam of North Yemen and head of the **Hamid al-Din** family who, during his long reign from 1904 to 1948, strengthened the imamate and extended its domain while he insulated and reinvigorated the traditional Islamic culture and society of Yemen. The first third of Imam Yahya's reign was largely devoted to ridding Yemen of its **Ottoman** Turkish occupiers, and the second third to the consolidation and territorial expansion of the **imamate** state, a process that concluded in the mid-1930s with conflicts and **border agreements** with **Saudi Arabia** to the north and **Great Britain** to the south. The revitalized imamate and a revived traditional Yemen, based largely on a self-sufficient subsistence agricultural economy, reached their apex in the last third of his reign. This period was also witness to the first serious intrusions of the modern world, the beginning of political opposition to the imamate and its incumbent, and, finally, the assassination of Imam Yahya by his political foes in the **1948 Revolution**.

Imam Yahya towered over North Yemen during the entire first half of the 20th century, and he held that century at bay to a remarkable degree. Stern, austere, and frugal, he devoted himself quite single-mindedly to the **Zaydi** imamate's charge of protecting and enhancing the Islamic character of Yemen, putting his political skills and considerable wisdom to this task. He did this at a time when key features of most traditional societies around the world were being dissolved in the solvent of modernity. Unlike his Saudi neighbors, he refused to open his domain to foreign oil companies, wary as he was of the imperialists—and the modern world in general. Not only did he never set foot outside Yemen, it is said that he never descended from the highlands to even set eyes on the **Red Sea** that bordered his domain.

YAM TRIBE. A tribe of the **Hamdan** that, although located in the **Najran** area in what is now **Saudi Arabia**, was deeply involved in the tribal and state politics of North Yemen for centuries before the **border** between the YAR and Saudi Arabia was drawn in the 1930s. Indeed, the **Saudi–Yemeni war** of 1934, which led to the demarcation of the border, was partly the result of a conflict between Yemen's **Zaydi** imamate and the Yam tribe in which the former's forces pursued the latter into Najran, territory then only recently claimed by Saudi Arabia. As a result of the Saudi–Yemeni Border Agreement of 2000, the Yam's base is firmly in Saudi Arabia. The Yam is unusual in that its members are **Ismailis**, and this was one basis of the **imamate's** conflict with it. Over the centuries, the Yam had supported their fellow Ismaili Hamdanis west of Sanaa.

YARIM. A major town in the highlands of North Yemen, located on the main road about halfway between Sanaa and **Taiz** and just before the **Sumara Pass** and the steep descent from the Zaidi northern highlands to the **Shafii** southern uplands of North Yemen. Yarim is also located near the northern end of Wadi **Bana**, an alternate route south to **Aden**. For cultural as well as geographic reasons, the town is considered part of what for centuries has been called the "middle region" of North Yemen. The ruins of Zafar, the capital of the ancient **Himyarite** kingdom, are on a nearby hill.

YATHUL. *See* BARAQISH.

YEMEN ARAB REPUBLIC (YAR). Created in 1962 in the wake of the **26 September Revolution** and the abolition of the Zaydi **imamate**, the YAR provided the framework for North Yemen's kaleidoscopic evolution for a generation and then ceased to be when the two Yemens merged to form the **Republic of Yemen** (ROY) in May 1990. The formation of modern North Yemen as a separate polity was largely a function of the interplay of the reoccupation of Yemen by the **Ottoman** Turks in 1849 and the resistance to this presence by an imamate increasingly supported by the Yemeni people, beginning in the early 20th century. Defeat in **World War** I forced the Turks to withdraw in 1918, and a resurgent imamate under Imam **Yahya** seized the opportunity to restore and extend its rule.

During the first six decades of the 20th century, Imam Yahya and his son Imam Ahmad acted to forge a king-state much as the kings of England and France had done centuries earlier. The two imams strengthened the state, thereby enabling them to secure Yemen's borders and pacify the interior to degrees rarely known over the past millennium. The imams used the strengthened imamate to revive North Yemen's traditional Islamic culture and society, and this at a time when traditional societies around the world were crumbling under the weight of modernity backed by imperial power. They were aided in their efforts to insulate Yemen by the degree to which its agricultural economy was self-contained and self-sufficient. The result was a "backward" Yemen, more frozen in time than not, and a small but growing number of Yemenis exposed to the modern world who wanted change—and blamed the imamate for its absence. This produced a fateful chain of events: the birth of the **Free Yemeni Movement** in the mid-1940s; the aborted **1948 Revolution** that left Imam Yahya dead; the failed **1955 coup attempt** against Imam Ahmad; and, finally, the 1962 Revolution that brought the YAR.

In retrospect, the history of the YAR can best be divided into three periods: (1) the **al-Sallal** era of 1962–1967, the wrenching first five years under President Abdullah al-Sallal marked by the revolution in 1962, the long **Yemeni civil war** and the quick **Egyptian** intervention that followed, and—above all—the rapid and irreversible opening of the country to the modern world, (2) a 10-year transition period (1967–1977) marked by the end of the civil war, the republican–royalist **reconciliation** under President Abd al-Rahman **al-Iryani**, and the attempt by President Ibrahim **al-Hamdi** to strengthen the state and promote development, and (3) the **Salih** era of 1978–1990, a 12-year period identified with both the long tenure of President Ali Abdullah Salih and the change from political weakness and economic uncertainty at the outset to political stability, the discovery of oil, and the prospect of oil-based development and prosperity in the late 1980s.

Of the many important changes that took place in the YAR since its birth in 1962, most of the positive ones were compressed into the years since its 15th anniversary in 1977. Nevertheless, the decade 1967–1977 was also important, a transition period in which much needed time was bought by a few modest but pivotal acts—and, most important, by economic good fortune. Above all, global and regional economic events over which the YAR had no control produced a huge flow of funds into the country in the form of foreign aid and **remittances** from Yemenis working abroad. This period of transition was much needed; the changes that had buffeted Yemen in the five years after the 1962 revolution had left it both unable to retreat into the past and ill equipped to go forward. The ability to advance rapidly in the 1980s was very much the result of the breather during the 1970s.

Given the isolation and the decentralized nature of North Yemen, it is not surprising that much of the YAR's first quarter-century would be taken up with the effort to establish sovereignty over the land and people. The Yemenis who made the revolution in 1962 were preoccupied from the outset with the need to create a state with the capacity to maintain public security and provide services. The long civil war that came on the heels of the revolution both increased this need and interfered with its being met. Yemeni state-building was more hindered than helped by the facts that the new state was largely built and staffed by Egyptians and that Egyptian forces did most of the fighting on behalf of the Yemenis.

The balance of power between the tribal periphery and the state at the center tipped back toward the **tribes** during the civil war. As a result, the reach of the YAR in 1967 extended little beyond the triangle in the southern half of the country that was traced by the roads linking the cities of Sanaa, **Taiz**, and **al-Hudayda**. The YAR, created in 1962, also lacked modern political organization, and its first 25 years consisted of attempts to fashion the ideas and organization needed to channel support and demands from society to the regime and, conversely, to channel information, appeals, and directives from the regime to society. The civil war caused the deferral of any major effort at political construction under President al-Sallal. Egypt's heavy-handed tutelage left little room for Yemeni national politics and politicians to develop. Indeed, it deformed the politics of the young republic.

As with other late-developing countries, the tasks of state-building in the new YAR went beyond the maintenance of order and security to include the creation of a capacity to influence, if not control, the rate and direction of socioeconomic change. The wrenching effects of the sudden end of isolation and self-sufficiency made state-building in all of its aspects greatly needed. No less than the viability and survival of Yemen in its new external environment depended upon the state-building that the civil war and the Egyptian presence had inhibited.

The Egyptian exodus in 1967 led to the quick overthrow of President al-Sallal and to the republican–royalist **reconciliation** that finally ended the civil war in 1970. Some state-building of importance was achieved thereafter by the new regime headed by President al-Iryani; the modern **1970 Constitution** was adopted, and some of the ministries and other agencies erected after the revolution were strengthened. Economic needs as well as political constraints caused Yemeni leaders during the al-Iryani era to focus on financial and economic institutions; only halting first steps were taken toward reform of the civil service and the **armed forces**, matters of great political sensitivity. President al-Hamdi, who forced President al-Iryani into exile in 1974, believed in the modern state and worked to realize it. He launched some efforts to reform state institutions at the center, initiated the first major reform and upgrading of the armed forces, and fostered the idea of exchanging the benefits of state-sponsored development for loyalty to the state.

The results of efforts by the al-Iryani and al-Hamdi regimes at political construction were modest. The price of reconciliation was the granting of office and influence in the state to leading tribal shaykhs for the first time and, after the **Sanaa Mutiny** in 1968, the expulsion of leftist modernists from the body politic. This price weakened the position of advocates of a strong state. The result was the narrowly based center-right republican regime that, with changes, persisted from the late 1960s through the 1980s. The chief institutional focus of politics during the al-Iryani era was the **Consultative Council** (CC), which convened after the YAR's first national **elections** in early 1971. However, political parties were banned, and, in the absence of explicit organizational and ideological ties, the council functioned as an assembly of local notables, including the shaykhs.

President al-Hamdi was unable to strengthen his position by translating his great popularity into political organization. Indeed, his major political achievement actually narrowed the political base of his regime and shortened the reach of the state. Aware that the shaykhs were using their new positions to protect the tribes from the state, al-Hamdi moved swiftly to drive them from the CC and from other state offices; to this end, he dissolved the council and suspended the 1970 Constitution. The tribes replied with virtual rebellion. Al-Hamdi's efforts to make up for this loss of support by reincorporating the modernist left were hesitant. In addition to maintaining ties to old leftist friends, he launched both the **local development association** (LDA) movement and the **Correction Movement**. Despite their initial promise, al-Hamdi seems to have had second thoughts, causing him to pull back from efforts to use these two initiatives as bases for a broad, popular political movement; his subsequent plans for a general people's congress were overtaken by his assassination in 1977. Frustrated by his failure to grant them re-entry into the polity, several leftist groups in 1976 created the **National Democratic Front** (NDF), which became the basis of the **NDF rebellion** that challenged the Salih regime a few years later.

The civil war finally behind it, the YAR underwent significant socioeconomic development in the 1970s based upon the rapid creation of a modest capacity to absorb generous amounts of economic and technical assistance from abroad and—most important—the massive inflow of workers' **remittances** that by itself fostered unprecedented consumption and prosperity. Whereas the remittances largely flowed into private hands, the modest strengthening of state institutions and the increase in their capacities were the critical factors in Yemen's growing ability to absorb significantly increased foreign aid. By the late 1970s, work on a broad array of state-sponsored, foreign-assisted infrastructure, agricultural, and human resource development projects existed side by side with high levels of remittance-fueled consumption and economic activity in the private sector.

President Salih's long term in office, which began in 1978, witnessed major gains in state-building. After a shaky start, the Salih regime slowly increased the capacity of the state in the provinces as well as in the cities, for the first time making the republican state more than just a nominal presence in the countryside. The armed forces were upgraded in 1979 and again in 1986 and 1988. Modest efforts were made to improve the functioning of the civil service, ministries, and other agencies.

The Salih regime increased its sway over lands controlled by the tribes, especially the large area that fans out north and east from Sanaa, the capital. However, the best evidence of the growing ability of the YAR to exercise power within its own borders was the political–military defeat of the NDF. The NDF rebellion, with its origins in the expulsion of the left from the republic in 1968, had finally burst into flame over a wide area in late 1978. This uprising was extinguished in 1982, and the state was able at last to establish a real presence in lands bordering South Yemen.

In 1979, the Salih regime had little political support outside the armed forces. After the failure of ad hoc efforts to change this, the regime put in place an impressive program of political construction during the first half of the 1980s. This sequential program began in early 1980 with the drafting of the **National Pact**. The pact then became the subject of a long national dialogue and local plebiscites orchestrated by the **National Dialogue Committee**. Elections to the **General People's Congress** (GPC) and its several-day session were held in mid-1982 in order to adopt the National Pact. This done, the GPC declared itself a permanent "political organization" that would be selected every four years, meet biennially, and be led by a 75-member Standing Committee headed by President Salih.

The key to the success of the Salih regime's political effort lay in the flexible, step-by-step process by which it moved the Yemeni polity from where it was in 1979 to the holding of the GPC in 1982. Moreover, by design and a bit of luck, this sustained initiative also provided a political process largely managed by the regime into which elements of the Yemeni left could be safely incorporated when the NDF rebellion was quelled in 1982. Two dialogues—one between the regime and the NDF as well as the more public one between the regime and the rest of the nation—converged in a structure that facilitated a second national reconciliation.

Although President Salih insisted that the GPC was not a political party, its activities clearly aimed at consensus-building, guidance, and control—typical functions of a party. In fact, the GPC did become an umbrella party, a loose organization of organizations in a society that was not well organized politically for many of the tasks required by modern life.

The Salih regime was also buttressed by constitutional change during the 1980s. The 1970 Constitution, suspended by al-Hamdi in 1974, had been reinstated confusingly in 1978 without its centerpiece, the CC, and with an amendment that formally created the presidency. Clarity and closure on a number of issues were not achieved until July 1988, when elections for a new Consultative Council were finally held. These elections, the first since 1971, were hotly contested and relatively fair and open; despite the continuing ban on parties, much partisanship was in evidence. In mid-July, the new council elected President Salih to a new term and then gave approval to the composition and program of the new government. As a result, for the first time since the al-Iryani regime was ousted in 1974, the head of state and the government were selected in accordance with the 1970 Constitution—namely, by a properly chosen CC.

The modest prosperity that the YAR enjoyed after the mid-1970s was paralleled by the modern sector's increasing vulnerability to negative economic and political forces both domestic and external. Domestic political uncertainty early in the Salih era threatened the limited capacity of the state to foster and manage development, and this was followed by the fall in oil prices and worldwide recession that led to sharp drops in aid and remittances to Yemen. Faced with economic crises, the regime in the early 1980s adopted austerity measures that had some success in forcing the country to live within more modest means in a less generous world.

The YAR's long-term development prospects improved abruptly when oil was discovered in commercial quantities in 1984. This event also placed severe demands on the still very limited capacities of the state. With the oil find, the twin tasks facing the Salih regime were to maintain the new discipline and austerity of the past few years and to gear up to absorb efficiently the oil revenues that were expected to start flowing in late 1987. Despite the politically difficult combination of rising expectations and continued hard times, the regime was able to limit imports and government expenditures during this period of transition. Although oil for export did begin to flow in late 1987, the regime was forced to reimpose austerity measures in 1989 that it had prematurely relaxed the previous year. Nevertheless, at the same time that it wrestled with these politically hard choices, the government proceeded as quickly as financing would allow with development of the oil sector, as well as with key infrastructure and agricultural projects.

In the 1980s, the increasing capacity of the Yemeni state for development also helped it perform its more traditional functions and was partly understood and justified in these terms. This was particularly the case when the regime stepped up efforts to extend its reach into NDF-influenced and tribal areas. Certain development efforts that made the periphery more accessible made possible the delivery of basic services to places where the state was regarded with suspicion or scorn, hence the emphasis on pushing roads into such areas as soon as they were pacified. President Salih came to justify development efforts in terms of nation-state building—in terms of national integration—as well as economic gains. The development activities of the second half of the 1980s, as well as the content of the Third Five-Year **Development Plan**, adopted in 1988, reflected the continuing influence of these ideas.

This third period of YAR history, spanning the 1980s, ended with the creation of the ROY in 1990, also headed by President Salih. It was the relative political and economic turnaround of the YAR after the 1970s, as well as the sudden weakening of the PDRY in the late 1980s, that made possible this YAR-initiated merger.

YEMEN BANK FOR RECONSTRUCTION AND DEVELOP-MENT. *See* BANKS.

YEMEN ECONOMIC CORPORATION. *See* MILITARY ECONOMIC CORPORATION (MECO).

YEMEN HUNT OIL CO. (YHOC). A subsidiary of Hunt Oil Company of Dallas, the company owned by Ray Hunt that in 1984 became the first to discover **oil** in commercial quantities in North Yemen. YHOC's 20-year production sharing agreement (PSA) became law in 1982. Partnering with Exxon and a Korean oil company, with major financing coming from Exxon, YHOC as operator rapidly developed the production-for-export capacity of the Alif and several other fields near **Marib** in the Marib/al-Jawf basin. It built a pipeline down to a terminus on the **Red Sea** at Ras Isa, and crude began to flow down to the terminus for export in 1987. A small refinery for petroleum products for domestic consumption was also soon built near Marib.

YHOC established the **United States** as a player in petroleum politics in Yemen. In the 1990s, as operator in another consortium, YHOC found, developed, and began producing oil in what, prior to Yemeni **unification**, was the "neutral zone" between the YAR's Marib/al-Jawf basin and the PDRY's **Shabwa** region. Called the Jannah field, this became a lesser (but still significant) contributor to oil production in the ROY.

YHOC also found Yemen's large natural gas deposits in the Marib/al-Jawf basis and began planning for their development in the early 1990s. After 2000, ending long delays caused by politics and market conditions for gas, a consortium headed by Total of France as operator, and including YHOC, signed the needed long-term marketing agreements for the provision of liquefied natural gas (LNG) to Korea and the United States. Construction of the collection facilities, pipeline, liquefaction plant and terminus on the Arabian Sea began in 2005, and it was projected that the first shipments of LNG to Korea would begin by late 2009.

Hailed from the mid-1980s to the mid-1990s as a partner and savior of Yemen, the YHOC later became something of a whipping boy in the oil sector in Yemen over such issues as the "Yemenization" of its work force and certain allegedly questionable accounting procedures. Partly based on the much greater productivity of its **Masila** field, **Nexen** succeeded YHOC as the model foreign oil company. After having negotiated and signed a five-year extension of its original oil agreement with YHOC for the Marib/al-Jawf basin in 2003, the Yemeni government broke the agreement in 2005, citing legal and constitutional reasons. It then seized YHOC's facilities in the basin and signed an oil production-sharing agreement for this area with a Yemeni firm, Safer Exploration Production Operations Company. In late 2005, Hunt Oil and ExxonMobil took the dispute to arbitration before the Paris-based International Chamber of Commerce—and lost.

YEMENI CIVIL WAR. The long, bitter, and costly internecine struggle in North Yemen between the republicans and the **royalists** supporting the **Hamid al-Din** imamate that began immediately after the **1962 Revolution** and the creation of the YAR and dragged on intermittently until the republican–royalist **reconciliation** of 1970. The second half of the civil war coincided with a long drought, and the two forces in combination caused hunger, economic hardship, social dislocation, and many deaths in most parts of the country. The struggle remains a defining memory for two generations of North Yemenis.

It was not until after the civil war that the Yemenis could really begin to take their destiny Yemen into their own hands. The war forced the deferral of most major efforts at development in the YAR until the 1970s. During that struggle, the republicans, who were committed to creating a modern state and using it to end Yemen's weakness and "backwardness," controlled little more than the third of the country defined by the triangle formed by the roads connecting Sanaa, **Taiz**, and **al-Hudayda**. Moreover, they shared control of that third with the Egyptian forces that intervened on their behalf; even much of the territory within the triangle was outside effective control by them or the Egyptians. The royalists and their tribal allies controlled another third of the country, and other **tribes** or local leaders concerned with their own autonomy, or willing to go either way if the price were right, controlled the last third. Clearly, the balance between the tribes and the state during these grim years was more in favor of the former than it had been under the **imamate** during the decades before the revolution.

The young Imam Muhammad **al-Badr**, son of just-deceased Imam **Ahmad**, escaped from Sanaa hours after the start of the revolution and went on to rally many of the northern tribes and others allies of the imamate. The civil war pitted the royalists, led by Imam al-Badr, against the republican regime, headed by President Abdullah **al-Sallal**. In 1968, however, Muhammad Ibn Husayn, the cousin of al-Badr who performed better in battle than any of the other princes, wrested leadership of the lagging royalist cause from a weary and ill imam. By this time, President al-Sallal had also been deposed by republican opponents in 1967 and replaced by Qadi Abd al-Rahman **al-Iryani**. The republicans broke the **Siege of Sanaa** in early 1968, and Qasim Munasser, the able and respected tribal leader and royalist commander, defected with his forces to the republican side near the end of the 1960s. These two events seemed to break the stalemate in the war, setting the stage for reconciliation in 1970—and the republic's survival.

The civil war had been regionalized when **Egypt** quickly came in strongly on the side of the republicans and **Saudi Arabia** sided with the royalists. It was then internationalized when the **Soviet Union** and East Europe supported Egypt and the new YAR even as **Great Britain** and then the **United States** deferred to the Saudis and their interests. As a consequence, the Yemeni civil war became a microcosm and a battleground of the "Arab Cold War" between the revolutionary Arab nationalist republicans and the conservative Arab monarchists and, to a lesser extent, of the global **Cold War** between the Soviet Bloc and the U.S.-led "Free World."

The Egyptians, who probably saved the republic in those first years, took control of fighting the civil war and ended up looking increasingly like occupiers; soon bogged down, they came to call the war "our **Vietnam**." Seen as a puppet of Egypt's President Gamal Abdul **Nasser**, the al-Sallal regime lost credibility and legitimacy. When Nasser withdrew his forces from Yemen in November 1967 in the wake of the sudden, total defeat of Egyptian and other Arab forces by Israel in the greatest of **Arab–Israeli conflicts,** the Six-Day War, the regime was toppled in a matter of weeks. This opened the way to the reconciliation that took more than another two years to consummate under Qadi **al-Iryani.**

From the outset, efforts were made to end the fighting and bring about reconciliation. In 1963 came the **United Nations'** brief and futile effort by Secretary General U Thant, Under Secretary Ralph Bunche, U.S. envoy Elsworth Bunker, and UN forces led by General Carl von Horn. Subsequently, the several efforts by the Yemeni republicans and royalists to find a solution were confounded by the conflicting interests and goals of the regional participants in the war, the Egyptians and the Saudis. Similarly, efforts by the Egyptians and the Saudis to extricate themselves were confounded by the conflicting interests and goals of the Yemeni republicans and royalists. On top of this, both the republicans and royalists were internally divided, with the pro-Nasser republicans versus the other republicans and Imam Badr versus his younger cousins and other royalists.

In an early peace effort, in September 1963, liberal republicans, among them Qadis al-Iryani and Muhammad **al-Zubayri** and both republican and royalist tribal shaykhs, convened a conference in **Amran,** north of Sanaa—and beyond the reach of the government. They proposed a peace council, drew up a set of demands for presentation to Presidents al-Sallal and Nasser, and sent a delegation to Cairo. The effort, which did not gain the support of the two presidents, came to naught. In the fall of 1964, the Erkowit Conference was held between moderate royalists and republicans, among them Sayyid Ahmad **al-Shami** and Qadi al-Zubayri. They arranged a ceasefire and called for a national conference. In the absence of enough common ground, the called-for conference failed to occur, the initiative ended, and fighting resumed.

Held in May 1965, the Khamir Conference was a major event and a clear indication that many Yemeni leaders were disillusioned with the course the revolution had taken and wanted to be free of the Egyptians, free to take their destiny into their own hands. Held in the "capital" of **Hashid** country north of Sanaa, and backed by Ahmad Muhammad **Numan** and Shaykh Abdullah ibn Husayn **al-Ahmar,** the YAR prime minister and interior minister, respectively, the conference brought together an array of republican leaders and powerful tribal shaykhs. Although supporters of the imam chose not to attend, the conference formed a committee to make overtures to the royalists and sent a message to Saudi King Faysal inviting talks. After the conference, when President al-Sallal and his military colleagues made clear their opposition to the initiative and President Nasser stepped up military activities in Yemen, many of the major shaykhs involved in the conference went into voluntary exile in South Yemen.

Qadi al-Zubayri's special project, the Khamir conference, had met a month after his assassination in the mountains to the northeast. He had only months earlier launched his Party of God, abandoned Sanaa, and begun promoting his ideas to the tribes to the north and northeast. Al-Zubayri and his new party were part of what came to be called "the Third Force," an assortment of groups that surfaced in the mid-1960s. Born of disgust with the virtual occupation of Yemen by Egypt, they advocated political alternatives to a restored Hamid al-Din imamate or the Egyptian-dominated republican regime. Most Third Force proposals sought to retain the republic, minus the al-Sallal regime and the Egyptian military, although the idea of a constitutional imamate without the Hamid al-Din family was also revived. With the Khamir initiative aborted, most of "the Third Force" activity became peripheral and moved abroad, particularly to Lebanon, where the **al-Wazir** clan and Ahmad Jabr **al-Afif** and his friends based their continuing efforts. Much of this ended up financed by the Saudis for their own purposes.

Efforts by Egypt and Saudi Arabia to find a way out of an increasingly dangerous confrontation in Yemen began at the Alexandria Arab Summit in September 1964, when President Nasser and King **Faysal** met and discussed the Yemen issue and stated publicly their common aim of ending all outside intervention. In August 1965, they met again, this time in Jidda. They fashioned the Jidda Agreement, a detailed blueprint for a ceasefire, Egyptian withdrawal, Saudi disengagement, a national conference of Yemeni republicans and royalists, and a transition regime for Yemen. The Egyptians and Saudis did not consult with the Yemenis on the terms of the Jidda Agreement, but the conference of republicans and royalists did convene at Harod near the Saudi border in late November 1965. Not surprisingly, they deadlocked from the start over the nature of the transition regime and other matters, and soon disbanded—and another initiative unraveled.

At the Khartoum Arab Summit in August 1967, after Egypt's defeat in the Six-Day War, President Nasser and King Faysal agreed to end their long confrontation and, in effect, implement the Jidda Agreement. Egypt agreed to withdraw its military forces from Yemen by December 1967 in exchange for the suspension of Saudi aid to the royalist side. The Egyptians did withdraw and, with the end of the Siege of Sanaa in early 1968, the Saudis ceased supporting the royalists. This was two years after the Jidda Agreement and two years before the republican–royalist **reconciliation** in early 1970.

Peace in Yemen was a long time coming. Although it put much state-building and socioeconomic development on hold and exacted an awful price in terms of human suffering, the Yemeni Civil War did open up a theretofore isolated and insulated North Yemen to a flood of new ideas, institutions, and practices. The YAR of the 1970s and later was able to grasp and use many of these new elements in ways, and to a degree, impossible in the mid-1960s and before.

YEMENI CORRECTIVE ORGANIZATION (TASHIH). *See* NASIRITES AND NASIRITE PARTIES.

YEMENI ISLAMIC JIHAD. *See* ADEN–ABYAN ISLAMIC ARMY (AAIA); AL-FADHLI; POLITICAL ISLAM, MODERN.

YEMENI JOURNALISTS SYNDICATE (YJS). *See* INTEREST (PRESSURE) GROUPS.

YEMENI–SAUDI BORDER DISPUTES AND AGREEMENTS. *See* BORDERS.

YEMENI SOCIALIST PARTY (YSP). The Marxist–Leninist vanguard party that was created in 1978 and that proceeded to rule the PDRY firmly and without legal opposition until the eve of Yemeni **unification** in 1990. The institutions, procedures, and practices of this Soviet-style party reflected the preferences of its first secretary general, **Abd al-Fattah** Ismail. It was he who pushed hard in the 1970s for the merger of the **National Liberation Front**, the **People's Democratic Union**, and the pro-Syrian **Baath Party** (the Vanguard) that resulted in the YSP. Despite considerable success in organizing political life in the PDRY into the mid-1980s, the YSP virtually decapitated itself in the course of the 1986 leadership fight, the **13 January events**. **Ali Nasir** Muhammad al-Hasani, who had replaced Ismail as YSP secretary general in 1980, was driven from office in the fight, and after the bloodbath his place was taken by Ali Salim **al-Baydh**.

In 1989, the weakened YSP under al-Baydh's leadership was swept up in the **unification** process. It joined the unification regime in May 1990 as co-equal partner with President **Ali Abdullah Salih** and his **General People's Congress** (GPC), providing for the transition period the vice president, prime minister, and speaker of the parliament. After a disappointing showing in the April 1993 **elections**, in which it trailed the GPC by a large margin and did only about as well as **Islah**, it formed a coalition government with those parties.

The YSP was torn asunder by the political crisis and **War of Secession** in 1994, after which most of its leaders and many of its cadre were forced to flee the country. The remnants of the party only hurt themselves further by boycotting the 1997 parliamentary **elections**, leaving the field wide open to the GPC and Islah. Thereafter, this former vanguard party of a one-party state slowly began to learn how to play democratic politics and to be an opposition party in a multiparty system. This transition was reflected in the two rounds of the YSP's 4th Party Congress, in 1998 and 2000, the first congress held since the 3rd Party Congress of 1985. The transition took place largely under the leadership of the late **Jarullah** Umar, who became deputy secretary general in 2000, and Dr. Yasin Said **Numan**, who became secretary general in 2005. In 2002, the party took a leading role with Islah in forming the **Joint Meeting Parties** (JMP), the five-party opposition coalition that put forward a candidate and made a respectable showing in the 2006 presidential **elections**. Thereafter, it continued with its partners to challenge and offer an alternative to President Salih and the GPC.

YEMENI UNIFICATION. *See* UNIFICATION AND UNIFICATION PROCESS, YEMENI.

YEMENI UNIONISTS. The vaguely defined, mostly young, heterogeneous, and growing group of Yemeni nationalists who in the early 1950s succeeded the **Free Yemenis** as critics of the Yemeni **imamate** and as advocates of various political and socioeconomic reforms for Yemen. Branches of the Yemeni Union were set up in 1952 in Aden and, with guidance from Ahmad Muhammad **Numan**, in Cairo just after the Egyptian Revolution. The large number of **Shafii** students and workers who joined and identified with the Yemeni Union distinguished it from the older Free Yemenis, which, established in Aden less than a decade earlier, had included very prominent **Zaydis**. Still, many of the Free Yemenis found their way to the union.

YEMEN NATIONAL OIL COMPANY. The PDRY's state agency created in the early 1970s through the amalgamation of five nationalized petroleum distribution companies for the purpose of buying petroleum products and distributing them throughout the country. The company, a subsidiary of the Petroleum and Minerals Board, was involved neither in bunkering at **Aden** port, which remained in the hands of a number of international **oil** companies, nor in the **Aden refinery**, which continued to be owned and operated (and, after 1977, just operated) by **British Petroleum.**

YEMEN PETROLEUM CO. (YPC). The old public corporation dating from the early years of the YAR that was revived in 1985 and made responsible for the procurement, marketing, and distribution of petroleum products. In the early 1970s, these tasks had been taken from the original YPC and combined with responsibility for oil and salt production near **Salif** in an important new public corporation, the Yemen Oil and Mineral Co. (YOMINCO). It was YOMINCO, under the direction of Ali Abd al-Rahman al-Bahr, that smoothed the way on the Yemen side for the **Yemen Hunt Oil Co.** and the subsequent discovery of oil near **Marib** in 1984. Under the 1985 reorganization, however, YOMINCO was dissolved and its duties were divided between the revived YPC and the newly created Ministry of Oil and Mineral Resources.

YEMEN PORTS AND SHIPPING CORPORATION. *See* ADEN.

YOUNGHUSBAND, SIR GEORGE. *See* GREAT BRITAIN.

YUFRUS. *See* IBN ALWAN AHMAD; RELIGION AND RELIGIOUS GROUPS IN YEMEN.

– Z –

ZABID AND WADI ZABID. A major inland town on the **Tihama** that was founded in the ninth century AD, a major political capital on two occasions, and, for a millennium down to the early 20th century, a major center of Islamic teaching and scholarship. Zabid was the capital of the Banu Ziyad dynasty, founded in 822 by Muhammad ibn Ziyad. Ruling much of Yemen for two centuries, this dynasty served to separate Yemen from the **Abbasid** Empire in distant Baghdad and to allow the distinctive character of the Yemenis and Yemeni society to reassert themselves and develop further. Zabid was also an important political center during the **Rasulid** dynasty in the 13th and 14th centuries.

Another legacy of the Ziyadi dynasty was Zabid's role as a major center of learning for more than the next millennium. It is said that at one time there were 230 colleges in Zabid, and that algebra was refined, if not conceived, there. Today Zabid is known for the many remnants of these schools and mosques, and, above all, for its distinctive, highly refined architectural style, which features baked brick and plaster surfaces broken by geometric trim and other detailing in baked brick. UNESCO declared Zabid a World Heritage Site in 1993, but only recently have plans been devised to conserve the old architecture and control invasive modern construction.

Zabid is located in Wadi Zabid, about halfway between **al-Hudayda** and **al-Mukha**. It depends upon Wadi Zabid, the major **wadi** in the southern half of the Tihama, which starts in the foothills of the mountains to the east and runs at a right angle to the **Red Sea**. Its groundwater is extensive and, during the rainy season, its runoff can reach to the coast. For millennia, these waters have supported extensive agriculture and a relatively large population, including that of Zabid. Beginning in the late 1960s, and even more so into the 1970s, it became the basis of the YAR's first moderately successful large-scale, integrated agricultural development project. The Wadi Zabid Project, first headed by Dr. Abd al-Karim **al-Iryani** and generously funded by international and Arab regional agencies, became the model for the several wadi development projects subsequently launched by the **Tihama Development Authority**.

ZAFAR (DHU RAYDAN). *See* HIMYARITE KINGDOM.

ZAKAT. See REVENUE.

ZANZIBAR. *See* TRADE ROUTES, ANCIENT.

ZARANIQ TRIBE. The largest and most formidable tribe on North Yemen's largely nontribal coastal desert, the **Tihama**. The Zanariq stood in the way of Imam **Yahya's** effort to extend the sway of the **imamate** state and submitted to the imam only after a savage two-year campaign in the late 1920s. An important actor in the history of the Tihama for many centuries, the Zaraniq was known in the past as the Maaziba tribe and, like other tribes on the Tihama, claimed descent from the **Akk** tribe.

ZAYD BIN ALI ZAIN AL-ABDIN. *See* ZAYDI SHIISM.

ZAYDIS AND SHAFIIS IN POLITICS AND SOCIETY. The great divide in Yemen is between the **Zaydi Shiism** and the **Shafii Sunnisn**, and this sectarian division has had a profound effect, political and otherwise, on historic and modern Yemen. The two communities established themselves in Yemen early in the Islamic era, more than a millennium years ago, and have been the two most dominant groups in most centuries since that time. The old myth of numerical parity notwithstanding, the Shafii community is and has probably been for a long time far larger than the Zaydi community in North Yemen. With Yemeni **unification** in 1990, the numerical superiority of the Shafiis increased to even an greater degree.

Over the centuries, the Zaydis in North Yemen have resided in the sparcely populated mountainous northern highlands as well as in the far north and northeast, whereas the Shafiis have populated the southern uplands, the **Tihama**, and the far south and east. The rough dividing line between the two communities is the same **Sumara Pass** that separates "Upper Yemen" from "Lower Yemen." **Ibb**, **Taiz**, and

al-Hudayda provinces are Shafii areas, whereas **Dhamar** province and the provinces to its north are Zaydi. Virtually all of South Yemen, the mountainous areas and the lowlands, is Shafii. As a result, the two terms do have geographic connotations, and reference is often made to the "Zaydi north" and the "Shafii south"—in the old YAR, and now in the ROY.

Although the Zaydis are Shii Muslims and the Shafiis are Sunni, the Zaydi branch of Shii Islam is more similar to the rationalist schools of Sunnism than it is to the mystical, millenarian sects typical of Shii Islam. Unlike Shiism in most Muslim countries, Zaydism in Yemen is an establishment religion, not one born of defeat and subjugation. As a result, the very real differences between the two communities in Yemen have been, and continue to be, less religious—less matters of dogma and ritual—than they are cultural, social, and political. The Zaydis of the northern highlands and the Shafiis of the rest of Yemen constitute separate subcultures, the main features of which were forged in the history of the past several centuries. Each community has viewed its relationship to the other in "us–them" terms. Segregated socially as well as geographically, the members of each community have tended to feel more comfortable with, and more easily understood by, their own kind.

In addition, the differences between the Zaydis and the Shafiis in North Yemen are perceived partly as matters of oppressors and oppressed, of warrior–rulers and subject peasants and merchants. The Zaydis have ruled the Shafiis more often than not over recent centuries, and Zaydi jurists and theologians developed an elaborate political theory that justified the rule of the Zaydi **sayyid** ruler, the imam, over non-Zaydi subjects as well as fellow Zaydis. Most of the counselors, judges, and administrators of the Zaydi **imamate** were drawn from the upper ranks of the Zaydi community, especially its sayyid minority, and it was the Zaydi tribes in the north that supported the Zaydi imams with tribal irregulars and as members in the imams' small armies. The Zaydi imamate patronized culture, learning, and the arts to a modest degree, and learned Zaydis dominated and were the arbiters of these matters, as well as of law and the legal system. At the top of society in North Yemen, the Zaydi leaders felt superior and found it easy to think themselves the best of the best in all known worlds. Largely confined to the highlands and cut off from the outside world, the Zaydis had little opportunity and inclination to compare their life with alternatives the outside world had to offer. They were a proud, inward-looking mountain people with a narrow, parochial perspective.

For its part, the Shafii community in North Yemen exhibited contradictory tendencies of submission and rebellion in the face of Zaydi power and claims to authority. More often than not, the Shafiis chose, or were forced, to accept, the imam as their secular ruler, though not as their religious leader. Denied political position and social status, some Shafii turned to trade and commerce, particularly in Taiz and al-Hudayda, in the 20th century. Beginning in mid-century, many more emigrated to Aden and sometimes far beyond as students, laborers, sailors, and merchants, thereby exposing themselves to the modern world and its ideas to a far greater degree than did the more isolated Zaydi highlanders. Many of the Shafii émigrés and their offspring returned to Yemen, bringing with them some of the skills learned in the outside world. Marginal men in a Zaydi-dominated society, the more able of the Shafiis were open to change and innovation. Increasingly aware of their marginality in the mid-20th century, these Shafiis felt more and more deprived, entitled to a fairer share, even as their Zaydi counterparts inclined toward conservation—particularly of their privileges—and often feared Shafii demands for change.

These notions informed politics in North Yemen just before and after the **1962 Revolution**. They also informed inter-Yemeni affairs and the question of Yemeni **unification**, since the latter had the potential to tilt the balance overwhelmingly in the Shafii direction. Most leaders, whether north or south, Zaydi or Shafii, have tried to submerge and dissolve the sectarian difference in the solvent of a stronger Yemeni nationalism. *See also* RELIGION AND RELIGIOUS GROUPS IN YEMEN; SOCIAL SYSTEM AND STRUCTURE.

ZAYDI SHIISM IN YEMEN. The sect and teachings of Shii Islam that have prevailed in the northern highlands of North Yemen since the 10th century A.D. The sect takes its name from Zayd bin Ali Zain al-Abdin, the son of the fourth Shii imam and the grandson of Husayn, who, in turn, was one of the two sons of Fatima, the daughter of the Prophet Muhammad, and Ali bin Abi Talib, the cousin and son-in-law of the Prophet. Shortly after the Prophet's death, the followers of Ali founded what became the heterodox Shii branch of Islam, which, in turn, took root in Yemen primarily in the form of the **Ismailis** and, more important, the Zaydis. The Zaydis accord special status to the Alids, the blood descendants of Ali and Fatima, and only **sayyids** who traced their descent from the Prophet by way of Ali and Fatima could lay claim to the Zaydi **imamate**.

The link between Ali and Yemen is made personal by a legend that has Ali being sent by the Prophet to Yemen in 631, where he converted to Islam all the members of the great **Hamdan** tribal confederation in a single day. Whether or not this really occurred, a link arose between the followers of Ali—the Zaydis and, in particular, their imams—and the **Hashid** and **Bakil** tribal confederations, which are descended from the Hamdan, that persisted into the 1960s.

The doctrine of the sect as developed by Zayd and his followers was pragmatic, rational, and open to extension by critical examination and interpretation and rejected such features of other Shii sects as the ideas of a "hidden" imam, an occult exegesis of the Koran, systematic dissimulation, and mysticism. Often referred to as the "fifth school" of Sunni Islam, Zaydism differs from Sunni orthodoxy primarily in the insistence on the institution of the imamate and the right of only descendants of Ali and Fatima to rule the world of Islam through that institution. Indeed, some learned believers in **Shafii** Sunnism claim to object only to this ascriptive feature of Zaydism.

The man who brought Zaydism to Yemen and founded the Zaydi imamate was al-Hadi ila al-Haqq Yahya ibn Husayn. He did so in 897 after being invited by tribes in the north around **Saada** to come from his native Medina to mediate a long and bitter dispute and govern them. Al-Hadi's 14-year reign established in the highlands of North Yemen the Zaydi imamate that was to persist, with numerous changes of fortune and breaks in continuity, until the establishment of the YAR in 1962, all the while maintaining many of the features that he and his immediate successors had decreed for it. Over the centuries, the imamate patronized learning, culture and the arts, albeit to a modest degree.

The strong imams of the first six decades of the 20th century, Imam **Yahya** and his son, Imam **Ahmad**, served as the spiritual leaders and temporal rulers and defenders of the community of Islam, much as their predecessors had a millennium earlier. They worked hard, and with considerable success, to isolate and insulate traditional Yemen from the outside world, the modern world, through these crucial decades.

AL-ZINDANI, ABD AL-MAJID (1938–). North Yemen's leading **political Islamist** from the 1970s through most of the first decade of the 21st century, who led the Muslim Brotherhood in North Yemen through much of the 1970s, recruited and served as religious guide for many **Afghanistan**-bound jihadists in the 1980s, and then became co-founder and spiritual leader of **Islah**, the opposition party formed at the time of Yemeni **unification** in 1990. Al-Zindani served as speaker of Islah's ruling Shura Council (its "central committee") from its beginning in 1990 until early 2007 and in this capacity had considerable influence in the party and the ROY. He was a member of the ROY's five-member **Presidential Council** from 1993, when Islah joined the ruling coalition after the 1993 **elections**, until it was replaced by the singular presidency in 1994.

Al-Zindani was under the patronage of the Saudis to varying degree throughout his career. They used him as leader of the Brotherhood in their efforts to rein in the YAR in the 1970s. Ousted from Brotherhood leadership in the late 1970s, al-Zindani spent most of his time in the 1980s teaching in Saudi Arabia, where he became known as a theorist on Islam and science. He became deeply involved in the recruitment and religious training of volunteers for jihad against the **Soviet** invaders in Afghanistan in the 1980s—and it was during this time that he allegedly played some part in shaping the religious perspective of Usama **bin Laden**. Still involved in the YAR affairs, al-Zindani mobilized Islamic fighters in the Salih regime's successful struggle against the **National Democratic Front** early in the decade.

Al-Zindani had returned to the YAR from Saudi Arabia at the end of the 1980s to wage jihad against the Marxist PDRY. With unification in 1990, he turned his efforts to influencing the course of events in the ROY through Islah. And when politics in the ROY turned to armed combat, he mobilized Islamic jihadists to fight against the southern socialist leaders and their forces in the **War of Secession** in 1994.

 With the First **Gulf War**, and especially since **9/11**, al-Zindani became increasingly hostile toward the **United States**. The hostility was reciprocated. The United States claimed that the large Al-Iman

University, founded and headed by al-Zindani, was a teaching ground for militant Islamists, both Yemeni and non-Yemeni. In 2004, the U.S. Treasury placed him on its list of persons providing support to terrorists and, in 2006, President George W. Bush asked the ROY's President Salih to arrest him for the same reasons. The ROY was quick to come to Al-Zindani's defense. However, he has become something of an embarrassment to the regime. Increasingly out-of-step with the pragmatic, moderate center of Islah and its goals, al-Zindani was voted out as chairman of its Shura Council in early 2007.

Al-Zindani is from a prominent family in **Ibb**, a major city in the **Shafii** heartland of the southern uplands. He went to Cairo to study pharmacy in about 1960, came under the sway of the Muslim Brotherhood, and reacted negatively to the secularism of **Nasserism**. He cut off his studies and returned to Yemen on the occasion of the **1962 Revolution**. Abd al-Majid, his younger brother, has a doctorate in international relations from Notre Dame University. A longtime bookstore owner, he was YAR minister of education in the mid-1980s and deputy minister of higher education in the first government after unification in 1990.

ZINJIBAR. *See* ABYAN.

ZIYADI STATE AND DYNASTY. *See* ZABID.

AL-ZUBAYRI, QADI MUHAMMAD MAHMUD (1919–1965). The **Zaydi** poet and writer from a prominent **qadi** family of Sanaa who helped to shape and serve the Yemeni nation from his days as a founder of the **Free Yemenis** in the mid-1940s to his political activities during the first years of the YAR. This ended with his assassination in April 1965. He first went to Cairo in 1940, where he initially teamed up with Ahmad Muhammad **Numan**. With Numan, he founded the Free Yemenis in Aden in 1944 and then spent years in exile in Egypt and elsewhere.

Like a growing number of other nationalists during the **Yemeni Civil War**, Al-Zubayri soon came to despair of the virtual **Egyptian** occupation of Yemen and the republican–**royalist** division of the nation that the regime of Egyptian-backed President **al-Sallal** seemed to be perpetuating. He then created part of "the Third Force," and his murder in 1965 in the mountains in the northeast occurred shortly after he had broken with the regime to found his Party of God and call for republican–royalist **reconciliation**, for which another failed attempt was made just after his death, at the Khamir Conference he had inspired. His Party of God, which called for reconciliation based on an Islamic consultative republic, did not long survive his murder.

Although his words and person inspired the men who carried out the **1962 Revolution**, al-Zubayri was a man of the previous generation. Indeed, he was a traditionalist, albeit one touched significantly by some of the features of the modern world that he had encountered in Cairo during his years of study and political activity in 1940 and thereafter.

ZWEMER, SAMUEL M. *See* TRAVELERS.

Bibliography

INTRODUCTION

The quantity and quality of the literature on Yemen, especially modern Yemen, has increased greatly in recent decades. The materials in Arabic by Yemeni scholars have become more varied and accessible, and there is much material available in English, French, and German. America's growing interest in Yemen, political and otherwise, has increased dramatically since the 1960s, and the increase in American scholarship on Yemen reflects this.

Robert W. Stookey's *Yemen: The Politics of the Yemen Arab Republic* (Boulder, 1978) remains a fine political history of Yemen in general for the two millennia prior to Britain's occupation of Aden in 1839 and of North Yemen through the Hamid al-Din imamate and the first decade of the Yemen Arab Republic (YAR). Three other books that deal with politics and society under the imamate in different decades of the 20th century are fascinating reading, in part because they reveal the extent to which Yemen and the Zaydi imamate at the time of the 1962 Revolution were so unchanged from earlier decades. They are Ameen Rihani's *Arabian Peak and Desert—Travels in al-Yemen* (New York, 1930); Hugh Scott's *In the High Yemen* (London, 1942), and W. Harold Ingrams's *The Yemen—Imams, Rulers and Revolutions* (London, 1963). Still worth reading to get a sense of the great continuity in place, people, and imamate rule is the earliest western account of North Yemen, Carsten Niebuhr's remarkable *Travels through Arabia and Other Countries in the East* (Edinburgh, 1792/Beirut, 1968). G. Wyman Bury's *Arabia Infelix or the Turks in Yemen* (London, 1915) provides an account of life during the last years of the second Ottoman occupation in the early 20th century.

The politics of North Yemen in the 20th century down to the 1962 Revolution and the first few years of the YAR are dealt with skillfully in Manfred W. Wenner's *Modern Yemen: 1918–1966* (Baltimore, 1966). For a detailed account of the YAR from the 1962 Revolution to the dawn of its age of oil in the mid-1980s, see Robert D. Burrowes's *The Yemen Arab Republic: The Politics of Development, 1962–1986* (Boulder, 1987), Wenner's *The Yemen Arab Republic: Development and Change in an Ancient Land* (Boulder, 1991) and J. E. Peterson's *Yemen: The Search for a Modern State* (Baltimore, 1982). A long chapter that evokes well the political tenor in the YAR in 1978 is found in Jonathan Rabin's *Arabia: A Journey through the Labyrinth* (New York, 1979).

The long history of Aden and the rest of South Yemen is sketched out in Robert W. Stookey's *South Yemen: A Marxist Republic in Arabia* (Boulder, 1982), and an overview of the British colonial era is afforded by R. J. Gavin's *Aden Under British Rule 1839–1967* (London, 1975). Three of last governors in Aden were uncommonly literate and insightful, and left fine accounts of that place and the rest of South Yemen during their tenures: Sir Tom Hickinbotham's *Aden* (London, 1958), Sir Charles Johnston's *The View from Steamer Point* (New York, 1964), and Sir Kennedy Trevaskis's *Shades of Amber: A South Arabian Episode* (London, 1968).

Several volumes by travelers and former colonial civil servants provide vivid, detailed pictures of the isolated interior of South Yemen during the decades of the 20th century prior to World War II, among them G. Wyman Bury's *The Land of Uz* (London, 1911), Bertram Thomas's *Arabia Felix* (London, 1932), Freya Stark's *Southern Gates of Arabia* (London, 1936), Daniel van der Meulen's *Aden to the Hadhramawt: A Journey in South Arabia* (London, 1947), W. Harold Ingrams's *Arabia and the Isles* (London, 3rd ed., 1966), and Doreen S. Ingrams's *A Time in Arabia* (London, 1970).

In addition to Stookey's *South Yemen: A Marxist Republic in Arabia*, two books on the politics of the People's Democratic Republic of Yemen (PDRY) are noteworthy: Helen Lackner's *P.D.R. Yemen: Outpost of Socialist Development in Arabia* (London, 1985) and Tareq and Jacqueline Ismael's *PDR Yemen: Politics, Economics and Society—The Politics of Socialist Transformation* (Boulder, 1986). The latter is crammed with information and sound analysis, and the former benefits from the author's having lived and worked for some years in the PDRY.

Several works deal with either or both the modern political history of the two Yemens and the unified Republic of Yemen (ROY). The best and most recent to do both is Paul Dresch's *A History of Modern Yemen* (Cambridge, UK, 2000). For a good analysis of changing state–society relations before and since unification, see Sheila Carapico, *Civil Society in Yemen* (Cambridge, Mass., 1998). Robin Bidwell's *The Two Yemens* (Boulder, 1983) spans two millennia and is most authoritative on the centuries up to and including the period of British rule in South Yemen, but becomes rather sketchy on the politics of the 1970s in both Yemens. Despite its revolutionary zeal, Fred Halliday's *Arabia without Sultans* (New York, 1975), the book on which many students of Yemeni politics cut their teeth, is still worth a read.

For Yemeni unification, see Robert D. Burrowes's "The Republic of Yemen: The Politics of Unification and the Civil War, 1989–1995," in Michael C. Hudson (ed.), *Middle East Dilemma: The Politics and Economics of Arab Integration (New York, 1999), 187–213. For the 1994 War of Secession and its aftermath, see Jamal S. al-Suwaidi (ed.), *The Yemeni War of 1994* (London, 1995) and E. G. H. Joffe, M. J. Hachemi, and E. W. Watkins (eds.), *Yemen Today: Crisis and Solutions* (London, 1997). For the politics of the ROY since 2000, see Sarah Phillips's *Yemen's Experiment in Regional Perspective: Patronage and Pluralized Authoritarianism* (New York, 2008) and Lisa Wedeen's *Peripheral Visions: Publics, Power, and Performance in Yemen* (Chicago, 2008).

Inter-Yemeni relations in particular and the foreign policies and international politics of the two Yemens in general are treated in Fred Halliday's *Revolution and Foreign Policy: The Case of South Yemen 1967–1987* (Cambridge, UK, 1990) and F. Gregory Gause III's *Saudi–Yemeni Relations: Domestic Structures and Foreign Influences* (New York, 1990).

For collections of essays on a broad array of topics pertaining to historical and contemporary Yemen, see Werner Daum (ed.), *Yemen: 3000 Years of Art and Civilization in Arabia Felix* (Innsbruck, 1987) and, more recently, Remy Leveau, Franck Mermier, and Udo Steinbach (eds.), *Le Yemen contemporain* (Paris, 1999). To learn just about all there is to know about Sanaa as well as a great deal about North Yemen in general, see Robert B. Serjeant and Ronald Lewcock (eds.), *Sanaa: An Arabian Islamic City* (London, 1983) and Lewcock's *Wadi

Hadramawt and the Walled City of Shibam (Paris, 1986). Selma al-Radi's *The Amiriya in Rada: The History and Restoration of a Sixteenth-Century Madrasa in the Yemen* (Oxford, 1997) recounts the successful restoration of a major cultural heritage site. For more on architecture, see Paolo Costa's and Ennio Vicario's aesthetically sensitive photo study of North Yemeni cities, *Arabia Felix: Land of Builders* (New York, 1977) and Fernando Varanda's excellent *Art of Building in Yemen* (Cambridge, Mass., 1982).

Many important studies of culture and society in North Yemen appeared in the last decade-and-a-half of the 20th century, among them Paul Dresch's *Tribes, Government, and History in Yemen* (Oxford, 1989), Steven Caton's *"Peaks of Yemen I Summon": Poetry as Cultural Practice in a North Yemeni Tribe* (Berkeley, 1990), Brinkley Messick's *The Calligraphic State: Textual Domination and History in a Muslim Society* (Berkeley, 1992), Thomas B. Stevenson's *Social Change in a Yemeni Highlands Town* (Salt Lake City, 1987), Bernard Haykel's *Revival and Reform in Islam: The Legacy of Muhammad al-Shawkani* (Cambridge, Mass., 2003), and Shelagh Weir's *A Tribal Order: Politics and Law in the Mountains of Yemen* (Austin, 2007). Two studies that focus on the role and significance of qat are Shelagh Weir's *Qat in Yemen—Consumption and Social Change* (London, 1985) and John G. Kennedy's *The Flower of Paradise—The Institutionalized Use of the Drug Qat in Yemen* (Dordrecht, Holland, 1987).

Abdulla S. Bujra's *The Politics of Stratification: A Study of Political Change* (Oxford, 1971) deals with South Yemen before and just after independence in 1967. Good, very recent studies of important aspects of the Hadhramawt include Linda Boxberger's *On the Edge of Empire: Hadhramawt, Emigration and the Indian Ocean, 1880s–1930s* (Ithaca, N.Y., 2002) and Engseng Ho's *The Graves of Tarim: Genealogy and Mobility Across the Indian Ocean* (Berkeley, 2006).

The finest travel guide to Yemen, one for the thinking person and serious traveler, is Joachim Chwaszcza (ed.) *Insight Guide: Yemen* (New York, 1992). This book and Costa's and Vicario's *Arabia Felix: Land of Builders* will have you calling your travel agent. Books that should add to this impulse are Tim MacIntosh-Smith's *Yemen: Travels in Dictionary Land* (London, 1997) and Steven C. Caton's *Yemen Chronicle: An Anthropology of War and Mediation* (New York, 2005). There is also Daniel McLaughlin's *Yemen* (Bradt Travel Guides) (Guilford, Conn.,

2008) and Pertti Hamalainen's *Yemen: A Travel Survival Kit* (Berkeley, 1999).

The World Bank remains a consistently good source of studies of economics and development in the YAR, the PDRY, and the ROY—e.g., see *People's Democratic Republic of Yemen: A Review of Economic and Social Development* (Washington, 1979) and *Yemen Arab Republic: Current Position and Prospects* (Washington, 1985). *The Economist Intelligence Unit (EIU)*, with its annual Yemen Country Profile and monthly Yemen Country Report, is perhaps the best source of economic information and analysis, as well as related political developments.

The two Yemens were not well covered in the newspapers and news magazines in the past, although it seems that events since the 1980s have drawn some increasing coverage. Perhaps the best newspaper sources are the *New York Times*, the *International Herald Tribune*, the *Christian Science Monitor*, the *Washington Post*, *The Wall Street Journal*, the *Times* (London), the *Sunday Times* (London), and *Le Monde*.

Among the general news magazines, the *Economist* (London) provides the most frequent coverage of Yemen, although these reports are few and far between and often superficial if not glib. Better and more regular reporting appears in the major regional news magazines, the monthly *Middle East* (London), and the biweekly *Middle East International* (London). The quarterly *Middle East Reports*, formerly the *Middle East Research and Information Project (MERIP) Reports*, occasionally contains excellent and unusual features on Yemen.

The best published source for monitoring Yemeni affairs in the 1980s and 1990s—for a regular chronology of events and timely features— was the *Middle East Economic Digest (MEED)*, the London-based weekly. (Thereafter, a change in format and mission greatly ended the usefulness of this source). Useful for a daily monitoring of the Yemeni and other Arab media on Yemeni affairs are the *Foreign Broadcast Information Service, Daily Report, Middle East* (Washington), and the BBC's *Summary of Foreign Broadcasts, Middle East and Africa* (London).

Internet resources and Web sites have grown dramatically in quantity and quality, especially since 2000. The Economist Intelligence Unit's annual Yemen Country Profiles and monthly Yemen Country Reports are online: http: //store.eiu.com/index.asp?layout.

Both of Yemen's English language newspapers, *The Yemen Times* and *The Yemen Observer*, appear on Internet sites:
www.yemen times.com/article.shtml?I=
www.yobserver.com/article-11595.php
    Other sources of good information online include:
www.al-bab.com/yemen/artic.htm
www.newsyemen.net/en/view_news.asp?sub
www.yemenmirror.com

Contents

General Surveys: Country/People in Words/Pictures

Adam, Paul. "Yemen: Toward Self-Sufficiency," *Geographical Magazine*, 60/7 (July 1988), 26–33.
Aithie, Charles and Patricia. *Yemen: Jewel of Arabia*. Northhampton, Mass.: Interlink, 2000

Damluji, Salma Samar. *A Yemen Reality.* London: Garnet Publishing, 1993.

Deonna, Laurence. *Yemen.* Washington, D.C.: Three Continents Press, 1991.

Gerard, Bernard. *Yemen,* translated from the French by Mostyn Mowbray. Paris: Delroisse, 1973.

Jargy, Simon. *Yemen,* photos by Alain Saint-Hilaire. Paris: Hachette Realites, 1978.

Jeffery, Richard Brooks (text), and Peggy Crawford (photos). *Yemen: A Culture of Builders.* Washington, D.C.: American Architectural Foundation, 1989.

Marechaux, Maria, Pascal Marechaux (photos), and Dominique Champault (text). *Arabian Moons: Passages in Time through Yemen.* Singapore: Concept Media, 1987.

Marechaux, Pascal. *Arabia Felix: Images of Yemen and Its People.* Woodbury, N.Y.: Barron's, 1980.

Ozeri, Zion M. *Yemenite Jews: A Photographic Essay.* New York: Schocken Books, 1985.

San Segundo, Gonzalo. "En el Reino de Saba," *Cambia,* 16 (4 November 1996), 68–71.

Searight, Sarah. "Fragile Unity in the Arab World," *Geographical Magazine,* 62/9 (September 1990), 10–14.

Smith, Tim. *Coal, Frankincense and Myrrh: Photographs of Yemen and British Yemenis.* Stockport, UK: Dewi Lewis, 2008.

Stark, Freya. *Seen in the Hadhramaut.* London: John Murray, 1938.

Wepf, Reinhold. *Le Yemen: pays de la reine de Saba.* Bern, Switzerland: Kummerly & Frey, 1967.

Handbooks, Surveys, Directories and Teaching Guides

Arab Report and Record (ARR). London economic and political biweekly, founded in 1965 and absorbed by the *Middle East Economic Digest (MEED)* in the 1990s.

Colburn, Marta. *From the Queen of Sheba to the Republic of Yemen: K–12 Resource Guide and Classroom Ideas.* Ardmore, Pa.: American Institute of Yemeni Studies, 2006.

Croken, Barbara, Lealan N. Swanson, and Manfred Wenner. *Libraries and Scholarly Resources in the Yemen Arab Republic.* Chicago: American Institute for Yemeni Studies, 1983.

The Economist. Economist Intelligence Unit (EIU). *Bahrain, Qatar, Oman, the Yemens.* Quarterly, London: 1978–85. *Oman, the Yemens,* 1986–89. *Yemen,* 1990–present. Monthly country reports and annual country profiles: eiu.com.

Green, Arnold H., and Robert Stookey. "Research in Yemen: Facilities, Climate and Current Projects," *Middle East Studies Association Bulletin*, 8 (1974), 27–46.

Middle East Contemporary Survey (MECS). Tel Aviv: Moshe Dayan Center, Shiloah Institute, Tel Aviv University, 1976–present.

Middle East Economic Digest (MEED). London: Middle East Business Intelligence, 1957–the present. www.meed.com.

Nyrop, Richard F., et al. *The Yemens: Country Studies*. Washington, D.C.: The American University, 1985.

Wenner, Manfred, and Lealan N. Swanson. *An Introduction to Yemen for Researchers and Scholars*. Chicago: American Institute for Yemeni Studies, 1984.

Personal Accounts: Adventure, Travel, Work, and Residence

Abercrombie, Thomas J. "Arabia's Frankincense Trail," *National Geographic Magazine*, 168/4 (October 1985), 475–513.

———. "Behind the Veil in Troubled Yemen," *National Geographic Magazine*, 125/3 (March 1964), 403–445.

Abdu, Rachid A., MD. *Journey of a Yemeni Boy*. Pittsburgh, Pa.: Dorrance Publishing, 2005.

Aithie, Charles and Patricia. *Yemen: Jewel of Arabia*. Northhampton, Mass.: Interlink Publishing, 2007.

Balsam, Francois. *Inquietude Yemen*. Paris: La Palatine, 1961.

Beckingham, Charles F. "Dutch Travellers in Arabia in the Seventeenth Century, Parts I and II," *Journal of the Royal Asiatic Society* (April 1951), 64–81; and (October 1951), 170–181.

———. "Some Early Travels in Arabia," *Journal of the Royal Asiatic Society* (October 1949), 155–176.

Beckinham, Charles F., and Robert B. Serjeant, "A Journey by Two Jesuits from Dhufar to Sanaa in 1590," *Geographical Journal*, 115 (January–June 1950), 194–207.

Belhaven, Lord. *The Kingdom of Melchior: Adventure in Southwest Arabia*. London: John Murray, 1949.

———. *The Uneven Road*. London: John Murray, 1955.

Bent, Theodore, and Mrs. T. Bent. *Southern Arabia*. London: Smith, Elder, 1900.

Bethmann, Erich W. *Yemen on the Threshold*. Washington, D.C.: American Friends of the Middle East, 1960.

Bidwell, Robin. *Travellers in Arabia*. London: Hamlyn, 1976.

Botting, Douglas. *Island of the Dragon's Blood*. London: Hodder & Stoughton, 1958.

―――. "The Oxford University Expedition to Socotra," *Geographical Journal*, 124/2 (June 1958), 200–209.

Boxhall, Peter. "Socotra: 'Island of Bliss,'" *Geographical Journal*, 132/2 (June 1966), 213–225.

Bury, G. Wyman (Abdullah Mansur). *The Land of Uz*. London: St. Martin's, 1911.

Caton, Steven C. *Yemen Chronicle: An Anthropology of War and Mediation*. New York: Hill and Wang, 2005.

Clarke, Harlan B, "Yemen: Southern Arabia's Mountain Wonderland," *National Geographic Magazine*, 92/5 (November 1947), 631–672.

Coon, Carlton. *Measuring Ethiopia*. Boston: Little, Brown, 1935.

Crawford, Peggy. *An American in Yemen: Travel Notes of a Photographer*. Paris: Editions Nicolas Chaudun, 2005.

Croskery, Sidney Elizabeth. *Whilst I Remember*. Dundonald, Northern Ireland: Blackstaff Press, 1983.

Deonna, Laurence. *Le Yemen que j'ai vu*. Lausanne, Switzerland: Heures-Imprimeries Reunies S. A., 1982.

Destremau, B. *Femme du Yemen*. Paris: Editions Peuples de Monde, 1990.

Eilts, Hermann F. "Along the Storied Incense Roads of Aden," *National Geographic Magazine*, 111/2 (February 1957), 233–254.

Farago, Ladislas. *Arabian Antic*. New York: Sheridan House, 1938.

Fayein, Claudie. *A French Doctor in the Yemen*, translated from the French by Douglas McKee. London: Robert Hale, 1957.

Fernea, Elizabeth Warnock, and Robert A. Fernea. *The Arab World: Personal Encounters*. Garden City, N.Y.: Anchor Press/Doubleday, 1985.

Fevrier, Louise. "A French Family in the Yemen," *Arabian Studies*, 3 (1976), 127–135.

Forbes, Rosita (Mrs. McGrath). "A Visit to the Idrisi Territory in Asir and Yemen," *Geographical Journal*, 62 (July–December 1923), 271–278.

Frankl, P. "Robert Finlay's Description of Sana in 1238–1239/1823," *British Society of Middle East Studies Bulletin*, 17/1 (1990), 16–32.

Freeth, Zahra, and H. V. F. Winstone. *Explorers of Arabia from the Renaissance to the Victorian Age*. London: Allen & Unwin, 1978.

Glaser, Edward. *Meine Reise durch Arhab und Haschid*, as translated into English by David Warburton, available from AIYS, Box 311, Ardmore PA 19003-0311.

Grove, Noel. "North Yemen," *National Geographic Magazine*, 156/2 (August 1979), 244–269.

Habshush, Hayyim. *Travels in Yemen: An Account of Joseph Halevy's Journey to Najran in the Year 1870*. Edited by S. D. Goitein. Jerusalem: Hebrew University Press, 1941.

Hansen, Eric. *Motoring with Muhammad: Journeys to Yemen and the Red Sea.* Boston: Houghton Mifflin, 1991.

Hansen, Thorkild. *Arabia Felix: The Danish Expedition of 1761–1767.* Translated from the Danish by James and Kathleen McFarlane. New York: Harper and Row, 1964.

Harris, Walter B. *A Journey through Yemen and Some General Remarks upon the Country.* Edinburgh: Blackwood, 1893.

Heard-Bey, Frauke. "The Society's Tour to the Yemen Arab Republic (YAR) and the People's Democratic Republic of Yemen (PDRY), *Asian Affairs,* 21, pt. II (June 1990), 174–186.

"Helfritz, Hans. "The First Crossing of Southwestern Arabia," *Geographical Review,* 25/3 (1935), 395–407.

————. *Land Without Shade.* Translated from the German by Kenneth Kirkness. London: Hurst & Blackett, 1935.

————. *The Yemen: A Secret Journey.* Translated from the German by M. Heron. London: Allen and Unwin, 1958.

Hoagland, Edward. "Arabia Felix," in Richard Bangs and Christian Kallen (eds.), *Paths Less Travelled.* New York: Atheneum, 1988.

Hoeck, Eva. *Doctor among the Bedouins.* Translated from the German by Mervyn Savill. London: Robert Hale, 1962.

Hoogstraal, Harry, and Robert E. Kuntz. "Yemen Opens the Door to Progress," *National Geographic Magazine,* 101/2 (February 1952), 213–244.

Horwitz, Tony. *Baghdad without a Map.* New York: Penguin Books, 1991.

Ingrams, Doreen S. "Excursion in the Hajr Province of the Hadramout," *Geographical Journal,* 98/3 (September 1941), 121–134.

————. *A Time in Arabia.* London: John Murray, 1970.

Ingrams, William Harold. *Arabia and the Isles.* 3rd ed. New York: Frederick A. Praeger, 1966.

————. "The Exploration of the Aden Protectorate," *Geographical Review,* 28/4 (October 1938), 638–651.

————. "From Cana (Husn Ghorab) to Sabbatha (Shabwa): The South Arabian Incense Route," *Journal of the Royal Asiatic Society* (October 1945), 169–185.

Jacob, Harold F. *Perfumes of Araby: Silhouettes of al-Yemen.* London: Martin Secker, 1915.

Johnston, Charles Hepburn. *The View from Steamer Point: Three Crucial Years in South Arabia.* New York: Frederick A. Praeger, 1964.

Kirkman, James, and Brian Doe, "The First Days of British Aden: The Diary of John Study Leigh," *Arabian Studies,* 2 (1975), 179–203.

de Landberg, Comte. *Arabica,* vol. 5. Leiden, Netherlands: Brill, 1898.

Lunt, James. *The Barren Rocks of Aden.* London: Herbert Jenkins, 1966.

Luqman, Farouk M. *Democratic Yemen Today.* Bombay, 1970.

————. *Yemen 1970.* Aden, 1970.

Macintosh-Smith, Tim. *Travels in Dictionary Land.* London: John Murray, 2000.

Mc Lean. Neil. "The War in the Yemen," *Royal Central Asian Journal*, 51/1 (January 1964), 102–111.

Macro, Eric. "William Leveson Gower in the Yemen, 1903," *Arabian Studies*, 5 (1979), 141–147.

Manzoni, Renzo. *El Yemen: tre anni nell'Arabia Felix.* Rome: Tipografia Eredi Botta, 1884.

Milligan, Charles. "Notes of a Journey in Yemen," *Proceeding of the Royal Geographic Society*, 18 (1874), 194–197.

Monroe, Elizabeth. *Philby of Arabia.* London: Faber & Faber, 1973.

Morris, Timothy. *The Despairing Developer: Diary of an Aid Worker in the Middle East.* New York: St. Martin's Press, 1991.

Mortimer, Peter. *Cool for Qat: A Yemeni Journey, Two Countries, Two Times (1930–2004).* Edinburgh: Mainstream Publishing, 2005.

Moser, Charles. "The Flower of Paradise: Ghat," *National Geographic Magazine*, 32/2 (August 1917), 173–186.

Newby, J. C. "South of the Empty Quarter," *Geographical Magazine*, 39/2 (June 1966), 92–101.

Niebuhr, Carsten. *Travels through Arabia and Other Countries in the East.* 2 vols., translated from the German by Robert Heron. Edinburgh: R. Morison and Son, 1792. (Reprinted Beirut: Librarie du Liban, 1968.)

Nizan, Paul. *Aden, Arabie.* New York: Monthly Review Press, 1968.

Philby, H. St. John B. *Arabian Highlands.* Ithaca, N.Y.: Cornell University Press, 1952.

————. *Arabian Jubilee.* London: Robert Hale, 1952.

————. "Halevy in Yemen," *Geographical Journal*, 102 (July–December 1943), 116–124.

————. *Sheba's Daughters, Being a Record of Travel in Southern Arabia.* London: Methuen, 1939.

Phillips, Wendell. *Qataban and Sheba.* London: Victor Gollancz, 1955.

Raban, Jonathan. *Arabia: A Journey through the Labyrinth.* New York: Simon and Schuster, 1980.

Rihani, Ameen F. *Arabian Peak and Desert: Travels in al-Yaman.* New York: Houghton Mifflin, 1930. (Reprint Delmar, New York: Caravan Books, 1983.)

Robertson, William. "San'a Past and Present," *Moslem World*, 33/1 (January 1943), 52–57.

Ruthven, Malise. *Freya Stark in Southern Arabia.* Reading, UK: Garnet Publishing, 1995.

Rushby, Kevin. *Eating the Flowers of Paradise: One Man's Journey through Ethiopia and Yemen.* New York: St. Martin's, 1999.

al-Salami, Khadija, with Charles Hoots. *The Tears of Sheba: Tales of Survival and Intrigue in Yemen.* Chichester, West Sussex, UK: John Wiley and Sons, 2003.

Scott, Hugh. *In the High Yemen.* London: John Murray, 1942. (Reprinted New York: AMS Press, 1975.)

———. "A Journey to the Yemen," *Geographical Journal,* 93/2 (February 1939), 97–125.

———. "The Yemen in 1937–38," *Journal of the Royal Central Asian Society,* 27 (January 1940), 21–44.

Seager, Basil W. "The Yemen," Journal of the Royal Central Asian Society, 42/3–4 (July–October 1955), 214–230.

Serjeant, Robert Bertram. "Notes on Subaihi Territory, West of Aden," *Le Museon,* 66 (1953), 123–131.

Smiley, David, with Peter Kemp. *Arabian Assignment.* London: Leo Cooper, 1975.

Somerville-Large, Peter. *Tribes and Tribulations: A Journey in Republican Yemen.* London: Robert Hale, 1967.

Stark, Freya. *Dust in the Lion's Paw.* New York: Harcourt, Brace, & World, 1961.

———. *East Is West.* London: John Murray, 1947.

———. "An Exploration in the Hadramaut and Journey to the Coast," *Geographical Journal,* 93/1 (January 1939), 1–17.

———. "In Southwestern Arabia in Wartime," *Geographical Review* (New York), 34/3 (July 1944), 349–364.

———. "Some Pre-Islamic Inscriptions on the Frankincense Route in Southern Arabia," *Journal of the Royal Asiatic Society* (July 1939), 479–498.

———. *The Southern Gates of Arabia: A Journey in the Hadhramaut.* London: John Murray, 1936.

———. *A Winter in Arabia.* London: John Murray, 1945 reprint.

Swayne, H. G. C. "Rock of Aden," *National Geographic Magazine,* 68/6 (December 1935), 723–742.

Tarcici, Adnan. *The Queen of Sheba's Land: Yemen (Arabia Felix).* Beirut: Nowfel, 1973.

Thesiger, Wilfred. *Arabian Sands.* London: Longmans, 1959.

———. "A New Journey in Southern Arabia," *Geographical Journal,* 108/4–6 (October–December 1946), 129–145.

Thomas, Bertram. *Arabia Felix.* New York: Charles Scribner's Sons, 1932.

Trench, Richard. *Arabian Travellers.* London: Macmillan, 1986.

Trevaskis, Sir Kennedy. *Shades of Amber: A South Arabian Episode.* London: Hutchinson, 1968.

Trevelyan, Humphrey. *The Middle East in Revolution*. London: MacMillan, 1970.

Twitchell, Karl S. *Saudi Arabia*. 3rd ed. Princeton, N.J.: Princeton University Press, 1958.

Valentia, Viscount. *Voyages and Travels*. London: W. Miller, 1809.

van der Meulen, Daniel, "Into Burning Hadhramaut: The Arab Land of Frankincense and Myrrh, Ever a Loadestone of Western Exploration," *National Geographic Magazine*, 62/4 (October 1932), 387–429.

———. *Aden to the Hadramaut: A Journey in South Arabia*. London: John Murray, 1947.

van der Meulen, Daniel, and H. von Wissmann. *Hadramaut: Some of Its Mysteries Unveiled*. Leiden, Netherlands: E. J. Brill, 1932.

Varthema, Ludovico di. *The Itinerary of Ludovico di Varthema of Bologna from 1502–1508*. London: Argonaut Press, 1928.

Wavell, A. J. B. *A Modern Pilgrim in Mecca and a Siege in Sanaa*. London: Constable, 1918.

Wellsted, J. R. *Travels in Arabia*, 2 vols. London: John Murray, 1838.

Villiers, Alan. "Sailing with Sinbad's Sons," *National Geographic Magazine*, 94 (1948), 675–688.

Zwemer, Samuel M. *Arabia: The Cradle of Islam*. New York: Fleming H. Revell, 1900.

General Histories

Hart, Jane Smiley. "Basic Chronology for a History of the Yemen," *Middle East Journal*, 17/1–2 (Winter/Spring 1963), 144–153.

Helfritz, Hans. *Al-Yemen: A General Social, Political and Economic Survey*. Cairo: Renaissance Bookshop, 1952.

Playfair, R. L. *A History of Arabia Felix or Yemen*. Photo reproduction of original edition, Bombay, 1859. Farnborough, UK: Gregg International, 1970.

Richards, D. S. (ed.). *Islam and the Trade of Asia: A Colloquium*. Oxford: Bruno Cassirer, 1970.

Sharafeddin, A. H. *Yemen*. Rome: Daily American Press, 1961.

Stookey, Robert W. *Yemen: The Politics of the Yemen Arab Republic*. Boulder: Westview Press, 1978.

Pre-Islamic History

American Schools of Oriental Research. "Chronology of Ancient South Arabia," *Bulletin of American Schools of Oriental Research*, 119 (October 1950).

Beeston, A. F. L. *Epigraphic South Arabian Calendars and Dating.* London: Luzac, 1956.

―――. "Kataban," in C. E. Bosworth, et al. (eds.), *Encyclopedia of Islam*, vol. 4. Leiden, Netherlands: Brill, 1976.

―――. "Kingship in Ancient South Arabia," *Journal of the Economic and Social History of the Orient*, 15 (1972), 256–268.

―――. "New Light on the Himyaritic Calendar," *Arabian Studies*, 1 (1974), 1–6.

―――. "Problems of Sabean Chronology," *Bulletin of the School of Oriental and African Studies*, 16.1 (1954), 37–56.

―――. "Some Features of Social Structure in Saba," *Studies in the History of Arabia*, vol. 1, pt. 1, *Sources for the History of Arabia*. Riyadh, Saudi Arabia: Riyadh University Press, 1979, 115–23.

―――. "Some Observation on Greek and Latin Data Relating to South Arabia," *Bulletin of the School of Oriental and African Studies*, 42/1 (1979), 7–12.

―――. "Temporary Marriages in Pre-Islamic South Arabia," *Arabian Studies*, 4 (1978), 21–25.

―――. *Warfare in Ancient South Arabia: 2nd–3rd Centuries A.D.* London: Luzac, 1976.

Bidwell, Robin, and G. Rex Smith. *Arabian and Islamic Studies.* London: Longman, 1983.

Bowen, Richard LeBaron, Jr., Frank P. Albright, et al. *Archaeological Discoveries in South Arabia.* Baltimore, Md.: Johns Hopkins Press, Publications of the American Foundation for the Study of Man, no. 2, 1958.

Brinton, J. Y, and A. F. L. Beeston. "Sculptures and Inscriptions from Shabwa," *Journal of the Royal Asiatic Society* (April 1954), 43–62.

de Maigret, A., and C. Robin. "Les fouilles italiennes de Yala (Yemen du Nord): nouvelles donnees sur la chronologie de l'Arabie du Sud preislamique," Academie des Inscriptions et Belles-Lettres, comptes rendus des seances del'annee 1989 (1989), 255–291.

Groom, Nigel St. J. *Frankincense & Myrrh: A Study of the Arabian Incense Trade.* London: Longman, 1981.

Inizan, M. L. "Prehistoire dans la region de Shabwa au Yemen de Sud," *Paleorient*, 13/1 (1987), 5–22.

Jamme, Albert. *Sabean Inscriptions from Mahram Bilqis (Marib).* Publications of the American Foundation for the Study of Man, no. 3. Baltimore, Md.: Johns Hopkins Press, 1962.

Montgomery, James A. *Arabia and the Bible.* Philadelphia: University of Pennsylvania Press, 1934.

Muller, Walter W. "Arabian Frankincense in Antiquity According to Classical Sources," in *Studies in the History of Arabia*, vol. 1, pt. 1, *Sources for the History of Arabia*. Riyadh, Saudi Arabia: Riyadh University Press, 1979, 79–92.

Munro-Hay, S. C. H. "The Coinage of Shabwa (Hadhramawt), and other Ancient South Arabian Coinage in the National Museum, Aden." *Syria*, 68 (1991), 393–418.

Periplus of the Erythraean Sea. Translated from the Greek and edited by G. W. B. Huntingford. London: Hakluyk Society, 1980.

Philby, H. St. John B. *The Background of Islam: Being a Sketch of Arabian History in Pre-Islamic Times*. Alexandria, Egypt: Whitehead Morris, 1947.

Pirenne, Jacqueline. *Le Royaume Sud-Arabe de Qataban et sa datation*. Louvain: Publications Universitaires, 1961.

———. *Paleographie des inscriptions sud-arabes: Contribution a la chronologie de l'Arabie du Sud antique*. Brussels, Belgium: Paleis der Academien, 1959.

———. "Recently Discovered Inscriptions and Archaeology as Sources for Ancient South Arabian Kingdoms." in *Studies in the History of Arabia*, vol. 1., pt. 1, *Sources for the History of Arabia*. Riyadh, Saudi Arabia: Riyadh University Press, 1979.

Redhouse, James W. *A Tentative Chronological Synopsis of the History of Arabia and Its Neighbors*. London: Trubner, 1887.

Retso, J. "The Earliest Arabs," *Orientalia Suecana*, 38–39 (1981990), 131–139.

Richer, Xavier. *Les hautes-terres de Nord-Yemen avant l'Islam*, 2 vols. Istanbul, Turkey: Nederlands Historisch-Archaeologisch Institute, 1982.

Robin, C. J. "Yemenite Tihama Before Islam: Notes on History and Historical Geography," *Arabian Archaeology and Epigraphy*, 6/4 (November 1995), 222–235.

Ryckmans, Jacques. *L'Institution monarchique en Arabie meridionale avant l'Islam*. (The Institution of Monarchy in Pre-Islamic South Arabia.) Louvain: Publications Universitaires, 1951.

Shahid, Irfan. *The Martyrs of Najran: New Documents*. Brussels, Belgium: Societe des Bollandistes, 1971.

Trimingham, J. Spencer. *Christianity Among the Arabs in Pre-Islamic Times*. London, New York: Longman, 1979.

van Beek, Gus W. "The Rise and Fall of Arabia Felix," *Scientific American*, 221/6 (December 1969), 36–58.

van den Branden, A. *Histoire de Thamoud*. Beirut: Lebanese University, 1960.

Whalen, N. M. "Early Mankind in Arabia," *Aramco World*, 43/4 (1992), 16–23.

Islamic History

Ahroni, R. "Some Yemenite Jewish Attitudes towards Muhammad's Propheth-ood (An Examination of Liberal Attitudes towards Islam from 'Muhammad's Writ of Protection')," *Hebrew Union College Annual*, 69/69 (1999), 49–99.

Balog, P. "Dinars of al-Mu'azzam Shams al-Din Turanshah and al-Aziz Tughtegin, Ayyubid Princes of the Yemen," *American Numismatics Society Museum Notes*, 9 (1960), 237–240.

Bashear, S. "Yemen in Early Islam: An Examination of Non-tribal Traditions," *Arabica*, 36 (1989), 327–361.

Bikhazi, Ramzi J. "Coins of al-Yaman, 132–569 A.H.," *Al-Abhath*, 23 (1970), 3–127.

Bishart, Mary. "The Collapse of Ottoman Authority in Yemen, 968/1560–976/1568," *Die Welt des Islam*, 19 (1979), 119–176.

————. "The Ottoman Penetration of Yemen: An Annotated Translation of Ozdemur Bey's *Fethname* for the Conquest of San'a in Rajab 954/August 1547," *Archivum Ottomanicum*, 6 (1980), 55–100.

Boxhall, Peter. "The Diary of a Mocha Coffee Agent," *Arabian Studies*, 1 (1974), 102–188.

Croken, Barbara. *Zabid under the Rasulids of Yemen 626–858 AH/1229–1454 AD*. Diss., Harvard University. Ann Arbor, Mich.: University Microfilms International, 1990.

Crone, P. "Were the Qays and Yemen of the Umayyad Period Political Parties? Tribal Confederations and Organization of the Early Arab Empire," *Islam Zeitschrift für Geschichte und Kultur des Islamischen Orients*, 71/1 (1994), 1–57.

Faris, Nabih Amin. *The Antiquities of South Arabia: Being a Translation from the Arabic with Linguistic, Geographic and Historic Notes of the Eighth Book of Al-Hamdani's al-Iklil*. Princeton, N.J.: Princeton University Press, 1938.

Gaimani, A. "Rabbinic Emissaries and their Contacts with Yemeni Jewry (An Evaluation of Ancient Rituals, Customs and Traditions in Conflict with Other Jewish Communities in the Diaspora)," *Hebrew Union College Annual*, 69/69 (1999), 101–125.

al-Hamdani, Husain F. "The Life and Times of Queen Saiyhidah Arwa the Sulaihid of the Yemen," *Journal of the Royal Central Asian Society*, 31 (1931), 505–517.

Hattox, Ralph S. *Coffee and Coffeehouses*. Seattle: University of Washington Press, 1985.

Haykel, Bernard. *Revival and Reform in Islam: The Legacy of Muhammad al-Shawkani*. Cambridge, UK: Cambridge University Press, 2003.

Jiwa, S. "The Genesis of Ismaili *da'wa* activities in the Yemen," *British Society for Middle East Studies Bulletin*, 15/1–2 (1988), 50–63.

Kay, Henry Cassels. *Yaman: Its Early Medieval History*. London: Edward Arnold, 1892.

Kazi, A. K. "Notes on the Development of Zaydi Law," *Abr-Nahrain*, 2 (1960), 36–40.

Keall, Edward J. "Drastic Changes in 16th century Zabid," *Proceedings of the Seminar for Arabian Studies*, 21 (1991), 79–96.

al-Khazraji, Shaikh Hasan bin Ali. *The Pearl-Strings: A History of the Resuliy Dynasty of Yemen*. Translated by J. W. Redhouse. London: Luzac, 1906–1907.

King, David A. "Mathematical Astronomy in Medieval Yemen," *Arabian Studies*, 5 (1979), 61–65.

Lerner, R. "Winged Words to Yemen ('Epistle to Yemen,' Maimonides, Political Philosophy)," *Revue de Metaphysique et de Morale*, 4 (October–December 1998), 479–493.

Lofgren, Oscar. "Adan," in H. A. R. Gibb, et al. (eds.), *Encyclopaedia of Islam*, vol. 1. Leiden, the Netherlands: Brill, 1957, 180–182.

———. *Al-Hamdani: Sudarabisches Mustabih*. Uppsala: Almqvist and Wiksells, Boktryckeri AB, 1953.

Macro, Eric. *Yemen and the Western World since 1571*. New York: Frederick A. Praeger, 1968.

al-Madaj, Abd al-Muhsin Madaj M. *The Yemen in Early Islam, 9–233/630–847*. London: Ithaca Press, 1988.

Margariti, Roxani Eleni. *Aden and the Indian Ocean Trade: 150 Years in the Life of a Medieval Arabian Port*. Chapel Hill: University of North Carolina, 2007.

Miles, G. C. "The Ayyubid Dynasty of the Yemen and their Coinage," *Numismatic Chronicle*, 9 (1949), 62–97.

Norris, H. T., and F. W. Penhey. "The Historical Development of Aden's Defenses," *Geographical Journal*, 121/1 (March 1955), 11–20.

Redhouse, James W. (ed. & trans.). *El-Khazreji's History of the Resuli Dynasty of Yemen*, 3 vols. Leiden, Netherlands: Brill, 1906–1908.

Schuman, Lein Oebele. *Political History of the Yemen at the Beginning of the Sixteenth Century*. Gronigen, Netherlands: V.D.R. Kleine, 1960.

Serjeant, Robert Bertram. "The Cultivation of Cereals in Medieval Yemen," *Arabian Studies*, 1 (1974), 25–74.

———. "Customary Law Documents as a Source of History," in *Studies in the History of Arabia*, vol.1, pt. 2, *Sources for the History of Arabia*. Riyadh, Saudi Arabia: Riyadh University Press, 1979, 99–103.

———. *The Portuguese off the South Arabian Coast*. Oxford: The Clarendon Press, 1963.

————. *Studies in Arabian History and Civilization*. London: Variorum Reprints, 1981.

————. "The Zaydis," in A. J. Arberry (ed.). *Religion in the Middle East*, vol. 2, *Islam*. Cambridge, UK: Cambridge University Press, 1969, 285–302.

Serjeant, Robert Bertram, and Claude Cahen. "A Fiscal Survey of the Medieval Yemen," *Arabica*, 4/1 (1957), 23–30.

Shoufani, Elias S. *al-Riddah and the Muslim Conquest of Arabia*. Toronto: University of Toronto Press, 1973.

Smith, Clive K. "Kawkaban: Some of Its History," *Arabian Studies*, 6 (1982), 35.

————. "The Dulrihid Dynasty in the Yemen," *Asian Affairs*, 68/new series 12 (1981), 19–28.

Smith, Gerald Rex. *The Ayyubids and Early Rasulids in the Yemen* (567–694/1173–1295). London: E.J.W. Gibb Memorial Trust, 1978.

————. "The Ayyubids and Rasulids: The Transfer of Power in 7th/13th Century Yemen," *Islamic Culture*, 43 (1969), 175–188.

————. "Ibn Hatim's *Kitab al-Simt* and Its Place in Medieval Yemenite Historiography," in *Studies in the History of Arabia*, vol. 1, pt. 2, *Sources for the History of Arabia*. Riyadh, Saudi Arabia: Riyadh University Press, 1979, 63–68.

————. "Lightning over Yemen: A History of the Ottoman Campaign (1569–1571), being a translation from the Arabic of Part III of 'Al-Barq al-Yamani fi al-Fath al-Uthmani' by Qutb al-Din al-Nahrawali al Makki as Published by Hamid al-Jasir (Riyadh 1967)," *Journal of Semitic Studies*, 49/1 (Spring 2004), 181–186.

————. "The Yemenite Settlement of Tha'bat: Historical, Numismatic and Epigraphic Notes," *Arabian Studies*, 1 (1974), 119–134.

Tibbetts, G. R. *Arab Navigation in the Indian Ocean before the Coming of the Portuguese*. London: Royal Asiatic Society, 1971.

————. "Arabia in the Fifteenth Century Navigational Texts," *Arabian Studies*, 1 (1974), 86–101.

Tritton, A. S. *The Rise of the Imams of Sanaa*. Oxford: Oxford University Press, 1925.

van Arendonk, Cornelis. *Les Debuts de l'imamat zaidite au Yemen*. Translated from the French by Jacques Ryckmans. Leiden, Netherlands: E. J. Brill, 1960.

Varisco, Daniel Martin. "A Royal Crop Register from Rasulid Yemen," *Journal of the Economic and Social History of the Orient*, XXXIV (1991), 1–22.

Voll, John O. "Linking Groups in the Networks of Eighteenth-Century Revivalist Scholars: The Mizjaji Family in Yemen," in Nehemia Levtzion and John O. Voll (eds.). *Eighteenth-Century Renewal and Reform in Islam*. Syracuse, N.Y.: Syracuse University Press, 1987.

Wilson, Robert T. O. *Gazetteer of Historical North-West Yemen in the Islamic Period to 1650.* New York: George Olms, 1989.

al-Yamani, Umara. *Yaman: Its Early Medieval History.* Translated from the Arabic by Henry Cassels Kay. London: Edward Arnold, 1892.

Modern History and Politics: North Yemen and the YAR

al-Abdin, al-Tayib Zein. "The Free Yemeni Movement (1940–48) and Its Ideas on Reform," *Middle Eastern Studies,* 15 (January 1979), 36–48.

al-Amri, Husayn bin Abdullah. *The Yemen in the 18th and 19th Centuries: A Political and Intellectual History.* London: Ithaca Press, 1985.

Baldry, John. "Imam Yahya and the Yamani Uprising of 1911," *Annali Instituto Orientale de Napoli,* 42/3 (1982), 425–459.

———. "Al-Yamam and the Turkish Occupation 1849–1914," *Arabica,* 23 (1976), 159–196.

Blumi, Isa. "Shifting Loyalties and Failed Empires: A New Look at the Social History of Late Ottoman Yemen, 1872–1918," in Madawi al-Rasheed and Robert Vitalis (eds.), *Counter-Narratives: History, Contemporary Society, and Politics in Saudi Arabia and Yemen,* N. Y.: Palgrave Macmillan, 2004, 103–118.

Brown, William R. "The Yemeni Dilemma," *Middle East Journal,* 17/4 (Autumn 1963), 349–367.

Burrowes, Robert D. "The Famous Forty and Their Companions: North Yemen's First-generation Modernists and Educational Emigrants," *Middle East Journal,* 59/1 (Winter 2005), 81–97.

———. "Prelude to Unification: The Yemen Arab Republic, 1962–1990," *International Journal of Middle East Studies,* 23/4 (November 1991), 483–506.

———. "State-Building and Political Construction in the Yemen Arab Republic, 1962–1977," in Peter J. Chelkowski and Robert J. Pranger (eds.). *Ideology and Power in the Middle East: Studies in Honor of George Lenckowski.* Durham, N.C.: Duke University Press, 1988, 210–238.

———. "The YAR's Legacy and Yemeni Unification," *Arab Studies Quarterly,* 14/4 (Fall 1992), 41–68.

———. "The Yemen Arab Republic and the Ali Abdullah Salih Regime: 1978–1984," *Middle East Journal,* 39/3 (Summer 1985), 287–316.

———. *The Yemen Arab Republic: The Politics of Development, 1962–1986.* Boulder: Westview Press, 1987.

Bury, G. Wyman (Abdullah Mansur). *Arabia Infelix or the Turks in Yemen.* London: Macmillan, 1915.

Carapico, Sheila. "Autonomy and Secondhand Oil Dependency of the Yemen Arab Republic," *Arab Studies Quarterly,* 10/2 (1988), 193–113.

————. *The Political Economy of Self-Help: Development Cooperatives in the Yemen Arab Republic.* Diss., State University of New York (Binghamton), 1984.

————. "Self-Help and Development Planning in the Yemen Arab Republic," in Jean Claude Garcia Zamor (ed.), *Public Participation in Development Planning and Management: Cases from Africa and Asia.* Boulder: Westview Press, 1985, 203–234.

Chaudhry, Kiren Aziz. "The Price of Wealth: Business and State in Labor Remittance and Oil Economies," *International Organization*, 43/1 (Winter 1989), 101–145.

————. *The Price of Wealth: Economies and Institutions in the Middle East.* Ithaca, N.Y.: Cornell University, 1997.

Corstange, Daniel. "Yemen (1962–1970)," K. DeRouen and U. Heo (eds.), *Civil Wars of the World*, vol. 2. Santa Barbara: ABC-CLIO (2007), 809–827.

Deffarge, Claude, and Gordian Troeller. *Yemen 62–69: de la revolution 'sauvage' a la treve des guerriers.* Paris: Robert Laffont, 1969.

Douglas, J. Leigh. *The Free Yemeni Movement 1935–1962.* Beirut: American University of Beirut, 1987.

Dresch, Paul. "Imams and Tribes: The Writing and Acting of History in Upper Yemen," in S. Khoury and J. Kostiner (eds.), *Tribes and State Formation in the Middle East.* Berkeley: University of California, 1990, 252–287.

————. "The Position of Shaykhs Among the Northern Tribes of Yemen," *Man*, 19/1 (1984), 31–49.

————. "Tribal Relations and Political History in Upper Yemen," in B. R. Pridham (ed.). *Contemporary Yemen: Politics and History.* London: Croom Helm, 1984, 154–174.

————. *Tribes, Government, and History in Yemen.* Oxford: Oxford University Press, 1989.

Dresch, Paul, and Bernard Haykel. "Stereotypes and Political Styles: Islamists and Tribesfolk in Yemen," *International Journal of Middle East Studies*, 27: 4 (November 1995), 405–431.

Fairchild, Ray. "Yemen Oil Hunt: A Gift from the Gods," in Allen G. Hatley, Jr. (ed.), *The Oil Finders: A Collection of Stories about Exploration.* Tulsa, Okla.: American Association of Petroleum Geologists, 1992.

Farah, Ceasar E. *The Sultan's Yemen: Nineteenth-Century Challenges to Ottoman Rule.* London: I. B. Tauris, 2002.

Gandy, Christopher. "The Yemen Revisited," *Asian Affairs*, 58/2 (1971), 295–304.

Ghaleb, Muhammad Anaam. *Government Organization as a Barrier to Economic Development in Yemen.* San'a, YAR, and Bochum, West Germany: Ruhr University Institute for Development Research and Development Policy, for the YAR National Institute of Public Administration, 1979.

Gochenour, D. Thomas. "Toward a Sociology of the Islamisation of Yemen," in B. R. Pridham (ed.), *Contemporary Yemen: Politics and Historical Background*. New York: St. Martin's Press, 1984, 1–19.

Haddad, George M. *Revolutions and Military Rule in the Middle East: The Arab States (Part II: Egypt, the Sudan, Yemen and Libya)*. New York: Robert Speller, 1973.

Heyworth-Dunne, J. (Gamel-Eddine). "The Yemen," *Middle Eastern Affairs*, 9/2 (February 1958), 50–58.

Holden, David. *Farewell to Arabia*. London: Faber & Faber, 1966.

Jacob, Harold F. *Kings of Arabia: The Rise and Set of the Turkish Sovranty in the Arabian Peninsula*. London: Mills & Boon, 1923.

Khadduri, Majid. "Coup and Counter-Coup in the Yaman 1948," *International Affairs*, 28 (January 1952), 59–68.

Kuhn, Thomas. "An Imperial Borderland as Colony: Knowledge Production and the Elaboration of Difference in Ottoman Yemen, 1872–1914," *MIT Electronic Journal of Middle East Studies*, 3 (Spring 2003), 5–17.

———. "Ordering the Past of Ottoman Yemen, 1872–1914," *Turcica*, 34 (2002), 189–220.

Labaune, Patrick. "Tribal Democracy and the Political System in the Yemen Arab Republic," *Revue Francaise de Science Politique*, 31/4 (1981), 745–768.

National Front. *al-Thawrah al-Wataniyah al-Demuqratiyah fi al-Yemen*. (The National Democratic Revolution in Yemen.) Introduction by Abd al-Fattah Ismail. Beirut: Dar Ibn Khaldun, 1972.

O'Ballance, Edgar. *The War in the Yemen*. London: Faber & Faber, 1971.

Omar, Garalla (Jarallah). "Northern Yemen: Working with Undiminished Vigour," *World Marxist Review*, 32/6 (June 1989), 67–70.

Omar, Sultan Ahmad. *Nazra fi Tatawwar al-Mojtam'a al-Yamani*. (A Look at the Development of Yemeni Society.) Beirut: Dar al-Tali'ah, 1970.

Pawelke, Gunther. *Der Jemen: Das verbotene Land*. Dusseldorf: Econ Verlag, 1959.

Pellas, Marc. "Armed Struggle in North Yemen," *MERIP (Middle East Research and Information Project) Reports*, 22 (November 1973).

Peterson, John E. "The Yemen Arab Republic and the Politics of Balance," *Asian Affairs*, 12 (1981), 254–266.

———. *Yemen: The Search for a Modern State*. Baltimore, Md.: Johns Hopkins University Press, 1982.

Pridham, Brian R. (ed.). *Contemporary Yemen: Politics and Historical Background*. London: Croom Helm, 1984.

al-Rashid, Ibrahim (ed.). *Yemen Enters the Modern World: Secret U.S. Documents on the Rise of the Second Power on the Arabian Peninsula*. Chapel Hill, N.C.: Documentary Publications, 1984.

———. *Yemen Under the Rule of Imam Ahmad.* Chapel Hill, N.C.: Documentary Publications, 1985.

Schmidt, Dana Adams. *Yemen: The Unknown War.* New York: Holt, Rinehart, and Winston, 1968.

Seager, Basil W. "The Yemen," *Journal of the Royal Central Asian Society,* 42/3–4 (July–October 1955), 214–230.

Serjeant, Robert Bertram. "The Yemeni Poet al-Zubayri and His Polemic against the Zaydi Imams," *Arabian Studies,* 5 (1979), 87–130.

al-Shami, Ahmad Muhammad. "Yemeni Literature in Hajjah Prisons, 1948–55," *Arabian Studies,* 2 (1975), 43–60.

Stookey, Robert W. "Social Structure and Politics in the Yemen Arab Republic," *Middle East Journal,* 28/3 (Summer 1974), 248–260; and 28/4 (Autumn 1974), 409–418.

———. *Yemen: The Politics of the Yemen Arab Republic.* Boulder: Westview Press, 1978.

Sultan, Nabel Ahmad. "Bureaucratic Corruption as a Consequence of the Gulf Migration: The Case of North Yemen," *Crime, Law and Social Change,* 19/4 (1993), 379–393.

Swagman, Charles F. "Tribe and Politics: An Example from Highland Yemen," *Journal of Anthropological Research,* 44/3 (Fall 1988), 251–261.

———. "Political Trends and Reorganization of Cooperatives," *Orient,* 28 (1987), 83–89.

Tutwiler, Richard. "Ta'awun Mahweet: A Case Study of a Local Development Association in Highland Yemen," in Louis Cantori and Illya Harik (eds.), *Local Politics and Development in the Middle East.* Boulder: Westview Press, 1984.

Vom Bruck, Gabriele. *Islam, Memory, and Morality in Yemen: Ruling Families in Transition.* New York: Palgrave, 2005.

Wenner, Manfred W. *Modern Yemen, 1918–1966.* Baltimore, Md.: Johns Hopkins Press, 1967.

———. "Yemen," in Frank Tachau (ed.), *Political Parties of the Middle East and North Africa.* Westport, Conn.: Greenwood, 1994, 611–639.

———. *The Yemen Arab Republic: Development and Change in an Ancient Land.* Boulder: Westview Press, 1991.

Zabarah, Muhammad Ahmad. *Yemen: Traditionalism vs. Modernity.* New York: Praeger, 1982.

Modern History and Politics: South Yemen and the PDRY

Abu-Amr, Zaid M. *The Peoples Democratic Republic of Yemen: The Transformation of Society.* Diss. Georgetown University. Ann Arbor, Mich.: University Microfilms, 1987.

Albergoni, G., and G. Bedoucha. "Hierarchie, mediation et tribalisme en Arabie de Sud: la *hijra* yemenite," *L'Homme*, 31/2 (1991), 7–36.

Ali, Hussein, and Ken Whittingham. "Notes Towards an Understanding of the Revolution in South Yemen," *Race and Class*, 6/1 (July 1974), 83–100.

al-Ashtal, Abdullah. "Politics in Command: A Case Study of the People's Democratic Republic of Yemen," *Monthly Review*, 27/9 (February 1976), 13–21.

Barbour, Nevill. "Aden and the Arab South," *World Today*, 15 (January–December 1959), 302–310.

Bell, J. Bowyer. "Southern Yemen: Two Years of Independence," *The World Today*, 26/2 (February 1970), 76–82.

—————. "South Arabia: Violence and Revolt," *Conflict Studies*, London, Institute for the Study of Conflict, no. 40 (November 1973), 1–14.

Bidwell, Robin. "The Political Residents of Aden: Biographical Notes," *Arabian Studies*, 5 (1979), 149–159.

—————. *The Two Yemens*. Boulder: Westview Press, 1983.

Bujra, Abdulla S. "Political Conflict and Stratification in Hadhramaut," *Middle East Studies*, 3/4 (July 1967), 355–376; and 4/1 (October 1967), 2–29.

—————. *The Politics of Stratification: A Study of Political Change*. Oxford: Clarendon Press, 1971.

—————. "Urban Elites and Colonialism: The Nationalist Elites of Aden and South Arabia," *Middle Eastern Studies*, 6/2 (May 1970), 189–211.

Burrowes, Robert D. "Oil Strike and Leadership Struggle in South Yemen: 1986 and Beyond," *Middle East Journal*, 43/3 (Summer 1989), 437–454.

Cigar, Norman. "Islam and the State in South Yemen: The Uneasy Coexistence," *Middle East Studies*, 26/2 (April 1990), 185–203.

—————. "State and Society in South Yemen," *Problems of Communism*, 34 (May–June 1985), 41–58.

Clarence-Smith, William G., and Ulrike Freitag (eds.). *An Indian Ocean People: Hadhramaut and Its Diaspora, 1750s–1960s*. Leiden: Brill, 1997.

Countryman, John R. "South Yemen: The Socialist Facade Crumbles," *Middle East International*, 7 February 1986, 12–13.

Cumming-Bruce, A. P. "The Emergence of Aden Since 1956," *Journal of the Royal Central Asian Society*, 49/3–4 (July–October 1962), 307–316.

Freitag, Ulrike. *Indian Ocean Migrants and State Formation in Hadhramaut: Reforming the Homeland*. Leiden: E. J. Brill, 2003.

Footman, David. *Antonin Besse of Aden*. London: Macmillan Press, 1968.

al-Habashi, Muhammad Umar. *Aden: Evolution politique, economique and sociale de l'Arabie du Sud*. Algiers: Societe Nationale d'Edition et de Diffusion, 1966.

Halliday, Fred. "Catastrophe in South Yemen: A Preliminary Assessment," *MERIP (Middle East Research and Information Project) Reports*, 16/139 (March–April 1986), 37–39.

———. "The People's Democratic Republic of Yemen: The 'Cuban path' in Arabia," in G. White, R. Murray, and C. White (eds.), *Revolutionary Socialist Development in the Third World*. New York: Harvester Press, 1983, 35–74.

———. "Yemen's Unfinished Revolution: Socialism in the South," *MERIP (Middle East Research and Information Project) Reports*, 9/81 (October 1979), 3–20.

Hawatmah, Nayif. *Azmat al-Thawra fi Janub al-Yaman* (The Crisis of the Revolution in South Yemen). Beirut: Dar al-Tali'a, 1968.

Hickinbotham, Sir Tom. *Aden*. London: Constable, 1958.

Hunter, Capt. Frederick M. *An Account of the British Settlement of Aden in Arabia*. 1st ed., 1877, new impression. London: Frank Cass, 1968.

Hunter, Frederick M., and C. W. H. Sealy. *An Account of Arab Tribes in the Vecinity of Aden*. 1st ed., 1909, facsimile. London: Darf, 1986.

Ingrams, William Harold. *Arabia and the Isles*. 3rd ed. New York: Frederick A. Praeger, 1966.

———. "Peace in the Hadramaut," *Journal of the Royal Central Asian Society*, 25 (October 1938), 507–541.

———. "Political Development in the Hadhramaut," *International Affairs*, 21/2 (April 1945), 236–252.

———. *A Report on the Social, Economic and Political Conditions of the Hadramaut*. London: HM Stationery Office, 1936.

Ismael, Tariq Y. *The People's Democratic Republic of Yemen*. New York: St. Martin's Press, 1992.

Ismael, Tarik Y., and Jacqueline Ismael. *The PDRY: Politics, Economics and Society: The Politics of Socialist Transformation*. Boulder: Lynne Rienner, 1986.

Ismail, Abd al-Fattah. "A New Vanguard Party," *World Marxist Review*, 22/1 (January 1979), 14–21.

———. *The Present and Future of the People's Democratic Republic of Yemen*. London: Embassy of the PDRY, 1977.

Johnston, Charles Hepburn. *The View from Steamer Point: Three Crucial Years in South Arabia*. New York: Frederick A. Praeger, 1964.

Kazziha, Walid. *Revolutionary Transformation in the Arab World: Habash and His Comrades from Nationalism to Marxism*. New York: St. Martin's Press, 1975.

Kelly, J. B. "Hadramaut, Oman, Dhufar: The Experience of Revolution," *Middle East Studies*, 12/2 (May 1976), 213–230.

Kostiner, Joseph. "Arab Radical Politics: Al-Qawmiyyun and the Marxists in the Turmoil of South Yemen, 1963–1967," *Middle Eastern Studies*, 17 (October 1981), 454–476.

————. *South Yemen's Revolutionary Strategy, 1970–1985*. Boulder: Westview Press, 1990.

————. *The Struggle for South Yemen*. New York: St. Martin's Press, 1984.

Kour, Zaki H. *The History of Aden*. London: Frank Cass, 1981.

Lackner, Helen. *P. D. R. Yemen: Outpost of Socialist Development in Arabia*. London: Ithaca Press, 1985.

Lawson, Fred H. "South Yemen's Troubles," *Orient*, 27/3 (September 1986), 441–449.

Little, Tom. *South Arabia: Arena of Conflict*. London: Pall Mall Press, 1968.

Muhammad al-Hasani, Ali Nasir. "Development of the Revolutionary Process and the Leading Role of the Party in Democratic Yemen," *Partiynaya Zhizn*, 12 (June 1983), 70–75.

————. "Fidelity to the Revolution," *World Marxist Review*, 24/3 (March 1981), 23–26.

Paget, Julian. *Last Post: Aden 1964–67*. London: Faber & Faber, 1969.

Ramotar, D., et al. "Democratic Yemen: After a Tragic Trial," *World Marxist Review*, 31/1 (January 1988), 132–139.

Smith, R. H. "Notes on the Kathiri State of Hadhramaut," *Middle East Journal*, 7/4 (Autumn 1953), 499–503.

Stanzel, Volker. "Marxism in Arabia: South Yemen Twenty Years after Independence," *Aussenpolitik*, 39/3 (1988), 265–288.

Stookey, Robert W. *South Yemen: A Marxist Republic in Arabia*. Boulder: Westview Press, 1982.

Stork, Joe. "Socialist Revolution in Arabia: Report from the People's Democratic Republic of Yemen," *MERIP (Middle East Research and Information Project) Reports*, 15 (March 1973), 1–25.

Trevaskis, Sir Kennedy. *Shades of Amber: A South Arabian Episode*. London: Hutchinson, 1968.

Unified Political Organization: National Front. *The Constitution of the Unified Political Organization, The National Front*. Nottingham, UK: Russell Press, 1975.

————. *Program of the Unified Political Organization, The National Front*. Nottingham: Russell Press, 1975.

Waterfield, Gordon. *Sultans of Aden*. London: John Murray, 1968.

Watt, D. C. "Labor Relations and Trade Unions in Aden 1952–1960," *Middle East Journal*, 16/4 (Autumn 1962), 443–456.

Wenner, Manfred W. "Ideology Versus Pragmatism in South Yemen, 1968–1986," in Peter J. Chelkowski and Robert J. Pranger (eds.). *Ideology and Power in the Middle East: Studies in Honor of George Lenczowski*. Durham, N.C.: Duke University Press, 1988, 259–273.

———. "The 1986 Civil War in South Yemen: A Preliminary Assessment," in Brian R. Pridham (ed.). *The Arab Gulf and the Arab World.* London: Croom Helm, 1988, 268–293.

Willis, John M. "Leaving Only Question Marks: Geographies of Rule in Modern Yemen," in Madawi Al-Rasheed and Robert Vitalis (eds.), *Counter-Narratives: History, Contemporary Society and Politics in Saudi Arabia and Yemen.* New York: Palgrave Macmillan, 2004, 124–127.

———. "Making Yemen Indian: Rewriting the Boundaries of Imperial Arabia," *International Journal of Middle East Studies,* 41/1 (February 2009), 23–38.

Zwemer, Samuel M. "Ingram's Peace in Hadhramaut," *Moslem World,* 33/2 (April 1943), 79–85.

Modern History and Politics: The Two Yemens and the ROY

Abdullah, Sami Ghaleb. "Internal Developments in Yemen'" in *Gulf Year Book 2005–2006* (Dubai: Gulf Research Center, 2006), 371–378.

Adams, Michael. "One Yemen or Two?" in Ian Richard Netto (ed.). *Arabia and the Gulf: From Traditional Society to Modern States: Essays in Honor of M. A. Shaban's 60th Birthday.* London: Croom Helm, 1986, 120–131.

Al-Akwaa, Khalid Mohsen. *The Policy Role of Senior Civil Servants in the Government of Yemen.* Diss. Portland, Ore.: Portland State University, 1996.

Anon. "New Government: Daring Step to Reform Yemen," *Middle East Reporter Weekly,* 99/1149 (2 June 2001), 16–17.

Anon. "Politics: Saleh Moves to Propel Yemen into 21st Century," *Middle East Reporter Weekly,* 102/1184 (9 February 2002), 16–18.

Anon. "Profiles of Yemen's Feuding Leaders," *Middle East Reporter Weekly,* 72 (14 May 1994), 14–15.

Anon. "Saleh Re-elected: Yemen's Fledgling Democracy Gets a Boost," *Middle East Reporter Weekly,* 93/1067 (9 October 1999), 9–10.

Anon. "South Yemen Tensions Signal National Crisis," *Middle East Reporter Weekly,* 128/1495 (15 March 2008), 16–17.

Anon. "Terrorism: Yemen Hunts Al Qaeda in Bid to Clear Image," *Middle East Reporter Weekly,* 102/1180 (12 January 2002), 14–15.

Anon. "Yemen: Cabinets," *Middle East Reporter Weekly.* 72 (11 June 1994), 14–15.

Anon. "Yemen Infighting: Muffling the Saada Violence," *Middle East Reporter Weekly,* 124/1453 (19 May 2007), 15–20.

Anon. "Yemen Marks 10 Years of Unity," *Middle East Reporter Weekly,* 95/1100 (3 June 2000), 17–18.

Anon. "Yemen Mediation: Yemen Initiative Opens 'Palestinian Dialogue of the Deaf,'" *Middle East Reporter Weekly*, 129/1499 (12 April 2008), 12–13.

Anon. "Yemen Seen Transforming into Monarchy in Disguise," *Middle East Reporter Weekly*, 98/1138 (3 March 2001). 14–15.

Anon. "Yemen: Spectre of Civil War Grows as Interim Period Nears Its End," *Middle East Reporter Weekly*, 70 (26 September 1992), 2–5.

Anon. "Yemen: The 2-Year-Old Union Is Still Two States in Some Ways," *Middle East Reporter Weekly*, 70 (8 August 1992), 11–13.

Anon. "Yemen: Tribal Society Enters Age of Democracy," *Middle East Reporter Weekly*, 70 (8 May 1993), 9–12.

Anon. "Yemen's Deadly Transition to Capitalism," *Middle East Reporter Weekly*, 88 (4 July 1998), 5–7.

Anon. Yemen's Numerous Islamist Groups Growing Stronger," *Middle East Reporter Weekly*, 77 (21 October 1995), 11–13.

al-Ashtal, Abdullah. "Politics in Command: A Case Study of the People's Democratic Republic of Yemen," *Monthly Review*, 27/9 (February 1976), 13–21.

Beatty, Sharon, Ahmad Noman al-Madhaji, and Renaud Detalle. *Yemeni NGOs and Quasi NGOs, Analysis and Directory, Part I.* Sanaa: Republic of Yemen, May 1996.

Be'eri, Eliezer. *Army Officers in Arab Politics and Society.* New York: Praeger, 1969.

Beuming, Floor. *The Merger of the Dagger and the Rifle: Failing Integration of Former South Yemen into the Unified Republic of Yemen.* M.A. thesis, University of Amsterdam, October 2004.

Bidwell, Robin. *The Two Yemens.* Boulder: Westview Press, 1983.

Blanche, Ed. "Al-Qaeda Resurgent," *Middle East Reporter Weekly*, 129/1507 (7 June 2008), 14–16.

Bonnefoy, Laurent. "Entre Pressions Exterieures et Tensions Internes, un Equilibre Instable au Yemen," *Far Eastern Economic Review*, 169/8 (October 2006), 6–7.

Braun, Ursala. "Yemen: Another Case of Unification," *Aussenpolitik (Hamburg)*, 43 (Summer 1992), 174–178.

Browers, Michaelle. "Origins and Architects of Yemen's Joint Meeting Parties," *International Journal of Middle East Studies*, 39/4 (November 2004), 565–586.

Burgat, Francois. "Normalisation du Yemen," *Le Monde Diplomatique*, 50/587 (February 2003), 22.

Burrowes, Robert D. "Ali Abdullah Salih and the Prospects for Democracy in Yemen," *Middle East Insight* (January–Febuary 2000), 35–38.

———. "Republic of Yemen," in David E. Long, Bernard Reich, and Mark Gasiorowski (eds.), *The Government and Politics of the Middle East and North Africa*, 5th ed. Boulder: Westview, 2007, 197–225.

————. "The Republic of Yemen: The Politics of Unification and Civil War, 1989–1995," in Michael Hudson (ed.), *Middle East Dilemma: The Politics and Economics of Arab Integration.* New York: Columbia University, 1999, 187–213.

————. "State-Building and Political Construction in the Yemen Arab Republic, 1962–1977," in Peter J. Chelkowski and Robert J. Pranger (eds.). *Ideology and Power in the Middle East: Studies in Honor of George Lenckowski.* Durham, N.C.: Duke University Press, 1988, 210–238.

————. "al-Yaman: History from 1960 to the Present Day," in *The Encyclopedia of Islam.* Leiden: Brill, 1998, 274–276.

————. "Yemen," *Microsoft Encarta 2000 Encyclopedia.* Seattle, Wash.: Microsoft, 2000.

————. "Yemen, Its Political Economy and the Effort against Terrorism," in Robert J. Rotberg (ed.), *Battling Terrorism in the Horn of Africa.* Washington, D.C.: Brookings Institution/World Peace Foundation, 2005, 141–172.

Burrowes, Robert D., and Catherine Kasper. "The Salih Regime and the Need for a Credible Opposition," *Middle East Journal,* 61/2 (Spring 2007), 263–280.

Burgat, Francois, and Mohamed Sbitli. "Les Salafis au Yemen ou la modernization malgre tout," *Chroniques Yemenites* (2002), 123–152.

Bury, G. Wyman (Abdullah Mansur). *Arabia Infelix or the Turks in Yemen.* London: Macmillan, 1915.

Carapico, Sheila. "Arabia Incognito: An Invitation to Arabian Peninsula Studies," in Madawi al-Rasheed and Robert Vitalis (eds.), *Counter-Narratives: History, Contemporary Society and Politics in Saudi Arabia and Yemen.* New York: Palgrave Macmillan, 2004, 11–34.

————. *Civil Society in Yemen: The Political Economy of Activism in Modern Arabia.* Cambridge, UK: Cambridge University, 1998.

————. "Elections and Mass Politics in Yemen," *Middle East Report,* 23/6, no. 185 (November–December 1993), 2–7.

————. "From Ballot Box to Battlefield: The War of the Two 'Alis,'" *Middle East Report,* 24/5, no. 190 (September–October 1994), 24–27.

————. "How Yemen's Ruling Party Secured an Electoral Landslide," *Middle East Report Online,* May 16, 2003. www.merip.org/mero/mero051603.html

————. "No Quick Fix: Foreign and State Performance in Yemem," in Nancy Birdsall, et al. (eds.) *Short of the Goal: U.S. Policy and Poorly Performing States.* Washington, D.C.: Center for Global Development, 2006.

————. "Pluralism, Polarization and Popular Politics in Yemen." In Bahgat Korany, Rex Brynen, and Paul Noble (eds.), *Political Liberalization and Democratization in the Arab World,* vol. 2. Boulder: Lynne Rienner, 1998, 241–266.

————. "Women and Public Participation in Yemen," *Middle East Report*, 21/6, no. 173 (November–December 1991), 15.

————. "Yemen Between Civility and Civil War," in Augustus Richard Norton (ed.), *Civil Society in the Middle East*, vol. 2. Leiden, Netherlands: E.J.Brill, 1996, 287–316.

————. "Yemen: Unification and the Gulf War," *Middle East Report*, 21/3, no. 170 (May–June 1991), 26.

————. "Yemen Unity: The Economic Dimension," *Middle East Report*, 23/5, no. 184 (September–October 1993), 9–14.

Carapico, Sheila, and Jemera Rome. *Human Rights in Yemen during and after the 1994 War*. Human Rights Watch, October 1994.

Carapico, Sheila, Lisa Wedeen, and Anna Wuerth, "The Death of Jarallah Omar," *Middle East Report Online*. December 31, 2002. www.merip.org/mero/mero051603.html

CIA World Fact Book, *Yemen*. 2006. www.cia.gov/cia/publications/factbook/geo/ym.html

Clark, Janine A. "The Conditions of Islamic Moderation: Unpacking Cross-Ideological Cooperation in Jordan," *International Journal of Middle East Studies*, 38 (2006), 539–560.

————. *Islam, Charity and Activism: Middle Class Networks and Social Welfare in Egypt, Jordan and Yemen*. Bloomington: Indiana University, 2004.

————. "Islamic Women in Yemen: Informal Nodes of Activism," in Quintan Wiktorowicz (ed.), *Islamic Activism: A Social Movement Theory Approach*. Bloomington: Indiana University, 2004, 164–84.

Clark, Janine A., and Jillian Schwedler, "Who Opened the Window? Women's Activism in Islamic Parties." *Comparative Politics*, 35/3 (April 2003), 293–313.

Colburn, Marta. *The Dynamics of Development and Democratization in Yemen*. Bonn, Germany: Friedrich-Ebert-Stiftung, 2002.

————. *The Republic of Yemen: Development Challenges in the 21st Century*. London: Catholic Institute for International Relations, 2002.

Coll, Steve. *The Bin Ladens: An Arabian Family in the American Century*. New York: Penguin, 2008.

Colton, Nora. "The Silent Victims: Yemeni Migrants Return Home," *Oxford International Review*, 3/1 (1991), 23–37.

Corstange, Daniel. "Drawing Dissent: Political Cartoons in Yemen," *PS: Political Science & Politics*, 40/2 (April 2007), 293–296.

————. "Yemen (1962–1970)," K. DeRouen and U. Heo (eds.), *Civil Wars of the World*, vol. 2. Santa Barbara: ABC-CLIO (2007), 809–827.

Da Lage, Olivier. "Les reves brises de l'unite yemenite: causes d'un conflit," *Le Monde Diplomatique*, 41 (July 1994), 8–9.

————. "Le Yemen entre democratisation et guerre civile," *Defense Nationale* (February 1993), 125–134.

Daair, Omar. *He Who Rides the Lion: Authoritarian Rule in a Plural Society: The Republic of Yemen*. MSc Diss. University of London, 2001. www.al-bab.com/yemen/pol/daair1.htm

Dabaghy, Jean. "Yemen: chronique d'une separation amorcee," *Arabies* (March 1994), 18–22+.

Dabaghy, Jean, and Samir Sobh. "Ou vont les Yemen(s)?" *Arabies* (July/August 1994), 10–13.

Day, Stephen. "Barriers to Federal Democracy in Iraq: Lessons from Yemen," *Middle East Policy*, 13/3 (Fall 2006), 121–139.

————. *Power-Sharing and Hegemony: A Case Study of the United Republic of Yemen*. Ph.D. diss.: Georgetown University, 2001.

————. "Updating Yemeni National Unity: Could Lingering Regional Differences Bring Down the Regime?" *Middle East Journal*, 62/3 (Summer 2008), 417–436.

————. *Yemeni Unification 1990–2005: Democracy, Power Sharing, and Central-Local Government Relations*, paper presented at the Middle East Studies Association, Washington, D.C., November 2005.

Detalle, Renaud. "Ajuster sans douleur? La methid yemenite," *Monde arabe Maghreb-Machrek*, 155 (January–March 1997), 20–36.

————. "Les elections legislatives du 27 Avril 1993," *Monde arabe Maghreb-Machrek*, 141 (1993a), 3–36.

————. "The Yemeni Elections Up Close," *Middle East Report*, 23/6, no. 185 (November–December 1993), 8–12.

Dresch, Paul. *A Modern History of Yemen*. Cambridge, UK: Cambridge University, 2000.

————. "The Tribal Factor in the Yemeni Crisis," in Jamal S. al-Suwaidi (ed.), *The Yemen War of 1994: Causes and Consequences*. London: Saqi Books, 1995, 33–55.

Dunbar, Charles. "Internal Politics in Yemen: Recovery or Regression?" in Jamal al-Suwaida (ed.), *The Yemeni War of 1994: Causes and Consequences*. London: Saqi Books, 1995, 57–70.

Dunn, Michael C. "Islamist Parties in Democratizing States: A Look at Jordan and Yemen," *Middle East Policy*, 2/2 (1993), 16–27.

————. "The Unification of Yemen: Process, Politics and Prospects," *Middle East Journal*, 46/3 (Summer 1992), 456–476.

————. "The Wrong Place, the Wrong Time: Why Yemeni Unity Failed," *Middle East Policy*, 3/2 (1994), 148–156.

Eraqi-Klorman, B. Z. "The Forced Conversion of Jewish Orphans in Yemen," *International Journal of Middle Eastern Studies*, 33/1 (February 2001), 193–208.

European Union Election Observation Mission 2006. "Final Report," January 5, 2007, www.eueom-ye.org/Final_Reports.html

Faqih, Abdullah M. *The Struggle for Liberalization in Egypt, Jordan and Yemen*. Ph.D. diss.: Northeastern University, 2003.

———. "Yemen between National Consensus or War," *Yemen Mirror*, 18 May 2006. www.yemenmirror.com/index.php?action=showDetails&id=19

Gandy, Christopher. "The Yemen Revisited," *Asian Affairs*, 58/2 (1971), 295–304.

Gause III, F. Gregory. "The Idea of Yemeni Unity," *Journal of Arab Affairs*, 6 (Spring 1987), 55–87.

———. "Yemeni Unity: Past and Present," *Middle East Journal*, 42/1 (Winter 1988), 33–47.

Glosemeyer, Iris. "The Development of State Institutions," in Remy Leveau, Frank Mermier, and Udo Steinbach (eds.), *Le Yemen contemporain*. Paris: Editions Karthala, 1999, 79–100.

———. "The First Yemeni Parliamentary Elections in 1993: Practicing Democracy," *Orient (Deutsches Orient-Institute)*, 34 (September 1993), 439–451.

———. "Local Conflict, Global Spin: An Uprising in the Yemeni Highlands," *Middle East Report*, 232 (Fall 2004), 44–47.

Gray, Matthew. "Electoral Politics and the 1997 Elections in Yemen," *Journal of South Asian and Middle Eastern Studies*, 21/3 (Spring 1998), 31–47.

Halliday, Fred. *Arabia without Sultans: A Study of Political Instability in the Arab World*. New York: Vintage Books, 1975.

———. "The Formation of Yemeni Nationalism: Initial Reflections," in Israel Gershoni and James Jankowski (eds.), *Rethinking Nationalism in the Arab Middle East*. New York: Columbia University, 1997.

———. "The Third Inter-Yemeni War and Its Consequences," *Asian Affairs*, 26 (June 1995), 131–140.

———. "The Yemens: Conflict and Coexistence," *World Today*, 40 (August/September 1984), 355–362.

———. "Yemen's Uneasy Elections," *World Today*, 53/3 (March 1997), 73–76.

Hamzawy, Amr. "The Key to Arab reform: Moderate Islamists," *Carnegie Endowment for International Peace* (August 2005), 7 pp.

Hartman, Rainer. "Yemeni Exodus from Saudi Arabia: The Gulf Conflict and the Ceasing of the Workers' Remittances," *Journal of South Asian and Middle Eastern Studies*, 19 (Winter 1995), 38–52.

al-Hassan, Bilal. "The Key to Yemen's Political Crisis Lies in One Word: Tribes," *Mideast Mirror*, 13 (July 5, 1999), 126.

Haykel, Bernard. "Rebellion, Migration or Consultative Democracy? The Zaydis and their Detractors in Yemen," in Remy Leveau, Frank Mermier, and Udo Steinbach (eds.), *Le Yemen contemporain*. Paris: Karthala, 1999, 193–201.

————. "The Salafis in Yemen at a Crossroad: An Obituary of Shaykh Muqbil al-Wadii of Dammaj," *Jemen Report*, 33 (2002), 28–31.

————. "A Zaydi Revival?" *Yemen Update*. Ardmore, Pa.: American Institute for Yemeni Studies, 28–31.

Henin, Nicolas. "Yemen: Un Pays Arme Jusqu'aux Dents," *Arabies*, no. 155 (November 1999), 50–53.

Hermida, Alfred, and Najm Jarrah. "Civil War Breaks Out in Yemen," *Middle East International*, 13 May 1994, 3–4.

Holger, Albrecht. "The Political Economy of Reform in Yemen: Privatisation, Investment, and the Yemeni Business Climate," *Asien Afrika Lateinamerika*, 30 (2002), 131–150.

Hudson, Michael C. "After the Gulf War: Prospects for Democratization in the Arab World," *Middle East Journal*, 46/3 (Summer 1991), 407–426.

————. *Arab Politics: The Search for Legitimacy*. New Haven, Conn.: Yale University Press, 1977.

————. "Arab Regimes and Democratization: Responses to the Challenge of Political Islam," *International Spectator*, 29 (October/December 1994), 3–27.

————. "Bipolarity, Rational Calculation and War in Yemen," in Jamal S. al-Suwaida (ed.), *The Yemeni War of 1994: Causes and Consequences*. London: Saqi Books, 1995, 19–32.

————. "Unhappy Yemen: Watching the Slide Toward Civil War," *Middle East Insight*, 10/4–5 (May–August 1994), 10–19.

Human Rights Watch/Middle East. *Yemen: Human Rights during and after the 1994 War*. New York: Human Rights Publications, 1994.

Ingrams, Doreen, and Leila Ingrams (eds.) *Records of Yemen 1798–1960*, 15 vols. inc. map box. Neuchatel, Switzerland: Archive International Group, 1993.

Ingrams, William Harold. *Arabia and the Isles*. 3rd ed. New York: Frederick A. Praeger, 1966.

————. *The Yemen: Imams, Rulers and Revolutions*. London: John Murray, 1936.

International Crisis Group. *Yemen: Coping with Terrorism and Violence in a Fragile State*. ICG Middle East Report, no. 8 (8 January 2003).

Ishiyama, John. "The Sickle and the Minaret: Communist Successor Parties in Yemen and Afghanistan after the Cold War," *Middle East Review of international Affairs*, 9/1 (March 2005), 7–29.

Jansen, G. H. "The Problems of South-west Arabia," *World Today*, 19/8 (August 1963), 337–343.

Al-Jawi, Omar. "We are the Opposition . . . but . . . ," in E. G. H. Joffe, M. J. Hachemi, and Eric W. Watkins (eds.), *Yemen Today: Crisis and Solutions.* London: Caravel Press, 1997, 83–88.

Joffe, E. G. H., M. J. Hachemi, and E. W. Watkins (eds.), *Yemen Today: Crisis and Solutions.* London: Caravel, 1997.

Johnsen, Gregory. "The Election Yemen Was Supposed to Have," *Middle East Report Online,* 3 October, 2006. www.merip.org/mero/mero100306.html.

————. "Profile of Sheikh Abd al-Majid al-Zindani," *Terrorism Monitor,* Jamestown Foundation, 4/7 (April 2006).

————. "Reprogramming the Imagination in Yemen: Hamoud al-Hitar and the Religious Dialogue Committee. Paper, annual meetings, *Middle East Studies Association,* 2005.

————. "Salih's Road to Reelection," *Middle East Report Online,* January 13, 2006, www.merip.org/mero/mero011306.html

Katulis, Brian, and David Emery. "Country Report: Yemen," *Countries at the Crossroads.* New York: Freedom House, 2006.

Katz, Mark N. "Breaking the Yemen-Al Qaeda Connection," *Current History,* 102/660 (January 2003), 40–43.

————. "Election Day in Aden," *Middle East Policy,* 5 (September 1997), 40–50.

Keating, M. "We Stand United," *Geographical Magazine,* 64 (March 1992), 38–43.

Kostiner, Joseph. *Yemen: The Tortuous Quest for Unity, 1990–1994.* London: Pinter Publishers, 1996.

La Gorce, Paul-Marie de. "Controverses a Washington," *Le Monde Diplomatique,* 48/572 (November 2001), 1 & 14–15.

Lata, Rafiq. *Yemen: Unification and Modernization,* London: Gulf Centre for Strategic Studies, 1994.

Lawless, Richard I. "Yemen: History," in *Regional Surveys of the World: The Middle East and North Africa 2005,* 51st ed. London: Europa Publications (2005), 1241–1265.

Lefresne, Bernard. "Les islamistes yemenites et les elections, *Maghreb Machrek* (July–September 1993), 27–36.

Lerner, George. "Yemen: Steps toward Civil Society," *Middle East Watch,* New York, 4/10 (November 1992), 1–26.

Longley, April. "The High Water Mark of Islamist Politics? The Case of Yemen," *Middle East Journal,* 61/2 (Spring 2007), 240–258.

Longley, April, and Abdul Ghani al-Iryani. "Fighting Brushfires with Batons: Analysis of the Political Crisis in South Yemen," *Middle East Institute Policy Brief,* no. 7, February 2008.

Mahdi, Kamil A. (ed.), *Yemen into the Twenty-First Century: Continuity and Change*. Reading, UK: Ithaca Press, 2007.

Makin, Patrick. "Drifting toward Dissolution," *Middle East (London)*, March 1994, 19–20.

Manea, Elham M. "Yemen, the Tribe and the State," paper presented at the *International Colloquium on Islam and Social Change*, University of Lausanne, 10–11 October 2005. www.al-bab.com/yemen/soc/manea1htm

al-Masudi, Abdul-Aziz ibn Qaid. "The Islamic Movement in Yemen," Middle Eastern Affairs Journal, 2/2–3 (1995), 26–55.

McGregor, Andrew. "Stand-off in Yemen: The al-Zindani Case," *Terrorism Focus*, Jamestown Foundation, 3/9, March 2006.

————. "Strike First," *World Today*, 58/12 (December 2002), 7–9.

Al-Mdaires, Falah. "Political Islamic Movements in Modern Yemen," *Journal of South Asian and Middle Eastern Studies*, 24/2 (Winter 2001), 73–86.

Mehra, Ram Narain. *Aden and Yemen, 1905–1919*. Delhi, India: Agam Prakashan, 1988.

Mermier, Frank. "L'islam politique au Yemen ou la 'Tradition' contre les traditions?" *Monde arabe Maghreb-Machrek*, 155 (1997a), 6–19.

————. "Yemen: L'Etat Face a la Democratie," *Monde arabe Maghreb-Machrek*, 155 (January/March 1997b), 3–86.

Metres, Katherine M. "Yemen Again on Path to Democracy, Economic Growth," *Washington Report on Middle East Affairs*, 15 (October 1996), 69–70+.

Middle East Watch/Human Rights Watch. *Yemen: Steps Toward Civil Society*. New York: Middle East Watch, 1992.

Miller, Derek B. *Demand, Stockpiles and Social Controls: Small Arms in Yemen*. Small Arms Survey, Occasional Paper No.9, May 2003.

Monroe, Elizabeth. *Philby of Arabia*. London: Faber & Faber, 1973.

al-Mutawakkil, Muhammad Abd al-Malik. "The Gap Between the Government and the Governed," in E. G. H. Joffe, M. J. Hachemi, and E. W. Watkins (eds.), *Yemen Today: Crisis and Solutions*. London: Caravel, 1997, 67–70.

Naana, Hamida. "Yemen: Les canons de la discorde," *Le Nouvel Afrique Asie* (June 1994), 34–37.

National Democratic Institute. *The April 27, 1997 Parliamentary Elections in Yemen*. Washington, D.C.: National Democratic Institute, 1998.

————. *The April 27, 2003 Parliamentary Elections in the Republic of Yemen*. Washington, D.C.: National Democratic Institute, 2004.

————. *Yemen: Political Party Capacity Building and Women's Participation*. Washington, D.C.: CEPPS/National Democratic Institute Quarterly Report (April–June 2005).

NewsYemen. "Al-Ahmar Refutes Announcement 'Leaving Yemen to Sons of President,'" 8 April 2006. www.newsyemen.net/en/view_newsasp?sub_no=3_2006_04_08_5978

Nonneman, Gerd. "The Yemen Republic: From Unification and Liberalization to Civil War and Beyond," Haifaa A. Jawad (ed.), *The Middle East in the New World Order*. London: Macmillan, 1997, 61–96.

Novak, Jane. "Bloody Protests in Yemen," *Worldpress.org*, 14 July 2008. www.worldpress.org/Mideast/2978.cfm

————. "Journalism in Yemen: A Battle for Truth in the Age of Terror," *Yemen Times* (April 2007) www.yementimes.com/article.shtml?i=876&p=report&a=1

————. "Al-Khaiwani, Democracy and Yemen," *Middle East Transparent* (19 January 2005). www.metransparent.com/texts/jane_novak_al_khaiwani_democracy_and_yemen.htm

Okruhlik, G., and P. Conge. "National Autonomy, Labor Migration and Political Crisis," *Middle East Journal*, 51/4 (Fall 1997), 554–566.

Ottoway, Marina, and Amr Hamzawy. "Fighting on Two Fronts: Secular Parties in the Arab World," *Carnegie Endowment for International Peace, Democracy and Rule of Law Project* (May 2007), 27 pp.

Ottoway, Marina, and Michele Dunne. "Incumbent Regimes and the 'King's Dilemma' in the Arab World: Promise and Threat of Managed Reform," Carnegie Endowment for International Peace, Middle East Program. (December 2007), 21 pp.

Paxton, Julian. "Bitter Memories," *World Today*, 56/12 (December 2000), 23–24.

Peterson, John E. "The Arabian Peninsula in Modern Times: An Historiographical Survey," *American Historical Review*, 96/5 (December 1991), 1435–1449.

Phillips, Sarah. "Cracks in the Yemeni System, *Middle East Report Online*, 28 July 2005. www.merip.org/mero/072805.html

————. "Evaluating Political Reform in Yemen," Carnegie Endowment for International Peace (February 2007), 23 pp.

————. "Foreboding About the Future in Yemen," *Middle East Report Online*, 3 April 2006. www.merip.org/mero/mero040306.html

————. "Yemen: Economic and Political Deterioration," *Arab Reform Bulletin*, 3/7 (September 2005).

————. *Yemen's Democratic Experiment in Regional Perspective: Patronage and Pluralized Authoritatianism*. New York: Palgrave Macmillan, 2008.

Pridham, Brian R. (ed.). *Contemporary Yemen: Politics and Historical Background*. London: Croom Helm, 1984.

Al-Qadhi, Mohammed. "WB Warns of Yemen's Reform Package Collapse," *Yemen Times* (October 14, 2004.)

Quin, Mary. *Kidnapped in Yemen: One Woman's Amazing Escape.* London: Mainstream, 2005.

al-Rasheed, Madawi, and Robert Vitalis (eds.). *Counter-Narratives: History, Contemporary Society, and Politics in Saudi Arabia and Yemen.* New York: Palgrave Macmillan, 2004.

Reilly, Sir Bernard. *Aden and the Yemen.* London: Her Majesty's Stationery Office, 1960.

Rouleau, Eric. "Grignotage islamiste au Yemen: mise a l'ecart des socialistes . . .," *Le Monde Diplomatique*, 42 (May 1995), 5.

Ryan, Missy. "States of Failure," *Bulletin of Atomic Scientists*, 63/3 (May–June 2007), 50–57.

Saif, Ahmad Abdul-Kareem, *A Legislature in Transition: The Yemeni Parliament.* Burlington, Vt.: Ashgate, 2001.

————. *The Yemeni Parliamentary Elections: A Critical Analysis.* Dubai: Gulf Research Center, 2004

Sanger, Richard. *The Arabian Peninsula.* Ithaca, N.Y.: Cornell University Press, 1954.

al-Saqqaf, Abou Bakr. "The Yemeni Unity: Crisis in Integration," in Remy Leveau, Frank Mermier, and Udo Steinbach (eds.), *Le Yemen contemporain.* Paris: Editions Karthala, 1999, 141–160.

Schmitz, Charles. "Civil War in Yemen: The Price of Unity," *Current History*, 94/588 (January 1995), 33–36.

————. "Transnational Yemen: Global Power and Political Identity in Peripheral States," *Arab World Geographer*, 6/3 (2003), 148–164.

Schwedler, Jillian M. "Democratization in the Arab World: Yemen's Aborted Opening," *Journal of Democracy*, 13: 4 (2002), 48–55.

————. *Faith in Moderation: Islamist Parties in Jordan and Yemen.* New York: Cambridge University, 2006.

————. "The Islah Party in Yemen: Political Opportunities and Coalition Building in a Transitional Polity," in Quintan Wikorowicz (ed.), *Islamic Activism: A Social Movement Theory Approach.* Bloomington: Indiana University, 2001, 205–228.

————. "Islam, Democracy, and the Yemeni State," paper presented at the CSID annual conference, Georgetown University, 7 April 2001.

————. "Yemen's Aborted Opening," *Journal of Democracy*, 13/4 (October 2002), 48–55.

Serjeant, Robert Bertram. "Perilous Politics in Two Yemen States," *Geographical Magazine*, 51/11 (August 1979), 767–774.

————. "The Two Yemens: Historical Perspectives and Present Attitudes," *Journal of the Royal Central Asian Society*, 60 (February 1973), 3–17.

Sharif, Abdu H. "Weak Institutions and Democracy: The Case of Yemeni Parliament, 1993–97," *Middle East Policy*, 9/1 (March 2002), 82–93.

Slater, Julia. "Why Is Yemen Falling Apart?" *Middle East International*, no. 477 (10 June 1994), 16–17; and no. 478 (24 June 1994), 16–17.

Smith, S. C. "Revolution and Reaction: South Arabia in the Aftermath of the Yemeni Revolution," *Journal of Imperial and Commonwealth History*, 28/3 (September 2000), 193–208.

Sobh, Samir. "Yemen an 1: ou est passe l'euphorie de l'unification? *Arabies* (June 1991), 46–53.

Stiftl, Ludwig. "The Yemeni Islamists in the Process of Democratization," in Remy Leveau, Franck Mermier, and Udo Steinbach (eds.), *Le Yemen contemporain*. Paris: Editions Karthala, 1999, 247–265.

Al-Suwaidi, Jamal S. (ed.). *The Yemeni War of 1994: Causes and Consequences*. London: Saqi Books, 1995.

Taheri, Amir. "Yemen: chronique d'une desunion announcee," *Politique Internationale* (Autumn 1994), 209–223.

Talib, Saadaldeen Ali. "A Decade of Pluralist Democracy in Yemen: The Yemeni Parliament after Unification," in Ali Sawi (ed.), *Parliamentary Reform*. Cairo: Konrad Adenauer Stiftung, 2003.

————. "Hadhrami Networking: Salvage of the Homeland," paper presented to the "International Conference on the Hadhramis in Southeast Asia: Identity Maintenance or Assimilation?" International Islamic University of Malaysia, Kuala Lumpur, August 2005.

Trevelyan, Humphrey. *The Middle East in Revolution*. London: Macmillan, 1970.

U.S. Agency for International Development. *Democracy and Governance Assessment of Yemen, 2004*. Washington, D.C.: Center for Democracy and Governance, February 2004.

U.S. Department of State. *Yemen Country Report on Human Rights Practices for 1997*. Washington, D.C.: Bureau of Democracy, Human Rights and Labor, 30 January 1998.

————. *Yemen: Country Report on Human Rights Practices*. Washington, D.C.: Bureau of Democracy, Human Rights and Labor, 8 March 2006.

Vom Bruck, Gabriele. "Being a Zaidi in the Absence of an Imam: Doctrinal Revisions, Religious Instruction, and the (Re-) Invention of Ritual," in Remy Leveau, Franck Mermier, and Udo Steinbach (eds.). *Le Yemen Contemporain*. Paris: Editions Karthala, 1999, 169–192.

————. "Evacuating Memory in Postrevolutionary Yemen," in Madawi al-Rasheed and Robert Vitalis (eds.). *Counter-Narratives: History, Contempo-*

rary Society, and Politics in Saudi Arabia. New York: Palgrave Macmillan, 2004, 229–246.

————. *Islam, Memory, and Morality in Yemen: Ruling Families in Transition.* New York: Palgrave, 2005.

Waterbury, John, and Ragaei el Mallakh. *The Middle East in the Coming Decade.* New York: McGraw-Hill, 1978.

Watkins, Eric. "Saleh Cracks Down on the Opposition: Despite His Military Victory in Last Year's Civil War, Yemen's President Ali Abdullah Saleh Continues to Experience Difficulties with Opponents of His Rule," *Middle East* (October 1995), 16–17.

————. "Still Looking for Unity: The Contest in Yemen Is Rigged: But the Game Goes On," *Index on Censorship*, 26 (November–December 1997), 162–163.

————. "Yemen: A Dark Winter's Day," *Middle East* (January 1998), 15–16.

————. "Yemen: Democracy against the Odds," *Middle East* (December 1992), 9–11.

————. "Yemen: Promise Them Anything," *Middle East* (September 1994), 8–9.

————. "Yemen: A Thin Veil of Democracy," *Middle East* (April 1997), 6–8.

Wedeen, Lisa. *Peripheral Visions: Public, Power, and Performance in Yemen.*

————. "The Politics of Deliberation: Qat Chews as Public Spheres in Yemen," *Public Culture*, 19/1 (Winter 2007), 59–84.

————. "Seeing Like a Citizen, Acting Like a State: Exemplary Events in Unified Yemen," in Madawi al-Rasheed and Robert Vitalis (eds.). *Counter-Narratives: History, Contemporary Society, and Politics in Saudi Arabia and Yemen.* New York: Palgrave Macmillan, 2004, 285–304.

Whitaker, Brian. "National Unity and democracy in Yemen: A Marriage of Inconvenience," in E. G. H. Joffe, M. J. Hachemi and Eric Watkins (eds.). *Yemen Today: Crisis and Solution* (London: Caravel, 1997), 21–27.

————. "'Armed' University," *Middle East International*, no. 742 (21 January 2005), 21–22.

Yadav, Stacey Philbrick. "Pen Battles Sword," *Cairo Magazine*, 21 April 2005.

al-Yemeni, Ahmed A. Hezam. *The Dynamics of Democratization: Political Parties in Yemen.* Bonn, Germany: Friedrich-Ebart-Stiftung, 2003.

External Relations and Foreign Policy

Abadi, Jacob. "Pragmatism and Rhetoric in Yemen's Policy toward Israel," *Journal of Third World Studies*, 16/2 (Fall 1999), 95–118.

Abir, Mordechai. *Saudi Arabia: Government, Society and the Gulf Crisis.* New York: Routledge, 1993.

Aliboni, Roberto. *The Red Sea Region.* Syracuse, N.Y.: Syracuse University Press, 1985.

Amadou, Fode. "Erythree-Yemen: Crise Explosive," *Le Nouvel AfriqueAsie* (March 1996), 17.

Anon. "Saudi-Yemen," *Middle East Reporter Weekly,* 88 (22 August 1998), 14–15.

Anon. "Saudi-Yemen: Tension Defused over 60-Year-Old Border Issue," *Middle East Reporter Weekly,* 75 (21 January 1995).

Anon. "Saudis, U.S. at Odds over Yemeni War," *Middle East Reporter Weekly,* 72 (21 May 1994), 4.

Anon. "What's behind the Closer Yemen–U.S. Ties?" *Middle East Reporter Weekly,* 87 (30 May 1998), 12.

Anon. "What's behind the Saudi–Yemen Border Pact?" *Middle East Reporter Weekly,* 96/1105 (8 July 2000), 16–17.

Anon. "Text of UN Council's Yemen Cease-fire Resolution," *Middle East Reporter Weekly,* 73 (2 July 1994), 15.

Anon. "Yemen Conflict Polarizes Arab World," *Middle East Reporter Weekly,* 72 (2 July 1994), 7–8.

Anon. "Yemen Crisis: Too Many Cooks Spoil the Broth," *Middle East Reporter Weekly,* 72 (23 April 1994), 14–15.

Anon. "Yemen: Foreign Intervention and Weapons," *Middle East Reporter Weekly,* 72 (4 June 1994), 14–15.

Anon. "Yemen Mediation: Yemen Initiative Opens 'Palestinian Dialogue of the Deaf,'" *Middle East Reporter Weekly,* 129/1499 (12 April 2008), 12–13.

Anon. "Yemen–Eritrea: Peaceful Settlement from The Hague," *Middle East Reporter Weekly,* 89 (24 October 1998), 14–15.

Arab Information Center. *British Imperialism in Southern Arabia.* New York: Research Section, Arab Information Center, 1958.

Anthony, John Duke. "Saudi–Yemeni Relations: Implication for U.S. Policy," *Middle East Policy,* 7/3 (June 2000), 78–96.

al-Ashtal, Abdullah. "Eventually There Can Only Be an Arab Solution," *Middle East (MERIP) Report,* 21/169 (March–April 1991), 8–10.

Badeau, John. *The American Approach to the Arab World.* New York: Harper & Row, 1968.

Badeeb, Saeed M. *The Saudi–Egyptian Conflict over North Yemen, 1962–1970.* Boulder: Westview Press, 1986.

Baldry, John. "British Naval Operation against Turkish Yaman 1914–1919," *Arabica,* 25/2 (June 1978), 148–197.

————. "Foreign Interventions and Occupations of Kamaran Island," *Arabian Studies*, 4 (1978), 89–111.

————. "Soviet Relations with Saudi Arabia and the Yemen 1917–1938," *Middle East Studies*, 20/1 (January 1984), 66–67.

————. "The Turkish–Italian War in the Yaman 1911–1912," *Arabian Studies*, 3 (1976), 51–65.

————. "The Yamani Island of Kamaran during the Napoleonic Wars," *Middle Eastern Studies*, 16/3 (October 1980), 246–266.

Balfour-Paul, Glen. *The End of Empire in the Middle East*. New York: Cambridge University Press, 1990.

Behbehani, Hashim S. H. *China and the People's Democratic Republic of Yemen: A Report*. Boston: Routledge & Kegan Paul, 1985.

Bidwell, Robin. *Affairs of Arabia 1905–1906*, 2 vols., London: Frank Cass, 1971.

————. "The Turkish Attack on Aden 1915–1918," *Arabian Studies*, 6 (1982), 171–194.

Bissell, R. E. "Soviet Uses of Proxies in the Third World: The Case of Yemen," *Soviet Studies*, 30 (1978), 87–106.

Boot, Max. "Retaliation for Me, but Not for Thee: A Foolish Inconsistency Is the Hobgoblin of the State Department," *Weekly Standard*, 8/10 (18 November 2002), 26–27.

Burrowes, Robert D. "The Other Side of the Red Sea and a Little More: The Horn of Africa and the Two Yemens," in David A. Korn (ed.). *The Horn of Africa and Arabia: Conference Papers*. Washington, D.C.: Defense Academic Research Support Program and Middle East Institute, 1990, 63–74.

————. "The Yemeni Civil War of 1994: Impact on the Arab Gulf States," in Jamal S. al-Suwaidi (ed.), *The Yemen War of 1994*. London: Saqi Books, 1995, 71–80.

Cigar, Norman. "South Yemen and the USSR: Prospects for the Relationship," *Middle East Journal*, 39/4 (Autumn 1985), 775–795.

————. "Soviet–South Yemeni Relations: The Gorbachev Years," *Journal of South Asian and Middle East Studies*, 12/4 (Summer 1989), 3–38.

Creekman, Charles T. "Sino–Soviet Competition in the Yemens," *Naval War College Review*, July–August 1979, 79–83.

Dawisha, A. I. "Intervention in the Yemen: An Analysis of Egyptian Perceptions and Policies," *Middle East Journal*, 29/1 (Winter 1975), 47–63.

————. "Perceptions, Decisions and Consequences in Foreign Policy: The Egyptian Intervention in the Yemen," *Political Studies*, 25 (June), 201–226.

Donini, Giovanni. "Saudi Arabia's Hegemonic Policy and Economic Development in the Yemen Arab Republic," *Arab Studies Quarterly*, 1/4 (1979), 299–308.

Duhs, Tom. "The War on Terrorism in the Horn of Africa," *Marine Corps Gazette*, 88/4 (April 2004), 54–60.

Dunn, Michael C. "Soviet Interests in the Arabian Peninsula: The Aden Pact and Other Paper Tigers," *American–Arab Affairs*, no. 8 (Spring 1984), 92–98.

El Azhary, M. S. "Aspects of North Yemen's Relations with Saudi Arabia," *Asian Affairs*, 15 (October 1984), 277–286.

Fabian Society. *Arabia: When Britain Goes*. London: Fabian Society, 1967.

Farid, Abdel Majid (ed.). *The Red Sea: Prospects for Stability*. New York: St. Martin's Press, 1984.

Gause III, F. Gregory. *Saudi–Yemeni Relations: Domestic Structures and Foreign Influences*. New York: Columbia University Press, 1990.

Gavin R. J. *Aden under British Rule: 1839–1967*. London: C. Hurst, 1975.

Gerges, F. A. "The Kennedy Administration and the Egyptian–Saudi Conflict in Yemen: Co-opting Arab Nationalism," *Middle East Journal*, 49/2 (Spring 1995), 292–311.

Gibbon, Scott. *The Conspirators*. London: Howard Baker, 1967.

Halliday, Fred. "The Arc of Revolution: Iran, Afghanistan, South Yemen, and Ethiopia," *Race and Class*, 20/4 (Spring 1979), 373–390.

―――. "Moscow's Crisis Management: The Case of South Yemen," *MERIP (Middle East Research and Information Project) Reports*, 18/151 (March–April 1988), 18–22.

―――. *Revolution and Foreign Policy: The Case of South Yemen, 1967–1987*. Cambridge, UK: Cambridge University, 1990.

Halliday, Fred, et al. "The Contest for Arabia," *MERIP (Middle East Research and Information Project) Reports*, 15/130 (February 1985), 3–22.

Hawthorne, Amy. "Yemen and the Fight against Terrorism," *The Washington Institute for Near East Policy*, Policy Watch 572, 11 October 2001.

Henderson, Simon, and Khairi Abaza. "Yemeni President Saleh Comes to Washington," *Washington Institute for Near East Policy* (7 November 2005), 3 pp.

Jones, Clive. "'Among Ministers, Mavericks and Mandarins': Britain, Covert Action and the Yemen Civil War, 1962–64," *Middle Eastern Studies*, 40/1 (January 2004), 99–126.

―――. *Britain and the Yemeni Civil War, 1962–1965: Ministers, Mercenaries and Mandarins: Foreign Policy and the Limits of Covert Action*. Brighton, UK: Sussex Academic Press, 2004.

Kaplan, Robert D. *Imperial Grunts: The American Military on the Ground*. New York: Random House, 2005, 17–38.

Katz, Mark H. "Five External Powers and the Yemeni Civil War," in Jamal S. al-Suwaida (ed.), *The Yemeni War of 1994: Causes and Consequences*. London: Saqi Books, 1995.

————. "North Yemen Between East and West," *American–Arab Affairs*, no. 8 (Spring 1984), 99–107.

————. *Russia and Arabia: Soviet Foreign Policy toward the Arabian Peninsula*. Baltimore, M.: Johns Hopkins University Press, 1986.

————. "Yemeni Unity and Saudi Security," *Middle East Policy*, 1/1 (1992), 117–35.

Kechichian, Joseph A. "Trends in Saudi National Security," *Middle East Journal*, 53/2 (Spring 1999), 232–253.

King, Gillian. *Imperial Outpost: Aden: Its Place in British Strategic Policy*. London: Oxford University Press, 1964.

————. "The Problem of Aden," *World Today*, 18 (January–December 1962), 498–503.

Koszinowski, Thomas. "Gesellschaftspolitische Veranderungen im Jemen nach dem Burgerkrieg," *Nord-Sud Aktuell*, 12/1 (1998), 144–152.

————. "Yemeni Foreign Policy since Unification and the Part Played by Saudi Arabia," in Remy Leveau, Franck Mermier, and Udo Steinbach (eds.), *Le Yemen contemporain*. Paris: Editions Karthala, 1999, 61–78.

Kour, Zaki H. "Why the British Took Aden," *Middle East International* (February 1976), 28–29.

Kutschera, Chris. "Erythree: La Guerre du Petrole," *Jeune Afrique Economie* (18 March 1996), 26–27.

Labrousse, Henri. "La Fin d'un Conflit en Mer Rouge," *Defense Nationale*, 56/4 (April 2000), 136–143.

Lang, Anthony F. "Punishment and Peace: Critical Reflections on Countering Terrorism," *Millennium-Journal of International Studies*, 36/3 (2008), 493–511.

Lathuilliere, Marc. "Erythree: L'Aventurier de la Mer Rouge," *Jeune Afrique Economie* (3 June 1996), 28–29.

Ledger, David. *Shifting Sands: The British in South Arabia*. London: Peninsular Press, 1983.

Lefebvre, J. A. "Red Sea Security and the Geopolitical Economy of the Hanish Islands Dispute," *Middle East Journal*, 52/3 (Summer 1998), 367–385.

Levitt, Matthew. "Targeting Terror: U.S. Policy toward Middle Eastern State Sponsors and Terrorist Organizations," *Washington Institute for Near East Policy* (2002), ix+141 pp.

Macro, Eric. "Fremantle at Aden in H.M.S. *Challenger* 1830," *Arabian Studies*, 6 (1982), 211–212.

————. *Yemen and the Western World Since 1571*. New York: Frederick A. Praeger, 1968.

May, Rupert. "Great Britain's Relations with Yemen and Oman," *Middle Eastern Affairs*, 11/5 (May 1960), 142–149.

McMullen, Christopher J. *Resolution of the Yemen Crisis, 1963: A Case Study in Mediation*. Washington, D.C.: Institute for the Study of Diplomacy, School of Foreign Service, 1980.

Monroe, Elizabeth. "Kuwait and Aden: A Contrast in British Policy," *Middle East Journal*, 18/1 (Winter 1964), 63–74.

Moore, John D. "The USS *Cole*: Implications for Long-term Counterterrorism Policy," *Journal of Counterterrorism and Security International*, 7/3 (2001), 26–33.

Muhammad al-Hasani, Ali Nasir. "Foreign Policy of Democratic Yemen and the Struggle against Imperialism," *Kommunist*, 10 (July 1985), 110–116.

Mylroie, Laurie. *Politics and the Soviet Presence in the PDRY: Internal Vulnerabilities and Regional Challenges*. Palo Alto, Calif.: Rand Corporation, 1983.

New York Times, The. "U.S. Broadens Terror Fight, Readying Troops for Yemen," 2 March, 2002.

Page, Stephen. "Moscow and the Arabian Peninsula," *American–Arab Affairs*, no. 8 (Spring 1984), 83–91.

———. *The Soviet Union and the Yemens: Influence in Asymmetrical Relationships*. New York: Praeger, 1985.

———. *The USSR and Arabia*. London: Central Asian Research Centre, 1971.

Peterson, John E. *Conflict in the Yemens and Superpower Involvement*. Washington, D.C.: Center for Contemporary Arab Studies, Georgetown University, 1981.

Phillips, James. *The Yemen Bombing: Another Wake-up Call in the Terrorist Shadow War*. Washington, D.C.: The Heritage Foundation, memo. no. 703, 25 October 2000.

Pieragostini, Karl. *Britain, Aden and South Arabia: Abandoning Empire*. New York: St. Martin's, 1991.

Pincus, Walter. "Missile Strike Carried Out with Yemeni Cooperation," *The Washington Post*, 6 November, 2006, A12.

Plaut, Martin. "A Clash for Control of the Shipping Lanes," *World Today*, 52/2 (February 1996), 46–47.

Pollack, David. "Moscow and Aden: Coping with a Coup," *Problems of Communism*, 35 (May–June 1986), 50–70.

Prados, Alfred S., and Jeremy M. Sharp. "Yemen: Current Conditions and U.S. Relations," *Federation of American Scientists* (4 January 2007), 6 pp.

Quandt, William B. *Saudi Arabia in the 1980s: Foreign Policy, Security, and Oil*. Washington, D.C.: The Brookings Institution, 1981.

Rahmy, Ali Abdel. *The Egyptian Policy in the Arab World: Intervention in Yemen*. Washington, D.C.: University Press of America, Inc., 1983.

Safran, Nadav. *Saudi Arabia: The Ceaseless Quest for Security.* Cambridge, Mass.: Harvard University Press, 1985.

Al-Saqqaf, Mohamed. "Le contentieux territorial entre le Yemen et l'Arabie Saoudite: Vers une solution?" *Maghreb Machrek* (July/September 1995), 56–71.

Schofield, Richard (ed). *Arabian Boundary Disputes,* vol. 13. Neuchatel, Switzerland: Archive International Group, 1992.

Schofield, Richard, and Gerald Blake (eds). *Arabian Boundaries: Primary Documents 1853–1960,* vols. 3–4. Neuchatel, Switzerland: Archive International Group, 1988.

Sicherman. Harvey. *Aden and British Strategy 1839–1968.* Philadelphia: Foreign Policy Research Institute, 1972.

Sinclair, Reginald W. *Documents on the History of Southwest Arabia, Tribal Warfare and Foreign Policy in Yemen, Aden . . . 1920–1929,* 2 vols. Salisbury, N.C.: Documentary Publications, 1976.

Stookey, Robert W., et al. *The Arabian Peninsula: Zone of Ferment.* Stanford, Calif.: Hoover Institution Press, 1984.

————. "Red Sea Gate-Keepers: The Yemen Arab Republic and the People's Democratic Republic of Yemen," *Middle East Review,* 10/4 (Summer 1978), 39–47.

Swayne, H. G. C. "The Rock of Aden: The Volcanic Mountain Fortress, the Sea Route from the Suez to India, Assumes New Importance," *National Geographic Magazine,* 68/6 (December 1935), 723–742.

Terrill, W. Andrew. "The Chemical Warfare Legacy of the Yemen War," *Comparative Strategy,* 10 (April/June, 1991), 109–119.

Tuson, Penelope, and Emma Quick (eds). *Arabian Treaties 1600–1960,* 4 vols. Neuchatel, Switzerland: Archive International Group, 1992.

U.S. Department of Defense. *DoD USS Cole Commission Report.* U.S Department of Defense, 9 January 2001.

U.S. Naval Institute, "USS Cole (DDG-67)," *U.S. Naval Institute Proceedings,* 126/12 (December 2000), 48–50.

Violli, Paul. "Politics in the Yemens and the Horn of Africa," in Mark V. Kauppi and R. Craig Nation (eds.). *The Soviet Union and the Middle East in the 1980s.* Lexington, Mass.: Lexington Books, 1983.

von Horn, General Carl. *Soldiering for Peace.* New York: David McKay, 1967.

Westing, A. H. "The Eritrean-Yemeni Conflict over the Hanish Archipelago: Towards a Resolution Favoring Peace and Nature," *Security Dialogue,* 27/2 (June 1996), 201–206.

Wilkinson, John. *Arabia's Frontiers: The Story of Britain's Blue and Violet Lines.* New York: St. Martin's Press, 1991.

Willis, John M. "Leaving Only Question Marks: Geographies of Rule in Modern Yemen," in Madawi al-Rasheed and Robert Vitalis (eds.). *Counter-Narratives: History, Contemporary Society, and Politics in Saudi Arabia and Yemen*. New York: Palgrave Macmillan, 2004, 119–150.

———. *Unmaking North and South: Cartographies of the Yemeni Past, 1857–1934*. London: C. Hurst, 2009.

Witty, D. M. "A Regular Army in Counterinsurgency Operations: Egypt in North Yemen, 1962–1967," *Journal of Military History*, 65/2 (April 2001), 401–439.

Worth, Robert. "Yemen's Deals with Jihadists Unsettle the U.S.," *The New York Times*, 28 January, 2008.

Zindani, Abdul Wahid Aziz. *Arab Politics in the United Nations*. New Delhi, India: Caxton Press, 1977.

Constitutions and Legal Systems

al-Abdin, al-Tayid Zein. "The Yemeni Constitution and Its Religious Orientation," *Arabian Studies*, 3 (1976), 115–125.

Al-Ahmar, K. "Intellectual Property Rights in Yemen: Proposals for Reforming the Legal Statutes and the Enforcement of Procedures," *IIC-International Review of Industrial Property and Copyright Law*, 34/4 (2003), 373–403.

Amin, Sayed Hassan. *Law and Justice in Contemporary Yemen: PDRY and YAR*. Glasgow: Royston Limited, 1987.

Bell, Gawain. "A Constitution for South Arabia," *Journal of the Royal Central Asian Society*, 55 (October 1966), 266–276.

Brinton, J. Y. *Aden and the Federation of South Arabia*. Washington, D.C.: American Society of International Law, 1964.

"Constitution of the People's Democratic Republic of Yemen, 1970," in Gizbert Flanz (ed.), *Constitutions of the World*, vol. 15, Dobbs Ferry, N.Y.: Oceana Publications, 1976.

Ghanem, Isam. "A Note on Law No. 1 of 1974 Concerning the Family, People's Democratic Republic of Yemen," *Arabian Studies*, 3 (1976), 191–96.

———. *Yemen: Political History, Social Structure and Legal System*. London: Arthur Probsthain, 1981.

———. *Zaydi Scholastics in Yemeni Commercial Shipping Disputes*. Dubai: Express Printing Services, 1989.

al-Hubaishi, Husayn A. *Legal System and Basic Law in Yemen*. London: Sphinx, 1988.

Kazi, A. K. "Notes on the Development of Zaydi Law," *Abr-Nahrain*, 2 (1960), 36–40.

Kretzmer, D. "Targeted Killing of Suspected Terrorists: Extra-Judicial Executions or Legitimate Means of Defense," *European Journal of International Law*, 16/2 (April 2005), 171–212.

Kwiatkowska, Barbara. "The Eritrea–Yemen Arbitration: Landmark Progress in the Acquisition of Territorial Sovereignty and Equitable Maritime Boundary Delimitation," *Ocean Development and International Law*, 32/1 (January/March 2001), 1–25.

McClintock, David W. *Constitutions of the Countries of the World: People's Democratic Republic of Yemen*. Dobbs Ferry, N.Y.: Oceana Publications, 1971.

————. *Constitutions of the Countries of the World: Yemen Arab Republic*. Dobbs Ferry, N.Y.: Oceana Publications, 1971.

Messick, Brinkley M. "Just Writing: Paradox and Political Economy in Yemeni Legal Documents," *Cultural Anthropology*, 4/1 (February 1989), 26–50.

Permanent Court of Arbitration. "Permanent Court of Arbitration (PCA): Eritrea: Yemen Arbitration (First Stage & Second Stage, 1998 & 1999)," *International Legal Materials*, 40/4 (July 2001), 900–1019.

Reisman, W. M. "Eritrea–Yemen Arbitration (Award, Phase II: Maritime Delimitation)," *American Journal of International Law*, 94/4 (October 2000), 721–736.

————. "Kissing Hands and Knees: Hegemony and Hierarchy in Shari'a Discourse," *Law and Society Review*, 22/4 (1988), 637–659.

————. "The Mufti, the Text and the World: Legal Interpretation in Yemen," *Man*, 21/1 (March 1986), 102–119.

————. *Transactions in Ibb: Economy and Society in a Yemeni Highland Town*. Ann Arbor, Mich.: University Microfilms International, 1979.

Rudolf, B. "The Government of the State of Eritrea and the Government of the Republic of Yemen: Award of the Arbitral Tribunal in the First Stage of the Proceedings (Territorial Sovereignty and Scope of the Dispute), *American Journal of International Law*, 93/3 (July 1999), 668–685.

Serjeant, R. B. *Customary and Shariah Law in Arabian Society*. Brookfield, Vt.: Ashgate, 1991.

Shamiry, Naguib A. R. "The Judicial System in Democratic Yemen," in B. R. Pridham (ed.), *Contemporary Yemen: Politics and Historical Background*. New York: St. Martin's, 1984, 175–194.

Yemen Arab Republic Government, "The Permanent Constitution of the YAR," *Middle East Journal*, 25/3 (Summer 1971), 389–401.

Public Policy

Bartelinck, Alexander (ed.). *Yemen Agricultural Handbook*. Eschborn: German Agency for Technical Cooperation, 1978.

Boustead, P. J. *A Market Consultancy Report to the Land Resources Division, Ministry of Overseas Development, on the Montane Plains/Wadi Rima Project, Yemen Arab Republic.* London: Tropical Products Institute, Ministry of Overseas Development, 1974.

Dobert, Margarita. "Development of Aid Programs to Yemen," *American–Arab Affairs*, 8 (Spring 1984), 108–116.

Eltigani, E. E. "Childbearing in Five Arab Countries," *Studies in Family Planning*, 32/1 (March 2001), 17–24.

al-Haddad, Abdul-Rahman. *Cultural Policy in the Yemen Arab Republic.* Paris: UNESCO, 1982.

Hermann, Jens. *Ambition and Reality: Planning for Health and Basic Services in the Yemen Arab Republic.* Frankfurt am Main: Peter Lang Verlag, 1979.

United Nations Education and Social Council. *National Science and Technology Policies in the Arab States.* Paris: UNESCO, 1976.

United Nations Industrial Development Organization (UNIDO). *PDRY: Enhancing Industrial Production Capacity.* New York: United Nations, 1989.

Economy and Economic Development

Abraham, Nabeel. "Detroit's Yemeni Workers," *MERIP (Middle East Research and Information Project) Reports*, no. 57 (May 1977), 3–9.

Addleton, Jonathon. "Economic Prospects in a United Yemen," *Journal of South Asian and Middle Eastern Studies*, 14 (Summer 1991), 2–14.

Albrecht, Holger. "The Political Economy of Reform in Yemen: Privatisation, Investment, and the Yemeni Business Climate," *Asien Afrika Lateinamerika*, 30 (2002), 131–150.

Al-Asaly, Saif Mahyoub. *Migration, Balance of Payments and Economic Growth: The Case of the Yemen Arab Republic.* Diss., University of South Carolina. Ann Arbor, Mich.: University Microfilms International, 1990.

Askari, Hossein, and John Thomas Cummings. *Middle East Economics in the 1970s: A Comparative Approach.* New York: Praeger Publishers, 1976.

Asquith, N. "Yemen: Cultivation Crisis," *Geographical Magazine*, 64 (March 1992), 40–41.

al-Attar, Muhammad Said. *Le Sous-developpement economique et social du Yemen: Perspectives de la revolution Yemenite.* Algiers, Algeria: Tiers-Monde, 1964.

Burns, P., and C. Cooper. "Yemen: Tourism and a Tribal–Marxist Dichotomy," *Tourism Management*, 18/8 (December 1997), 555–563.

Chami, Saade, S, Elekdag, T. Schneider, and N. B. Ltaifa. "Can a Rule-Based Monetary Policy Framework Work in a Developing Country? The Case of Yemen," *Developing Economies*, 46/1 (March 2008), 75–99.

Chami, Saade, S. Elekdag, and I. Tchakarov. "What are the Potential Benefits of Enlarging the Gulf Cooperation Council?" *International Economic Journal*, 21/4 (December 2007), 521–548.

Cohen, John M., and David B. Lewis. "Capital–Surplus, Labor Short Economies: Yemen as a Challenge to Rural Development Strategies," *American Journal of Agricultural Economics*, 61/3 (1979), 523–528.

Cohen, John M., and David B. Lewis. *Rural Development in the Yemen Arab Republic: Strategy Issues in a Capital Surplus Labor Short Economy*. Cambridge, Mass.: Harvard Institute for International Development, 1979.

Cohen, John, Mary Hebert, David B. Lewis, and Jon C. Swanson. "Development from Below: Local Development Associations in the Yemen Arab Republic," *World Development*, 9/11–12 (1981), 1039–1061.

Colton, Nora. "Homeward Bound: Yemeni Return Migration," *International Migration Review*, 27/4 (Winter 1993), 870–882.

————. "The Silent Victims: Yemeni Migrants Return Home," *Oxford International Review*, 3/1 (1991), 23–37.

Committee for Middle East Trade. *Market Opportunities and Methods of Doing Business in the Yemen Arab Republic*. London: Committee for Middle East Trade, 1978.

Cooper, John. "Yemen Squares Up to Reform," *Middle East Economic Digest*, 39 (21 April 1995), 4–5.

Couland, Jacques, and Blandine Destremau (eds.). *Arabie de Sud: Le Commerce comme facteur dynamisant des changements economiques et sociaux*. Paris: Cahiers de GREMAMO 10, 1991.

Denes, Marco. "Yemen Special Report," *Petroleum Argus*. 27 June 2005, 7–10.

Destremau, Blandine. "L'economie de Yemen: quelle sortie de la crise?" *Cahiers de GREMAMO*, 11 (1993), 129–148.

Dobert, Margarita. "Development of Aid Programs to Yemen," *American–Arab Affairs*, 8 (Spring 1984), 108–116.

Edge, Simon. "Yemen: Special Report," *Middle East Economic Digest*, 27 July 1990, 9–13.

Farouk-Sluglett, M. "Problems of Agricultural Production in the Yemeni Tihama with Special Reference to the Role of Unpaid Family Labor," *Cahiers de GREMAMO*, 11 (1993), 45–83.

Gazzo, Yves. "The Specifics of the Yemeni Economy," in Remy Leveau, Frank Mermier, and Udo Steinbach (eds.), *Le Yemen contemporain*. Paris: Editions Karthala, 1999.

Kemp, Peter. "Special Report: Oil and Gas," *Middle East Economic Digest*, 42 (24 July 1998), 11–20.

Kopp, Horst. "Oil and Gas in Yemen: Development and Importance of a Key Sector within the Economic System, in Remy Leveau, Franck Mermier, and

Udo Steinbach (eds.), *Le Yemen contemporain*. Paris: Editions Karthala, 1999, 365–380.

Longrigg, Stephen Hemsley. *Oil in the Middle East*, 3rd ed. London: Oxford University Press, 1968.

el-Mallakh, Ragaei. *The Economic Development of the Yemen Arab Republic*. London: Croom Helm, 1986.

Melamid, Alexander. "Economic Changes in Yemen, Aden and Dhofar," *Middle Eastern Affairs*, 5/3 (March 1954), 88–91.

———. *Oil and the Economic Geography of the Middle East and North Africa*. Princeton, N.J.: Darwin Press, 1991.

Mills, S. J. "Oil Discoveries in the Hadramaut: How Canadian Oxy Scored in Yemen," *Oil and Gas Journal*, 10 (1992), 49–52.

Saqqaf, Abdulaziz Yassin. "Energy Production and Consumption in the Yemen Arab Republic," *Journal of Energy and Development*, 11/1 (1986), 105–118.

———. *The Structural Transformation of the Yemeni Economy*. Diss., Fletcher School of Law and Diplomacy, Tufts University. Ann Arbor, Mich.: University Microfilms International, 1980.

Thirumalai, Srinivasan, and Thilakaratna. *Coping with Oil Depletion in Yemen: A Quantitative Evaluation, 2005*. www.ecomod.net/conferences/middle_east_2005_papers/Thirumalai.doc

Van Hear, Nicholas. "The Socio-economic Impact of the Involuntary Mass Return to Yemen in 1990," *Journal of Refugee Studies*, 7/1 (1994), 18–38.

Vincent, L. *The Politics of Water Scarcity: Irrigation and Water Supply in the Mountains of the Yemen Republic*. London: Overseas Development Institute, 1990.

Vogel, Horst. "Terrace Farming in Yemen," *Journal of Soil and Water Conservation*, 42 (1987), 18–21.

Wagenaar, Arnout, and Marijke D'Haese, "Development of Small-Scale Fisheries in Yemen: An Exploration," *Marine Policy*, 31/3 (May 2007), 266–275.

Wilson, Robert T. O. "Hajjah Market," *Arabian Studies*, 2 (1975), 204–210.

———. "Regular and Permanent Markets in the San'a Region," *Arabian Studies*, 5 (1979), 189–191.

World Bank. *Economic Growth in the Republic of Yemen: Sources, Constraints and Potential*. Washington, D.C.: World Bank, 2000. http://inweb18.worldbank.org/mna/mena.nsf/Attachments/Judicial$file/BB-5.pdf

———. *People's Democratic Republic of Yemen, A Review of Economic and Social Development*. Washington, D.C.: World Bank, 1979.

———. *Yemen Arab Republic: Current Position and Prospects*. Washington, D.C.: World Bank, 1985.

————. *Yemen Arab Republic: Development of a Traditional Economy.* Washington, D.C.: World Bank, 1979.

Yacoub, Salah M., and Akil Akil. *Socio-economic Study of Hojjuriyya District, Yemen Arab Republic.* Beirut: American University of Beirut, 1971.

Culture and Society

Abdulmalik, H. A., and D. W. Chapman. "Teacher Nationality and Classroom Practice in the Republic of Yemen," *Teaching and Teacher Education,* 10/3 (May 1994), 335–344.

Addleton, Jonathon. "Economic Prospects in a United Yemen," *Journal of South Asian and Middle Eastern Studies,* 14 (Summer 1991), 2–14.

Adra, Najwa. "The Concept of the Tribe in Rural Yemen," in N. S. Hopkins and S. E. Ibrahim (eds.), *Arab Society: Social Science Perspectives.* Cairo, Egypt: American University of Cairo Press, 1985.

————. "Dance and Glance: Visualizing Tribal Identity in Highland Yemen," *Visual Anthropology,* 11 (1998), 55–102.

————. "Tribal Dancing and Yemeni Nationalism: Steps to Unity," *RE.M.M.M.,* 67/1 (1993), 161–167.

Adwa, Najwa, and Daniel Martin Varisco. "Affluence and the Concept of the Tribe in the Central Highlands of the Yemen Arab Republic," in R. Salisbury and E. Tooker (eds.), *Affluence and Cultural Survival.* Washington, D.C.: American Ethnological Society, 1984, 134–149.

Ahroni, Reuben. *Yemenite Jewry: Origins, Culture, and Literature.* Bloomington: Indiana University Press, 1986.

Al-Jumly, M. S., and J. B. Rollins. "Emigration and the Rise of the Novel in Yemen," *World Literature Today,* 71/1 (Winter 1997), 39–47.

Alzubaidi, A., G. Upton, and B. Baluch. "Express Concerns of Yemeni Adolescents," *Adolescence,* 33/129 (Spring 1998), 193–207.

Alzubaidi, A., B. Baluch and A. Moafi. "Attitudes towards the Mentally-Disabled in a Nonwestern Society," *Journal of Social Behavior and Personality,* 10/4 (December 1995), 933–938.

Alzubaidi, A., and A. Ghanem. "Perspectives on Psychology in Yemen," *International Journal of Psychology,* 32/5 (1997), 363–366.

Anon. "Yemen 1991/92: Results from the Demographic and Maternal and Child Health Survey," *Studies in Family Planning,* 25/6, pt. 1 (November–December 1994), 368–372.

Ashuraey, Nadeem Muhammad. *Adolescents and Culture in Yemen.* Diss., Boston University. Ann Arbor, Mich.: University Microfilms International, 1986.

Beckerleg, Susan. "Special Issue on Khat: Use, Users and Unresolved Issues," *Substance Use & Abuse,* 43/6 (2008), 749–761.

Beddoucha, G. "Domestic Government, Kinship, Community and Polity in North Yemen: Review of M. Mundy," *Homme*, 37/144 (October–December 1997), 184–188.

Bishart, Mary. "Yemeni Farmworkers in California," *MERIP (Middle East Research and Information Project) Reports*, no. 34 (January 1975), 22–26.

Bornstein, Annika. "Some Observation on Yemen Food Habits," *Nutrition Newsletter*, 10/3 (July–September 1972), 1–9.

Boxberger, Linda. *On the Edge of Empire: Hadhramawt, Emigration and the Indian Ocean, 1880s–1930s*. Ithaca, N.Y.: SUNY Press, 2002.

Boyd, Douglas A. *Broadcasting in the Arab World*. Philadelphia: Temple University Press, 1982.

Capwell, C. "Contemporary Manifestations of Yemeni-derived Song and Dance in Indonesia," *Yearbook for Traditional Music*, 27 (1995), 76–89.

Carapico, Sheila, and Cynthia Myntti. "A Tale of Two Families: Change in North Yemen, 1977–1989," *Middle East Report*, 21/3, no. 170 (May–June 1991), 24–29.

Carapico, Sheila, and Richard Tutwiler. *Yemeni Agriculture and Economic Change*. Richmond, Va.: American Institute for Yemeni Studies, Box 311, Ardmore PA 19003-0311, 1981.

Caton, Steven C. "Icons of the Person, Lacan Imago in the Yemeni Males Tribal Wedding," *Asian Folklore Studies*, 52/2 (1993), 359–381.

———. *'Peaks of Yemen I Summon': Poetry as Cultural Practice in a North Yemeni Tribe*. Berkeley: University of California Press, 1990.

———. "The Poetic Construction of Self," *Anthropological Quarterly*, 58 (1985), 141–151.

———. *Yemen Chronicle: An Anthropology of War and Mediation*. New York: Hill and Wang, 2005.

Chelhod, Joseph (ed.). *L'Arabie du Sud: Histoire et Civilisation*, 3 vols. Paris: Editions Maisonneuve et Larose, 1984–1986.

———. "Les ceremonies du marriage au Yemen," *Objets et Mondes*, 13 (1973), 18.

———. "L'Organisation sociale au Yemen," *L'Ethnographie*, 64 (1979), 61–86.

Chistov, Y. K. "Anthropometry of the South Yemen Population: Between Groups Multivariate Analysis," *Homo*, 47/1–3 (June 1996), 3–22.

Clark, Janine. "Social Movement Theory and Patron–Clientism: Islamic Social Institutions and the Middle Class in Egypt, Jordan and Yemen," *Comparative political Studies*, 37/8 (October 2004), 941–968.

Dahbany-Miraglia, Dina. "Yemenite Jewish Migration and Adaptation to the United States, 1905–1941," in Eric J. Hooglund (ed.). *Crossing the Waters:*

Arabic-speaking Immigrants to the United States, Washington, D.C.: Smithsonian Institution Press, 1987.

Doe, D. Brian. *Socotra, Island of Tranquility.* London: Immel, 1992.

Dorsky, Susan. *Women of Amran: A Middle Eastern Ethnographic Study.* Salt Lake City: University of Utah Press, 1987.

Dostal, Walter. "Sozio-okonomische Aspekt der Stammesdemokratie in Nordost-Yemen," *Sociologus,* 24/1 (1974), 1–15.

Dresch, Paul K. "A Fragment of the Yemeni Past: Ali Nasir al-Qardai and the Shabwah Incident," *Journal of Arabic Literature,* 26/3 (October 1995), 232–254.

―――. "Imams and Tribes: The Writing and Acting of History in Upper Yemen," in Philop S. Khoury and Joseph Kostiner (eds.). *Tribes and States.* Berkeley: University of California Press, 1990, 252–287.

―――. "The Position of Shaykhs among the Northern Tribes of Yemen," *Man,* 19/1 (1984), 31–49.

―――. "The Several Peaces of Yemeni Tribes," *Journal of the Anthropological Society of Oxford,* 12/2 (1981), 73–86.

―――. "The Significance of the Course Events Take in Segmentary Systems," *American Ethnologist,* 13/2 (1986), 309–324.

Dyer, Caroline. "Working Children and Educational Inclusion in Yemen," *International Journal of Educational Development,* 27/5 (September 2007), 512–524.

Elsner, J. "The Coastal Music of Southern Arabic Countries: Yemenite Songs and Dances from the Coast of the Arabic Sea," *Lied and Populare Kultur-Song and Popular Culture,* 46 (2001), 242–247.

Ewald, Janet J. "Crossers of the Sea: Slaves and Migrants in the Western Indian Ocean, c. 1800–1900," *American Historical Review,* 105/1 (2000), 69–91.

―――. "The Economic Role of the Hadhrami Diaspora in the Red Sea and Gulf of Aden," with William G. Clarence-Smith, in William G. Clarence-Smith and Ulrike Freitag (eds.), *An Indian Ocean People: Hadhramawt and Its Diaspora, 1750s–1960s.* Leiden: Brill, 1989, 281–296.

Fleurentin, Jacques, and Jean-Marie Pelt. "Repertory of Drugs and Medicinal Plants of Yemen," *Journal of Ethnopharmacology,* 6 (1982), 85–108.

Friedlander, Jonathan (ed.). *Sojourners and Settlers: The Yemeni Immigrant Experience.* Salt Lake City: University of Utah Press, 1988.

Gerholm, Tomas. *Market, Mosque and Mafraj: Social Inequality in a Yemeni Town.* Stockholm, Sweden: University of Stockholm, 1977.

Gingrich, Andre. "How the Chiefs' Daughters Marry: Tribes, Marriage Patterns and Hierarchies in North-west Yemen," in Andre Gingrich, et al. *Kinship, Social Change and Evolution: Proceedings of a Symposium Held in Honor of W. Dostal's 60th Birthday.* Vienna, Austria: Verlag Ferdinand Berger & Sohne, 1989, 75–85.

Gingrich, Andre, and J. Heiss. *Beitrage zur Ethnographie der Provinz Saada (Nordyemen)*. Vienna: Austrian Academy, 1986.

Goitein, S. D. "The Jews of Yemen," in A. J. Arberry (ed.). *Religion in the Middle East*, vol. 1, *Judaism and Christianity*. Cambridge, UK: Cambridge University Press, 1969, 226–239.

Glander, Annelies. *The Queen of Sheba's Round Table: A Study of the Most Favored Daughters of Eve*. Frankfurt am Main: Peter Lang, 2004.

Gunaid, A. A., N. A. Hummad, and K. A. Tamim. "Consanguineous Marriage in the Capital City of Sanaa, Yemen," *Journal of Biosocial Science*, 36/1 (January 2004), 111–121.

Halliday, Fred. *Arabs in Exile: Yemeni Migrants in Urban Britain*. London: I. B. Tauris & Co. Ltd., 1991.

Han, Carolyn, and Kamal Ali al-Hegri. *From the Land of Sheba: Yemeni Folk Tales*. Northhampton, Mass.: Interlink Publishing Group, 2005.

Harrower, Michael J. "Hydrology, Ideology, and the Origins of Irrigation in Ancient Southwest Arabia," *Current Anthropology*, 49/3 (June 2008), 497–510.

Hashim, Abd al-Mumin. "Food Security and the Nutritional Gap in the Republic of Yemen," in Remy Leveau, Frank Mermier, and Udo Steinbach (eds.), *Le Yemen contemporain*, Paris: Editions Karthala, 1999, 419–436.

Khawaja, Marwan, M. al-Naour and G. Saad. "Khat (Catha Edulis) Chewing During Pregnancy in Yemen: Findings from a National Population Survey," *Maternal and Child Health Journal*, 12/3 (May 2008), 308–312.

Ho, Engseng. *The Graves of Tarim: Genealogy and Mobility Across the Indian Ocean*. Berkeley, Cal.: University of California, 2006.

———. "The Two Arms of Cambay: Diasporic Texts of Ecumenical Islam in the Indian Ocean," *Journal of the Economic and Social History of the Orient*, 50/pt. 2–3 (2007), 347–361.

Hofman, Michael. *Development Potential and Policies in the South Arabian Countries: Yemen Arab Republic, People's Democratic Republic of Yemen, Sultanate of Oman*. Berlin: German Development Institute, 1982.

Horgan, James. "Akhdam Tribe in Servitude," *Geographical Magazine*, 48/9 (June 1976), 533–539.

Ingrams, Doreen S. *Survey of the Economic and Social Conditions in the Aden Protectorate*. Asmara, Eritrea: Government Printer, British Administration, 1949.

Ingrams, William Harold. "Education in the Hadhramaut," *Overseas Education*, 16/4 (July 1945), 145–151.

———. "The Hadhramaut: Present and Future," *Geographical Journal*, 92/4 (October 1938), 289–312.

———. "House Building in the Hadramaut," *Geographical Journal*, 85 (January–June 1935), 370–372.

Ingrams, William Harold, and Doreen S. Ingrams, "The Hadramaut in Time of War," *Geographical Journal*, 105/1,2 (January–February), 1–29.

Johnston, T. M. "Folklore and Folk Literature in Oman and Socotra," *Arabian Studies*, 1 (1974), 7–23.

Jurdi, R, and P. C. Saxena. "The Prevalence and Correlates of Consanguineous Marriages in Yemen: Similarities and Contrasts with Other Arab Countries," *Journal of Biosocial Science*, 35/1 (January 2003), 1–13.

Katz, Marion Holmes. "Women's *Mawlid* Performances in Sanaa and the Construction of Popular Islam," *International Journal of Middle Eastern Studies*, 40/3 (2008), 467–486.

Keall, Edward J. "Smoker's Pipes and the Fine Pottery Tradition of Hays," *Proceedings of the Seminar for South Arabian Studies*, 22 (1992), 29–46.

Keddi, Nikki, Ron Kelley, Tony Maine, Milton Rogovin, and Jon Swanson. "Sojourners and Settlers: Yemenis in America: A Photoessay," *MERIP (Middle East Research and Information Project) Reports*, 16/139 (March–April 1986), 3–36.

Kefaya, Najwa A. "Yemen: Country Case Study," UN Educational, Scientific and Cultural Organization (UNESCO), 2007, 27 pp.

Kennedy, John G. *The Flower of Paradise*. Dordrecht, Holland: D. Reidel, 1987.

———. "A Medical Evaluation of the Use of Qat in North Yemen," *Social Science Medicine*, 17/12 (1983), 783–793.

Kennedy, John G., James Teague, and Lynn Fairbanks. "Qat Use in North America and the Problem of Addiction: A Study in Medical Anthropology," *Culture, Medicine, and Psychiatry*, 4 (1980), 311–344.

Klorman, Bat-Zion Eraqi. "Jewish and Muslim Messianism in Yemen," *International Journal of Middle East Studies*, 22/2 (May 1990), 201–228.

———. *The Jews of Yemen in the Nineteenth Century: A Portrait of a Messianic Community*. Leiden, Netherlands: E. J. Brill, 1993.

———. "Muslim Supporters of Jewish Messiahs in Yemen," *Middle Eastern Studies*, 29 (October 1993), 14–25.

Knysh, A. "The Tariqa on a Landcruiser: The Resurgence of Sufism in Yemen," *Middle East Journal*, 55/3 (Summer 2001), 399–414.

Kunitzsch, P. "Medieval Agriculture and Islamic Science: the Almanac of a Yemeni Sultan," *Islam-Zeitschrift fur Geschihte und Kultur des Islamischen Orients*, 74/2 (1997), 374–378,

———. "Southwestern Arabian Astronomical Calendars: An Ethnological Study of the Structure, Context and regional Comparison of the Tribal Agrarian Calendars of the Munibbeh of Yemen," *Islam-Zeitschrift fur Geschihte und Kultur des Islamischen Orients*, 74/2 (1997), 369–374.

Lambert, J. "Musical and Social Time in Yemen: The Musical Suite and the Magyal in Sanaa," *Homme*, 171–72 (July–December 2004), 151+.

————. "The 'Yemen Tihama, Trance and Dance Music from the Red Sea Coast of Arabia': Topic-Records-TSCD-920 (Anderson Bakewell)," *Yearbook for Traditional Music*, 35 (2003), 234–235.

Lambert, Louise. "HIV and Development Challenges in Yemen: Which Grows Fastest?" *Health Policy and Planning*, 22/1 (January 2007), 60–62.

Leveau, Remy, Franck Mermier, and Udo Steinbach (eds.), *Le Yemen contemporain*. Paris: Editions Karthala, 1999.

Lewis, Herbert S. *After the Eagles Landed: The Yemenite Jews of Israel*. Boulder: Westview Press, 1989.

Lewis, Jim R. "People's Democratic Republic of Yemen: Struggle for Survival," *Geography*, 72/4 (October 1987), 360–363.

————. "Land Reform or Socialist Agriculture? Rural Development in PDR Yemen 1967–1982," in Dean Forbes and Nigel Thrift (eds.), *The Socialist Third World: Urban Development and Territorial Planning*. Oxford: Basil Blackwood, 1987, 169–193.

Lichtenthaler, G., and A. R. Turton. *Water Demand Management, Natural Resource Reconstruction, and Traditional Value Systems: A Case Study from Yemen*. Occasional Paper no. 14, Water Supply Group, School of Oriental and African Studies, University of London, 1999. www.ciaonet.org/wps/lig03/index.html

Luqman, Ali Muhammad. "Education and the Press in South Arabia," in Derek Hopwood (ed.), *The Arabia Peninsula: Society and Politics*. London: George Allen & Unwin, 1972, 255–271.

MacPherson, S. "Goals for Social Integration and Realities of Social Exclusion in the republic of Yemen: Review of Muna Hashem," *Journal of Social Policy*, 26/pt. 4 (October 1997), 533–541.

Mahda, Kamil A., Anna Wurth, and Helen Lackner (eds.). *Yemen into the Twenty-First Century: Continuity and Change*. London: Ithaca, 2007.

Makhlouf, Carla. *Changing Veils*. Austin: University of Texas Press, 1979.

Makhlouf, Carla, and Gerald J. Obermeyer. "Women and Social Change in Urban North Yemen," in James Allman (ed.), *Women's Status and Fertility in the Muslim World*. New York: Praeger, 1978, 333–347.

Makin, Patrick. "Yemen: Marital Breakdown," *Middle East* (June 1994), 17–18.

al-Maktari, Abdullah M. A. *Water Rights and Irrigation Practices in Lahj*. Cambridge, UK: Cambridge University Press, 1971.

Meissner, Jeffery R. "Tribes at the Core: Legitimacy, Structure and Power in Zaydi Yemen." Ph.D. diss., Columbia University, 1987.

Meneley, Anne. "Fashions and Fundamentalisms in Fin-de-Siecle Yemen: Chador Barbie and Islamic Socks," *Cultural Anthropology*, 22/2 (May 2007), 214–243.

———. *Tournaments of Value: Sociability and Hierarchy in a Yemeni Town.* Toronto: University of Toronto, 1996.

Messick, Brinkley M. *The Calligraphic State: Textual Domination and History in a Muslim Society.* Berkeley: University of California Press, 1992.

———. "Just Writing: Paradox and Political Economy in Yemeni Legal Documents," *Cultural Anthropology*, 4/1 (February 1989), 26–50.

———. "Kissing Hands and Knees: Hegemony and Hierarchy in Shari'a Discourse," *Law and Society Review*, 22/4 (1988), 637–659.

———. "Literacy and the Law: Documents and Document Specialists in Yemen," in Daisy Hilse (ed.), *Law and Islam in the Middle East.* New York: Bergen and Garvey (1990), 61–76.

———. "The Mufti, the Text and the World: Legal Interpretation in Yemen," *Man*, 21/1 (March 1986), 102–119.

———. "Textual Properties: Writing and Wealth in a Sharia Case," *Anthropological Quarterly*, 68/3 (July 1995), 157–170.

———. *Transactions in Ibb: Economy and Society in a Yemeni Highland Town.* Ann Arbor, Mich.: University Microfilms International, 1979.

———. "Written Identities: Legal Subjects in an Islamic State (The Emergence of Modern Political Forms in Twentieth-Century Yemen), *History of Religions*, 38/1 (August 1998), 25–51.

Miller, W. Flagg. "Metaphors of Commerce: Trans-valuing Tribalism in Yemeni Audiocassette Poetry," *International Journal of Middle Eastern Studies*, 34/1 (February 2002), 29–57.

———. *The Moral Resonance of Arab Media: Audiocassette Poetry and Culture in Yemen.* Cambridge, Mass.: Harvard University, 2007.

———. "Of Songs and Signs: Audiocassette Poetry, Moral Character, and the Culture of Circulation in Yemen," *American Ethnologist*, 32/1 (February 2005), 82–99.

———. "Public Words and Body Politics: Reflections on the Strategies of Women Poets in Rural Yemen," *Journal of Womens History*, 14/1 (Spring 2002), 94–122.

Moghadam, Valentine M. "Gender, National Identity and Citizenship: Reflections on the Middle East and North Africa," *Comparative Studies of South Asia, Africa and the Middle East*, 19/1 (1999), 137–157.

Molyneux, Maxime D. "Legal Reform and Socialist Revolution in Democratic Yemen," *International Journal of the Sociology of Law*, 13 (1985), 147–172.

———. *State Policies and the Position of Women Workers in the People's Democratic Republic of Yemen, 1976–77.* Geneva: International Labour Organization, 1982.

———. "Women and Revolution in the PDRY," *Feminist Review*, 1 (1979), 5–20.

———. "Women's Rights and Political Contingency: The Case of Yemen, 1990–1994," *Middle East Journal*, 49/3 (Summer 1995), 418–431.

Mundy, Martha. *Domestic Government: Kinship, Community and Polity in North Yemen.* London: I.B. Tauris, 1995.

———. "Women's Inheritance of Land in Highland Yemen," *Arabian Studies*, 5 (1979), 161–187.

Myntti, Cynthia. "Hegemony and Healing in Rural North Yemen," *Social Science and Medicine*, 27/5 (1988), 515–520.

———. "Notes on Mystical Healers in the Hugariyya," *Arabian Studies*, 8 (1990), 171–176.

———. "Social Determinants of Child Health in Yemen," *Social Science Medicine*, 37/2 (July 1993), 233–240.

———. *Women and Development in the Yemen Arab Republic.* Eschborn, GFR: German Agency for Technical Cooperation, Ltd, 1979.

———. "Yemen Workers Abroad: The Impact on Women," *MERIP (Middle East Research and Information Project) Reports*, 14/124 (June 1984), 11–16.

Naim-Sanbar, S. "L'habitat traditionnel a San'a': Semantique de la maison," *Journal Asiatique*, 275/1 & 2 (1987), 79–113.

———. "'S'asseoir': comment dire, comment faire a San'a,'" *Technique et culture*, 13 (1989), 103–125.

Naumkin, Vitaly. *Island of the Phoenix: An Ethnographic Study of the People of Socatra.* London: Ithaca Press, 1993.

Nini, Y. *The Jews of Yemen 1800–1914.* Philadelphia: Harwood Academic Publishers, 1991.

Numan, N. "Exploration of Adverse Psychological Symptoms in Yemeni Khat Users by the Symptoms Checklist-90 (SCL-90)," *Addiction*, 99/1 (January 2004), 61–65.

Owens, Geoffrey R. "The Shomvi: A Precursor to Global Ethnoscapes and Indigenization in Precolonial East Africa," *Ethnohistory*, 53/4 (Fall 2006), 715–752.

Penney, D.S., "Meeting Women's Health Needs in Yemen: A Midwifery Perspective," *Journal of Midwifery & Women's Health*, 45/1 (January–February 2000), 72–78.

Pike, Ruthven W. "Land and People of the Hadhramaut, Aden Protectorate," *Geographical Review (New York)*, 30/4 (October 1940), 627–648.

Prados, E. "Indian Ocean Littoral Maritime Evolution: The Case of the Yemeni Huri and Sanbuq," *Mariners Mirror*, 83/2 (May 1997), 185–198.

Pridham, Brian R. (ed.). *Economy, Society and Culture in Contemporary Yemen.* London: Croom Helm, 1985.

Pritzkat, Thomas. "The Hadhrami Community in Saudi Arabia and the Rationale of Investing in the Homeland," Remy Leveau, Franck Mermier, and Udo Steinbach (eds.), *Le Yemen contemporain.* Paris: Editions Karthala, 399–418.

de Regt, Marina. *Pioneers or Pawns? Women Health Workers and the Politics of Development.* Syracuse: Syracuse University, 2007.

————. "Preferences and Prejudices: Employers' Views on Domestic Workers in the Republic of Yemen," *Signs: Journal of Women in Culture and Society*, 2007.

Riphenburg, Carol J. "Changing Gender Relations and Development in Yemen: Education, Family, Health and Cultural Expression," *Southwestern Political Review*, 28/4 (December 2000), 715–743.

————. "Gender Relations and Development in Yemen: Participation and Employment," *Peacekeeping and International Relations*, 28/3 (May–June 1999), 5–18.

Sarroub, Loukia K. *All American Yemeni Girls: Being Muslim in a Public School.* Philadelphia: University of Pennsylvania, 2005.

Scheepers, L. M. "Jidda: The Traditional Midwife of Yemen?" *Social Science and Medicine*, 33/8 (1991), 959–962.

Schopen, Armin. *Das Qat.* Wiesbaden: Franz Steiner Verlag, 1978.

Schuyler, Phillip D. "Hearts and Minds: Three Attitudes toward Performance Practice and Music Theory in the Yemen Arab Republic," *Ethnomusicology*, 34/1 (1990), 1–18.

————. "Music and Tradition in Yemen," *Asian Music*, 22/1 (1991), 51–71.

————. "Qat, Conversation, and Song: A Musical View of Yemeni Social Life," *Yearbook for Traditional Music*, 29 (1997), 57–73.

————. "Yemen: Songs from Hadramawt: UNESCO Records D8273 ((Scheherazade Qassim Hassan), *Yearbook for Traditional Music*, 30 (1998), 210.

Serjeant, Robert Bertram. "Folk-Remedies from Hadhramawt," *Bulletin of the School of Oriental and African Studies*, 18/1 (1956), 5–8.

————. "A Judeo-Arab House-Deed from Habban (With Notes on the Former Jewish Communities of the Wahidi Sultanate)," *Journal of the Royal Asiatic Society* (October 1953), 117–131.

————. "The Man 'Gypsies' of the West Aden Protectorate," *Anthropos*, 56 (1961), 737–749.

————. "The Mountain Tribes of the Yemen," *Geographical Magazine*, 15/2 (June 1942), 66–72.

————. "The Quarters of Tarim and Their Tansurahs," *Le Museon*, 63/1–4 (1950), 277–284.

————. "Recent Marriage Legislation from al-Mukalla with Notes on Marriage Customs," *Bulletin of the School of Oriental and African Studies*, 25/3 (1962), 472–498.

————. *The Saiyids of Hadramawt*. London: University of London School of Oriental and African Studies, 1957.

————. "Some Irrigation Systems in Hadramawt," *Bulletin of the School of Oriental and African Studies*, 27/1 (1964), 33–76.

————. *South Arabian Hunt*. London: Luzac, 1976.

————. "The 'White Dune' at Abyan: An Ancient Place of Pilgrimage in Southern Arabia," *Journal of Semitic Studies*, 16/1 (Spring 1971), 74–83.

Serjeant, Robert Bertram, and Robin L. Bidwell (eds.), *Arabian Studies 8*. Cambridge, UK: Cambridge University Press, 1990.

Al-Serouri, A.W., S. M. Grantham McGregor, B. Greenwood, and A. Costello. "Impact of Asymptomatic Malaria Parasitaemia on Cognitive Function and School Achievement of Schoolchildren in the Yemen Republic," *Parisitology*, 121/4 (October 2000), 337–345.

al-Sharki, Amatalrauf. "An Unveiled Voice," in Margot Badran and Miriam Cooke (eds.). *Opening the Gates: A Century of Arab Feminist Writing*. Bloomington: Indiana University Press, 1990, 375–385.

Shryock, A. C. "The Rise of Nasir al-Nims: A Tribal Commentary on Being and Becoming a Shaykh," *Journal of Anthropological Research*, 46 (Summer 1990), 153–176.

Smith, Gerald Rex. "Lahdj," in C. E. Bosworth (ed.), *Encyclopedia of Islam*, vol. 5, Leiden, Netherlands: Brill, 1982, fascicules 87–88, 601–602.

Sollers, P. "Rimbaud's Rifle: New Revelation on the Life of Arthur Rimbaud in Aden, Yemen," *Infini*, 75 (Summer 2001), 3–5.

Stephens, Robert. *The Arab's New Frontier*. London: Temple Smith, 1973.

Stevenson, Thomas B. "Migration, Family, and Household in Highland Yemen: The Impact of Socio-economic and Political Change and Cultural Ideals on Domestic Organization," *Journal of Comparative Family Studies*, 28/2 (Summer 1997), 14.

————. *Social Change in a Yemeni Highlands Town*. Salt Lake City: University of Utah, 1987.

————. "Yemen Workers Come Home: Reabsorbing One Million Migrants," *Middle East Report (MERIP)*, no. 181, 23/2 (March/April 1993), 15–24.

Stevenson, Thomas B., and Abdul Karim al-Aug. "Football in Newly United Yemen: Rituals of Equity, Identity and State Formation," *Journal of Anthropological Research*, 56/4 (Winter 2000), 453–475.

Stone, Francine (ed.). *Studies on the Tihamah: The Report of the Tihamah Expedition of 1982 and Related Papers.* London: Longman, 1985.

Sukkarystolba, S., and J. T. Fullerton. "Task-Analysis in Education and Evaluation: An Application among Midwives in the Republic of Yemen, *Midwifery,* 10/2 (June 1994), 104–111.

Swagman, Charles F. *Development and Change in Highland Yemen.* Salt Lake City: University of Utah Press, 1988.

———. "Fija: Fright and Illness in Highland Yemen," *Social Science and Medicine,* 28/4 (1989), 381–388.

Swanson, Jon C. *Emigration and Economic Development: The Case of the Yemen Arab Republic.* Boulder: Westview Press, 1979.

———. "Some Consequences of Emigration for Rural Economic Development in the Yemen Arab Republic," *Middle East Journal,* 33/1 (Winter 1979), 34–43.

Taminian, Lucine. "Persuading the Monarch: Poetry and Politics in Yemen," in Remy Leveau, Franck Mermier, and Udo Steinbach (eds.), *Le Yemen contemporain.* Paris: Editions Karthala, 1999, 203–220.

———. "Rimbaud's House in Aden, Yemen: Giving Voice(s) to the Silent Poet, *Cultural Anthropology,* 13/4 (November 1998), 464–490.

Tibawi, Abdul Latif. *Islamic Education: Its Traditions and Modernization into the Arab National Systems.* London: Luzac, 1979.

Tutwiler, Richard. "Taawun Mahweet: A Case Study of a Local Development Association in Highland Yemen," in Louis Cantori and Illya Harik (eds.). *Local Politics and Development in the Middle East.* Boulder: Westview Press, 1984.

———. "Tribe, Tribute and Trade: Social Class Formation in Highland Yemen." Ph.D. diss. Binghamton, N.Y.: SUNY Binghamton, 1987.

Underwood, P. "Barriers to Health in North Yemen: What Is the 'Evidence' and What 'Evidence' Is Wanted?" *Health Transition Series (Canberra),* 2 (1990), 602–608.

———. "Cultural Change, Growth and Feeding of Children in an Isolated Region of Yemen," *Social Science and Medicine,* 25 (1987), 1–7.

UN National Human Development Report Project. *Yemen: Human Development Report 2000/2001.* New York: United Nations Publications, 2001. www.undp.org.ye/nhdr.htm

UN Development Programme. *Arab Human Development Report 2003: Building a Knowledge Society.* New York: United Nations Publications, 2004. www.sd.undp.org/HDR/AHDR%202003%-%20English.pdf

UN Development Programme. *Arab Human Development Report 2004: Toward Freedom in the Arab World.* New York: United Nations Publications, 2005. www.sd.undp.org/HDR/AHDR%202003%-%20English.pdf

Varisco, Daniel Martin. "The Agricultural Marker Stars in Yemeni Folklore," *Asian Folklore Studies*, 52/1 (1993), 119–142.

———. "The Future of Terrace Farming in Yemen: A Development Dilemma," *Agriculture and Human Values*, 8 (Winter-Spring 1991), 166–172.

———. "Green Arabia: Continuity and Change in North Yemen," *The World and I*, 3/5 (May 1988), 514–523.

———. "Land Use and Agricultural Development in the Yemen Arab Republic," in M. Salem Murdock and M. Horowitz (eds.). *Anthropology and Development in North Africa and the Middle East*. Boulder: Westview Press, 1989, 292–311.

———. "On the Meaning of Chewing: The Significance of Qat in the Yemen Arab Republic," *International Journal of Middle East Studies*, 18/1 (1986), 1–13.

———. "Sayl and Ghayl: The Ecology of Water Allocation in Yemen," *Human Ecology*, 11/4 (1983), 365–383.

———. "Terminology for Plough Cultivation in Yemeni Arabic," *Journal of Semitic Studies*, 49/1 (Spring 2004), 71–129.

Van Hear, Nicholas. "The Socio-economic Impact of the Involuntary Mass Return to Yemen in 1990," *Journal of Refugee Studies*, 7/1 (1994), 18–38.

Venter, Al J. "Arabia's Curse: The Qat Drug Problem Moves West," *Middle East*, no. 294 (October 1999), 35–37.

Vom Bruck, Gabriele. "Elusive Bodies: The Politics of Aesthetics among Yemeni Elite Women," *Signs*, 23/1 (Fall 1997), 175–214.

———. "A House Turned Inside Out: Inhabiting Space in a Yemeni City," 2/2 (July 1997), 139–172.

———. "The Imagined 'Consumer Democracy' and Elite (Re)production in Yemen," *Journal of the Royal Anthropological Institute*, 11/2 (June 2005), 255–275.

Wagner, Mark S. *Like Joseph in Beauty: Yemeni Vernacular Poetry and Arab-Jewish Symbiosis*. Leiden: Brill, 2009.

Walker, G. J. A., et al. "Evaluation of Rational Drug Prescribing in Democratic Yemen," *Social Science and Medicine*, 31/7 (1990), 823–828.

Walters, Dolores M. "Cast among Outcasts: Interpreting Sexual Orientation, Racial and Gender Identity in the Yemen Arab Republic," Ellen Lewin and William L. Leap (eds.), *Out in the Field: Reflections of Lesbian and Gay Anthropologists*. Urbana: University of Illinois, 1996, 58–69.

———. *Perceptions of Social Inequalities in the Yemen Arab Republic*. Ann Arbor, Mich.: University Microfilms, 1987.

Warfa, Nasir, A. Klein, K. Bhui. G. Leavey, T. Craig, and S. A. Stansfeld. "Khat Use and Mental Illness: A Critical Review," *Social Science and Medicine*, 65/2 (July 2007), 309–318.

Weir, Shelagh. "A Clash of Fundamentalisms: Wahhabisms in Yemen," *Middle East Report*, 204 (July–September 1997), 22–26.

————. *Qat in Yemen: Consumption and Social Change.* London: British Museum Publications Ltd, 1985.

————. "Trade and Tribal Structures in North-west Yemen," *Arabie di Sud: Cahiers du GREMAMO*, 10 (1991), 87–101.

————. *A Tribal Order: Politics and Law in the Mountains of Yemen.* Austin: University of Texas, 2007.

————. "Tribe, Hijra, and Madina in North-west Yemen," in Kenneth Brown (ed.). *Middle Eastern Cities in Comparative Perspective.* London: Ithaca Press, 1986, 225–39.

Weiss, M. "The Children of Yemen: Bodies, Medicalization, and Nation-Building," *Medical Anthropology Quarterly*, 15/2 (June 2001), 206–221.

Willemsen, T. M., and A. van Lenning. "Women's Studies Project in Yemen: Experiences from the Counterpart's Viewpoint," *Womens Studies International Forum*, 25/5 (September–October 2002), 515–527.

World Bank. *Governance Research Indicator Country Snapshot Comparison within Yemen for All Six Governance Indicators.* May 2005. http://info.worldbank.org/governance/kkz2004/sc_chart.asp

"Yemen/South Yemen: Women's Rights at Risk," *International Labour Review*, 132/1 (1993), 26–28.

Geography, Demography, Manpower, and Human Resources

Allman, James, and A. G. Hill. "Fertility, Mortality and Family Planning in the Yemen Arab Republic," *Population Studies*, 32/1 (March 1978), 159–171.

Birks, J. S., C. A. Sinclair, and J. A. Stocknat. "Aspects of Labour Migration from North Yemen," *Middle Eastern Studies*, 17 (January 1981), 49–63.

Cerny, Viktor, C. J. Mulligan, J. Ridl, M. Zaloudkova, Christopher M. Edens, M. Hajek, and L. Pereira. "Regional Differences in the Distribution of the Sub-Saharan, West Eurasian, and South Asian mtDNA Lineages in Yemen," *American Journal of Physical Anthropology*, 136/2 (June 2008), 128–137.

Colton, Nora A. "Homeward Bound: Yemeni Return Migration," *International Migration Review*, 27/4 (Winter 1993), 870–882.

————. "The Silent Victims: Yemeni Migrants Return Home," *Oxford International Review*, 3/1 (1991), 23–37.

Demeny, Paul. "Population Policy Dilemmas in Europe at the Dawn of the Twenty-first Century," *Population and Development Review*, 29/1 (March 2003), 1–28.

Fritz, Hermann M., and Emile Okal. "Socotra Island, Yemen: Field Survey of the 2004 Indian Ocean Tsunami," *Natural Hazards*, 46/1 (July 2008), 107–117.

Keddi, Nikki, Ron Kelley, Tony Maine, Milton Rogovin, and Jon Swanson. "Sojourners and Settlers: Yemenis in America: A Photoessay," *MERIP*

(Middle East Research and Information Project) Reports, 16/139 (March–April 1986), 3–36.

Lucet, Marc. "Les rapatries de la crise du Golfe au Yemen: Hodeida quatre ans apres," *Maghreb Machrek*, no. 148 (April/June 1995), 28–42.

Meyer, Gunter. "Labour Emigration and Economic Development in the YAR: The Case of Employment in the Building Sector in Sanaa," *Applied Geography and Development*, 23 (1984), 55–71.

Rouaud, Alain. *Les Yemens et leurs populations*. Brussels: Editions Complexe, 1979.

Steffen, Hans. *A Contribution to the Population Gegraphy of the Yemen Arab Republic*. Wetzikon, Switzerland: Druckerei Wetzikon, 1979.

Steffen, Hans, et al. *Final Report on the Airphoto Interpretation Project of the Swiss Technical Cooperation Service*. Berne, Switzerland: Swiss Technical Cooperation Service, 1978.

Tabutin, D., and B. Schoumaker. "The Demography of the Arab World and the Middle East from the 1950s to the 2000s. A Survey of Changes and a Statistical Assessment," *Population*, 60/5–6 (September–December 2005), 611–724.

Thirugnanasambanthar, S., et al. "Water Resources in Yemen and their Degradation: The Risk for an Extensive Desertification," *Desertification Control Bulletin*, no. 32 (1998), 51–61.

Zain, Mohammad Gaffar. "The Brain Drain in the Context of Social Change to Democratic Yemen and Problems in High Level Manpower Training at Aden University," in A. B. Zahlan (ed.). *Arab Brain Drain: Proceedings of UN Seminar, Beirut 1980*. London: Ithaca, 1981, 43–58.

Van Hear, Nicholas. "The Socio-economic Impact of the Involuntary Mass Return to Yemen in 1990," *Journal of Refugee Studies*, 7/1 (1994), 18–38.

Language and Literature

Cline, Walter. "Proverbs and Lullabies from South Arabia," *American Journal of Semitic Language and Literature*, 57/3 (July 1940), 291–301.

Dahbany-Miraglia, Dina. "How to Address Your Spouse in Judeo Yemeni: Syllable as Discourse," *Semiotica*, 146/1–4 (2003), 307–349.

Dobzynski, C. "Lapidaires du Yemen," *Europe-Revue Litteraire Mensuelle*, 73/794–95 (June–July 1995), 155–159.

Ghanem, Muhammad Abduh. *Aden Arabic for Beginners*, 2nd ed. Aden, 1958.

———. "The Language of al-Gades. The Main Characteristics of an Arabic Dialect Spoken in Lower Yemen," *Le Museon*, 73 (1960), 351–394.

Greenman, Joseph. "A Sketch of the Arabic Dialect of the Central Yamani Tihamah," *Zeitschrift fur arabische Linguistik*, 3/3 (1979), 47–61.

De Landberg, Comte. *Glossaire Datinois*, 3 vols. Leiden, the Netherlands: Brill, 1920–1942.

Piamenta, Moshe. *Dictionary of Post-Classical Yemeni Arabic*, 2 vols. Leiden, Netherlands: E. T. Brill, 1990 & 1991.

Qafisheh, H. A. "Major Phonological Processes of San'ani Arabic," *Journal of King Saud University*, 5 (1993), 39–54.

———. *Yemeni Arabic Reference Grammar.* Kensington, Md.: Dunwoody Press, 1992.

———. *Yemeni Arabic I*. Beirut: Librairie de Liban, 1990.

Serjeant Robert Bertram. "The Yemeni Poet al-Zubayri and His Polemic against the Zaydi Imams," *Arabian Studies*, 5 (1979), 87–130.

al-Shami, Ahmad Muhammad. "Yemeni Literature in Hajjah Prisons, 1948–55," *Arabian Studies*, 2 (1975), 43–60.

Smith, G. R. "Dictionary of Postclassical Yemeni Arabic: review of M. Piamenta," *Journal of Semitic Studies*, 38/2 (Fall 1993), 349–355.

Watson, J. "'Mubtada and Khabar with Reference to San'ani Arabic," *BRISMES Proceedings* (1991), 292–301.

Art, Architecture, and Urban Design

Centre for Middle Eastern and Islamic Studies, University of Durham. *North Yemen: Images of the Built Environment.* Durham, UK: Centre for Middle Eastern and Islamic Studies, University of Durham, 1982.

Costa, Paola M., and Ennio Vicario. *Arabia Felix: Land of Builders.* New York: Rizzoli, 1977.

Damlugi, S. S. *The Valley of Mudbrick Architecture.* Reading, UK: Garnet Publishing, 1992.

———. *A Yemen Reality: Architecture Sculptured in Mud and Stone.* Reading, UK: Garnet Publishing, 1991.

Davey, P. "The Yemen's Mud Brick Buildings," *Architectural Review*, 211/1265 (July 2002), 70–75.

Daum, Werner (ed.). *Yemen, 3000 Years of Art and Civilization in Arabia Felix.* Innsbruck, Austria: Pinguin, 1988.

Doe, D. Brian, and R. B. Serjeant. "A Fortified Tower-house in Wadi Jirdan (Wahidi Sultanate)," *Bulletin of the School of Oriental and African Studies,* 38/1–2 (1975), 1–23, 276–295.

Golvin, Lucin, and Marie Christine Fromont. *Thula: architecture and urbanisme d'une cite de haute montagne en republique arabe de Yemen.* Paris: A.D.P.F./Recherche sur les civilisations, 1984.

Kia, B., and V. C. Williams. "Saving Sanaa," *Geographical Magazine*, 61/5 (May 1989), 32–36.

King, Geoffrey, and Ronald Lewcock. "Key Monuments of Islamic Art: Arabia," in George Mitchell (ed.). *Architecture of the Islamic World: Its History and Social Meaning*. London: Thames & Hudson, 1978, 209–211.

Kirkman, James (ed.). *City of San'a*. London: World of Islam Festival Trust, 1976.

Lewcock, Ronald. *Wadi Hadramaut and the Walled City of Shibam*. Paris: UNESCO, 1986.

Lewcock, Ronald, and Gerald Rex Smith. "Three Medieval Mosques in the Yemen," *Oriental Art*, 20/1–2 (Spring/Summer 1974), 75–87, 192–203.

———. "Two Early Mosques in the Yemen: A Preliminary Report," *Art and Architectural Research Papers*, 4 (1973), 117–130.

Marechaux, Pascal. *Sanaa: Parcours d'une Cite d'Arabie*. Paris: L'Institut, 1987.

Porter, Venetia. "The Architecture of the Tahirid Dynasty of the Yemen," *Proceedings of the Seminar for Arabian Studies, Twenty-second Seminar*, 19 (1989), 105–120.

———. "Conservation in Yemen," in Cecil Hourani (ed.). *The Arab Cultural Scene*. London: Namara Press, 1982, 132–134.

al-Radi, Selma. *The Amiriya in Rada: The History and Restoration of a Sixteenth-Century Madrasa in the Yemen*. Oxford: Oxford University, 1997.

———. "The National Museum, Sana, YAR," in Cecil Hourani (ed.). *The Arab Cultural Scene*. London: Namara Press, 1982, 132–133.

Raikes, R. L. "Marib Dam," *Antiquity*, 51 (1977), 239–240.

Rathjens, Carl. *Jewish Domestic Architecture in San'a, Yemen*. With an intro. and append. by S. D. Goitein. Jerusalem: Israel Oriental Society, 1957.

Saqqaf, Abdulaziz Y., Ali Oshaish, and Fritz Piepenberg. "The Modernization of an Islamic City: The Case of Sana'a," in Abdulaziz Y. Saqqaf (ed.). *The Middle East City, Ancient Traditions Confront a Modern World*. New York: Paragon House, 1987, 85–144.

Schulze, J. "Restoration of the Samsarat-Al-Mansuriah of Sanaa and Traditional Yemeni Architecture," *Denkmalpflege*, 53/1 (1995), 76–80.

Serjeant, Robert Bertram (ed.). *The Islamic City*. Paris: UNESCO, 1980.

Serjeant, Robert Bertram, and Ronald Lewcock (eds.). *San'a: An Arabian Islamic City*. London: World of Islam Festival Trust, 1983.

Spicer, D. "Restoring Tradition (Restoration of a Yemen Tower House by Marco Livadiotti)," *Architectural Review*, 203/1213 (March 1998), 61–63.

Turner, Geoffrey. "South Arabian Gold Jewelry," *Iraq*, 1/2 (Autumn 1973), 127–141.

Um, Nancy. *The Merchant Houses of Mocha: Trade and Architecture in an Indian Ocean Port*. Seattle: University of Washington, 2009.

Varanda, Fernando. *Art of Building in Yemen*. Cambridge, Mass.: MIT Press, 1982.

Archaeology

Antonini, S. "Statuettes from the Excavations of the Temple of Nakrah (Temple A) at Baraqish (Republic of Yemen)," *Arabian Archaeology and Epigraphy*, 10/1 (May 1999), 58–68.

Barbanes, E. "Domestic and Defensive Architecture on the Yemeni Plateau: Eighth Century BCE–Sixth Century CE," *Arabian Archaeology and Epigraphy*, 11/2 (November 2000), 207–222.

Breton, J. F. "Archaeological Excavations in Shabwa (Yemen): Semitic Traditions and External Influences," *Comptes Renud Des Seances de L'Academie des Inscriptions & Belles-Lettres*, 2 (April–June 2000), 849–882.

Breton, J. F., A. M. McMahon, and David A. Warburton. "Two Seasons at Hajar-Am-Dhabiyya, Yemen," *Arabian Archaeology and Epigraphy*, 9/1 (May 1998), 90–111.

Chistov, Y. K. "Human Cranial Remains from South Yemen," *Homo*, 45/1 (June 1994), 8–30.

Clapp, Nicholas. *The Road to Ubar: Finding the Atlantis of the Sands*. Boston/ New York: Houghton Mifflin, 1999.

Cleveland, Ray L. *An Ancient South Arabian Necropolis: Objects from the Second Campaign (1951) in the Timna' Cemetery*. Baltimore, Md.: Johns Hopkins Press, Publications of the American Foundation for the Study of Man, no. 4, 1965.

Costa, Paola M. *The Pre-Islamic Antiquities at the Yemen National Museum*. Rome: "L'Erma" di Bretschneider, 1978.

Deutsches Archaologisches Institut San'a. *Archaologische Berichte aus dem Jemen*. Mainz: Verlag Philipp von Zabern, 1982.

Doe, D. Brian. "Husn al-Gurab and the Site of Qana,'" *Le Museon*, 74 (1961), 191–198.

———. "Pottery Sites Near Aden," *Journal of the Royal Asiatic Society* (October 1963), 150–162.

———. *Socotra: An Archaeological Reconnaissance in 1967*. (Miami: Field Research Projects, 1970.

———. *Southern Arabia*. New York: McGraw Hill, 1971.

Dreibholz, Ursula. *Early Quran Fragments from the Great Mosque in Sanaa*. Sanaa: Deutsches Archaologisches Institut Orient-Abteilung Sanaa, 2003.

———. "Preserving a Treasure: The Sanaa Manuscript (in Yemen)," *Museum International*. 51/3 (July–September 1999), 21–25.

Edens, Christopher, T. J. Wilkinson, and G. Barratt. "Hammat al-Qa and the Roots of Urbanism in Southwest Arabia," *Antiquity*, 74/286 (December 2000), 854–862.

———. "Southwest Arabia during the Holocene: Recent Archaeological Development," *Journal of World Prehistory*, 12/1 (March 1998), 55–119.

Fakhry, Ahmad. *An Archaeological Journey to Yemen*, 3 vols. Cairo: Government Press, 1951–1952.

Francaviglia, V. M. "Dating the Ancient Dam of Marib (Yemen)," *Journal of Archaeological Science*, 27/4 (July 2000), 645–653.

Hayjaneh, H. "An Old Sabaic Inscription from Thula, Yemen," *Arabian Archaeology and Epigraphy* (May 2000), 24–27.

Hamilton, R. A. B. "Archaeological Sites in the Western Aden Protectorate," *Geographical Journal*, 101 (January–June 1948), 110–117.

Giumlia, A., Edward J. Keall, A. N. Shugar, and S. Stock. "Investigation of a Copper-Based Hoard from the Megalithic Site of al-Midamman, Yemen: An Interdisciplinary Approach," *Journal of Archaeological Science*, 29/2 February 2002), 195–209.

Gorsdorf, J., and B. Vogt. "Radiocarbon Dating from the Almaqah Temple of Bawan, Marib, Republic of Yemen: Approximately 800 cal BC to 600 cal AD," *Radiocarbon*, 43/3 (pt. 3) (2001), 1363–1369.

Harding, C. Lankester. *Archaeology in the Aden Protectorates*. London: HM Stationery Office, 1964.

Lane, Arthur, and R. B. Serjeant, "Pottery and Glass Fragments from the Aden Littoral with Historical Notes," *Journal of the Royal Asiatic Society* (October 1948), 108–31.

Maigret, A. D., and C. Robin. "The Temple of Nakrah at Yathill (Today Baraqish), Yemen: The Results of the Italian Mission's First Two Excavating Seasons," *Comptes Rendus des Seances de L'Academie des Inscriptions & Belles-Lettre*, 2 (April–June 1993), 427–496.

Mallory-Greenough, L., J. D Greenough, and C. Fipke. "Iron Age Gold Mining: A Preliminary Report on Camps in the Maraziq Region, Yemen," *Arabian Archaeology and Epigraphy*, 11/2 (November 2000), 223–236.

Maraqtan, M., and Yusef Abdullah. "A Recently Discovered Inscribed Sabean Bronze Plaque from Mahram Bilqis Near Marib, Yemen," *Journal of Near Eastern Studies*, 61/1 (January 2002), 49–53.

McCorriston, J. "Early Settlement in Hadramawt: Preliminary Report on Prehistoric Occupation at Shib Munayder," *Arabian Archaeology and Epigraphy*, 11/2 (November 2000), 129–153.

Norris, H. T., and F. W. Penhey. *An Archaeological and Historical Survey of the Aden Tanks*. Aden: Government Press, 1955.

Prados, E. "An Archaeological Investigation of Sira Bay, Aden, Republic of Yemen," *International Journal of Nautical Archaeology*, 23/4 (November 1994), 297–307.

Al-Radi, Selma, and Francine Stone. "Surveys of the North Yemen Tihamah," *Proceedings of the Seminar for Arabian Studies, Sixteenth Seminar*, 13 (1983), 101–102.

Ryckmans, Jacques. "A Bust of a South Arabian Winged Goddess with Nimbus in the Possession of Miss Leila Ingrams," *Arabian Studies*, 3 (1976), 67–78.

Shinie, P. L. "Socotra," *Antiquity*, 34/134 (1960), 100–110.

Thompson, Gertrude Caton. *The Tombs and Moon Temple of Hureidha (Hadramaut)*. Oxford: Oxford University Press, 1944.

Um, Nancy. "Spatial Negotiations in a Commercial City: The Red Sea Port of Mocha, Yemen, during the First Half of the Eighteenth Century," *Journal of the Society of Architectural Historians*, 62/2 (June 2003), 178–193.

————. *Indian Ocean Currents: Commercial Life, Urban Space, and Architecture in the Yemen Port of Mocha, 1686–1748*. Seattle: University of Washington, 2009.

van Beek, Gus W. *Hajar bin Humeid: Investigations at a Pre-Islamic Site in South Arabia*. Baltimore, Md.: Johns Hopkins Press, Publications of the American Foundation for the Study of Man, no. 5, 1969.

Whalen, N. M., and K. E. Schatte. "Pleistocene Sites in Southern Yemen," *Arabian Archaeology and Epigraphy*, 8/1 (May 1997), 1–10.

Wilkinson, T. J., Christopher Edens, and M. Gibson. "The Archaeology of the Yemen High Plains: A Preliminary Chronology," *Arabian Archaeology and Epigraphy*, 8/1 (May 1997), 99–142.

Wilkinson, T. J., and Christopher Edens. "Survey and Excavation in the Central Highlands of Yemen: Results of the Dhamar Survey Project, 1996–1998," *Arabian Archaeology and Epigraphy*, 10/1 (May 1999), 1–33.

Yaseen, G. T., M. M ElGamili, and A. M. Shalan. "Unpublished Terracotta Figurines in the Museum of the Archaeology Department, Sann University, Yemen," *Arabian Archaeology and Epigraphy*, 7/2 (November 1996), 287–303.

Geography, Flora, and Fauna

Ambraseys, N. N., and C. P. Melville. "Seismicity of Yemen," *Nature*, 303/5915 (May 1983), 321–323.

Bagnold, R. A. "Sand Formations in Southern Arabia," *Geographical Journal*, 117 (January–December 1951), 78–86.

Beydoun, Z. R. *Geology of the Arabian Peninsula: Eastern Aden Protectorate and Part of Dhufar.* Washington, D.C.: U.S. Government Printing Office, 1966.

Cockrane, R. A. "An Air Reconnaissance of the Hadhramaut," *Geographical Journal,* 77/3 (March 1931), 209–216.

Defense Mapping Agency Topographic Center. *People's Democratic Republic of Yemen: Official Standard Names Gazetteer.* Washington, D.C.: U.S. Board on Geographic Names, 1976.

————. *Yemen Arab Republic: Official Standard Names Gazetteer.* Washington, D.C.: U.S. Board on Geographic Names, 1976.

Fleurentin, Jacques, and Jean-Marie Pelt. "Repertory of Drugs and Medicinal Plants of Yemen," *Journal of Ethnopharmacology,* 6 (1982), 85–108.

Forbes, Henry O. (ed.). *The Natural History of Sokotra and Abd-el-Kuri.* Liverpool: Museums Committee, 1903.

Geukens, F. *Geology of the Arabian Peninsula: Yemen.* Washington, D.C.: U.S. Geological Survey, 1966.

Greth, A. "Gazelles in Yemen and Southern Saudi Arabia," *Bulletin of the Ornithological Society of the Middle East,* 27 (1991), 39.

Gwynne, M. D. "The Possible Origin of the Dwarf Cattle of Socotra," *Geographical Journal,* 133 (1967), 39–42.

Harrison, David L. *The Mammals of Arabia.* London: Ernest Benn, 3 vols., 1964–1972.

Hepper, F. Nigel. "Arabian and African Frankincense Trees," *Journal of Egyptian Archaeology,* 55 (1969), 66–72.

Hopkins, I. W. J. "The Maps of Carsten Niebuhr 200 Years After, *Cartographic Journal,* 4/1 (June 1967), 115–118.

Kopp, Horst. *Agrargeographie der Arabischen Republik Jemen.* Erlangen: Palm and Enke, 1981.

Menzies, M. et al. "Lithospheric Extension and the Opening of the Red Sea: Sediment-Basalt Relationship in Yemen," *Terra Nova,* 3 (1992), 340–350.

University of Aden, Faculty of Education. *Socotra Island: Flora, Fauna, and Geography.* Madrid, Spain: Editorial Oriental, S. D., n.d.

Varisco, Daniel Martin. "Beyond Rhino Horn: Wildlife Conservation for North Yemen," *Oryx,* 23/4 (October 1989), 215–219.

Werdecker, Josef. "A Contribution to the Geography and Cartography of North-west Yemen," *Bulletin de la Societe royale de Geographie d'Egypte,* 20 (1939), 1–160.

Wood, J. R. I. *A Handbook of Yemen Flora.* New York: Kegan Paul Int'l, 1989.

Current Travel and Guide Books

Chwaszcza, Joachim (ed.). *Insight Guide: Yemen.* Singapore/New York: Apa Publications (HK)/Houghton Mifflin, 1992.

Fayein, Claudie. *Yemen.* Paris: Seuil, Collections Microcosme Petite Planete, no. 49, 1975.

Hamalainen, Pertti. *Yemen: A Travel Survival Kit,* 4th ed. Berkeley, Calif.: Lonely Planet Publications, 1999.

McLaughlin, Daniel. *Yemen.* (Bradt Travel Guides). Guilford, Conn.: Globe Pequot, 2008.

Walker, Jenny, et al. *Oman, UAE and Arabian Peninsula,* 2nd ed. Berkeley, Calif.: Lonely Planet Publications, 2007.

Bibliographies

Blackburn, J. R. "Arabic and Turkish Source Material for the Early History of Ottoman Yemen 945/1538–976/1568," *Studies in the History of Arabia,* vol. 1, pt. 2, *Sources for the History of Arabia.* Riyadh, Saudi Arabia: Riyadh University Press, 1979, 197–210.

Buringa, Yoke. *Bibliography on Women in Yemen.* Westbury, N.Y.: American Institute for Yemeni Studies (also available from Middle East Studies Association, Tucson, Ariz.), 1993.

Hopwood, Derek. "Some Western Studies of Saudi Arabia, Yemen and Aden: Bibliographical Survey," in Derek Hopwood (ed.). *The Arabian Peninsula: Society and Politics.* London: George Allen & Unwin, 1972, 13–27.

Labaune, Patrick. *Bibliographie de la Peninsule Arabique,* vol. 2, *La Republique Arabe de Yemen.* Paris: C.N.R.S., 1985.

Landau, Jacob M. "Soviet Books on the Yemen," *Middle East Studies,* 10 (May 1974), 234–237.

Littlefield, David W. *Islamic Near East and North Africa: An Annotated Guide to Books in English for Non-specialists.* Littleton, Colo.: Libraries Unlimited, 1977.

Macro, Eric. *Bibliography on Yemen and Notes on Mocha.* Coral Gables, Fla.: University of Miami Press, 1960.

———. "The Yemen: Some Recent Literature," *Royal Central Asian Journal,* 45/1 (January 1958), 43–51.

Marchand, T. H. J. *Yemen. Revised Edition (World Bibliographical Series, vol. 50), Bulletin of the School of Oriental and African Studies-University of London,* 61/pt. 3 (1998), 546.

Meghdessian, Samira Rafidi. *The Status of the Arab Woman: A Select Bibliography.* London: Mansell, 1980.

Mondesir, Simone Luchia (ed.). *A Select Bibliography of the Yemen Arab Republic and the People's Democratic Republic of Yemen.* Durham, UK: University of Durham Centre for Middle Eastern and Islamic Studies, 1977.

Nagi, Sultan (ed). *Biblioghrafia Mukhtarah wa Tafsiliyah 'an al-Yamam.* (Selected and Annotated Bibliography on Yemen.) Kuwait: University of Kuwait, 1973.

Sayyid, Ayman Fuad. *Sources de l'histoire du Yemen a l'epoque Musulmane.* Cairo: Institut Francais d'Archeologie Orientale de Cairo, 1974.

Serjeant, Robert Bertram. "Regional Bibliographies, Arabia," in Diana Grimwood-Jones and Derek Hopwood (eds.). *Middle East and Islam: A Bibliographic Introduction.* Zug, Switzerland: Inter Documentation Company, 1979, 181–187.

Smith, Gerald Rex. *The Yemens: The YAR and the PDRY.* Santa Barbara, Calif.: Clio Press, World Bibliographical Series 50, 1984.

Stevenson, Thomas B. *Studies on Yemen, 1975–1990: A Bibliography of European-Language Sources for Social Scientists.* American Institute for Yemeni Studies, Box 311, Ardmore PA 19003-0311, 1994.

About the Author

Robert D. Burrowes was an adjunct professor in the political science department and Henry M. Jackson School of International Studies (JSIS) at the University of Washington from the beginning of the 1990s until his retirement in 2003, and he continues to maintain ties with the JSIS. Dr. Burrowes taught at New York University from 1961 through 1972, after which he departed to teach at the American University of Beirut from the beginning of 1972 until late 1975, early in the Lebanese civil war. Thereafter, he lived, researched, and worked in development projects in North Yemen most of the period between the fall of 1975 and late 1981. He returned briefly in 1990 to what had just become the Republic of Yemen and has gone back frequently for research purposes and good living since that time, particularly between 2003 and 2009. Dr. Burrowes is the author of *The Yemen Arab Republic: The Politics of Development, 1962–1986* (Westview Press, 1987), as well as many articles in professional journals and books on North Yemen (the YAR), South Yemen (the PDRY), and the Republic of Yemen (the ROY).